Bronislava Nijinska:
Early Memoirs

BRONISLAVA NIJINSKA:
Early Memoirs

TRANSLATED AND EDITED BY
Irina Nijinska
AND ### Jean Rawlinson

WITH AN INTRODUCTION BY

AND IN CONSULTATION WITH

ANNA KISSELGOFF

HOLT, RINEHART AND WINSTON   NEW YORK

Copyright © 1981 by Irina Nijinska
Introduction copyright © 1981 by Anna Kisselgoff
All rights reserved, including the right to reproduce this
book or portions thereof in any form.
Published by Holt, Rinehart and Winston, 383 Madison Avenue,
New York, New York 10017.
Published simultaneously in Canada by Holt, Rinehart and
Winston of Canada, Limited.

LIBRARY OF CONGRESS CATALOGING IN PUBLICATION DATA
Nijinska, Bronislava, 1891–1972.
Bronislava Nijinska—early memoirs.
Includes index.
1. Nijinsky, Vaslav, 1889–1950. 2. Ballet dancers—
Russia—Biography. I. Nijinska, Irina. II. Rawlinson,
Jean. III. Kisselgoff, Anna.
GV1785.N6N5713   792.8'092'4 [B]   80–21825
ISBN 0–03–020951–X

FIRST EDITION

Designer: Anthea Lingeman
Endpaper photograph: *L'Après-Midi d'un Faune*, photograph
published in anticipation of the Paris premiere in
Comoedia Illustré, June 15, 1912.
Printed in the United States of America

1   3   5   7   9   10   8   6   4   2

Contents

Contents

Contents

List of Illustrations

Introduction
by Anna Kisselgoff

IT IS HARDLY an exaggeration to suggest that this is the book about Vaslav Nijinsky for which the world has waited for more than half a century. Written by the person closest to Nijinsky in his formative years, Bronislava Nijinska's early memoirs provide an unprecedented insight into the personality and creative development of this great dancer and choreographer.

As his sister, she writes totally and most revealingly from the inside—from the heart of the Nijinsky family as it has never been revealed before. At the same time, she speaks as an internationally known creative figure in her own right, opening up new aspects in the history of Russia's Imperial Maryinsky Ballet and Serge Diaghilev's Ballets Russes. It is important to remember that the young dancer in this volume became one of Diaghilev's choreographers, sealing her distinguished reputation with *Les Noces* in 1923 and *Les Biches* in 1924.

A loving sister and a major artist with a firm aesthetic viewpoint, Bronislava Nijinska might be expected to approach her subject with no more objectivity than Nijinsky's other biographers. His contemporaries and colleagues, with few exceptions, have left self-servingly inaccurate accounts, colored by the vested interests of their own reputations. Others who did not know him—recent historians, chiefly—have been prone to concern themselves with illustrating artistic or psychological theses.

Nijinska's own account is certainly subjective. Its very value rests precisely upon its highly personal nature. No secondhand narrative could match the intimacy of her detailed eyewitness recollections. In human terms, this is a profoundly moving book. Its emotional range has the breadth of a Russian novel.

The enormous amount of information that Nijinska conveys at so many levels also turns this book into a prime historical source. One of its important disclosures is embodied in the actual descriptions of Nijinsky's dancing. For the first time, this technical information has survived into print. Nijinska names not only the steps in his performances but also describes how they were executed. Coached and taught by her brother in private classes, Nijinska is uniquely qualified to analyze the physical basis of his extraordinary technique. Those who ascribe to mere legend the report that Nijinsky could perform the rare virtuoso feat of *entrechat-dix* need only refer to the many occasions when Nijinska saw him execute these multiple leg beats in the studio.

Nijinska is capable of explaining the previously unexplainable—the special training and anatomical features that enabled her brother to acquire his exceptional jump. She is always concerned, however, with communicating the artistic intent and imagery of her brother's dancing.

If there is an overriding theme in this book, it is Nijinska's insistence upon the aesthetic creed of the Nijinskys—namely, that artistry and creativity must not be sacrificed to technique.

This was the emblem as well of the great artistic enterprise known as Diaghilev's Ballets Russes. Yet an important leitmotiv of Nijinska's story is her belief that she and Vaslav instinctively sought an artistic direction before either ever encountered Diaghilev.

This complex assertion rests upon four major aspects of these memoirs. The first is the picture of Vaslav Nijinsky himself. The second is Nijinska's portrait of Diaghilev, involving eyewitness accounts that flesh out this other legendary figure's character. Another major element of this story is the insider's view of a crucial period in the history of ballet—the transition from the nineteenth-century academicism of Marius Petipa to the expressiveness of Mikhail Fokine and the modernism of Nijinsky's choreography. Although this ground has been well trod, Nijinska freshly records the atmosphere in the Imperial Theatres and in the Ballets Russes, directing attention to the personalities and ballets supplying that atmosphere. Finally, these are the memoirs of Bronislava Nijinska, documenting her own growth as an artist, and replete with personal revelations.

There are also two special aspects to this volume that reach beyond its focus on the Nijinsky family. The first is contained in new information about ballet in provincial pre-Revolutionary Russia, and the second is its picture of life in Russia at the turn of the century.

In chronicling her parents' careers as itinerant dancers in the Russian Empire, Nijinska fills an important gap in ballet history unfamiliar to the West. English-language biographies of Italian dancers such as Virginia Zucchi and Enrico Cecchetti, who appeared in Russia's private theatres, have already demonstrated that a degree of ballet activity existed outside the Imperial Theatres. Yet the common image of nineteenth-century Russian ballet is that of the Imperial Ballet, restricted to two official government ballet academies attached to two ranking companies—the Maryinsky in St. Petersburg and the Bolshoi in Moscow—and all supported by the Imperial household. The idea that Russian ballet was an aristocratic entertainment stems from this administrative network. But it does not take into account the kinds of ballet to which Russians of other classes were exposed.

In vivid descriptions of the ballets and ballet pantomimes choreographed and performed by her parents, Nijinska reveals the wide-ranging state of the art form within Russia. It was common to find ballet in the municipal opera houses of major provincial cities such as Kiev and Odessa; in resort towns with their summer theatres; and even, as her father's career amply demonstrated, in the circuses.

It is doubtful that the level of dancing and choreography in these private companies met the highest standards of the Imperial Theatres, yet such conclusions must be tempered by Nijinska's own esteem for these performances. As she points out, such touring companies were often headed by the same Italian ballerinas who appeared at the Imperial Theatres. Her mother had danced in a troupe with Carlotta Brianza, the first Aurora in *The Sleeping Beauty*, and had absorbed a degree of Italian training. Nijinska's appraisal of her father—from the viewpoint of adoring daughter but also, perhaps, of an artist—ranks him as a great character dancer who chose not to enter the Imperial Theatres. It should also be remembered that the Warsaw Great (Wielki) Theatre, which supplied these private touring companies with their *corps de ballet*, would later provide Diaghilev with many of his own dancers.

The repertory on this touring circuit was on a popular level, but the classics could filter down in different versions. This was the period when the Imperial Ballet was going into decline. Nijinska's enthusiasm for her father's choreography is thus understandable beyond the context of filial attachment. Thomas Nijinsky knew how to hold an audience. His ballets were not classical, but the variety of idioms he incorporated into his presentations left its imprint upon his children.

Indeed, another significant discovery of this book is its proof of the amazing extent to which Bronislava and Vaslav Nijinsky were exposed at a young age to nonclassical forms of dance. It is not so surprising that they learned Ukrainian and Polish dances, social dances, and a variety of character dances from their parents. But an unexpected encounter is their exposure to a black American tap-dancing team named Jackson and Johnson, complete with cane and tails, in the same theatre in which their father worked. And circus life, as Nijinska notes, provided a valuable store of idiosyncratic movement that she could utilize creatively much later in her ballets for Diaghilev.

It would be wrong, then, to think of the sheltered life of the Maryinsky School as the only dance world the Nijinsky children had experienced. Unlike their classmates, they had seen more open horizons. In view of the modernist choreographers they became—in view of their break with academic forms—we can now take into account their early awareness of a multitude of movement possibilities.

Although of Polish descent, Nijinska writes as a Russian. She has a typical love for the Russian countryside, whose beauty she captures in vivid nature descriptions. St. Petersburg is her beloved city, and her picture of everyday urban existence is a kaleidoscope of carefully observed detail. Her view of Russian life is panoramic: the colorfulness of a summer spent next door to gypsies and Cossacks is juxtaposed with the splendor of a princely mansion belonging to Vaslav's benefactor.

Although these memoirs constitute the first part of Nijinska's autobiography, they serve largely as a new biography of Vaslav Nijinsky. The usual depiction of a slow-witted youth, silent or sullen, molded artistically by Diaghilev, is at odds with Bronislava's portrait. The Vaslav in this book is a child filled with excess energy, deeply marked—like his sister—by the emotional trauma of his parents' separation and, later, by his elder brother's mental illness.

Vaslav's development cannot be separated from the family background here provided for the first time in anything close to such depth. Nor should one overlook the insights Nijinska offers into her brother's personality. His early aloofness in the Maryinsky, she asserts, was actually an attempt to avoid putting on airs. He is shown to have grown up well-read and with a perfect ear for music. There is no doubt in Bronislava's view that he was as creatively inclined in his dancing as in his choreography. His reinterpretation of the Blue Bird *pas de deux*, involving his adoption of a new costume, showed his independence even within the fossilized traditions of the Imperial Ballet.

Among the most valuable pages in this volume are those concerned with Nijinsky's work on his first three ballets, *L'Après-Midi d'un Faune*, *Jeux*, and *Le Sacre du Printemps*. It is Nijinska's brilliant insight that this was the first time a choreographer had demanded total exactitude from his dancers, requiring that every part of the body be aligned to gain maximum expressiveness. Her image here is of a sophisticated creative artist, knowing exactly what he wished to accomplish.

Nijinska presents new versions of certain episodes crucial to Nijinsky's life. Her account of his dismissal from the Imperial Theatres, with its implication that Mathilda Kshessinska's entourage was involved, differs from earlier narratives. The disclosure that Nijinsky was classified as a deserter because he could not gain exemption from military service explains why he could not return to Russia. Of further illumination is Diaghilev's inactivity on her brother's behalf on this issue.

While Nijinska was not a member of Diaghilev's inner circle, her personal account contributes new and valid information, particularly with respect to the artistic impetus of the Ballets Russes' first years, and its director's later treatment of her brother. In this regard, Diaghilev's avant-garde reputation emerges as less adventuresome than usual. This is the Diaghilev uneasy about Nijinsky's choreographic innovations and all too ready to listen to advice that Nijinsky's ballets are bad box office and should be withdrawn.

Yet in her comparison of the lack of artistic ambience in the Imperial Theatres and the stimulation of the Ballets Russes, Nijinska recognizes her generation's debt to Diaghilev. These are pages replete with information about the Petipa ballets and the genesis of works that became part of the Diaghilev repertory. It was Bronislava, for example, who suggested to Fokine that the Street Dancer's solo in *Petrouchka* be a parody of Kshessinska.

Among the book's personal revelations, Nijinska's relationship with Feodor Chaliapin emerges as a motif to her development as an artist during the first years of the Ballets Russes. The full autobiographical story of her own career, however, is contained in another set of her memoirs, continuing from the 1914 close of this book.

Despite her attraction to Diaghilev's modernism, Nijinska's choreography proved her eventually to be a pioneer of twentieth-century neoclassicism. Many of her theatrical concepts were taken over by others. She did the original ballet versions of Ravel's *Bolero* and *La Valse*, also Stravinsky's *Le Baiser de la Fée*, and she danced the role of the Faune in her brother's ballet after the period described here. In 1934, she portrayed Hamlet in her own ballet of the same name.

After leaving Diaghilev, she worked in a variety of ballet companies in South America, Europe and the United States. She headed her own company, the Théâtre de la Danse, in Paris in 1932–34 but she did not, in the end, attach herself to a permanent institution whose artistic profile would be identified with her own. Nonetheless, if the public could not always be sure to find her ballets in the same place, her influence was keenly felt by the key figures of contemporary ballet. Among them was Frederick Ashton, who was a young dancer in Ida Rubinstein's company in 1928 when Nijinska was its choreographer. Today, as one great neoclassical choreographer paying tribute to another, he reaffirms the unwavering opinion of Nijinska he has held since that initial encounter: "She was a genius, one of the very few."

Editors' Foreword

BRONISLAVA NIJINSKA, sister of the legendary Vaslav Nijinsky, began to plan these memoirs in the 1920s. Herself a dancer and choreographer, she felt it would be important for the history of dance to write her own recollections of her brother and his artistic accomplishments.

Only a dozen years earlier, as a young dancer with the Ballets Russes in Paris in 1909, Nijinska had witnessed her brother's overnight rise to fame. But, in 1921, on rejoining the Ballets Russes de Serge de Diaghilev, she had been amazed to realize how little the dancers in the company had assimilated from their work with Nijinsky. This became all the more evident to her when she was asked by Diaghilev to revive her brother's first ballet, *L'Après-Midi d'un Faune*. As she rehearsed with Diaghilev's dancers she was distressed to see how little they had retained of her brother's first choreographic creation. This was especially painful to her as she feared his mental illness would keep Nijinsky from resuming his artistic career. During the 1920s, not only had the dancers apparently erased Nijinsky's ideas from their work, there was also little mention of him in ballet literature. By the early 1930s Nijinsky's fame had faded to a point where it appeared that even his reputation as a performer was destined for oblivion.

At the end of 1934, Nijinska was invited to Hollywood to mount the ballet sequences for Max Reinhardt's *A Midsummer Night's Dream*. Her second visit to the United States was in 1936 when she came to New York to present a revival of her ballet *Les Noces* at the Metropolitan Opera House. She was astonished on both occasions by the interest in Nijinsky shown by the American press.

Repeatedly reporters asked her questions about her brother. They were, however, either trivial questions—"How many lumps of sugar did he like in his coffee?"—or they were concerned with her brother's personal life and mental illness. Hardly any were about Nijinsky the artist, or Nijinsky the choreographer. Reporters also wanted to know her reaction to the recent publications: *Nijinsky* by his wife, Romola Nijinsky, and *Tragedy of Nijinsky* by Anatole Bourman.

Her daughter, Irina Nijinska, acting as her interpreter in 1936 in New York, well remembers Nijinska's answers: "The books are filled with half-truths and outright fantasies not only about my brother, but also about my mother and father." Nijinska further declared that she was working on her own book and, as Vaslav Nijinsky's sister and fellow artist, would present a true description of his early life and his artistic creativity.

Already Nijinska had drawn up a draft summary, under topic or chapter headings, of materials covered in her diaries and notebooks. As well as keeping a personal diary since her schooldays, 1900–08, she had also, since becoming an Artist of the Imperial Theatres, been jotting down her impressions and opinions of different ballets, choreographers, and dancers in a set of notebooks; the habit had probably grown out of a custom in the Imperial School whereby each student was given a notebook in which to record the details of each of their own performances in the Imperial Theatres.

Throughout her career as dancer, choreographer, and teacher, Nijinska continued to make entries in her personal diary and to write commentaries in her notebooks. Her career as a choreographer spanned five decades, and saw the creation of more than seventy ballets, including many contributions to operas. In moments snatched from this busy artistic life she also found time to compose fuller recollections about Vaslav and their life and work together, recollections written, according to the summary topic headings she had already drafted, in what she called her "cahiers" —exercise books bought in whichever city her engagements took her.

By the early sixties she was planning to retire from most of her choreographic engagements. She had already moved into a new home in Pacific Palisades, built to accommodate her library and collection of programs and theatrical memorabilia, which had been stored in Paris since the beginning of the war. Surrounded by the materials she deemed necessary for the writing of her memoirs, she was at last able to concentrate on that task. She began to write a preliminary draft of her first manuscript, a narrative account covering her childhood years in the Imperial School and her artistic life with her brother up to 1914. At the same time she drafted the skeleton of another manuscript concerning her own choreographic career following World War I.

The "cahiers," written since the mid-twenties, were the primary source from which she composed that first manuscript, and they also contributed to her draft of the second. They were augmented by material from both her diaries and her notebooks, as well as her letters. The earlier manuscript, typed by herself on a portable Russian typewriter, was almost completed by the mid-sixties.

However, her writing was interrupted in 1964 when Nijinska was invited by Frederick Ashton to mount her ballet *Les Biches* for the Royal Ballet, at Covent Garden; *Les Biches* (music by Poulenc), a witty satire and precursor of neoclassical ballet, had been created in 1924. Then, in 1966, she was invited to the Royal Ballet to mount her ballet *Les Noces;* first created in 1923, *Les Noces* (music by Stravinsky) is today considered one of the most important dance works of our century.

The writing of her book was further delayed in 1967 when she suffered a stroke and was temporarily paralyzed on her left side. Feeling that her health was failing, she wrote a detailed synopsis of the work remaining. She discussed this synopsis with her daughter, pointing out those items she wanted to include in the first book of her memoirs, essentially about Vaslav, and those she wanted to retain for her memoirs about her career as a choreographer.

Following the death in 1968 of Bronislava's second husband, Nicholas Singaevsky, who was also her manager, Irina Nijinska became her mother's constant companion and assistant. As a dancer herself, she was already familiar with more than twenty of Nijinska's ballets and had taught in the Nijinska Studio in Hollywood. She now accompanied her mother on all her engagements both in the United States and abroad.

Interest in Nijinska's choreography led to several engagements for 1969 and 1970, the last being in Venice, at the Teatro Fenice, where she celebrated her eightieth birthday onstage, while conducting rehearsals of *Les Noces*. Before leaving the city she took a gondola with Irina to visit the tomb of Sergei Diaghilev. Undeterred by the icy winter weather, she wished to pay homage to the memory of Diaghilev and to offer thanks for the opportunity he had given her almost fifty years earlier to create *Les Noces* with Stravinsky. "At first," she reminisced to Irina, "Stravinsky was confused and disturbed. But Diaghilev had confidence in me. 'Let her finish it,' he said. 'Maybe we will be understood twenty years from now.' "

In February 1971, on returning home to Pacific Palisades, she postponed several other engagements abroad to work uninterruptedly on her memoirs. Her Russian manuscript, about 180,000 words, was completed towards the end of that year. She was preparing to leave for Europe, where she had accepted engagements in Düsseldorf, Vienna, and Paris, when she died of a heart attack on February 21, 1972.

IRINA NIJINSKA, as her mother's literary executor, had been entrusted with the responsibility of rendering the Russian manuscripts into English. When Nijinska, in the last years of her life, had talked with her daughter about her writings, she had explained that any extra information necessary would be found in her library. This was no idle boast. Despite the loss of precious items during the upheavals of two world wars, Nijinska had collected (and catalogued) a rare and comprehensive library of more than 2,500 volumes in English, French, Italian, Russian, Polish, Ukrainian, and other languages. Not only was it concerned with dance and dance history but, as she would often point out, it was a *choreographer's* library, with works on such subjects as anatomy, perspective, sculpture, painting, music, history, and the literature of many cultures. She had already designated those books containing background materials pertinent to her manuscripts, sometimes even placing bookmarks in specific pages.

Nijinska had a flair for discovering rare books, engravings, and lithographs, finding many of her treasures in Paris in the stalls of the *bouquinistes* along the Seine. Her daughter remembers one time in Edinburgh, for an engagement with the Markova-Dolin Company, when during a ride through the city Nijinska unexpectedly stopped their tram in a little side street and proceeded to discover, in a secondhand book shop, first-edition copies of Dickens's *Bleak House* and *Nicholas Nickleby*.

It was Nijinska's range of interests that brought the present editors together—a chance meeting through an exhibition of antique Japanese prints that included some that Bronislava Nijinska had bought as a young dancer in London in 1911.

Jean Rawlinson, a writer then engaged in research for a historical novel set in Tsarist and Revolutionary Russia, was interested in the writings of Nijinska for the light they could shed on that period, but soon became fascinated by the writings for themselves and their revelation of Nijinska's life and choreography. Irina had just returned from Düsseldorf where, with the cooperation of the Royal Ballet, she had fulfilled Nijinska's engagement to mount *Les Biches*, in May 1972. Before leaving Germany, she had agreed to act as artistic advisor to the Stuttgart Ballet for their planned production of *Les Noces*, working with Robert Mead, formerly of the Royal Ballet. She wanted to have for the Stuttgart dancers copies of a chapter written by Nijinska in the later memoirs concerning the creation of *Les Noces* in 1923, and Jean agreed to prepare an English version.

Initially, both editors also being fluent in French, a word-for-word translation was made in a combination of English and French. This initial translation was then reviewed and from it an English first draft composed, then refined through further drafts until both editors were satisfied. By the time of the performance in Stuttgart the article had not only been distributed to the company but also had been accepted for publication by *Dance Magazine*, where it appeared in December 1974.

The working pattern for that article was to lay the foundation of the later and larger task, rendering into English the whole of Nijinska's memoirs.

The general procedure was for Irina to be responsible for the accuracy of the initial literal translation and, where necessary, to compare the manuscript with Nijinska's handwritten papers and "cahiers," as well as with original Russian documents. Jean was then entrusted with the task of rendering this literal translation into idiomatic English. The first material to be translated was the detailed working synopsis, prepared by Nijinska in 1968, so that Jean as well as Irina would be aware of the total scope of the manuscript. This synopsis was also a worksheet against which sections of the literal translation were checked before being drafted into an idiomatic and fluent version.

Comparing manuscript with synopsis proved fruitful. For one example, in the synopsis the name Sarah Bernhardt was mentioned for the year 1908 but no details were found in the manuscript. The reference in the synopsis indicated that Nijinska had intended to include something, but what? According to the date she was still a resident student of the Imperial Theatrical School. Had she actually seen Bernhardt or merely heard about her in the School? After first ascertaining that Sarah Bernhardt did indeed have an engagement in St. Petersburg in 1908, a thorough search of the "cahiers" revealed a few lines giving details of the performance to which Bronislava went with her brother Vaslav. It was then possible to include this paragraph in the text as designated by Nijinska.

The manuscript included some sections under separate headings— "Mother," "Father," "Our Parents," "Stanislav," "Nijinsky's Military Service." Wherever the order of these sections in the manuscript seemed to break the main narrative flow, we used the synopsis as our guideline to move the appropriate descriptions to their chronological positions.

One would expect to encounter problems in such transpositions in a manuscript prepared over so many years and covering such a varied extent of biographical and historical material; nevertheless, though the "cahiers" were written at different times and away from home—that is, away from Nijinska's library and source materials—there was a remarkable consistency not only of style but also in the use of particular words and phrases, so that only minor rearrangements of the manuscript were necessary.

The descriptions of individual dances were written by Nijinska so that the reader unfamiliar with ballet terms would be able to follow the sequences and envision the dance movements. At the same time, in her descriptions of classical ballet steps and dance sequences, she used accepted French terminology as found in *Fundamentals of the Classic Dance*, by Agrippina Vaganova, translated by Anatole Chujoy, New York, 1947.

Working together on the preparation of Nijinska's manuscript, the editors found that their areas of responsibility continually overlapped. Their real collaboration extended into an exchange of ideas and interpretations in the search for fluency and accuracy, and the deeper insight gained thereby into Nijinska's own ideas and nuances of expression.

Arnold Haskell, the English ballet critic, once wrote of Nijinska that "her particular trait is an artistic integrity that makes all compromise loathsome and impossible." This integrity was both an inspiration and a challenge in the translation and editing of these memoirs of a great creative artist.

> *Irina Nijinska and Jean Rawlinson*
> Pacific Palisades, California
> August 1980

Acknowledgments

THE EDITORS are pleased to express their thanks to Anna Kisselgoff, Dance Critic of *The New York Times*, for the comprehensive introduction and informative footnotes she has contributed to this book. We are grateful, too, for the time she has spared from her busy schedule in order to read the advance copies of our manuscript and provide consultations with the publisher, Holt, Rinehart and Winston, in New York.

We are also most appreciative of the ongoing patient and sympathetic support given us during the preparation of this manuscript by Donald Hutter, Executive Editor of Holt, Rinehart and Winston, whose pertinent comments and questions have been most helpful in clarifying our rendering of Nijinska's writings.

—

WITH REGARD to this book's illustrations, we are particularly grateful to Mrs. Parmenia Ekstrom through whose good offices several photographs, including the early costume designs sketched by Nicholas Roerich for *Le Sacre du Printemps*, were made available from the collection of the Stravinsky Diaghilev Foundation.

Thanks must also go to The New York Public Library at Lincoln Center for permission to use some of their collection of photographs, including those from the collection of Boris Kochno.

We are also grateful to Roland John Wiley for permission to reproduce the portrait of Col. V. A. Telyakovsky, from his personal collection.

The sources of these illustrations are all acknowledged in the captions.

All the other illustrations, 117 in number, have been selected from the Nijinska Archives, and the special task of photographing them from diverse materials—including diminutive and faded old photographic prints, various precious artworks, and fragile old documents—was kindly performed by Irina's husband, Gibbs Raetz.

Bronislava Nijinska:
Early Memoirs

Preface

WHENEVER PEOPLE talk to me about my brother Vaslav Nijinsky, so many questions are raised. Very often I am asked, "How did he become a dancer?" . . . or, "How and when did he know that he must dance?"

In these, my early memoirs, I want to describe, year by year, from childhood on, how we lived within our family . . . and what I knew and shared closely with Vaslav as a sister and as a friend.

Our parents were ballet artists, dancers. We were born artists of the dance. We accepted without question our birthright from our parents —our dancing bodies. The theatre and the dance were a natural way of life for us from birth. It was as if, in the theatre, we were in our natural element, where everything responded in our souls.

In recounting here the story of our childhood and of the years when I danced with Nijinsky as a ballet artist and performed the choreography of his own ballets, I want to re-create for the reader my image of Nijinsky as a person and as an artist. . . .

1 Mother and Father

OUR MOTHER, Eleonora Nicolaevna Bereda, was born in Warsaw on December 15, 1856.* She was only seven when she and her two sisters and two brothers became orphans. The family was living at the time in a modest apartment, deep in a courtyard of one of the large houses in Warsaw. The parents did not leave anything to their children, not even a close relative.

Her father, Nicolas Bereda, was a skilled cabinetmaker, but he was also a compulsive gambler, which brought great sorrow to his young wife and their children. He continually lost large sums of money in card games and became more and more despondent because he could no longer provide adequately for his family. Then, one day, he suffered a heart attack and died.

In the weeks following the death of her husband, the grieving widow did not leave her room and refused to eat. One morning the children were unable to wake her. They called the doctor and were told that their mother was dead. For the three days until the funeral the children could not believe that she was dead. As their mother lay among the flowers, illumined by the glow of candles so that her fair complexion seemed to retain its natural color, she appeared to be asleep. In secret from each other, the children stuck pins into her and talked to her in the hope of bringing her back to consciousness.

When I asked my mother, "How did you manage to live alone without your mother and father?" she told me, "At first the godmother of my

*This is the date according to the Julian (Old Style) Calendar officially used in Russia until 1923. The date according to the Gregorian (New Style) Calendar of general Western usage would be twelve days later in the nineteenth century and thirteen days later in the twentieth century. All biographically important and cross-cultural dates that follow will be expressed both ways (New Style second, in brackets). Single dates for events occurring in Russia and Poland are Old Style. (IN/JR)

sister Theodosia helped us. She was quite well-to-do. She even took all of us to live in her house . . . but soon, I don't know what happened, my brothers quarreled violently with her. Refusing her charity, they made us leave her house. And so we returned to our own apartment where we lived on our own, with my elder brothers Adam, seventeen, and Henryk, fifteen, taking care of us. I was the youngest in this family of orphans. Theodosia was eleven and my other sister, Stephanie Marie, was nine.

"My brothers were still students and received government scholarships to enable them to continue in school. The regulations stipulated that out of the scholarship money they had to provide themselves with school uniforms, keep themselves decently dressed, and buy their own school textbooks. Because they were among the best students in the school they were asked to give private tutoring lessons on the side, and this enabled them to earn money for the upkeep of the family and to pay for the apartment. They were only able to spare five kopeks a day for their three sisters.

"Theodosia, we called her Thetya, took care of the whole family. Thetya was pretty, kind, and wise. She kept everything clean and mended, made dresses and hats. She was extremely thrifty and even managed to buy shoes for the girls from the household allowance. We called her 'little Mama.' "

Stephanie, without telling her brothers, entered the Theatrical Ballet School at the Wielki Theatre in Warsaw.* A little later, Liota, as Eleonora was called in the family, was also accepted by the School. But as general subjects were not taught there, the sisters continued to attend public school each morning.

"In the ballet school we not only studied dancing but also appeared in the ballets and operas."

In the last year of her life when she was seventy-five years old, my mother remembered those performances with pride. "We were paid a *zlotouvke* [fifteen kopeks, called a *zolotoy* in Russian] for each performance. So Stephanie and I were soon contributing something to the household. Sometimes, I was able, myself, to collect six zlotouvke a month."

Somehow the brothers found out their sisters were going to ballet school—"a shameful thing for a decent family." They followed Stepha and Liota one day and caught them at the stage door. They made them come back home, and there a real storm broke out.

*This Theatre was officially ranked as a State Theatre and not, as according to Enrico Cecchetti, an Imperial Theatre. Its ballet school, where he taught, dates from 1785 and was reestablished in 1818. (AK)

"You are disgracing us before the entire school and in the eyes of the households where we teach . . . we are decent boys . . . and now suddenly our sisters are discovered to be dancers . . . we shall lose our private students . . ."

The brothers forbade them ever to go back to the ballet school. They were very strict with them, checking their homework and giving them extra work to keep them at home.

It was almost a year before both sisters, in secret, managed to go back to the ballet school. Maybe the brothers decided to turn a blind eye because they were struggling to create their own lives and every zlotouvke helped.

By the time she was thirteen, Stepha was already outstanding in classical ballet technique, even more so in character dances. She had a good stature and was the beauty of the family. Young as she was, she was engaged as a member of the *corps de ballet* of the Wielki Theatre at a salary of eight rubles a month. The ballet company was made up of eighty artists in addition to the students who also took part in the operas and ballets.

The ballet in Warsaw by the middle of the nineteenth century was especially strong and flourishing. The repertoire in the Wielki Theatre was in many ways similar to that of the St. Petersburg Imperial Theatres. Many choreographers from Paris, Vienna, and Milan staged their ballets in Warsaw before they were seen in St. Petersburg. Carlo Blasis had spent a year in Warsaw where he choreographed his ballets *Venus* and *Faust*. Marie Taglioni, during her engagements in Russia, appeared for guest performances in Warsaw, in 1837 and in 1838 and then in 1841. Her father Filippo Taglioni was the ballet master at the Wielki Theatre for five years, 1841–46, during which time she danced *La Sylphide*, *La Fille du Danube*, and other ballets mounted by him. In the 1850s, Carlotta Grisi danced *Giselle*, *La Esmeralda*, and *Paquita*.

The heritage of the Wielki Theatre was formed by the contributions of these world-famous dancers and choreographers, as well as by the works of choreographers Jules Perrot and Arthur Saint-Léon. This heritage surrounded the students of the school—among them my aunt, my mother, and later my father—through its excellent teachers and choreographers.

Many of the ballet masters, soloists, and *corps de ballet* in private and provincial opera theatres in Russia were drawn from artists trained in the Warsaw Wielki Theatre.

In the summer of 1868, the year after Stepha joined the *corps de ballet*, Kviatovsky, a Polish ballet master, came to Warsaw to recruit dancers for a ballet troupe for the Russian Opera Season organized by the Ferdinand

Berger Enterprise at the newly opened City Opera Theatre in Kiev.* He talked mainly with the younger artists, as the established artists in the Wielki Theatre were not tempted by the higher salaries in the provincial theatres in Russia. They preferred to remain as artists of the Warsaw Government Theatre with a secure pension, living at home with their families and making extra money by giving private lessons or by dancing occasionally in the cities around Warsaw. After all, they reasoned, in a private enterprise in Russia there was always the risk of being "left without a crumb of bread."

And so Stephanie, though only fourteen, signed a contract with Kviatovsky to dance with the Berger Enterprise as a first soloist. She also asked that her sister Eleonora be accepted as a member of the company as of December, when she would be twelve, and that in the meanwhile she be considered part of the company and that her fare to Kiev be paid.

Even though at this time Poland was part of Russia, many Poles considered going there to be like going to a foreign land. But the sisters were not afraid. They intended to go together, all three of them, and were convinced that no matter what might happen, nothing could be worse than their life in Warsaw. Besides, the salary that Stepha would be getting, eighty rubles a month, seemed like a fortune, even for three of them. They left without telling their brothers. Only after they reached Kiev did they write to disclose their whereabouts and their good fortune.

Upon their arrival the sisters decided they did not have "an artistic appearance." Their attire was sadly inadequate considering Stepha's position in the company. If she and Eleonora were to present themselves to the director, dressed as they were, their whole future careers in the theatre could be jeopardized. Thetya immediately ran to Kviatovsky to receive the promised advance on Stepha's salary. With this money the sisters went shopping . . . knowing hardly a word of Russian.

When they returned with all their purchases they set to work for the rest of the day. Thetya sent her two younger sisters to bed early that

*The first City Opera Theatre in Kiev was opened in 1803. A new larger theatre was opened in 1856 and until 1863 it was leased by Russian, Ukrainian, or Polish theatrical enterprises. Then, for three years, the Theatre was rented to an Italian opera company. The first permanent private Russian Opera Theatre began in 1867, and it continued most notably under the famous Josef Yakovlevitch Setov, promoter and stage manager of the Russian Opera-Ballet Season from 1874 to 1883, and again from 1892 to 1893. In 1896 the Theatre burned down; it was rebuilt in 1901.

The Kiev Theatre was important in the lives of the Nijinsky family. Eleonora Bereda danced there in her first engagement in Russia in 1868. Thomas and Eleonora Nijinsky worked there for several seasons, including the twenty-fifth anniversary season of 1892 under Setov. And Bronislava Nijinska during the years 1915–21 was herself dancing on the stage of the rebuilt Theatre. (IN/JR)

evening so that they would get a good night's rest—she especially wanted Stepha to look fresh next morning for her first day's work in the theatre—and then stayed up all night to finish Stepha's dress, saying "After all, she can't go to the theatre dressed like a schoolgirl. She is a *first* soloist."

Mother never forgot that next happy day. "The first time we all three went from the house to the theatre we were dressed like dolls. It seemed to us that nothing more beautiful could have been created than our dresses. Indeed there was not one person in the street who did not turn and look at us. How could they help but notice us with our happy young faces? Picture for yourself how proudly we walked down that street in an unknown city, taking our first steps to the theatre, to our independence, with all the excitement, joy, and anticipation of our new artistic life."

Stephanie and Eleonora were the youngest girls in the ballet troupe that season. They spoke only Polish. The other artists, mostly Russian, welcomed them with open hearts, these young Polish girls who were living on their own with their elder sister, herself only sixteen. Many sincerely tried to help them in a new theatre, in a foreign land, but a few of these new friends amused themselves by teaching the young sisters vulgar phrases in Russian. The poor little ones found themselves in many embarrassing situations until they caught onto the mean pranks some of the artists were playing.

The season in Kiev, as was usual in Russia,* opened with Glinka's opera, *A Life for the Tsar*. In the Polish act, Stephanie and the ballet master Kviatovsky danced as the first couple for the *mazurka*. Eleonora also took part in the performance and was quickly noticed. She was blonde and had a small head with fine features and a long neck. Her feet were tiny, and she was so slender and graceful that her friends in the ballet troupe nicknamed her "Gazelle." She was very talented and was soon dancing in the *corps de ballet*. After her twelfth birthday she became a member of the company, receiving at first a salary of thirty-five rubles; for the second season she signed a contract for sixty rubles.

It was not hard for talented young dancers like Stephanie and Eleonora Bereda to find work in the Russian theatres. One simply had to choose the best terms and find reliable employers and directors. Life for such young provincial artists was being on the move from one season to another, like migrating birds. Friends were lost, new friends were made, there was no time for deep attachments, always moving from city to city—Kiev . . .

*The only exception during this period was in the Revolutionary year of 1905, when the Kiev season opened with *Eugene Onegin* rather than the usual tribute to the Tsar. (AK)

7

Tiflis . . . Odessa . . . Kharkov. Fortunately the three sisters were bound together by their great love, friendship, and devotion to each other. They had a motto for their love and family devotion: "One for another through fire and water . . ." Mama passed this motto on to her children as a basic principle for their lives.

In 1874 Stephanie and Eleonora were again working with the City Opera Theatre in Kiev where the Russian Opera Seasons were now under the direction and management of Josef Yakovlevitch Setov.*

When Eleonora was nineteen, in 1876, she became engaged to a Russian captain of an artillery regiment. She believed so much in her happiness—that she had met her "destiny"—she decided to leave the stage forever.

The wedding was to take place in the summer, when the sisters returned to Warsaw, where only their eldest brother Adam was living, their second brother Henryk having died of pneumonia the previous year. A few days before the wedding the engaged couple were driving through the city when the fiancé pointed out one of Warsaw's Catholic churches with traces of bullets on its walls, saying, "There at that wall more than one Pole was shot in '63–'64." Perhaps forgetting that his bride-to-be was Polish, he went on to describe how he himself, as a young officer, had taken part in the repression of the Polish Insurrection. Eleonora did not say anything, but she realized now that she could not marry a Russian officer. The next day she sent her engagement ring back to her fiancé and left Warsaw.

They did not meet again until many years later, after Mother was married, even though he searched for her in theatres throughout Russia. As she told us this story Mother showed us his photograph: a full-length portrait of an officer with a long saber at his side, his face kind and serious. But we children never regretted not being born into a military family. We were proud that we were born artists.

Eleonora rejoined the ballet troupe working in Setov's Russian Opera Enterprise, which besides the seasons in Kiev also had engagements in St. Petersburg, Moscow, Odessa, and other cities in Russia. The life of the

---

*Josef Yakovlevitch Setov (real name Setgofer)—1826–1894—was of Hungarian descent. After studying voice in both Paris and Milan, he was an opera singer from 1855 to 1868 with the Imperial Theatres in St. Petersburg and in Moscow. From 1868 to 1872 he staged operas at the Maryinsky Theatre in St. Petersburg. In 1874 he organized his own private Opera Enterprise and worked continuously there until his death. Setov's Opera Enterprise had regular engagements in the Kiev Opera Theatre from 1874 to 1883, and Setov is sometimes described as the Stage Manager of the Kiev State Theatre. Setov's Opera Enterprise also arranged performances and/or seasons in Moscow and Odessa and in 1886 and 1887 in the Summer Theatres in St. Petersburg. (IN/JR)

three sisters continued as before, until Eleonora met a young Polish dancer . . . Thomas Nijinsky.

———

THOMAS LAVRENTIEVITCH NIJINSKY was born in Warsaw on March 7 [N.S. 19], 1862. Like our mother, though at a later time, he was a pupil at the Ballet School of the Warsaw Wielki Theatre. When he began going to preparatory school in 1870 he discovered that some of his young friends were also studying dancing at the Wielki Theatre School. Thomas would run off with them and join them at the dance class during free periods from the preparatory school. Thus Father was only eight when he chose his lifelong artistic path, and he did so quite on his own, for his family did not have anything to do with the theatre.

Both his grandfather and his father devoted their lives to political activity—the liberation of Poland from Russian rule. Thomas's grandfather had participated in the Insurrection of 1830 and had been deprived of all his rights, small estates, and landed property by the Russian government. Thomas's father, Lavrenty Lavrentievitch Nijinsky, was employed by the railroad and lived with his family in Warsaw. During the Polish Insurrection of 1863 he served with the cavalry, and as an active revolutionary he carried out a number of dangerous assignments. From the Polish Communications Headquarters where he worked, he made his way through Russian troop lines and ambushes with secret papers sewn in the soles of his boots, to establish connections between headquarters and the different insurgent groups. He was wounded but managed to avoid arrest by the Russians.

Father's younger brother, Eugenius, followed in his father's and grandfather's footsteps. He too was an active member of the Polish Revolutionary Party of the Liberation. Thomas, however, although always an ardent patriot, did not take an active part in politics. His whole life was absorbed by the theatre.

In the Wielki Theatre School, Thomas was seen to have talent and was soon promoted to the front of his class. On March 6, 1880, Thierry's ballet *Wesele w Ojcowie* was performed by the students of the Warsaw Ballet. Mateusz Glinski in his monograph *Dance II*, published in Warsaw in 1930, mentions that the name Nijinsky appeared for the first time on a theatre playbill when Thomas Nijinsky danced the role of Stanislav for that performance in 1880.

After his graduation, Thomas was enrolled as a ballet artist in the Wielki Theatre in Warsaw. He was nineteen when the Theatrical Administration agreed to let several dancers, including Thomas, go to Odessa to be part of the ballet troupe for the Opera Season.

Thomas quickly made many friends in the ballet troupe. They called him Foma, the Russian for Thomas. From his new friends he learned how easy it was for a dancer to find employment in Russia. There were many other theatrical enterprises, besides the Opera Theatres, that often needed ballet and character dancers. After the season in Odessa, Foma went to work in Tiflis. He was expected to return to the Wielki Theatre after one year out of Poland, but when he was offered a contract with the Setov Enterprise to perform as a soloist dancer with the Odessa Opera Theatre, he accepted immediately. He realized that in the Wielki Theatre it would be many years before he would be promoted to the rank of *premier danseur* and gain an increase in salary. He journeyed to Warsaw and only stayed long enough to submit his application for a leave of absence. He did not wait for an answer.

He kept the document, dated May 18/30, 1882 [Illustrations 3 and 4], sent him by the Theatrical Administration of the Warsaw Theatres, signed by the Director, a Colonel . . . [illegible]. In it he was not granted a leave of absence but instead was dismissed "with the proviso that henceforth you will not be accepted for employment in the Warsaw Theatres." He used to tell us how happy he felt at this release from the Russian Military Theatrical Administration, which had turned even more oppressive that year since the assassination, in 1881, of Alexander II by the Pole Grinevetski.*

Thomas Nijinsky had another reason for wishing to return immediately to Russia. He had met and fallen in love with Eleonora Bereda, who was also working with the Setov Enterprise in the Odessa Opera Theatre. He dreamed of marrying her and was working hard to secure the position of *premier danseur*. But, within a year, he had to face a great obstacle to both marriage and dancing—military service.

Military service was compulsory in Russia for young men between the ages of twenty-one and twenty-four. For a dancer to be called to military service was a real tragedy. For three crucial years one had to give up one's artistic life and inevitably lose one's dancing technique. To be subjected every day to military drill made the whole body coarse, the muscles lose their elasticity; it spoiled the body for the dance.

Military service had been especially hard for Poles since the Insurrections of 1830 and 1863. They were sent to military units as far as possible

---

*On March 13, 1881, two members of the People's Will movement were involved in the assassination of Tsar Alexander II—Ryssakoff, a Russian, and Grinevetski, a Pole. An explosive device thrown by Ryssakoff exploded near the royal coach, but it was another thrown five minutes later by Grinevetski that killed the Tsar. (IN/JR)

from Poland, even to Siberia, so that a soldier did not get to see his family, or his friends, for the whole three years.

Foma Nijinsky, now twenty-one years old, was going to Warsaw with a heavy heart to answer the call for military service as the eldest son in his family. His whole life was threatened—his theatrical career, his love for Liota. His only hope was to draw a lucky number. Since not all those eligible for military service could be used, exemptions were drawn by lottery. Those called for military service went into both their medical examinations and the drawing of the lots completely naked, leaving their clothes in the dressing room.

Foma was lucky . . . he drew a surplus number . . . he was exempt. He rushed like a madman from the reception hall to the dressing room, his one thought to get out of there before anyone tried to take his lot away from him. He pulled on his trousers and coat, pushed his feet into his shoes without bothering to lace them, forgot his underwear in the military office, rushed out into the street away from the horrible place, and burst like a whirlwind into his parents' apartment. Father always said that never in his whole life did he experience a greater joy.

Now our father could formally propose to Liota. Her sisters had hoped for a well-to-do husband for her but admitted that Foma was exceedingly talented and handsome. Father was broad-shouldered, above average height, and also very strong. His hair was jet black and he had large hazel eyes with long black lashes. Though our mother was attracted by his ardent sincerity and fervor, and was indeed in love with him, it was two years before she consented to marry him. She was unwilling because she was five years his senior. Foma proposed often, and both of them were tormented by her hesitancy to accept his hand in marriage.

One day he said he had come to propose for the last time and drew a revolver out of his pocket. Liota knew that among his colleagues he had a reputation of *narwany* [a Polish expression suggesting a man of strong emotions and impulsive actions]. So fearing what he might do, Liota accepted.

They were married in May 1884, in Baku in the Caucasus. Eleonora was then twenty-seven years old and Foma was twenty-two. An enterprising young man, energetic, intelligent, and full of life, he was working not only as a *premier danseur* but also as a ballet master* in the

---

*The ballet master at this time was an important figure in theatrical enterprises. He was responsible for the administration and management of the troupe of dancers, whom he hired. He then looked for engagements in different theatrical productions—drama, opera, ballet, circuses, summer theatres—and provided the needed ballet performances in operas or *divertissements* in the intermission between drama performances; sometimes he mounted short

Setov Opera Enterprise, and Eleonora was a great help to him in his theatrical work. My parents' first years of married life passed in great happiness, and their eldest child, Stanislav Fomitch (Stassik), was born on December 17 [N.S. 29], 1886, in Tiflis.*

Mother and Father were again working in the Caucasus, touring from town to town. As they drove through the mountains, the coachdrivers, afraid of being ambushed by brigands, would drive their horses at full speed, never slowing down as they approached the narrow, twisting corners. Just before Stassik's birth, Mother became terrified during a particularly dangerous drive when the coach lurched from side to side and the wheels seemed to hang over the edge of the road above the steep abysses. She was afraid that the shaking of the coach might harm her unborn child. The birth was indeed difficult, but the baby was healthy and strong. When the season ended, the parents immediately took their first child to Warsaw to be baptized.

Their second child, Vaslav Fomitch (Vatsa), was born two years later in Kiev on the night of February 27–28 [N.S. March 12], 1889. Mother often told us he was "born in the shirt [a Russian expression for "born in the caul," and an omen predicting a happy life for a child]."

Vatsa was about fifteen months old when Eleonora realized she was again carrying a child. She was distressed—a third baby . . . how would they be able to care for three children? She did not dare tell Foma for some time. For married artists without a permanent home, it was a hardship to have a large family. The managements in the private theatres were reluctant to offer engagements to artists encumbered with many children. When Liota finally told Foma, he did not want the company to know another child was on the way, and since he was the ballet master he was able to arrange Mother's roles and dances during the season so that they kept their secret.

At Christmas time they had an engagement at the Opera Theatre in Minsk and were performing one evening in Glinka's opera, *A Life for the Tsar*. They led the stately *polonaise*, but then Eleonora felt that she could not continue and dance the *mazurka* and the *cracovienne* in the Polish act.

---

ballets to complete a program. He was thus also a choreographer, though the word *choreographer* was not in common use in Russia before the twentieth century. Such great choreographers as Jules Perrot, Marius Petipa, and later Mikhail Fokine were called ballet masters in Russia. (IN/JR)

*The birthdates of the Nijinsky children have been a subject of confusion in most biographies. The earliest, by Romola Nijinsky, has Vaslav born in the year 1890 while, Richard Buckle's *Nijinsky* erroneously gives Vaslav's year of birth as 1888 in an attempt to correct previous inaccuracies. However, Vera Krassovskaya, the Soviet ballet historian, has the dates correct in her recent *Nijinsky* (1979). (AK)

Assisted by a stagehand, she left the Theatre while a substitute was instructed to take over for the remainder of the performance. Foma simply told the company that his wife was indisposed and had had to go home.

The curtain had just fallen on the last act, the artists were still onstage or in the wings, when a messenger from the nearby hospital rushed into the Theatre, looking for Foma Nijinsky. Excitedly, Foma called everyone back onto the stage and, to their great surprise, announced the birth of his daughter. And so I, Bronislava Fominitchna (Bronia), was born during a performance, on the evening of December 27, 1890 [N.S. January 8, 1891], one hour after my mother and father danced together on the stage of the Opera Theatre in Minsk.

Mother and Father wanted all three of their children to be baptized in Warsaw so that they would, like themselves, be inscribed in the civil records there. But they had not yet been able to take Vaslav. It was not until after I was born that the opportunity arose for the whole family to go to Warsaw, the city where both our parents had been born and baptized and where both had studied at the Wielki Theatre. We went at the end of the Opera Season in Minsk, and on the same day, April 18 [N.S. 30], 1891, Vaslav and I were baptized in the Roman Catholic Church of the Holy Cross, where the heart of Chopin is kept in a silver urn. We had the same godparents: Father's younger brother, Eugenius Nijinsky, was our godfather, and Bronislava Gousekevitch, a Polish dancer and an artist with the Wielki Theatre, was our godmother.

Vaslav was two years old and already walking and talking. Mother often told us how all through the solemn rites of the baptism it was impossible to keep him still. When the priest bent over him, Vaslav pulled his beard, and when, according to the rite, the priest patted him on the cheek, Vaslav protested loudly, "Don't you dare slap me!" He could be heard all over the church to the embarrassment of our parents, their families, and friends.

In the fall our parents returned to Kiev, but it was always our mother's dream that each of her three children would some day dance on the stage of the Wielki Theatre in Warsaw.

2 My Earliest Memories

IN THE FALL of 1892, and then in 1893, Mother and Father were again working with Setov in the City Opera Theatre in Kiev. Father was the ballet master and Mother was a first soloist. The winter and spring Opera Seasons in Kiev lasted from September to the end of May. For the summer months our parents had to find work in other theatrical enterprises, and for the two summers of 1892 and 1893 they worked in the Summer Theatre on Trukhanov Island, in the Dnieper, across from Kiev.

My earliest memories are of those summers spent on Trukhanov Island. From the first summer I remember standing in the garden, holding an armful of toys, looking for a place to hide and play alone. I ran to the far corner of our garden and there, hidden behind thick bushes, I built tall towers with my blocks. Soon Stassik and Vatsa came looking for me. Vatsa discovered my hiding place, and as he pulled me by the arm to go play with him and Stassik, he knocked down my "castles." When he saw my tears he tried to console me, and then he took me by the hand and together we ran around the garden. Both my brothers liked to play with me, and whenever I couldn't keep pace with them they would stop and wait for me, or if I fell over they would rush to help me; but always I heard, "She's only a girl," or, "She's a crybaby."

From our second summer on the island when I was nearly three, many incidents remain clearly in my mind. The Theatre and its large gardens were enclosed by a high fence, and the dacha we were staying in for the summer was just outside the Theatre grounds. My brothers and I were so happy on the island with its meadows, away from the city.

Each morning Mother and Father would leave for the Theatre for rehearsals, leaving us in the care of our Niannia, as we called our nanny. We also had a girl to do the cooking. Our parents had been earning substantial salaries for some years and could afford to have live-in servants. In those days it was easy to find peasant girls who were glad to come to live in the city and work for a family for "room and board." Our Niannia had been with us since I was born; she had been my wet nurse, her own baby having died at birth. She became very attached to our family and remained with us for several years.

In the afternoons Mother and Father would bring home some of their fellow artists who would remain with us until the evening. We were the only theatre family staying on the island. All the other artists and musicians came daily by boat from Kiev. Our cook, a young peasant girl, would serve a light meal before they all went back to the Theatre for the performance.

When it grew dark Niannia was supposed to put us to bed, but sometimes with our cook she would take us out in secret. We would sneak along the fence, hiding behind trees and bushes so as not to be seen, to a side gate into the gardens, the artists' entrance leading to the stage door. I recall being hardly able to keep up with them and trembling with fear at the thought that I might be left behind, alone in the dark. It was my first time out in the dark night—there above me was the black sky with big bright stars. I caught up with the others just in time. Inside the gardens, the gate closed behind me. I was dazzled by the myriad fairy-tale lights. I don't remember the music or the stage show, only the magic of the lights. I suppose I must have fallen asleep in Niannia's arms.

Years later Vaslav would tell me of his delight in that mysterious night walk and how he used to run in front of everyone to see the lights of the many colored paper lanterns, hanging on so many chains in so many directions.

We were not allowed to wander away from the dacha on our own but had to stay with Niannia. Often in the mornings she would take us to play in the Theatre gardens. We used to walk along the shaded paths around the Summer Theatre. One day Niannia took us to the Open-Air Theatre. While she sat on a bench knitting or sewing, Stassik and Vatsa began playing among the benches in front of the stage and running around the stone rotunda where the orchestra played in the afternoon and evening. Vatsa called me to come and play Blind Man's Buff with them. He tied a handkerchief over my eyes to blindfold me, turned me around and around, and then he and Stassik ran away. I could hear their voices and rushed forward only to hit my head on the stone rotunda just where a large nail protruded from the wall. My eyes and my face streamed with blood. Niannia and my brothers rushed towards me screaming even more loudly than I. Niannia carried me home, and Vaslav and Stassik ran in front of us crying all the way. When Mama saw our procession she thought something had happened to Stassik and Vaslav, the way they were coming home in tears, until she saw Niannia carrying me, my white blouse stained with blood. The wound on my forehead was washed and dressed, and soon I calmed down and it was my turn to comfort the others. But the scar remained near my right eyebrow.

Around our dacha stretched an enormous meadow, and not far away was the wide Dnieper with its swift and dangerous currents. To make sure that we would stay near the dacha, Mother would tell us there were bears on the island and crocodiles in the river. She even showed us pictures of them in our books. We often saw fishermen in boats on the river, and towards the end of the summer we heard shooting on the island and began to see hunters as well.

One of our Father's colleagues, a dancer named Boutchinsky, would often come hunting on Trukhanov Island. When we saw him in his complete hunter's outfit—brown leather suit, rifle on his shoulder, his boots high above his knees for wading in the swamps, and the dead birds slung at his belt—we would rush delightedly to meet him. The boys would hang on his neck and pull him along to our dacha, all the while asking him, "Did you kill a bear yet?" or "Where's the bear?" Vatsa wanted to learn to shoot, and to Mother's distress would try to take the rifle, but fortunately it was too heavy for him to lift.

Boutchinsky loved us children and would sometimes take us to the river. One day we went crayfishing with him along the shore. We walked barefoot in the water, catching crayfish and playing with them. Vatsa had learned how to catch them between his thumb and forefinger. Once in a while a crayfish would catch and nip him, hanging on to his forefinger. Vaslav would then shake his hand to make the crayfish fall off, and we would watch it trying to get back into the water. I remember taking a great part in this catching game, even though I knew my fingers would be sore afterwards from the crayfish attacks. We returned home with a pail half-filled with crayfish. Cook threw them into a pan of boiling water. How I cried when I saw the crayfish turn red—at the terrible pain, I thought. Vaslav then amused himself by continuing to play with the red, cooked crayfish, teasing and frightening me with them.

Towards the end of that summer on Trukhanov Island, Vatsa became alarmingly ill. The local doctor diagnosed both scarlet fever and diphtheria. As I remember, Stassik and I were immediately separated from him, all the rooms were darkened, and the cottage was hushed. As soon as the danger to Vaslav's life passed and he started to recover, the sun and joy appeared in our house again. Though we were not yet allowed to go into his room, his bed was near the window so that Stassik and I could just peek in from the garden and see him.

As he got better Vaslav became bored alone in his room. During the daytime when our parents were out at the Theatre and Niannia was busy, I would quietly creep into his room and sit with him. Vatsa was still on a strict diet and always complained of being hungry. He would tell me what things he wanted me to bring him . . . "so that I won't be sick again!" He loved berries, pears, cherries, green apples from the garden, fresh small cucumbers, candies, sweet rolls and jam, and most of all he loved wild strawberries. I managed to find most of the things he asked for, or I got them by pretending that I wanted them for myself. I was too small to understand the possible harm fresh fruits could do. One day Mother found me in Vaslav's room with a green apple in my hand. No more visits, no more offerings.

—

At the end of their engagement with the Summer Theatre our parents did not go back to the Kiev Opera, but instead signed a contract with the Odessa Opera Theatre for the 1893–94 season.

I remember our apartment in Odessa as being large with light rooms. Our favorite room had large leather sofas in the corners, and we used to love to climb on them in the twilight and listen to Niannia tell us stories. There was always something frightening in her stories, and we used to snuggle up together against the cozy back of the sofa. If Mama was not busy in the Theatre we would persuade her to tell us stories, too. One of our favorites was about Vaslav's lucky silver cup.

"We were living in Kiev in a house on Kreshtchatik Prospekt," Mother would begin. "It was Carnival and your father was appearing in a charity masked-ball at the Opera Theatre. At the end of the ball there were several prizes left over from the lottery. They were 'surprises' and the organizers threw them into the air for the public. Everyone tried to catch one and your father, leaping highest of all, caught a small sterling silver cup. When he came home and saw Vaslav, his newborn son, he was overjoyed and said that winning the little cup would be a lucky gift for his new son."

Along the entire length of the apartment was a glassed-in balcony leading from the dining room to the kitchen. Although it was forbidden, one of our favorite games was to run and race each other there. One day when we were all sitting at the table in the dining room, Mama sent Stassik to tell the cook it was time to serve dinner. Stassik rushed to the kitchen, delighted to have a chance to run along the balcony. Cook appeared at the doorway with a tureen of hot soup and Stassik ran into her. The tureen fell from her hands and the hot soup poured over poor Stassik's head. I remember everyone jumping up from the table scream-

17

ing. We were all terribly frightened. Stassik had to wear a bandage around his head for several days.

Unfortunate accidents always seemed to happen to Stassik. His worst had occurred before I was born, when he was only two and a half. The family was living in Moscow in a third-floor apartment. Everything in the house was comfortably arranged, and the children were well looked after. Stassik had a nanny, Vaslav was only a few months old and had a wet nurse, and there was also a cook. Father and Mother were in the dining room with several invited guests, and the cook was serving dinner. Nastia, the wet nurse, was putting Vaslav in his crib in the children's room. Stassik's nanny was preparing his bath and had left him alone in the drawing room.

A military band passed on the street below on its way to the nearby zoological gardens. Stassik was a bright child and already extraordinarily musical, and as soon as he heard the music he quickly pushed a chair under the window. He climbed up and onto the broad windowsill, pressed his hands on the windowpane, and looked out onto the street below. The window suddenly opened outwards, and Stassik fell from the third floor onto the cobbled street below. Just at that moment the nanny entered the drawing room and saw him fall. She screamed. Father rushed down to the street. He didn't run from step to step but jumped in single leaps from landing to landing. Mother followed quickly behind him. They found Stassik on the ground, unconscious, blood running out of his ears, nose, and mouth. The doctors who came were astonished not to find any broken or dislocated bones, but the boy did not regain consciousness for three days. When the doctor arrived on the fourth morning Stassik was sitting up in bed, laughing and playing. It seemed like a miracle.

The Opera Season in Odessa, as in Kiev, lasted longer than other theatre engagements, seven or eight months. Father and sometimes Mother were able to supplement their work in the theatre by teaching at home in our large drawing room. There was no demand for classical ballet lessons at this time, but to take ballroom dancing lessons with renowned dancers was very fashionable. As Mother and Father were well-known performers with the Odessa Opera and with Setov's Enterprise, they had many adult pupils as well as a children's class.

Stanislav and Vaslav studied in the class with the children. I sat quietly in a corner near the grand piano and sang to the music in a low voice. A pianist from the Opera came to play for the dancers. The children loved the lessons. They danced polkas, galops, quadrilles, and thoroughly enjoyed the Russian round dances with songs. Vatsa, though not yet five, stood out among the older children, as he was the only one who could dance the mazurka and the waltz. He felt himself to be quite a hero.

That Christmas in Odessa, Father brought home a magnificent Christmas tree. Many of the children came and gathered around it. The tree reached up to the ceiling and sparkled with silver stars, silver thread, chains, and lighted candles. Then a marvelous thing happened. An enormous Father Frost with a long white beard and covered with snow appeared at the door. He was dressed all in red, with a red hat and white mittens. He carried a bag full of toys on his shoulder and gaily started to distribute the presents to the children. We walked with him around the tree, singing and dancing. He lifted us up one by one so that we could choose what to take from the Christmas tree, an apple, a golden nut, a bag of candy, a little angel, a chimney sweep . . . then we all sat around the tree. Father Frost told us about his life in a fairy-tale silver forest where golden squirrels would jump from branch to branch, and about the fluffy white rabbits running about the forest, and about his tame, shaggy bear cubs who would play around the foot of his special silver Christmas tree. We were in an enchanted fairyland.

This was the first and the best Christmas that I remember. Later we learned that Father Frost of the Christmas Fairyland was Chalif,* a seventeen-year-old *figurant* [extra] from the Opera, using a costume from the Theatre wardrobe. Father had been teaching him classical ballet and character dances to help him improve his standing in the Theatre. Finding Chalif to be talented, Father had begun to employ him in his ballets and dances in the Opera.

At the beginning of 1894, Stassik and Vatsa began to learn to read and write, in both Polish and Russian. Stassik was seven, and Vatsa was almost five. Their teacher, Lestovsky, was an artist from the Warsaw Ballet who was working with Father in the Odessa Opera. They would not let me study with the boys. No matter how hard I pleaded, they said I was too young. Before each lesson I would go and hide under the table. One day the teacher discovered me but let me stay and sit near my brothers. I could listen to the lessons and look into the boys' copybooks. Mother and Father were quite surprised in the spring to find that I knew

---

*Louis H. Chalif left Russia in 1904 by steamer from Odessa and was one of the first to open a ballet school in New York, in 1907. I met him there in 1935, and he enthused about my father, his teacher, and what an extraordinary dancer he was.

Chalif had seen Vaslav Nijinsky in the Russian Ballet in 1916, and he felt that Vaslav's jump did not equal in height that of Thomas Nijinsky. Chalif assured me that as a choreographer, too, Thomas Nijinsky surpassed Fokine—his dances and staging of *The Fountain of Bakhchisarai* were many times superior to those of *Schéhérazade*.

No doubt his words must be taken as reflecting the early theatrical impressions of a seventeen-year-old student of Thomas Nijinsky. (BN)

all of the Russian alphabet. The teacher, as a reward for my diligence, gave me a small slate, and that very same day I wrote on it in alphabetical order all the Russian letters, the capitals as well as the small ones. This small slate on which you could write letters and then wipe them off and then write new ones seemed to me the greatest treasure. I would not part from my slate all that first day, not for a minute. I was afraid something might happen to it. Before I went to bed I decided to hide it carefully. A far corner of the drawing room seemed to be the safest place for my treasure. There on the seat of one of the armchairs I put my slate, with all my letters written on it, safe for the night. In the morning I found it broken and crushed. One of the artists had come to visit my parents and had sat on my treasure. I cried bitterly. Mama immediately bought me another slate, but I was inconsolable and did not copy any more letters while we stayed in Odessa.

At this time only children of artists or young *figurants* like Chalif studied ballet. Father gladly taught them free of charge and sometimes took Stassik and Vaslav to these ballet lessons in the Theatre, also to his rehearsals with the dancers.

Later in that spring of 1894, Father began to teach Stassik and Vaslav a Ukrainian dance, the *hopak*. In the largest room of our apartment Vatsa and Stassik held hands, jumped and threw their legs very high, and then turned separately. First Stassik would jump up high and then squat down low near the ground. Then Vatsa, holding a red handkerchief, would whirl quickly and with a high jump put his hands on Stassik's shoulders, who would then lift him high in the air.

At Easter the boys danced the *hopak* in a children's performance. The costumes were sewn and fitted at home. I remember their lovely red knee-high boots, the smell of fresh leather. Stassik was the Cossack boy and was dressed in wide blue pantaloons, belted with a broad red sash, its long ends hanging by his side. His white Ukrainian shirt was embroidered with cross-stitching and had a red ribbon at the neck. On his head he wore a high gray lambskin cap and, most beautiful of all, the red leather boots. Stassik with his blond hair and gray-green eyes looked just like a young Cossack boy.

Vatsa danced the part of the girl. With his slightly dark skin, big brown eyes, and long fluffy eyelashes, it was impossible to tell that he was a boy. He looked like a little Ukrainian girl in his white cross-stitch embroidered shirt with wide sleeves, and a Ukrainian dress, decorated with spangles. On his head was a garland of artificial cornflowers, poppies, and long blue and yellow ribbons, and around his neck he wore many multicolored beads. Like Stassik he had a pair of red leather boots. Mama touched up their cheeks with a little rouge, using a hare's foot to apply it.

The boys were to dance on the stage in the middle of the auditorium. I was standing at the side well below the stage. "How will I be able to see Stass and Vatsa dance?" I asked. Then Mama lifted me in her arms and I clapped my hands with delight.

Stassik and Vatsa were a tremendous success. To the shouts of "Bravo" and "Bis," they had to repeat their dance once, and then again.

It was for that performance in Odessa, Easter 1894, that Vaslav Nijinsky, just five years old, made his first public dancing appearance.

3   From Town to Town
Across Spacious Russia

AT THE END of the Opera Season in Odessa, Father joined a light opera company for a season in the Crimea. With the death of Setov at the beginning of the year, the Setov Enterprise had now disbanded, and so Father as the ballet master found other theatrical engagements for his small ballet troupe. Many of the artists had worked with Father and Mother for many years and had become attached to them. His troupe included twelve excellent dancers from the Warsaw Wielki Theatre and a few of his own students, among them Chalif. For this season Father also engaged the Italian Prima Ballerina, Maria Giuri.*

Every summer people would come from all over Russia to the towns and sea resorts of the Crimea. But in 1894 there were rumors that Tsar Alexander III was dangerously ill and the public, many of them officials from Moscow and St. Petersburg, stopped going to the theatre. The light opera enterprise had been successful up until then, but now it disintegrated and the artists were left without work or money.

Father wanted to give a ballet concert with his small troupe, but nobody had enough money to rent a hall or a theatre. He decided to pawn some of the precious gifts he and Mother had received over the years from their Benefit Performances.† These included gold and silver cigarette cases, watches, cuff links, pearl tie pins, gold bracelets, diamond rings, precious stones, and silver flatware. Theatregoers in Russia were very generous and tried to outdo each other with the lavishness of the gifts they presented onstage.

---

*According to Carlotta Zambelli, longtime ballerina of the Paris Opera Ballet, Giuri performed multiple *fouetté* turns before Pierina Legnani made her celebrated introduction of this innovation in technique in St. Petersburg in 1893. Born in Trieste, c. 1845, Maria Giuri studied with Carlo Blasis at La Scala Royal Ballet Academy and was a star of the Warsaw Ballet in the 1880s. (AK)

†Benefit performances, in which theatrical artists received gifts and money from their admirers or their management, existed in many European cities but were particularly common in Russia. The pretext was usually but not necessarily an anniversary. (AK)

With the money from the pawnshop, a theatre was rented and a small orchestra engaged. Father ordered posters and handbills to be printed, and at night when the town was asleep he and his artists hung the posters all over town. The performance was an artistic and financial success but it was not possible to find other work in the Crimea, and the artists began to move away.

From that time on our parents had to take short engagements, the longest being three or four months, in various theatres. This took our family wandering from town to town, across Russia, from the Crimea in the south to as far as St. Petersburg in the north.

I remember clearly our embarkation on the ship leaving the Crimea. We were in a tiny boat rocking from side to side, and above us the ship loomed high and from it a narrow rope ladder reached down to us. Suddenly a sailor in our boat grabbed me and started to climb the ladder. I was trembling with fear as I looked over his shoulder and saw the anxious faces of Mama, Papa, and Stassik still in the boat. Close behind me Vatsa was quickly scrambling up the rope ladder on his own. Suddenly he missed his footing and dangled at the side of the ladder. I gasped, frightened that he would lose hold and fall into the sea. The sailor put me down on the deck and turned and caught Vatsa and pulled him up onto the deck, too. We gripped each other's hands as we waited alone on the deck for the others.

From the Crimea we went first to Novorossiysk and then to Ekaterino-dar [now Krasnodar], where the theatre engagement on which our parents had counted was canceled. There was no work. We lived in half-dark lodgings, and this was very frightening. A low window overlooked the street, and on the outside the windowpanes were entirely covered with insects, maybe flies or moths, so thickly that the light could not penetrate into the rooms. My aversion to insects, particularly flying insects, probably dates from those dark days.

We did not stay long in Ekaterinodar. In August our parents obtained work in a theatre in Vladikavkaz for the fall and winter season. We lived in a one-story house on the outskirts of Vladikavkaz. In front of the house a wide, usually deserted road led straight to the Military Georgian Highway, and in the distance we could see the majestic mountains of the Caucasus.

Through the light evening mist, just before sunset, the mountains assumed the soft, iridescent colors of mother of pearl. Gradually the colors changed to violet and then to bright purple. We especially liked to watch the mountains on clear, bright nights when their serene, snowy summits would shine under the brilliance of the stars and the moonlight. Sometimes before a storm the outlines of the mountains were dark and

23

threatening among the gathering clouds. I was fascinated by the mountains. They dominated the view far away in the distance, but on clear days the huge mass seemed to grow and I could almost believe that the mountains were alive and breathing and drawing closer to us.

Mama told us many times about her travels with her sisters and later with our father over the mountains of the Caucasus. How dangerous it was to go from Vladikavkaz to Tiflis traveling by horse-drawn carriage over the Military Georgian Highway! As we listened to her, we could see in our imaginations the peaks of the mountains, the deep abysses, the bad weather, the storms all around the carriage. We could also see the brigands who lived in the mountains and the coachdrivers who kept their horses at a gallop through the narrow passes so as not to be caught in ambush.

Our house in Vladikavkaz had large rooms, so large that I remember the light from the kerosene lamp did not reach into the corners. Those dark corners frightened me as there was hardly any furniture in the house, making the rooms seem empty. I did not have a bed or a crib but slept in our big traveling trunk. The lid was always completely open, but I was still afraid that it would suddenly slam shut. In the evenings when we were left alone while our parents were at the Theatre, the boys would light a candle on the table and I would climb out of the trunk and we would roast pieces of sugar over the flame of the candle.

One time Father came home in the middle of the day with a special present for us. He was carrying a package out of which he pulled a long string, which in turn pulled a long sausage covered with a white powder. Something showed green, yellow, red, and white through the powder. It did not look at all appetizing. "Children, here is something delectable for you." He put it on a plate and cut it into small slices. It looked like spoiled sausage, and I could not be persuaded to taste it. Mother and Father laughed and Vatsa, emboldened, tried it. One taste and he could not be kept away from it. Still doubtful, I approached the plate and sniffed. It smelled of flowers. I touched it and put my finger to my mouth, and to my surprise and joy it tasted sweet. It was the Caucasian type of Turkish Delight, filled with nuts and almonds. From then on no other sweet could compare with this delicacy; many years later, as an adult, I would try to find Turkish Delight in the hope of recapturing the delicate flavor I remembered from childhood, but I was always disappointed. The taste was always too sweet and the artificial smell of roses overpowering.

In the yard outside our house, a doe with large eyes was kept. She had tiny hooves, and I remember one day I was on the ground and she walked, stamping all over me. The boys and I used to feed her watermelon rinds and vegetables. At the far end of the yard was a separate building where our cook lived. A small piglet lived with her, even slept on her bed. We used to love to play with him. The cook was so attached to the piglet that when the time came that she was told to prepare him for dinner, she burst into sobs, and we children with her. To our relief the piglet was given a reprieve and continued to live in the cook's room.

Suddenly, on October 20 [N.S. November 1], the news came that Tsar Alexander III had died. Mourning was declared for All the Russias, and every theatre had to close. It was a terrible time for artists, and our parents found it difficult to earn any money. Even their ballroom lessons, which were usually well paid, came to an end during the mourning period as families considered it improper to learn to dance at such a sad time. Throughout our childhood this would happen—one day prosperity, the next anxiety.

We left Vladikavkaz and went to Nijni Novgorod where Mother and Father worked in a Café-Chantant. Café-Chantants were popular in Old Russia, and the management would pay the artists quite well. The public was served with lavish food and wines while watching entertainments presented onstage. Musical, vocal, and dancing numbers would follow each other at a fast pace, and from time to time gypsies and popular musicians would wander among the tables. The public was lighthearted and animated, the champagne flowed in abundance. The stage show would conclude at around two o'clock in the morning, but the gypsies would continue their wonderful singing and dancing until later hours of the morning.

Of course we never went to these performances, but Father often brought the performers home. We especially loved Jackson and Johnson,* two young Negro music-hall artists, tap dancers, well-known throughout Europe as well as in their homeland, the United States of America. We developed a deep friendship with them. My first dancing lessons were from these two American tap dancers. They brought a small plank to our home one day, spread sand on it, and taught me how to tap dance on the plank. Stassik was not interested in tap dancing, but when Vaslav saw how quickly I picked up the routine and its rhythms he joined the lessons. He was surprised to find it was not as easy as it looked.

Vaslav and I were fascinated by the diamond rings Jackson and Johnson wore on their little fingers. As they showed us the routines, we loved to watch how the rings sparkled on their black hands. We kept a photograph

---

*Scholars of American Black Theatre history point out that many black entertainers who toured Western Europe after the 1860s went on to perform in Russia. (AK)

of Jackson and Johnson for a long time.* It showed them standing one behind the other, in white satin tailcoats with black lapels and shiny top hats. Each held a cane in one hand while the other hand rested on a hip so that the big diamond rings shone brilliantly in the photograph.

Father was regularly teaching Stassik and Vatsa the ballet positions and the first easy *pas* of classical dance. When the Theatre asked him to prepare a children's Christmas show he rehearsed them in the dances they already knew, the *hopak* and the *mazurka*. I was very hurt that I was not going to take part, too. Mama, who had seen how well I had learned my tap dancing with Jackson and Johnson, began to teach me the Sailor Dance. When we showed Father that I could do it, he agreed to let me dance with the boys in the performance.

That Christmas of 1894, just before my fourth birthday, I was to make my very first appearance on the stage and even dance a solo.

For many days before the performance I was completely oblivious to everything going on around me. All my thoughts were centered on my own dances—the Chinese Dance and the Sailor Dance. I practiced by myself, pestering Stassik and Vatsa to go over the dances with me, but they were too busy preparing their own new dances. Stassik was practicing the *mazurka* with a girl partner. Vatsa was going to have his own first solo performance. He was to dance the *hopak*, and was working diligently to master the difficult steps of the Ukrainian dance. Father, renowned throughout Russia and most particularly in the Ukraine for his breathtaking and exhilarating execution of the *hopak*, had prepared a simplified version for Vaslav's first solo. Vaslav was determined to be worthy of his father's renown.

New costumes were made for the new dances. I especially liked my sailor costume, preferring it to the Chinese, and I enjoyed the fittings and posing in the costumes in front of the mirror. For the *hopak* Vaslav was to wear the Cossack costume made for Stassik in Odessa. The high gray astrakhan hat was very becoming on him.

The first number of the performance was Vaslav's solo, the *hopak*. The audience applauded for a long time and he had to repeat the dance as an encore. How high he jumped, throwing his legs from side to side and touching the heels of his boots with his hands, striking his heels together, crouching down to dance the *prissyatka*, flinging his legs forward faster and faster, and finishing by whirling around in a spinning *prissyatka* close to the ground! Father was so pleased with Vatsa. He later said that not every adult dancer could manage all those difficult stunts of the *hopak*.

* This photograph, like many other family mementoes, was left in Petrograd in 1915 and was lost during the Russian Revolution. (IN)

Then came the Sailor Dance, for which we were all three dressed alike. Over long blue bell-bottom trousers we wore white blouses with wide blue sailor collars. On our feet were black pumps, and on our heads round sailor hats tilted low over our right ears.

First Stassik and Vatsa danced the *matelot gigue*. In this joyful and vivacious dance the two brothers, their faces glowing with excitement, tried to surpass each other. After each stanza the boys were applauded loudly, but when they finished their dance my brothers did not spend any time taking bows. They ran towards the back of the stage and stopped, clicked their heels and bowed low, and extended their right hands forward as a gesture of invitation to their sister, Bronia, for her entrance.

I ran out onto the stage from the last wing and danced the four stanzas of the *matelotte*. Then Stassik and Vatsa and I together danced the *bravura coda*. We mimed rowing a boat, lowering and raising the sails, and taking our stance to pull in the mooring line. Our dance ended with a double *pirouette* on heel, at the same time we threw our sailor hats into the air, and as we finished the *pirouette* we caught our hats and made a low bow to the audience.

The Sailor Dance was a great success with the children, and we had to repeat it several times. We were thrown boxes of candy, oranges and nuts, toys and gifts that the children had received from the Christmas tree. I was literally knocked off my feet by the ovation—either a box of candy or an orange hit me, and I fell over. We artists, of course, gathered up the "laurels" of our success.

The final number of our children's performance was the Chinese Dance. Besides us three Nijinskys there were five other children, all older than Vaslav, taking part in the dance. We were all dressed in bright yellow shorts with loose overblouses made of shiny red sateen. To make our heads look shaven we wore pink stocking caps over our own hair, with a long braid of black wool fixed to the cap at the crown. Our costumes only remotely resembled those of Chinese coolies, and our dance was just as far from being a Chinese dance.

Stassik, Vatsa, and I came onstage with small mincing steps. Throughout the dance we held both forefingers up in front of our faces, bowing repeatedly to each other in a "Chinese Ceremony." We thrust our forefingers in all directions, up and down, side to side, and then we ran in quick mincing steps in a figure eight. The little copper bells that were sewn to each pointed end of the cut-out scalloped edges of our costumes jangled and jingled. Then the other children joined us in the dance. Again we bowed to each other repeatedly. We crisscrossed in lines and formed different groupings while Vaslav danced several short solos.

I remember each of his entrances was greeted with laughter. His face was made up so that he looked old and Chinese. The funny expressions on his face and the grimaces that he used to turn himself into an old wrinkled Chinaman made the children in the audience laugh. He ended all his solos with the same *pas*—jumping up very high, his legs turned out and his feet pulled up underneath him, in first position. He repeated it several times, turning and bending and poking his fingers. On the last jump he crossed his legs in midair and came down on the floor in sitting position—*à la turque*, as we called it.

Our public, the little children, liked the Chinese Dance enormously and showed their enthusiasm by loud shouts and thunderous applause, but it was Vaslav as the comical old Chinaman who was the hit of the show. He was called back after each solo and took several curtain calls on his own.

After the performance Father and Mother praised our execution of the dances and rejoiced with all three of us over our success with the audience.*

Next we went to Saratov, where our parents were performing in the Summer Theatre. A sad event occurred there that overshadows all my other memories of Saratov.

Vladimir Dourov,† the famous Russian clown and animal trainer, was working in the Open-Air Theatre. His performance drew great crowds. A piglet was sent up in the air in the small gondola of a balloon. The balloon was held by a long rope, and when it had floated as high as it could go the piglet was ejected from the gondola. Usually the descent went off well, as he had a small parachute on his back. But one day something went wrong, the parachute did not open, and the piglet fell like a stone to the ground and was smashed to pieces.

How angry the crowd was. They all shouted that Dourov was a monster, a torturer of animals. The remains of the pig were put on a cart and taken off somewhere. Dourov wept. All of us gathered around him, and we children cried too and embraced Dourov. We grieved deeply for many days.

—

AFTER SARATOV we went to Nijni Novgorod. We sailed there on a large steamer up the Volga. As soon as we had boarded and were settled in

---

*This performance was important to Vaslav, who in an interview with *T.P.'s Magazine*, in London, May 1911, described it as his "first appearance in public." (IN/JR)

†Dourov (1863–1934) became internationally famous and beloved for his brilliance in animal acts. He was associated with Albert Salamonsky's Circus, a major enough enterprise by 1880 to open its own permanent quarters in a stone building in Moscow. (AK)

our cabin, Vaslav and I ran back to the top deck to watch the sailors cast off. Then we walked round and round the deck and watched the shore from both sides of the steamer. It wasn't until we wanted to go back to our cabin that we realized we hadn't noticed which door we had come through onto the deck. Mother found us wandering around trying to find the right door.

During the day our cabin was hot and stuffy, and Mother would take us up to the top deck for a breath of fresh air. My brothers and I loved to watch the traffic on the water, the flat barges transporting all kinds of goods up and down the river. We would wave to the men on the barges and they would wave back to us. There was always a struggle when Mother announced it was time for us to go back to our cabin.

At dusk balalaikas could be heard all along the river, and both passengers and sailors would join in and sing together. Each evening we were lulled to sleep by this Russian music and by the soft splashing of the water against the sides of the steamer.

None of us children ever came back to this wonderful river after we grew up. And so this was the only time that we made a trip on the Volga.

4 The Great Annual Fair of Nijni Novgorod

Since 1816 the Great Annual Fair was always held between July 15 and September 1 in Nijni Novgorod, bringing many rich merchants, manufacturers, and traders from all over Russia and from many parts of Asia. Large transactions were made involving millions of rubles, and special offices were opened to negotiate bulk sales of Russian grains, tea, coffee, and wine. The traders would be busy buying and selling bales of cotton, wool, and linen, leather and furs from Siberia, or precious gems and metals from the Urals.

Each large store would have a special display for the Fair. In one would be beautiful handmade rugs and carpets, in another rare imports from Persia—silver, turquoises, porcelains, and silks—or in yet another, ancient ikons of gold and silver, set with precious stones. Each day more barges came up the Volga bringing new supplies of fish and caviar, or general merchandise for the stores, or specialties for the stalls set up in the streets—decorated handmade wooden pails, basins, bowls, spoons, earthenware and painted pottery, sheepskin coats, felt boots and *lapti* [Russian peasant straw shoes].

It was the beginning of August when we arrived in Nijni Novgorod, and the Fair was in full swing. The colorful crowd was in continuous motion as we drove through in our droshky. Flashing past us were elegant carriages drawn by beautiful horses with streaming tails and fancifully dressed manes.

Father and Mother took us to see the Fair. We felt excitement in the air as we were surrounded by a multitude of people of many races, all wearing their own colorful costumes. I was overwhelmed by the noise, the sounds of the accordions, the whooping of the coachmen, the ringing of bells, the drunken songs, and I marveled at everything there was to see. Outside an expensive restaurant stood a black lacquered landau. Sprawled in the back was a merchant with a large black beard and wearing a Russian coat and cap. At his side was a lady wearing a chic dress and a hat with long ostrich feathers. Along the stalls numerous vendors were wandering about offering trays of cakes, candies, fruits, and pies to passersby. Someone told us that there were over six thousand stalls and sideshows, and of course Stassik, Vatsa, and I wanted to see every one.

We saw magicians, jugglers, weight lifters, strongmen, midgets, man-lions, and other freaks, but our special joy and delight was the puppet show—"Petrouchka." Our parents took us back to the Fair several times and I believe that we did indeed see most of the sideshows. But each time we visited the Fair we made sure not to miss seeing our beloved, unhappy Petrouchka. Along with everyone else, children and adults alike, we shouted to Petrouchka, encouraging him in his fight with the puppet-soldier. We laughed and we cried.

The Annual Fair in Nijni Novgorod was unique in the world. In addition to the sideshows and the booths, there was an excellent opera theatre featuring the best Russian and Italian singers. Nearby was another theatre presenting plays and dramas. Concert singers and musicians would also come to Nijni Novgorod to give concerts during the Fair.

The year we were there, 1895, M. V. Lentovsky* was staging his grandiose spectacle in the circus—Jules Verne's *Around the World in 80 Days*. Our parents had previously worked with Lentovsky in the Kin Grust Theatre, one of the St. Petersburg Summer Theatres, and valued his talent for organization and his artistic taste. He would bring artists from the very ends of the earth if necessary for his productions. He would have ships sinking in the ocean, cataracts from high cliffs, wild animals, forest fires, the Flood . . . But this year, having lost most of his money, he brought only one tribe of Indians from South America.

For the first few days our parents took us with them to the rehearsals. Vatsa soon got tired of watching the same thing repeated over and over again and would disappear. He found so many other interesting things in

---

*Mikhail Valentinovitch Lentovsky, 1843–1906, an actor in the Maly Theatre in Moscow, became a theatrical entrepreneur in 1878, founding the *Fantastic Theatre*—later known as *Antey*—in Moscow in 1882 and at the same time presenting operettas and spectaculars in the Summer Theatres in St. Petersburg. There, in 1885, at the Kin Grust, he introduced the Italian ballerinas, Virginia Zucchi and Maria Giuri, to Russian audiences. In 1894, at the Arcadia Theatre, a young and as yet unknown singer, Feodor Chaliapin, starred in the Lentovsky Enterprise. Lentovsky lost most of his money through the lavishness of his productions, and from 1895 he was engaged to stage smaller spectacles for other Enterprises, as in the Theatre-Circus in Nijni Novgorod, described here. Later, from 1898 until 1901, he was the Regisseur for Mamontov's Private Opera Enterprise in Moscow, where in December 1898 he staged Mussorgsky's opera *Boris Godunov* with the title role sung for the first time by Feodor Chaliapin. (IN/JR)

31

the circus behind the arena—the horse stalls, cages with wild animals, the props, rifles, lances, sabers, drums, and dressing rooms with costumes hanging ready. Best of all he found he could run backstage, which in a circus meant all the way around the arena. During the installation of the machinery for the scenic effects, we were supposed to keep out of the way so that we wouldn't be hurt, but Vaslav was curious and wanted to watch how everything was done, and I followed him. Naturally the stagehands did not appreciate having children under their feet, and so after the first few days we were no longer taken to the rehearsals.

Our hotel was next to the circus, and many of the artists—singers, actors, and musicians—also lived there. We became well acquainted with many of them. We were supposed to stay in our room, but Vaslav would run in the corridors and halls or drop in for a visit with some of the artists. Soon he became familiar with "our neighborhood" and began to explore farther away.

First he discovered a side gate into the circus field, and once through that he found another gate leading into a large yard, and from the yard a back entrance to the hotel. He came rushing back to our rooms with a look of mysterious excitement on his face.

"There are *wild Indians* living here!"

In no time at all, all three of us were down in the yard. In the middle was a large barn. It had no windows and was dark inside, the only light coming from the gates across the doorway. We squatted low and approached cautiously, peering around the corner of the barn. There, standing, or sitting, or lying on the earthen floor, were the Redskins. Their entire bodies were tattooed in different colors and shone like polished wood. Hanging down over their chests were many necklaces with large teeth among the beads. Their jet black hair was adorned with clusters of colored feathers, their nostrils and ears were pierced with white sticks and rings, their hips were girded with leopard skins, and on their arms and ankles they wore brass bangles. Lances and hatchets with long handles were leaning against the walls of the barn. The place reeked with a repugnant, suffocating smell. Frightened, we did not linger, and ran away.

We were later taken by one of the artists to see the Indians, who were indeed the tribe brought from South America by Lentovsky to take part in the spectacle. We were surprised to see that they did not eat from plates but from white pottery bowls; we were afraid that they might eat us, and that this wild tribe might burst into the hotel at night and attack us. However, they were soon taken away. We imagined, I don't know why, that the wild Indians must have left treasures buried in the yard, and straightaway we ran to search. There was no trace of buried treasure in the yard and we could not find anything of their multilayered necklaces, not one bead or brass ornament, not even one tiny red feather. They had taken everything with them. The barn was swept clean except for a few pieces of broken white bowls in the corner.

Now that the Indians had gone we were attracted back to the circus yard. Over by the wall a large, round wooden platform was stored, standing upright on its rim. Whenever there was to be a dancing or pantomime performance, this platform was used to cover the circus ring and provide a stage. On the back of the platform, around the rim and in the center, were long spikes to set the stage firmly into the sand of the ring. One day Vaslav took it into his head that he could make the platform roll on its edge by walking along the spikes, climbing them toward the top. He was able to do this sort of thing with an extraordinary innate balance, but when Stassik's turn came to walk the spikes, he did not get up fast enough and the platform tipped over and began to fall. Vatsa and I ran out of the way, but Stassik fell to the ground and the heavy platform fell on top of him. Fortunately he was not seriously hurt, but after this accident we had to spend most of our time sitting in our room.

Like Mother and her sisters, Stassik, Vatsa, and I were "ready to go through fire and water for each other," and there was deep friendship and love between us, but now that we were confined together in our room, quarrels and fistfights broke out often. Stassik never started a fight, but Vaslav would tease both Stassik and me, and then Stassik would turn from a quiet boy into a violent fighter while I, the youngest, would be caught in the middle as my two brothers desperately thrashed at each other.

One day Mother came home, tired after a rehearsal, and found such a scene. Angrily, she screamed at us, "You are not like children at all. . . . You are like Petrouchka at the Fair!"

The fighting stopped. Vaslav's eyes were shining . . . how happy he was to be described as Petrouchka!

That evening when we were alone we prepared our own performance of "Petrouchka." We pulled the sofa out from the wall, and Vaslav announced the parts. "Petrouchka—Vatsa; the Soldier—Stassik; Matreoshka—Bronia." Stassik had a wooden ruler in his belt as a saber, Vatsa had a roll of newspapers as Petrouchka's stick, and Matreoshka wore a kerchief on her head, tied under her chin. The back of the sofa was our puppet stage; Vatsa and Stassik let their bodies hang over it from the waist with their arms dangling and swinging. It was too high for me to do that, so I could only jump up and down to show my face.

First to appear is Petrouchka, jumping from one end of the sofa to the other and then back again, waving his arms about and then finally falling overboard. From the other end of the sofa Matreoshka arrives, dancing with turns and jumps. She sees Petrouchka and is frightened and moves back to her end of the sofa. As Matreoshka disappears she blows kisses to Petrouchka, who now revives and runs towards her with outstretched arms. But the Soldier appears at the end of the sofa and swings his saber with a display of courage. Matreoshka comes back, and the Soldier puts his saber away in his belt. Putting their hands on each other's shoulders, Matreoshka and the Soldier dance and kiss.

Suddenly Petrouchka appears and Matreoshka jumps away from the Soldier. An unequal fight begins between the saber and the stick; soon the saber flies aside, the Soldier runs away, and Petrouchka, the victor, kisses Matreoshka and they dance together. But, again, the Soldier appears; a violent fistfight breaks out between Vatsa and Stassik. Now the Soldier, now Petrouchka, fall overboard, and Matreoshka dashes between them.

The noise and commotion in our room soon brought the maid and the floor valet running. They were our first audience. Later we showed our "Petrouchka" to our parents and friends. At the end of the performance the artists, Matreoshka in the middle, took their bows, and the grown-ups applauded and praised us.

Soon the Great Annual Fair came to an end, and the streets of Nijni Novgorod looked deserted with their stores and restaurants closed. We got ready to go to Kazan for the Opera Season, and then to Narva for the following summer.

The rich theatricality of the Fair and its folklore left its imprint deep in our minds. I recall the creation of our "Petrouchka" so well. Long after we left Nijni Novgorod we continued to perform it for ourselves.

5 Coronation Season: 1896

As WITH ALL artists in the private theatres in Russia, our life had its ups and downs. Sometimes we could live in a large apartment with two or three servants, while at others Mother would have to divide her time between the theatre and looking after her three children herself. Though Mother and Father were talented artists, they had to work continuously in order to make a reasonable living, one that could afford us a good and comfortable life. We were used to long travels across the great expanse of Russia, but with each new theatrical engagement it was not always possible to find a good apartment or live-in servants. So it was in Narva, a small town on the Baltic, where our parents signed a contract for the Coronation Season of 1896. The hotel where we were lucky enough to find accommodations was far from first-class. On the ground floor next to the restaurant was a pool hall. It was not possible to find a servant to come and stay with us during the daytime.

In the Theatre-Circus* Father was staging a pantomime ballet, *The Fountain of Bakhchisarai*,† using Polish and Russian music. Mother was performing the role of the Princess Maria and so would go with Father to the rehearsals. She did not like leaving Stassik with Vaslav and me, as the two boys together would play rough games and get into trouble, so Stassik was often taken along to the rehearsals and took part in some of the *mises en scène*.

---

*The term Theatre-Circus is particularly apt for the theatrical scope of the Russian circus, which went beyond today's circus bills. The idea that ballet existed only on one level, at the Imperial Theatres, is belied by the exposure to various dance idioms for the population at large as provided by the popular theatres and circuses. The degree of dance varied, however, in each pantomime ballet. In 1905, for the Krutikov Circus, Thomas Nijinsky made the arena three-quarters beach and one-quarter sea for a comic pantomime, *By the Seaside*, whose performers suddenly danced a cakewalk. (AK)

†*The Fountain of Bakhchisarai*, based on Alexander Pushkin's poem of the same name, remained a favorite theme in Russian ballet. The most famous staging is Rostislav

This meant that Vaslav and I were frequently left on our own in the hotel. Our room was on the third floor, at the front, looking out onto the square. But we could not open the windows—they were kept locked and bolted, top and bottom. The hotel was such an old building that our parents were afraid of fire and so did not want to lock the door of our room. Instead they told us we had to stay in there, quietly, and not go out, not even into the corridor. I was afraid of disobeying my parents, perhaps because I was the youngest, but for Vaslav there was no resisting the urge to explore. As soon as we were left alone, Vatsa took me by the hand and led me out of the room. The corridor windows were high, but we soon found a stool, and by standing on it we were able to look out of them and see the back of the hotel . . . there below us was the most exciting yard—dirty, untidy, with hens wandering everywhere, and in the middle mounds of dirt around a freshly dug hole filled with milky water. There were two sheds by the wall, a gate that opened out onto a street, and a carriage standing in the corner.

"There may be some horses," Vatsa whispered hopefully, "only we can't see from here. . . . Let's go down and find out."

I don't remember how we found our way down to the yard, but I do remember that at each corner we promised each other, "We won't go any farther, otherwise we might get lost."

There were horses in the yard, we discovered, but they were locked in the shed. We were about to return when we suddenly heard the grunting of pigs in the next yard. We remembered our piglet in Vladikavkaz, and Dourov's trained pig that had perished so tragically in Saratov during the parachute fall. On hearing the grunting, Vaslav immediately forgot his resolution "not to go any farther" and said, "Bronia, I will go alone to see what is happening in the next yard." He found a short stump of a log and set it up on a mound of dirt near the hole. "Bronia, you sit here quietly and don't go away. If I get lost I'll call you and you will answer me so that I can find my way back."

With that Vatsa left me alone and went exploring on his own. For a long time he did not come back. I grew bored and was gently rocking myself backwards and forwards when suddenly the log shot out from under me. I screamed as I rolled down the slope and plunged into the hole. Vatsa came running back to find me standing up to my neck in the thick, white, milky liquid. To my distress as I looked up I could see Mother's frightened face looking down at me from the third-floor window. She was down quickly,

Zakharov's 1934 production, with Galina Ulanova as Maria, the Polish princess abducted by the Tartar Khan Guirei. She is killed by Zarema, the harem favorite of the Khan, and he erects a fountain in Maria's memory. (AK)

36

then she and Vatsa pulled me out of the hole. Lime—slaked lime, fortunately for me—was clinging all over me. Mother carried me upstairs, and then for hours I was alternately soaked and scrubbed to get rid of the sticky stuff.

For a long time afterwards, I was terribly ashamed and didn't want anyone to know that I had fallen into the lime pit. Mother had only to threaten to tell someone how I "bathed" in slaked lime to make me behave immediately. The same threat also made Vaslav behave, afraid as he was to have people learn that because of his disobedience his sister had almost drowned.

Vaslav had a strong fear of being punished, in spite of which he never could resist a need to "explore new lands" and make his own discoveries in every new place we went. Mother always said it had started in Odessa when Stassik took him for a walk. She and Father had gone to the theatre to introduce themselves to the management, and we children—I was only a few months old—were left in the care of my wet nurse. As soon as our parents left, the nurse began my toilet and the unpacking. Stassik, just five, took Vaslav, not yet three, outside. Somehow they got hold of long stalks of wheat, threw them over their shoulders like rifles, and hand in hand walked along the street. A policeman near the house noticed the wheat stalks moving through the crowd and spotted the two little boys in their gray cloth sailor suits. He did not stop them, however, as they seemed to be walking with some adults in front of them. Later it was easy to trace the explorers by their wheat-stalk rifles and find them on the outskirts of the city.

Throughout my childhood I can remember many occasions of Vaslav disappearing, but whenever he was supposed to be looking after me he would take me along with him. In Narva, only a few days after that first exploration which ended so unhappily, he again took me by the hand. I didn't want to go this time, but he dragged me down to see another yard he had found. What a delightful yard it was for us city children. There were cows, hens, a sow with piglets, and horses. Vatsa had become friends with the stable boy, and he let him sit on the horses.

One day Vatsa confided to me that late in the evening, after Father, Mother, and Stassik had left for the theatre, he would leap out of bed and run downstairs to join the stable boy, who let him ride bareback to the river to water the horses. Vatsa even stayed on his horse while it went into the river. He made me promise to keep his secret.

At the time we arrived in March, the square in front of our hotel was quite empty, but soon it was buzzing with preparations for the fair to be held there to celebrate the coronation of Tsar Nicholas II in May. The entire small town was getting noisier and noisier. Mama would warn us about "suspicious characters," saying, "The gypsies are here . . . they steal little children . . . who are then lost for ever . . ."

One morning Vaslav disappeared. He was nowhere in the hotel. I was questioned, and frightened at what might have happened to Vaslav, I revealed all our secrets—the barn . . . the yard . . . the animals . . . Vaslav's friendship with the stable boy . . . his going to the river to water the horses. But still Vaslav was nowhere to be found. Even his friend the stable boy did not know where he was.

This time I think Mother herself believed that Vaslav had been taken by the gypsies. Stass and I were sure that we would never see Vaslav again. By evening Mother, Stassik, and I had been weeping so much that our faces were red and our eyes swollen with tears. Finally Father decided he should go and report to the police that a child had been lost, when suddenly Vaslav appeared, accompanied by a stagehand from the theatre. He didn't look at all frightened. On the contrary, he looked happy and pleased with himself, as though he had accomplished some great feat. It turned out that Vaslav had gone along with the theatre van to hang posters all over town. His new friend the stagehand declared that he had met Vaslav in town and, when he recognized him as Nijinsky's son, had taken him along so that he could bring him home after hanging the posters. Mother, however, was quite sure that somehow Vaslav had arranged the trip after becoming friends with the theatre worker. Few adults could resist Vaslav when he looked at them appealingly with his enormous dark eyes fringed with dark lashes.

Mother and Father were so happy and relieved to see Vaslav alive and unharmed that there was no mention of punishment. Perhaps, also, Father saw how proud Vatsa was of having "worked for the theatre," and did not want to dampen his enthusiasm.

Many amusements for the fair were arranged by both the City and the Provincial Government. I remember vividly the high, greased mast poles, installed in the square for the festivities. On the top of each mast were flat baskets filled with prizes—an accordion, a pair of boots, a Russian shirt, a cap, a comb, packs of tobacco, a belt, a mug with the Coronation emblem. Throngs of people gathered around the poles and drew lots to see who would be the first to climb and take the best prize from the top. How the watching crowd laughed whenever a contestant slid back down the slippery pole, or couldn't even climb his own height. Vatsa must have already tested his ability to climb the poles on one of his explorations, for when the crowd left he ran over and suddenly began to climb one of the poles like a fly. Mama was frightened and had just enough time to catch him by his legs and pull him down.

The square in front of our hotel was becoming more and more of a fair in itself. It was filling with drunks and vagabonds, and Mother grew concerned about the streets being safe. She was also suspicious of the people who lived in the basement of our hotel. They often came into the hotel restaurant and once even played pool there with Father. He remarked that one of them had very long elegant fingers. One day our hotel was suddenly surrounded by policemen. Vaslav and I watched from the window of our room and saw three men brought out of the basement in handcuffs. They were counterfeiters, it turned out, and had been printing money in the basement. We were horrified to realize that so close under us in the same hotel had lived dangerous criminals.

We left the hotel soon afterwards and rented an apartment on the outskirts of the town. A cleaning woman came in the mornings, but most of the time we children were alone. The apartment was wonderful during the day. It was obviously a painter's studio with a high, wide skylight jutting out of the sloping ceiling. That window was like a show for us, a show filled with sky. Once in a while it would be all blue, and then from the corner would appear billowing clouds that would gradually fill up the whole window like a flock of fleecy white sheep. A storm was frightening. The black thunder clouds would flash with lightning and the sheets of rain would close off the window like a curtain. In good weather the window would be full of sun and we could look out onto the colored roofs of the nearby houses.

Vaslav soon devised a new game for us. He began to tame the birds on the roof by throwing bread onto the ledge of our window. First the sparrows would fly to our window, and then the pigeons would stroll about with them. Unfriendly black crows usually stayed on the ground, but once in a while they would attack the window ledge, drive away the smaller birds, and carry away pieces of our bread. We did not like them.

The pigeons soon got used to us. They would sit on the window ledge and look inside and take bread from Vaslav's hand. Some even flew into the room and came and pecked at the bread crumbs on the floor. Other times Vaslav climbed out the window after the pigeons. Stassik and I followed him and we all three sat on the sloping roof below the window and basked in the sun. Soon Vaslav began to explore farther across the roof. I pleaded and begged him not to go so far away but could make no impression on Vaslav. He would not abandon his exploration and even crossed over to the adjoining roof. One day our parents came home and saw us outside the window, and then Vaslav's dangerous adventures on the roof had to stop.

During the summer nights when the sun barely set there was no need of a lamp or candle as the light poured in through our window. These were the White Nights. We lay dozing on our beds trying not to fall asleep. It would be late by the time Mother and Father came home after the performance, and we had to open the door for them. Mama always brought us something tasty—a pastry, candied fruit, halva, pears, or an apple . . .

As we listened to every noise, hoping to hear the sound of their footsteps on the stairs, I was filled with a terrible fear. Even though we had no neighbors and our apartment had its own entrance from the street and we knew that only our parents could come up the steep flight of stairs from the downstairs door, still we were afraid. Whenever we heard the sound of footsteps on the stairs, we jumped out of bed and ran over to the door. As we huddled there listening, all sorts of scary thoughts came into our childish heads: *Maybe it is not Mother and Father. . . . Maybe it is some kind of evil monster . . .*

A loud knock on the door. Before we opened the heavy bolt our three voices would ask "Who is there?" Once Father amused himself by speaking in a terrible voice, saying, "Open quickly, or I will eat you all up!" Then we heard Mother's voice reassuring us, "It's Mama and Papa." When they saw how very frightened we were—for we were, after all, still quite small children; I was five and a half, Vatsa was seven, and Stassik was nine and a half—they promised, "Tomorrow we will take you to the performance!"

They had promised us this for a long time, that one day they would take us to the performance, and impatiently we waited all the next day for the evening. Mama again told me the story of the ballet, as she did not want me to be frightened.

I can see us that evening, high above the arena, I sitting next to Vaslav. A ball is taking place in the palace onstage, and some of the guests come down to the arena and stroll around. Onstage they are dancing Polish dances—*mazurkas, cracoviennes* . . . "I can dance that . . . and that too!" Vaslav keeps exclaiming.

Suddenly a terrible Tartar on a horse leaps out and whirls in a pirouette, the bright lights turn blood red, and terrified guests run in all directions. I am writhing in my seat, but Vaslav is gazing at the arena with fascination, and when more raiding Tartars rush in on horseback to battle the Poles with swords, Vatsa becomes even more excited. But then the Tartar grabs Mama, the Polish Princess Maria, throws her across his horse in front of him, tears around the arena in a furious gallop, and repulses all the Poles who chase after him. . . . I cling to Vaslav. Together we whisper, "Lord save Mamoussia. Matka Boska [Mother of God], save Mamoussia!"

The lights went out and after a minute the upper stage was lit. The harem. Now there was soothing oriental music and dancing, until the terrible Tartar appeared again and threw Mama down at the feet of Khan Guirei. The Khan immediately fell in love with Mama—the Princess Maria—but she did not return his love. All the girls in the harem looked on Mama with angry eyes—especially one, the most beautiful, Zarema.

We became more and more carried away by the ballet, so immersed in the performance we forgot the real world outside. My heart was beating wildly, I could hardly breathe. I tried to force myself to remember what I had been told at home, that this was only make-believe and that Mama was only pretending to be the Princess Maria, asleep on the oriental rugs and pillows. But when I saw Zarema, sneaking in to bend over the sleeping Princess, whispering something to her and then lifting her arm with a dagger in hand . . . I screamed, sobbed, and cried, "She wants to kill Mama . . ." For many days after that performance I was happy only when I could see that Mama was alive and near me. Vatsa teased me for a long time. "Bronia can't go to the theatre—she is a crybaby—she doesn't understand anything yet." I could not leave this unanswered and reminded him that he too had prayed, "Lord save Mamoussia, Matka Boska save Mamoussia!"

The Fountain of Bakhchisarai was last on the program, following several circus acts. The acrobats and jugglers made a tremendous impression on Vaslav, and for days afterwards he worked hard to master some of the acrobatics. Father helped by holding his legs while Vaslav tried to keep his balance standing on his head. Soon he was able to walk on his hands as well as stand on his head, both on his own. Stassik had been more taken with the musical clown who played skillfully on an ocarina—a wind instrument—all the time he was performing his antics. Father gave Stassik an ocarina, and while Vaslav was doing his somersaults and cartwheels all around the room, Stassik would play his new instrument and try to render familiar tunes on it. Vaslav also taught himself how to juggle, first with two apples and then three. He could also balance a plate on the end of Father's walking stick. I wanted to do everything the boys did, so Father taught me to tumble head over heels on my bed. I also practiced standing on my head by propping my back and legs against the wall. Picking up all these acrobatics from the circus proved useful to me eventually in my choreography: *Le Renard, Le Train Bleu, Impressions de Music Hall,* and other ballets. Even now the memories of those happy days attract me to the circus.

The Coronation Season in Narva did not last long. In a few weeks we left for Vilno.

6   Vilno: 1896

EACH SUMMER our parents would work in either summer theatres or circuses, where pantomime ballets would be performed. Father preferred to work in the circuses where he had the opportunity to stage large spectacular ballets. At the end of the Coronation Season in Narva we returned to Poland, to Vilno, where our parents had an engagement with Salamonsky's Circus. I do not remember at all what parts in the program they performed, as Vatsa and I became wholly engrossed in our own performances.

The great Vladimir Dourov was with Salamonsky's Circus. For his pantomime he used children and animals. In the center of the ring was a small house with a gallery or balcony. The "residents" of the house—mice and rabbits in hats and little skirts—looked out of the windows and then strolled on the gallery.

I was a bridegroom and wore short black satin pants and a red satin tailcoat. Another girl, even smaller than I, was the bride dressed in a traditional white wedding dress with a veil and carrying a large bouquet. We rode together in a miniature lacquered open wedding carriage. I held the reins, driving a team of four dogs. They ran around the edge of the ring while Dourov stood in the middle cracking his whip. Our carriage tore along faster and faster to the music: "I will harness a troika of swift speed . . ." The bride and bridegroom waved to the people on all sides, and when they arrived at the house got out of the carriage. We bowed to the audience who applauded us loudly, then we turned and went into the house, which suddenly appeared to catch fire. Steam illuminated with red lights poured out of it, looking like smoke. The bride and bridegroom had to jump out of the house and run away as though frightened by the fire.

Animals dressed up as firemen came into the ring with their fire brigade, ringing the bells on their tiny vehicles, bringing their equipment

—barrels of water, ladders, and fire hoses—and then proceeded to extinguish the burning house. Dogs in firemen's helmets rolled a barrel of water; monkeys watered the house with the fire hose; mice, cats, piglets, puppies, rabbits in bonnets and skirts could be seen in the windows dodging the flames.

Vaslav was a chimney sweep, all dressed in black, with a black skullcap on his head, his hands and face covered with soot, carrying a short ladder over his shoulder. He, too, ran around the fire, then climbed his ladder to help in the rescue from the roof. First he would throw down a dog to Dourov, next a piglet would be saved from the fire, and finally a white fluffy rabbit. He grabbed the rabbit, jumped down from the roof into the ring, and passed the rabbit over. Then he ran to the monkey-fireman and snatched the fire nozzle from him. The monkey jumped up onto his shoulders as Vaslav excitedly extinguished the flames of the burning house.

Vaslav was in action until the fire was out, performing his part of the chimney sweep, the hero, the savior of the inhabitants of the burning house, with enthusiasm. I watched everything he did on the roof with admiration, though sorry that I too was not taking part in this scene in which he was having so much fun.

At the end of each performance Dourov would take his bow before the delighted audience, then he would take Vaslav by the hand and they took a bow together.

This experience in Vilno, of being in the wings of the circus—for the first time "artists" on equal footing with adult artists—was the height of bliss for us. It affected Vaslav very deeply. I remember after each performance how uncommonly quiet and pensive he would be as he walked home ahead of Mother and me. Vaslav was still immersed in the experience and was thinking about the next day's performance, what should be improved or added.

In Vilno we lived with our aunts Stepha and Thetya. Aunt Stepha was extraordinarily beautiful. She was no longer dancing in theatres but was teaching ballroom dancing in the government high schools. This appointment entitled her to a rent-free apartment. She also taught at a private school, the Institute for Young Ladies.

Aunt Theodosia, the eldest sister, was now a widow and, with her daughter, Stanislava, was living with Aunt Stepha. The apartment was large enough so there was plenty of room for our family of five to stay there as well. Our cousin Stassia was already in the upper grades of the High School. She was very attractive and talented, and was studying music and singing. She taught Stassik and Vaslav to play the piano. Vatsa was her special favorite and she spoiled him. She would intercede for him in all his pranks, for she always considered that whatever the misdemeanor he was unjustly accused.

That summer Father and Mother were offered a three-month contract with a revue in Paris, and both aunts tried to persuade them to leave us in Vilno. "The children," they suggested, "could have a quiet family life here with us. They will not suffer any hardship and later can go to the *Gymnasium* and get a good education, instead of traveling from town to town."

Father was gladly ready to agree to the offer, and we children also loved the idea. We felt we had a home in Vilno and adored our dear aunts and cousin as much as they loved us. But Mama would not even discuss it. She felt her maternal responsibilities very deeply and would not part with her children. And so, to please Mother, Father reluctantly had to refuse the offer.

Our mother's deep devotion and attachment to her children was a strain on our parents' relationship and harmful to their artistic careers. There were many interesting engagements Father couldn't accept because he always had to give first consideration to the comfort and needs of the children.

Once or twice Mother and Father danced at Krasnoe Selo. This was before I was born, but I remember a poster featuring their performance that was kept in our home. Usually only artists from the Imperial Theatres appeared during the summer in Krasnoe Selo, but Father was such a success that he was invited to join the Maryinsky Theatre as a character dancer. It was when Stassik was little and the salary was only one hundred twenty-five rubles a month, which would not have been enough to support his family.

Later he also received an offer to join the Imperial Theatres in Moscow as a dancer, and there the salary was only one hundred rubles a month. At this time Father was already a ballet master earning four hundred rubles a month in the private theatres. He had also choreographed two very successful ballets, *The Fountain of Bakhchisarai* and *Zaporozheskaya Tcharovnitza*, and as a choreographer his salary was an additional eight hundred rubles a month. He refused the Imperial Theatres' offer for he doubted, inasmuch as they had their own ballet masters who had studied in the Imperial Theatrical School, that he would ever be asked to mount a ballet there. Instead he recommended a colleague, Boutchinsky, a bachelor whose only ambition was to be a dancer.

Aunt Stepha's apartment in Vilno looked out on Ostra Brama Street, which led up the hill to the ancient gate of the city. Above the gate was the

Catholic chapel with the miraculous Ikon of Ostra Brama. The apartment was quite near the chapel, and sometimes with Mother and Stassik, but more often on our own, we would go up to the chapel to pray. Vaslav and I liked to go there in the mornings. The chapel would be filled with people, some kneeling, others prostrate on the floor, praying in whispers before the Holy Ikon with its priceless decoration. There were always many candles, large and small, illuminating the Ikon, so that the precious stones shone brightly. The Ikon was something extraordinarily beautiful. Here was our first encounter with Beauty in Art.

Vaslav would kneel in prayer, his hands together, close to his chest. I do not know what occupied his prayers. I never asked him whether, as his eyes lifted to the face of the Mother of God, he repeated prayers learned by heart, or whether words inspired by the Ikon sprang together into prayers in his mind, or whether he found himself, as I did, in his thoughts, far from earth and on the very brink of heaven . . .

7   Moscow: 1896–1897

FROM VILNO we went to Moscow where Father signed a contract with the Oman Variety Theatre, a Café-Chantant. As Father was now drawing a large salary, more than one thousand rubles a month, Mother decided to stay home with her children and not work with Father in the Theatre. Mama was always quite thrifty and we often heard her say, "We must think about the future and the children." But our parents were never able to save because Father loved to be with painters, writers, actors, and musicians and would usually end up paying the bill for everyone. He also loved to discuss politics and would often get together with Polish patriots. Mama did not like such gatherings in smoke-filled rooms where many rounds of drinks were served. She preferred to stay home with us rather than go with Father for dinner or supper with his colleagues and friends.

Father was himself a light drinker and only once did I ever see him drunk. That was in Moscow, where he was brought home after supper by his friends who had gotten him drunk. I remember how frightened Mother looked when she saw Father with his eyes closed and not able to stand unaided. Immediately they put Father to bed, but they could only let him rest for a short while as he soon had to be sobered up for the evening performance at the Oman Theatre.

For that entire Moscow winter season of 1896–97, a teacher came to us every afternoon. Along with Stassik and Vatsa, I learned to read, write, and do a little arithmetic. Each of us had a copybook with a blotter, attached by a narrow ribbon. Next to our hotel was a stationery store, and when we bought our copybooks we received a free little picture. I invariably chose lacquered pictures, but Vatsa loved transfers as he was expert with them.

We were never bored in Moscow, being always busy doing something. Near our hotel were many large houses with enormous courtyards that Vaslav loved to explore. He found many friends there. In one house lived a family of ballet artists, Shearer-Bekefi, related to Alfred Bekefi, the well-known Artist of the Imperial Theatres. We became friends with the children. There were two girls older than Vatsa and Stassik, and a very tiny girl, Maroussia, as well as a good-looking boy, Fedya, about my own age. They often came to visit us. Later Fedya Shearer and his sister Maroussia were students at the Imperial School at the same time as Vaslav and myself. We also came to know their uncle, Alfred Bekefi, who taught the character classes in the School until 1905.

At night Father would return home late from the Theatre and have the supper Mama had prepared for him along with a cold beer. One evening we children had just gone to bed when one of Father's colleagues, who was living in our hotel, knocked at the door. Mother opened the door and unwillingly let him into the hall but did not invite him into the living room, saying it was late and she was preparing the children for bed.

He was not to be put off and said, "I have some guests I would have liked to bring over, but if you don't care to let us in to wait and have supper with Foma, then the least you can do is lend me a few bottles of beer."

Nervously Mother answered him, "I'm very sorry but I have nothing to offer you, not even a beer."

Suddenly Vaslav, having jumped out of bed, appeared in the hall. "Mama, you forget, there are two bottles on the window." And to the embarrassment of our mother he brought the two bottles and handed them to the "guest."

Mother was at a loss for words, while the "guest" patted Vaslav on the head and disappeared with the two bottles.

Mother then told Vaslav that he should have kept quiet and not made his mother look like a liar. Vaslav defended himself. "But I told the truth. I saw the two bottles on the window and thought you had forgotten them."

"You are a stupid boy. I did not have any beer to spare. Now your father will come home late and tired, and instead of beer he will have only cold water to drink. You gave away the beer I was cooling for him, and now the stranger will enjoy it with his friends."

Vaslav started to cry and ran back into the bedroom he shared with Stassik.

When Father finished his contract with the Oman Theatre, he assembled a small company including the ballerina Gousekevitch, Vaslav's and my godmother. They went to Finland for a short season, and we remained in Moscow. It was the first time we had been separated from Father. Mama, we could see, was very upset. After Father's departure we children quieted down, especially Vaslav, who stopped playing pranks and began to work diligently with our teacher.

8   Novaya Derevnia

FOR THE SUMMER of 1897 Mother and Father had an engagement together in St. Petersburg to dance in the operas at the Arcadia Theatre in the Summer Gardens, in Novaya Derevnia—"The New Village," a summer resort for St. Petersburg on the islands in the delta of the Neva. There were two other theatres as well as the Arcadia—the Livadia and the Kin Grust. All three were equipped to stage elaborate productions of operas and other spectaculars. Konstantin Skalkovsky, a contemporary critic, commented in his book, *In the Theatrical World*, published in St. Petersburg towards the end of the nineteenth century: "At the Maryinsky it is impossible to effect the simplest changes of scenery without lowering the curtain, while at the theaters of the Summer Gardens, in the course of one act, five to six changes of scenery *à vue* are a common occurrence."

Mother and Father had previously worked in all three of the Novaya Derevnia theatres. In 1885 they had appeared in Lentovsky's fantastic spectacular, *Trip to the Moon*, staged in the Kin Grust Theatre, when Virginia Zucchi and Maria Giuri* had danced for the first time in Russia. And in 1886 my parents had danced in the Arcadia Theatre where Setov had staged *Wiener Walzer*, a spectacular depicting the evolution of the waltz since its introduction in 1795. Father was the ballet master for this rich production with magnificent sets and costumes, and Mother was a first soloist.

---

*Both ballerinas had studied with Carlo Blasis at La Scala and were now at the peak of their careers, but, according to Skalkovsky, although Giuri surpassed Zucchi by the brilliance of her technique on toe the public gave greater acclaim to Zucchi, whom Skalkovsky described as dancing with "soul and fire." Following the Lentovsky spectacular at Kin Grust, Zucchi was invited to dance for the Royal Family at the Krasnoselsky Theatre and the Director of the Imperial Theatres invited her to dance at the Maryinsky, where the "Divine Zucchi," as she came to be called, stayed for seven years. Giuri, meanwhile, was invited to dance in America. On her return she was engaged to dance in Milan, and later she danced in Russia with various companies, including that of Thomas Nijinsky. (IN/JR)

Italian ballerinas like Virginia Zucchi, Antonietta Dell'Era, and Carlotta Brianza became famous in St. Petersburg on the stages of the Arcadia, Livadia, and Kin Grust before they were engaged by the Maryinsky Theatre. Mother often used to tell me how in the summer of 1886, on May 24, in the Arcadia Theatre, she had seen the debut of Antonietta Dell'Era.

The following summer, 1887, Mother and Father again performed in Novaya Derevnia, where Setov was staging the monumental spectacular ballet *Excelsior** in which Carlotta Brianza made her Russian debut. The dances were mounted by the ballet master Giorgio Sarraco.

Now in 1897 they were once again dancing in Novaya Derevnia, and for Vaslav and me it was our first time in St. Petersburg. We arrived in May but did not stay in the city; we went directly to Novaya Derevnia. Almost immediately Mama tried to submit an application for both Stanislav and Vaslav to the Imperial Theatrical School in St. Petersburg. She was distressed by her cold reception. She could not see any official and was simply told that both boys needed to go to school first to learn to read and write in Russian and that in any case Vaslav was too young.

When Mother returned to Novaya Derevnia, she and Father talked to Cleopatra Alexandrovna Karatyguina and Joachim Victorovitch Tartakoff, two Russian artists whose acquaintance they had renewed during the performance at the Arcadia Theatre, and with whom they had previously worked in Kiev. Tartakoff had been a young singer then, at the beginning of his career, and now he was a soloist at the Maryinsky Theatre. Mme Karatyguina had starred in a comedy at the Summer Theatre in Kiev and Father had mounted a short ballet to complete the program. She had graduated in 1866 from the Imperial Theatrical School and was a very talented dancer. However, Cleopatra Gluharova (Karatyguina) preferred to be an actress. In the first year after her graduation she starred in a French play being performed in St. Petersburg and, following her marriage to A. A. Karatyguin, a member of a famous family of actors, she acted in many private theatres throughout Russia. She was a person of great influence who knew everyone in the theatrical world of St. Petersburg, and she promised to speak to Ivan Vsevolojsky, the Director of the Imperial Theatres, about the Nijinsky children. Mama depended very much on Karatyguina and Tartakoff, convinced that her children had no chance of even being admitted to the entrance examination without their influence.

*The theme of *Excelsior* was the triumph of industrial progress. The original version by Luigi Manzotti in 1881 at La Scala extolled contemporary scientific achievements such as the building of the Suez Canal. The ballet was a huge success, and was produced also in Paris and London. (AK)

That summer in Novaya Derevnia, we lived in a small two-story dacha with its own garden not far from the Arcadia Theatre. We had a nanny to look after us—Klavdia, a young widow who had recently lost "my boss," as she called her late husband. She was good-hearted and became very attached to our mother and didn't want to distress her or worry her about the children. So it was easy to persuade Niannia, as we children called Klavdia, not to tell Mother about Vaslav's escapades, and there were many that summer.

Next door, separated only by a vacant lot, was a large three-story house where several families of gypsies lived. *"Real live gypsies!"* we would say to each other, fascinated by the bright, multicolored costumes they wore. They were the popular St. Petersburg Gypsy Chorus, and I believe they were working in a theatre on Krestovsky Island. They had many famous soloists, both singers and dancers.

We could hear the gypsy singing from our garden, but Vatsa wanted to get closer and see them as well, so he took to wandering around their house. He would tell me about the beautiful black horses he saw in their stables. Very soon he made friends with the gypsy boys, who were a little older than he and even more mischievous.

Mama was so displeased with Vatsa's friendship with the gypsies that she forbade us to play with them and would not allow them to come into our garden. Niannia would often catch Vatsa and rebuke him, "Vassia, why do you go on playing with the gypsies when you know your mother will be angry and punish you?" He would plead in reply, "Niannia, they sing so well. I'm not doing anything wrong. I sit quietly and just listen to their songs. Besides, they have such wonderful satin-smooth horses. They are so gentle and they let me stroke them."

Stassik and I also loved horses and with our pocket money would buy little wooden toy horses with manes and tails made of straw, for three kopeks each. In our garden we made our own stable with a long row of stalls. We dyed some of the horses' manes and tails with ink.

Probably it was at the gypsies' that Vatsa met a bird catcher and became fascinated by the world of birds. He started to bring home little birds in small wooden cages—siskins and bullfinches. Soon Stassik and I came to share his new passion. We spent all our savings on these little birds that would always fly away, and then we would grieve until we could buy another one. One day Vatsa brought home a new bird, a bluetit. Suddenly Niannia came up to the cage and before our very eyes set the bird free.

We rushed towards her. "Niannia, what have you done? . . . Our very new bird! . . . We have hardly seen her . . ." I remember as clearly as if it were yesterday, the severe look on Niannia's face and her serious tone of voice. "How could you bring a bluetit into the house? Now a misfortune will come about. . . . Someone will die!"

We shuddered at the thought, and this proved the end of our passion for pet birds. Niannia's prophecy did indeed come true—for herself.

Whenever Vaslav was not running away to join the gypsies he would practice acrobatic stunts in the garden. He was particularly good at inventing new tricks. He would climb the tallest trees and cross from one to the next over the branches. I would stand on the ground beneath him, trembling with fear that he might fall and hurt himself badly. Then Vatsa taught me how to climb the trees so that I could sit in the branches with him, and gradually I ceased to be afraid.

In the garden there was a high swing mounted on strong wooden posts. We loved to swing on it. It was always frightening to be with Vatsa on the swing, he flew so high. Once I was alone on the swing and Vatsa came and moved me to one side of the board and told me to grip the ropes tightly with both hands. He then stood on the other side of the board and started to swing higher and higher until the board was straight up in the air. Suddenly I realized that Vatsa and I were upside down. For a moment the swing seemingly froze in the air. Vatsa curved his body in an arc as if hurling himself forward and we were swiftly thrown over the crossbar. Still swinging high, I saw that Vaslav was holding on to one rope, and indicating with his other hand for me to turn around. Obediently I did so, moving to the other side, and the trial by fear was repeated. Once more we flew high, now in the other direction, and were thrown back over the crossbar so that the ropes that had twisted over the bar in our first flight now were back in place and no trace of our escapade could be seen.

How Vatsa loved to climb! Whenever he was at the top of a tree, on a high post, on the swing, or on the roof of our house, I noticed a rapturous delight on his face, a delight to feel his body high above the ground, suspended in midair. He would climb out of the attic window onto the sloping roof, walk to the very edge, boasting how brave he was, or he would stand on one leg and stretch out his arms, extended like wings, pretending he wanted to take off in flight. Or he would crouch down as if ready to jump off. I used to implore him to come down, but my fright and the joy of having an audience would urge him on to even more outrageous stunts. It is astonishing that no misfortune happened to us that summer.

During one of his excursions onto the roof Vatsa suddenly saw our parents in the distance. They were coming home early. In a panic, for he had been punished more than once for his gymnastics, and without hesitating a single second, he jumped down from the second-story roof onto a pile of sand. I was certain he had crashed to his death. He remained crouched on his knees for only a second or so, then stood erect, as white as a sheet of paper, and went with me to meet Mama and Papa, telling me on the way, "Bronia, keep quiet. I'm all right, I don't hurt at all. Don't say anything to Mama. If you don't cry, she will never know." To placate me he added, "I will give you all the horses in my stable!"

This was not the last of Vaslav's adventures in Novaya Derevnia. Wanting very much to keep up with the gypsy boys when they went fishing, he was busying himself with a fishing line. The river was not far away, and though it was not very wide it was deep, and its name—Black River—frightened me. Not one of us could swim at that time, and so we did not dare go bathing in it. I was sure, though, that Vaslav dreamed of going on the river in a boat, and that he would find a way of doing so. I tried to talk him out of any excursion on the water, stressing the river's name, so ominous to me. Vaslav was not frightened by the ominous name nor was he afraid of the river itself. On the contrary, he seemed to be excited and fascinated by it. One day, when our parents were not expected back until evening, Vaslav disappeared.

He did not come home for lunch. Niannia went to the gypsies' house. The younger boys were home but said they had no idea where Vaslav might be. Stassik and I rushed to look for Vatsa on the banks of the river, but did not find him there. We began to question a boatman who rented out boats on the small pier, and he told us that the big gypsy boys had rented a boat from him and that they had had a little Russian boy with them. Scared, Stassik and I ran home. We decided not to say anything to Niannia and stayed quietly in the garden waiting for Vaslav, hoping he would be back any minute. I imagined him in a boat on the threatening river and my heart nearly stopped beating. As the time for dinner drew near, all I could do was pray that Vaslav would get home before Mama and Papa.

Our parents, when they returned, were so busy talking about their day they did not immediately notice Vaslav's absence. When they did, they first questioned Niannia, and then very sternly questioned Stassik and me. We had to reveal the truth, that Vaslav was in a boat on the river with the gypsies. Mama was in despair. What if the boys played pranks in the boat, suppose they overturned it? . . . Vatsa did not know how to swim! Seeing our parents' grief, I felt Vaslav's danger even more keenly.

It was getting dark and nearly time for our parents to go to the Theatre for their evening performance. I went out and stood looking down the road, waiting for Vatsa. At last I saw him far in the distance. Forgetting everything else, I ran to meet him, as though he had been rescued from certain death. His first words were, "Bronia, how is Mama? Is Papa home? What will they do to me for this?" I told him quickly what concern there had been at home.

"It's terrible, Vaslav, Mama is crying, she believes you to be drowned. Aren't you ashamed? Papa is at home and he is very angry. Why didn't you come home earlier?"

"The gypsies weren't ready to come, and I couldn't jump out of the boat." He caught my hands. "Dearest Bronia, will you go and tell them that I will never do it again. I am so afraid."

"Vatsa, how can you be? Let's go together. Think about Mama, she is so worried. Maybe Papa and Mama will be so happy and relieved to see you that they will not punish you."

I took Vaslav by the hand but still he pulled back and resisted. "I am afraid to go home . . . you see, one of the gypsies ordered me to bring some money or they would not let me go on the boat. I took a ruble from the dresser."

I knew no one had discovered that yet and so I suggested, "When Mama is alone, it would be best if you told her about that yourself, Vaslav."

"I will do anything for you, Bronia, if Mama and Papa will not be too angry with me. Here, take this." He pulled out of his pocket a cut-glass Easter egg he never would part with. "I don't want this anymore."

When we reached the house little Vatsa looked so pitiful and crushed. Our parents were just ready to leave for the Theatre. Vatsa fell to his knees, crying and weeping, and implored them, "Tatous, Mamoussia, forgive me. I will never again be so bad, so wicked." Father pushed him away. "Get out of my sight. Go, wash yourself and go to bed. I will deal with you tomorrow morning!"

Vaslav was terribly frightened, and I couldn't understand what kind of punishment he was imagining. Mother and Father rarely punished us. Vaslav usually looked so unhappy after an offense and implored forgiveness so pitifully, that Mother, who suffered if we were punished, would happily seize on whatever pretext for forgiveness could be found. And Father, as I look back on our childhood, was more often full of admiration for Vaslav rather than distressed and angered by the daring and fearlessness of his son. Nevertheless, he was not easily moved by our tears and would begin his punitive ritual. Sternly, he would say to Vaslav, "Take your pants down!" Trembling and weeping, Vaslav would beg for forgiveness, but Father would continue, "Lie down on the chair!" Vaslav would then fall to his knees, "Forgive me Papa, forgive me!" Stassik and I would begin to cry too, and beg Father not to punish Vaslav. But Father was not to be moved, and he would repeat, "Lie down on the chair!" Then Mother would catch Father's hand and intercede for Vaslav, saying,

"Look, he knows he is a bad boy and promises this will be the last time!" Father would finally relent and tell Vaslav, "Go and stand in the corner!"

As I remember, Father did not resort to this punitive ordeal often, and it was indeed an ordeal for us children, even though the threatened punishment was never carried out. Vaslav's fear of punishment was always strong, but this time it was especially so, as Mother and Father had met him with stern faces and harsh voices, concealing their happiness at seeing him unharmed. I tried to console him, "Why are you afraid? . . . nothing will happen to you!"

The next morning began full of gloom for Vaslav. But, instead of carrying out the expected punishment, Father declared, "Come with me to swim in the deep Neva."

The Great Nevka had closed bathing huts, separate ones for men and women, and you had to pay to enter them. After they got undressed Father told Vatsa to get in the water and he showed him how to swim, for Father was an excellent swimmer. The bathing hut was very deep for an eight-year-old boy. Vatsa sat on the wooden deck, lowered his feet into the water, but could not bring himself to get right into it, saying, "Papa, I will drown, it is very deep here." Then Father got out of the water, caught Vatsa up in his arms, and threw him in, shouting "Swim!"

"I was covered at once by water over my head and found myself on the bottom," Vatsa told us when they came back. "I quickly jumped to my feet and, not knowing what to do, opened my eyes and walked forward on the wooden floor of the bathing hut. The water was so transparent, I could see everything. There was so much water over my head that I got terribly frightened and began to strike the water with my hands and legs. I suddenly came to the surface and *I was swimming*!"

Vaslav was incredibly happy as he told us how he learned to swim that very first day. Regularly after that, Father took Vaslav and Stassik to the bathing huts on the Neva. One morning he took them to Sestroretzk on the Gulf of Finland, twenty-five or thirty versts from Novaya Derevnia, to bathe in the sea. When the boys returned they told me all about bathing in the sea, in the open air, not enclosed in a bathing hut. How they loved the beach, where they had turned somersaults on the sand!

Sometimes our parents took us to the Theatre in the evenings. We loved to walk through the gardens, the paths illuminated by Chinese lanterns, the music of a military orchestra in the distance, the elegantly dressed ladies and gentlemen wandering through the gardens on their way to the opera. We especially enjoyed the performances of short ballets and *divertissements* on the open-air stage.

Stassik and Vaslav were often taken to the Opera Theatre and had heard several performances, but I can only remember being taken to see the ballet in one opera. I remember that I liked the name: *L'Africaine.** We sat in the front row of the stalls, and the Theatre was almost empty. I do not remember the dances, only a "brown" ballet in which all the artists wore brown, heavy, wool-knitted tops and tights, big brass earrings, and enormous black woolen wigs. Their lips were outlined broadly in red paint and their eyes in white and black paint. The weather was intensely hot and the Theatre was stifling. I did not follow the plot of the opera or the ballet, being tormented by the thought, "How hot they must be in their heavy costumes!" I could see the perspiration streaming down their makeup, and their badly fitting, wrinkled tights were covered with dark spots. It was easy to see where their costumes ended and their own non-African bodies began. Neither Vaslav nor I liked the ballet; mostly we examined the scenery, for it was the first time we had seen life-size palm trees painted on the sets.

After the performance Mama asked me, "Well, how did you like the ballet? Did we dance well?" I answered with the candor of a six-year-old, "No. The dancers did not look like the real savages we saw in Nijni Novgorod."

"But those savages certainly couldn't dance as well as we do here in the theatre. It doesn't need to be real. In the theatre it is make-believe."

Mama had been sure that we would like the dances of the "savages" —the tropical scenery, the full chorus, and the large cast with lots of *figurants*—and was astonished when Vaslav added, "They had very bad makeup. Their faces looked like the apprentice clowns who roll up the carpets at the end of the clowns' act."

"But did you enjoy the performance?" Mama insisted.

"No, Mama," I replied. "All the time I was sorry for them. Why did they have to wear long, warm, costumes in the summer? I don't want to see the African ballet anymore. I don't like it. I want to see again and again that gay ballet. The one where you and Father dance so wonderfully."

This favorite of ours was a Ukrainian ballet staged by our father from the book *The Evenings in a Hamlet near Dikanka,*† by Gogol. The ballet was called *Zaporozheskaya Tcharovnitza*, and was full of humor. We laughed during all the *mises en scène* and loudly applauded and cheered our father's

*Opera in five acts, music by Giacomo Meyerbeer, with the fourth act a ballet by Louis Mérante. First performed in Paris, 1865. (IN/JR)

†These stories are set in the Ukraine and Thomas Nijinsky utilized Ukrainian dances in his staging. (AK)

dances, especially the *hopak*. He would jump so high that his tall lambskin hat would disappear into the frieze of the set, and then he would drop down like a stone, landing with both legs extended sideways in a split. Immediately he would jump up again and execute many other spectacular stunts, bringing tumultuous applause from the audience.

Father had been trained in classical ballet and as a young artist had often danced with Italian ballerinas in the private theatres, but his genius was revealed in character dances. He created many new steps and was imitated by numerous popular Russian dancers. Mother, in her character dances, displayed the fiery spirit of her Polish ancestors, while in her classical dance technique she had assimilated much of the Italian School, having worked with many Italian ballerinas who were engaged for the Opera Seasons in Kiev, Odessa, and Tiflis. Mother was particularly proud that when dancing in the Summer Theatres in St. Petersburg, 1885–87, she had had the opportunity, during the daily ballet classes attended by the whole ballet company, of studying with Virginia Zucchi and Carlotta Brianza.

But that summer at the Arcadia, in Novaya Derevnia, was the last time she worked together with Father in the theatre.

—

THE OPERA SEASON continued into September even though it was growing cold and damp and it often rained. Many of the artists had left, and the wind wailed around the empty houses. It seemed as though with the end of summer my carefree, happy childhood was also coming to an end.

We children knew that the time had come to enroll Stassik and Vaslav in regular school and that we should be going to St. Petersburg in the fall with Mother, who was planning to enter Stanislav and Vaslav for the Imperial Theatrical School examination. She had already started looking there for an apartment for us. Father, however, had signed a contract with a theatre in Moscow, and so was not going to live with us.

During his work in Finland just before we had come to Novaya Derevnia, Father had met a dancer named Rumiantseva. He was now spending all his free time with her. Mother and Father never talked in front of us about their personal relationship, but I could sense that some important, sad changes were happening within our family. Even Father noticed my awareness. "Bronia is an incredibly mature child," he once said to a friend, whispering so that I would not hear. This sentence remained in my mind for a long time because I did not understand the word *mature* and felt that because Father talked about it in a whisper it must be some terrible vice in me.

Each day Mama would go with Father to the rehearsals but would return alone for dinner and then go back for the performance. We began to see less and less of Father, as we were usually in bed when he returned at night. My room was on the ground floor and sometimes, when I could not fall asleep, I would hear their arguments when they came in together. Those long agonizing nights, lying awake in my bed, listening to Mother's trembling, tormented voice and Father's agitated tones, hearing the unbearable grief of my mother, all tore at my child's heart. I learned that some abominable woman had stolen our father and was taking him away, and that he was abandoning Mama and his children.

I could not conceive of living without my adored father. I did not look to blame anyone, for Mother and Father were equally dear to me. I never saw my mother crying, but I knew she was suffering and trying to hide her emotions from us. I loved her very much and would keep telling her, "Mama, you are so beautiful, more beautiful than ever," but she would only smile sadly at me and then cover her eyes with her hand.

Stassik and Vaslav were as disturbed as Mama and I by the impending separation from Father. Stassik grieved in silence and was unusually quiet. Vaslav responded differently; that summer his behavior was specially stormy. His reckless escapades and disobedience, which Klavdia tried to hide from Mama or to blame on the gypsies, I can see now, were to mask his inner suffering over the events in our family. Mother's grief pained Vaslav and he spoke out often, taking Mother's side, which aggravated the already tense situation. Mother told him not to interfere, and so during those last summer days in the dacha Vaslav would simply avoid Father and try not to look in his direction. It was as if he were throwing Father out of his heart.

Every evening until our parents returned from the Theatre we were left alone with Klavdia, who would tell us stories about the "brownie," a mischievous goblin who lived in the house. After I was put to bed I would hear footsteps and moaning and sighing. I tried to overcome my fear of the "brownie," but one night I could bear it no longer. I started to scream and call for Niannia. She came running, leaned over my bed, and began to soothe me. "Sleep baby, quiet, it's nothing to be afraid of. It is our good brownie moaning, but if he sees that you are afraid of him and you do not go to sleep, then Lord save us, that will be bad luck."

We did not know it then but Niannia was already seriously ill. Like most Russian peasants she was mortally afraid of going into a hospital, and so she was trying to conceal her illness. But one morning Mama noticed her looking extremely pale and strange and asked her, "Klavdia, dear, what is it? You don't look well."

"No, no, Gospojha [Mistress], I am perfectly well. But there is something wrong with this house. I didn't want to tell you about it as it is a bad omen for me."

Mama was exasperated. "Now, Klavdia, what are you inventing? With stories like this no wonder the children are so frightened they can't get to sleep until we return from the Theatre. Soon we shall be moving from this house and going to St. Petersburg. Then everything will be all right."

"No," interrupted Klavdia, "I will not be coming to St. Petersburg with you. Death is coming for me here. Last night he even knocked at the door. I thought it was you, come home from the Theatre early. I wouldn't open the door until I heard your voice, as you've told me. But you didn't say anything. I went to the window and saw the figure of a man leaving the porch. Suddenly he turned his head. My God, I see it is my boss. I wanted to turn away from the window but I couldn't take my eyes away from him. He was walking away from me but one hand beckoned me until he disappeared. That's my death. That's my boss come for me!"

Niannia told this story with such simplicity and conviction that I believed her completely and was quite indignant for her when I heard Mama say, "Now Klavdia, is this a dream, a story you are telling?" I resented Mother's words and thought to myself, "Why is it grown-ups never believe anything?"

For some time Stassik and I had not been well and Mama had noticed that whenever the doctor came to see us, Niannia was never around and impossible to find. She decided that the next time the doctor came he should see Klavdia too. When he finally did see her, he discovered that she had an advanced form of typhoid and had been ill for a long time. He immediately put her in the hospital and, as she had feared, she died three days later. And so we lost our poor, dear Niannia.

Later Mother told me that at the very hour of Klavdia's death I screamed out in a delirium, "Good-bye Niannia. Go away! Go away! I don't want to go with you."

Stassik and I had both been infected by Niannia and were running high fevers. Stassik was moved into my room downstairs and we were not allowed out of bed. I did not sleep at all during those nights. Every part of me ached—my head, my body, and my heart. When our parents came home I was again able to hear them talking together. None of the sorrows of later life made me suffer as deeply as did those long painful nights of overhearing the parting talks between Father and Mother. Children no less than adults feel the profound catastrophes of the heart.

I do not remember our moving to St. Petersburg, into the new apartment. I cannot remember Father's departure. For six weeks Mama never left our bedside, she fought for our lives. It is difficult to imagine what she went through at this time. Separation from her husband, two children near death, and in this sorrow all alone, no relatives near, no close friends, as she began a new life for us in an unknown city, in St. Petersburg, the capital of Russia.

9   Our First Year
in St. Petersburg

STASSIK AND I were still ill with typhoid fever when we arrived in St. Petersburg, so Vaslav was the only one of us able to go to school. Mama enrolled him in a preparatory school, nearby on our own street.

Our recovery from the illness went slowly, and we were confined to our bedroom for a long time. Vaslav was not permitted to enter our room but would stick his head around the door and amuse us with funny grimaces. Sometimes when the door was shut he would push the dining-room table close to our bedroom door, get up on the table, and talk to us through the transom above the door. He would bring an apple, orange, or some chocolate, and tease us by eating it with gusto.

From the stories Vaslav told us, Stassik and I received our first information about St. Petersburg. As he walked to school Vaslav had begun to familiarize himself with our house and its neighborhood. We lived at 20 Mokhovaya Ulitza [Street]. The house was a large one, with four stories. Each floor had one main apartment, occupying three-quarters of the area, and an additional small apartment, like ours, Apartment 9, with three rooms and a kitchen. The house was built around three sides of a huge courtyard, and on the fourth side rose the enormous windowless wall of the five-story house next door. There were no trees or shrubs in the courtyard, which was paved with cobblestones and had a wooden walk from our entrance to the gateway. In winter the high neighboring wall served as a shelter for black crows cawing stridently all the time. The entire courtyard was painted with chalky yellow paint, which made it look bright and gay in any kind of weather.

We lived on the third floor and Vaslav told us about the rest of the house. The first floor was occupied by a store in which upright and concert grand pianos were rented and sold. On the second floor lived old Countess Perovska, and on the third General Kokhanovsky. I believe the owner of the house, whom none of us ever saw, lived on the fourth floor. The whole place was managed by the head custodian, Moukhin—he let the apartments, collected the rents, and supervised the cleaning of the house, the courtyard, and the street in front of the house.

There were deep cellars where the firewood was stored for the winter, and above the fourth floor was a high attic where the tenants' laundry was hung to dry. Vatsa had soon thoroughly examined the whole house, the cellars, and, of course, the attic, where he found a small window through which he could climb out onto the roof. Whenever he played with his black cast-rubber ball in the courtyard and bounced it onto the roof, he would go up to the attic, climb out through the window, and collect the ball from the very edge of the roof, where it had usually caught in the drainpipe.

The windows of each apartment overlooked the courtyard. General Kokhanovsky's were high and arched, while the Countess Perovska's were lower, except for one that was huge and square, extending over the entire gateway and all beautiful plate glass. Vatsa got into trouble over this—his hard rubber ball broke it. Luckily only a corner was broken, so the man gave Mama credit for the rest of the plate glass. But she still had to pay twenty-five rubles to replace the window.

Even when Stassik and I began to get better, Mama would not let us go out of the apartment because of the thick fogs, strong winds, and rainy days. From the windows of the drawing room overlooking the back courtyard, Stassik and I could see the coach-houses of Countess Perovska and General Kokhanovsky and the stables with the horses. The harnessing and hitching of the horses to the carriages all took place in the back courtyard. Soon we knew all the horses, grooms, and coachmen, and as we sat on the wide windowsill of the drawing room we would try to guess, "Which horses will be harnessed today? The black, or the dapple-gray pair? The single golden one? Will the coachman put on his blue coat, or the dark raspberry, or the gray? On the horses, will it be net or cloth? Will it be blue or raspberry, or the festive white with the tassels?"

The back courtyard provided us with great entertainment. It was a real show to watch the coachman being dressed. He seemed to us to be an extraordinarily important person, what with two grooms fussing around him, helping to put one garment on top of another. The coachman grew fatter and fatter; finally they wrapped a sash of brocaded braid about him and helped him climb on the coachman's seat of the carriage. At last the carriage would move away, and we would run to the other side of the apartment to see it entering the big courtyard. The horses, held back by the coachman pulling the checkreins to arch their necks, advanced smartly as if on parade, and we would listen to the clatter of their horseshoes on the cobblestones. Then the sound would change as the horses started over the wooden pavement of the entrance, and when the carriage drove out through the gates into the street, the sound of hoofs ceased completely.

The gateway for our house was wide and long; it stretched like a curved tunnel through the front wing of the house, from the courtyard to the street, and had an arched oval ceiling that merged with the walls. The gateway looked very massive, and during the night its big, heavy, wooden gates were closed. We felt protected by this enormous gateway, by its strong oak gates and stern custodian, as if we were in an impenetrable fortress, far from the fears and apprehensions of robbers and spirits of Novaya Derevnia. The custodian slept on a bench near the closed gates, to guard them, as was the custom in St. Petersburg. When the street bell rang, he would open the small side wicket-gate. He slept out there even through the bitter frosts of winter, wearing an enormous black sheepskin coat with a high sheepskin collar and warm felt boots.

During the time when Mama had been looking for an apartment in St. Petersburg, she had collected some folders and illustrated booklets, printed on the occasion of the State Visit of Félix Faure, President of France, in August of that year. As soon as Stassik and I were able to get up we looked avidly through the pages of these albums to find out about our new home city. Vaslav was given a map from his school and we studied that too in great anticipation of the day when we would be able to go out and see for ourselves all the marvels of St. Petersburg.

By Christmas Dr. Reshetnikov, who had attended us during our illness and had become our family doctor, pronounced us well. Mother wanted to do something special for us during the holidays, beyond the traditional Christmas tree with gifts. She suggested she take us to a children's show. Our usual favorite was the circus, but somehow we had heard of a troupe of Lilliputian Artists. We had never seen such a troupe, and Mother said there was one performing in a theatre on Nevsky Prospekt, within walking distance from home. I was excited at the idea of going out; this would be my first outing since our illness, and my first time to see St. Petersburg.

Vatsa and I walked hand in hand while Mother and Stassik followed us. It was growing dark, and the streetlights glimmered faintly through the thin fog. It was snowing. When we came onto Fontanka Street I was dazzled by the bright lights. People were thronging the street and crowding over towards the granite embankment. Suddenly the air reverberated with the sound of a military brass band, coming from the other side of the embankment wall. In less than a moment, forgetting everything around us, Vaslav and I dashed across, pushing our way through the crowds trying to get close to the wall. Lights and music seemed to be coming from the frozen Fontanka below the embankment. I grabbed the iron railing and lifted myself up to look over. I stared at the fascinating spectacle. On the translucent blue ice, beautifully dressed men and women were creating fantastic patterns with their shining steel skates as they raced and whirled over the ice to the sound of the music.

On each side of the skating rink steep "Ice Mountains" had been erected, two tall, wooden structures facing each other across the frozen river. Small sleighs were hurtling all the way down them with the speed of wind. I do not know how much longer I would have remained there, transported into this wonderful fairyland, if I hadn't suddenly felt a sharp pain in my hands as they gripped the icy railing. Only then did I look around for Vaslav, thinking he would be just by my side. To my horror he was not there. He had disappeared. I hurried back through the crowds to the sidewalk, looking for Mother and my brothers. I couldn't find them. I waited for a while and then decided to continue walking in the same direction we had taken from home. I came to a bridge and climbed the steps, stared at a statue of a man on a horse, but when I came to the street at the end of the bridge I didn't know which way to go and didn't have the courage to cross the street. It would be impossible now to catch up with Mother and the boys. Besides, where was the theatre? I decided to go back home.

It was my first time out alone on the streets of St. Petersburg—I had just had my seventh birthday—and I was sure that I remembered my way back. The most difficult part was crossing the streets by myself. It was holiday time and many fancy carriages drawn by beautifully dressed horses were flying up and down the street like arrows. I was held by the scene but I was also frightened as I kept hearing the coachmen shout, "Watch out!" to the passersby. How could I cross these mad streets?

I devised a plan. I would go up to some people about to cross the street and stay very close, as though I was with them, until I reached the other side. I did this on each street corner until I arrived home, and that was how I became acquainted with St. Petersburg on my own.

It was quite late when I got home, and there was no answer when I pulled the doorbell to our apartment. Our servant must have left for her night off. I came back down and sat on the bench under the archway leading to our entrance. I don't know whether at that time St. Petersburg had yet gotten its Belgian Corporation electric power station, but our gateway did have its own electric motor in a large wooden box to light all the stairways of the house. I was fascinated by the motor, which buzzed mysteriously.

I did not have to wait long; soon Mama and my brothers arrived back looking very worried. Mama had already notified the police of my disappearance. But they were all so happy to see me, and once inside the house we children quickly recovered our spirits and begged Mother to take us to the performance. She made us change our clothes and, after we had downed a drink of hot milk, she agreed. This time we took a sleigh. How we enjoyed the ride along the embankment and the sights of the frozen Fontanka!

When we arrived at the Ponopticum Theatre, the performance had already started and the only chairs we could find in the stuffy hall were right in front of the stage, a simple narrow platform on which a huge, overweight, half-naked, ugly, fat woman was lifting weights. With every movement rolls of fat bulged through her pink tights decorated with multicolored sequins. Her eyes were underlined with thick black makeup and her tightly curled red hair was frizzed up high and held on top of her head with a brass clip. She was covered with perspiration, and as she lifted her heavy weights each of her extra chins quivered.

Next came the man-lion. His face was so completely covered with thick hair that not an inch of skin could be seen. He had a long beard and long mustache. His thick mane was dyed a bright yellow color. He wore a purple Russian shirt, a black vest, and a large gold medal on his chest. He sat on a stool in the middle of the stage, plucking the strings of a balalaika and rhythmically turning from side to side. He was followed by a ventriloquist who made a deep muffled voice come out of his stomach. All these acts, one after the other, frightened me. I didn't like the show at all, I wanted to go home, my mood was no longer joyful. I was tired and felt a physical revulsion for the performance. Even the magician in his black top hat and red cloak, pulling coins and cards out of thin air and making them disappear just as mysteriously, failed to distract me.

The troupe of Lilliputians appeared. I was disappointed at the sight of the little people; they looked so old. The skin on their faces was yellow and wrinkled. I do not remember the plot of their act at all, only that there was a bride and a groom and that the guests were dressed in black tailcoats and evening gowns. I kept turning my head away from the stage, not wanting to watch them. They acted more like children than adults, but they were all so old that I felt sorry for them and begged Mother to take me away from that awful place. I wept. I wanted to go home. Mama was afraid that I had caught a cold and was ill again, and she hurried us all home. That is how I ruined a Christmas treat for my brothers.

⌣

After Christmas our aunts came from Vilno to visit us. They rented an apartment not far away, on the same street. Stanislava, Aunt Thetya's daughter, was not with them because she was now married and had moved with her husband to Marijampole. It had been just over a year since we had seen our aunts, but I couldn't recognize Aunt Stepha. She had lost weight and her beauty had faded. She was very ill and had to be confined to bed. We were told she was suffering from "a bad heart" and needed peace and quiet around her.

Mother went to see her sisters when Vaslav was in school. I always wanted to be near Mama and suffered whenever she went out of the house, imagining all sorts of accidents if she was ever late returning; and so Mother took me with her to our aunts, leaving only Stassik at home.

Over Aunt Stepha's bed hung a large portrait of General K. [no further identification], in full uniform, wearing all his decorations and medals. We had seen him frequently at our aunt's house in Vilno, arriving in his carriage drawn by beautiful thoroughbred horses. He had been Aunt Stephanie's friend and protector for many years. Because of his high rank he could not marry Stephanie, a dancer, without handicapping his military career. Stephanie had left the stage for him, and through his influence—he was the Governor of Vilno—she had been appointed to teach dancing in the government high schools.

But now the General had abandoned Stephanie.

As Mother and Aunt Stepha talked together about their lost loves, I felt deep in my little heart how unhappy my mother must be and listened closely to every word they said. I understood, although they talked cryptically and in whispers, that the General had gone to Warsaw on business, and that after a few days Stephanie had received a letter from him saying he would not be returning to Vilno, because he had been assigned an important position. I think he became Governor of the Province of Warsaw. Stephanie did not receive another letter from the General, and soon after he left Vilno she read in the newspaper about his sumptuous wedding in Warsaw to a beautiful young socialite.

On another day when Vaslav must have been home on holiday, Mama took him along with us. He was bored having to sit quietly without disturbing Aunt Stepha. He played in the living room with her small fluffy lap dog, but soon he had it barking and so Aunt Thetya gave him an album of photographs to look at. I was with Mother in the bedroom playing on the bed with Aunt Stepha's cat. After a while Mama, with a worried expression, broke off her conversation with Aunt Thetya and Aunt Stepha. "I wonder what Vaslav is doing, so quiet all this time?" I went with Mother to the living room and to our horror we saw that Vaslav had been pulling the threads out of the Persian rug on the table. Already there was a big, bare patch. Mother was very embarrassed, knowing the rug was especially precious, as it had been a gift from General K. Aunt

Theodosia came in and called Vatsa *psota*. It was the first time we heard the Polish word *psota*—a wrecker or spoiler—and it sounded very offensive.

Soon after Christmas Mama arranged for a teacher to come two hours each afternoon to prepare Stassik and me for school in the fall. Each day after lunch we would clear the table quickly so that Stassik and I could work with our teacher in the dining room. At night the square oak table and chairs were pushed against the wall to make room for the two folding beds where Vaslav and Stassik slept. On the wall, over the table, hung a large ikon.

Vaslav had been attending school ever since we had arrived in St. Petersburg, and from the beginning his weekly grades, which he brought home on Saturdays, had not been very good. In the spring they were still low, and now for some days the reports showed no grades at all. After Mama mentioned this to Vaslav there was a sudden improvement, though some of the grades appeared oddly written over. At first Mama did not say anything, believing them to be corrections by the teacher. But one day the page was rubbed thin, nearly through, in several places. Mama realized what was going on and told Vaslav she would go to the school and ask about his grades, hoping this would discourage him from altering them again. She did not expect what actually happened. Vaslav was so frightened that he stayed away from school altogether.

One day when Mama was out she met Vaslav walking gaily along a St. Petersburg street. Mama was very angry. "You will never be a real artist unless you mend your ways!" Mother took him back to school, where she found that he had been absent for a whole week. He was punished severely and made to do extra lessons at home with the teacher who came for Stassik and me.

Father, during that year, was working in Moscow. Mama corresponded with him often and punctually received the agreed amount of money, two hundred rubles a month. We lived well and had one servant, Mania, a nice Polish girl who managed our household. She was very attached to us and stayed for two years, until she left to get married. She had her own "room," a curtained alcove in the kitchen. On the wall over her bed were various cheap popular prints, left behind by previous servants in the apartment. One of them depicted a fiery hell showing devils—terrible creatures with long claws on their hands and feet—pursuing sinners with iron pitchforks.

One day Mania, seeing me writing to Father, confidingly told me her secret. She was in love with a young Russian sailor. She asked me to read his letters out loud to her and to write down her reply in Russian. For a whole year I wrote her letters to her fiancé for her, all the time keeping it a secret from Mama.

With spring the weather grew warmer and the sun shone more often. The winter shutters and seals were removed, and we could open the windows overlooking the courtyards, allowing us to feed the many pigeons that would gather near the windows.

In the back courtyard beside the stables was another separate building where hired laundresses would do the washing for the tenants of the apartments. Billows of white steam escaped from the many open vents, and from our apartment we could quite clearly hear the laundresses singing as they worked. We loved to hear them and learned all their songs. Vatsa and I would sing them together while Stassik accompanied us on his harmonica and Vatsa plucked the strings of his balalaika.

The main courtyard on the other side of the house was often visited by organ-grinders. One of these was a hunchback who hobbled along carrying a brightly colored organ on his back. Alongside him walked a thin little girl bearing a heavy wooden gilded harp on her shoulder. The stick that the old man used as a crutch became the stand for the organ. He started to turn the handle and from the organ came loud hoarse sounds. When the sweet voice of the little girl joined the squeaking notes of the organ, many windows would open to hear her sing "Parting, parting is such sweet sorrow, leaving for far-off lands" or "Our bonfire shines through the fog, the crescent shines over the river." The barrel organ had a variety of popular melodies and also a few arias from old operas. To finish the show the little girl always sang "The moon has hidden behind the clouds and refuses to shine for us tonight." The old man and the little girl looked so pitiful and tired, we felt very sorry for them, and whenever it was cold and rainy, and only a few windows would open and not many coins would be thrown down to them, we were concerned for them. We asked Mama to give us a few coins, and wrapping them in paper we threw them down to the courtyard, aiming as close as we could. If our aim was wide we would worry and watch until we saw that the little girl had found and picked up the coins.

There was another organ-grinder who carried a bird in a cage on top of his organ. For two kopeks the bird would pull a card from a box with a fortune written on it. This organ-grinder gave us other popular Russian melodies. Soon we were familiar with each of the repertoires—the laundresses', the organ-grinders', and the little girl's—and were able to sing all their songs.

Mama had no friends when we first moved to St. Petersburg, but now with her sisters there she did meet some Polish families. I remember particularly Stanislava Zemnitzka, who was also a friend of my godmother, Bronislava Gousekevitch. We became very fond of Stanislava and often visited her house, where we occasionally met Stanislav Gillert.

The previous summer in Novaya Derevnia Mother and Father had renewed their friendship with Gillert, a Polish dancer whom they knew from the Warsaw Wielki Theatre.* Both Gillert and my godmother, Gousekevitch, had been students there, and later leading dancers. When Mucharsky, Gousekevitch's husband, went to Poltava as an officer in the Russian Army, she became a ballerina in the private theatres and operas in Russia. She danced in Kiev, Odessa, and Tiflis, often working with Eleonora and Foma Nijinsky.

Stanislav Gillert told us how he had gone to the same *Gymnasium* in Warsaw where Mucharsky and our Bereda uncles, Mother's brothers, had studied. He also talked with Mother about the Polish satirical journal *Mucha* [*The Fly*], which Mucharsky had published before he went into the Army. Our uncle Adam had worked as an editor for the journal.

Gillert was older than Mother and Father and had been in Russia for many years. He had first worked as a soloist and a leading dancer in the Imperial Theatres in Moscow, where he had partnered his wife, the Russian ballerina Anna Sobeshchanskaya. He had been brought to St. Petersburg by Petipa as a leading dancer in the Maryinsky. Now he was also a teacher in the Girls' Division of the Imperial Theatrical School and assistant to Enrico Cecchetti. And so when the time came to submit the application for Vaslav's entrance examination for the Imperial Theatrical School, Stanislav Gillert helped Mama prepare it.

In May the summer vacations came and Vaslav's school closed. The teacher also stopped her lessons with Stassik and me, and so we were all three free from schoolwork. This summer of 1898 was our first to be spent in St. Petersburg itself, and we set out to familiarize ourselves with the city. Every morning after breakfast Mama took us to some park—"to breathe fresh air," as she used to say—to the Summer Garden, the Alexandrovsky Park, or somewhat farther away, the Tavritchesky

*Victor Stanislav Gillert, 1851–1907, came from a family of Polish dancers, including Alexander Gillert, who had begun his career in 1844 by dancing in the ballets staged by Filippo Taglioni in Warsaw, and Arnold Gillert, born in 1823, an excellent character dancer and mime who worked in the Bolshoi Ballet in Moscow from 1856 to 1885.

Stanislav Gillert danced in Paris in the 1870s in the ballets of Saint-Léon and Mérante; in the 1880s he was a *premier danseur* in the Warsaw Wielki Theatre, partnering Maria Giuri in the premiere of *Coppélia* and also in the Mendez ballets, *India* and *Flic-Flac*, before becoming a member of the Bolshoi Ballet in Moscow. During the time he was both a teacher in the Imperial Theatrical School in St. Petersburg and a member of the Imperial Ballet, he returned many times to Warsaw as a guest artist. (IN/JR)

1. Eleonora Bereda, at the age of sixteen.
Photograph taken in Kiev, 1872.

2. Thomas Nijinsky, at the age
of twenty-three. Photograph
taken at the time of his marriage
to Eleonora Bereda.

3, 4. Dismissal of Thomas Nijinsky from the Warsaw Theatres. Main text, written in Russian, reads:

In answer to the application submitted by you on April 22/May 4 this year for resignation from your service, the Directorate of the Warsaw Theatres advised you on 24/6 same month and year, that according to the existing theatrical laws, your dismissal from the duties of dancer at the Warsaw Corps-de-ballet cannot occur earlier than four months after the day of the application for resignation, that is on August 23/September 4 this year.

In spite of this and of the renewed memorandum to you, you ceased to report for work from the day of presentation of the aforesaid application, thus hampering the regular course of the theatrical performances.

Following the report of this to the Supreme Chief of the Territory and on the basis of the resolution by His High Excellency attached to the reference by the Office of the General-Governor, dated May 7 of this year no. 6018, the Directorate of the Warsaw Theatres notifies you that you are excluded from April 22/May 4 of this year from the rolls of the Corps-de-ballet Dancers of the Warsaw Theatres, with the proviso, that henceforth you will not be accepted for employment in the Warsaw Theatres.

5, 6. Thomas and Eleonora Nijinsky
onstage in Ekaterinodar, c. 1884,
and at the Kiev City Opera Theatre,
c. 1886.

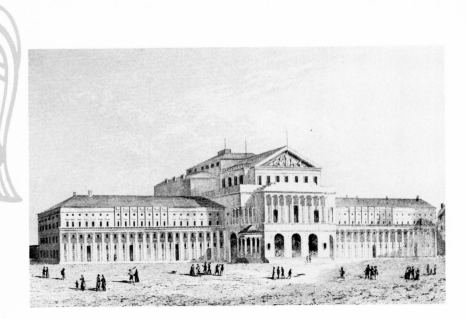

7. The Wielki Theatre in Warsaw. This French engraving
published in 1840 shows the Drama Theatre on the left, the Concert
Hall on the right, and the Opera Theatre in the center.

8. St. Isaac's Cathedral, St. Petersburg, a view across
the frozen Neva. Engraving, c. 1850.

9. Grille of the Summer Garden bordering the Neva Embankment, with the bridge over the Fontanka Canal and the Summer Palace of Peter the Great amid the trees. Engraving, 1840.

10. Ice Mountains on the Neva. Engraving, 1840.

11. Theatre-Circus in Old Russia about 1890, showing
the different stage levels with fountains and the flooded
arena for sea battles.

12. The Arcadia Summer Theatres in Novaya Derevnia,
St. Petersburg, 1890.

13. The Nijinsky children: Stanislav, aged eleven; Bronislava, aged seven; and Vaslav, aged eight and a half. Photograph taken in St. Petersburg.

14. The main façade of the Alexandrinsky Theatre.

15. Teatralnaya Ulitza (Theatre Street) with the Imperial Theatrical School on the right and, at the end of the street, the back of the Alexandrinsky Theatre.

Garden. Usually we spent the morning in the Summer Garden, as it was the nearest. We walked along Panteleimanskaya past the Baron Stieglitz Museum, and after crossing the bridge over the Fontanka we came to the Engineer's Mikhailovsky Palace. From there the Summer Garden extended all the way to the Neva Embankment, enclosed by the most magnificent wrought-iron railing, twelve feet high, interspersed with huge granite columns each surmounted with a gilded urn. The garden was divided down the middle by a wide avenue lined on each side with ancient marble statues, Greek gods and muses, and Roman emperors. Between the statues were granite benches, but we never sat in this part of the garden; we always hurried on to the small square where, behind a low railing, was the statue of Kriloff, the fable-teller.

We loved to visit Grandfather Kriloff. There were benches placed all around the square, and we liked to rest there for a while facing the statue of the seated Kriloff. At his feet and around the pedestal were the sculptured characters from his fables—the monkey with the dozen pairs of spectacles, a crow, a fox, and "the quartett." All the children who came to the park loved to climb over the railing and look at the animals. After some of the monkey's spectacles got broken off, a park attendant began to watch over the statue and would stop us from climbing over the railing.

Along one side of the square was a terrace where a young city teacher had an apartment in a small narrow house. We often used to shelter from the rain on her terrace. Like other children who came to the park, we became great friends with this young teacher. She told us that rather than breaking pieces from the statue of Grandfather Kriloff we should all learn his fables. She asked which ones we already knew, and straightaway I answered with the "Monkey and the Spectacles" and recited the whole fable.

Vaslav then began "The Quartett":

> *A roguish Monkey,*
> *A Goat, and Donkey,*
> *With a great clumsy Bear,*
> *Agreed in a Quartett to share.*
> *They got their notes, two fiddles, flute, and bass,*
> *And on a grass plot sat, under some limes,*
> *Fain to enchant the world with skill and grace;*
> *But how they struck up can't be told in rhymes.*
> *"Stop, brothers, stop," the Monkey cries, "Be quiet!*
> *Your music ends in riot,*
> *Because you are all seated wrong . . ."* *

---

*From *Kriloff's Original Fables*, translated by I. Henry Harrison, published by Remington & Co., London, 1883. (IN/JR)

Vaslav was embarrassed when he forgot the lines that followed, and a girl of his own age continued to recite the fable for him. He did finish with her, in unison, reciting the last lines spoken by a nightingale:

"But ye, my friends, whatever seats ye take,
Musicians all your lives will never make." *

Our teacher friend often led the children in games in Grandfather Kriloff's square. I had a big hoop and would run with it along the garden paths. Another girl had a big ball. One day Vaslav grabbed the ball and began to jump with both feet in time with the bouncing of the ball. It seemed that the ball lifted his body up. All the other children were delighted and the ball was snatched from Vaslav; we all wanted to try this marvelous game. Not one of us could achieve Vaslav's bouncing tempo or the height of his jumps. For the first time I saw the extraordinary ability of my brother to hold himself in the air at the height of his leap, just like the ball before it falls back to the ground. That same day Mama bought us a big ball for ourselves.

Along one side of the garden, behind the magnificent railing bordering the Fontanka, was a paved stone walk. The shrubbery beside the walk arched over to the high railing forming a long narrow corridor that led to another of our favorite places. There, at the end of the Summer Garden where the Fontanka and the Neva met, through the high railings and between the granite columns, we could see all the way across the Great Neva to the Petropavlovsky Fortress on the far shore.

We watched with fascination whenever we saw a small steamboat pull a big barge from the Neva into the Fontanka. Loaded with firewood or watermelons, earthenware crockery or woodenware, the barges would be going to the center of the city where everything would be sold. We could see people on board, barefooted lads in patched pants, and in patched Russian shirts or naked to the waist, pushing long boat hooks against the bottom of the river as they walked along the edge of the barge, to help the small steamboat move the barge.

Each barge had a small half-hut with one window, a door, and a tin smokestack. We knew the barges came from far away, from the Volga itself, and that the people we could see lived on the barges, constantly afloat. Vaslav was delighted whenever one came past us, and he would greet the barge-boys, shouting and waving his little hat. Sometimes there would be hens on the barges and we could hear them clucking, or dogs would run along the deck barking at us.

At noon a cannon was fired from the Fortress, and that was our signal to

* Ibid.

return home for lunch. All day afterwards, Vaslav could talk only about how wonderful it would be to live on a barge.

Whenever Mama went to buy firewood from the barges, where it was cheaper than in the woodyards, Vatsa made sure that he went with her. He would always run over to the barges to make friends with the people living on them. Mama was afraid that Vaslav might run away with them, and she would tell us all about the hard life of the barge people, often drenched with rain, sleeping on bare boards, and, when necessary, hauling the barges. She even showed us a reproduction of Repin's picture *The Volga Boatmen*.

On Thursday and Sunday afternoons also we went to the Summer Garden. Regimental bands would give concerts in one or another of the squares, and we loved to listen to the music. We tried to learn the tunes so that we could sing them ourselves at home.

Sometimes we strolled through the Garden to the Lebiagiya Kanavka, where a small stream ran through a ditch between two quite steep slopes. On the other side stretched an enormous field, the Marsovo Polye, where military exercises were often held. On special ceremonial days there were parades attended by the Tsar, at which the cavalry and infantry regiments would pass before him. The infantry, their rifles on their shoulders, marched in formation, and the cavalrymen, astride beautiful horses, in handsome uniforms and cuirasses, with plumes on their headgear, swung around in different formations with not a single horse breaking line in the crossings. The Cossacks showed their daring in fancy riding. We were enraptured at this spectacle as at a theatrical show and wanted to stay all day. How marvelous it was there in the Summer Garden!

In the middle of the summer, for one month, Mama worked as a ballet master in an operetta. I don't remember the name of the theatre, which was on Basseynaya, but it was a summer theatre in a garden. Mornings and afternoons when Mama went for rehearsals, we were left to our own devices. Little by little we won permission from Mama to go for independent walks. She set down only one condition, that we should go only to the Summer Garden. We would study the map of St. Petersburg that Vaslav had been given at school, and then start our walks around our house and down the street to the Summer Garden, which was so near that it was almost next door. Through the railings of the Garden we could see the Neva and the embankment. How could we keep our promise not to go beyond the Garden! From the parapet of the granite embankment, at intervals, granite steps went down in a half-circle to a small landing dock at the water's edge. We could not resist the temptation; we came down the steps to look for fish, to dip our hands in the water and imagine how nice it would be to bathe and swim there.

As we walked along the parapet of the embankment our real initiation to the marvels of our neighborhood began. We admired the magnificent palaces, the Marble Palace, the Hermitage, and the Winter Palace. We were amazed at the breadth of the river but did not dare venture out over the long bridges to the other shore of the Neva. After we passed the Admiralty Building we continued until we reached the statue of Peter the Great, and then we turned back and came home. Each time we went out we extended the radius of our exploration.

We were not interested in going to the theatre this summer and did not pester Mama to take us with her. We saw one performance, in the afternoon, of the ballet that Mama staged. I think we came to the theatre only for the last act of the operetta, as I do not recall its plot or its name, but we liked the ballet very much; especially well-mounted, we thought, were the march of the tin soldiers and the dance of the white rabbits. The tin soldiers marched in skillfully arranged formations, and the white rabbits paraded proudly as they beat on their drums. Dolls in short frilly dresses whirled on their toes, and we were amused by the antics of the mischievous imps frolicking around a big scary bear. And how we laughed when the awkward bear danced a solo, the *trepak*.

For the finale the entire cast came onstage, and together the singers and the dancers took part in a lively galop and farandole. The audience applauded enthusiastically. But Mama was disappointed and chagrined when the director declared that her ballet was too naïve for their theatre and the summer public. We didn't see the ballets she staged later, but the administration was very pleased and she finished the season with success.

On one of her free days Mama took us to Teatralnaya Ulitza—exquisite Theatre Street. Nowhere in the world is there a more beautiful street! From beginning to end, on each side, stretch two identical architectural lines. They are locked in the distance by the Alexandrinsky Theatre. The yellow buildings and the white pillars, even on a gloomy St. Petersburg day, create the impression of sunny weather—they shine. The street looks like an enormous festive palace hall.

The square where the Alexandrinsky Theatre is situated, the Theatre itself, and the Theatrical School together form a complete, exquisite architectural composition, the work of the architect Carlo Rossi, one of the creators and builders of St. Petersburg.

Rossi was born in St. Petersburg in December 1775, the son of an Italian dancer, Gertrude Rossi. Carlo was reared in a ballet family and returned to Russia in 1786 with his mother and his stepfather, Charles Felix Reinhard Auguste Le-Picq, who was a star of the first magnitude of the dance in Europe, having made his debut in Paris in 1776, where he had been the favorite student of Noverre. In St. Petersburg he choreographed a whole series of his own ballets and staged many ballets by Gardel, Didelot, and Noverre. He greatly contributed to the development of ballet in Russia.

The theatrical era of these magnificent ballets of Le-Picq and the highly artistic performances of Charles and Gertrude Le-Picq were undoubtedly a strong influence on young Carlo, who grew up to be a remarkable architect. The environment in which Rossi lived, his acquaintance with the theatre and the ballet, served to foster his perfect creation of the Theatrical School and the Alexandrinsky Theatre.*

I remember when we children first came to Teatralnaya Ulitza—what a fairyland it seemed to us! The possibility of living and studying and dancing in this magnificent building, the Imperial Theatrical School, was like a dream.

---

*Teatralnaya Ulitza is now called Zodchevo Rossi Ulitza (Architect Rossi Street). (BN)

10   Vaslav's Entrance into the Imperial Theatrical School

MAMA HAD no doubts that Vaslav had all the qualifications needed to pass the dancing aptitude test in the entrance examination for the Imperial Theatrical School, but she worried about getting her application accepted. She had been counting on the promises of Mme Karatyguina and Joachim Tartakoff to contact the Director, Vsevolojsky, on her behalf, but now she learned that both would be out of St. Petersburg for the whole summer. But then Stanislav Gillert said that he would speak to the members of the Commission and to Enrico Cecchetti.

Mama herself knew Cecchetti, as she and Father had worked with him during the summer of 1887, taking part in the performance at the Arcadia Theatre, where Cecchetti had staged *Le Pouvoir d'Amour* and *L'Illusion d'un Peintre* for Giovannina Limido and the Imperial Ballet Company. My parents had appeared in dance numbers in the *Divertissements* staged by my father. That same summer my mother had also taken part in Setov's spectacular ballet in six acts, *Excelsior*, with Carlotta Brianza, and also in *Sieba*, with Virginia Zucchi. In both ballets Cecchetti had also danced with Limido, and Mother had often seen him during the rehearsals. So now she visited Cecchetti and asked him to put in a good word for Vaslav with the members of the Commission and with the Director of the Imperial Theatres.

When Mama heard that the application was accepted and that the audition was scheduled for August 20, she added an extra prayer every night: "Matka Boska, help Vaslav. Let him be admitted to the Imperial Theatrical School!"

Vaslav's entrance to the Imperial Theatrical School would determine his future path in life. Once accepted, there would be no more uncertainty or financial anxiety about his education. He would become an Artist of the Imperial Theatres, a permanent government position. If, God willing, he should advance to the rank of *premier danseur*, and Mother had no doubt that he would, then he would be assured not only of a large salary but also of a distinguished and honorable position in the Imperial Theatres and, at age thirty-six, a life pension almost equal to his salary.

Mama knew that at the audition there was to be a general examination in addition to the dancing aptitude test and the medical examination. Vaslav did not appear at all concerned; he seemed to take it for granted that he would be accepted. Mama, however, was afraid that during the summer Vaslav would forget everything he had learned in the preparatory school, and so she told him that now he must study for at least one hour every day. Vaslav considered "book work" a punishment, but at Mother's insistence he obediently sat at the table, though his face expressed suffering and impatience. He moved restlessly in his chair, his pencil broke often, and it was obvious that he could not concentrate on his books. Mama was worried that if Vaslav was not accepted by the Imperial School his only future would be as an artist of the private theatres. "You will be like your mother and father, always 'on the road' . . ." She implored Vaslav to study diligently: "The Theatrical School is not an ordinary school. There is not another like it in the whole world. For you to be accepted there will bring us all great happiness." Vatsa loved Mother very much, and so he would embrace her and sit down again with a book, saying: "I will study!" But very soon he would be on his feet again, announcing, "Mamoussia, I already know everything, let me go for a walk!"

By nature Vaslav was a very lively and adventurous boy. He longed to dash out of the apartment to play in the courtyard or to explore farther away—to go to parks, or to the embankment and watch the barges on the Neva. It was not easy for him during the nice summer weather to toil indoors over his lessons, but Mother would encourage him: "If you study well, you will be an Artist of the Imperial Theatres and will always perform on a big stage. Then I can die peacefully."

Vatsa could not listen calmly to talk of Mother's death and answered with emotion: "Mamoussia, you will live for a long time. I will be accepted in the Theatrical School, you will see! And when I am an Artist, I will buy you everything—a velvet dress, a fur coat, hats with ostrich feathers . . ."

One day Mama would be confident that her son would pass the entrance examinations, the next she would be full of doubts and seem discouraged. She would tell us: "There will be so many children at the audition, maybe a hundred. And no more than eight or ten will be admitted to the School. Maybe some of the others will have stronger 'pull'!"

Stanislav Gillert did intercede for Vaslav by telling several members of the Commission that here was a very talented child and son of Foma Nijinsky, a well-known dancer and ballet master of the Russian private theatres. Gillert had a certain influence in the selection of the children to be admitted to the School, and Cecchetti promised him that he would pay special attention to Vaslav. Afterwards Gillert told us that Sergei Legat, a dance instructor in the Boys' Division, had promised to accept Vaslav.

As the first selection was based on physical appearance, Mama consulted with her sisters as to how she should dress Vaslav for the entrance examination so that he would make a good impression. Aunt Thetya and Mama took Vaslav shopping and he himself carried all the packages home; he would not let anyone else carry them. He held them with both arms, pressing them close to his chest, pleased to receive so many new things.

At home every purchase was tried on several times, and we admired each new item. Dress was important to Mama. As she always impressed upon us: "Remember, as you are seen, so are you judged."

Finally the wardrobe was complete, and Vatsa looked as if "dressed for a wedding." Everything was new for this occasion, even his underwear, made from fine Holland linen. He wore a blue sailor suit; the short pants with gold buttons down the side and the cream-colored knee socks were flattering and showed to advantage the well-developed muscles of his dancing legs. The black patent leather open pumps looked very elegant on his high-arched feet. Below the wide sailor collar a blue silk tie, fastened in a knot, accentuated his long graceful neck and small head.

Vaslav was proud of his new outfit, and most of all he liked his light blue sailor hat. He was continually trying it on before the mirror. The hat had to be worn so that the gold letters RUSSIA on the dark blue ribbon band would remain well centered over his forehead, and the gold anchors at the end of the two ribbons had always to lie neatly over the collar at the back. He would stand in front of the mirror and try it this way or that, pulled right down over his eyebrows, or pushed right back on his head, then pulled over one ear, then over the other, but always keeping RUSSIA correctly in the center.

Mama, of course, never left Vaslav alone during his fittings or let him admire himself too long in the mirror. She wanted to keep everything fresh and new. Over the summer Vaslav had acquired a beautiful tan, and then, on the day before the examination, his hair was cut with a short and very becoming fringe.

And so came August 20, the day of the entrance examination of the Imperial Theatrical School.

Usually it was difficult to wake Vatsa—he was a sound sleeper and loved to sleep late—but this day he got up quickly, washed and combed his hair, and wanted to put on his new outfit straightaway, even though it was still early. He only drank a glass of tea, despite Mama's urging him to eat, with the audition sure to last several hours.

I knew that in two years I would also be applying for entrance to the Theatrical School, and so I begged Mama to take me with them to let me see everything and get to know how to be admitted to the Theatrical School. Mama agreed.

Before leaving the house, Vatsa had to show Mama one more time how he would bow to everyone at the examination, as she had taught him: "Draw your feet together, then, without bending your back, bow your head low and hold your arms in line with the seams of your trousers. Smile so you will look pleasant. And don't you dare play any pranks there."

We all looked at Vaslav, and I thought he was the most handsome boy with his dark brown hair . . . his long, thick, black eyelashes . . . his high cheekbones. His face was radiant, his expressive, slanted, dark brown eyes sparkled with excitement, and his almond-shaped teeth flashed in spontaneous smiles.

Then Mama crossed herself and blessed Vaslav, and we were ready to go.

Teatralnaya Ulitza was usually quiet, but when we arrived on the morning of the audition the street was full of carriages. We went up several steps of the wide staircase under a large awning to enter the wide doors of the Theatrical School. There stood a doorman with a long gray beard and wearing a gray uniform—the uniform of the Court, with gold Imperial Eagles on a double-breasted jacket.

In the entrance hall we were shown another wide staircase leading to the upper floor, to the Boys' Division. Vatsa kept his sailor hat pressed tight to his breast as we rushed upstairs, so fast that Mama could hardly keep up with us. We were asked to enter a large hall with high semicircular windows. One wall was covered by a huge mirror, and along the others were *barres* for dancing exercises. In one corner stood a grand piano. The floor was gently slanted, at the same degree as the slope of the Maryinsky Theatre. Around the hall were portraits of Nicholas II and other Tsars.

Several boys and their parents were already in the hall, and more and more were gathering at the far end near the doors leading to a second hall. The Directorate of the Imperial Theatres, the Administration of the School, Teachers, and Artists began to move into the second hall. Two old gentlemen appeared and everyone made way and bowed low; one of them looked very old, but the other seemed hale and hearty and had a beautifully combed beard. I learned later that they were Christian Petrovitch Johannson and Marius Ivanovitch Petipa.

The doors to the second hall were then closed. The head clerk of the Imperial Theatrical School, wearing a uniform with gold buttons, announced that he would call the boys on the list to go into the second hall. When Vaslav's turn came, Mama took his sailor hat, which he was still clutching nervously to his breast.

Many of the other boys came back from the second hall, but Vaslav did not.

The head clerk came out with a large sheet of paper and read a list of names. Vaslav's was one of them. "These boys must wait for the medical examination and the general examination. Those boys not named on the list must consider themselves not admitted to the Imperial Theatrical School."

It made me very sad to see the hurt, disappointed faces and the tears of some of the boys and their parents as they left the hall.

Vaslav described for us later how he was examined by various members of the Commission and how his aptitude for dancing was tested. "At first we stood in a long line as they all looked at us, then they told us to turn our backs and walk away from them, then turn once more and walk forward. Then we stood and waited. I and several other boys were told to move aside and wait; the others were told to leave.

"We were put in line again and ordered to take off our shoes. They examined our feet, arching them to see our insteps, and tried the 'turn-out' of our legs. I immediately stood well in the first position. Then some more boys were told to leave, and only a few of us remained. We were told to run around the big hall; I outran them all. Then they asked me to jump several times, and praised me very much."

The admission procedure continued. The selected boys were taken to the infirmary for the medical examination, and the hearing and sight tests.

"I was very embarrassed," admitted Vatsa. "They ordered us to strip. They measured my height, my chest, legs, hips, weighed me on the scales, listened to how I was breathing and how my heart was beating. Then we each had to go alone into another room and they talked to me in a whisper through a closed door. Next came an eye examination. Large and small letters were shown at a distance. How good it was that I knew them. One boy could see very well, but made mistakes with his letters."

Again the head clerk appeared in our hall with his list. He explained that after the medical examination three more boys were considered unsuitable candidates for the strenuous program of the Imperial Theatrical School.

Finally, after the general examination the head clerk again appeared with his sheet of paper and announced: "These boys are admitted to the Imperial Theatrical School for one trial year. If during the school year they show progress in Dance and General Subjects, they will be enrolled next year as pupils in the School. The boys' parents are asked to come tomorrow to the office of the School to obtain the necessary information about the beginning of studies, school uniforms, books, et cetera."

Vaslav's name was on the list.

When he heard his name, knowing that he would be studying in the Imperial Theatrical School, Vaslav was filled with unspeakable joy. Mama had difficulty restraining him as he immediately wanted to explore all over the School. She very firmly put his sailor hat on his head and, very tired, but happy and excited, we came down the stairs. . . .

The entrance examination had lasted several hours, and since Vaslav had been on his feet all this time and had not eaten anything all day, Mama wanted to get home quickly. As we came out onto the street, Vaslav suddenly turned pale, staggered, and could barely stay on his feet. The doorman got us a carriage and helped us in. Riding in the fresh air, Vatsa soon recovered. We came to Mokhovaya Ulitza where Stassik was waiting for us at the door. Inside Mania had spread the table with a white cloth and prepared a festive dinner.

11 Vaslav's First Year in School: 1898–1899

ONLY A FEW days remained before September 1, when studies would begin, and Mama had to get new school clothes for Vaslav. His short knee pants had to be replaced by long gray woolen trousers, the sailor jacket by a gray woolen shirt with a wide, black patent leather belt fastened with a square copper buckle, and the elegant sailor cap by a blue cap with a patent leather visor. He also had to have high-topped boots. This was the official uniform for day pupils of the Theatrical School.

Mama tried to get boots made of the softest, lightest leather. She chose Vaslav's clothes to allow for growth, so the gray trousers—long and wide, worn outside his boots—made his legs look heavy, as though they were carved of wood. He was transformed from a little boy into a rather awkward, ordinary-looking school pupil. But he liked his new suit; he felt grown-up in it. For the first few days he strutted with military steps, until he got used to his uniform and no longer wore it like a theatrical costume.

Stanislav and I also started school that September, so all three of us went to bed no later than nine o'clock now that we had to get up early to get ready for school. Vaslav had to be in the Theatrical School and changed into his dancing costume, ready for the lesson that began at nine each morning. His school was a half hour's walk from home; he could run there in twenty minutes if he was late, but Mama always tried to make sure that he left the house on time so he should walk calmly and not tire his legs before the lesson. The schools for Stassik and me started at eight-thirty but were nearby, and so we all three left the house together and then separated to go to our own schools.

Stassik and I stayed in school only for the morning, returning home for lunch, but the Imperial Theatrical School lasted all day. Vaslav used to take his lunch with him—two round buttered rolls with ham, meat, sausage, or cheese. At lunchtime the day pupils like Vaslav were given hot tea with sugar.

When Vaslav returned home late in the afternoon he was very hungry. He would ring the doorbell of the apartment impatiently, and when someone opened it he would burst in and shout loudly: "Mamoussia, I want to eat, I want to eat! What is for dinner?"

But first he had to wash his hands. We all crossed ourselves and sat down at the table, which was covered with a white tablecloth, and Mania brought the dinner. Vaslav ate with great appetite and would often glance at Stanislav's plate to see if he had been given a larger portion.

"Why does Stass get a bigger helping than me?"

"He is eleven and you are only nine!"

I usually ate very little, and with every bite I took Mama would say: "Eat for Mama . . . eat for Papa . . . eat for Stass . . . eat for Vatsa . . . so we won't get sick!"

Vaslav would tease Stassik at dessert time. He would eat very slowly so that he would still be eating his dessert long after Stassik had finished his, and then with exaggeration he would tell him how good and sweet it was. But Mama did not approve of such teasing.

After the table had been cleared, we would sit with our books and copybooks to do our lessons for the next day. Because I had completed the lower first grade with our tutor at home, I had been admitted into the upper first grade. Vatsa, like all the Imperial Theatrical pupils, had to start with the lower first grade, which meant he was repeating the work he had done at the preparatory school. Stanislav was also starting with the first grade, and so all three of us, despite the differences in our ages, were doing similar school work and could help each other.

We all went to bed at the same time. Together we would kneel and repeat the prayers after Mama. As she put us to bed Mama blessed and kissed each one of us.

Every Sunday, around eleven o'clock in the morning, we went to the Roman Catholic Church and stayed there until one o'clock. In the afternoon we did our homework to be ready for Monday.

As winter ended, after the snow had melted and the weather grew warmer, we were allowed to play in the courtyard. There was only one other child living in our house, a boy named Shura. He was about the same age as Vaslav and liked to play with him, though he would not follow Vaslav to the parks or to the embankment without his parents' permission; he was an obedient child, like Stassik. When the weather was bad and we had to remain indoors, Shura would visit us and play checkers or dominoes with Vaslav. Sometimes all of us, including Mama, would play a game of lotto together.

But the weather had to be very bad indeed to keep Vaslav inside. At the first opportune moment, even if it was raining, he would dart out of the front door and run across the courtyard to play with his black rubber ball, bouncing it against the vaulted walls and ceiling of the arched carriage entrance leading from the street.

Every spring and fall during the time we were in St. Petersburg, Vaslav would catch a cold or influenza or have a sore throat, and so Mama always worried whenever he was out—had he dressed warmly, fastened his sheepskin coat, wrapped his scarf well around his throat, put on his felt boots and his lambskin cap. She would continually look through the big dining-room window into the courtyard, and if she could not see Vaslav then Mania would have to run out and search for him to bring him home.

I liked playing with Vaslav. He was fun to be with—cheerful, ingenious, good at inventing new games to play. Most of his games tended to be lively and energetic, even boisterous. Sometimes Vaslav brought home new ideas for games that he must have learned from the "street boys" on his way home from school. I remember one he taught Stassik and me to play in the drawing room, during our first winter in St. Petersburg when Stassik and I were not allowed to go outside. The drawing room did not have all its furniture then, so there was room for us to play the rough game of "tip-cat"—swinging the wooden broomstick in the wild pursuit of a low-flying wooden block—and one of the window-panes got broken.

The handyman who had to come to replace the window soon became very familiar to us, carrying his big box of glass panes. I remember how the smell of putty used to linger in the apartment. We would manage to get some putty from the handyman, and though at first we might pretend that we were imitating him and fixing the windows, we usually ended up playing with it instead and making little model figures.

By spring Aunt Stepha was feeling better, but because the damp St. Petersburg weather did not agree with her she did not venture out of the house. When Mama accepted an engagement to work with a summer theatre, which meant she would have little time to spend with her sisters, they decided to return to Vilno, though Mama promised to visit them sometime in the summer. Mama had been asked to work with some members of the Warsaw Ballet who were coming to St. Petersburg to take part in two productions staged by V. Baldo in the Zoological Gardens' Theatre. The first performance took place on May 10 with the presentation of the *Tale of Tsar Saltan*, after the story by Pushkin. The second production that summer was *The Secret of the Dense Forest*, after "Hansel and Gretel" by the Brothers Grimm.

Our schools closed at the end of May. The first year in the Imperial Theatrical School had passed well for Vaslav. Everything had come easily for him, even the general subjects, which of course were a repetition of all that he had learned at his preparatory school. The knowledge that this was a trial year in the School, as Mama often reminded him, had restrained him from many pranks. His first ballet teacher in the school was Sergei Legat, who from the very first day appreciated Vaslav and made him his favorite pupil. Vaslav, for his part, adored Legat and studied under him with zeal and enthusiasm.

Again I found myself with Mama and Vaslav in the large hall in the School, which this time was filled with pupils, students, and their parents. In the front, facing us, the officials of the School sat at a long table. The Inspector stood up and read a list of names, starting with the youngest class. When we heard "Nijinsky, Vaslav Fomitch, is enrolled as a pupil of the Imperial Theatrical School," Mama sighed with relief. We had to stay a long time while the promotions from each class were read out and the awards and diplomas given to the graduating students. As soon as the ceremonies ended Vaslav pulled Mama's arm to go out instantly and buy a uniform cap. Now that he was a pupil of the Imperial Theatrical School he was entitled to wear the official uniform cap with silver insignia—the Imperial Crown on a lyre in a wreath of laurel.

Stassik and I were also let out for the summer vacation until September 1. None of us was to have any tutoring or assignments for the summer. Vaslav quickly escaped to join his neighborhood friends.

Whenever we went to the parks, the Summer Garden or the Tavritchesky Garden, Mama was very strict and careful to see whom we played with. Whenever she considered a group too old or too noisy and rough she would forbid us to play with them. She was afraid we might pick up bad habits or undesirable traits from such children. She had already noticed to her despair that the "street boys," as she called children who were allowed to play in the streets without supervision, were having a bad influence on Vaslav. To her increasing concern, she was finding it more and more difficult to make Vaslav mind her. But Vaslav's new friendships were soon cut short. Father arrived in St. Petersburg for the summer.

It had been two years since we had seen Father, and now he was to work as a ballet master in the operetta of the Theatre Bouffe. One day we visited the Theatre Bouffe with Mama. In the large garden there was an enclosed summer theatre where performances of an extensive repertoire of operettas were presented. There was also another theatre with an outdoor stage that had a music-hall program, and in the garden there was a restaurant with an orchestra. An entrance ticket for the garden permitted one to visit the open stage with its program of different acts, and to visit the restaurant and stroll through the gardens. A separate entrance fee was charged for performances of the operetta.

While Father was working with the Theatre Bouffe he did not stay with us; Mother simply said that our apartment was too crowded and there was no separate room for Father. But Father did often come for dinner, and sometimes he brought his friends from the theatre.

Mama had gradually been adding new furniture to our apartment, and when she heard that Father was coming to St. Petersburg she bought a new oblong table and six chairs for the dining room. She moved our square oak table into the drawing room and had the four chairs upholstered in pale magenta velours to match the sofa and the two armchairs.

There was one evening I especially remember. Mama had offered the guests cherry brandy and cognac with their after-dinner coffee. We children could have a taste of the cherry brandy by touching the rims of the small glasses with our lips. Mama then took her guests into the drawing room. She was very proud of her elegant room, upholstered in the latest fashionable color, pale magenta, and with several souvenirs of her and Father's past successes on display. There was a poster featuring both of them in a performance at Krasnoe Selo. On a small table by the window she had placed dried flowers in her "sailboat." The boat and sails were made of spongy sea bast, and the "sailboat" had contained beautiful fresh flowers when she had received it on stage for one of her own benefit performances. Father had brought a cut-crystal tobacco jar with a silver lid, and Mother placed it next to the "sailboat." The handle of the jar was a tiny statue of Father dressed as a Cossack and the inscription read: "Dance Cossack! Be an Ataman! [title of a Cossack leader]" He was proud to have received it in Moscow from the Director of the Oman Theatre.

Mama wanted to show her guests her own latest acquisition, a tall pier mirror standing between the windows with a mirror display shelf below. Everyone had their backs to the dining room, admiring the mirror, when in it they saw the reflection of the open door to the dining room. There was Vaslav kneeling on a chair, leaning across the table, reaching for one of the bottles. Mama rushed into the dining room but not before Vaslav had taken a large gulp straight from the bottle. His face turned bright red, then purple as he spat it out. Mama snatched the bottle from Vaslav's hand—it was not the sweet cherry brandy he had expected, but cognac. From that time Vaslav never cared to drink cognac—or whiskey or vodka.

During the time Father was working in St. Petersburg we were made even more keenly aware of the break between our parents. I think that Stassik and Vaslav, as I, felt Father's absence from our family and his separation from us children very deeply, and we knew that Mother, though she tried to hide her emotions from us, was suffering even more. Father's presence in St. Petersburg did keep Vaslav out of a lot of mischief. He became very quiet and stayed close to Mother, seeming to blame Father and wanting to stay out of his way and attract as little attention as possible; he actually tried to avoid Father. Maybe because Father was always affectionate with me, I felt he was unduly stern with the boys and particularly harsh with Vaslav.

Mama saw how this family drama was upsetting us and after a short while she decided to leave St. Petersburg for the rest of the summer and take us to visit her sisters in Vilno.

We were excited at the prospect of returning to Vilno. Riding to the railway station on the splendid thoroughfare of Nevsky Prospekt, we admired the symmetrical beauty of the new city of St. Petersburg, barely a hundred years old. Then there was the thrill of the locomotive, the railway carriages, and the journey through the countryside—the fields and woods—before we found ourselves transported back in time to the thousand-year-old city of Vilno. We saw again the narrow streets, the quaint houses, the different styles of architecture, reflecting the passing of the centuries. It was difficult to believe that we were still in Russia. All around us many different dialects were being spoken, some Russian and some Lithuanian, but mostly we heard Polish. In addition to all the Orthodox churches, there were also many Catholic ones, and naturally we returned to the Ostra Brama Chapel. We asked the *isvostchik* [both the driver of a horse-drawn cab and the cab itself] to stop in front of the Chapel, built into the archway over the street. The shining beauty of the Ikon could be seen from the street below. On both sidewalks people were kneeling in prayer. The driver slowed down as we approached the Chapel and took off his hat. We stopped for a moment and bowed our heads in prayer. This day we did not go up to the Chapel, for Aunt Stepha was still weak and tried to avoid going up and down stairs.

We soon saw how happy Mama was to be in Vilno with her sisters. Our aunts loved us very much and pampered us children in every possible way. They drove us through the city to visit many new places as well as those we already knew. We were taken to some friends who lived on the shores of the river Vilia. Stassik and Vaslav swam in the river, taking care to stay near the bank. We also went out on the river in a rowboat. Vaslav took the oars and rowed quite well.

Only now during our holidays, as Vaslav and I spent more time together, did he tell me something about his life in the Theatrical School, complaining that his classmates pestered him at dance lessons, pushed him in the back, and teased him, saying things like, "Are you a girl, to dance so well?"

Vaslav was burning inside as he went on to tell me, "There are so many of them. But one day I will show them. I will punch them so hard they will flee in all directions!"

But from his stories it seemed that when in his fury he attacked them they would all pounce on him and beat him brutally.

"Why don't you tell Mama, then she can complain to the head tutor."

"Oh, no, no, that's impossible. I would be called a tattletale! Look, Bronia, don't say anything to Mama!" he implored.

I could keep a secret. Vaslav only mentioned three of them by name—Georgi Rosai, Anatole Bourman, and Grigori Babitch. How I wished I could protect Vaslav from these monsters! They could harm Vaslav in such fights. I tried to find out more about them. I learned from Vaslav that only in exceptional cases did the pupils of the Boys' Division care for dancing. Most were enrolled by their parents to take advantage of the free education and care. During the dancing lessons the majority only went through the motions of the exercises and would tease those who were working hard.

When the time came for us to return to St. Petersburg for the beginning of the school year, our aunts gave each of us a gift. They gave Stassik an accordion and Vaslav a balalaika. The old balalaika he had bought for five rubles saved out of his pocket money was now broken, the strings torn and the wood dried and split. They gave me a doll, but I never liked dolls; I really wanted a zither. I had always wanted to play an instrument so that I could accompany the boys as we played and sang our favorite songs, but I had never told anyone this; it remained my secret hope to be given a zither, as there was no way that I could save enough money to buy one.

We returned to St. Petersburg where Father had been staying in our apartment while we were away. When the time came for Father to leave, Mother took him into the dining room and heartily reproved him. The boys were out playing in the courtyard but I was in the drawing room; I was hidden in the corner, playing with my new doll. Isolated words, half sentences, reached me through the closed doors.

". . . how could you . . . bring her . . . in the house where our children live . . . where I live . . ."

Then Father's loud voice: "Ah, Liota, don't make a scene . . ."

At last the boys were called in from the courtyard; I was in a flood of tears. We said good-bye to Father and he left for Odessa.

12   1899–1900

WHEN WE WENT back to school the first Monday in September, Vaslav proudly put on his new cap with the silver lyre as a pupil of the Imperial Theatrical School. A few days after the beginning of classes he came running home from the School and announced excitedly: "Tonight I am employed in the Maryinsky Theatre! I must return to school no later than seven-thirty. They will take us to the Theatre in a coach! I will receive sixty kopeks!"

Vaslav's enthusiasm knew no bounds. Mama could not quiet him down. He ate little at mealtime and was afraid he would be late. Mama started to get ready to take him back to the School, to find out when the students would arrive back from the Theatre after the performance. Vaslav protested: "I will go there alone and will come back on my own. Only girls walk to school accompanied by their mothers. They will all laugh at me and call me a girl if they see me walking with you, Mama."

Still Mama walked part of the way with Vaslav, then waited awhile to give him time to get inside the School before going up to the doorman and asking him when the carriage from the Theatre usually returned to the School.

I fought to stay awake for Vaslav's return, but fell asleep and was awakened by the sound of Vaslav singing an aria. I could hear Mama, Vaslav, and Stassik in the dining room where Mama had prepared a light supper for Vaslav. In an excited voice Vaslav was telling them something. I wanted so much to hear about the performance but I was too tired to get up out of bed. I tried to listen but could not make sense out of what Vaslav was telling them. I must have dozed off and fallen back to sleep.

Next morning Vaslav ran to school though still half asleep. When he returned home he described with rapture how the opera artists sang. He struck different attitudes, lifting now one arm, now the other, and singing or humming tunes I did not know. Mama laughed hard as she recognized them; it seemed there were no operas she did not know. During the evening Vaslav broke off from his homework again and again. He told us what costume they gave him to wear, what kind of wig he had on, and how all the boys lined up to have their cheeks rouged. Then the pupils were instructed on their entrances and how to take part in the crowd scenes.

"I guess I did it all well. I was even praised by one artist for my acting 'in the crowds.' "

I was anxious to hear about the ride to the Theatre in the coach. It seemed to me out of a fairy tale—a coach in which the prince rides. But Vaslav did not mention the coach. When I asked about it, he complained: "Only the resident students get to ride in the coaches. We day pupils were driven in a kind of wide, closed, droshky lined with several benches. We were cramped, about sixteen to twenty boys. I was sitting with my back to the horses and did not even see the coachman. I could hear only the clatter of the horses' hoofs on the wooden pavement."

Vaslav was used more and more often in the opera performances, not only in crowd scenes with the other pupils but also to dance with the older students in the operas. Unlike the other pupils he was already familiar with many Russian and Polish dances. Whenever he appeared in a different opera he would sing new arias to us at home. Feodor Chaliapin's performance in *Faust* had so impressed Vaslav that as he sang Mephistopheles's aria he would deepen his voice and wrap a cloak around himself, and taking a stick for a rapier he would imitate Chaliapin's facial expressions, gestures, and monumental poses in the role of Mephistopheles.

He was also chosen for ballet performances. He was a mouse in *The Nutcracker* and a page in both *Sleeping Beauty* and *Swan Lake*. After seven performances he would receive a total of three rubles and fifty kopeks. He was so proud. He clutched the money tightly in his hand, then put it in a money-box and gave the key to Mama so that he wouldn't squander the money. He wanted to buy himself a mandolin.

Whenever Vaslav was busy at the Theatre in the evenings, Stassik would impatiently wait up for him. Mama would try to calm him and put him to bed before Vaslav's return, but since both boys slept in the dining room, Vaslav would disturb Stassik and wake him up when he came home late at night. So Mama moved Vaslav into the drawing room. Before each performance Mama gave Vaslav twenty kopeks for a cab, but he would run home and put the twenty kopeks in a special safe place he had found in the drawing room—Mother's "sailboat." The tall dried flowers that Mother had arranged in the metal-lined sailboat made a perfect hiding place.

One evening after I had been in bed for some time I heard Vaslav shouting from the drawing room, "Fire, fire, we are burning." I jumped out of bed and grabbed the pitcher of water from the washstand; I ran through the dining room and across the corridor to the drawing room, spilling water all the way. There were Mama, Vaslav, Stassik, and Mania standing around the sailboat on the rug in the middle of the floor. The tall dried flowers were still burning, and nearby was a smoking curtain. Vaslav had been bending over the little sailboat with a lighted candle, sorting through his treasure, when the flowers had caught fire and their flame set fire to the tulle curtain. Instantly Vaslav had carried the precious sailboat with the burning flowers carefully to the middle of the room, then Mama had come and pulled the curtain down and tried to stamp out the fire just as I entered with the water. I threw the water onto the flames, and then Stassik and Mania ran to the kitchen to bring more water. The sailboat was saved and for a long time afterwards continued to stand on the table in the corner of the drawing room.

For two years I had been writing letters in Russian for Mania to her fiancé, the sailor. But it was only now, when we both went to Mama and announced Mania's plans to marry, that Mama learned how much of a role I had played in their love letters. Mama gave Mania her bride's trousseau and on the day itself we helped her to dress in her wedding gown. Mama also helped her to fix up her new home.

In December Mama took part in a pantomime staged by Ivan Asselyn, a young Artist of the Imperial Theatres. Besides dancing with the ballet company in the Maryinsky Theatre, he also worked at the young age of twenty-two as ballet master at the Mikhailovsky Manège where, for this Christmas, he was presenting his own pantomime with dances, *In Love with the Moon*. Asselyn also worked in the Theatre Bouffe and the Tavritchesky Garden, and later in Narodny Dom,* which opened December 25, 1899.

During the Christmas holidays Vaslav was also busy, with many matinees as well as evening performances. When he was home we often sang together from our growing repertoire, now including some of the arias Vaslav had taught us from the operas. Stassik played his own variations on his new accordion, and Vaslav practiced different tunes on his new balalaika. Mama did not care for some of the popular songs we had picked up from the laundresses, but she was content to see the two boys busy together at home with their music and was especially pleased that Stanislav seemed happy. She sometimes gathered us together in the

---

*Literally, People's House. It was a popularly priced arts institution and theatre supported by a philanthropic society in St. Petersburg. (AK)

drawing room and taught us new folk dances—the Polish *mazurek*, *krakoviak*, and *oberek*, the Hungarian *czardas*, the Italian *tarantella*. These lessons pleased us very much, but they were really for Stassik.

Stanislav had always been a very quiet boy, but suddenly he began to shout at Mama: "Why am I not in the Imperial School together with Vaslav?" She would calm him by saying that he would enter the School later, when he caught up. But I think she already knew that he was too old to apply, having just celebrated his thirteenth birthday. Yet Mama did everything she could so he wouldn't feel left out.

Up to then Vaslav and I had not noticed anything different about Stassik. Now, however, we learned that he would not return to school, being unable to adjust to the discipline or keep up with the work of children his own age. Stanislav's misfortune grieved Mama terribly, and she tried to do her best for him. She arranged for a tutor to come to our home and for Stassik to have flute lessons, as he liked to play musical instruments. Possibly Mama hoped that he might become a musician or a dancer in the provinces. He had shown some skill in music when he was quite young. From going to the theatre with Mother and Father, he had taught himself to play the flute and the clarinet by picking up instruments of the orchestra during rehearsals. We all loved Stassik very much—he was quiet and gentle and ready to give us anything he owned.

After Christmas Mama was also concerned about my forthcoming entrance examination for the Imperial Theatrical School. Twice a week she took me to dancing lessons with Enrico Cecchetti, to his home on Officerskaya Ulitza. The Cecchetti apartment seemed enormous to me. In addition to the rooms where the family lived there was a large hall with mirrors and practice *barres* and special dressing rooms, two for girls and one for boys.

The lessons, at eight o'clock in the evening, were given by the Maestro himself or by his wife, Giuseppina Cecchetti, who was also an Artist of the Imperial Theatres. There were three or four girls in the class, and we worked mostly on *barre* exercises in preparation for the entrance examination in August.

This was in the middle of winter, so after each class I had to wait to cool off and not go out immediately into the frost. From Officerskaya Ulitza it was quite a long walk to the horse trolley at Sadovaya Ulitza. The trolley made many stops, picking up and letting off passengers. When it came to a certain high arched bridge it stopped and two extra horses were hitched to it, then with a running start the trolley would fly over the bridge before stopping again to unhitch the horses. I would often fall asleep on the trolley, as it took half an hour or longer to reach Nevsky Prospekt. From there we had to walk home. We never got there before eleven o'clock at night. I would then sit up to finish my homework and Stassik would practice his flute. Vaslav was often still at the Theatre.

In the spring, three boys, Cecchetti's sons, would sometimes join the dancing class. All three were handsome. Nini, the eldest, was ten, had jet black hair and enormous black eyes, and was well built. Riccardo was nine, slender, with brown hair, and was very friendly. The youngest, Lolo, was seven, with a blond curly head like a cupid, and was everybody's pet. None of the boys spoke Russian well; they all had strong Italian accents. Once, in the presence of Mama and Cecchetti, Riccardo passed a note to me written in Russian—"I love you very much." All three boys entertained us girls before and after the lessons.

Vaslav didn't study with Cecchetti when I took lessons there, but once he asked Mama to take him with us. I don't recall that he even once looked at my class, which, anyway, was mainly *barre* work and a different method of teaching. Vaslav simply declared: "Mine's the best." His real purpose in coming was not to see the class but to see Nini Cecchetti, who was also a pupil in the Imperial School and a great friend of his. That day when Vaslav came Nini did not study with us girls and his brothers, but instead went off to play with Vaslav. They ran round and round the apartment, making lots of noise. Mama was very angry that Vaslav's presence disturbed my class and reprimanded him. After that she never again took him to the Cecchettis'.

Though Vaslav had the highest possible mark for dance—a 12—Mama was concerned that his participation in the performances might be affecting his other studies. She was worried lest his general marks be too low to permit his admittance as a resident student. It was Vaslav's dream to be a resident student and he applied himself to his studies, but there was not enough time after the performances to prepare his lessons, and even then he was often very tired from lack of sleep. I used to help him with his homework, and many times he would ask me to do it for him so that he would not get a failing grade.

Finally the school year ended. Vaslav was admitted as a resident student and was awarded the Didelot Scholarship. This Scholarship was established for the children of ballet artists from the proceeds of the estate of Charles Louis Didelot. Vaslav was so proud of his Didelot Scholarship. Didelot [1767–1837], whose teachers had been Auguste Vestris and Jean-Georges Noverre, had been associated with the St. Petersburg Imperial Ballet Company for more than thirty years—from 1801—as ballet master, teacher, and choreographer. His work as head of the Imperial Ballet School was remarkable, and it revolutionized the entire system of teaching. Alexander Pushkin declared that there was more poetry in a Didelot ballet (and he choreographed more than fifty) than in the entire French literature of the day.

Vaslav was also anxious to show himself to Father in his new uniform as a resident student of the Imperial Theatrical School. We were expecting Father back in St. Petersburg from Paris, where he had been dancing during May and June with Maria Nikolaevna Labounska* at the Folies-Bergère Theatre during the International Exhibition of 1900.

At this time the Folies-Bergère was a variety theatre with a program of ballets, pantomimes, and music-hall numbers featuring foreign artists, and it had one of the best orchestras in Paris. In his letters Father described Labounska with admiration and told us how thoughtful she was on our behalf, even going shopping with him in Paris to buy gifts for his wife and children.

Labounska and Nijinsky had received an invitation to dance at the Krasnoe Selo Theatre. It was considered a great honor to perform there during the summer maneuvers of the Imperial Guard. The audience consisted of the elite from St. Petersburg, including the Grand Dukes, the high-ranking officers of the Guards Regiments, and often the Tsar himself.

Mother looked more relaxed this summer, her face was less sad. She had ordered a new dress with bouffant sleeves at the dressmaker's and she came back from the hairdresser with a new hairdo. She looked very graceful and beautiful.

Mother liked Labounska, Father's new partner, and hoped secretly that his love affair with Rumiantseva was over. One evening Mama was invited with Father to the gala supper after the performance, and she told me later how amiable and considerate she had found Labounska, who had chosen to wear a blouse and skirt with a wide leather belt so that Nijinsky's wife should not be the only one there not wearing a gala evening dress.

Labounska was very beautiful, with fine aristocratic Russian features, delicate skin, large expressive eyes, luxuriously long, ash-blonde hair, and a charming smile. Although she was a classical ballet dancer, her success on the stage was due to her fiery temperament and her flamboyant style of dressing. I saw a photograph taken in Paris in which Father, dressed as a toreador, was kneeling on his left knee; Labounska's right foot was on his

---

*Maria Labounska, born in 1868, was the subject of rumors in 1890 that she had been assigned to instruct the future Nicholas II, then the heir to the throne, in the "art of love." As a result, the mother of the officer to whom she was engaged tried to break off the engagement. Officially, Labounska left Russia to study and dance in Paris in 1892 on a leave of absence. She was dismissed from the Imperial Ballet in 1894, while still on leave. (AK)

other knee, and she was holding out the skirts of her sumptuous Spanish costume so that layers and layers of laces were displayed behind him. She was wearing many ornaments—jewels in her hair, earrings, necklaces, bracelets, rings . . .

Labounska felt that to be invited for that summer of 1900 to dance at the Krasnoe Selo Theatre was her "pardon." She told my mother that she had graduated from the Imperial Theatrical School in 1886, and I believe it was at that time that she had been introduced to the Tsarevitch, when they were both eighteen years old. In 1890 she was promoted to *coryphée*, the same year that Mathilda Kshessinska had graduated from the School. Two years later Kshessinska became the official mistress of the Tsarevitch and Labounska was exiled from Russia, being falsely accused of spreading gossip and slander about the Royal Family. She felt the source of these cruel allegations was Kshessinska, her rival for the attentions of the Tsarevitch.

While Father had been working in Paris, Mother had become even more worried about Stassik and had consulted Professor Bekhterev, the famous psychiatrist. Bekhterev felt that Stassik needed the supervision of a man, his father. At the end of his engagement at Krasnoe Selo it was planned that Father take Stassik with him. By now Mama seemed to have accepted the inevitability of separation from her husband, as she knew he was returning to his former partner, Rumiantseva; but the additional separation from her son was a new cause of grief, and she began to worry whether Stassik would have the care and attention he needed. As the time approached for him to leave with Father, Vatsa and I realized how dearly we loved Stassik, and we worried whether he would be happy living away from us. Mother, naturally, was even more saddened to have her son leave her.

All summer Vaslav had been parading up and down in his new summer uniform issued to him as a resident student. It was only the everyday uniform. The blue dress uniform with the silver lyres he would not receive until the beginning of the school year. The tailor had already taken his measurements to have the uniform ready for September 1, but Father would not be in St. Petersburg then and Vaslav was very disappointed that he would not be able to present himself to his father in his full dress uniform.

After Father left, Mama danced in a spectacular pantomime, *Histoire d'un Pierrot*, in three acts with music by Mario Costa. Several artists from the Warsaw Wielki Theatre were invited to come to St. Petersburg to take part in this production at the Aquarium Theatre, the first performance being August 2.

That summer, instead of going to Cecchetti's for my dancing lessons in the evenings, I went three times a week from eleven to twelve in the mornings. With the Imperial School closed, Maestro himself taught our class. In August, just before my entrance examination, Cecchetti told me I should take five lessons a week. Because I had made progress, and perhaps because I was his favorite in his "baby" class, he let me come twice a week for *barre* exercises in his "ballerina" class. Many artists from the Imperial Theatres studied with Cecchetti in his private school, and here I was at nine years of age in the same dancing class with two prima ballerinas, Olga Preobrajenska and Mathilda Kshessinska. Sometimes Cecchetti allowed me to do center floor exercises as well. He put me in the middle of the front line, and before the mirror he demonstrated the positions of the body and arm movements, *port de bras*. My view of myself was blocked by Cecchetti, but I was fascinated to watch the dancers beside me in the mirror; on one side there were Lubov Egorova and Julia Sedova, and on the other the recently graduated Elsa Will and Anna Pavlova. At the end of the center floor exercises I was allowed to stay in the room and watch the entire lesson. I was spellbound.

One day, just before the entrance examination, I remember Mama worriedly asking Cecchetti, "Will they accept Bronia in the School?"

Cecchetti patted me on the head, saying, "Of course they will accept her, don't worry."

Then the mother of another girl in the class, Maroussia Dobrolubova, also asked Cecchetti, "Will they accept Maroussia?" Cecchetti pondered, and then reluctantly answered, "Maybe."

Maroussia's mother became very angry: "Why are you so sure for Bronia but not for Maroussia?"

Cecchetti flew into a rage and in his strong Italian accent shouted, "You do not understand anything. Brroo-nia is Brroo-nia and you are doo-rra [*Dura*—Russian for a silly woman]."

Finally the day came for my entrance examination. This time the vestibule in the Imperial Theatrical School was filled with girls and their parents. There were 214 candidates, many more than for the boys' entrance examination. We were told to go upstairs to the Girls' Division and were then invited into the classrooms. As we took off our hats and coats we eyed each other carefully, inspecting the others' outfits. I was wearing a dress Father had bought for me in Paris, one that Labounska had helped him choose. It was all white with an embroidered bodice and ruffles around the skirt. I wore a wide sash around my waist. Most of the other girls were neatly and modestly attired, but here and there one had been strikingly dressed up to catch an examiner's eye.

Our parents remained in the classrooms, sitting on the benches of the school desks, as the candidates were taken into the large hall. It was the dancing hall with two large windows overlooking the street. One wall was taken up with a mirror. In a nearby corner stood a piano, and across on the other wall hung a life-size portrait of the Tsar Nicholas II in a wide gold frame. All around the perimeter of the room was a double row of exercise *barres*. As we waited for the examination we examined each other, trying to assess who would be the strongest competition.

We were divided into groups of twenty to twenty-five, and each group was taken in turn into a second hall. I remember when my name was called I felt weak at the knees. We were led into the other hall that was just like the first but with a long narrow table, covered with a green cloth, running the length of one wall. Sitting at the table were about twenty-five people. First we walked in pairs, and then we were put in a long line facing the table. Several examiners were in full dress uniforms with all their medals and decorations, and on the table in front of each one was a large sheet of paper and a well-sharpened pencil. Later I learned who some of the examiners were. There was Prince Volkonsky, the Director of the Imperial Theatres; the ballet masters Marius Petipa, Nikolai and Sergei Legat; also Enrico Cecchetti and Stanislav Gillert, whom I already knew. I recognized the two ballerinas Mathilda Kshessinska and Olga Preobrajenska from Cecchetti's classes. Kshessinska took no notice of me, but Preobrajenska smiled at me.

Finally twelve girls were accepted, including me and my two friends from Cecchetti's classes, Efrosima Georgievskaya, "Frossia," and Maria Dobrolubova, "Maroussia."

13 My First Year in the Imperial Theatrical School: 1900–1901

I WAS so happy now that I too was a pupil of the Imperial Theatrical School. Each morning Mama took me to the School, and I climbed the marble staircase up to the lobby of the Girls' Division on the second floor. My first lesson was the dancing class with Stanislav Gillert, and so I made my way to the cloakroom to find Frossia and Maroussia and our new friends, Lydia, Zina, Tina, Nina, and the others.* We changed into our gray dancing dresses, ready for nine o'clock.

When I entered the Imperial Theatrical School I was already well prepared in dancing. I had been studying with Cecchetti for a whole year, but since Maestro had not used French terminology in his beginners' classes, I did not find the lessons in the School easy to follow. It was not only the French that was new to me; sometimes I was also confused by the instructions given to the class. In one of the first lessons I heard Gillert say in a stern voice, "Hold your heel forward!" I was at a loss. My heel would not move forward as my leg was already turned out and I was concentrating all my force on the pointed toe for the *battements tendus*. At the end of the lesson, unhappily, I changed into our school uniform, the brown ankle-length skirt and long-sleeved blouse with the white fichu collar, and put on my black apron ready for the rest of the day. For lunch I had brought, as usual, my rolls filled with cheese or ham, but I was not hungry; I just drank the tea with sugar provided by the School for day pupils. During our supervised walk in the small inner courtyard after lunch, all I could think about was why my heel did not move forward.

*Lydia Shiraeva and Zina Puyman, both of whom graduated in 1907, entered the School with Bronislava Nijinska in 1900 and were her friends throughout her school years. The other girls, Tina and Nina, cannot be identified and possibly were among the girls who were accepted as pupils following the entrance examination but who later were not accepted as students at the end of the trial period. (IN/JR)

At the end of the afternoon, after our general subject classes, I went to meet Mother in the lobby, where she waited each day with the other mothers. I could not wait to get home to tell her about my dancing problem.

Mother told me to assume the first position and explained, "Your legs are fully turned out. It's not your heel . . . it's here . . . it's your pelvis." She put her hand on my hip and turned my leg. "Feel the movement—it begins here in your pelvis—then your heel will be correctly forward."

That way the movement came very naturally. Mother's lesson was imprinted in my memory so that years later, in my own teaching, I remembered her skills and studied the anatomy of the body to understand the relationship of movements.

Life at home was quiet now that both my brothers were away. Stassik had gone with Father, and Vaslav was now a resident student of the Imperial Theatrical School. It was the first time in my life that I had lived alone with Mama; we often talked about dancing, but more often we remembered the summer, when Father had come from Paris and we had been a family together again.

As a resident student Vaslav had the privilege of coming home on weekends when he was not used in the theatres. Sometimes he brought his friend, Kolya, home—Nikolai Issaev, the boy who shared his desk with him. Kolya's mother had died when he was quite small, and with his father being an alcoholic and a compulsive gambler Kolya had been raised by his grandmother. Later he had been placed in an orphanage, and then in a military band school. He loved musical instruments and sometimes brought his *domra*, a Russian stringed instrument, and played tunes on it for Vaslav and me, and Vaslav would accompany him on his balalaika.

But whenever Vaslav came home by himself he never played his balalaika. As I did, he missed Stanislav.

One day Gillert was ill, and so we day pupils had to join some of the other dancing classes. Maestro Cecchetti spoke in flattering terms about me and took me in with some of the advanced students. But his "Brroonia" whose dance talents he praised, still only nine years old, had difficulties keeping up with the tempo of the advanced students. Maestro Cecchetti then lost his temper and threw his cane at "Brroonia." The cane broke, and the little ballerina cried. Afterwards he spoke to me in the corridor, trying to comfort me and saying he was sorry.

After Christmas Pavel Gerdt and Enrico Cecchetti began preparing a Student Performance. "In the Kingdom of Ice," a tableau from Gerdt's ballet *L'Etincelle d'Amour*, was to be presented on March 13 in the School Theatre. One day Frossia and I were surprised to read our names on the call board, along with the names of several students, for rehearsals with Enrico Cecchetti. As a rule first-year day pupils were not scheduled to take part in Student Performances. At the rehearsal Maestro first worked on a dance with a group of girls from his advanced class. Frossia and I were wondering why we had been called; maybe it was a misunderstanding.

I was dumbfounded when I heard, "Brroonia, Frroossia—now it is your solo." Maestro Cecchetti smiled as he added, "Get your toe shoes ready."

Then I knew Maestro was joking. We were first-year day pupils, and according to the School program "Beginners' Toe Exercises, at the *Barre*" was taught only to the second-year day pupils.

But no, Maestro Cecchetti told us to come out on each side of the stage from the last wing and advance towards each other *pas de bourrée*, on toe. When we met in the middle of the stage we were to turn towards the audience and then, still on toe, *pas de bourrée*, move side by side towards the footlights. Here Maestro got up from his chair and, on half-toe, his arms raised above his head in a circle, daintily and with grace, demonstrated a deep curtsy. He added, "Now you disappear into the wings. Brroonia, you to the right, Frroossia to the left."

For the next few days it seemed as though everything were illumined by a bright light. It was a small, brief solo, but I never felt happier or more proud. I had been chosen to dance on the stage of the Imperial School Theatre. Cecchetti had made an exception to the School rules by choosing two day pupils, still on trial, for a ballet he was to stage for the Student Performance. I was overjoyed to find that Maestro still believed in my talent. I had been so afraid that I had disappointed him the day he threw his cane at me, when I couldn't keep up with the tempo of his advanced class.

I determined not to disappoint him this time. I practiced on toe at home with Mama, and at the School Gillert worked with both Frossia and me. He kept us for additional instruction *sur pointe* after our regular dancing classes, and then worked diligently with us at the rehearsals, taking two or four bars of the music at a time. Frossia and I also worked together by ourselves practicing our "solo" whenever we had the chance.

Sometimes our rehearsals took place on the small stage of the School Theatre, and occasionally we would be allowed to stay and watch the rehearsal of the ballet, staged by Pavel Andreevitch Gerdt and danced by the graduating student Evgenia Eduardova. The girls in the School were not allowed to speak to the boys, not even in dancing classes or rehearsals, so it was only at home that Vaslav could tell me about his part. There were no dancing parts for the first-year resident students in the ballet, but

Pavel Andreevitch had wanted to use several boys from Sergei Legat's class in the *mises en scène*. One day I saw Vaslav onstage with a group of boys from his class. I thought Vaslav stood out from the others; he seemed to be more actively involved in the performance. Later he told me that Pavel Gerdt had explained to them the plot of the ballet, and where and when they should be onstage. "In the *mises en scène*, Pavel Andreevitch encouraged us to use our imaginations, and several times during rehearsals he praised me."

The dress rehearsal came. Mama had checked my toe shoes the night before to make sure they were correctly broken in and that the ribbons were sewn on tightly and that I had darned the tip.

I was too involved with thinking about my first appearance to look for Vaslav in his costume or to watch Gerdt's ballet at the dress rehearsal. As I stood in the wing, waiting for Gillert to give us the cue for our entrance, my heart was beating fast. I looked across at Frossia; she was crossing herself again and again. Our solo was a success. We were even applauded.

On March 13, from early in the morning, there was a festive atmosphere at the School, we were all so excited about the performance that evening in the School Theatre. Student Performances were presented before the Administration of the Imperial Theatres, and occasionally members of the Royal Family also attended. We wondered who would be there that night—"Perhaps the Tsar himself will come?"

I waited impatiently for the end of the school day so that I could go home, wash, change, and be back at the School by six o'clock. But when I hurried to the lobby by the stairway where Mama should be waiting for me, a chambermaid stopped me. "Wait, your mother is in with Varvara Ivanovna." The other mothers were there waiting in the lobby, which was on the same landing as the apartment of the Inspectrice, Varvara Ivanovna Lihosherstova [the Principal of the Girls' Division]. *Why my mother? Why she alone?* These thoughts had barely flashed through my mind as I approached the doors leading to Varvara Ivanovna's apartment and saw Mama coming out in tears, followed by Vladimir Pisnyatchevsky, the Inspector of the Theatrical School. *Could it be that Vaslav was expelled?* I rushed to her, asking: "What has Vaslav done?" Her response was barely audible: "It is bad. Vatsa is in the hospital."

As we made our way out through the group of mothers waiting in the lobby, I did not ask Mama anything more, only snuggled to her tightly. We hurried down the stairs and took an *isvostchik*.

"The Court Hospital—Malaya Koniushennaya."

We were met by a nurse in the large, well-lighted corridor of the hospital. A doctor soon came out of the ward where Vaslav was lying. Mama rushed to him.

"The boy is unconscious. Probably an internal hemorrhage. He is in very critical condition. I cannot tell you anything more now, but come again this evening and I will be here."

On the way home Mama told me what Vladimir Pisnyatchevsky had told her. During a recess the students had organized a high-jump contest in the large dancing hall. They had put a heavy wooden music stand, which could be adjusted in height, in the middle of the hall. As he jumped Vaslav slipped, and his stomach hit the wooden rib of the music stand; he fell together with the music stand, hitting the floor full force, and was found there unconscious.

Mama took me back to the School for the performance and then returned to the hospital.

In the Theatrical School, as if in a daze, I changed into my costume, but what I had on I still don't remember. I went with the other girls into the large dancing hall where the Administration of the Theatrical School and the guests were already gathered. They were awaiting the arrival of members of the Royal Family to begin the performance. I saw Maestro Cecchetti, purple in the face, speaking sharply to Prince Volkonsky, the Director of the Imperial Theatres. When he turned away he looked agitated. Just before the performance began I learned that Cecchetti had resigned from the Imperial Theatres. To my grief and concern for Vaslav was now added the realization that Cecchetti would not teach me anymore. I would no longer see him at the lessons in the Imperial Theatrical School. I suddenly realized how much I had loved him, even loved his very strictness with me. I felt grieved for him.

I found out later that Cecchetti's wife, an Artist of the Imperial Theatres, had not been invited to the Student Performance, and Cecchetti had seen the wife of Pavel Gerdt among the invited guests.

The performance itself passed as if in a fog. My only thoughts: *How soon can I see Mama? Has Vaslav regained consciousness? What more has the doctor told her at the hospital?*

But at the end of the performance Frossia and I had to stay with the resident students for the gala supper with the Grand Dukes, the Administration, and the guests. The dining room of the Theatrical School had two long tables along the sides and a small table at the end forming the letter "П." I remember that the Grand Duke Vladimir Alexandrovitch was sitting at the middle table flanked by two beautiful students, Alexandra Baldina and Tamara Karsavina. Vladimir Alexandrovitch's voice thundered over the entire dining room, and everybody responded with loud laughter. This laughter echoing through me while Vaslav was lying near death in the hospital filled me with fear.

When supper ended all I wanted to do was change and go home. But first, we had to listen to the announcement: "By order of the Grand Duke Vladimir Alexandrovitch the School will have three days free from studies."

This announcement was followed by instructions from Varvara Ivanovna explaining to the resident students that they could go home for the three days and the subsequent weekend provided that their parents were in town and that arrangements could be made to pick them up. All this I had to listen to.

At last I was able to change, but here again I was delayed; my stockings were missing. Dressed but barefoot, I searched for them with the wardrobe keeper. Only one stocking was found, among the ballet costumes, and so I had to put a bare foot into one shoe. All this delay was annoying and made me nervous, with poor Mama waiting for me. At last I ran towards the exit. Mama was there, her face drawn and ashen; she could not tell me anything more.

Next morning Vatsa was still unconscious. At the hospital I heard the doctor tell Mama, "You must be prepared for the worst. The boy's condition is hopeless. It is doubtful that he will live, and if he does it will be a miracle."

Mama begged the doctor to let her at least look at Vaslav, so she could bless him. She went into the ward and I waited in the corridor.

From the hospital we went to the Catholic church nearby and prayed there for a long time. When we returned to the hospital Vaslav was still unconscious.

I remember how tenderly and attentively the doctor talked with Mama every day, trying to explain to her that all his medical knowledge and experience as well as the concerned care of the hospital staff were being applied to save the life of her son. He visited his patient several times each day and a nurse was at Vaslav's bedside at all times.

There were no X rays at this time, and so the diagnosis had to be made on the basis of Vaslav's symptoms and the doctor's experience and intuition. On the day after the accident the doctor called three students —Rosai, Bourman, and Babitch—to question them in detail and learn exactly how Vatsa fell. I remember the three frightened boys in the hospital. One even appeared with his mother, who then and there, in our presence, rebuked all three of them: "Look what your cruel pranks have done to Vaslav. The poor boy is dying." Mama was so overcome with distress that she could only say "Please leave, go home." Then she and I left the reception room.

Four days passed and Vaslav did not recover consciousness. On each of these days we went to the hospital early in the morning and waited near the door to Vaslav's ward, to talk to the doctor when he came out. He would try to comfort Mama. "We must wait. As long as the boy is breathing there is hope." Then sadly we went from the hospital to the church, to pray until midday. We came home for lunch and then hurried back to the hospital, stopping on the way to light a candle in the church and say a short prayer. We stayed in the hospital until evening.

Not until the fifth day did Vaslav regain consciousness. Mama and I were allowed to see him only for five minutes. Vatsa was lying on his back; he looked up with enormous eyes and smiled at us. The white ward was full of light; the sun was shining through a high window. Vatsa did not say one word to us, but for Mama and me it was as if he had returned to life. The doctor, however, did not consider the danger over; he was afraid of complications and internal bleeding.

We were soon to realize how dangerous internal bleeding could be. In the bed next to Vaslav's was a young man, a groom from the Royal Stables, who had been kicked in the stomach by a horse and admitted to the Court Hospital almost the same time as Vaslav. He talked to us, and his condition seemed less serious than Vaslav's, who on that first visit did not utter a word and only looked at us. The next day when we came the bed was empty, and we were told the groom had died during the night. Then we realized that Vaslav was indeed still in danger.

All Mama could tell was that Vaslav had an ice bag on his stomach and that several times a day a teaspoonful of almond milk was poured in his mouth. She had witnessed more than one accident in the theatre and the circus arena, and she was very worried that Vatsa might have other injuries besides the blow in the stomach. "What if his spine is injured? Will Vatsa be able to dance again?"

As soon as Vaslav was allowed other visitors, Rosai, Bourman, and Babitch came to see him. They did not enter the ward right away but waited until Mama and I had left Vaslav's bed. We lingered in the corridor; Mama was afraid the boys might disturb Vaslav too much. We watched them through the door of the ward; they bent over Vaslav and whispered something to him. It was obvious to me that they begged his forgiveness and implored him not to betray them. We waited until the boys left.

Later, when I asked Vaslav what had happened during the recess, he told me that the other students had egged him on. "We know you can jump far, over seven benches, but now let's see if you can jump as high. Come on, jump over this music stand." Just as Vaslav began his jump, Lukyanov, the oldest boy in the dancing class, had pulled him back by grabbing his leg from behind.

Kolya Issaev also told us that the whole idea had originated with Bourman, Rosai, and Babitch. They had first suggested the high-jump contest and then, at the last moment, when Vaslav was not looking, they had raised the music stand so high that if Vaslav had seen it he would not have jumped. Other students told me that they had also rubbed the floor in front of the music stand with soap.

Only after the special holiday did the Administration begin to investigate the accident and try to find out why the boys had scattered and hidden in the classrooms, leaving Vaslav unconscious on the floor. Bourman, Rosai, and Babitch all denied any guilt—it was impossible to get anything from them—and Vaslav said that he remembered nothing. They had agreed with Vaslav to spare Iliador Lukyanov. Vaslav felt sorry for Lukyanov. The boy's parents had separated before his birth, and though his father, Sergei Lukyanov, was a leading dancer at the Maryinsky Theatre, his mother was very poor. Lukyanov had begged Vaslav not to reveal his name, for if he were to be expelled it would cause his mother additional hardship. So the name of Lukyanov was never mentioned during the investigation. The punishment meted out to Rosai, Bourman,* and Babitch was limited to a bad mark for conduct and the loss of one Sunday's leave.

Fortunately Vaslav had no broken bones, and towards the end of the school year he was allowed to leave the hospital, though he had to remain at home on a special diet for a long time.

During his stay in the hospital both Stanislav Gillert and Sergei Legat visited him often. Of the students from the School only Kolya Issaev ever came to visit Vatsa.

At the end of the school year Vaslav was promoted with the boys in his class on the basis of his dancing lessons, but not for his general subjects. His grades even before the accident had not been good, and also because he had missed a lot of school he was kept for the second year in the lower second grade. I finished the school year at the top of my class in all subjects and was accepted as a pupil of the Imperial Theatrical School.

---

*Bourman, in *The Tragedy of Nijinsky* (1936), places the blame on Rosai. As is often noted, Bourman's attempts to portray himself as Nijinsky's protector and close friend lack credibility. (AK)

14   1901–1902

VASLAV AND I were not told that while he was recovering from his accident Father also had been hospitalized, nor did we know anything of the money troubles that our mother was facing. During a rehearsal Father had been trying to perfect a new stunt for the *hopak* when he had fallen on the stage and broken his leg. His dancing engagement for the summer had to be canceled, and he was not able to send us his full promised allowance. The rent had not been paid, and money was owing to the local shops. To help Mother, Cousin Stassia invited us to spend the summer with her. Mama said she herself had to remain in St. Petersburg, but she insisted to Vaslav and me that we go to Marijampole without her, saying that a few weeks away from the city in the fresh air of the countryside would be good for both of us. We assumed that Mama would be working in one of the Summer Theatres.

We were thrilled to travel alone on a train for a long journey, all the way from St. Petersburg to Marijampole, which was near the Prussian border. Cousin Stassia, her husband Alex, and Aunt Thetya were all waiting for us at the station. Immediately we recognized Alex, whom till then we had known only from wedding pictures. He was tall and had sandy hair and blue eyes.

Marijampole was a small town surrounded on all sides by fields and farmlands. Stassia and Alex lived in a large, two-story house surrounded by its own garden. They loved to entertain in their beautiful home and would often seat six to ten guests for dinner at the long table in the dining room, in addition to us five. We liked our new "uncle," as we called Alex. He was jovial and always in a good mood.

There was a grand piano in the drawing room and Vaslav immediately wanted to play on it, but I was more attracted by Alex's study, where the walls were lined with glass-fronted bookshelves. I was fascinated by the rows and rows of books in their beautiful leather bindings, tooled in gold, and at once asked to borrow a book. Aunt Thetya would not allow me to read, and she discouraged Vaslav from playing the piano. "You did not come here to study, but to have a good time. Go and play outside in the garden."

Aunt Thetya and her daughter Stassia did not let us stay up late. They had promised Mother that Vaslav would get plenty of rest and fresh air so as to regain all his strength after the accident. They were both marvelous cooks and made all sorts of sweets that Vaslav liked—fruit cakes, nut tortes, candied fruits, cookies—and thoroughly spoiled him. In the orchard behind the house they had many fruit trees, and they also grew their own vegetables, which they then canned. They made jams and jellies to last them all year. There was always fresh fruit on the table, and every evening in our bedrooms upstairs we always found a small dish of compote—apple or cherry or plum—on the night table beside our beds. Vaslav usually ate his at night before going to sleep, but I preferred to eat mine first thing in the morning before I ran downstairs to help feed the hens, ducks, and geese kept in a pen beside the orchard.

Stassia and Alex had many friends and acquaintances, and whenever they went on a visit they would take us along. We went on several outings and picnics, and sometimes we went to the river to bathe. One day Alex, who was a Government Tax Inspector, took us to the Town Hall and showed us the courtroom.

It was Sunday, and the courtroom was empty. Vatsa ran around the room and between the benches. He urged me to join him, to come and play hide and seek, and when he jumped up into the Judge's chair and yelled my name, I could hear "Bronia, Bronia, Bronia" coming at me from all directions as Vaslav's voice echoed around the big hall. Alex tried to stop him but Stassia, who had come with us that day, was happy to see Vaslav run and jump and play, with no sign of injury to his back or legs.

On our own Vaslav and I soon explored the small town of Marijampole, which was like a large garden. There were only two main streets and a few stores or business buildings. Each house had its own garden with tall trees and flowers. We enjoyed our daily walks along the shady streets. There was a fragrance in the air; the lilac bushes were in bloom. And there was color everywhere; masses of climbing roses covered the walls of the houses, and along the street fences were multicolored sweet peas.

As the weeks passed, the green fields around Marijampole turned golden yellow. Whenever we rode in the countryside it seemed that as far as the eye could see, the tall ripe golden wheat was moving in the wind like ocean waves. The time for the harvest was approaching, as was the time for us to return to St. Petersburg. We were sorry to have to leave before the harvest festivals that would soon be celebrated in the villages.

It was mid-August when we returned home, and only then did Mama tell us that her hopes of working in a Summer Theatre production had not been realized, and so she had had to dismiss the girl who had been working for us after Mania got married. She had also had to rent three rooms of the apartment to a couple of friends, dancers who used to work with her and Father. She had fixed up a room for herself near the kitchen and had done all the cleaning and cooking herself during the summer. She had made sure, though, that the dancers were gone by the time we came home. We both felt terrible realizing that we had lived in comfort at our cousin's, unaware of how Mama was economizing in every possible way to save every kopek to pay off her debts and to put aside enough money to get us ready to go back to the School.

My trial year was over. I was still a day pupil, but now that I was officially enrolled as a pupil of the Imperial Theatrical School I was eligible to be used in the performances. I was eagerly looking forward to taking part in operas, ballets, and dramas on the stages of the Imperial Theatres: the Maryinsky, the Alexandrinsky, the Mikhailovsky, and others. We were each given a little notebook in which we were to record all our appearances on the stage. For each appearance we would be paid fifty kopeks, and if we ever had a speaking part, even if we spoke only two words, then we would receive one ruble fifty kopeks. We were told that at the end of each month the Inspectrice would check our notebooks and pay us our salaries. I was so proud that now I would be able to bring home my very first earned money.

But the joy of my first few days in the School was soon marred. We heard that Aunt Stepha had suffered a heart attack and died. Mama arranged to go to Vilno for the funeral, and at the same time she planned to see Stassik, who was studying music there. Father, while in the hospital after his accident, had placed Stassik in care of a dancer, a former member of his company, and had asked her husband, a bandmaster in Vilno, to give Stassik music lessons, promising them a handsome fee. In Marijampole Aunt Thetya had also told Vaslav and me that she had heard that Stassik was in Vilno, and that she hoped to see him when she went back home.

After Aunt Stepha's funeral, Mama and Aunt Thetya went to see Stassik. The bandmaster and his wife lived in a new house on the outskirts of Vilno, on the shore of the river Vilia across from the military camp. Mama was very disappointed when they did not find anyone at home, for she had been planning to return to St. Petersburg that same evening. She went around the house to see if she could find somebody to leave a message with and discovered Stassik in a storeroom, the door bolted on the outside. Stassik cried with joy when he saw his mother and his aunt.

He told them how cruelly he had been treated, never being allowed in the house, made to sleep in that dark storeroom on a thin mattress on the bare dirt floor. He was often beaten, and for his meals had to swim across the river to get a soldier's ration in the barracks.

Later Mama found out that because Father had not worked that summer he had not been able to send the money for Stassik's keep, and so these heartless people had neglected the boy completely and the bandmaster had not bothered to give him even one music lesson. When confronted they denied everything and demanded full payment for Stassik's stay with them. They accused Stassik of lying and insisted that he was locked in the storeroom that afternoon as a punishment. They also claimed that he had to be locked up for his own protection whenever they went out, for he could not be left alone in the house.

Mama brought Stassik home with her. I was overjoyed to be reunited with Stassik and to have him living at home with us again.

In the School too a joyous time began for me as I took my first steps on the stage of the Maryinsky Theatre. In the ballet *Coppélia* I was used in the *mises en scène*. We did not have any rehearsal, but on the evening of the performance we were taken to the Theatre and, already dressed in our costumes, were brought onstage just before the beginning of the ballet to have the *régisseur* show us where to stand or walk.

The Italian dancer, Carlotta Zambelli, ballerina of the Paris Opéra, was making her debut in St. Petersburg in her famous role in *Coppélia*. As I stood onstage in the first act in a group with the other pupils, I admired the brilliance of her technique. I was fascinated by her spectacular *manège*, as she kept circling the stage at a fast speed, her body remaining low during the quick turn, *déboulé en plié*, and then thrusting forward, far and low, in an extended *jeté arabesque*. I was seeing this *pas* for the first time and it differed so much from the *manèges sur pointe* with "straight backs" in the Cecchetti classes. To this day I can see Zambelli vividly, flashing like an arrow, circling the stage close to the ground in one continuous line *en arabesque*.

This performance of *Coppélia* took place on October 10, and was staged by Lev Ivanov. In the School we were told that it was the same version he had mounted in 1894 with Enrico Cecchetti, and that the ballet *Coppélia* was seen for the first time in Russia in 1884 when it was staged in St. Petersburg by Petipa. Mama told me that she had seen excerpts of the Petipa version in 1885, at the Arcadia Theatre with Dell'Era, but she also told me that the first performance of *Coppélia* in Russia was not in St. Petersburg in 1884 but in Warsaw* in 1882, when it was mounted by José

*Poland was then part of the Russian Empire. (IN/JR)

Mendez. She went on, "If you don't believe me, then ask Stanislav Gillert. He was the leading dancer at the Warsaw Wielki Theatre that season partnering Maria Giuri, the Italian ballerina. Only last summer he was reminiscing with your father about the Warsaw production of *Coppélia*. Gillert thought it was closer to Saint-Léon and Mérante's original creation, which after all he also saw in the repertory of the Paris Opéra when he was there as a young dancer."

In school Mlle Verchault read to us in French "Le Marchand de Sable," the translation of the tale by Hoffmann that was the source of the libretto for *Coppélia*. After the ballet classes we all tried to execute Zambelli's *manège*.

The new Director of the Imperial Theatres, Vladimir Arkadievitch Telyakovsky, announced that the ballet *Camargo* was to be scheduled for October 21, with Olga Preobrajenska. It was generally recalled that a performance of the very same ballet, with Mathilda Kshessinska, had caused the resignation of Telyakovsky's predecessor, Prince Volkonsky. In January of 1901, *Camargo* had been restaged by Lev Ivanovitch Ivanov for the farewell performance of Pierina Legnani. When Kshessinska came to dance the ballet in April she refused to wear the costume as designed for Legnani, and against the orders of the Directorate she removed the hoops from the dress, a copy of a Louis XV style worn by Catherine the Great for a masked ball. When fined by the Directorate, she had retaliated, with the support of the Tsar, by demanding that the fine be lifted and a public announcement posted to that effect. Prince Volkonsky naturally had to accede to the Tsar's wishes, but thereupon resigned.

We were intrigued that his successor should announce so soon another performance of *Camargo*, not with Kshessinska, who was absent from St. Petersburg, but with Preobrajenska—for we knew how jealous Kshessinska was of her starring roles.

As well as working on *Coppélia* with Carlotta Zambelli and *Camargo* with Olga Preobrajenska, Ivanov was also staging *Sylvia* for Preobrajenska. Ivanov was energetic and appeared to be in good health, but in November we heard that he was ill and that Pavel Andreevitch Gerdt had taken over rehearsals and was putting the finishing touches to Ivanov's *Sylvia*. The ballet was presented as scheduled on December 2, and in the program the choreography was credited to both Ivanov and Gerdt. A few days later we were shocked to hear that Ivanov had died from a liver ailment at age sixty-seven. During the Christmas holidays Ivanov's masterpiece *The Nutcracker* was performed.

I shall always remember my opera stage "baptismal," as I called my very first appearance in an opera, Gounod's *Faust*, at the Maryinsky

Theatre. As I stood onstage in the crowd with other students and pupils, I was enthralled listening to the rich and beautiful basso voice of Feodor Chaliapin and was captivated by the figure of Mephistopheles as portrayed by this great artist.

Since the days of my early childhood I had heard the name of Chaliapin. I saw him for the first time in Moscow when I was not quite six years old. Father took me to a dress rehearsal of *Faust* at the Private Russian Opera Theatre. Chaliapin was singing Mephistopheles. It was September 1896. Father had met Chaliapin three years before in Tiflis, where the twenty-year-old singer had made his opera debut. At that time Chaliapin was singing mainly in secondary roles, and his performances had hardly been noticed by the press or the public.

In Moscow, Father took me backstage with him during the intermission to congratulate Chaliapin on his recent successes on the stages of the Imperial Theatres in both St. Petersburg and Moscow.

I must have been greatly impressed by the performance of Chaliapin in *Faust*, for I remember that for several days afterwards I would mold figures of Mephistopheles from clay. And now, four years later in St. Petersburg, for my first appearance in an opera I had been on the stage of the Maryinsky when Chaliapin had been singing Mephistopheles.

The next day I was still under the spell of Chaliapin's unforgettable performance when, on the way home from the School, Mama stopped at the *confiserie* to pay her bill. Imagine my surprise and joy when the shopkeeper gave me a gift, a small box of "Caramels Chaliapin"! The top of the box depicted Chaliapin in the role of Mephistopheles, and on the wrapper of each caramel was a picture of Chaliapin in other roles from the many operas he sang. Mama told me about those she had seen. I saved every wrapper.

—

IN THE THREE or four weeks after Stassik's return, Vaslav stayed at the School over the weekends. He told Mama that he was busy in the Theatre on Sundays, both in ballet and opera. This provoked stormy outbursts of resentment from Stassik, who would shout again and again, "Why do I not study in the Theatrical School together with Vaslav?"

Mama invited Kasimir Loboyko, an Artist of the Imperial Theatres, to give Stassik ballet lessons, but this did not satisfy him.

Again Mama asked the psychiatrist, Professor Bekhterev, to examine Stassik. Dr. Bekhterev visited us two or three times, and on his last visit he told Mama that he felt it was dangerous to keep Stassik at home and that for the sake of her other children she should place him in a sanatorium. It seemed that the year's separation from us, instead of helping Stassik, had affected him adversely. This came as a great sorrow. Unhappy Stassik, so affectionate and good when calm, was doomed to a life of loneliness, away from his family, in a psychiatric hospital. Mama and I visited Stassik often, but whenever we were getting ready Vaslav would turn pale and be reluctant to come with us. He visited Stassik with us very rarely.

Now that Stassik was in the sanatorium Vaslav did not care to play his balalaika alone. Nor did he come home as often, and when he did he no longer brought Kolya with him. I missed my brothers, and I missed Kolya too. I missed our evenings together with the songs we sang and the music we played, and I was lonely.

When I asked Vaslav about Kolya he said he no longer found him interesting, and that anyway Kolya was not in his ballet classes, and they were no longer in the same classroom for general subjects. One day Mama ran into Kolya who told her that Vaslav's new friends, Rosai, Bourman, and Babitch, were getting him into mischief. They were deliberately giving him a bad reputation in the School, to ensure that they would pass him in grades. By nature Vaslav was quick-tempered, so it was easy to tease him to the point where he would start a fight, and then the others would leave him to take the blame.

Mama found that Vaslav's marks in both conduct and general subjects were so low that he was losing his home privileges. She was able to draw some consolation from his high grades in Dancing, Music, and Drawing —always among the highest in the class—but she found it very hard to influence his behavior or encourage him to do better in his general subjects, inasmuch as she hardly ever saw him. Once when he did come home she asked him why he was no longer friendly with Kolya, and Vaslav simply said, "He doesn't play the piano like Bourman. He doesn't dance very well, but you should see Rosai . . ."

During the Easter holidays I came down with chicken pox and missed three weeks of school. Going on my weekly grades I should have been promoted without examination, but because of my absence I was asked to take the test. I was given some difficult problems in arithmetic and did them well, explaining the last one so quickly that the teacher gave me, not the maximum mark of 12, but 12+. I was promoted to the lower second grade and accepted as a resident student. Vaslav was also promoted, into the upper second grade.

For the summer vacation we again went to visit Cousin Stassia in Marijampole, and this time Mama came with us.

15   1902–1903

We returned to St. Petersburg on August 1 to prepare for the new school year. In mid-August I was one of sixteen girls recalled from vacation. We were told to come to the Theatrical School on the morning of August 19, ready to be driven to Peterhof for rehearsals and a Gala Performance of *Swan Lake*, part of the celebrations for the marriage of the Grand Duchess Princess Elena Vladimirovna to Prince Nicholas of Greece, which was to take place at Tsarskoe Selo on August 16. I was excited and looked forward to the festivities as I had heard that in 1897, probably for the visit of the French President, a stage had been built in the middle of the small ornamental lake on Olgin Island at Peterhof and the paths through the gardens had been strewn with gilded sand.

Early in the morning we were taken to Peterhof for a rehearsal onstage with Alexander Victorovitch Shiraev. He was Petipa's assistant ballet master and was in charge of student rehearsals for operas as well as ballets; we all loved him very much. We were sixteen extra swans and he arranged us in groups, sometimes kneeling and sometimes standing holding a pose. Afterwards we were taken for a walk, in pairs, to look at the marvels of Peterhof Park. All the fountains were playing and each was a spectacle in itself. There was the Big Cascade, Samson Opening the Jaws of the Lion, and another that was called the Chessboard Mountain. From the mouths of three dragons water came pouring down over the black-and-white chessboard steps of the mountain. There were so many cascades and avenues of fountains that I cannot remember all their names, but I do remember how beautiful they were.

For lunch we were taken to a restaurant in the park and Mlle Verchault, a governess from the School, explained to us very carefully how we were to behave and to remember that we were students of the Imperial Theatrical School. After lunch we were taken back for another rehearsal.

In the afternoon we rehearsed with the whole *corps de ballet* to piano accompaniment. Shiraev showed us how to make our changes from one ornamental grouping to another, smoothly with the music, and indicated the cues we would have to watch for during the performance. He told us he would be standing in the orchestra pit, just below the conductor's podium, and would be giving us the cues himself. After the rehearsal we tried on our costumes, which were identical to those worn by the girls in the *corps de ballet*. A seamstress from the Maryinsky Theatre adjusted the costumes on us and made the necessary alterations on the spot.

Act II of *Swan Lake* was danced by Mathilda Kshessinska, and I believe it was her first appearance onstage after the birth of her son in June. For the whole of the performance we extra swans remained on the *avant-scène* placed so that at all times we were facing the public (and could keep our eyes on Shiraev). I could not see the dancers on the stage behind me but I was totally enraptured by the beautiful music of Tchaikovsky's *Swan Lake* that I was hearing for the first time.

After the performance we returned to St. Petersburg. Riding in the carriages, we could see the illuminations of the gardens as the celebrations in the Palace continued into the night.

———

ON THE FIRST Monday in September Mama took me to the School. When the time came to leave me, she wept as she hugged and kissed me. I felt a lump at the back of my throat but held my own tears back; I was so happy and proud to be a resident student of the Imperial Theatrical School. Mama promised to come and see me on Thursday afternoon during the visiting hour, from four to five.

It took me several hours to fall asleep that first night. I felt quite alone in the enormous dormitory with the long rows of beds, and now I gave way to tears.

At eight o'clock in the morning we were awakened by a loud bell. After we had washed and brushed our teeth we had our hair combed by a maid. My hair had not grown back much since being shaved off when I had typhoid. It was still too thin and short to be combed in the regulation style, tightly drawn back in braids from a center part. I looked with envy at several of the other girls in my class with their long thick hair reaching below their waists.

When we were ready—dressed in our uniforms of long, wool, cornflower-blue gathered skirts, thick stockings, and flat, laced shoes —we had to pass one by one in front of the governess sitting at her desk. We had to make a curtsy and slowly turn around as she examined us to see if we were dressed correctly. We then gathered in the next room, where one of the older students recited a morning prayer in front of the Ikon, before going to the dining room for breakfast, which consisted of a cup of tea and a buttered bun. From nine we had almost an hour's study period to prepare our homework for that afternoon's general studies classes. We then promptly went to change into our gray dance practice dresses for the dancing lesson, which lasted until ten minutes before noon. At that time we changed back into our school uniform dresses, which we then had to wear for the rest of the day.

After lunch we were taken for a twenty-minute walk around the inner courtyard of the School, in pairs and in a line. We were then ready for our general subjects classes, which lasted until four or sometimes five.

Dinner was at five, and then we were "free" until six when, depending upon the day of the week, there were either fencing or music lessons. Vaslav and I both studied the piano twice a week, and there were also special periods for those students, like Kolya, who wanted to study the violin as well as the piano. Vaslav had to prepare his assignments during that time, but I was able to choose a reading period in the library. Then some evenings there was needlework for the girls and military drill for the boys. At eight we had a light supper, and by nine we were in bed. The older students were allowed to stay up a half hour or an hour longer.

Just as in any other boarding school we had to do everything together. We got up, we went for walks, we went to bed: always together and always under supervision. Our lives were so restricted. There was no chance of any individual life. The Inspectrice and the governesses were very strict and insisted on discipline, but our own governess, Mlle Verchault, had a kind heart beneath her stern manner.

During our free time and after dinner the older students told us of the customs and regulations of the School and described all the ballerinas and teachers. They imitated them so well that I immediately recognized Christian Petrovitch Johannson when I saw him in the corridor. He was tall and lean and always carried a violin under his arm. By then eighty-five years old, he walked with some difficulty. When he ascended the stairs he was usually assisted by Nikolai and Sergei Legat, both of whom regularly attended his class for the leading dancers of the Imperial Ballet.

He came once to watch a class, and we were all amused by the old-fashioned dress and appearance of the octogenarian: the high, stiffly starched collar of his shirt, the unusually wide cravat, his long coat reaching below his knees, and of course his famous red handkerchief, its two pointed ends protruding from his back pocket through the vent of his long coat. We knew he had lost the sight in one eye, but as he sat on the upholstered chair in front of the mirror watching our class, nothing seemed to escape his good eye.

From time to time he would reach into his breast pocket and take out his snuffbox, open it to take a pinch of snuff, then rise from his chair and reach into his back pocket, pull the red handkerchief out by the two ends, and sneeze. Afterwards he would meticulously refold the handkerchief and return it to his back pocket with the two points arranged just so, ready for his next pinch of snuff.

Soon it was announced that Marius Petipa was preparing a new ballet. The previous year he had remounted only one ballet, *La Bayadère*, but now rehearsals were to begin for *The Magic Mirror*. Several names were called; I was delighted to hear mine. How thrilled I was at the opportunity to participate in this new ballet by Petipa!

We came to the rehearsal hall with the *répétiteur*, Shiraev. Petipa was already there, a distinguished old man in his eighties. His hair, his short beard, and his neatly combed mustache were all white. Impeccably dressed, he sat in a chair to watch us. Shiraev told us to stand one behind the other in a straight line, facing forward. Being the smallest girl in the group, I was put at the head. After a while Petipa rose stiffly and started to walk towards me. I was nervous and frightened at his approach. Petipa said a few words to Shiraev and then showed us the sequence of dance steps he wanted us to execute. He said, "*Répétez!*" and looking straight at me, "*Vous!*" The *pas* were already quite familiar to me from our classes, and despite my nervousness and fear I danced the required sequence correctly. Marius Petipa smiled and putting his hand on the top of my head said to me, "*Bien.*" I was so proud of his praise.

During my years in the School, I also danced in some of Petipa's other ballets. In *The Daughter of Pharaoh*, in the scene called "Beneath the Nile," I danced with several girl students. We were a stream, and we danced holding hands around the stage in an undulating line like water flowing in a stream. There were also several rivers. The Neva was Maria Petipa, who had a great success in her Russian dance; Olga Tchumakova as the Guadalquivir danced a Spanish dance with fire; and there were other national dances for the rivers Thames, Rhine, Congo, and Tiber. I recall finding it difficult to understand how all these rivers could be at the bottom of the Nile. It also bothered me that the Russian river from cold, northern St. Petersburg could find its way to the Sahara, to the deserts of Egypt. But I was amused to hear when the ballet was remounted by Alexander Gorsky in Moscow that the Neva then became the Moskva.

I also took part in *The Sleeping Beauty*. In Act I, "The Christening," I was part of the cortege of the Lilac Fairy. There were six of us little girls who carried her train as she entered the King's palace. We advanced slowly on a red carpet towards the gilded thrones where the King and Queen were seated. Beside them was an ornate gold crib. The costume department did not have ballet shoes small enough to fit me, and so a special pair had to be ordered. They were made of light lilac satin and were my very first pair of satin ballet shoes.* As I carried the train of the Lilac Fairy, danced by Maria Petipa, I could see that she was wearing shoes with a tiny heel, like a real lady.

I knew that Maria Mariusovna Petipa had created the role of the Lilac Fairy—the youngest of the seven fairy godmothers, according to Perrault's fairy tale—when her father had choreographed *The Sleeping Beauty* twelve years earlier, in 1890. At that time she was already established as a successful character dancer. Petipa believed that his daughter's beauty contributed greatly to his ballets.

As we walked behind her one of the girls whispered, "Look at Maria Mariusovna. She must be at least forty-five and she still has her part as the Lilac Fairy, the youngest fairy invited to the christening."

Following the Lilac Fairy as she approached the King and Queen to bestow her gift on the Princess, I kept looking for Vaslav. I was sure he would be one of the pages, but I could not see him among the Princes or Princesses standing or sitting in the palace, all wearing their beautiful court dress costumes designed by Ivan Vsevolojsky, the retired Director of the Imperial Theatres. I could recognize nearly all our teachers. There were the two Legat brothers, Pavel Gerdt, Mikhail Oboukhov, Stanislav Gillert, and Mikhail Fokine.

During rehearsals we were told to act frightened when the Wicked Fairy Carabosse entered in fierce anger at not having been invited to the christening, but on the night of the performance I did not have to act. Suddenly there were flashes of lightning and peals of thunder, and when the Wicked Fairy came riding onto the stage in a carriage drawn by rats I was truly frightened.

Finally the curtain came down on Act I and we were taken back to the School. How I wished I could have stayed and watched the whole ballet!

Later when I told Vaslav that I had looked for him among the pages he told me he was no longer in Act I but was in one of the scenes in "The Wedding," Act III. He was one of Tom Thumb's brothers in "Petit Poucet et ses Frères." Vaslav said that their number was more mime than dancing and that he also appeared in "Ogre and Ogress." Because he was in the last act it was well after midnight before he was back in the School.

---

*The ballet shoes worn in the School were of heavy, unbleached cotton. (IN/JR)

In December Olga Preobrajenska danced in Saint-Léon's *La Source*. Though the ballet had first been performed in Paris in 1866, it had never been presented in St. Petersburg. Achille Coppini, appointed ballet master as recently as August, choreographed this St. Petersburg premiere of *La Source* . . . much to the annoyance of Petipa.

During the performance I watched Preobrajenska with adoration; she had been the first ballerina to encourage me, when she smiled at me during my entrance examination, and now I was fascinated by her dancing and her dainty *pizzicato pas*. How happy I was when I was chosen to stand in for her in the apotheosis . . . to pose as Naïla, the Spirit of the Spring, high on a pedestal in the center of the fountain surrounded by jets of water. I remained there as Preobrajenska received her applause until the last of the curtain calls. Preobrajenska and the whole ballet company were re-called over and over again.

During the Christmas vacation Vaslav and I met one of Mama's friends, a small hunchbacked woman whose name, I believe, was Maria Lenorman. She had once managed the wardrobe for Father's company but now was employed in the Imperial Theatres. She had traveled the length and breadth of Russia and seemed to know everyone in the theatrical world. She was a wise and good-hearted woman, and as she talked I felt that she missed her life with the traveling companies and had settled in the costume workshop at the Imperial Theatres in her old age so as to retain some contact with the life of the theatre. Vaslav and I loved to listen to her talk with Mama. It was like a living history of the theatre.

They recalled the dramatic performances of the Karatyguins and then turned to opera, talking of the Italian operas performed in Russia with Adelina Patti and Marcella Sembrich, and were sad that both great artists were no longer in Russia. The famous soprano, Patti, had retired from the stage, and Sembrich had not returned from the United States of America where in 1898 she had been engaged by the Metropolitan Opera in New York. Mother had known Sembrich well, for she was Polish—her real name was Kochanska. Of course they also remembered the early performances by a young, then unknown singer—Chaliapin. We enjoyed hearing about the work of Mother and Father in the Setov Enterprise at the beginning of their careers as artists on the Russian stage.

Equally fascinating to us was the information this hunchback brought about Father. We learned that he was concentrating on working in circuses, which Mother had never liked. Father loved using the whole enormous arena for spectaculars, with elaborate sets and effects.

Often Maria would bring a set of tarot cards with her and tell Mother's fortune. She also gave Mother addresses of fortune-tellers who claimed to see the future in tea leaves or by gazing into a crystal ball. From Mother we heard tales of dark mysterious lodgings as she visited them all, expecting some miracle or news of some great change in her life. We could see how much she was missing Father. At times her visits to the fortune-tellers would inspire her with hope, and after others she would be filled with despair. She was tormented and suffering greatly, until one day, quite suddenly, she abandoned all fortune-tellers forever. I think it was after she had gone to confession and talked to the priest.

After the Christmas vacation we continued working on the new ballet by Petipa, *The Magic Mirror*. During the dress rehearsal, at the beginning of Act I, the King, Pavel Gerdt, presented a Venetian mirror to the Queen, Maria Petipa. The Queen began to admire herself in her new mirror as the King introduced the Prince, Sergei Legat, to the Princess, Mathilda Kshessinska, whose image was supposed to appear in the mirror. At that very moment the mirror cracked and broke on the stage: a bad omen for the ballet.

Nevertheless all the seats for the first performance on February 9 were sold. It was a benefit for Marius Petipa, attended by the Tsar and the Royal Family.

I cannot remember the story of the ballet very well, but I do especially recall two scenes. The first was a dance of gnomes, with Vaslav as one of them. A group of boys dressed as old gnomes came out of a cave, and in the middle of the stage there was an anvil. As the boys danced around it they beat upon the anvil with their hammers. The audience enjoyed the dance, and the boys were applauded loudly. They were told to remain onstage, and the Tsar came and asked the leader of the gnomes, Leonid Gontcharov—whose beard was the longest, stretching to his knees—how old he was.

"I am eighty-five, Your Majesty." For a boy to make a joke when talking to the Tsar was considered an impertinence, and Leonid could have been expelled for this breach of etiquette. But I remember somebody on the stage coming to his defense, saying the boy was still "living" the role he was portraying, and Leonid was forgiven.

In one of the later scenes the sets showed a dense forest, and in the center was a glass coffin suspended on golden chains. The inside of the coffin was lined with silver and decorated with flowers. Around the coffin we girls were flowers also; we were immortelles. It was like being part of a beautiful fairy tale.

We knew that Petipa had been very angry that the immortelles were dressed in tunics like nymphs, and then we heard that he did not like any of the costumes. These had been designed by Mme Telyakovsky, the wife of the Director and a close friend of the painter Golovine, who designed the sets. Mme Telyakovsky considered herself an authority on modern art and enjoyed collaborating on her husband's productions. *The Magic Mirror* had been commissioned by Prince Volkonsky just before he resigned, and Petipa blamed its lack of success in St. Petersburg on the new administration of the Imperial Theatres. He too resigned.* *The Magic Mirror* was the last ballet choreographed by Marius Petipa, and I am so happy and proud that I was chosen to dance in it. The ballet was later performed successfully in Moscow.

On February 7, I also took part in the Court Performance at the Hermitage Theatre—*The Fairy Doll*, choreographed with dances and *mises en scène* by Nikolai and Sergei Legat.† There were lots of toys and dolls in a toy shop. Anna Pavlova was a Spanish Doll and Vera Trefilova was a Japanese Doll. The Fairy Doll was, of course, Mathilda Kshessinska. Dressed as pierrots, my teacher, Mikhail Fokine, and Vaslav's teacher, Sergei Legat, danced a *pas de trois* with Mathilda Kshessinska. Alfred Bekefi and Alexander Shiraev were two black dolls, and they danced a tap dance. . . .

Even now I can relive the enchanted memory of the costumes. It was our first contact with the painter, Lev Samuilovitch Bakst, watching him create his designs. Before this I had worn only stock costumes from the wardrobe, but for *The Fairy Doll* each costume was individually designed and we were all specially measured. I was a pink doll, and I remember what a delight it was for me as a child as I put on each detail: the pink openwork socks over white tights, ruffled pantalettes showing beneath the short, full, ruffled, white muslin skirt of the dress. I had a wide pink ribbon over one shoulder tied in a bow below the waist, and tiny pink bows tied on each wrist just above the short white gloves. Over my golden curly locks I wore a light, lacy bonnet tied with a ribbon under my chin.

Bakst was not only meticulous about each costume, he also designed our makeup and applied it himself. I had two bright red round spots on my cheeks and long eyelashes that Bakst had drawn on my face. We children had to admire each other, and I cannot remember feeling happier or more proud in any costume in the theatre. Vaslav was a wooden soldier and wore a blue jacket and black trousers, designed so that the soldiers really looked as though they had been carved out of wood. Their trousers and boots made one triangle and their blue jackets made another. Their

*Officially, his contract was not renewed. (AK)

†This was a private performance; the official premiere took place in the Maryinsky Theatre several days later, on February 16. (IN/JR)

noses were made up to look like round buttons, and each soldier had a thin painted line for a mouth. For eyebrows, one line pointed downwards and the other flew upwards.

As I stood with the other dolls in the shop window and looked out at the set, I recognized it as the Arcade on Nevsky Prospekt. The shoppers in the ballet, going past the toy shop, made me remember the time I had gone with Mama and Vaslav to Skorokhod [The Seven League Boots Shop], the fashionable shoe shop on this very Arcade, when the School had given Mama a voucher to buy Vaslav some boots, not having any regulation ones small enough to fit him.

At the end of my first year as a resident student I took part in the Student Performance at the Mikhailovsky Theatre on May 2, 1903. Klavdia Kulichevskaya* mounted the scene "Masquerade" from Act III of Petipa's ballet *Ordre du Roi* for her graduating student, Leontina Pugni. Five of us younger students danced with Leontina, and we were all listed by name in the program. I felt quite close to Leontina, who had been assigned to look after me at the beginning of the year. She came from an artistic family; her grandfather, Césare Pugni,† had composed the music for many ballets, several of which were performed in the Imperial Theatres. Her younger sister, Julia, had also started to study in the School, and both came with Vaslav and me to attend the Catholic Instruction Class, once a week in the music room in the School.

This Student Performance was the first time my name appeared on an Imperial Theatrical School Program. It was the culmination of a very happy and successful year for me. But 1902–3 was not such a good year for Vaslav. He was still doing poorly in his general studies, and his grades for conduct were also bad. Once they were as low as 5, and Mama was asked to go and see Pisnyatchevsky, the Inspector of the Imperial Theatrical School. He issued a warning: "If your son, Nijinsky, continues to behave badly and to do so poorly in his general subjects, he could be expelled from the Imperial Theatrical School. Nijinsky is only holding on to his place now because of his excellent grades in dancing."

Vladimir Porfiryevitch Pisnyatchevsky had been Inspector of the School since 1887 and was considered quite a balletomane. His severity

*Klavdia Kulichevskaya (1861–1923) graduated from the Maryinsky School in 1880. She was promoted to First Dancer in 1889, specialized in classical roles, and resigned in 1901 to teach, replacing Cecchetti as instructor in the advanced girls' class. She choreographed many of the school's annual performances, teaching there through 1916. Olga Spessivtseva was one of her students. (AK)

†Another descendant of Césare Pugni was Ivan Puni, a leading figure in Russian modernist painting after 1910. Following his emigration, he was known in France as Jean Pougny. (AK)

towards Vaslav and his threat of expulsion astonished and frightened Mama. She tried to explain, as best she could in Russian, that her son was not only talented in dancing but also a good-hearted boy.

"Vladimir Porfiryevitch, my son is inventive at games, and perhaps he is rowdy and noisy. That I know only too well. But his pranks are not malicious, merely the usual sort of mischief for a boy of his age and energy. I have already been told that Vaslav repeatedly breaks the Theatrical School rules and has to be punished and deprived of weekend leave at home, for running and playing in the stairways and corridors and for bringing personal items from home."

One "personal item" was probably the black cast-rubber ball that Vaslav never parted with, since he had found that by squeezing the hard ball he developed flexibility in his fingers and strengthened the grip of his hand.

Mother went on, trying to convince the Inspector. "I do not know what he has done; I can only guess. I have prohibited him at home from sliding down the banisters and from swinging the front door open and closed by standing on both handles of the door. But I can see very well how here in the School the highly polished wooden banisters down the stairways and the tall massive doors of the classrooms offer an irresistible temptation to my son. Yes, I do agree Nijinsky is perhaps often unrestrained in his energetic temperament, but I am sure he is always polite in his manners and that his language when addressing his teachers or tutors is never rude."

What the Theatrical School considered Vaslav's bad conduct was really his continuing attempt to find ways to use his excess energy. At home, in our apartment, he would run along the corridors so that the ceilings of the lower floors would shake, making the other apartment-dwellers complain. Little did they, or Mother, know that Vaslav used the corridor as an ice rink. He would add a coat of wax to the already highly polished wood floor and then, standing on the edge of his shoes so that the sole made a skate, he would slide back and forth along the corridor, or take a running jump and slide the full length on his "skates."

One of his gymnastic stunts particularly delighted me. He would throw off his shoes, press his hands against one wall of the corridor and his feet against the opposite one, and raise himself so that he walked with giant strides all the way up to the ceiling; then he would slowly let himself slip down. Later, when I was in the Upper Classes, I showed this gymnastic stunt to my friends. In the corridor between the washroom and the dormitory I "walked" up to the ceiling this way. I was just getting ready to come down when a governess appeared. I froze. She passed by not noticing me above her, but as she turned and came back she lifted her head and suddenly saw that somehow there was a body on the ceiling. In a frightened voice she called the maid: "Fima, Fima, get her down from the ceiling." I slipped down, mumbling an excuse. Even though Anna Ludvigovna was a very strict governess, she didn't lower my grade for conduct. But Vaslav would not have been so lucky.

I don't know if Mama was aware of all the problems arising from our participation in the opera and ballet performances. I remember how even in my first year as a resident student we had to use every available minute to prepare our assignments, and there was just not enough time. After classes finished at five we would have our dinner, and by six-thirty we would already have been taken away to the theatre. Whenever we had to perform in the last act we would not return to the School before midnight. In the Alexandrinsky Theatre, which was almost next door to the School, the performances did not finish until around one in the morning. After such plays as *Midsummer Night's Dream* and Goethe's *Faust*, or such operas as Rimsky-Korsakov's *Snow Maiden*, where the students were used extensively in several acts, we would have to change, take off our makeup, then walk back to the School. We would be tired and hungry and wouldn't get to bed until we had eaten, sometimes not before two in the morning. Rehearsals the next day often saved us from having to attend classes with an unprepared assignment, but that also meant missing the teacher's explanations for the next assignment.

Some of this Mama must have explained in her spirited defense of Vaslav, drawing attention to the fact that Vaslav was chosen so often to participate in the opera and ballet performances. The Inspector himself now remarked on the contrast in the grades earned by Nijinsky. They were always among the highest in the class in Dancing, Music, Art, Drawing, and Gymnastics, whereas in the other subjects they were very low. The Inspector began to see Nijinsky in a more favorable light. And of course Mama promised that Vaslav would reform.

Towards the end of the school year his marks for conduct did improve significantly, and for the last quarter he even received 10. But his general grades were still poor and so he had to remain in Class II, Upper Division, for a second year. I was promoted from Class II, Lower Division, to Class II, Upper Division, which meant that we were now both in the same class for General Subjects.

For the summer vacation we again went with Mama to Marijampole. Aunt Thetya had moved there to live with her daughter Stassia and her son-in-law after Aunt Stephanie died. Mama wanted to go with us as she had not seen her sister since Aunt Stephanie's funeral.

One Sunday morning after Mass, we were all walking across the square to the building where Uncle Alex, as we called Stassia's husband, had his office as Tax Inspector. He wanted to show Mother the place where he worked. Along the wall behind his desk were rows of books in the same beautiful bindings he had at home in his study. He showed some of them to Mama, and only now did I realize that they were all reference or law books and understand why I had been forbidden to touch any of the books in his study.

The previous summer Stassia had encouraged Vaslav to play her concert grand in the drawing room. Even as a small child Vaslav could play any musical instrument that he came across. Without any lessons he had been able to play his brother's accordion, clarinet, and flute. He would also play the domra and the mandolin, and on the balalaika he achieved a virtuoso technique. In the School and also in our individual lessons with Stassia we had, of course, both learned to read notes, but Vaslav had no patience for sitting at the piano and trying to read the music in front of him; it was so much easier for him to play a piece of music by ear.

With his perfect ear for music Vaslav was able to memorize entire overtures from the operas he heard at the Maryinsky—Tchaikovsky's *Eugene Onegin* and *The Queen of Spades*, Glinka's *Ruslan and Ludmila*, Gounod's *Faust*, Boito's *Mefistofele*. Cousin Stassia and Uncle Alex had many friends—town officials, cavalry officers and their wives, the young cadets, students from the private Girls' School where Stassia taught music—and Vaslav entertained them all when we went visiting, or when we received guests at home. Mama was very proud when she saw how her fourteen-year-old son amazed everyone with his brilliant technique, but only Stassia and I knew that he was playing everything by ear. Sometimes he also sang arias from the operas at the Maryinsky, accompanying himself on the piano. I liked everything he did, but most of all I liked the way he sang and played the aria "Evening Star" from *Tannhauser*.

16   1903–1904

THE BEGINNING of the school year 1903–4 was filled with difficult trials and sufferings for Vaslav. He was expelled from the School. The incident was serious and involved the police, an unbelievable thing to happen at the Imperial Theatrical School.

Several Theatre carriages were taking a group of students from the School to the Maryinsky Theatre for the matinee performance. The youngest boys were in the first carriage. Vaslav and his friend Georgi Rosai were in the second carriage with four older, graduating students —Alexander Batcharoff, Nikolai Dmitriev, Pavel Gontcharov, and Alexander Matiatin. In the last carriage rode the tutor; he was supposed to keep an eye on all the carriages as well as the students in his own carriage.

Vaslav and Georgi and several of the other boys had taken along their handmade slingshots and darts. The slingshots were made of thin strips of elastic pulled out of a dancing stocking garter, looped at each end to slip on the thumb and index finger of the left hand. The darts were pieces of paper rolled tightly and bent over the center of the taut elastic. With the right hand the two ends of the bent paper were grasped firmly, pulled back, and then the dart was quickly released. I also had one of these slingshots and often played with it at home.

As they rode to the Theatre the boys would fire at various targets such as lamp posts or street signs—always careful not to be seen by the tutor in the last carriage. Later Vaslav told me that the older students in his carriage, instead of trying to stop him or Georgi from shooting their paper missiles, actually egged them on and eventually took over the slingshots themselves, firing the darts aimlessly as they moved along Bolshaya Morskaya, one of the most fashionable streets in St. Petersburg. Just as they turned into Isaakyevskaya Ploshchad [St. Isaac's Square] one of the darts hit the top hat of a passerby and almost knocked it off his head. He was an important government official.

It was most likely that the dart had come from the first carriage, which had gone past and disappeared, but the angry official stopped the second carriage. Closest to the window sat Nijinsky, pale and mute with fear. The government official pointed him out as the guilty one to the policeman standing nearby. The tutor came up and tried to smooth things over, but the angry official took no notice and ignored the pleading eyes of the boys. Then and there he insisted that the tutor make an official report to Telyakovsky, the Director of the Imperial Theatres. He also threatened to make his own report to Telyakovsky and said he would demand that the guilty boy be expelled.

Back at the Theatre, confused and frightened at the thought of the punishment in store for them, the boys discussed what they should do. The older students decided that instead of everyone confessing his guilt and participation in the affair, they should all deny everything; no one should confess. The students who were graduating that year had the most to lose, for the possibility of being expelled in their final year could mean the end of their artistic careers. If no one confessed and they all denied any knowledge of the incident, then the worst that could happen would be a severe remonstration for Nijinsky, whom the official had mistakenly pointed out, and as one of them said, "They will not expel you, Nijinsky, you dance better than all the other students . . ."

When they returned from the Theatre to the School they found the Administration already waiting for them to begin the interrogation. Everyone persistently denied his guilt. The culprit could have been in any one of the three carriages, for witnesses were found who had seen darts flying from all three. But an example had to be made, and so they turned to the statement of the official who had put the blame on Nijinsky. It also emerged from the questioning that Nijinsky was considered the best shot with a homemade sling. So it seemed perfectly plausible that Nijinsky should be the only one responsible, especially in light of the fact that only a year earlier he had been threatened with expulsion because of bad conduct.

Then the Administration decreed that Nijinsky was to be permanently expelled from the Imperial Theatrical School. Vaslav was sent home and told never to return to the School. Mama wept for two days. Finally, still weeping, she went to see Inspector Pisnyatchevsky and implored him to intervene on her son's behalf, begging that Vaslav be forgiven. Pisnyatchevsky as well as Vaslav's teachers, Sergei Legat and Mikhail Oboukhov, interceded for him with the Director, and Telyakovsky finally agreed to lessen the punishment: Nijinsky was to be demoted to the status of nonresident pupil and would be allowed to attend classes.

The decision taken by the Director was communicated to Mother by Inspector Pisnyatchevsky, who added, "Before Vaslav Nijinsky can be allowed back in classes he must be severely punished at home. I order corporal punishment: several hard strokes with a leather belt."

Mama was distressed. "I have never punished Vaslav in this way, even when he was a little boy, and now he is nearly fifteen."

The Inspector, however, was adamant. "For this matter you must then call your *dvornik*." The *dvornik* [the yard man], the bearded man who usually carried the wood up to our kitchen, came up to our apartment. He, Mama, and Vaslav went into the living room and closed the door. Mama later told me that Vaslav had endured his punishment bravely.

That punishment at home was not the end of Vaslav's humiliation. He was ordered to return his uniform and books and all other items supplied by the School. Mama was at a loss. Now she would have to clothe Vaslav from head to toe. From the time Vaslav and I became resident students Father had been cutting down the money he sent each month; there were even times, when he was not working, when he did not send anything at all. Mother had earned some money by teaching and by renting out one of the rooms when we were away, but it was barely sufficient for herself and certainly not enough to feed an extra mouth, and a growing boy at that. She did not see how she could possibly find enough money to outfit Vaslav as well as feed him.

With a heavy heart, Mother forced herself to go again to the office of Inspector Pisnyatchevsky and explain her difficult situation. She begged him that Vaslav at least be allowed to wear the School uniform and be given textbooks, notebooks, and dancing shoes. Pisnyatchevsky respected Mother's request . . . but when Vaslav returned to the School, before he was allowed in the classroom, he was stripped of his own uniform. He had to return his beautiful jacket with the two lyres on the blue velvet collar, the dress cap with the silver lyre, his winter coat with the astrakhan collar, even his underwear, socks, and shoes. Then Vaslav was given another uniform. But what a uniform: a used one, wrinkled, old, torn, and full of holes.

All Mother's efforts to repair, to iron, and in any way try to make Vaslav's clothing look presentable were in vain. I recall how shocked I was when I came home on Saturday and saw Vaslav dressed in such shabby and wrinkled clothes.

Seeing me, Vaslav looked embarrassed, but I had the impression that he wanted to look like a tramp, that he was obviously not making any effort to improve his appearance. His hair was disheveled and his clothes put on carelessly so as to look their very worst. I believe Vaslav hoped that the guilty boys, instead of calling him their hero, would feel their guilt at having placed him in this predicament. And by walking in the streets of St. Petersburg in an old worn-out School uniform, Vaslav was also trying to embarrass the Administration of the Imperial Theatrical School. But I could see how deeply my brother was suffering at having to come to rehearsals for performances at the Maryinsky Theatre dressed like that. To deprive him of the Theatrical School privileges, his residence, uniform, books—everything he had become used to for the last five years—was a cruel punishment and out of all proportion for such a trivial and innocent childish prank.

After only one month Nijinsky was pardoned and reinstated to the status of resident student of the Imperial Theatrical School. When Vaslav returned to the School after his humiliating experience, he concentrated on his class work and his grades became more satisfactory. He learned to control his temperament and could no longer be roused to quick outbursts of anger.

—

WE WERE very excited to hear that *Paquita* was planned for the spring of 1904. Ever since Petipa, who always liked to use the students of the School in his ballets, had remounted *Paquita* in 1881, it had become the tradition for the *mazurka* in that ballet to be danced by the younger students. As we rehearsed, I recalled Mother's dance lessons from when she had taught Stassik, Vaslav, and me during our first years in St. Petersburg. One day Alexander Shiraev noticed me among the other girls and chose me to dance in the front pair with Vaslav. Over the previous two years Vaslav had become quite renowned in the School for his performances of this Polish dance, which he had been taught by Father long before he joined our lessons with Mother. It was the first time I ever danced with Vaslav in the Imperial Theatrical School, and with what exuberance we danced together, both in rehearsals and in the performance itself at the Maryinsky. Holding Vatsa by the hand I seemed to fly through the air like a whirlwind!

I knew my brother danced well, and this seemed perfectly natural to me. But the first person in the School to speak to me about the rare dancing talent of Nijinsky was Mikhail Mikhailovitch Fokine. I was studying in his class, and one day he was late for the lesson. The boy students were taking their dancing examination in another room at the time, and Fokine, as a teacher, had to attend. The governess told us not to wait to begin our exercises at the *barre*.

To this day I can remember the very steps we were practicing when

Fokine entered the dance hall. He came right over to me and said, "Bronislava Fominitchna, you have such a brother that I must congratulate you!"

Teachers didn't usually talk with students about personal matters, particularly not in front of the whole class and before the governess. We continued in *battements frappés*, but Fokine paid no attention to our exercises. "Your brother dances remarkably!" he went on. "All of us examiners gave him a mark of 12. But this was unfair. For other examinations we have given students 12, but there has never been anyone who danced like Nijinsky."

With great animation Fokine continued to tell us about Vaslav. "How lightly he jumps . . . how high he jumps, higher than a meter from the floor straight up for the *changement de pieds*, and other *pas* even higher. . . . All the difficult *pas* are so easy for him . . . three *tours en l'air* and *entrechat-dix* effortlessly . . . as a bird in the air. . . . For Nijinsky today we should have come up with a new grade. If anybody had suggested it, I would have given a 20 or even a 30. He surpassed anything we have seen so far . . . wonderful . . .

"After all the boy students had danced the *allegro pas* in a group, Nijinsky was asked to repeat the dance sequence by himself. And then something happened that never happens at examinations . . .

"Suddenly we all, everyone, applauded. The Director, Telyakovsky, his assistant, Krupensky, and all the teachers applauded Nijinsky as if at a performance. I'm late because we could not leave right away; we were all talking about Nijinsky. A great future awaits your brother."

Mikhail Mikhailovitch Fokine was completely enchanted with Nijinsky. When I told Mama what he had said, her worries and doubts about Vaslav's future finally lifted and she began to hope to see him as a *premier danseur* in the Imperial Theatres.

For five years Vaslav had been Sergei Legat's student, until, in September 1903, he had been promoted to the Advanced Class taught by M. K. Oboukhov. Mikhail Konstantinovitch had soon appreciated the extraordinary talent and unusual quality of Nijinsky's dancing, but apart from Legat and Oboukhov no one had expected such a brilliant performance from Nijinsky in the examination.

⁓

THE SUMMER vacations began at the end of May and lasted until the end of August. We were given no lesson assignments and were not even told to do ballet exercises at home. The boy students were provided with a summer uniform for the vacation. Except for dancing shoes, the smallest detail was provided: shoes, underwear, even hankerchiefs. We girl students on the other hand did not receive any uniform at all; when we went home for the vacation we had to wear our own clothes. It was an extra problem for Mother.

When Father had heard from Mother's letters about Vaslav's success in the dancing examination, he had sent a hundred rubles. We began to beg Mother to take us to a dacha in the suburbs of St. Petersburg for the summer. My friend in the School, Zina Puyman, had told me that it was possible to find a small *izba* [peasant house], quite cheap, near Dudergoth. Mama had informed us that she would have to give up our apartment on Mokhovaya Ulitza and move to a smaller one, now that we were both residents in the Imperial School and Stassik was in the sanatorium. She figured that if she put the furniture that we would not need in the country into storage, and not rent an apartment in St. Petersburg until the end of the summer, she would save money. An apartment in St. Petersburg would cost one hundred twenty rubles for three months.

To our joy Mama did find a newly built peasant house near Dudergoth. It had two rooms and a kitchen, and the rent for the whole summer was twenty-five rubles.

We were happy to go to Dudergoth but also sad to be leaving our beautiful apartment on Mokhovaya Ulitza where we had lived for seven years, ever since we first came to St. Petersburg. It had always been special to us as our very first home, and we loved the beautiful high windows and the courtyards with all their activity. I remembered how after Countess Perovska's funeral we saw our house as more special and distinguished from all the other houses on the street. It was a solemn funeral. The main entrance to the house from the street, the steps of the staircase, and the sidewalk were all covered with wide red carpeting. Vaslav and I joined the onlookers on the street watching the various carriages drive up. There were many members of the aristocracy, and they all went up the red-carpeted entry into our house. We recognized the Grand Duke Vladimir Alexandrovitch, the brother of Tsar Alexander III. His enormous, spectacular figure was familiar to us from the Imperial Theatres. He was wearing a uniform of the Imperial Guards with a white lambskin cap with a red insert and gold tassels.

Vaslav had another attachment to our house on Mokhovaya Ulitza —Liza, his first sweetheart. She lived on the floor below us. Her mother, who was a seamstress, had taken a small room there. Liza had fine features, light blue eyes, red hair, and was a little younger than Vaslav. I was only slightly acquainted with her but had noticed her tenderness towards Vaslav. When we were leaving the apartment to go to Dudergoth,

I unexpectedly came upon them on our staircase; Vaslav embraced and kissed Liza, and she gave him her photograph.

Leaving St. Petersburg on the train we could see the countryside spread over the lowlands of the delta of the Neva. But very soon, about sixteen miles to the south, the scenery changed abruptly. High hills rose up in the middle of the low-lying countryside. The Pulkovo and Dudergoth Mountains, as the hills were called, were considered to be an unexplainable natural phenomenon.

The train began to slow down and Mama said we were approaching Krasnoe Selo, where she and Father had danced together. Krasnoe Selo was a lively summer town and had a small theatre. The programs were often attended by the Tsar and his retinue, the Grand Dukes, and the Officers of the Guards Regiments who came to Krasnoe Selo for the summer military reviews and parades.

Many passengers alighted at the station, and Vaslav and I recognized some familiar faces—employees of the Maryinsky Theatre. We did not see any artists, though we knew that many dancers and singers appeared on the stage of the small theatre in the summer and that it was a great honor to be invited to perform at Krasnoe Selo.

"Some day I too will be arriving here from St. Petersburg to dance at Krasnoe Selo as an Artist of the Imperial Theatres," Vaslav said with great assurance.

Mama told us to get ready because the next stop was Dudergoth, only two miles farther on. In front of the railway station was a large lake fed by underground springs, and on its shores swamp grass was growing wild. Across the lake stood the summer barracks for the Cavalry Officers. The small community of Dudergoth was made up of four villages about a mile apart on the road from the railway station. Three of the villages were used to house the men of the Don Cossacks Squadron of the Imperial Guard. Our village was the only one on a hill and had no soldiers quartered in it. There were also some expensive dachas and a park on another hillside.

Several other families from St. Petersburg were also staying in our village for the summer. In addition to the family of my friend Zina Puyman there was the choirmaster from the Maryinsky Theatre and his family. Our village was about two miles from the railway station and the stores where we went to buy our provisions. The peasants of the community were either Finns or Estonians, and though they were very poor their homes, like the one we were renting, were neat and clean, both inside and out.

On one side of our village were fields and vegetable gardens with potatoes and turnips growing in them. At the bottom was a dirty pond for watering the cows and horses and to irrigate the gardens. Vatsa soon discovered there were no fish in the pond, only fat black leeches; we did not try to swim there.

Not far off we could see two redoubts—earthen fortifications built in the time of Peter the Great. We imagined that the officers and men who had been engaged in combat here a long time ago must have buried their valuables somewhere around, and so Vatsa and I would search for buried treasure.

Beyond the fortifications stretched a swamp full of small hillocks of grass. To get through the swamp we would jump from one hillock to the next, and large birds, grouse or partridges, would fly up from under our feet. Alongside the swamp was a dense forest where we would gather mushrooms and wild strawberries. We liked to stay in the forest all day, until nightfall. As we walked home we found a few late lily of the valley decorating the roadside with their white bells, so delicate and fragile as they grew deep in the shadow under the low branches of the hazelnut trees. They were too beautiful to be picked.

The First Squadron of the Don Cossacks had its barracks near Dudergoth. In the square courtyard in front of the barracks was an exercise pole for their horses, and we used to run and swing on the ropes, and often played our game of "Giant Steps." This game was not without danger, especially when Vaslav would fly very high, half-sitting in the loops of the ropes. I could sense his elation at this freedom to experiment with flight. I enjoyed running around with the ropes, but I was scared that if I didn't run fast enough to keep up with them I would be dragged into the center around the pole and crack my head.

Sometimes a horse would bolt out of the Cossack camp and tear at full gallop along the road towards our village. We were taught not to be afraid but to stand in the middle of the road with our arms outstretched, and then the horse would turn and bolt back to the camp.

As I remember them, the Cossacks of the First Squadron were all tall and huge, and all had thick beards and wore their hair in a heavy lock on one side of their caps. They would often ride past our village in full military uniform with their spears and sabers. We would run out to the path beside the road and try to make friends with them, even though they did look rather frightening. In the Cossack camp we used to buy black bread, several pounds for six kopeks; the bread had a rare, delicious flavor.

We knew that Japan had started the war against Russia in February of 1904, but beyond that we were not told anything in the School. When we asked the Cossacks about it, they would laugh and say something like, "At one throw we will bury the little Japanese under our hats . . ."

As Vaslav made friends with the Cossacks he learned more about their way of life. Each Cossack, when he enlisted in the Imperial Guard, had to provide himself with two horses that had to be exactly the same color and height as all the other horses in the squadron. The Cossacks themselves also had to be of a certain height—the tallest possible, it seemed to me.

Vaslav was greatly attracted by the Cossack horses; he watched how they were groomed, their manes and tails thoroughly combed. Sometimes the hair was braided at night so that in the morning the mane and tail tossed around the horse in waves. We both loved to stroke the horses on the neck or, better still, around their soft nostrils. To give the horses a piece of sugar was always a thrill for us. Vaslav would have loved to ride on the Cossack horses, but he was not allowed to even sit on one. He did help lead the horses of the villagers to the meadow for their night grazing, riding an unsaddled horse. Whenever I went with him I would ride a horse too, and then in the dark we would run back, hurrying to get home so that Mother would not find out about our forbidden sport.

Like parents in most dancing families, Mother had always warned us about the dangers of sports. We recognized her concern and fear that in sports it is possible to injure the body so that one can no longer dance. At that time we did not understand how indulgence in any one sport can overdevelop certain muscles and interfere with the correct development of a dancer's body. Riding on horseback, bicycling, and ice-skating all spoil and distort the normal form of the leg, while rowing a boat overdevelops the shoulders.

Zina, who had been to Dudergoth before, introduced us to some of her friends there. They were all girls, so Vaslav was the only boy among us. We played several games together—catch, *lapta* [a ball game], and *gorodki* [a game similar to skittles]. *Gorodki* was a new game for us, but Vaslav grasped it quickly to the point where he could knock down all the wooden pieces with one shot no matter how they had been arranged.

One day I was standing behind the *gorodki* box while Vaslav was far away behind the line. He took aim with the heavy stick and swung with all his might for the throw, but the stick slipped in his hand and instead of following its path went a little to the side and struck me . . . not directly on the knee, fortunately, but just below it. Vaslav was afraid he had broken my leg, and I grew frightened when I saw his face turn white and his lips go blue. In a house nearby was a nurse, who took a look at my leg, bandaged it, and calmed everyone down. She declared the bone not broken and the swelling due merely to the force of the blow. The skin was only grazed.

For another game Zina and I would stand facing each other with a rope stretched between us, held as high in the air as we could reach. With a little run Vatsa easily leaped over the rope, amazing all those who had gathered around to watch. Each time he jumped he took smaller and smaller runs, until finally, almost standing next to the rope, he was able to fling himself over it.

Our young servant Pasha, who had been working for us for more than a year, had come with us to Dudergoth, and it was from her that we learned how to look for mushrooms in the forest. She taught us to distinguish the fields of rye from fields of barley or wheat, the leaves of potatoes from swedes or beets. Pasha was a wonderful country girl with a small turned-up nose and a face so thickly covered with freckles that they seemed to blend into one spot on her nose and cheeks. One time, after she had been living with us for a while in St. Petersburg, she saw Vaslav washing his hands in the kitchen and using a pumice stone to clean the ink stains from his fingers. "Master," Pasha asked, "what is this stone? Does it take stains from the skin? Can it remove anything?" "Of course, anything . . ." Vaslav answered on his way out of the kitchen. The next day, Pasha wouldn't answer Mama's call to come into the dining room. She was hiding in the kitchen, her hands over her face. She had scraped the freckles from her skin with the pumice stone until her face was all raw and bleeding. We were sorry for Pasha, but it was impossible not to laugh. Mother washed the girl's face with alcohol and dusted it with talcum powder. To Pasha's chagrin the freckles came back with the new skin.

The weather that summer in Dudergoth was quite good, though we were pleased to see it rain sometimes so that afterwards we could go and look for mushrooms in the forest. Then when we were out of sight of the house we would take off our shoes and walk through the puddles on the road in our bare feet. Mama had strictly forbidden us to walk in our bare feet, not so much because of the possibility of catching cold or injuring our feet but because she believed that to go barefoot coarsened and widened the feet. She even thought we should wear narrow shoes to keep our feet small and narrow.

In the middle of August we returned to St. Petersburg. Mama took an apartment on Gagarinskaya Ulitza, parallel to Mokhovaya and very near the Baron Stieglitz Museum. The new apartment was less expensive because there were only two rooms and a kitchen—on the first floor, level with a small yard. But very little sunshine came through the windows, and after the large well-lighted apartment on the third floor of the large house on Mokhovaya, we did not like the new apartment on Gagarinskaya Ulitza at all.

Mama began to get our things ready for our return to the School. She was putting Vaslav's clothes in order when suddenly she discovered in the jacket pocket of his uniform a photograph of a young girl with the tender inscription, "Do not forget me." It was the photograph I had seen Liza give to Vaslav. The photograph horrified Mama. She called Vaslav to her, tore up the photograph, and reminded him of his promise to concentrate on his studies. But it was the move to Gagarinskaya Ulitza that really brought the romance of Liza and Vaslav to an end.

17   1904–1905

I WAS STARTING my fifth year in the Imperial Theatrical School. For the last three I had studied dance with Mikhail Mikhailovitch Fokine. I had been one of his first pupils in 1901 after Fokine, then only twenty-one years old, had accepted a teaching position in the School. I had loved Fokine's classes and was sorry that I was no longer going to be studying with him. I was assigned to the advanced class taught by Klavdia Mikhailovna Kulichevskaya. I had already had some lessons with her. In 1901 Kulichevskaya had replaced Enrico Cecchetti as Head Teacher in the Girls' Dance Division. She was then forty years old and an excellent teacher who upheld the tradition of classical dance established by Johannson and Petipa. She was very strict with her students and paid attention to the minutest detail. I realized that under Kulichevskaya I would concentrate on developing the necessary discipline to perfect my dance technique, and I looked forward to studying with her.

Vaslav was starting his seventh year in the Imperial Theatrical School. Because he had repeated two school years he had only this year completed, at the same time that I had, the program of General Studies in the Lower Division, and we were both promoted to the Upper Division, Class III. But Vaslav had already been studying for two years in the advanced ballet class. In 1902, while still a student in the Lower Division, he had, because of his perfect grades in dancing, been promoted to the advanced ballet class of Nikolai Legat, taught that year by his brother Sergei Legat. For the next year he had been assigned to the class taught by Mikhail Konstantinovitch Oboukhov, with whom he was to continue studying this year. Vaslav was very happy that now, at last, having been admitted to the Upper Division, he was entitled to the same privileges enjoyed by other students in the advanced dance division.

On the first day back after the vacation we had to be weighed and measured and have a complete medical checkup. My height and weight had not changed since the last checkup, six months before, which meant that for both my age and my height I was underweight. The School doctor examined me from head to toe and told me I was too thin. "You will have an egg for breakfast and a glass of milk at lunch and eat all that is on your plate." I said that I could never eat all the food served to me at dinner, and so the doctor told me to go to the infirmary just before the evening meal and each day the nurse would give me a small glass of wine—to stimulate the appetite. The wine was sweet and tasted like Marsala.

Vaslav, since his last checkup in the School, had grown taller, his muscles had grown stronger, and he had gained eight pounds. He was looking forward to the time when he could study in the mime and adage class under the guidance of Pavel Gerdt. For more than forty years Gerdt had been dancing on the stages of the Imperial Theatres as a *premier danseur*, partnering all the great ballerinas, as well as teaching the *classe d'adage* to the advanced graduating students. In September, when we returned to the School, Vaslav was very disappointed to learn that Pavel Gerdt had retired from the Imperial Theatrical School.*

There were other changes that were disturbing to both the students of the School and the Imperial Ballet Artists. Many of us were shocked to learn that Shiraev had been asked to resign by the Director, Telyakovsky. There had been tension between Telyakovsky and Shiraev ever since Petipa had resigned and left the Imperial Theatres. Shiraev had been Petipa's assistant and ballet master and had participated in the mounting and rehearsing of all Petipa's ballets. He knew them well. Telyakovsky kept asking Shiraev to remount and choreograph new dances for Petipa's ballets, but Shiraev repeatedly refused. Besides, he was a dancer and not a choreographer. He went abroad to dance, in Berlin and London, returning from time to time to dance in private performances. Later he returned to teach in the Imperial Theatrical School, but only to the drama students and not in the Ballet Division.

Later that year Alfred Feodorovitch Bekefi also resigned. Bekefi, like Shiraev, was an outstanding character dancer and teacher. Together they had developed exercises for a character-dance class later adopted by the Theatrical School.

In a short time, a period of three years, the Imperial Theatrical School had lost many of its great teachers—Cecchetti, Johannson, Ivanov,

---

*From 1909 Gerdt taught the *classe de perfection* to the Artists of the Imperial Ballet. It was attended by both Vaslav Nijinsky and Bronislava Nijinska until 1911. (IN/JR)

Petipa—and now with the retirement of Pavel Gerdt and the resignation of Shiraev, and later Bekefi, there was an unsettled, anxious atmosphere among both the Artists and the students.

Now that Vaslav was in the Upper Division he began to study well. The classes were smaller than in the Lower Division, five to eight students, and we had different teachers for each subject, whether French, Geography, History, Literature, Mathematics, or Science. Our teachers all had University degrees and were specialists in their subjects. Our art classes were taught by fine artists from the Academy of Art, and our music classes by musicians from the Conservatory. There was also a marked change in Vaslav's behavior. He broke with his former friends —Babitch, Bourman, and Rosai—and made a new friend, Leonid Gontcharov.

Leonid, or Leni, came from a family of artists. His sister was a ballet artist with the Imperial Ballet, as was his brother, Pavel, who had just graduated from the Imperial Theatrical School. Now that Pavel was living at home, Leni saw his brother only rarely and missed him very much. The friendship between Leni and Vaslav was to last until they both graduated. Leni was a serious student of music and dreamed of entering the Conservatory after graduating. His interest in music and his serious application to his piano were a good influence on Vaslav's studies.

In spite of Vaslav's improved grades for both conduct and studies, it did seem to him at first that the tutors and inspectors were unduly strict with him, but after a few months this attitude seemed to change and improve. Vaslav told me of one incident, but really to please me with a compliment more than anything else. He was sitting one day at the piano practicing fingering and speed exercises when the new inspector, Missovsky, approached and remarked, "Nijinsky, you should take an example from your sister. Bronislava Fominitchna is two years younger than you are and is in the same class as you, and she studies magnificently. Instead of playing your arpeggios you would do better to get out your books and study!"

"I was very annoyed," Vaslav commented to me, "and I answered sharply, telling him I was sitting at the piano studying the music, and that I was preparing myself to be an artist and had to study music no less than any other subject . . ."

Vaslav knew that such a reply would have brought a reprimand from the former inspector, but Missovsky didn't say anything and walked away.

Although Vaslav and I were in the same class, the Girls' Division was completely isolated from the Boys' Division, and so I hardly ever saw

Vaslav in school. I was only able to catch rumors about my brother, about the dancing of the remarkable Nijinsky, from my friends Tonya Tchumakova, Frossia Georgievskaya, and Lydia Lopukhova, all of whom had older sisters who were Artists of the Imperial Theatres. Mama, too, heard from our friends, Gillert and Loboyko, both Artists of the Imperial Theatres, that reports of the sensation caused by Vaslav at the previous year's dance examinations had reached the Imperial Ballet Company. The Board of Examiners had been so impressed by Nijinsky that they had begun to talk about him a great deal—the discovery of a new talent . . . a dance phenomenon . . . Nijinsky. Artists began to attend Oboukhov's classes to see this young prodigy of a dancer for themselves. Oboukhov, both an excellent classical ballet artist and a great teacher, asserted enthusiastically that Nijinsky's talent was unique, though he did not show Vaslav off in his classes, adhering rather to the routine classroom exercises. As might be expected, the comments expressed by the dancers, some of whom recognized Nijinsky as an upcoming competitor, were contradictory and not always favorable.

THE WAR had been going on since February but did not affect us in the School, since it was taking place so far away from St. Petersburg. After our return that summer from Dudergoth, where we had heard the Don Cossacks speak laughingly of this war with Japan, I went to look at the large maps on our geography classroom walls. I could see the vast expanse of Russian territory, and somewhere far away to the east were the little islands of Japan. As nobody in the School told us anything about the war, I did not think any more about it until we were given an assignment to knit socks for the soldiers.

In December, just before the Christmas holidays, Olga Andreevna, one of our governesses, also our new needlework teacher, told us of the great need for warm clothing to be sent to our soldiers fighting the Japanese in Manchuria. She said we should all do our part by knitting during the holidays. We had begun to learn to knit the previous year, in the Lower Division, but many of the other girls already knew how to knit. I believe Frossia and I were the only two beginners. I did not care for knitting. During our knitting lessons one of the students would read aloud from French or Russian literature. I recall that I always volunteered to go and fetch the book from the School Library and read to the class when it was time for a knitting lesson.

On the last day of school before the holidays, the governess distributed a ball of wool and a set of four knitting needles to each of us, saying,

"Each of you will knit one sock." Frossia and I were given enough yarn to knit one sock each, to make a pair. We promised each other that we would get together to work on our socks, and Frossia told me her mother would help.

But during the holidays I did not see Frossia, and it was not until New Year's Eve that I realized I had not yet started on my sock. I had never knitted a sock before, and did not know how to knit on four needles, like the set given to us with the yarn. But Pasha came to my rescue. She told me not to worry, that she would have the sock ready for me before I had to go back to the School. Pasha's brother was in the Army, and she had already made several pairs of socks for him.

As we came into the classroom we handed our socks to Olga Andreevna, who told us they would be collected later that day to be distributed to the soldiers leaving for the front. There were no marks given for this assignment, and so when she picked up my sock and said "Very good, Bronia," I did not feel it was necessary to tell her that I had not knitted it myself. But later I felt terrible when Frossia entered the classroom and handed in her sock and I heard the governess say, "Look, Frossia, your sock is supposed to match Bronia's. Her sock is perfect but yours is out of shape and not the right size." She then turned to me. "I'm sorry, Bronia, that we will not be able to send your one sock as there is no time now to knit another one. Because of Frossia's carelessness one poor soldier will not have a pair of socks for the cold months ahead . . ." I did not say anything, and I was later so angry with myself for remaining silent.

We soon learned that Port Arthur had been captured by the Japanese. We also heard rumors of unrest throughout Russia. We tried to understand what was happening but sensed a feeling of danger. We did not know what to expect. In the School at night all lights were dimmed and the drapes drawn tightly closed. We were forbidden to look out of the windows at Teatralnaya Ulitza. There were strikes and demonstrations in St. Petersburg and revolutionary outbreaks in other cities.

I recall that when we were taken to the Maryinsky Theatre the governess made sure that the curtains in the carriage were pulled closed. On the way to the Theatre we heard loud shouts and strident whistles. It was Sunday, January 9, 1905, and we were taking part in the ballet *Caprice du Papillon* in a Benefit Performance for Olga Preobrajenska. Though all the tickets had been sold out well in advance, the Theatre that night was only half full. At the Alexandrinsky Theatre the performance was interrupted by a demonstration, and the Mikhailovsky Theatre closed early, about nine-thirty. We later learned that many people had been killed that day, which came to be known as Bloody Sunday. The Theatres canceled their performances and remained closed for the next several days.

For the rest of January we were not allowed to go home on Saturdays because of the disturbances in the streets of St. Petersburg. Mama did not come to see us on visiting days, Thursdays and Sundays, because she had a bad cold and was not feeling well. Sometimes I saw Vaslav during a rehearsal, but we could not talk. Waiting for our turn to dance, the girls stood along one wall of the large rehearsal hall and the boys stood along the opposite wall. Even if a boy and girl danced together they were not allowed to talk to each other, and as soon as the dance was over each had to return to his or her place along the wall.

The only opportunity I had to talk with Vaslav was during the Catholic Instruction that we attended once a week, and then he told me only that he was enjoying working individually with Oboukhov. I remembered that Vaslav, even after a short break from his regular ballet exercises, like the two-week Christmas or Easter holidays, would complain that his legs were "stiff" and that the muscles in his whole body did not respond. He needed at least two weeks of intensive and vigorous training to put himself back in shape after the holidays. Since Vaslav started studying with Oboukhov the previous year, I had noticed how conscious he had become of the importance of a well-built body and the need for physical exercises in addition to the ballet exercises. Oboukhov was very athletic and believed in daily workouts to keep fit. Vaslav worked every day with Oboukhov in the School gymnastic hall, lifting weights and working on the parallel bars in order to develop his musculature, also to acquire the agility and force so essential to a dancer in the perfection of his technique.

By the end of February calm had returned to the city, and in the School we began rehearsals for the Student Performance. The Annual Student Performance was a big event for the whole School. All the students participated, and the excitement began to grow long before the time of the performance. For the graduating students this program in the Maryinsky Theatre was both a theatrical experience and a contest. Their future careers as artists depended upon it.

Each year the program consisted of two one-act ballets and the *Divertissement*. This year K. M. Kulichevskaya staged *The Parisian Market*, music by C. Pugni, and M. M. Fokine choreographed *Acis and Galatea*, music by A. V. Kadletz. For the *Divertissement* Fokine and Kulichevskaya mounted several dance numbers for their advanced and graduating students, and N. G. Sergeyev, instructor of the Stepanov System of Dance Notation, mounted a *pas de trois* from *The Blue Dahlia*, music by C. Pugni.

Fokine had been promoted the year before to *premier danseur*, and at the beginning of the school year had been appointed *professeur de danse*. As his first choreographic work he chose *Acis and Galatea* from Ovid's *Metamorphoses*. This ballet, first choreographed by Lev Ivanov in 1896, had been dropped from the Maryinsky Theatre repertory.

I envied my friends who studied with Fokine, they were so interested in their work with him. They told me about the rehearsals and that Fokine had just seen Isadora Duncan in her first performance in St. Petersburg and been greatly impressed by the exhilarating freedom of her dance. I was sorry that our rehearsals with Kulichevskaya were held on the same day and at the same time, keeping me from seeing theirs.

Fokine told his students that for the style of the ballet he had been inspired by the frescoes he had seen in Pompeii, during his visit to Italy the previous year. My friends, Zina and Maroussia, excitedly told me that though all their dances were *sur pointe*, Mikhail Mikhailovitch had introduced many innovations in his choreography. He had placed his students in new asymmetric groupings—sitting on the rocks, lying on the grass, or standing by the brook—and had explained that in contrast to the rigid classical ballet poses they must relax their bodies when not dancing. However, he was almost apologetic that he had not been able to obtain permission from the inspector, Missovsky, for the nymphs to dance in sandals. Missovsky insisted that the students must show the progress they had made in classical technique *sur pointe*. Though Missovsky rejected Fokine's request that the nymphs dance in sandals, he did agree to let them dance in Grecian tunics.

Fokine used twelve boys for his completely innovative "Dance of the Fauns," including both Nijinsky and Rosai, who each danced a solo against the background of the dancing fauns. In his own memoirs, *Against the Tide* (Leningrad, 1962), Fokine comments that when using the boy students he was "free." He points out, "boys do not dance on toe and they are not my students, and so I do not have to demonstrate their progress. They are dancing my composition." The fauns looked like animals and, at the end of their dance, tumbled head over heels—certainly not a *pas* of the classical ballet. But Fokine claimed it was "well in conformity with the animal characteristics of the dance." I, who always spoke against the use of acrobatics in the ballet, made use of somersaults in my very first ballet, Stravinsky's *Le Renard* (1922). But there was no contradiction. I did not use those steps as a trick but to achieve an artistic aim.

The ballet *The Parisian Market* had first been choreographed by Marius Petipa in St. Petersburg in 1859. For the Student Performance, Kulichevskaya produced her own version of the ballet and used all her students and some of the boys from Oboukhov's class. Twelve of us from her younger advanced class were flower girls, and in the finale we danced with the boys. I was disappointed that Vaslav was not one of the boys chosen to come to our rehearsals. Kulichevskaya had distributed all the important roles and the solo dances among the graduating students and her older advanced students. The leading roles were assigned to Nadejda Soboleva and Feodor Lopukhov. New costumes and sets were specially made for the performance.

It was only after Kulichevskaya had completed mounting her ballet with us that we learned there was to be a *pas de deux* we had not seen. Kulichevskaya had mounted it for her graduating student, Anna Fedorova, partnered by a young student, Nijinsky.

I knew Anna Fedorova slightly; I had seen her in our dance classes. Though not pretty, she was lively and danced well; her technique was strong and precise. She was two years older than Vaslav and as a graduating student had already studied for over a year in the *classe d'adage* with Pavel Gerdt. Though Vaslav was in the advanced dance class, he was still two years away from his own graduation, and to distinguish a young student in a *pas de deux* for the Student Performance was exceptional for the School.

Although I was dancing myself in *The Parisian Market*, I did not see their *pas de deux* until the full rehearsal. Fedorova and Vaslav rehearsed separately from us. In fact no one was allowed to see their rehearsals; Oboukhov wanted the first appearance of Nijinsky on the stage of the Maryinsky to be a surprise.

The *pas de deux* was mounted by Kulichevskaya in the style and form of Petipa, consisting of an *adagio, male variation, female variation,* and *coda*. Vaslav told me that Oboukhov participated in the mounting of his *variation*, and that since Vaslav had not yet studied the art of partnering, Oboukhov also worked with him and Fedorova on their *adagio* and *coda*. Anna Fedorova welcomed the opportunity of working with Oboukhov, who had just been named *premier danseur* of the Imperial Theatres.

Oboukhov mounted the *variation* for Vaslav on a double-measure time, so that any slight adjustments in the tempo to allow for Nijinsky's unusual elevation would not change the rhythm or the musical sonance; this also added a wider range of nuances to Nijinsky's interpretation.

The full rehearsal for *The Parisian Market* began. It was time for the *pas de deux*. My eyes followed Vaslav's performance of the *adagio* with Fedorova, spellbound. As he began his own *variation* my heart suddenly stood still with happiness. With great emotion I lived each of Vaslav's *pas*, each line of his body in the movement of his dancing . . . both in the air and on the ground.

AT LAST the day we were all waiting for came. On April 10, 1905, we were taken to the Maryinsky Theatre two hours before the performance. Usually we students had to go up to the very top floor, to the dressing rooms of the *corps de ballet*, to change into our costumes, but on this important day we were taken to the artists' foyer, on the same level as the stage, and told we were to change there. Our costumes had already been brought there for us. The foyer, with its grand piano, large wall mirror, and upholstered chairs, reminded me of the *foyer de danse à l'Opéra* of the ballet lithographs in the School. The doors of the ballerinas' dressing rooms opened into the foyer, and the graduating students were given those dressing rooms. The air was thick with a mixture of stage smells . . . powder, eau de cologne, face cream, burned hair . . . immediately creating for us the atmosphere of "established artists." Wishful conversations could be heard as to which dressing rooms we would have for our own use when we became ballerinas like Preobrajenska and Kshessinska.

I combed my hair, put on my makeup, pulled on my pink tights, tried on my toe shoes, but I wasn't dreaming of my own future. I was worrying about Vaslav. . . . *How is he doing his makeup? . . . How is he fixing his hair? . . . How will he look in his costume? . . . Will he "freeze" just before stepping out onto the stage . . . Will he be flustered in the excitement of his first appearance in a classical* pas de deux? . . .

I prayed silently and knew that Mother would be praying too, even more fervently than I. She would be terribly anxious. This was the first time she would be seeing Vaslav dance in the Maryinsky Theatre.

The Theatre was overflowing with guests invited for the program. In addition to the relatives and friends of the students, the Administration of the Imperial Theatres, and critics from the St. Petersburg newspapers, there were musicians and artists from the Ballet, Opera, and Drama.

The curtain opened.

I was onstage from the beginning of *The Parisian Market* but was not aware of anything until Nijinsky and Fedorova were onstage dancing the *adagio*. I could detect no sign of nervousness in Vaslav. He was handsome and looked elegant in his costume, which fitted him well. He partnered Fedorova splendidly, and while with a light touch of his hand he assured her balance and imperceptibly assisted her in the pirouettes and lifts, he was always dancing and sustaining his own continuity of movement.

Fedorova and Nijinsky were warmly applauded after the *adagio*.

But now, Nijinsky is onstage alone.

A short pose, *5ème position*, and suddenly a tremendous jump straight up, *grand échappé*, his legs firmly locked together. As he remains thus poised in midair, a rustle of appreciation is heard from the audience. He drops quickly, strikes the ground, *2ème position*, to rebound straight up like a ball thrown hard against the floor, and once again Nijinsky is seen for a split second suspended in midair. He drops down slowly, lightly touching the ground, *5ème position*, and a barely perceptible preparation, on half-toe, lifts him high in the air in a spiral movement, three *tours en l'air* on the ascent. After the third *tour*, he stops the spiral movement with an ascent of the whole body reaching upwards and then, *en face*, comes down. Smoothly, maintaining the flow of the dance, he glides in a short *glissade*, lightly touching the floor, and then Nijinsky flies across the whole width of the stage with *grand assemblé entrechat-dix*. He beats the *entrechats* high above the center of the stage and continues his flight in the air to the other side of the stage. There, as he seems to linger two or three seconds in the air before coming down, the audience explodes with applause. Vaslav repeats the *enchaînement de pas* to an ever-mounting storm of applause. He continues to dance—the audience continues to applaud.

For the second musical phrase of the *variation* Nijinsky soars from the depth of the stage. In his dance he flies diagonally across the whole stage with the following *enchaînement de pas:* a short preparation *pas*, *petit assemblé devant*, then he soars high in a *sissonne soubresaut*, the body arched back, suspended in midair; he holds the fishlike pose, then smoothly the lines of his body flow into a new form as he descends on *attitude effacée;* he touches the floor lightly on the right foot, quickly bringing the left leg to the floor front for a *coupé preparation* to spring and fly onward, continuing his diagonal trajectory; *grand brisé volé entrechat-dix*, his torso leaning forward, his hands and head almost touching the fluttering legs raised high in front of him swiftly beating the *entrechat-dix;* once more the same *enchaînement de pas*, bringing him to the ramp; he ends the *variation* with a *prestissimo pirouette*, the contour of his body disappearing in the increasing momentum of the ten *pirouettes en dehors*.

In the *coda* solo Nijinsky dances as effortlessly as in his *variation*. In all of his dancing movements, even the most difficult technical steps, no effort or forcing can be discerned in Nijinsky's body. When Nijinsky soars upward he takes off from the ground as lightly as a fly, or he rebounds like a ball to articulate briskly the *pas battu*. He ends his solo with twelve *pirouettes à la seconde*.

Fedorova and Nijinsky had danced the *coda* brilliantly. At the end of the *pas de deux* there was a storm of applause, but when Vaslav came onstage alone the audience greeted his appearance with a frenzy of enthusiasm. I was experiencing a totally new sensation of happiness. I was immeasurably proud and happy for Vaslav.

I had never seen Vaslav dance in any rehearsal the way he danced this night. Nijinsky, onstage, was transfigured, an elated being overcoming the limitations of the human body. The radiance of his inner flame touched my soul with the same magic that was arousing the audience to its enthusiastic frenzy.

In the *Divertissement*, when Nijinsky came out to dance the *pas de trois* from *The Blue Dahlia* with Maria Gorshkova and Elena Smirnova, he was immediately recognized by the audience and applauded. The *pas de trois* had been remounted by Sergeyev after the Stepanov notations of the original Petipa choreography. When working and rehearsing with Vaslav, he had adhered strictly to the tempi established by previous dancers in *The Blue Dahlia*. Even so Nijinsky danced brilliantly, adapting his technique to the tempi of the notations.

Mother was so happy as she sat in the audience, hearing around her, "Nijinsky has surpassed them all." . . . "The graduating students were hardly noticed." . . . "Nijinsky has overshadowed everyone tonight."

Maria Gorshkova and Feodor Lopukhov, the graduating students, were both excellent dancers and did not get the appreciation that their talents deserved that night, for by comparison with Vaslav their presentations paled, possibly adversely affecting their later dancing careers.

After the program the St. Petersburg newspaper *Russ* wrote:

[Fokine] succeeded best in his mounting of the *variations*, very interesting dances and groupings of the fauns. . . . The student Nijinsky had a great success with his high jumps and fast turns, which he executed with ease and without any sign of acrobatics. With confidence we can predict a future of ballet laurels for this young artist . . .

In *Slovo* the critic did not single out Vaslav but did comment that in the *Divertissement* "Maria Gorshkova, Vaslav Nijinsky, Iliador Lukyanov and Anna Guimelman were outstanding . . ."

Another critic expressed the enthusiasm of the audience:

The student Nijinsky amazed everyone: the young artist still has two years ahead of him in the School. It is all the more pleasant to see such exceptional talent. His lightness and elevation together with his remarkably fluid and beautiful movements were striking. Here is a worthy future partner for Mesdames Pavlova and Sedova. . . . It only remains to wish that this 15* year old artist does not remain a child prodigy but rather continues to perfect himself.

---

*Vaslav had just had his sixteenth birthday a little over a month before the Student Performance. (BN)

18 Our Second Summer in Dudergoth

THE SCHOOL YEAR had finished well for Vaslav. After his success in the Student Performance he had worked hard at his studies and was promoted to Class IV without having to take any examinations. Father was very satisfied with Vaslav's progress in his academic studies and even happier when he read all the laudatory reviews of Vaslav's dancing in the St. Petersburg newspapers. At that time ballet was not accepted on equal terms with other branches of the performing arts, so the performance of a dancer was usually not considered important enough for a full review. Naturally, then, Father was very proud when he saw his son acclaimed in the reviews of the Student Performance. He promised to come to St. Petersburg for next year's program to see Vaslav dance.

Father also sent us some money and wrote that he had a good contract for the summer and that we could be sure of going to Dudergoth, for he would be sending us money promptly every month.

Vaslav and I got out our book about St. Petersburg published for the visit of President Faure of France in 1897 and made our plans to visit some of the palaces and parks in the countryside around Dudergoth. We looked at the pictures of Gatchina and Peterhof, both of which we could reach by train. Gatchina, about nine miles beyond Dudergoth on the same line, had been the eighteenth-century estate of a favorite of Catherine the Great, Grigori Orlov. There was a small theatre at Gatchina, but no programs from the Imperial Theatres were given there. The main summer programs took place in Krasnoe Selo and Tsarskoe Selo, and for special occasions there were performances in Peterhof, the pearl of Russian culture. Fairy-tale Peterhof was already familiar to me from the time when I, as a very young student, had taken part in a performance there. I told Vaslav all about the various fountains and sculptures I could remember. Vaslav had never been to Peterhof, so we planned to go there as well as to Gatchina.

The apartment where we had been living on Gagarinskaya Ulitza had turned out to be damp, cold, and gloomy, and so before leaving for Dudergoth Mother found another one on Nikolaevskaya Ulitza, in a good area near Nevsky Prospekt. The new apartment was in a larger house, off the inner courtyard and on the first floor. In order to hold it for us so that we could move in directly after our vacation, Mother paid for the month of August in advance. We were going to the same peasant house we had stayed in the summer before, and she had to pay that rent in advance, also the driver who was going to transport our furniture and things to Dudergoth on his wagon, and lastly she had to outfit me for the summer. Vaslav, like all the boy students, was provided by the School with a gray summer uniform that it was strictly forbidden to modify. But Mama knew that the jacket was uncomfortable for the summer and thought that its open collar looked quite sad and dejected on Vaslav. So she decided that as long as we were going to the country it would be all right to let Vaslav wear a Russian shirt instead, and she bought him three white ones. After all these considerable expenses there was just enough money left to get by on until we received some money from Father, and so Vaslav and I had to let our trips to Gatchina and Peterhof wait awhile.

This summer we were the only vacationers in our village. There was one family who lived there all year round—an artist from the chorus of the Maryinsky Theatre with his wife and daughter. We had become slightly acquainted with them our first year in Dudergoth, when my friend Zina had introduced us to several families. Since then the chorister had taken early retirement from the Maryinsky because of ill health and they had come to live permanently in their large dacha, which was near ours.

Vaslav became quite friendly with the artist and visited his home almost daily. From our terrace it was possible to see the dacha just down and across the road. Often the sick man would be lying in a hammock in the garden or sitting back in an armchair on the terrace, and we would be able to see Vaslav sitting beside him, listening to his stories about operas, composers, conductors, and artists. Vaslav loved his tales about the theatre, but was saddened by his friend's illness. The man had tuberculosis, and Vaslav was afraid that he might soon die, as indeed he did the following winter. Sometimes, in order to distract him, Vaslav took his Italian mandolin with him and would play arias from the operas.

Vaslav spoke warmly about the whole family. The singer's wife was a teacher in the preparatory class of the high school, and their daughter, who was older than Vaslav, was a high school student. They were a cultured and educated family, and Vaslav loved to visit them in the evenings when they would gather together and someone would read aloud from Turgenev, Pushkin, or Gogol, or from the work of some other writers in the large library in their home. Vaslav's friendship with this family was responsible for my introduction to the works of Dostoyevsky. He would borrow books for me to read, and the previous year he had brought me *Crime and Punishment*. I remember with what enthusiasm I read it; I couldn't put it down but read it day and night—those were the White Nights when I could read in bed by the light through the window. This summer he continued to bring me more books by Dostoyevsky, who has ever since been one of my favorite writers along with Tolstoy and Pushkin.

Vaslav also introduced me to some of the games he had learned from the family. He taught me chess and beat me like a virtuoso. Then we took up a new diversion. We covered the table with a large sheet of paper with widely scattered letters written on it. A saucer was placed on it, turned upside down and with an arrow drawn on its base in black ink, and one of us would put a hand on it and begin to ask questions. They were always the same: "Will Father write soon and send us some money?" The saucer slipped about on the paper, stopping at various letters, and almost always it gave a comforting answer. But there were no letters from Father, and no money either. Nor did Father answer our letters. We began to imagine something terrible must have happened to him. (Eventually we learned that Father had suffered a complex fracture of his arm and had been in the hospital for several weeks.)

Our vacation was taking a bad turn. Day by day the money was running out. At first we had the food that Mother had bought at the beginning of our vacation: macaroni, rice, semolina, pearl barley, and buckwheat . . . but these supplies could not last forever and we had no money left to buy coffee, tea, even salt and matches. In St. Petersburg we could have found something to pawn or sell, but here in Dudergoth we had nothing, not even the money for a train ticket back to St. Petersburg.

Our servant Pasha, who had again come with us to Dudergoth for the summer, turned out to be very resourceful and borrowed potatoes, flour, vegetables, eggs, and milk from the owner of our house. She even got hold of matches and salt. Mother prepared *kefir*, which we ate with boiled potatoes and fried mushrooms we had gathered in the forests, or she made milk soup with dumplings. But Vatsa could not drink milk, he could not tolerate it, so for him Mama made *drachena*, a kind of pancake from flour and eggs.

The baker who carried around his goods in a large basket on his back let us have bread on credit. We would get a *sitnik*, a whole-meal bread sold by the pound, and two or three flat cakelike pies covered with sugar icing. Mama was very inventive with these; she cut them into small equal pieces and shared them among the four of us so that instead of sugar we had these with tea or the "coffee" we made out of fried acorns and barley grain.

We had never been so badly off. We had neither fish nor meat. Mother was in despair as she knew we children were in a period of growth and needed to eat well. I had always been an indifferent eater, but Vaslav loved good food. Our main concern, however, was whether we would be able to return to St. Petersburg, though we pretended not to worry in front of Mama and increase her own despair.

One day Vaslav announced optimistically that he would go to St. Petersburg on foot and there find something to do to make money, but it was obvious that in the course of such a journey he would wear out the soles of his boots and have to return home barefoot. His next idea was to dig up earthworms in the evening and then, instead of sleeping late in the morning as he loved to do, he got up very early, put on his Russian shirt, and with his fishing rod over his shoulder, a bucket for the fish, and a large piece of bread wrapped up in a bundle, he set off to go fishing in the big lake by the railway station. Before noon he would return tired, hungry, and disillusioned, and no fish in the bucket. The lake was fed by deep underground springs and was icy cold, and quite possibly no fish lived in it at all. Vaslav never confessed to Mother that when he couldn't catch any fish he would swim for a long time in the lake.

On other days we would go into the forests to gather berries and mushrooms. We also collected pinecones to light under the samovar, and dry twigs and branches to fuel the stove.

It always seemed to happen in our family that just when there appeared to be no way out of misfortune, some stroke of good luck would rescue us. Pani Kirst, a childhood friend of Mother's and a former artist of the Warsaw Opera, came to visit us in Dudergoth. Vaslav and I had known her since we were young children, and as she was part owner of a food store she always brought many "gifts" with her whenever she came to visit. This time she brought some splendid foods: ham, sausages, a piece of bacon, Swiss cheese, Ukrainian lard, sprats, a ring of Polish sausages, and a box of fruit-drop candies. Pani Kirst stayed with us for a few days, with she and Mother spending much of the time talking together, for Pani Kirst had also been deserted by her husband not long before. When she left to go back to St. Petersburg she loaned Mother several rubles.

Usually the summer military maneuvers were held near Krasnoe Selo, but this year they were transferred to Dudergoth, to a large field between the first and second villages and on both sides of the road. Tsar Nicholas II was present and often rode quite near our house, and sometimes he even walked on foot with his officers.

The maneuvers were quite an event, and for the occasion Vaslav would specially put on his blue dress uniform, with the golden lyres and the Tsar's crown on the collar, so as to be allowed to observe everything as closely as possible. The artillery thundered on the big field, so strongly that we had to tape up the windows to keep them from breaking. Soldiers with rifles lay on both sides of the road and shot at each other with blanks. We loved to move fearlessly down the street between the shots. Vaslav, of course, went right out onto the field, quite close to the center of the maneuvers, where he said there was a long line of cannons, and he would watch how they were fired.

On the edge of our village they put up a tent for the Tsar. Next to it was erected a large flagpole—for the Tsar's standard—and in front of the tent they set up a long table. Since Vaslav was in uniform they let us come quite close to the tent, enough so that we could watch everything quite clearly. Around the table were gathered the Tsar and his retinue of generals and other officers, all studying a map of the area. Later the same table was covered with a white tablecloth, and there the Tsar and his officers ate, while a military brass band played nearby. We immediately recognized the conductor, a well known military music director from St. Petersburg whose band, placed in the wings or onstage, often played the brass section for ballets and operas at the Maryinsky Theatre.

One soldier from the orchestra climbed up a tree and played a virtuoso solo on his cornet. When the Tsar approvingly clapped his hands, everyone around joined in applause. It seemed to Vaslav and me that the two of us clapped louder than all the others. Later in the evening, after the Tsar again gathered his retinue around the tent, the same soldier-musician played "Evening Sunset," and the maneuvers ended.

At the end of our vacation Mama wrote to Aunt Thetya and Cousin Stassia, telling them of our misfortune. They sent us some money, enough so that Mama could pay our debts to the owner of the dacha and the baker and buy our train tickets back to St. Petersburg. When the wagon arrived in the evening bringing Pasha back from Dudergoth, Mama had just enough money to pay the driver.

Looking ahead, we became more concerned than ever about money. How were we going to live? I suggested that we pawn Vaslav's mandolin. He made a face, but then immediately gave the instrument to Mother. It was decorated with a butterfly of inlaid tortoiseshell and mother-of-pearl. The Italian maker's mark was burned into the bridge, and it had a good case, lined with raspberry velvet. Vaslav had saved up twenty-five rubles to buy the mandolin, but Mother was doubtful whether they accepted musical instruments at the pawnshop.

At the same time, saying nothing to Mama and Vaslav, I collected up a set of books I had received as Christmas or Easter gifts—a series called Our Golden Library, in handsome red bindings with golden decoration. There weren't many: *David Copperfield* by Dickens, *Don Quixote* by Cervantes, *Twenty Thousand Leagues Under the Sea* by Jules Verne, Andersen's fairy tales (with my favorite story "The Snow Queen"), and stories by Vladimir Nemirovich-Danchenko and one or two others. I tied them together with a rope and carried them to a bookstore near Nevsky Prospekt, where I had seen a sign: SALE AND PURCHASE OF OLD BOOKS. But all my books looked like new, I had taken such care of them. With agitation and fear—would they buy my books?—I entered the store. The owner began to tell me that he didn't buy children's books, but then he untied the rope, took a look, and agreed to buy them. I got five rubles from him and joyfully returned home. A second piece of good news was waiting for me there; the pawnshop had paid fifteen rubles for the mandolin. Our total of twenty rubles gave us wealth. Because of my ideas as to what we should pawn and sell, Mama and Vaslav nicknamed me "Minister of Finance."

By now it was time to return to the School. During summer vacations Vaslav seemed to forget all about the School, so at the beginning of the year it was always difficult for him to get back into the habit of working at his studies. He would always complain, "They give us so many lessons that there is no time to prepare them."

Once Vatsa brought so much assigned work home for the weekend, we knew he couldn't possibly do it all. He worried most over having to write a composition: "How I Spent My Vacation."

"What can I write? How we sat without any money and wondered what would happen to us?"

I said I would try and write a composition for him while he prepared his history, geography, and French lessons. I began to recollect some of the things Vaslav had told me during the summer; then I wrote a composition about how early in the morning, at dawn, Vaslav set off to go fishing, walking down the road between the fields of ripening rye, towards the lake with his fishing rod on his shoulder. As he walked along he became immersed in thoughts about the future and forgot about the fishing. A slight mist covered the ground so that he seemed to be walking in a cloud. Suddenly everything was illuminated by the sun. A gentle breeze sprang up and the entire field with its tall rye began to sway and stir, the stalks bent before the wind as if running ahead of it; they ran like waves on a large body of water. . . . Suddenly he remembered himself and hurried his steps towards the lake . . . and so forth. Vaslav was very pleased and copied the composition into his notebook in his beautiful fine hand. He received exceptional praise from his teacher of Russian Language.

He also had some mathematics to do, and since arithmetic problems had been my "specialty" from early on, I quickly solved the rest of Vaslav's assigned work. In this way I was able to help Vaslav get off to a good start for the school year. Later he had no difficulties himself and received good grades all year for his studies.

19 1905–1906

DURING SUMMER vacation we had read in the newspapers official reports of the war and the tragic losses inflicted on the Baltic Fleet in the straits between Japan and Korea. We felt tremendous pity for the soldiers and sailors obliged to go to war.

Following the news of a treaty signed with Japan in September 1905 and the loss of the eastern part of the Trans-Siberian Railroad, strikes and disorders broke out in St. Petersburg. On October 10 the Nikolaevskaya Railroad went on strike, and other railroads were expected to follow. Many people feared shortages and began to hoard food. Often the streets were not lit in the evenings, and with so few people venturing out the audiences at the Imperial Theatres became small and the private theatres had to close down.

One Saturday as he was on his way home, Vaslav came upon a crowd of demonstrators, workers, and students going along the middle of Nevsky Prospekt. I remember that Mama and I were already home when Vaslav, out of breath, rushed into the apartment.

"I was on Nevsky near Anichkov Palace when I saw a dense crowd being scattered by Cossacks. They were riding among the demonstrators and beating them with whips. A row of soldiers were following, shoulder to shoulder, firing into the crowd, and people were falling to the ground. I quickly climbed a lamp post." Vaslav was agitated, and his voice trembled with emotion. "A Cossack probably mistook me for a demonstrating student. He hit me with a whip so hard that I almost fell under the horse's hooves."

Vaslav's coat had been slashed along the bottom as though by a saber. Fortunately the blow had been absorbed by his overcoat and the upper part of his boot. Mother, frightened and in tears, begged him to stay away from any other demonstrations. Poles in Russia were always under suspicion of being involved in revolutionary activities, and she was afraid that he could be expelled from the Imperial School on the slightest excuse—particularly now, just after we had heard that Uncle Eugenius, Father's younger brother and Vaslav's and my godfather, had been exiled on suspicion of being involved in some uprising in Poland.

Vaslav and the other boys in the School learned what was happening from the drama students, who were nonresidents and so were not as isolated from the outside world as we ballet students were, the girls more so than the boys. The drama students were also older, having completed their high school studies and, at seventeen or more, begun their drama courses. Their classrooms were on the top floor of the School, on the same corridor as the academic classrooms where Vaslav studied. During class breaks the advanced dance students would meet and talk with the drama students, who gave them news of what was happening in St. Petersburg and throughout the country. The drama students themselves were also discontented and would voice criticisms of their drama teachers and talk of plans to demand changes in the teaching system.

Then suddenly agitation broke out among the ballet artists. Everyone was talking about a stormy meeting attended by about three-quarters of the ballet troupe. They had gathered in the rehearsal hall to choose a delegation to discuss their complaints with the Directorate. The meeting had lasted six hours and had produced a confrontation between Sergeyev and Fokine, with Sergeyev leaving the hall to the accompaniment of whistles and shouts.

The meeting had chosen Pyotr Mikhailov as chairman and a delegation that included Fokine, Pavlova, and Karsavina. They demanded the return of Marius Petipa, Alexander Shiraev, and Alfred Bekefi. They also demanded that the ballet troupe should have the right to reapportion the budget, with a raise for themselves, to have a say in the choice of the *régisseur* of the company, and to be allowed one additional free day besides Saturdays. In addition they called a strike of the next day's matinee performance of the opera, *The Queen of Spades*. Upon urging from the delegates, many ballet artists did not show up for the performance, so that all the ballet scenes had to be cut and the ballroom act shortened, and the singers of the chorus had to improvise a few ballroom dances.

In the Imperial Theatrical School the older boy students, following the example of the drama students and the ballet artists, presented their own demands to the Director. Vaslav was one of the students at this meeting, and I remember their "revolutionary demands": the improvement of education, instruction in theatrical makeup, permission for the graduating students to smoke, and permission for the advanced students to wear their own shoes and their own starched collars and cuffs under the School jackets.

Most of these student demands were met, but Telyakovsky tried first to discourage and then to prevent any further meetings of the artists. From the windows of our classrooms we could hear the uproar in the courtyard below when the artists were refused permission to enter the rehearsal hall for another meeting. Our classes were interrupted as several students opened the hinged ventilation panels in the windows to yell their greetings to the artists, until the police arrived and ordered everyone to disperse. Thereupon the artists went over to the Alexandrinsky Theatre to hold their meeting.

While the ballet performances for that day, October 17, were not canceled, the previously striking artists, the "mutineers," were barred from the Theatre, and students were chosen to replace them. Mikhailov and the artists tried to persuade the students to refuse to replace the professional artists, but the temptation to appear on the stage of the Maryinsky as real artists proved too great.

Disagreements and arguments began to break out among the artists, many of whom didn't approve of the strike and the demands made upon the Directorate. As they were not supported by the opera and drama artists, there was panic lest they be fired. Many began to withdraw their signatures.

Suddenly there came the shocking news that Sergei Legat had committed suicide, slashing his throat with a razor. Athletically built and handsome, with dark hair and blue eyes, Legat had been a leading performer in the ballet. With his brother, Nikolai, he had choreographed the splendid ballet *The Fairy Doll*, and was also an instructor in the School. Sergei Legat had been Vaslav's first teacher of dancing, and even after Vaslav had been promoted to the Upper Advanced Class, Legat had continued to follow his progress closely. On several occasions, together with Oboukhov, Legat had saved Vaslav from harsh punishment. Vaslav had worshiped Legat, and he wept bitterly when he came home on Saturday and told us about his death. Many felt it had been caused by Maria Petipa, Legat's common-law wife, when she made him renege on his fellow artists and remove his signature from the protest to the Directorate of the Imperial Theatres.

His funeral took place on October 21, and the students were not allowed to attend. There was only one representative from the Directorate, but Legat was mourned widely by his fellow artists, many of whom now regarded him as their martyr.

Meanwhile there were other incidents and outbursts in the Theatres, and also throughout the city. A performance of *Lohengrin* was stopped at the end of the first act. Vaslav told us that someone had shouted "Down with the Autocrats," and there had been a terrible outcry. The audience had jumped up from their seats, officers pulled out their swords, chairs were thrown from the loges, artists and musicians had scattered, and the program could not continue.

Some students of the Conservatory of Music staged a private performance of a new opera by Rimsky-Korsakov, *Kostchei the Immortal*. Rimsky-Korsakov was considered a "revolutionary" and the Tsar had banned some of his operas from the Imperial Theatres. The performance was interrupted and closed by the police, and a struggle ensued.

There were no further major outbreaks for the rest of the year, but an atmosphere of political unrest remained in St. Petersburg. In the Imperial Theatres a commission of inquiry was conducted that lasted until Christmas. For their participation in the disturbances both Pyotr Mikhailov and Josef Kshessinsky, the brother of Mathilda Kshessinska, were dismissed, though through his sister's influence with the Imperial Court, Kshessinsky did not lose his pension. Mikhailov left Russia and went to Paris where he studied law. Many of the other artists involved were eventually dismissed without cause, or were not given the chance to dance good roles, or simply were not duly promoted.

In the fall Mama began giving dancing lessons in our home, in the large drawing room of our new apartment on Nikolaevskaya Ulitza. Father, though not always on time, was also now sending some money fairly regularly. And so by Christmas Mama was able to redeem Vaslav's mandolin and return to me the five rubles from the books I had sold. I saved the money for the summer vacation. Mama also gave Vaslav a gift. Now that the students were permitted to wear their own shoes, collars, and cuffs, she bought him some shoes like the ones worn by law students, made of very fine kid leather, smoothly stretched over the foot and with long pointed toes. In all the School only Vaslav had such beautiful shoes. She also bought him starched collars and cuffs for his blue jacket. The thin line of a mustache was beginning to show above his lip, and in his dark blue jacket and white starched collar and cuffs he looked very grown-up and handsome.

At the end of January 1906, on the occasion of the 150th anniversary of Mozart's birth, a splendid program was announced for the Maryinsky Theatre—the opera *Don Juan*. For the opera's ballet, four ballerinas, three *premier danseurs*, and the student Nijinsky were chosen to perform. I am not sure of all the ballerinas, but I do remember that Vaslav danced with Trefilova. I think the other ballerinas were Preobrajenska, Vaganova, and

Egorova. When I met Trefilova later in Europe, she reminisced about that evening when she had danced in *Don Juan* with the student Nijinsky, and described the dance "Roses and Butterflies" mounted by Nikolai Legat.

The intention of the Directorate to put Nijinsky, a student with a year and a half before his graduation, on the stage at an equal level with established artists caused a sensation. Vaslav was himself stunned at such an unexpected honor. Perhaps it was an unofficial debut, so that the Directorate could evaluate his artistic and dancing achievement alongside the great Artists of the Imperial Theatres and answer those who had pointed out that Nijinsky's previous success had only been in a Student Performance.

Probably because of the unrest in St. Petersburg, neither the Boys' Division nor the Girls' Division were taken to the Maryinsky to watch the dress rehearsal of *Don Juan*. So I was not able to see how Vaslav, at sixteen, shone in the same setting as those other precious jewels of the Imperial Ballet.

After the program I could see that Vaslav was happy, but as usual he did not speak of himself but only of the other dancers and how much they had all been applauded. During the intermission Alexander Krupensky, the manager of the Imperial Ballet Company, had come backstage and told Vaslav how splendidly he was handling his part and that he was showing himself to be an excellent artist of the ballet. Mother and I were touched by this recognition of Vaslav and showed more happiness and talked more about the performance than he did. A few days later there was a second performance of *Don Juan*, with Anna Pavlova replacing Trefilova as Vaslav's partner. This was the first time Vaslav danced with Anna Pavlova.

Not long afterwards Mother was called to the office of the Imperial Theatrical School, for a matter they said needed her consent. Mother was worried—*Has Vaslav not been keeping up with his studies?* What unpleasant news was she going to hear this time? But instead she was told of the decision of the Directorate of the Imperial Theatres to release Nijinsky in 1906, a year ahead of his graduation, and allow him to become an Artist of the Imperial Theatres at a salary of sixty-five rubles a month.* This would be on condition that Nijinsky take the examination for the academic subjects at the end of the school year, 1906–7, in order to complete the last required year in the School.

Mother answered that although she was happy and grateful for this flattering offer for her son, she could not give her consent, explaining that Vaslav was too young—he had only just had his seventeenth birthday—to

---

*The usual starting salary was fifty rubles a month. (IN/JR)

find himself among the Artists of the Imperial Theatres. One more year of study could only strengthen him in his dancing discipline and achievement. As Mother saw it, for Vaslav to have to divide his attention between the responsibilities of an Artist and the effort to keep up his studies would be a tremendous load. Still being attached to the School would mean that he would not be the equal of the other Artists; it would deprive him of the freedom to express himself as an Artist and hamper his progress in his work. Mama felt that for his own self-esteem he should finish the School like the other students.

Vaslav, however, was greatly irritated at the prospect of having to sit for still another year at his desk in class. Mama simply asked him one question: "Imagine, Vaslav, that you are already an Artist of the Imperial Theatres and tell me if you would even glance at your textbooks. Would you go at all to the classes in the School to prepare for your examinations?"

"Never" was Vaslav's answer. "I dream only of the time when these textbooks will fly up to the ceiling and no longer weigh me down and oblige me to study, study . . . as an Artist I will study something else; I will dance a lot, and I will study not merely to be a *premier danseur* but to become an Artist of the Dance!"

I wanted to tell Vaslav that he already was an Artist of the Dance, but I held back, sensing that he was speaking of his own personal ideal. Mama was satisfied with Vaslav's answer. "Vaslav, you said what I expected you to say . . ."

In February Kulichevskaya started to mount a new ballet for the Annual Student Performance—*The Prince Gardener*, a one-act ballet with music by A. A. Davidov. The libretto was by Valerian Svetlov after the Andersen fairy tale, "The Swineherd." Svetlov, a dean of ballet critics, came often to watch the rehearsals of his ballet. The leading parts were distributed among Kulichevskaya's graduating students, and three graduating students from Oboukhov's class were distinguished by being given solo dances: Nikolai Issaev, Anatole Bourman, and Grigori Babitch. The leading role of the Prince-Swineherd was given to a student, Vaslav Nijinsky, who would be dancing with a graduating student, Ludmila Schollar.

Our rehearsals were interrupted for the first week of Lent, when there were no classes in the Imperial Theatrical School. All the Orthodox students fasted, went to the Chapel in the School, made their confessions, and took communion. Since Vaslav and I were Catholics we were allowed to go home for the whole week, so that we could go to confession in the Catholic church.

For the Orthodox, confession means simply answering the priest with

"We are sinners, Father," and the sins are forgiven. But Catholic confession is stricter. You, yourself, must tell the priest about your sins. I would assiduously write down all my sins on a scrap of paper, lest I forget something. Each time before we went to confession Mama would tell us that to take communion and then later recall some sins that had not been confessed was itself a mortal sin. Every confession was a great burden for me, but for Vaslav it was more than that. He would ask me, "Why must I tell my sins to a priest I do not know? How can a man believe that simply by being consecrated to the priesthood he has the holy right and power to forgive me all my sins? Better that I confess all my sins with prayer and remorse to God Himself. When I partake of communion, then I feel as if all in me is purified with the Holy Sacrament and on that day I am 'holy' and pure." Vaslav never mentioned these thoughts to Mama, who was very religious.

Not counting the summer vacation, that first week in Lent was one of the longest times Vaslav and I were at home together. We would talk about our dreams for the future and how we would arrange our lives when we became artists. Most of all we talked about how life could be made easier for Mama. Her rheumatism was getting worse, and there was no money for treatments.

We were also aware that whenever we came home she was finding it difficult to feed the two of us as well as herself and the servant. We could see her distress when she could not offer us the special fish dishes for Lent, as she would have liked. We had yet to taste red or black caviar, or salmon. But Vaslav assured Mama that everything that she prepared for us was delicious.

When it came time to return to the School we were obliged to take with us a "church certificate" stating that we had been to confession and had received communion. In a whisper, so as not to upset Mother, Vaslav said to me, "This is not free belief in God, but religious coercion . . ." The next year when we were home for Lent, Vaslav's last before graduating from the School, his confession did not go well. The priest asked him several questions and then began to reproach him for his lack of Polish patriotism, saying that he should go fight for Poland and help the struggle for Poland's independence and freedom. Vaslav answered him sharply: "I am not a Pole, I am Russian. I don't know Poland. I grew up and studied in Russia and I will always be a Russian. I came here to confession and not to hear a political exhortation!" In order to get the necessary "church certificate" Vaslav had to go to another priest for confession.

After the incident with the Polish patriot priest, Vaslav cooled completely towards religion, and from then on Mother could not persuade him to go to confession. But I have always felt that a belief in an Almighty Creator never left Vaslav. Over the many years we worked together I never saw Vaslav cross himself before going onto the stage, like the other dancers, but I did notice how before a dance he always took a deep breath and held it for a long time, and perhaps in this moment of meditation he reached God.

Rehearsals for the Student Performance resumed immediately upon our return to the School. For the program Mikhail Fokine choreographed the one-act ballet, *A Midsummer Night's Dream* (first choreographed by Marius Petipa in 1876), music by Mendelssohn-Bartholdy. His graduating student, Elena Smirnova, was to dance "Andante," a *pas de deux*, with the student Vaslav Nijinsky. Fokine also mounted a *pas de deux* for Smirnova and Nijinsky in the *Divertissement—The Valse-Fantasia*, music by Glinka.

The rehearsals took place in the dance hall of the Girls' Division. During our class breaks, and at other times when we were not in rehearsals ourselves, we could hear the music in the distance. I was especially taken by Glinka's music, *The Valse-Fantasia*.

The program was to take place on March 26, and during the weeks beforehand we looked forward to the arrival of Father, whom we hadn't seen for several years. We were at once excited and apprehensive, though we did not voice our feelings. I loved Father very much, and despite the enormity of Mother's grief I could not judge him. Mother had taught us, "That which takes place between a father and a mother should not affect the love of the children for their parents." But Vaslav did judge Father. Taking Mother's side, and in anticipation of Father's visit, he told her proudly, "Let Father look at me and see how I grew up without him; with only you, Mamoussia. Let him see me on the stage!"

Indeed Vaslav did look splendid, not only onstage but all the time. He carried his head slightly thrown back on his long neck. His hair was smoothly combed and his dress immaculate, with his snow-white collar and cuffs, his elegant simple boots. In school, from my friends as well as from the graduating students, I was continually hearing things like "Bronia, tell Vaslav that I adore him," or "Nijinsky, what a nice fellow . . . he is a *doushka* [darling]."

As he had promised, Father arrived in St. Petersburg for the program, but I did not see him until the day of the performance. A reception was given that afternoon for all the parents, in the large dance hall. I was seated with Mama. The chairs were all around the edge of the hall; ours were beneath the portrait of the Tsar, facing the entrance. When Father came in and saw us, he had to walk across the entire hall to join us. He had come straight from an audition held in the Theatre Bouffe for the A. A.

Briansky production of Lehar's operetta *The Merry Widow*, for which he had worn his evening clothes. And so he arrived at the reception in his tuxedo, with diamond cuff links and three diamond studs in the front of his dress shirt, and black patent-leather shoes. All heads turned in his direction as he crossed the room.

It was very painful for me to have to greet my beloved Father, for the first time after several years of separation, in the presence of all these people. My heart was beating fast; I was overwhelmed by great emotion, a burning love for my dear Father.

When Vaslav came in a little later, he greeted Father casually, but then he had already seen him the evening before at home. Vaslav looked paler than usual, and he seemed nervous; probably his mind was on the performance. He stayed away from Father, as if, like me, somewhat embarrassed that Father should appear so overdressed among the other parents.

The reception lasted only half an hour and then I had to say good-bye to Father and get ready for the evening performance. We had to go to the carriages that were waiting to take us to the Maryinsky Theatre. On the way, I appreciated what an effect Father's entrance into the hall had created on all the girls, who told me how handsome he was, ". . . and how elegant!"

As we arrived at the Theatre I could feel my head spinning. My knees felt wobbly. Having heard that our ballerinas, after a light lunch at twelve o'clock, ate nothing more until the end of the program, so as to be light and dance well, I had myself not eaten anything since morning. Besides, I was disturbed by Father's arrival; my mind was full of thoughts about Father being in the audience and watching us for the first time.

That evening I was to dance in "The Whisper of the Flowers." This was an important dance number in the ballet *The Prince Gardener*, for most of the six girls dancing it were graduating students. We depicted a bouquet of lilac flowers, white and purple, in lovely new costumes, but that evening I had not thought about getting myself ready, particularly how to comb my hair and arrange the sprays of lilac in it. Around me all the dancers were busy with themselves. I became nervous and anxious. One of the graduating students, Antonina Nesterovskaya, a kind and generous girl, took me into her dressing room and combed my hair. She noticed that I was unduly excited and tried to calm my anxieties, but suddenly I felt dizzy and slumped limply in the chair. Ninotchka revived me with smelling salts and, realizing that I was weak from hunger, made me eat a large orange, then continued to help me get ready for the performance.

I barely remember the performance itself, but I do recall Father in the intermission hugging and embracing me tenderly, and saying, "You were very good and you must continue to work hard."

Of Vaslav's dancing in the Student Performance I remember more from the rehearsals than from the evening itself. In *A Midsummer Night's Dream* he had a very impressive solo. Fokine's choreography inspired Nijinsky. His dancing did not try to astonish or amaze by emphasizing the technical difficulties. Nijinsky illumined the whole stage, flashing and scintillating in the air like a shooting star. One critic declared that "Vol des Papillons" was a masterpiece in which Fokine had featured his graduating student, Smirnova, and Oboukhov's student, Nijinsky. "They fluttered above the stage in their *pas de deux*, their dance interlaced in uninterrupted flight . . ."

I thought that seeing his son dancing on the stage of the most famous Theatre in all Russia and hearing the praises and applause would make Father proud, but to my surprise he did not seem at all astonished. He was stingy with his praise and even quite severe in his criticism. While admitting that Vaslav had great talent, he felt that he had a long way to go to perfect his dancing and would have to work a great deal more in order to attain the title of *premier danseur* in the Imperial Theatres.

Suddenly he added, "Remember, Vaslav, that in a *pas de deux* you do not have to show yourself off as an adroit *porteur* . . ."

Inside myself I knew that this word *porteur* must have wounded Vaslav, but he answered quite calmly, "On the stage, I do not try to show myself off at all. I am inspired by the dance and *I also am dancing* in the *pas de deux*. I perform what is mounted for me by my teachers—the *premiers danseurs*, Fokine and Oboukhov."

Perhaps Father's criticism was deliberate, so that Vaslav would not become self-satisfied, but his words were not well chosen and only hurt Vaslav's feelings. It also seemed to me that Father did not understand the nature of Vaslav's talent, though it must be pointed out that neither did Vaslav's partners at that time. In the minds of the two graduating students, Elena Smirnova from Fokine's class and Ludmila Schollar from Kulichevskaya's class, Nijinsky was simply the male partner in the *pas de deux*, whose only role was to support them well and comfortably *sur pointe*, to assist in their *pirouettes*, and to follow each of their *pas*. Each of them was noted for the purity of her ballet technique, though each had her own style. Smirnova created the impression of being a little severe and harsh, while Schollar was soft and coquettish. As graduating students in the Annual Student Performance of 1906, both were tensely occupied with the execution of their own difficult *pas* and with the purity of their technique, as could be seen on their faces, whereas Nijinsky's ease and individual style had been strikingly apparent through both Fokine's and Kulichevskaya's choreography.

The next morning Vaslav offered to show Father the Imperial Theatrical School where we had spent so many years. I went with them. We entered through the artists' entrance and came to the large rehearsal hall. We climbed the narrow stairs leading up to the open gallery overlooking the hall and walked along it to the boys' section of the School. It was the beginning of Holy Week, and everyone had been dismissed for the Easter vacation. The dancing halls were empty.

In the advanced ballet classroom Father paused in front of the mirror. He began humming a tune and casually traced a few dancing steps.

"Vatsa, yesterday you showed yourself to be an excellent classical dancer, and though you seem to know quite a lot about dancing, . . ." Father chuckled, "I want to show you some of *my own* dances and *pas*. Perhaps someday, who knows, they may be of some use to you."

I had not seen Father dance on the stage since the performance in Novaya Derevnia at the Arcadia Theatre in 1897. Now I watched spellbound, one dance after the other of a technical difficulty I had never seen before, and even to this day I cannot understand the mechanics of some of his dancing movements. It was impossible to tell the inception of a *pas* from its follow-up movement, given the force and speed of the dance he executed so effortlessly and with such clear-cut precision. There was no end to our amazement at the virtuosity displayed in the classical *pirouettes*, or the character turns, all at a whirlwind speed, crouched down close to the ground where, as he rotated faster and faster, the outlines of his body blurred until they disappeared like the blades of a rotating fan.

Father's jump, like Vaslav's, was enormous, and he too possessed that special gift, the ability to linger or hover in the air and then drop down at will, either softly and gently or as hard and fast as a stone. In a Russian dance, Father astonished us when he covered half the room in one leap—he started this huge jump from the right corner, diagonally across from where we were watching him. He landed in the middle of the room, in the crouched position of the *prissyatka*, then he glided onwards on the inside edge of the soles of his boots, as if on ice skates. We were startled to see him rushing towards us at an ever-increasing speed, which he controlled so that he pulled up short, barely missing, it seemed to us, the front of the piano bench where we were sitting.

Father then demonstrated with great virtuosity some *pas* from the *lezginka*, the dance that had made the name of Nijinsky famous in Tiflis and Baku many years ago, before we children were born. Mother had often told us how thrilled she had been to dance the *lezginka* with Father on the stages of the theatres of the Caucasus. She would recall their tremendous successes there and describe the many beautiful and valuable gifts, since lost to the pawnshop, that had been presented to them on the stage. But, she told us, their greatest reward had been the approbation and applause from the people of the Caucasus who had packed the theatres to see their native dances performed by the Polish dancers, the Nijinskys.

Father also showed us several other amazing *pas* seemingly impossible within the routine mechanics of dancing. Vaslav was genuinely surprised, but later after Father had left he said, "These dancing tricks are of no use to me . . . they bring dancing closer to acrobatics than to art."

While watching Father dance, I had noticed how some of his physical traits had passed to both Vaslav and me. Our legs and feet had the same strength and shape of musculature.

The next day, before leaving, Father went alone to visit Stassik in the sanatorium. The following Sunday was the Orthodox Easter, and Mama and I planned to go on that day when there would be lots of visitors. We did not want Stassik to be alone and feel that he had been forgotten. Vaslav also promised that he would come with us then.

Sometime during his short visit Father told me about a pantomime he had staged for the Benefit Show for the Firemen's Brigade in Kiev the previous year. The show had taken place in the Hippodrome Palace, and though it had been scheduled for only two performances the tickets had been sold out well in advance. It proved so successful that it was repeated eight more times.

The first part of the show featured equestrian numbers with all the horses trained by Pyotr Krutikov, who owned both the Hippodrome Palace and the Circus in Kiev, where Father also worked. The second part of the show was a demonstration of gymnastics and acrobatics by the firemen on their tall ladders, followed by a fire drill when the heavy equipment driven by a steam engine rolled around the arena.

The third part of the show was the pantomime staged by Foma Nijinsky. Father told me that while he was staging the pantomime and during each of the shows he would think about us, his children, and remember our pantomime in Vilno. "You, little Bronia, riding around the circus arena, dressed like a boy in your coach drawn by dogs and then frightened by the fire—you ran across the arena pulling by the hand a little girl dressed as a bride. You were sensational. In my pantomime I had a young child sitting in a baby carriage being pushed around the arena by a nurse dressed in a colorful Russian costume. Suddenly the baby, wearing only his diaper, jumped out of his carriage and ran across to join the firemen and help to put out the fire. He always got roars of laughter from the audience, but not as much as you did in Vilno.

"Do you remember," Father asked me, "Stassik dancing a Russian dance to the accompaniment of the accordion?" Father then told me how he had mounted that same Russian dance, Stassik's dance, for one of his pupils, a son of one of the clowns working in the Krutikov Circus. Father had used all his pupils in the Firemen's Show, many of them children of the circus artists. "I ended the show by having a small boy dressed in a fireman's outfit run across the arena and help put out the fire, just as Vaslav did in Vilno."

I was deeply touched by Father's story of his recent work in Kiev and realized that he did care for his children, and was missing us too and thinking about us when he was working with the children of the circus artists.

Soon Father heard the result of his audition—he was ecstatic to be offered a contract to dance in Briansky's Moscow production of *The Merry Widow*. After his departure for Moscow I cried for three days. Frequently Vaslav would say to me, "Stop crying! What are you crying for, Bronia? It's better that such a father is no longer with us." Mother left me alone with my crying, until at length she asked, "Bronia, why do you go on crying so long? . . ." I told her how I felt: "I am sorry that Father is not with us."

"Your Father himself wanted to live apart from his family, often forgetting about us completely." Mother spoke sadly, and I calmed down.

The school year finished at the end of May, and after all the examinations there was the official *Akt*, the annual prize-giving ceremony. The entire Administration of the School attended, also the Directorate of the Imperial Theatres and most of the parents. First were announced the names of those graduating from the School, then the different prizes and certificates were awarded. The Inspector made a speech of congratulation and advice for the future artists, and the priest bestowed his counsel and blessing.

Next came the list of promotions for each class in the School, both in general subjects and in dancing. When it was announced that Nijinsky was being promoted to Class V (the final class for Academic Subjects), it was also announced that his Charles Didelot Scholarship for his education was ending and that he would be transferred to the Government Account. Mama had begun to grow hard of hearing, especially when she was nervous, and simply heard that the Didelot Scholarship was coming to an end; she thought this meant that Vaslav would no longer be able to study in the School. It was only afterwards that Vaslav could explain to her that everything would remain as before.

In the Girls' Division for Class IV, it was announced that despite my excellent progress—I had already been in the advanced class for dancing for over a year—I was too young, only fifteen, to be transferred to the last Academic Class, Class V. And so I was left for a second year in Class IV. This meant that for the next year Vaslav and I would not be preparing the same lessons at home on weekends.

20   Summer: 1906

We spent the summer vacation of 1906 in St. Petersburg, staying in our apartment on Nikolaevskaya Ulitza. After so many months of living at the School, from morning to night under the vigilant eyes of the inspectors and teachers, the summer vacation seemed to Vaslav like an escape from a cage into the wide open space outside. He would disappear from the house for long walks all around St. Petersburg, walking on the boulevards along the banks of the Neva, crossing the bridges to the islands on the other shore. Enchanted with St. Petersburg he would return home tired, hungry, and happy. He liked to go on his own and would walk for two or three hours without stopping, then sit for a while on a granite bench beside the Neva or in one of the parks before setting off again, having forgotten all about his tiredness or the long walk home.

On one of his walks he noticed a pier on the Neva, a landing dock for a passenger boat that regularly traveled all along the Neva, across Lake Ladoga, along the Svir River, and into Lake Onega as far as Petrozavodsk before returning to St. Petersburg. He announced that he wanted to take that round trip on the boat and he had the money for it, since Father had given him twenty-five rubles. There were often storms on these large lakes, but this was Vaslav's dream—to be in a storm on a lake. The boat was small and did not look very reliable, but Vaslav assured Mama that it always remained near the shore between its many stops.

It was Vaslav's first journey by himself, and when he returned he was overjoyed at having sailed the huge expanse of water across the large lake, though he did admit that it could be dangerous. As they approached Petrozavodsk, Vaslav told us, a strong wind had come up and the boat had swayed from side to side a great deal. But he had not been seasick like the other passengers, and the swaying had not frightened him. Vaslav loved sailing, and after that he often took me with him on short trips along the

Neva as far as Novaya Derevnia. As we sailed along we admired the splendid landscapes of St. Petersburg and the shores of the Neva.

Our house on Nikolaevskaya Ulitza stood well back from the street with a garden behind a cast-iron railing. There were several tall shade trees and yellow-sanded paths and a few comfortable benches for the residents of the house, though the garden was always empty.

I had bought, with my savings, a croquet set with heavy mallets made of Karelian birch. Vaslav and I stamped out a smooth level playing area and played the game. For some time Vaslav always won, but eventually I acquired a skill like his and could pass through all the wickets and the "mousetrap." Then we lost interest in the game, until it was revived with the appearance in the garden of a student from my class, Antonina Tchumakova. Tonya had only recently joined my class, so at this time I knew her just slightly. She was a pretty girl, a brunette with big blue eyes framed by long black eyelashes. Though not very tall, she had a Ukrainian build, robust and sturdy. She had a reputation as a mischievous girl with bad grades in conduct. I knew that she was Vaslav's *simpatiya*, as special boy or girl friends were called in the School, and that he liked her very much for her splendid dancing. Tonya was the younger sister of the famous character dancer of the Imperial Ballet, Olga Tchumakova, for many years the common-law wife of Nikolai Legat. For this summer Tonya was staying with them in their apartment, which was also on Nikolaevskaya Ulitza.

Vaslav stopped going out for long walks on his own, and now strolled more often with me along Nikolaevskaya Ulitza, or we waited for Tonya in our garden. The three of us would play croquet together or wander up and down Nikolaevskaya Ulitza, talking about dancing, artists, and ballet. Vaslav was amused by Tonya's jokes and stories about the School; he was always cheerful with us.

I remember one day he bought a bag of red currants for five kopeks at a fruit stall. He offered a bunch to Tonya and me, and we opened our mouths wide and pulled the currants from their stems with our lips. Vaslav would make a face when he got back a bunch that was nearly all stems, hardly any fruit left at all. We laughed loudly whenever he drew from the bag a bunch that was so big we couldn't get all the berries in our mouths.

During the year Mama had been giving dancing lessons in our apartment, and she continued during our summer vacation, allowing us to watch them. She told us that since there were not enough dancers for the private theatres, girls who had never been to dancing school were employed to perform in the "ballets" of light operas and operettas. Their performances were more those of *figurantes* than of dancers.

There were two ballet masters, Lyuzinski and Zhabchinski, who had trained in the Warsaw Wielki Ballet and were former colleagues of both Mother and Father, and whenever they had problems in the Opera Theatres with their "self-taught dancers," as Mama called them, they would ask Mother to help them. Mother would say with indignation that to enter the "ballet" of the Opera Theatres it was only necessary to be young and attractive. Only rarely did one see actual dancing skills. However, in one troupe she did find some girls who really wanted to study dancing. Eight of them became her students, and she taught them by an accelerated method.

At the Imperial Theatrical School the only lessons in the Teaching of Dance were for Ballroom Dancing, and that was only taught in the last year before graduation from the School, so Vaslav and I were particularly interested in watching Mother's classes. She taught her students the basic classical ballet steps—*glissade, chassé, pas de basque, ballonné, pas de bourrée*. She then explained to us that these steps are the basis of all other nonclassical dances, whether character or ballroom dances. She soon taught her class to dance a polonaise, a polka, a waltz, a mazurka, a quadrille, a minuet, a galop, and Hungarian and Spanish dance steps. She also worked very hard on their grace—the movements of their hands, arms, and bodies, and how they walked. Within two years Mother's students were considered the "elite" of the ballet in light opera and musical comedies.

Another reason for Vaslav's interest in watching Mother's lessons was that he had already begun giving preparatory dancing lessons to the seven-year-old sister of Elena Sechenova-Ivanova. Vaslav had met Elena in the School, where she was a drama student. The boys of the advanced ballet classes were always invited to the drama students' classes for ballroom dancing, character dancing, movement, and fencing, to be an example to the male drama students, many of whom were rather stiff onstage.

In these classes with the drama students Vaslav was the regular partner of Sechenova-Ivanova, so I heard all about her from him: her beauty, her theatrical talent, her intelligence, her education, and her understanding of all the arts, especially ballet. She was indeed beautiful. Two years older than Vaslav, she was tall and slender, with ash-colored hair, very fine features, and big gray-blue eyes. She was both feminine and graceful, stately and aristocratic. She was also the very first admirer of the young Nijinsky. She had seen his dancing at the Student Performance of 1905 and been delighted with his unusual talent. Her father, a General, was the Supervisor of the Circuit Court in St. Petersburg. Their home, where

Vaslav used to go to give his lessons to her young sister, was a government apartment in the Circuit Court Building.

The second month of the vacation, Vaslav also began to give lessons in classical dancing. At the end of the School year, the mother of a student in my class had approached Vaslav and asked him to give her daughter, Lydia Alexandrovna Shiraeva, lessons to help her get her pink dress, the second-highest dancing award in the School. Vaslav agreed on the condition that his sister Bronia, who had already had her pink dress for a year and a half, attend the class and study with Lydia.

Though she did not display great ability in her dancing, Lydia Shiraeva did very well in academic subjects. She was a jolly girl who wrote short, clever, humorous verses about the students. She surprised us by her ability to choose appropriate rhymes for each student's characteristics and personality.

Before we began our lessons with Vaslav, I had to buy dancing shoes. Vaslav accompanied me to Lifshted, the supplier of dancing shoes to the School, and watched attentively as I tried on the dancing shoes made of coarse, gray unbleached linen, with hard soles and the semi-hard "box" toe that we wore to dance in the School. He took the shoe in his hand, looked it over inside and out, tried to bend the sole, and told me decisively that I must instead buy men's black soft leather shoes like the ones he himself wore.

It was impossible to convince Vaslav that one could not exercise on toe in men's soft ballet shoes. His answer was short: "As you wish. . . . I am not going to teach you to dance in these shoes that are as hard as boxes!" I had to submit. Only later did I understand that Vaslav was right and appreciate how great is the significance of dancing shoes in the quality of dance.

Our classes took place every day from eleven o'clock until one in the afternoon. The room in the Shiraeva apartment where we studied was on the first floor, so we did not have to worry about knocking plaster from the ceilings below on anyone's head and could jump freely. However, the room itself did not have a very high ceiling, and whenever Vaslav showed us *pas* with jumps he had to hold back on the height of the jump.

A great deal in Vaslav's lessons was new for us, especially preparation for jumps. In the School we took all the power for the jump from the knees, from the *demi-plié*, and only as we left the floor were the instep and foot stretched. Vaslav taught us to feel the floor not only with the foot but also with the toes, and then, simultaneously, the quickly stretched body and the power of the arch and the instep would throw the body upwards for the jump.

I made great progress and improved the quality of my elevation as

Vaslav, in his exercises for jumps, developed the elasticity and strength of my arch and instep. I no longer needed the hard inner sole of the toe shoes to keep my toes from bending over. I stood well on toe and by the end of the vacation I was able to turn two or three *pirouettes* and could do sixteen *fouettés sur pointe* in my soft men's shoes.

During our lessons I often felt that Vaslav picked on me, continuously making me repeat the same *pas* and giving me many more instructions, while with Shiraeva, who was not his sister, he was polite and patient and let her wear the same hard gray toe shoes that we wore in the School without saying anything about them.

I did not realize the progress I was making during those summer lessons with Vaslav until I returned to the School and saw the amazement of my teacher, Kulichevskaya. Then I understood and valued what Vaslav's lessons had done for me. Those two months of Vaslav's classes were full of dancing discoveries and were to lay the foundation for the development of my technique and dancing achievements. Within three months, before Christmas, I received the white dress—the School's highest award for dancing, usually not given before graduation year. For this year in Kulichevskaya's class, only two white dresses were awarded. The other girl to be so honored was my friend Frossia Georgievskaya.

Lydia Shiraeva's dream also came true when, at the very beginning of the school year, she received the pink dress.

For ballroom and character dancing lessons, the boy students would join us in the Girls' Division, and at the beginning of the year Vaslav always went up to his *simpatiya*, Tonya Tchumakova, for a partner in the pairs. His pleasure in dancing with Tchumakova did not last very long . . . after one unpleasant incident in the fall, he was no longer allowed to dance with her.

It happened just after the Catholic Instruction Class. A Catholic priest came to the School to teach Vaslav, Julia Pugni,* and me. We met for the class in the music room in the Girls' Division. At the end of the lesson the priest and Vaslav left the room. I was standing with Julia when Vaslav came back and quickly slipped a narrow envelope into my hand, saying, "It's for Tonya," and left the room again. I had no time to hide the envelope before the governess, Julia Popova, grabbed me by the arm and sternly demanded that I give her the letter. Then I realized the seriousness of infringing the rules of the Imperial Theatrical School. I got scared thinking what could happen to Vaslav and me. We were both

---

*Julia Pugni, a year younger than Bronislava, was also an accomplished student who took part in the Annual Student Performances of 1907 and 1908, but of whom there is little other record. She died in 1909, her graduation year. (IN/JR)

guilty of violating the strict rule prohibiting communications between the Girls' and the Boys' Divisions. I tried to tear up the envelope, but Julia Popova seized both my hands. "Give me that letter." I was still desperately trying to tear it up. She then added, "I promise not to read it, I will destroy the letter myself." As I continued to resist she swore that she would not even open the letter. Finally I had to give in. She put the envelope in her pocket and sharply ordered me back to my classroom. I was upset, not knowing whether I could believe her. We did not like Julia Popova, and had always distrusted her.

I was called to the office of the Inspectrice. She was sitting at her desk, and I could see that she had in her hand Vaslav's pink letter—open. I was asked where the meetings between Vaslav and Tchumakova had taken place, what they had talked about, and how they had behaved. My voice was trembling and I began to cry as I told about our summer meetings, our games of croquet, and that we three were always together, that Vaslav and Tonya were never alone. Then it was Tchumakova's turn to come in and face the questions, and her answers were the same as mine.

I never asked Vaslav what was written in the pink letter, but judging by the punishment, the contents were quite proper. Vaslav only got a severe reprimand from the Inspector and was forbidden to dance with Tchumakova in classes. This did not seem to sadden Tchumakova at all. At this time she was spending all her free time and weekends with her sister, Olga, and Nikolai Legat. She began to praise the teaching and artistic qualities of Legat and to criticize Fokine and the other artist-dancers, including Nijinsky. She graduated in 1908, at the same time I did. Though she surpassed everyone in the Maryinsky with her dancing mechanics on toe, her ballet career was quite short. She married Nikolai Legat in 1910, and after the birth of her child grew so stout that she had to leave dancing and she resigned from the Imperial Theatres.

Vaslav soon forgot about Tchumakova. It was enough for me to tell him that another girl student, Inna Neslukhovskaya, worshiped and adored him, for her to become his *simpatiya* for the rest of the school year. Inna came from a cultured and educated family. Her father was a military engineer, and her mother, who was very beautiful, was now remarried to an actor, Trukhanov, the director-producer of the Souvorinsky Theatre in St. Petersburg.

Inna Neslukhovskaya was also a graduating student like Vaslav and did well in her academic studies, and in the mime and character dance classes, but she was not very strong in classical dancing. Sometimes when she went home for the weekends, accompanied like all the girl students by her mother or a maid, Vaslav would wait for her and walk home with them.

21   1906–1907

FOR THIS YEAR, which was to be Vaslav's last in the School, Mama decided
to move into a smaller apartment, with only two rooms. This way she was
able to save twenty-five rubles a month, which she put aside for Vaslav's
graduation outfit. From the lessons he was giving, Vaslav was earning
quite a bit of money, and though he kept a fair amount for himself he gave
the rest to Mama to be saved for his "outfitting." Upon graduation he
would have to dress himself, "from head to toe" as they say, instead of
wearing the uniform provided by the School.

From the start of his graduation year, Vaslav seemed very grown-up;
both at home and in the School he acted as though he were already an
Artist. The company of adults began to attract him, and he spent a good
deal of time in discussions with one of the strictest teachers in the
School—Grigori Grigorievitch Isaenko. With Father's absence while
Vaslav was growing up, and no other male relatives at hand, Mama had
turned to this teacher, Isaenko, asking him to associate with Nijinsky and
pay attention to him, to be his mentor not only in the School but also
in the life awaiting Vaslav as a man. Vaslav began to frequent the
teacher's apartment and spoke about him as a truly inspiring teacher and
influence.

In the School Vaslav preferred the drama students, who were also older
than he was. He listened to stories about their studies, and their criticisms
of this or that play. Ever since he had been promoted to the Upper
Division in 1904, Vaslav had been moving away from his old friends. He
had told me that he was no longer interested in playing pranks or tricks.
Some of the older ballet students began to pick on him and laugh at his
new serious application to his studies. They taunted him, saying that he
already imagined himself an Artist, until finally he was forced into a big
fight to put an end to such treatment.

The jealousy of some of the students towards Nijinsky was enormous,
in proportion to their recognition of his talent. This atmosphere of

malicious envy poisoned Nijinsky's life in the School. Vaslav told me then and later that living in the School was repugnant to him. He hated the School and couldn't wait to finish it and leave forever.

"Only when I am dancing in the School or at the Maryinsky can I breathe . . ."

But most of the boys in Vaslav's class for his last year in the School were serious students. Two of them, Leonid Gontcharov and Andrei Khristapson, were preparing to enter the Conservatory of St. Petersburg, in the piano division, while Alexei Erler was planning to enter the Institute of Civil Engineering. All were excellent students, but none of them was interested in dancing.

The only other student in Vaslav's class who had dancing talent was Georgi Rosai, who later proved to be an excellent character dancer in several ballets by Fokine. Rosai's ambition was to be a classical dancer and to dance leading roles, and for a long time he had been considered the student with the most promising career before him. But in the 1905 Student Performance of Fokine's ballet *Acis and Galatea*, both Rosai and Nijinsky had danced their own solo in the "Dance of the Fauns" and Rosai had been jealous and resentful that only Vaslav had been mentioned in the press: "The most successful number in *Acis and Galatea* was 'The Fauns' in which a student, Nijinsky, distinguished himself." Rosai had also been disappointed that in the same Student Performance he had been given only one short semiclassical number, mounted by Fokine, a polka with Smirnova, whereas Vaslav, that same evening, had performed as a classical dancer in the ballet *The Parisian Market* and had also danced a classical *pas de trois* in the *Divertissement*.

In the Upper Division Rosai had continued to associate with Bourman and Babitch, even though they had been promoted to a higher class, and possibly it was they who encouraged his hostility towards Vaslav. I thought and hoped that now that both had graduated from the School and Rosai was on his own, he would not annoy Vaslav.

During the year I saw very little of Vaslav. On Saturday evenings and midday Sunday, he gave social dancing lessons to children. By the time he came home there would be only an hour or two before it was time for us to return to the School. Vaslav liked the lessons he gave, and the families where he taught were delighted with him.

During his visits to the Sechenova-Ivanova home in the Circuit Court Building he met a young twenty-two-year-old student from the St. Petersburg Conservatory, Boris Vladimirovitch Asafiev,* whose father

*Asafiev (1884–1949) became a leading Soviet composer. His own ballet scores include *Flames of Paris* and *The Fountain of Bakhchisarai*. His writings include two often-quoted essays on *The Sleeping Beauty* and *The Nutcracker*. (AK)

was also an official of the Circuit Court and had a government apartment in the Court Building. Asafiev had written a children's opera, *Cinderella*, and planned to produce it that year at Christmas with children of the employees of the Circuit Court and their acquaintances. He asked Vaslav to work with him both in staging and mounting the dancing for the children, and so Vaslav, still a student himself in the School, became a choreographer and staged the dances and the *mises en scène* for Asafiev's opera *Cinderella*.

The performances took place in the hall of the Circuit Court Building and were a great success. Unfortunately I was still in the School and could not see the program, but at home Vaslav animatedly recalled for me all his own rehearsals and classes, and laughingly called himself the ballet master. His leading pupil, the little sister of Sechenova-Ivanova, distinguished herself in *Cinderella*.

Every year just before Christmas all the government schools in St. Petersburg, including the Imperial Theatrical School, were taken to the Maryinsky Theatre to see a performance of the ballet *The Nutcracker*. Traditionally the roles of the Nutcracker and the King of the Mice were assigned to graduating students. That year Leni Gontcharov danced the role of the Nutcracker, and Vaslav danced the role of the King of the Mice.

Vaslav had worked out his role well, and he was splendid. He wore a gray cloak with red lining, and as he expertly flung it around himself the bright red accentuated the gray mouse costume and the crown on his mouse head. Majestically he commanded his army of mice as they attacked the forces of the Nutcracker. His magnificent gestures were obviously copying Chaliapin, while his steps and movements remained mouselike. The forces battled together fiercely until at last the King of the Mice was vanquished and died, wounded by the Nutcracker.

Everyone was delighted with Vaslav. All the artists onstage praised him during the intermission, saying they had never seen such an artistically perfect rendering of the King of the Mice. Vaslav was considered the best student in the School in fencing, and he told me later that he and Leni had practiced a lot together on their own, with Vaslav teaching Leni to fence and fight with the short swords.

Sometimes Vaslav took me with him to the Islands, to the home of the Englund family, where he gave lessons. The house was in Novaya Derevnia near Sestroretzk Station. It was like a villa, with three stories occupied entirely by the Englunds and their servants. There were two children—a daughter, Zina, who was in her last year of high school, and her younger brother, Kolya. Several of Zina's friends from school attended Vaslav's class in the Englund home. The Englunds were very hospitable people, and for every holiday—Christmas, Easter, birthdays, and name days—they would arrange parties with dancing and invite many young people. In addition to attending these parties, Vaslav and I often visited the Englunds when they did not have other guests. Then with Zina and Kolya we would entertain ourselves like little children, running around in their large home, up and down the stairs from floor to floor, chasing each other noisily. Zina and Vaslav became very close friends. They always danced together at parties, and sometimes Vaslav would sit at their grand piano and play something with bravura. Zina also played the piano well and would occasionally play with Vaslav.

The Englunds manufactured cosmetics that were well-known and highly successful in St. Petersburg. In the yard behind their home was the laboratory where they made creams, powders, soaps, and lotions. Vaslav and I were interested in the laboratory, and Zina's father showed us around. He explained how face creams and other cosmetics were made. I wrote down the recipes and tried to make them myself at home. I even bought a pestle and mortar to crush the rose petals for the cream.

We continued to visit the Englunds even after we had both graduated from the School. In the winter we would run in the snow and throw snowballs, or we would hire coachmen with good horses to ride on sleighs around the Islands. The Zimmerman brothers were also regular guests at the Englunds. They had a music store in St. Petersburg on Nevsky Prospekt. I remember its sign: THE BROTHERS YULI AND HENRY ZIMMERMAN. Vaslav had long been a regular customer. He had bought his expensive Italian mandolin from them, and that was where he always got new strings for his balalaika. Later Zina married one of the Zimmerman brothers, and she and I corresponded whenever I went abroad. She was always interested in Vaslav's successes and was happy for him. After the Russian Revolution, she and her husband left for Sweden and I lost contact with them.

After Christmas vacation, Vaslav was chosen to take part in a Charity Performance for the Society for the Prevention of Cruelty to Children, to take place on February 10, 1907. The event was organized by Victor Dandré, who was later to marry Anna Pavlova. Fokine was to mount *Eunice*, a ballet in two acts with music by Nikolai Scherbachev and a libretto taken from *Quo Vadis*, the Polish novel by Henryk Sienkiewicz.

I saw this ballet during the dress rehearsal when, as was the custom, the resident students were taken to the Maryinsky Theatre. The title role of the slave Eunice was danced by Kshessinska and included one dance that she performed around eight daggers thrust into the floor of the stage.

Pavlova was another slave, Akthea, and she performed a dance of the seven veils. Pavel Gerdt was a Roman patrician.

I did not like the sets, which were obviously borrowed from the Theatre's opera warehouse, nor did I care for the ballet itself, which was staged like an old ballet with many *mises en scène*, while much of the choreography was à la Duncan, in a pseudo-Greek style. I was disappointed, and during the intermission, despite my devotion to Fokine, I had to admit that I did not like *Eunice*. A "battle" ensued as I was attacked by Fokine's own students, all of whom admired the ballet. But to me *Eunice* lacked artistic taste; it was like the scenes pictured on the top of chocolate boxes.

At the very end of the ballet came the most effective scene, a dance of torches. The dancers suddenly came on carrying lighted torches and leaped across the stage, which soon filled with the smoke of the torches. The success of the dance was enormous, and Fokine received an ovation at the end of the ballet.

To follow *Eunice* Fokine had mounted *Chopiniana*, five short, independent scenes presented in the form of a *divertissement*.

While browsing in a music shop Fokine had come across a score, *The Chopiniana Suite*—an orchestration by A. G. Glazounov of four piano pieces by Frederic Chopin: "Polonaise," "Nocturne," "Mazurka," and "Tarantella." Since all four were essentially character dances, Fokine asked Glazounov to orchestrate an additional piece suitable for classical dancing. Glazounov agreed and included the "Valse" in his suite, and Fokine used it for the scene "Moonlight Vision."

The first scene, "A Ballroom in Warsaw," opened with a *polonaise* and was followed by a dramatic scene, "Nocturne," in which the ailing Chopin was magnificently portrayed by Alexei Bulgakov. (Bulgakov had graduated in 1889 from the Imperial Theatrical School, where like Vaslav he had received a Didelot Scholarship.) The composer was seated at the piano in a monastery, surrounded by visions of dead monks and muses in long flowing white gowns.

The two scenes with character dances were: "A Peasant Wedding in a Polish Village," with Julia Sedova as the bride dancing a *mazurka*; and the final scene, "A Square in Naples," with Vera Fokina and the ensemble, where Fokina danced the *tarantella* with fire—she had learned the authentic dance with Mikhail Fokine during their visit to Italy in 1905, following their wedding. Since then Vera had danced it often at home with Fokine playing for her on his mandolin.

But the memory that fills my mind is of Anna Pavlova as she danced in the scene "Moonlight Vision" with Mikhail Oboukhov. Her costume was designed by Léon Bakst after an 1840 lithograph of Marie Taglioni in the ballet *La Sylphide*. Oboukhov wore a black velvet costume with a white flowing bow at his neck, also designed by Bakst, though two years earlier for *The Fairy Doll*.

In the short scene Pavlova, light and ethereal, seemed to float in the air. When I left the Theatre, all I could see was the image of Anna Pavlova.

Immediately after the performance of *Eunice* and *Chopiniana*, Fokine started to prepare for the Annual Student Performance. He had already begun to work on a new ballet, *Le Pavillon d'Armide*, using music by a young Russian composer—Nikolai Nikolaevitch Tcherepnine, a pupil of Rimsky-Korsakov. For the Student Performance of 1907, Tcherepnine agreed to let Fokine mount one tableau from the new ballet under the title *L'Animation des Gobelins*.

Since there were not enough students in his own advanced class for this ballet, Fokine used several students from Kulichevskaya's class, and I was one of them. I was so thrilled to be working with Fokine, who had been my teacher in the Lower Division, and also to have the opportunity of seeing Vaslav working with Fokine. Vaslav had already told me that he liked dancing with my friend Zina Puyman, who had been promoted to Class V and was one of the strongest students in Fokine's graduating class. In the adagio class taught by Nikolai Legat I could see for myself that they looked well together, and I hoped that Zina would be chosen to dance a *pas de deux* with Vaslav in the Student Performance.

I remember how distressed I was to find out that because Zina had been absent from the School during February and March, and had missed many rehearsals, she had been dropped from participation in the Annual Student Performance. Her absence was due to a family illness. I can't remember whether it was her father or her mother who was critically ill and died that spring. By April Zina was back in the School, but she did not dance in the Student Performance. However, because of her good grades, and as she had taken all the required examinations, she was allowed to graduate that year, 1907.

Without Zina I was worried. Who would now dance with Vaslav in his graduation performance? It was important that he be able to show to advantage his skill in partnering. The *pas de deux* in the Student Performance was specifically designed to define the artistic capabilities of the graduating students for their future work in the ballet of the Maryinsky Theatre. I could not see among the other graduating students anyone who was outstanding in classical dancing, unlike the year before when Vaslav had partnered the graduating students Smirnova and Schollar, both of whom were now promising young Artists of the Imperial Theatres.

And indeed for his ballet, *L'Animation des Gobelins*, Fokine did not choose any of his graduating students for the role of Armida, but rather one of the day pupils of the School who was still a year away from graduation—Yelizaveta Gerdt. She was not a resident student, but being the daughter of Pavel Gerdt, she lived at home. She was in the same class as I for Academic Subjects, Class IV, and we also studied together in the pantomime and adagio class taught by Nikolai Legat. At home she was taught by her father, and in the School she had already received her white dress.

In our earlier rehearsals with Fokine, Yelizaveta had appeared to me a little too tall among the other students when dancing with us in the "Grand Pas d'Action" and the "Petit Galop," and I was concerned how she would look beside Vaslav in a *pas de deux*. But when I saw her dancing with Vaslav in the rehearsal, they looked well together. Yelizaveta had assimilated the noble style of her illustrious father.

For her new ballet *Salanga*, music by Peter Schenck, Kulichevskaya had chosen her graduating student Lydia Soboleva to dance the title role, and Vaslav was also to dance in this ballet as Prince Sing, the only principal male role. Rehearsals had begun sometime before, and all Kulichevskaya's graduating students were dancing important roles.

Frossia and I, though we both had our white dresses, were not given any solo in *Salanga*, as we were not graduating students. We were placed in front of the other dancers and given the responsibility of leading them, so we were in about half the scenes in the ballet. Several scenes included the entire ensemble of forty-seven girls and seven boys, six little boys—in their first year as students—and the graduating student, Nijinsky. At rehearsals Vaslav looked very elegant. He wore his new dancing trousers specially made for his graduation. They were fastened from his ankles over his calves with mother-of-pearl buttons. Each day he came in a freshly laundered shirt of fine Holland linen, and his dancing shoes always looked new.

As several of us danced in both ballets, we were constantly called for rehearsal with either Fokine or Kulichevskaya. The call often came in the afternoon in the middle of one of our academic classes. I enjoyed the rehearsals and did not mind missing classes, for I was repeating this year anyway in Class IV, but I felt sorry for some of the others who were in Class IV for the first time. We were given no extra time to study or prepare the next day's assignment.

Though rehearsals for *Salanga* and *L'Animation des Gobelins* were in progress, we were still waiting to hear about the *Divertissement*. Everyone wanted to have a place in the *Divertissement*, where in each number the attention of the audience would center on the individual dancers, thus giving them more notice than when appearing in a ballet. The *Divertissement* was mounted by Kulichevskaya and Fokine, and by Sergeyev as the teacher of the Stepanov System of Dance Notation, and all the solo numbers were given to the graduating students. It was not customary to distinguish advanced students before their graduation year, but four of us—Georgievskaya, Gerdt, Tchumakova, and I—hoped that our professors would choose us, as we had all received our white dresses, the highest distinction in dancing, a year earlier than usual, while some of the graduating students only had the second highest, the pink dress.

During the ten-minute break between academic classes, all the students gathered in the big dance hall while the classrooms were aired. The atmosphere was electric; maybe today would be the day that the program for the *Divertissement* would be announced.

The four of us were standing together when I told Tchumakova that I doubted that I would be chosen for the *Divertissement*; there were so many graduating students, I did not expect there would be a place for me. But the others reassured me saying that I was considered the best pupil in Sergeyev's Theory Class and that they were sure I would be used. But I still felt doubtful for I did not have the kind of "influence" the three of them had. Yelizaveta's father, Pavel Gerdt, held the rank of Soloist to His Imperial Majesty, the highest distinction for an Artist of the Imperial Theatres. Tonya had the protection of both her sister, Olga, and Nikolai Legat. And Frossia's elder sister, Zenaida Georgievskaya, was also an established Artist of the Imperial Theatres.

Just at that moment somebody came up behind me and hit me hard on the head. I heard the voice of one of my classmates, Maroussia Dobrolubova, "Don't lie. Don't pretend you don't know you have a place in the *Divertissement*."

I was dumbfounded. I had always been well-liked in the School and had never imagined I might have enemies. I had known Maroussia ever since we attended Cecchetti's classes before entering the Imperial Theatrical School. She was a pretty, quiet girl, and I never thought her capable of mean feelings. Maybe her mother had found out that Maroussia was not to be distinguished in the Student Performance, for unlike my mother she often came to the School to check how her daughter was progressing. Possibly, then, Maroussia was boiling inside with resentment to a point where she was unable to control her feelings, even though she must have known that she could be expelled for such behavior.

The governess on duty that day was Olga Andreevna Molass, and though she saw the incident, to the surprise of everyone Olga Andreevna did not intervene. Maroussia was her pet. The bell rang for us to return to our classrooms. Everything inside me was burning; I could not forget the incident; I could not concentrate on the lesson. I had been called a liar, and in front of all the students and the governess too.

At the next break the program was read out, and in fact I did receive a place in the *Divertissement*, in a *pas de quatre*. Sergeyev gave me a roll of paper with notations for the dance, which I had to read and then demonstrate to the other three students—Frossia Georgievskaya, Georgi Rosai, and Alexei Erler—before the first scheduled rehearsal.

But I did not experience any sense of happiness. I was sick with hurt. Possibly because of the Polish pride that was part of my ancestry, I was by nature oversensitive to insult, often to the point of injury.

Each evening the governess marked our grades for conduct in the journal. If a mark was not satisfactory—that is, below 10—then an explanation was also written in and the offending student was called to the desk of the governess. The following morning the Inspectrice would check the marks and then call the offender to her office.

But that evening though Maroussia was given a 6, no reason was written beside the grade, and the next morning the Inspectrice did not call her to account for her misbehavior, or make her apologize to me. As well as hurt, I was now angry, but to whom could I complain and pour out my indignation at this injustice?

During our day off at home, I told everything to Vaslav. He promised, "I will not let the matter rest. No one should dare offend you without cause!"

The discipline in the School was strict and specific. The Inspector and the Inspectrice of the Imperial Theatrical School were subject to the authority of the Director of the Imperial Theatres, but as far as we students were concerned they were our highest authority. And we were never allowed to speak to them, except in answer to their questions.

So, naturally, I could not imagine that Vaslav had gone to speak to the Inspector. As I learned later, the Inspector listened to his story and then explained that he could do nothing. The only jurisdiction he had over the Girls' Division was in the area of General and Academic Studies. It was the Inspectrice who, through the governesses, was solely responsible for conduct in the Girls' Division.

Suddenly I heard that Vaslav, a student, without considering the personal consequences, had gone to the Office of the Directorate of the Imperial Theatres and asked to see Telyakovsky himself. Normally the Directorate was entirely out of the reach of the students. We only saw them at our examinations and the Annual Student Performances. Probably, though, it was through Inspector Missovsky that Vaslav got an interview with the Director. Indignantly Vaslav told Telyakovsky what had happened to his sister and demanded that Dobrolubova apologize in the presence of the whole School, and that there be some punishment.

The next day all the students were called into the rehearsal hall and the Inspectrice asked Dobrolubova and me to approach her. She reprimanded Dobrolubova and told her to apologize to me.

Then an unheard-of thing happened. The Inspectrice began to talk to me, excusing herself in front of the whole School and asking, "Why did your brother not come to me instead of going with a complaint to the Director? I did not know anything about this."

"How is that possible?"

"Nobody told me anything."

"But you saw the mark in the journal."

"For that mark she was deprived of home leave."

But I persisted with my questions. "Why was there no explanation next to the mark? Why was she not called to your office for a reprimand?"

"For misbehavior calling for that, Dobrolubova should have been expelled. Do you want that?"

"No, I do not want her to be expelled, but no one should dare call me a liar." And firmly I added, "I could not bear it that you, Varvara Ivanovna, let the matter go without consequence and accepted Dobrolubova's statement as fact. I always tell the truth."

That's about all I said, but I remember well the effect of my words on the students, and how Vaslav became a hero to the whole School through his courageous defense of his sister. I noticed particularly the warm regard which Neslukhovskaya directed towards Vaslav. Later in rehearsals all the girls told me how much they admired Vaslav.

The Annual Student Performance was now quite near, and so we had extra rehearsals for the *Divertissement*. My partner for the *pas de quatre* was the graduating student Georgi Rosai, and Frossia's was another graduating student, Alexei Erler. For our rehearsals the boys wore regular practice clothes, white shirts, and black pants narrow at the ankles. Frossia and I wore our white dresses with their knee-length full tulle skirts. My partner Rosai often came late, having been detained at another rehearsal. And if we ever asked him to stay and go over the *pas de quatre* with us at the end of our rehearsals with Fokine, he would be unwilling, claiming that he was very tired.

"Danse des Bouffons," which Fokine had mounted for Rosai and six other boys, was a very difficult dance, and Fokine called many extra rehearsals. Rosai said it was the most difficult dance he had ever seen. "There is one *pas* where I have to jump very high holding both legs bent under me and then land on one knee. Fokine sometimes makes me repeat this *pas* over and over again."

Rosai felt that Mikhail Mikhailovitch was merciless almost to the point of cruelty in his demands from the boys for perfection in the execution of the individual *pas*.

"We have to learn to jump straight up, cross both legs under in the air, and come down in this sitting position, to the floor—*à la turque*."

I had seen that dance at the rehearsals and there were many complicated *pas*, all done at very fast tempo. After the dance the boys would be all out of breath. Rosai was enthusiastic about his rehearsals with Fokine, but when the time came for our rehearsals he was dull and bored. Once he said to me, "I don't understand why they had to put me in a classical *pas de quatre*. I thought the teachers had long ago decided that your brother, Nijinsky, was to be a classical dancer while, I, Rosai, was to be a character dancer."

Rosai also resented having to dance a classical *pas de quatre* between his two other dances, for the classical dance used quite different muscles from those in the two character dances he was performing. He also felt that the *pas de quatre* was not as important for his career as the Hungarian Dance, which he was to dance with Neslukhovskaya only two numbers after our classical dance in the *Divertissement*. Consequently he did not put his full effort into our rehearsals; often he would only mark the steps.

I also thought that he, a graduating student, resented the fact that Frossia and I were only advanced students, whereas Lydia Soboleva and Maria Leontieva, Vaslav's partners in the *pas de trois*, also mounted by Sergeyev, were both graduating students. The *pas de trois* was the next number in the program after our *pas de quatre*.

The day of the Annual Student Performance came: April 15, 1907.

We were expecting Father again, but he was late and missed the reception. He arrived only just in time for the evening performance, explaining that his train had been delayed.

The first ballet was *Salanga*, described in the program as "A Fantastic Ballet," in one act, to the music of Peter Schenck and choreographed by Klavdia Kulichevskaya. Even though I was dancing in it, this ballet did not impress itself on my memory, neither the libretto nor the choreography. Nor did I care for the music, which seemed to me to be unsuitable for ballet. In *Salanga* Vaslav danced the leading male role, Prince Sing, partnering the graduating student Lydia Soboleva, in addition to his own *variation* from the ballet *Bluebeard*, also by Peter Schenck.

The second ballet was *L'Animation des Gobelins*, a tableau from *Le Pavillon d'Armide*, music by Nikolai Tcherepnine and choreography by

Mikhail Fokine. Again Vaslav had the leading role, Le Marquis, and danced a short *pas de deux* in the "Grand Pas d'Action" with Yelizaveta Gerdt, who had the role of Armide. I liked Tcherepnine's music from his suite for the ballet, *Le Pavillon d'Armide;* it was both melodic and original.

For this Student Performance there was no special scenery. Black drapes served as the wings and the backdrop was a light blue sky. Deep at the back, across the full width of the stage, was a large wide platform about three to four feet high, covered at the front with black linen. This long black strip stood out unpleasantly, forming an unattractive background to the stage and cutting off the figures of the dancers. The costumes were all provided from the Theatre's wardrobe.

All the *variations* were effective and proved a success with the audience. Tchumakova distinguished herself in her virtuoso *variation sur pointe,* which was full of playful sparkle. Even more effective was the "Danse des Bouffons." Rosai was an immediate success with the difficult character *pas,* as he had expected. For Nijinsky, Fokine mounted a new rendering of the classical ballet *pas, changement de pieds.*

Nijinsky surprised everyone when, after jumping straight up in the air from fifth position, he did not return to the same spot but instead leaped sideways across the stage. Immediately he repeated this amazing sideways *changement de pieds* that had never been executed in this manner before, jumping from side to side several times. With each *pas* he covered a wider span of the stage until with his fourth and last jump he flew more than fifteen feet.

The audience was amazed by this new rendering of an old classical *pas,* appreciating such a sportive display of distance jumping. But I was more surprised by the *préparation,* which was not the customary *glissade* or *pas couru* [the gliding or running steps that usually impart force to any wide leap]. For his sideways *changement de pieds,* Nijinsky used a *demi-pointe préparation.*

After *L'Animation des Gobelins* came the *Divertissement,* in which Frossia and I danced the *pas de quatre* with Rosai and Erler. We were well applauded but I was disappointed in our *pas de quatre,* feeling that Rosai had been saving himself for his Hungarian dance with Inna Neslukhovskaya.

That evening after the performance, Father joined us at home for supper and complimented me, but again he did not have much to say about Vaslav's performance. He simply commented, "They showed you in the program as a jumper, but you must work to become a dancer."

Vaslav told us that the *variation* he had danced in *Salanga* was originally mounted for Pavel Gerdt by Petipa in his ballet *Bluebeard,* first performed in the Maryinsky Theatre on December 8, 1896, on the occasion of Maestro Petipa's fiftieth anniversary of his work with the Imperial Theatres. Vaslav also told us that the music for both *Salanga* and *Bluebeard* was written by the same composer, Peter Schenck, who had begun composing as early as the age of seven, when he was admitted to the St. Petersburg Conservatory.

Father commented on the coincidence that he himself had also staged a pantomime ballet—in an Opera Bouffe, *Barbe Bleue*, music by Offenbach —which was performed in St. Petersburg in August of 1896, at the Zoological Gardens' Theatre. I wanted to ask Father more about his ballet but hesitated as Mother looked so sad. Then she remarked, "Yes, that was the summer I remained with the children at my sisters' in Vilno and you went alone to St. Petersburg. I have always been sorry that I never saw your performances in the Zoological Gardens' Theatre. . . . We rejoined you later in the fall, in Moscow."

I remembered then that Mother had not worked with Father in Moscow either, and that immediately afterwards had come the sad days at Novaya Derevnia. Vaslav must have shared my thoughts, for he too did not ask Father about his work in St. Petersburg or *Barbe Bleue*.

Later that evening I noticed again how many of Father's physical traits Vaslav and I had inherited. With our hands side by side on the table it was uncanny to see how alike they were. Our hands were the same shape, the little fingers had the same curve inward, and our nails were the same elongated almond shape. In movement, also, the expression of our hands and our gestures were identical.

Vaslav had also inherited Father's dark complexion, dark hair, and hazel eyes, and his long dark eyelashes. My features were like Father's, too, though I was blonde and had green eyes like Mother, while Vaslav's fine features, particularly his small head, were like Mother's. Vaslav and I had inherited our long necks from both our parents, which had caused us both to be called "long-neck" in the School.

The next day Mother and Father went together to see Stassik in the sanatorium and to obtain from the doctor there some signed document or letter that they could submit with a petition of dispensation from military service for Stassik, who would be twenty-one on his next birthday. Afterwards Father returned with Mother to have tea with us. As they came in Father was humming a lively, catchy, tune. I asked him what it was, and immediately Mother answered, "It's from *Belle Hélène* . . ." But Father interrupted her, "You're half right, Liota. It is by Offenbach, but it's not *Belle Hélène*, so familiar to you from our work in the Odessa Opera Theatre. It's from *Barbe Bleue*."

I asked Mother about this later and she told me that operettas by Offenbach were popular in all the Summer Theatres where she and Father had worked, as well as in Odessa. Most of the more than one hundred operettas were short one-act pieces for a cast of four to five actors and had been written by Jacques Offenbach for his own theatre in Paris, Bouffes Parisiens. Many had then become popular in Europe, America, and Russia.

Before leaving St. Petersburg Father gave Vaslav one hundred rubles. This made us very happy, since now it would be possible to make plans for the summer and order the rest of Vaslav's equipment in time for his graduation. Vaslav and Mama, whenever Vaslav was home on a Saturday or Sunday, had already made up a list of what he would need, both for his graduation and as an artist. Vaslav's first concern was not his everyday clothing but for his dancing clothes. He wanted everything ordered early enough so as to be sure that on the very day of his graduation he would be ready to start his work as an artist. With some of the money saved from his dancing lessons he already had his dancing clothes, and had in fact begun to wear them at the School in the rehearsals for the Student Performance. Mama had bought some fine Holland linen and had had his dancing shirts sewn by a seamstress. Vaslav had ordered three pairs of black dancing pants.

On our days off from the School we had gone to various stores and had looked over shirts, ties, hats, and gloves and had found out the price of everything. Vaslav loved good and elegant things. He preferred the shop on Nevsky Prospekt called The Jockey Club, where the clothes all came from London. Though they were expensive, Mama did not object as she herself had taught us that it was important for an artist to be well dressed.

Already in the School Vaslav had become very conscious of how he was outfitted, and he dressed impeccably. He had given his School uniform to a tailor to alter for a better fit. He wore his own boots, of fine kid leather, and his own white, well-starched collars and cuffs under his jacket. Every day all his clothes were freshly brushed, and on Saturdays they were well pressed by a servant in the School, who also polished Vaslav's boots daily. Naturally Vaslav gave him an extra tip for this.

We knew that on graduation each student was to be given one hundred rubles for outfitting, and Mama and Vaslav had been waiting for that to order a summer suit, coat, hat, and shoes. Father's gift meant that these clothes could be ordered now and be ready for the summer. When Vaslav and Mama went to choose the material for his first grown-up outfit, Vaslav asked me to go too because he trusted my taste. We ordered a light beige summer suit that would be appropriate for the summer season at Krasnoe

Selo. My teacher, Kulichevskaya, had already promised Vaslav that he would dance there that summer, and Vaslav was hoping that the extra money he would earn there would go towards his autumn and winter outfits. He had learned that the Artists of the Imperial Theatres had their own tailor who fortunately allowed the Artists to pay over several months.

After the Student Performance there were final examinations, and then graduation day. The graduation ceremony, the *Akt*, was very formal. Behind a long table, placed beneath the portrait of the Tsar, sat the Director of the Imperial Theatres, Vladimir A. Telyakovsky, the members of the Administration of the Imperial Theatrical School, the Inspector, the Inspectrice, and our professors.

The graduation awards in the Ballet Division of the Imperial Theatrical School were not given for dancing alone but were also based on success in academic subjects and on conduct marks. Though Nijinsky in Dancing, Art, and Music had the highest possible grade, a 12, his overall average grade was 11, and so he was second in the graduating class. He received his diploma, the New Testament in Polish, and the complete works of L. N. Tolstoy, also the one hundred rubles given to each graduating student; and then to his joy Vaslav received an additional one hundred rubles from his Didelot Scholarship.

At the end of the ceremony the young men and women, no longer students, left the School, and in their elegant graduation outfits got into the waiting cabs to be driven around St. Petersburg to show themselves off before returning home to a gathering of friends and a celebratory meal, which in our small, two-room apartment got rather crowded.

Vaslav was filled with joy and feeling magnificent. He submitted his application to the Imperial Theatres and on May 25, 1907, he was accepted as an Artist of the Imperial Theatres, as a *coryphé*, one rank below soloist, at a salary of seven hundred and eighty rubles a year.*

---

*The usual starting salary, for the *corps de ballet*, was six hundred rubles a year. (in/jr)

22 Summer: 1907

WITH VASLAV engaged to dance at Krasnoe Selo this summer, he and Mama decided to give up our small apartment in St. Petersburg and to go again, as we had two summers before, to Dudergoth, which was only two miles away from Krasnoe Selo. We rented a dacha with three large rooms and a kitchen, and so were able to take most of our furniture from the apartment and some of our books. Mama hung sheer curtains everywhere and put flowers in vases in the living room. In Vaslav's room she put down a carpet on the bare floor. She made everything pleasant and comfortable.

Our dacha was on top of a hill overlooking Dudergoth. A narrow winding path led down to an unpaved road that went alongside the railroad tracks to Dudergoth Station. Every morning Vaslav would go either to St. Petersburg or to Krasnoe Selo, and as I sat finishing my breakfast by the window I could see him running down the hill, then walking briskly to the station. Whenever it was rainy and the road became muddy, he walked carefully on the rails so as to keep his shoes out of the mud. If he was late or afraid that he might miss the train, he would jump from one railroad tie to the next with great agility and ease. I often watched him until he disappeared from view.

Vaslav was going to St. Petersburg three mornings a week to attend the ballet classes for Artists in the rehearsal hall of the Imperial Theatrical School. The classes were taught by leading dancers of the Imperial Theatres; that year I believe they were taught by Nikolai Legat. From St. Petersburg Vaslav would go directly to Krasnoe Selo for the afternoon rehearsal and stay there for the evening performance. Other days he went to Krasnoe Selo first thing in the morning to practice on his own, and usually he remained there all day.

The small theatre at Krasnoe Selo was under the jurisdiction of the Imperial Theatres, and the stage, though not large, was adequate for a ballet performance by a small troupe of dancers. The auditorium consisted simply of a *parterre* with a few semicircular loges at the side. The audience was drawn mainly from the elite community of Krasnoe Selo, the officers of the Imperial Guards, who had come for the summer maneuvers, and their families. Tsar Nicholas was often present at these maneuvers and would come to the theatre in Krasnoe Selo. Several titled families and some of the balletomanes and critics from St. Petersburg also attended the performances.

Vaslav was dancing at Krasnoe Selo with Julia Sedova, a *première danseuse* who had danced leading roles in the Imperial Ballet both in Moscow and in St. Petersburg since her graduation in 1903. She had an exceptional classical ballet technique, with great elevation, but to my mind she was not very feminine in appearance, and she was too tall for Vaslav. From Vaslav, however, I heard that they had a great success with the Krasnoe Selo audiences. Vaslav, too, enjoyed his own personal success, and many admirers would invite him to supper after the performances—to the Pavillion Restaurant, next to the theatre. The food was prepared by one of the best chefs in St. Petersburg and everyone would gather there—the officers, the critics, the balletomanes, the artists, and the performers. Sometimes Vaslav would dine with Julia Sedova and her husband, Schedlovsky, who was a ballet critic for a small St. Petersburg newspaper. His reviews of the Krasnoe Selo season, signed Vidi, were always favorable and praised the artistic qualities of Sedova and her partner, Nijinsky.

One day when Vaslav had gone to St. Petersburg for a rehearsal, suddenly, without having been invited, Anatole Bourman arrived at our dacha. He expressed a wish to wait for Vaslav and to spend a few days with us. Mama and I were surprised; we were not accustomed to having my or Vaslav's friends from the School come to visit our home. We wondered why Bourman, also an Artist of the Imperial Theatres, had come to Dudergoth on his own and had not tried to meet Vaslav in St. Petersburg.

In his early years in the School Vaslav had sometimes gone to Bourman's house—but not to visit, only to play ball in the courtyard. Then, once they were no longer in the same class, Vaslav did not consider Bourman one of his friends. Recently, however, he had taken up with him again, and had asked him to play the piano for the dancing lessons he gave. But this was only occasionally when either of his regular accompanists, Leni Gontcharov on the piano or Kolya Issaev on the violin, was not available.

Bourman stayed a whole week, sharing Vaslav's room. He accompanied

Vaslav everywhere, trying to establish new contacts for himself among Vaslav's admirers in Krasnoe Selo. Mama did not like Bourman. She felt he could be a bad influence for Vaslav, for he liked to frequent fast company in restaurants and nightclubs. He was also a gambler, especially in card games. Mother considered card games a vice, and they were taboo in our home.

At last Bourman left, and Mama sighed with relief. Vaslav too. He had been bored with Bourman; they had nothing in common. Vaslav did not like Bourman's behavior in the ballet company, where he was always borrowing money to cover his gambling and card game losses, or to pay for extravagant restaurants that he could not afford on his salary of fifty rubles a month.*

During that summer, his first as an Artist, Vaslav did not seem very exuberant or excited, and Mama became worried that he was tiring from his daily journey to St. Petersburg and Krasnoe Selo. What Vaslav told me was that he was unhappy among the flashy officer set surrounding the Artists. More than that, he was disappointed with the season at Krasnoe Selo and getting no joy or pleasure from the performances, which he felt were only aimed to please the royal entourage and the officers of the Imperial Guards.

"At the beginning of the program Kulichevskaya puts on one of her own ballets, the ones we know from the Student Performances. Fortunately this year's ballet, *Salanga*, which I don't care to dance, was a failure, and so we don't do it very often. Then the last part of the program is the *Divertissement*, made up of comedy numbers and character dances. There is a polka from *The Parisian Market*, you remember, where the coquettish grisette hiding behind her parasol is flirting as she dances with an amorous student. Or there are sentimental waltzes and gypsy and Hungarian dances, and in the middle of these comes my *pas de deux* with Sedova.

"Not even the presentation is artistic. The sets and costumes are chosen at random from different ballets; it is a far cry from what we are accustomed to at the Maryinsky. Even when the best Artists of the Imperial Theatres take part, it still gives one the impression of an amateur performance. There is one good thing though: I get to dance many *pas de deux*, which will help me for my debut on the stage of the Maryinsky. But it's too bad that performances such as these are pleasing to the public; it's an insult to the art of ballet!"

Those evenings when Vaslav was late returning from Krasnoe Selo,

---

*This account suggests a motive for Bourman's appearance and contradicts the version in his book that he spent an entire and happy summer as part of the Nijinsky family. (AK)

Mama and I would feel quite frightened alone in the dacha, being surrounded by military camps and having heard of several robberies committed by the soldiers. However, all was calm for us until the last few days before the end of the summer maneuvers. Then, as the soldiers began to leave their billets and camps, they would wander past the dachas singing lewd songs, pilfering from sheds, and stealing laundry hanging out in the gardens. One evening as I was sitting in Vaslav's room, on the floor beside the bookcase, picking out something to read, a bullet whistled through the window and lodged in the wall, just above the bookcase and my head. Some soldiers had raided a wine cellar and one of the drunken men was going around shooting at lighted windows.

The season at Krasnoe Selo had finished by then, and we began packing our things ready to move back to St. Petersburg so that Vaslav would not have to travel there every day for rehearsals and classes. For his performances at the Krasnoselsky Theatre that summer he received a special distinction, a gift from the Tsar: a gold watch with the Imperial Eagle on the cover. He had also earned two hundred fifty rubles for the season and, with his salary of sixty-five rubles a month as an Artist of the Imperial Theatres, which had been paid since June, Vaslav was able to give Mama some money towards a new apartment in St. Petersburg.

During the summer we had not received any money from Father, though he had sent us several letters and was pressing an invitation for Vaslav to visit him in Nijni Novgorod. Vaslav was reluctant but Mother insisted: "Your father will be hurt and disappointed if you do not go. He is very proud of you and wants to introduce you to his colleagues, and he hopes you will dance for them now that you are an Artist of the Imperial Theatres."

I did not like the idea of Vaslav making such a visit to Nijni Novgorod, anticipating trouble if he should happen to meet Rumiantseva, Father's partner and the woman with whom he was living. I thought it would be better if Vaslav wrote Father a good long letter. Vaslav agreed with me that a letter would suffice and tried to convince Mother. But she still insisted, saying that while he could refuse to make the acquaintance of that woman he should not refuse his father, and that besides Father had come to St. Petersburg for Vaslav's Student Performance.

We decided that Mama and I should move back to St. Petersburg and get the new apartment ready while Vaslav went to Nijni Novgorod to visit Father. I wrote a long letter to Father for Vaslav to take with him. He left planning to stay for a week, but actually he only stayed in Nijni Novgorod for one day.

He came back very upset and told us he had quarreled with Father and had broken with him forever.

Mama wanted to know every detail and made Vaslav repeat over and over again every word he had exchanged with Father.

When he had arrived in Nijni Novgorod he found that Father had reserved a room for him in his own hotel. Vaslav preferred not to stay in the same hotel, and so he went to another and invited Father to join him there for dinner. At the table Father ordered some wine, saying, "We will have dinner later. First I want to talk with you. You are no longer a child; now you are a man; you should understand something. I have been living with my partner, Rumiantseva, for many years now, and I have asked her to come and join us for dinner so that you can meet her . . ."

Vaslav was startled and made as if to leave the table, exclaiming, "I have no wish to meet this odious and immoral woman who was the cause of such deep sorrow for Mother and for us children, stealing our father away from his family, his wife and three small children . . ."

Father broke in, "You are insulting me. A son should not speak this way to his father."

Father was angry but Vaslav was angry too; he told us how he answered: "A father should not introduce his mistress to his son. If I sat at the same table with her, how could I ever look my mother in the face again?"

Hoping to calm Vaslav, Father began to compliment him on his appearance and his elegant outfit. But Vaslav was not to be deterred. "The matter is not that I am standing before you wearing an elegant outfit that you helped me buy. The matter is that for all the years when we never saw you, Father, my dear Mother was sacrificing herself for me. Alone, Mother took care of us children and brought us up. She gave me my education so that I could become an Artist . . ."

Nothing could stop Vaslav now. He poured out all the anger that had accumulated in his heart over the years, telling Father how many anxious moments Mama had faced when she could not pay the rent or the local shopkeepers while he, Father, was earning good money and living with his mistress and forgetting about us. How many times Mama would scrimp on food for herself during the week so that on Saturdays and Sundays she could serve a good meal to her children. How many times when there was no money to buy food Mama would sell what she could from the household, or even her own clothes . . .

Angrily Father interrupted again, "That's enough. I don't want to hear any more . . ."

Just at that moment Vaslav noticed an elegantly dressed woman approaching their table. With a start he leaped to his feet and, without saying another word to Father, walked out of the restaurant. That same evening he left Nijni Novgorod.

After that neither Vaslav nor I ever saw Father again. He stopped writing to us. He sent no money at all, not even for my graduation.

Later Vaslav told me more of his last conversation with Father, something he had kept from Mother. Father had told him that there was a child, and that he also loved his second family. According to Vaslav, Mother knew about the child but did not believe it was Father's. He remembered hearing conversations between Mother and Father in Novaya Derevnia, that awful nightmarish summer when in my sickness I too heard unhappy, angry voices. Vaslav remembered Mama telling Father, "She says that you are the father. How can you believe that woman? Everyone knows her reputation and her many lovers in Moscow . . ."

But no matter how much Mother wanted to know every word exchanged between father and son in Nijni Novgorod, Vaslav never mentioned to her what was said about the child, or the child's name: Marina.

I was so distressed at what Vaslav told me about Father that I could not ask him what happened to my own letter that he had taken with him to Nijni Novgorod. I think Vaslav in his anger must have forgotten all about it or destroyed it.

23   Nijinsky: Artist of the Imperial Theatres

THE NEW APARTMENT that Vaslav and Mama found for us in St. Petersburg was on Torgovaya Ulitza. It was a three-room apartment on the third floor. I was worried that this would mean a lot of stairs for Mama to climb, but Vaslav proudly told me that they had chosen an apartment in a newly built house that had an elevator.

In the very small apartment that Mama had taken the year before, Vaslav had had to sleep in the living room whenever he came home from the School, but now that he was living at home all the time he had a room of his own. It was quite a small room, but he arranged it very well. He placed his desk under the only window, with one of our black lacquered bookcases on one side and, on the other, the wardrobe with a mirrored door, where he kept his new outfits as an Artist of the Imperial Theatres. His bed was along the wall facing the window, leaving just enough room for a chest of drawers and a washstand.

Vaslav loved to walk through the streets of St. Petersburg and had been very happy to find an apartment that was within easy walking distance of the Maryinsky Theatre. This would mean he could walk to the Theatre and stand in the wings to watch the ballets and the operas even when he was not participating in a performance. The walk to Teatralnaya Ulitza, where he would have to go every day for both the morning *classe de perfection* for the Artists, and also for rehearsals, was quite a long one, but it was only a short walk to Sadovaya Ulitza where he could catch a streetcar to take him quite near to Teatralnaya Ulitza.

In all our time living in St. Petersburg, Vaslav had never been able to get used to the cold, damp weather and had often caught colds. Though he loved to walk to the Maryinsky, he was not accustomed to having to walk there in bad weather, for as students in the School we had always been taken in special carriages. Mama was continually concerned during the fall and winter that Vaslav be dressed warmly and that he always wear his galoshes. Vaslav couldn't stand galoshes and was forever leaving them someplace.

On wet days she did not like Vaslav to walk to the Theatre and would persuade him to take a cab. But this ate into his budget so that at the end of the month he would have to borrow from Mama. Now that Father was no longer sending us money, we had only Vaslav's earnings to live on. In addition to his salary of sixty-five rubles from the Imperial Theatres he was also getting about a hundred rubles from the classes he was teaching. However, his expenses as an Artist were considerable, and so he and Mama both balanced their budgets carefully.

The season of ballet and opera in the Maryinsky Theatre began this September with the opera, *A Life for the Tsar*. The ballet performances were given on Sundays and sometimes on Wednesdays. Nijinsky's debut as an Artist of the Imperial Theatres came in *La Source*, the first ballet performance of the season.

La Source was an old ballet in three acts and four tableaux by Saint-Léon, to music by Minkus and Delibes. It had been remounted in 1902 by Achille Coppini in an attempt to produce a ballet that was different from the style of Petipa. There were thirty-three dance numbers in the ballet, and many students were used, as well as the whole ballet company. Throughout the performance the *corps de ballet* marched from one end of the stage to the other, in perfect alignment, performing all kinds of gymnastics.

Coppini had staged spectaculars for the Zoological Gardens' Theatre, and though *La Source* would have been more appropriate for such an outdoor theatre, rather than in the Maryinsky, nevertheless I was happy to be chosen to participate in the last act where I would be able to watch Vaslav's debut—a *pas de deux* with Julia Sedova, "Jeux des Papillons." It had been mounted for them by Kulichevskaya, to music by Waldteufel, during the season at Krasnoe Selo, and was now inserted into the last act of *La Source*.

For us students there was not a single dancing step; all we had to do was come onstage each carrying a stool. We placed the stools behind the *corps de ballet* and then, standing on the stools, would assume poses to complement theirs.

During the rehearsals of the last act, when the whole company was onstage, Nijinsky and Sedova would only mark their *pas de deux*. As I watched I became worried about this debut for Vaslav; I did not think it would be a very promising beginning for his career as an Artist of the Imperial Theatres. Sedova, as she stood on toe, was half a head taller than

Vaslav. She also seemed too broad in the shoulders beside him. I was concerned: How would they look together when Vaslav lifted her?

To my surprise when they came out for the performance they looked good together. When Sedova jumped for Vaslav to catch her in a "fish" pose, he caught her low and effortlessly. Then I understood how well Sedova and Nijinsky had become adjusted to each other during the season at Krasnoe Selo.

Later Vaslav told me that he found Sedova lighter to lift than many other smaller dancers who did not use their bodies correctly, in harmony with the beat of the music. Some dancers "sat" during lifts, and that made them heavier for their partners, but Sedova was as straight as an arrow and resounded like the string of a violin.

Though Vaslav had a great personal success, he would have preferred to have made his debut in a more advantageous *pas de deux*. Still, the first month of his work at the Maryinsky was most auspicious. He was soon chosen to dance two other *pas de deux*. In mid-September he danced with Lydia Kyaksht, "Andante Religioso," to music by François Tome, mounted by Nikolai Legat and inserted in the ballet *Paquita*. A week later his partner was Elena Smirnova, with whom he had danced so well in the Student Performances of 1905 and 1906; they danced a *pas de deux* in the last act of *La Fille Mal Gardée*.

In an apartment on the same floor as ours lived a ballet artist, Anna Domershikova. Mother was surprised to notice Vaslav going to visit our neighbor and taking flowers, boxes of chocolates, and French pastries. I became curious too when I came home for the weekend and saw that each of his visits was lasting longer than the one before. I learned from Vaslav that the real attraction was not Domershikova but her very close friend, the beautiful Maria Gorshkova. During the summer Gorshkova also had been dancing at Krasnoe Selo, and she and Vaslav had met there often. Vaslav had known Maria since 1905, the year she had graduated, when he had danced with her in the Annual Student Performance.

Gorshkova was two years older than Vaslav, and her ambition was to obtain the position of ballerina. To this end she followed Anna Pavlova like a shadow, claiming to be one of her admirers but in fact seeking Pavlova's influence for the furtherance of her own career.

Mama was concerned when she realized how often Vaslav saw Gorshkova. She talked to him one day when they were having tea together and tried to warn him against getting too involved. Vaslav was furious and declared that he loved Maria and was going to marry her. But Mama told me later that she did not think Gorshkova was sincere, and so she had said to Vaslav, "Gorshkova cannot be serious about you and your love, an eighteen-year-old boy. She is only trying to turn your head for the sake of her career. You will see. One day you will try to take her in your arms and she will make it a condition for her love that she dance with you."

Vaslav became very pale and tense; he gripped the heavy cut-crystal glass so hard that it cracked and spilled tea all over the tablecloth.

Not long afterwards we noticed that Vaslav's visits next door had stopped. Nothing was said at the time, but later Vaslav casually mentioned to Mama, "Mamoussia, how right you were about Maria. It happened exactly the way you said it would. I had my arms around her and was about to kiss her when she coyly whispered, 'Vatsa, promise me that you will insist on dancing a *pas de deux* with me . . .' Now I am cured of love. Mamoussia, will you forgive me for the bitter time you went through?"

At the beginning of September I had returned to the Imperial Theatrical School for my last year there, my graduation year. Now I was to share the room for graduating students. Though there were seven of us who were to graduate that year, Yelizaveta Gerdt was not a resident student, so there were only six of us sharing the room, which was very comfortable and enjoyable in its privacy after the long narrow dormitory of fifty students. We each had our own table with drawers beside our beds. We could study and read in our room, were allowed to stay up later than the younger students, and could have a half hour longer in bed in the mornings. And we were able to use our room to change into our practice dresses for our dancing classes or rehearsals.

I recall that I often helped Lubov Tchernicheva, "Luba," who now shared my desk with me since Zina Puyman had been promoted to Class V. Luba and I spent a lot of time together, studying and reading aloud to each other. We became close friends, and I even helped her compose her love letters to Sergei Leonidovitch (Grigoriev), whom she was to marry in 1909, a year after our graduation. Luba was also my partner when we were taken for our daily walks in the School courtyard and on the Sunday walk along Nevsky Prospekt, whenever there was a Sunday performance in the Maryinsky Theatre and we were kept in the School.

Whenever we were not assigned to a Sunday performance we could go home like the other students on Saturday, when we were allowed to leave at five o'clock in the afternoon. I would quickly change out of my uniform and into my own clothes, then wait impatiently for my mother. Unlike the boys, we girl students were never allowed to leave the School unaccompanied. But soon a maid would call, "Bronislava Fominitchna, your mother is here."

I then had to stop by the governess's desk to pick up my pass card,

16. The Maryinsky Theatre, c. 1890. *(Stravinsky Diaghilev Foundation)*

17. Interior of the Maryinsky Theatre looking from the stage towards the Imperial Royal Box.

18–23. Artists of the St. Petersburg
Imperial Ballet Company, c. 1899.
Clockwise from upper left: Marius Petipa;
Pavel Gerdt; and Enrico Cecchetti . . .

. . . and clockwise from left:
Mathilda Kshessinska, as Aspicia in
Petipa's ballet *The Daughter of Pharaoh;*
Lubov Egorova; and Julia Sedova.

24. Vaslav Nijinsky in the
uniform of a resident student
of the Imperial Theatrical School
in St. Petersburg. Photograph
taken in 1900.

25. Silver insignia of the
Imperial Theatrical School from
Vaslav's own uniform. Photograph
of original insignia preserved
in the Nijinska Archives.

26–28. Vaslav Nijinsky in the uniform of the graduating class of 1907, and his report card for the first quarter of the school year 1906–7. The report card is signed by his mother (Nijinskaya) and the school Inspector (Missovsky). Nijinsky's grades were 12 (highest) for Conduct, Religious Studies, and Ballet Dancing (under three headings—aptitude, application, and progress), and also in Ballroom Dancing. Pantomime was 11, with 10 for Music, Russian language, History, and Drawing. His two 9 scores were for French and the Theory of Notation. Photograph of original document in the Nijinska Archives.

ЗНАЧЕНІЕ БАЛЛОВЪ:

12 — отлично.

11 ⎱
10 ⎰ очень хорошо.

9 — хорошо.

8 ⎱
7 ⎰ удовлетворительно.

6 — не вполнѣ удовлетворительно.

5 ⎱
4 ⎰ не удовлетворительно.

3 ⎱
2 ⎰ худо.

1 — полное незнаніе.

1906/07 уч. годъ.

СВИДѢТЕЛЬСТВО

ОБЪ УСПѢХАХЪ И ПОВЕДЕНIИ

воспитанника V класса

С.-Петербургскаго ИМПЕРАТОРСКАГО Театральнаго

УЧИЛИЩА.

Нижинскаго Вацлава

	Законъ Божій.	Устный.	Письмен-ный. Русскій языкъ.	Ариѳметика.	Французск. языкъ.	Исторія.	Географія.	Выразит. чтеніе.	Рисованіе.	Чистописаніе.	Способ-ность. Бальныя танцы.	Прилежа-ніе.	Успѣхи.	Бальные танцы.	Мимика.	Теорія балетнаго искусства.	Музыка.	Поведеніе.	Средній балл.	Подпись родителей.
I-я четверть.	12	10	10	10	9	10	—	—	10	—	12	12	12	12	11	9	10	12		Нижинская
II-я четверть.																				
III-я четверть.																				
IV-я четверти.																				
Годовой. . .																				
Экзаменный .																				
Общій																				
Замѣчанія:																				

Инспекторъ П. Миссовскій

29–31. Anna Pavlova in *Chopiniana*, in *The Swan*, and as Papillon.

32. Vaslav Nijinsky in *Raymonda* in 1907. This was the first photographic portrait of Vaslav as an Artist of the Imperial Theatres.

33. Vaslav Nijinsky in *Eunice*, 1908.

ПОХВАЛЬНЫЙ ЛИСТЪ

По постановленію Конференціи ИМПЕРАТОРСКАГО
С.-Петербургскаго Театральнаго Училища данъ сей похвальный листъ
воспитаннику онаго Училища *Нижинскому Вацлаву*
за успѣхи: *очень хорошіе* въ наукахъ и *отличные*
въ балетныхъ танцахъ. С.-Петербургъ *Мая, 20* дня 190*7* года.

Инспекторъ *Т. Миссовскій*

34. Nijinsky's diploma from the Imperial Theatrical School. It reads:

> By decree of the Committee of the Imperial Theatrical School of St.
> Petersburg is issued this testimonial to the student of the above school
> *NIJINSKY VASLAV* for progress, *very good* in studies and *excellent* in
> ballet dancing. St. Petersburg, May 20, 1907.
>
> (signed) *Missovsky*.

This large document, 43 × 34 cm., was carried out of Russia by Nijinsky's
mother in 1921, and the marks on the reproduction are the crease lines where
she had to fold the document to hide it during their six-week journey.
Photograph of original document in the Nijinska Archives.

dated and stamped valid until eight o'clock on Sunday evening, before I could run down the wide staircase towards Mama. We would embrace and immediately hurry out to the street, for I was always so anxious to get away from the School and its strict rules, away from the watchful eyes of the Inspectrice and the governesses and even the maids. Usually we walked home, but if Mama was tired or if it was raining, we rode part of the way on the streetcar.

The ballet rehearsals for the Maryinsky always ended by five o'clock on Saturdays, so Vaslav arrived home about the same time as Mama and I did. We all had dinner together. Mother never skimped on food, no matter how carefully she was trying to balance her budget. She wanted to be sure that Vaslav always had the right food to give him strength for his dancing. She cooked steaks and vegetables and avoided macaroni and kasha, for though Vaslav liked such starchy foods he would gain weight if he ate them. For dessert we either had a compote or fresh fruits or French pastries; Vaslav's favorite was a *mille-feuille*.

Now that Vaslav was an Artist and no longer a student in the School, I was eager to share with him my experiences there. But whenever I mentioned anything concerning the School he would invariably stop me quite abruptly, saying he found it unpleasant to hear anything about the School as it reminded him of his own stay there. I was always surprised by his antagonistic attitude towards the School because however much I looked forward to my weekend and enjoyed coming home I still loved being a student of the Imperial Theatrical School.

Vaslav explained to me that in the School he had always been bored and lonely; among the other boys he did not have a really close friend. He had felt confined and imprisoned. "Only when I was dancing, did I feel free . . ."

I also knew that Vaslav had been very unhappy since his break with Gorshkova and was keeping to himself in the theatre, where he had not found any close friends among the artists.

I was pleased when Mama told me that Pavel Dmitrievitch, Prince Lvov, had recently become friends with Vaslav. Mama used to come to the School every Thursday afternoon to visit me, and during one of her visits she told me how wonderful Prince Lvov was and how kind he had been to her. She told me of one incident when she had been deeply touched by his tactful concern.

One day Vaslav had come in, accompanied by Prince Lvov, when Mama was sitting in the living room crying, a court summons on the table beside her. As Lvov came across the room to greet her she put her hand over the summons to hide it. When he took her hand to kiss it, he saw the sheet of paper and immediately recognized its meaning. He realized what Mother had been trying to hide, the cause of her grief.

"Do not get upset over this Eleonora Nicolaevna . . . you do not need to do anything about it. I will give this paper to my lawyer, and he will take care of everything."

To explain the incident of the summons, I must go back to 1904. That summer we had left Mokhovaya Ulitza, the expensive apartment where we had lived for seven years, ever since we had first moved to St. Petersburg in 1897. Mama never told Vaslav or me that when we moved to Dudergoth, having put our furniture into storage, she was several months behind with the rent.

During that summer Vaslav had gone to Kiev to visit Father, and Mother, who also owed money to the local tradespeople, had given Vaslav all the unpaid bills to take with him and give to Father. Since then Mother had not heard any more from her creditors, so she was sure that Father had paid the bills.

Now, three years later, not long after the beginning of Vaslav's first season as an Artist, when notices about him began to appear in the newspapers, Mama suddenly received demands for bills from 1904. Almost after the first review mentioning Nijinsky's name, she received a notice about the unpaid rent on Mokhovaya Ulitza. The demands increased until soon she received threats that if she did not pay in full her creditors would take her to court so that they could collect. They said that now that her son was earning he should be able to pay off his mother's debts completely.

But Mama knew that out of Vaslav's sixty-five rubles a month it would be absolutely impossible to pay off all the debts at once. She felt the only thing she could do was ignore the demand notices.

But then she received a summons to appear in court. This would be a terrible disgrace; she was also afraid that Vaslav would be called to testify, which would provide a "story" for the newspapers. She was also worried that the court might order the sale of her furniture, which was still in storage.

This was the court summons that Prince Lvov had taken care of. Mama never knew how much was paid, nor how the lawyer straightened things out with the creditors. When she asked Prince Lvov how much she owed, he said he had paid much less than the creditors had demanded and there was no need for her to think about it as Vaslav could settle with him later, "when he is making extra money from guest appearances."

When Mother told me this story I too was deeply moved by Prince Lvov's kindness, and so when I met him one evening in our home I felt that I had known him for a long time and greeted him like a close family friend.

Prince Lvov, Chamberlain of His Highness and secretary of the Minister of Transport and Communications, was then about thirty-five years old, six feet tall, and had dark brown hair, which he wore smoothly combed and parted. He was clean shaven except for a small mustache above his rather full lips. His highly arched eyebrows above his slightly bulging blue eyes and his long face with a narrow, high-bridged nose all gave him an air of aristocratic distinction. The Prince, however, had such tactful and friendly manners that he made everyone feel at ease in his presence and not at all uncomfortable because of any difference in social rank.

I think it was through Mikhail Fokine and his brother, Alexander, that Vaslav first met Prince Lvov. Alexander Fokine was not a dancer; he was a sportsman and an athlete who competed in many championship events. He was a champion oarsman and for a time held the title of World Champion in long-distance bicycle racing.

As Prince Lvov, who was a patron of many sports and athletic organizations, was interested in all kinds of competition, he would often take Vaslav, and sometimes me, to watch a sporting event. Though I went to both bicycle races and horse shows, I preferred the latter. I enjoyed watching the Concours Hippique, with the women dressed in scarlet riding outfits, jumping over all the obstacles as they rode sidesaddle on their beautiful thoroughbred horses. I also liked the display of the Imperial Guards in their magnificent, colorful uniforms.

I believe Prince Lvov was the very first person in St. Petersburg to own a car. He possessed both a sedan and a four-seater coupe in which he often took us out for a ride. I remember one day when we were driving out to the Islands. How cold the wind seemed to be blowing, the car was going so fast! Lvov and Vaslav were sitting in the front seats, while Mama and I were in the back. I was wearing a thin coat and was shivering in the corner under a blanket. Prince Lvov turned to tell us something, and when he saw how cold I was he gave me his fur coat and sheltered me from the wind, even though he risked getting cold himself. Soon he stopped the car in front of a restaurant, The Ernest, and said we must go in to warm up. I was not the only one who was cold, for even Vaslav, in spite of his winter coat with an astrakhan fur collar, was rubbing his face and ears.

As we entered The Ernest, which reminded me of a Café-Chantant, I tried to hide behind Vaslav. I was afraid that if I were seen and recognized I could be expelled from the Imperial Theatrical School. Prince Lvov, noticing my uneasiness, took us into a private room. He made me drink a rowanberry brandy; I had difficulty swallowing it, and afterwards could hardly stand on my feet. After we had supper he called his chauffeur to bring more blankets and another car to take us home.

Almost every Saturday evening Vaslav and Prince Lvov attended a symphony concert at the Dvorianskoye Sobranie, Salle de la Noblesse. The concerts were the same ones that had just been presented in Paris, by Sergei Diaghilev—concerts of Russian music, with Rachmaninoff and Rimsky-Korsakov playing their own works. There were other famous artists and conductors of international renown, such as Arthur Nikisch and Felix Mottl, and also a young pianist, Josef Hoffman. I went only once and then asked Vaslav not to invite me again. It was not that I did not enjoy the program, but I felt very uncomfortable in the beautiful concert hall in the middle of such an elegantly dressed audience. All the ladies were in evening dress, with white gloves, precious jewels, and fancy hairdos. I was modestly dressed in a white batiste embroidered blouse and a navy skirt that came only just below the knee. My hair was tightly pulled back in a braid tied with a silk ribbon. It seemed to me that I was attracting the attention of everyone in the *parterre*, though probably they only noticed "a schoolgirl who liked music."

After that, whenever they went to a concert, Prince Lvov always brought me a box of chocolates or marzipan or petits fours, or sometimes a basket of fresh fruit. He often gave Mother gift boxes filled with all kinds of delicacies—caviar, salmon, pâté de foie gras, cheeses—and French white wine.

On the evenings when Vaslav was going to a concert he would change as soon as we had finished dinner. After he had put on his white starched shirt he would ask me to knot his bow tie. I was always nervous about this, apprehensive lest I not succeed the first time, for I knew it would annoy Vaslav if he was not ready when Prince Lvov came, usually around seven o'clock. They liked to leave almost immediately, not wanting to be late for the concert that began at eight o'clock.

At this time Vaslav did not yet have a tailcoat but wore his dinner jacket for the evening. I admired how handsome he looked and thought to myself how much better evening clothes suited him than his everyday suit. I was so anxious to learn how to knot a man's bow tie so that it would be just right for Vaslav, that I would practice during the week in our room at the School by tying a bow on the end of my braid.

It would be late by the time Vaslav returned from the concert, and though I wanted to hear all about it I would already be asleep. On Sunday mornings Mama and I would go to church early, and Vaslav would often still be asleep when we came home from Mass. It was always difficult to get him up in the morning; he would be angry at being disturbed and want to stay in bed longer.

But over our light breakfast, the same as we usually had in the School—tea, hot rolls, and butter—he would tell us all about the concert the evening before: the music he had heard and who he had seen. I never seemed to have enough time with Vaslav on a Sunday, for soon he would leave to teach his classes. I wanted him to tell me all about the performances in the Maryinsky Theatre.

In October he danced a peasant dance with Tamara Karsavina, a semiclassical *pas de deux* from Act I of *Giselle*. As soon as he came out onto the stage for his *variation* the audience applauded him. Afterwards he told me that though he was happy and proud to be dancing with soloists like Sedova, Kyaksht, and Karsavina, he was dreaming of the day when he would dance a *grand pas de deux* in *Giselle*, *Swan Lake*, or *Sleeping Beauty*.

But despite his youth, more and more ballerinas and *premières danseuses* wanted to dance with Vaslav. Anna Pavlova often invited him to join her practice sessions with Maestro Cecchetti. She had an apartment, not far from us and on the same street, Torgovaya Ulitza, and Cecchetti used to go there every day to work with her. Vaslav was thrilled to have the opportunity to study with Maestro Cecchetti and to go over many *pas de deux* with Pavlova under his careful direction.

The young Nijinsky was soon accorded a special distinction in the Maryinsky Theatre. It was announced that on the same night, Wednesday, October 16, he would dance the leading roles in two ballets: *La Fille Mal Gardée* and *The Prince Gardener*.

The Prince Gardener, choreographed by Kulichevskaya, had first been presented for the Student Performance of 1906 and was to be danced now by the same performers, all young Artists of the Imperial Theatres who had graduated in 1906 and 1907. So Vaslav would again be dancing with Ludmila Schollar.

He was immeasurably proud that on that same evening he was to dance the leading role of Colin in *La Fille Mal Gardée* with the *prima ballerina assoluta*, Mathilda Felixovna Kshessinska.

I had seen *La Fille Mal Gardée*, actually taken part in it, many times. One occasion in particular remained in my memory: the performance of February 4, 1904, announced as the Farewell Performance of the Prima Ballerina Assoluta, Mathilda Kshessinska. She had chosen for that "farewell performance" the same ballet in which she had made her stage debut at the Maryinsky Theatre in 1890.

I will never forget that night. The atmosphere was electric in the Theatre, and backstage emotions were high among the artists, the students, even the stagehands. Kshessinska's decision to leave the Imperial Theatres had been a complete surprise. Ever since 1895 when she had become a ballerina, she had reigned supreme at the Maryinsky. Kshessinska had wielded extraordinary influence and power owing to her proximity to the Imperial Court and Tsar Nicholas II.

Following her "farewell performance," Kshessinska had returned the next season to dance at the Maryinsky, by "popular demand," but she had refused to sign a long-term binding contract. She preferred to retain her independent status of a guest artist and to dance only occasionally in the Imperial Theatres in St. Petersburg and Moscow. She would then be free to accept various engagements abroad as she chose. She had regretted very much that in 1903, when she had danced in Vienna, she had not been able to accept the invitation of an American impresario to dance in the United States of America.

I would have liked to have seen the performance in 1907 when Vaslav was to dance with Kshessinska in *La Fille Mal Gardée*, but none of the graduating students were used in the performance.

Mama always collected the newspaper reviews that mentioned Vaslav, and then when I came home on Saturdays I would read them all before pasting them in a special album. It had a green velvet cover and Vaslav's own monogram in silver, a gift from his first admirer, Elena Sechenova-Ivanova, after she saw Vaslav for the first time, in the Student Performance of 1905.

In the *St. Petersburg Gazette*, the critic Valerian Svetlov, who had also written the libretto of *The Prince Gardener*, wrote about Vaslav, ". . . his elevation, ballon and brilliancy were astonishing, as for instance in the amazing *entrechat-huit* in the *variation* of the *pas de deux* in *The Prince Gardener*. He also proved himself to be a gifted mime in the role of Colin and if there were some flaws in the interpretation of the role it was only due to shyness."

Another critic declared, "the hero of this performance is the young dancer, Nijinsky . . . our ballerinas must not take offence if his success overshadows them . . ."

Following *La Fille Mal Gardée*, Kshessinska asked Vaslav to dance with her in the *Divertissement* for the Farewell Benefit Performance for Maria Petipa, to be given in the Maryinsky Theatre on November 11, 1907. The program was also to include the ballet *Raymonda*, and Vaslav was excited to be chosen to dance in the "Pas Classique Hongrois." For this performance the dancers would be Nikolai Legat, Mikhail Fokine, Mikhail Oboukhov—all *premiers danseurs*—and Vaslav Nijinsky, the young artist and newly graduated student.

For the *Divertissement* Kshessinska had asked Kulichevskaya to mount a *pas de deux*, to music by Chopin, for her and Vaslav. Kshessinska had greatly admired Isadora Duncan since seeing her dance in an all-Chopin concert in Vienna in 1903. The following year Kshessinska had been instrumental in bringing Duncan to Russia for her first visit.

The *pas de deux* called "Nocturne" that Kulichevskaya mounted used both a nocturne and a valse by Chopin. Vaslav wore a costume of the Romantic period and Kshessinska danced in a flowing, ankle-length, silk tunic, à la Duncan; both costumes were designed by Bakst.

Though Vaslav did not care for Kulichevskaya's interpretation and rendition of Chopin's music in "Nocturne," he was nonetheless pleased when Kshessinska invited him to dance another performance of "Nocturne" in Moscow for the Benefit Performance for the Corps de Ballet of the Bolshoi Theatre, in December.

Before that, however, both Kshessinska and Vaslav would be dancing in November at the Maryinsky when the whole of *Le Pavillon d'Armide* was to be presented as a one-act ballet. I was able to watch the ballet during rehearsals, since I was taking part in the first tableau. This scene had not been included in the performance Fokine had mounted for the Student Performance of 1907, so it was new to us. According to the plot of the ballet, at midnight, just before the Gobelin tapestry comes to life, twelve of us students, representing the twelve hours, were to come out of the face of the monumental clock standing beneath the tapestry. We each carried a lantern painted with the number of our hour, and we danced in a clockwise circle, then returned back inside the clock.

It did not seem to me that Fokine had brought any innovations to his new ballet. He still retained the same style as Petipa with *mises en scène* and pantomime. Though the many dances were well choreographed, they did not relate to each other, and the ballet looked like a big *divertissement*.

The real interest for me was in watching the painter Alexandre Benois, whose work I was observing for the first time. He painted a backcloth to look like a Gobelin tapestry and copied a photograph of Kshessinska for the face of Armide and one of Pavel Gerdt for the face of René, her lover. A light gauze scrim in front of the painting gave it the effect of a tapestry. The dancers were placed behind the gauze and were carefully schooled by Benois in the same poses and groupings as the figures in the tapestry, so that they would really look as though they had come to life. He also directed the lighting of the stage.

There were several rehearsals onstage with the orchestra and the sets, but the costumes for *Le Pavillon d'Armide* were not to be worn until the day of the dress rehearsal, Friday, November 16. The costumes were kept locked up in the Theatre wardrobe, and Krupensky, the manager of the Imperial Ballet Company, would not allow any artist or student to try them on much less to dance in them. He was afraid that the hand-painted costumes might be ruined before the public saw them at the premiere, on Sunday, November 18.

On the evening of the dress rehearsal there was great confusion. Benois gave everyone detailed instructions for all the makeup and indicated how the Louis XIV costumes and headgear were to be worn, but the artists did not have time actually to learn how to put on their complicated costumes or how to wear their headdresses properly.

At the back of the stage was the platform where the artists were placed in their groupings for the tapestry. The large monumental clock was in front of the platform, and we students were placed behind the clock, under the platform. Confined in this small narrow space, in total darkness, we waited our turn to come out onto the stage.

On the stroke of midnight we were to come out of the clock one by one. I was the first hour and the light inside my lantern was lit by a stagehand so that the numeral "I" became visible the moment I emerged from the clock. The girl student who was to follow me missed her entrance because the stagehand had trouble lighting lantern numeral "II." Then there were further delays as the students, standing in the dark narrow space, could not recognize each other, being dressed as pages in identical silver costumes, with their faces darkened and hair hidden under gold lamé turbans.

Fokine was furious and stopped the rehearsal, making us repeat our number, much to the obvious annoyance of Tcherepnine, the conductor of the orchestra and composer of the music. After our number, as we were standing in the wings, I saw Alexandre Benois looking very distressed and saying that the performance could not go on without another dress rehearsal the next day, Saturday. Krupensky refused, saying it would be impossible to arrange another dress rehearsal on such short notice and that the budget was already too stretched and this would mean additional expense.

The following morning we were all surprised to read in the *St. Petersburg Gazette*, the newspaper most widely read in theatrical circles, an interview of Alexandre Benois by I. S. Rosenberg, a regular contributor, albeit in a small way, to one of the paper's daily columns. Rosenberg was also the brother of Léon Bakst.

The interview was written mostly by Benois himself, and in it he accused the Directorate and Administration of the Imperial Theatres of refusing to provide the conditions essential for the success of the new ballet, *Le Pavillon d'Armide*, declaring that ". . . in consequence the Directorate alone is responsible for making the complete failure of my work almost inevitable . . ."

Later that Saturday we were informed that the premiere had been postponed for a week and that there would be two more dress rehearsals onstage. Then, on top of everything else, Kshessinska refused to go on with the role of Armide. She had been pleased at first to participate in the premiere of a new ballet choreographed by the promising young choreographer, Mikhail Fokine, but after the difficulties of the dress rehearsal and the lack of faith in their own ballet expressed by the authors, Tcherepnine, Fokine, and Benois, the latter even going so far as "to put it on paper" with his interview, she had become uncertain and had decided to withdraw. Anna Pavlova immediately offered to replace her, and by the time of the next dress rehearsal had learned the role of Armide.

The first performance of *Le Pavillon d'Armide* took place on Sunday, November 25, 1907, following the performance of *Swan Lake* with the prima ballerina Vera Trefilova. Although the role of Armide was danced by Anna Pavlova, Benois had not repainted the features in the tapestry where the face of Armide still bore the likeness of Kshessinska.

Vaslav, the student, had been the Marquis in *L'Animation des Gobelins* in the spring of 1907, but now in the fall I saw Nijinsky, the Artist, in *Le Pavillon d'Armide* in the role of Armide's slave, wearing an elaborate costume designed by Benois with a string of pearls encircling his long neck. He danced the same *variation* in both roles, but as I watched him dance now it seemed to me to be done differently from the Student Performance. At that time, as the Marquis, the new sideways *changement de pieds* had just been a sportive exercise, but now in the role of Armide's slave he brought the whole of his body into play with the new *pas*. Vaslav was radiant on the stage. The glow did not leave him even when he was simply standing in a pose next to Armide.

The ballet, Fokine's first choreography to be danced by the Artists of the Imperial Theatres on the stage of the Maryinsky Theatre, was a tremendous success. Usually when a one-act ballet followed a main attraction it was only presented to complete the program. It was not "taken seriously," but served simply to allow the audience to leave the theatre at leisure. But this evening most of the audience chose to see the whole of *Le Pavillon d'Armide*, staying to the end, close to one o'clock in the morning.

A second performance was arranged to be given two weeks later, on Sunday, December 9. For that performance Fokine himself took the dual role of the Vicomte de Beaugency and of René, Armide's lover. He did not bother to have the faces on the tapestry repainted, and so in the Maryinsky Theatre the smiling face of Armide that appeared to glow on the tapestry in the first scene continued to bear the resemblance to Mathilda Kshessinska, and René, her lover standing beside her, retained the handsome features of Pavel Gerdt.

24   Nijinsky Dances
the Blue Bird

THREE DAYS after the first performance of *Le Pavillon d'Armide*, Vaslav's dream was realized. On Wednesday, November 28, 1907, he was to dance the *grand pas de deux*, "Princess Florine and the Blue Bird," in Act II of *The Sleeping Beauty*.

Nijinsky was only eighteen years old when he was chosen to appear as the Blue Bird on the stage of the Maryinsky Theatre. It was most unusual that such an important dancing part as the Blue Bird should be entrusted to an Artist in his very first ballet season in the Imperial Theatres.

Princess Florine was to be danced by Lydia Kyaksht. I was not familiar with this excellent classical dancer, for soon after her graduation from the School, in 1902, she had been transferred to the Bolshoi Theatre in Moscow. She had only just returned to St. Petersburg, and one of her first appearances in an important role was to be Princess Florine in *The Sleeping Beauty*.

Ever since the brilliant performance and the creation of the Blue Bird by Enrico Cecchetti on January 3, 1890, the *grand pas de deux*, "Princess Florine and the Blue Bird," had been danced by the best Artists of the Imperial Theatres. Over the years an unshakable routine had been established for the presentation and execution of this *pas de deux*, though the artistic interpretation of the Blue Bird was left to the dancer himself.

As students of the Imperial Theatrical School we had seen the Blue Bird danced by such leading Artists as Nikolai Legat, Georgi Kyaksht, Mikhail Oboukhov, and Mikhail Fokine. Though each dancer was free to give his own artistic rendering of the Blue Bird, most of them were satisfied to leave everything "as it was" and not bring any artistic innovation to the dance.

Vaslav had also seen the Blue Bird many times from on the stage of the Maryinsky, ever since the time when he had taken part in "Le Petit Poucet et ses Frères" in the last act of *The Sleeping Beauty*. No doubt each time something wonderful had resounded in his dancing body. He had not tried consciously to memorize the dance, but the melody of the music and the choreographic image of Petipa's Blue Bird had merged and left an everlasting impression on the young student.

It was the custom that young artists should learn their assigned parts from their older colleagues, and that the leading dancers and soloists should work on their roles and the preparation of their dances independently of the ballet master and the *régisseur*.

Nijinsky could have asked his former teacher Oboukhov to show him the *variation* and the solo from the *coda* of the Blue Bird, but being already familiar with the dance, he was creating his own dance-image of the Blue Bird. So he worked alone a great deal. He did not turn to anyone to give him artistic direction.

I had seen Fokine dance the Blue Bird at the same time that he was introducing new artistic expressions and innovations in the ballets he was mounting for the Annual Student Performances, but even he, like all the others, performed the Blue Bird traditionally, interpreting the role as that of a Prince, dressed as a Blue Bird, performing with the Princess Florine as guests at the ball on the occasion of the marriage of Princess Aurora and Prince Desiré.

Fokine's Blue Bird did not fly but danced in a classical ballet manner, assuming striking poses and using prolonged pauses to emphasize the end of a sequence of *pas*. Only the large rigid wings mounted on a wire frame served to identify the character as a bird.

All the costumes for *The Sleeping Beauty* had been designed by Ivan Vsevolojsky, Director of the Imperial Theatres from 1881 to 1899. The costume for the Blue Bird was similar in style to the ballet costume worn by Louis XIV in his court ballets at Versailles. The full-skirted coat was in two shades of blue, and both the dark top and the lighter blue skirt were richly ornamented. A wide blue ribbon was caught on the left shoulder and then draped across the chest and the back to tie in a bulky bow above the right hip. The large wings extended upwards from the shoulder in a curved shape and covered the arms and the hands. A crown of blue feathers completed the costume.

I never knew how Vaslav, only eighteen years old, persuaded the Administration of the Maryinsky Theatre to alter the original design and make a new costume for him. Instead of the elaborate full-skirted coat Vaslav wore a regular ballet tunic and short trunks over tights. The entire costume was blue, a slightly deeper blue than the darker shade of the original coat. For Vaslav's Blue Bird there was no supporting wire frame for the wings. In the original costume a dancer could only perform the *pas* with his legs; his body was encumbered by the large rigid wings. In the new costume Vaslav's arm-wings and his body moved together, as do the wings and body of a bird—freely in the air.

I saw Vaslav during one of the final rehearsals of the last act of *Sleeping Beauty* when Legat and Sergeyev were rehearsing all the participants. All the artists except Vaslav were wearing their usual practice clothes, but Vaslav was trying out his dance wearing his new costume for the Blue Bird.

The birdlike wings were part of his dancing body; his arms did not bend at the elbow, but the movement as in the wing of a bird was generated in the shoulder; the movements of the dancing body were the movements of a bird in flight. A flittering motion of the hands at the wrist and the Blue Bird's wings trembled and fluttered; the Blue Bird was soaring and singing its bird's song, and Nijinsky's body was singing in his dancing flight. He was creating his dance-image of a Blue Bird, an image that had become a living entity, part of himself and his dancing body.

Nijinsky was following his creative path on his own at this time; there was no one to give him artistic direction; neither Diaghilev nor Bakst nor Benois was at his side to guide him.

The performance of *The Sleeping Beauty* took place on November 28, 1907. The appearance of Nijinsky in the Blue Bird was unforgettable.

Nijinsky flies on in an enormous leap, a prolonged *grand assemblé*. The arm-wings are open wide, extended. The Blue Bird soars—two light motions of the shoulders, a flutter of the wings, and the Blue Bird seems to linger in its flight. A slow sweeping movement of the arm-wings, as if gathering new strength, and then a strong upsweeping movement of the wings create the impression that the Blue Bird is rising still higher in its flight. Then smoothly, imperceptibly, Nijinsky comes down on half-toe only to fly upwards again.

One of the amazing features of Nijinsky's dance was that it was impossible to perceive when he was finishing one *pas* and when he was starting the next. All the preparations were concealed in the shortest possible time, the very instant of the foot touching the floor of the stage. On a background of persistently repeated *entrechat-six, entrechat-huit, entrechat-dix*, a whole range of movements played in the body of Nijinsky: vibrating, trembling, fluttering, flying. It seemed that after each *entrechat* Nijinsky did not come down to touch the floor but was flying higher and higher like a bird soaring upwards. It was one continuous *glissando* in which all the *entrechats* flowed together in an upward flight.

The admiring audience burst into an unrestrained thunder of applause and shouts of "Bis." Their enthusiasm was aroused not only by the unprecedented virtuosity in the technique of the *pas*, or the height and lightness of the jumps. To all this was added something else—magic—the dancing-image of the Blue Bird.

His *coda* solo, the *pas brisé volé*, was an absolutely extraordinary dancing phenomenon.

How can one find words to capture the essence of Dance? How to bring it to reality? How to describe the dancing-image created of a bird in flight?

A vision-impression—as if the Blue Bird is flying low over the swift current of an impetuous stream . . . plays in the spray of water, splashes around in the stream, shakes itself with a flutter of trembling wings . . . then again flies upwards and hovers, rocking backwards and forwards in flight over the stream. As both legs are lifted high in front and flutter in *brisé volé*, they are covered by a fast passing movement of the trembling wings as the body bends half-forwards. Another fast movement and the wings swing aside; Nijinsky changes position during the jump to arch his body backwards to the utmost. It seems that Nijinsky's body is continuously suspended in the air, without touching the floor, now bent forwards, now arched backwards, swinging backwards and forwards in the air. The arm-wings in wide movements, now folded, now open, seem to hold him in the air, in his own atmosphere, his own element. This movement of the *brisé volé* in the *coda* is repeated twice on the diagonal of the stage from the last wing to the first wing, ending in a great number of *pirouettes*, ten to twelve, at top speed, *prestissimo*.

The regular audience of the Maryinsky Theatre knew the performance of *The Sleeping Beauty* by heart. Each dance was so familiar to them in every detail that they could well judge and appreciate each performer and reward him accordingly with their applause. The triumph of Nijinsky as the Blue Bird was overwhelming.

Nijinsky had in no way changed the choreography of Petipa; it had served him as a theme for his dancing *variation* so that his performance had become his own composition. In creating his dance—its movements, rhythm, expression, and character—Nijinsky had created a whole new theatrical image of the Blue Bird. Here everything in his creative work was remarkably and newly found—the artistic technique of the dance, the makeup, the costume. Nijinsky was guided by innate genius. His every movement sang the music of Tchaikovsky. The body of Nijinsky had seemed to lose its human contours and design a bird's flight in the air, the flight of the enchanted bluebird of Perrault's fairy tale.

25   Christmas: 1907

IMMEDIATELY AFTER the performance of *The Sleeping Beauty*, Vaslav left for Moscow with Kshessinska for the Benefit Performance for the Corps de Ballet of the Bolshoi Theatre. The program in Moscow was to be a new production of Petipa's *La Bayadère*, staged by Alexander Gorsky after Stepanov's notations, and was also to include a *pas de deux* originally mounted by Nikolai Gustavovitch Legat for Kshessinska and himself and inserted into Petipa's ballet, several years before. Since then Legat had been the regular partner of Kshessinska for this *pas de deux*, but in Moscow she had chosen to dance it with Nijinsky. They were also to dance in the *Divertissement*, the "Nocturne" they had performed at the Maryinsky on November 11.

Before leaving, Vaslav had been quite nervous and upset. He felt he had not been getting enough rehearsals with Mathilda Kshessinska and that Nikolai Legat had been reluctant, to say the least, to show him the *pas de deux* for *La Bayadère*. "Nikolai Gustavovitch told me that he was very busy and did not have any time to spare for rehearsals with me."

Upon his return from Moscow Vaslav seemed tired, but he danced in the second performance of *Le Pavillon d'Armide* with the same lighthearted nonchalance and ease as for the premiere. I was able to see him during rehearsals but was not able to talk to him; I wanted to hear all about his trip to Moscow, but even at home I barely saw him, for during the month of December he was always rushing into the house for just a few minutes before dashing out again. He was busy with the children's social dancing classes he was teaching, and the rehearsals with Asafiev for the Christmas performance of the children's opera, and he was also working with Anna Pavlova on the *pas de deux* from *Swan Lake*. About all he had time to tell me was that the violin accompanist for the *Swan Lake* rehearsals was his old friend Kolya Issaev.

I was looking forward to the Christmas holidays; there was so much I wanted to ask Vaslav. But, on December 22, Mama came to collect me from the School in an *isvostchik*, and on the way home she told me she was in a hurry, as she was expecting the doctor for Vaslav. I knew he had been bothered by a lingering cold ever since he returned from Moscow, but now Mama said that he was quite ill and was running a high fever.

When we got home we found that the doctor had already arrived and had examined Vaslav. Dr. Reshetnikov had been our family doctor ever since we first arrived in St. Petersburg and had seen Stassik and me through our typhoid fever. All three of us children had become fond of the doctor. He was a military doctor and had lived quite close to our first apartment on Mokhovaya Ulitza. He was young, tall, and handsome. He had a small beard and mustache and was very affectionate towards us. His medicines were never disgusting; in fact, his fever prescription was quite tasty, both sweet and sour, and raspberry-colored! Mama's usual prescription at the beginning of any illness was castor oil. What a drama that would provoke! We would plead with Mother until finally she placed a few drops of lemon juice on our tongues, and then we would hold our noses to keep out the obnoxious smell as she gave us the oil. After swallowing we would suck on the sour lemon to get rid of the oil in our mouths and on our lips. But Dr. Reshetnikov saved us from this unpleasant ordeal; he substituted castor pills for the liquid castor oil.

The doctor now told Mama that Vaslav would have to remain in bed for several days and was not to go out until he had regained his strength. Vaslav was terribly upset; he insisted that he must dance that night at the Charity Performance organized by Mikhail Fokine at the Maryinsky Theatre. "I must dance tonight; Anna Pavlova is counting on me; we are dancing a *pas de deux* from *Swan Lake*. I don't care if I am ill. I will dance tonight!"

At that moment Prince Lvov arrived to drive Vaslav to the perform-ance. When Mama told him that Vaslav was ill, he joined the doctor in persuading Vaslav that he could not possibly dance with such a fever. They had great difficulty, but finally Vaslav agreed. Prince Lvov sent his chauffeur to the stage door of the Maryinsky to deliver two messages, one to Anna Pavlova and one to Mikhail Fokine, together with a note from the doctor certifying Vaslav's illness.

The next morning Vaslav sent me out to get all the newspapers, as most of the St. Petersburg newspapers carried reviews of the performances at the Maryinsky. In one of them I read that a change in the program had been announced at the beginning of the performance: "Mme Pavlova will not dance the *pas de deux* from *Swan Lake* due to the illness of her partner.

Instead Mme Pavlova will perform 'The Swan' by Saint-Saëns." Vaslav's name was not mentioned.

Some critics praised Tamara Karsavina for the "Danse Assyrienne," mounted by Fokine. Others commented on the success of Feodor Lopukhov in the Ukrainian *hopak*. All the critics, however, agreed that the highlight of the evening was a masterpiece by Fokine, "The Swan" danced by Anna Pavlova.

Vaslav felt relieved and delighted that because of his illness Fokine's *The Swan* had been performed at the Maryinsky Theatre. He explained that Fokine had mounted it for Anna Pavlova two years before, also for a charity performance, but because it had been danced in a private hall and not at the Maryinsky it had not received any publicity.

Later I found out that because Vaslav was unable to dance, Fokine and Pavlova had decided on the spur of the moment that she should dance Fokine's "The Swan," performing it in the costume she would have worn for the *pas de deux* from *Swan Lake*. Fokine had hummed the tune for her as they went over the dance together backstage. Fortunately, the violinist who was to have played the violin solo in *Swan Lake* was also familiar with Saint-Saëns' "The Swan," from "Carnaval des Animaux."

Though Vaslav was happy that Anna Pavlova had danced "The Swan" that night he was also disappointed that he had not been able to dance the *pas de deux* from *Swan Lake* with her. The opportunity was never to arise again for Nijinsky to dance in *Swan Lake* with Pavlova.

While Vaslav was recovering from his cold and fever I was able to ask him about the performance in Moscow. I had felt that he was somewhat disappointed and had not had the same successful reception that he was getting in St. Petersburg. He wondered if one explanation might be that Kulichevskaya's choreography of "Nocturne," while highlighting Kshessinska's brilliance and virtuosi *pas*, did not reveal his own.

He had brought back with him the newspapers from Moscow where the majority of the critics had been somewhat harsh in their evaluation of Kulichevskaya's "Nocturne," although one critic had declared Kshessinska to be "a real prima ballerina . . . endowed with the gift to lend to each dance the appropriate characteristic mood. Her wonderful partner, Nijinsky, greatly contributed to the success of this dance."

Vaslav felt that the balletomanes and audiences of the Bolshoi Theatre expected something different from a ballet performance than did the Maryinsky audience. He wondered whether the Muscovites preferred demonstrations of theatrical brilliance to refinement of dance technique.

I asked him about the notice in the *St. Petersburg Gazette* after the performance of "Nocturne" in November, which said that Nijinsky would probably be Kshessinska's partner in Paris in February. He told me that she had indeed asked him to be her partner for the Paris engagement but it was not to be until later in the spring. Vaslav asked me not to talk about it until it was officially announced as he expected it would anger Nikolai Legat, Kshessinska's usual partner. "I am sure he did not help me with *La Bayadère* because he considers it 'his ballet' and he was resentful that Mathilda Felixovna had chosen me to go to Moscow with her."

"But," I pointed out, "she doesn't always dance with Legat. Remember, last year she danced with Fokine in Moscow."

"That's true. But I realized just how difficult Legat is being towards me when I saw how helpful Alexander Gorsky was in Moscow. He told me I should familiarize myself with every new stage, wherever I dance, and he helped me to do so with the stage of the Bolshoi Theatre.

"You know," Vaslav went on, "I get nothing out of the classes with Legat. I wish I could study more with Cecchetti. But now that our rehearsals for the *Swan Lake pas de deux* are finished I never know when Anna Pavlova is going to invite me to join her classes with him."

—

JUST BEFORE Christmas, on December 17, Stassik turned twenty-one and was transferred from his juvenile sanatorium on the outskirts of St. Petersburg to the Psychotherapy Sanatorium, Novoznamenskaya Dacha, near Ligovo. This was on the same Baltic Railroad as Dudergoth, about fifteen miles south of St. Petersburg, and Mama and I planned to go and visit him. Vaslav, who was feeling much better, offered to come with us to help find the sanatorium, which was about two miles from the Ligovo railway station, but Mama said he should stay inside for a few more days as the weather was cold and snowing. Vaslav was concerned about Mama and I going on our own, unescorted, and offered to speak to Pavel Dmitrievitch, who, he was sure, would be only too happy to drive us to Ligovo. Mama refused absolutely, saying she did not know how the change and the new environment might affect Stassik, and she did not care to have Prince Lvov meet her son for the first time when Stassik might be in a nervous state.

So, despite Vaslav's protests, Mama and I went alone on the train to Ligovo and then walked the two miles from the station to the sanatorium. The snow was deep, but we wore high boots and were warmly dressed; Mother had bundled us both up with scarves over our winter coats, and we also wore our fur hats. But I felt sorry for Mama, seeing how difficult it was for her to walk in the deep snow; she was suffering so from her rheumatism.

Stassik was in a new wing of the sanatorium, and his room, which he shared with several other adult patients, was light and airy with a high ceiling. We came into his room and Stassik smiled as he saw us. He was also happy to receive his Christmas and birthday gifts. Vaslav had sent him a wool sweater and I had brought him some hand-knitted wool gloves, and from Mama he received a wool scarf and hat. He immediately wanted to put them on, and as it was not snowing just then, the sun shining pleasantly, we went for a short walk in the gardens of the sanatorium. Then Mama and I left to return to St. Petersburg.

A few days later, when Vaslav was sufficiently recovered to begin going out again, Mama felt we were now able to accept Prince Lvov's invitation. He had invited Mama, Vaslav, and me to dinner, to celebrate my birthday. We arrived at his home on the elegant Bolshaya Morskaya Ulitza, and the heavy oak doors opened slowly before us. We were greeted by two tall footmen wearing gray tailcoats decorated with yellow braid and brass buttons. Their trousers were also gray and had a wide yellow stripe down the side. We were escorted up the short, wide, marble stairs to the vestibule, where they helped us take off our fur coats and boots.

Pavel Dmitrievitch welcomed us and took us into a large room where the entire wall facing the door was dominated by an organ. The organ pipes reached up to the ceiling and filled the whole wall. In the middle of the room was a billiard table with a blue-green felt top; the room seemed to me to be somewhat somber, and then I noticed that the two side walls were lined with dark armoires where the collections amassed by Lvov were displayed. They reminded me of my favorite museum, the Baron Stieglitz Museum, and I rushed towards the armoires. Lvov described his collections to us. I was very interested and attentive, but perhaps because I was still young, just seventeen, or because I was so overwhelmed by the atmosphere here in this princely mansion, I did not always understand the origin or significance of the pieces collected by Prince Lvov.

However, I do remember a beautiful china service with each plate decorated with a different scene showing the cavalry of the Imperial Guard at the time of Alexander I. There was also a small manicure case that had belonged to Napoléon and a large traveling dressing-case bearing his monogram, also a fan that had belonged to Marie Antoinette as well as a collection of rare coins and medals. One armoire contained nothing but books, all rare first editions. There were also several bronze busts, of Napoléon, Alexander I, Beethoven, and others whom I do not remember.

Pavel Dmitrievitch then asked us to come through to his study. Walking through the doors on the right side of the billiard room, as I had named the first large room, we soon found ourselves in another large room with a high ceiling. The floor was covered with a beautiful thick rug and the four high windows were draped with heavy silk, and on one wall was the portrait of a beautiful woman. The Prince told us she was the wife of the Grand Duke Konstantin Pavlovitch; I understood too that she was a member of Prince Lvov's family.

Close by the door was a large concert grand piano. As Vaslav quickly approached the piano and lifted the lid to reveal the keyboard, he mentioned to us that he had heard the pianist Josef Hoffman play on it. He extended his hand as if he wanted to caress the keyboard lightly with his fingers, then suddenly withdrew his hand without touching the keys and quickly closed the lid, as if afraid that his touch might obliterate the imperceptible traces left by the fingers of the celebrated pianist.

I was reminded of how elated Vaslav had been after he had heard Josef Hoffman play at one of the concerts in the Salle de la Noblesse. Even the next morning he was still as excited as if he had just come out of the concert, telling me he had never heard such music before.

"He has the most extraordinarily beautiful hands . . . and to play the piano like that, Hoffman cannot be an ordinary mortal, he must be an angel . . ." Vaslav had then described how the public had adored Hoffman, giving him ovation after ovation following his return from the successful concerts in Paris organized by Diaghilev.

"How I wish I could attain his artistry . . ."

Little could Vaslav imagine then that in the very near future the fame of his own artistry would surpass that of Hoffman.

As we continued our tour of the house, we returned through the billiard room where Lvov suddenly opened one of the armoires and took out a collection of old laces, Venetian and Valenciennes. They were yellow with age and had belonged to his grandmother. Pavel Dmitrievitch wanted me to have them as a birthday gift. But I refused, saying I could not possibly accept such a precious collection and that they should remain with him where they could be safely and carefully preserved.

Lvov then took us into a smaller room where the decoration was in the oriental style. The walls and the floor were covered with ceramic tiles, and the ceiling was painted blue with gold stars. At the end of the room was a large alcove filled with tropical plants and illuminated with fantastic green electric lights; in front of the alcove was a fountain spouting from the center of a round pool where goldfish were swimming. The high jet of water from the fountain was illuminated with a red light. All around the pool were more plants, mainly evergreens.

I was completely entranced to find a pool with a fountain and goldfish and living plants in the middle of a house where people actually lived.

There were no words to express my feelings of wonder and enchantment.

From this garden room a narrow wooden stairway, as if on board a ship, led up to the dining room, reminding me of a captain's cabin, for the windows were round like portholes.

The dining room was paneled in dark oak, and around it were shelves on which were displayed gold and silver platters, goblets, and vases, and precious china services. I was astonished by the size of the fireplace. The opening was so large that the footman who was adding logs to the fire was able to stand right inside it. The oval table was covered with a fine lace tablecloth, and in the center was a bowl filled with sprays from fruit trees with their fruits and leaves still on them. In front of each of our places there were individual small vases holding sprigs of mimosa and violets. It was winter outside, but here inside the air was marvelously filled with the delicate scent of spring.

The dinner was served by two footmen in black tailcoats and wearing white gloves. In front of each of us they set a gold plate and on it served assorted hors d'oeuvres of caviar, sturgeon, marinated mushrooms, and every possible delicacy.

At the table, the plates and dishes kept changing. At the fireplace, the footmen keep going in and out of the brick-lined hearth, adding more logs to keep the flames aglow.

By nature I was a shy person, and that on top of the unaccustomed luxury made everything inside me shrivel up. I couldn't swallow the food; I was miserable. I was apprehensive lest I not pick up the correct knife or fork or spoon for each dish placed in front of me. During the entire dinner I had an unbearable pain in the pit of my stomach.

At last the dinner was over. Mama and Lvov went to the study where their coffee and liqueurs were served while Vaslav, who was quite familiar with Prince Lvov's home, took me to the billiard room and showed me how to play billiards. We did not stay much longer, and just before we left the Prince again tried to persuade me to accept his collection of old laces. I was adamant in my refusal, saying that I was still a young girl and would not know how to take care of them and that his grandmother's collection should remain there in the home of Prince Pavel Dmitrievitch Lvov.

We were taken home in the Prince's automobile. I was still overwhelmed by the magnificence of the Prince's home and his surroundings. I wondered how Vaslav had felt the first time he had been there. This evening he had certainly not looked as stupefied as I felt. He had seemed to be completely relaxed and at ease, and he had also looked rather proud to have a friend showing such courtesy, respect, and kindness to his mother and sister.

A few days later, when Prince Lvov was visiting our home, we talked more about Josef Hoffman. Pavel Dmitrievitch knew him well and had introduced Vaslav to him. Vaslav told us again how much he admired the pianist.

"He has only to enter a room and his presence and personality brighten everyone and everything around him."

Seeing how impressed Vaslav was by Hoffman, Lvov talked to him at length, trying to encourage Vaslav's ambition and stressing how important it was for him to have continuous training in dancing and that he should take every possible lesson with Cecchetti. I think Lvov must have known that Vaslav did not feel that Legat's classes had much to offer him and that Vaslav took advantage of the slightest excuse in order to miss them.

Lvov also advised Vaslav that he should stop teaching the social dancing classes; they took well over four hours, a waste of precious time and strength that he should be using for his own dance training. Naturally Lvov understood very well that it was necessary for Vaslav to teach with his salary insufficient to cover even our essential living expenses.

He offered to pay for Vaslav's lessons with Cecchetti. He talked with Mama, asking us to support him in his efforts to convince Vaslav to accept his offer. Lvov said that Vaslav was a gifted young man and that this was not just his own opinion but was shared by all who had seen Nijinsky dance.

"But Vaslav is still a boy—a youth who must continue to strive towards perfection. It would make me proud for the rest of my life to know that I had contributed to the development of this great talent by making it possible for him to continue with his own training instead of having to waste time, strength, and energy in teaching social dancing. Vaslav is proud, I know, but his pride should be guided to the unfolding of his unique artistic talent."

Lvov also said that he felt it was the duty of every truly honorable man as wealthy as he was, to encourage talent such as Vaslav's.

Such patrons of art were not unusual in Russia. They supported talented artists, musicians, painters, and singers, and they financed theatrical productions and contributed to museums and scientific research. We had often heard from our parents about such patrons and their generosity.

Mama and I agreed with Lvov when he suggested that people who engaged Vaslav to give social dancing lessons were similarly motivated, inasmuch as the payments of one hundred rubles that Vaslav received for these lessons far exceeded the regular fees paid for social dancing classes. So some people were already coming to his aid. We said we were surprised that Vaslav should willingly accept money from strangers but refuse the help offered by a sincere, close friend of the family.

Soon Vaslav accepted. He began his own daily lessons with Cecchetti, for which Lvov paid the one hundred rubles a month. He was also considerately aware of Vaslav's material needs and would anticipate them in such a way that Vaslav never had to ask him for assistance. To satisfy Vaslav's pride, Pavel Dmitrievitch assured him that once he was famous, he could pay him back.

Little by little Vaslav dropped many of his private lessons, but he continued to teach the young sister of Elena Sechenova-Ivanova, for Vaslav and Elena were close friends and she would have been very hurt if he discontinued teaching her sister. Vaslav also felt that the girl could be a talented dancer. She was always the success of the evening in the performances of the children's operas where he mounted the dances. Later Vaslav was able to persuade her father that she should be entered in the Imperial Theatrical School to train as a dancer—something considered quite improper at that time for the daughter of an aristocratic family.

Vaslav also enjoyed his continuing work with Asafiev, mounting the dance sequences for the new children's opera, *The Snow Queen*, from the fairy tale by Hans Christian Andersen. Vaslav loved working with children.

26   Early Months of 1908

IN JANUARY the *St. Petersburg Gazette* announced: "During the forthcoming engagement of Mathilda Kshessinskaya at the Grand Opéra in Paris . . . her partner will be the young dancer, Vaslav Nijinsky."

The announcement, which was also printed in several other newspapers in Russia, made Nikolai Legat, the ballet master of the Imperial Ballet in St. Petersburg, extremely jealous. He had been Kshessinska's regular partner for several years, and up to now, in the eyes of both the public and his fellow artists, he had been her preferred partner. He resented being replaced by "the young dancer, Vaslav Nijinsky." Legat also felt that his privileged position as the leading *premier danseur* in the Maryinsky was being threatened, seeing that the other ballerinas —Preobrajenska, Trefilova, Egorova, and Pavlova—all wanted to dance with Nijinsky.

When he first heard that Kshessinska had chosen Nijinsky to dance with her, Legat had rephrased the uncomplimentary Russian saying "One fisherman can see another fisherman from far away" by remarking "One Pole can see another Pole from far away"; he was referring to the fact that Kshessinska's father, Felix Kshessinsky, had, like our father, Thomas Nijinsky, and our mother, Eleonora Bereda, been born in Warsaw and had studied at the Wielki Ballet School, and had also been a dancer at the Warsaw Wielki Theatre before coming to Russia.

The early success of the young Nijinsky was also arousing resentment among the other dancers. They were jealous when they saw the way the public was recognizing him and that he was being greeted when he appeared onstage with the sort of applause customarily accorded only to great and well-established artists.

Vaslav told me that when he had been working on the Blue Bird he had had to listen to the sneers of two dancers in particular: Georgi Kyaksht, who graduated in 1891, and Samuil Andrianov,* in 1902. Both had danced the Blue Bird and considered Nijinsky's Blue Bird less an artistic creation than an ostentatious innovation. Vaslav also told me that they had both tried to interfere during his *pas de deux* rehearsals with Lydia Kyaksht, the younger sister of Georgi Kyaksht. Andrianov had graduated at the same time as Tamara Karsavina and Lydia Kyaksht, and he felt that by right he should have been chosen for many of the first soloist's roles that were being given to Nijinsky, especially since he had been promoted to *premier danseur* in 1908, while Nijinsky was only a *coryphé*.

In 1906 Kyaksht had organized a provincial tour in Russia with a company including Andrianov, Tamara Karsavina, and Lydia Kyaksht. Then, in the summer of 1907, he had hoped to get an engagement at one of the Summer Theatres in St. Petersburg and had put all his own money into the enterprise. His company had again included Andrianov and Lydia Kyaksht. Among the dances they had rehearsed had been the Blue Bird from *Sleeping Beauty*, which was to have been danced by Andrianov and Lydia Kyaksht. Unfortunately the venture failed, and all the money put into it was lost and the artists were bitterly disappointed.

Kyaksht had been the first artist to dance the Blue Bird after Cecchetti, by whom he had been personally taught, and so he considered himself the expert interpreter of the role; he resented Vaslav's independent interpretation and unwillingness to ask for assistance. Kyaksht claimed that he could teach Nijinsky to improve his technique and execute more *pirouettes* in the *coda*, saying that Maestro Cecchetti, when he taught him the Blue Bird, had also passed on to him "the secret" of Cecchetti's famous twelve to sixteen *pirouettes*. But Vaslav did not need "the secret"; I had seen him in Cecchetti's classes and knew that he often did fourteen and sixteen *pirouettes* there. But on the stage I never saw him do more than twelve *pirouettes;* he never used up all his strength in leaps, *tours*, or *pirouettes*, lest they become forced and the effort show.

Vaslav also realized that the ballet master, Nikolai Legat, did not appreciate him, in fact had been against him from the first time that Kshessinska had asked Vaslav to dance with her in *La Fille Mal Gardée*, a ballet that Legat considered his own. This became more noticeable after the announcement in the St. Petersburg newspapers that Nijinsky was to accompany Kshessinska to Moscow and later to Paris. Legat did not schedule Vaslav to appear in the ballet program at the Maryinsky very often early in 1908.

---

* Andrianov (1884–1917) became one of George Balanchine's principal teachers at the Maryinsky School. (AK)

But this did not disturb Vaslav unduly at the time, as he was being kept quite busy. Even though they were not going to perform in Paris until May, Vaslav was already rehearsing occasionally with Kshessinska and was also working with Fokine, who was mounting two programs for Charity Performances in the Maryinsky Theatre in February and March. Vaslav was proud that for the first program, to be given on February 16, Fokine had chosen him to dance in *Eunice* in the role of the Greek slave, a role created the year before by Alexander V. Shiraev, considered one of the best character dancers in St. Petersburg. For the same performance, Vaslav was to dance "Nocturne" with Kshessinska in the *Divertissement*.

Since the beginning of January he had been going to the studio of Anna Pavlova for his daily lessons with Maestro Cecchetti. When Anna Pavlova had persuaded Cecchetti to return to St. Petersburg in 1905, insisting how much she needed lessons from him, she had made her large, forty-five-by-thirty-foot studio available for him to give private lessons to other artists.

In addition to studying with Cecchetti in the evenings, Vaslav also worked occasionally with Anna Pavlova in the mornings. She was scheduled during January and February to dance in three performances of *Sleeping Beauty*, and each time she was to appear in a different role. On January 6 she was to dance, for the first time, the leading role of Princess Aurora; two weeks later she was to be the Lilac Fairy; and in mid-February she was to take the role of Princess Florine in the *grand pas de deux*, "Princess Florine and the Blue Bird." For this performance her partner was to be Vaslav Nijinsky.

Pavlova also asked Vaslav to rehearse the two *grand pas de deux* danced by Princess Aurora and the Prince. Maestro Cecchetti was often present at their rehearsals and worked with both of them together. Vaslav was happy for the opportunity to learn the role of the Prince with Pavlova and Cecchetti. The role of the Prince was of course new to him, not only because he was a recent graduate but also because such principal roles in the Imperial Theatres were by tradition given to *premiers danseurs*, and it would normally be several years before Nijinsky might expect to dance it.

Vaslav told me what a joy it was for him to work with Pavlova and how creative and imaginative was her interpretation of Princess Florine. He asked me to be sure to watch the performance of *Sleeping Beauty*, when he would be dancing the Blue Bird with Anna Pavlova.

———

THE DUET of Pavlova and Nijinsky in the Blue Bird was unforgettable. The voices, heard in Tchaikovsky's music, calling to one another, were duplicated in the dance. Pavlova and Nijinsky, as two musical voices, responded to each other, and their movements reverberated and resounded in unison . . .

Princess Florine runs out onto the stage and the lightness of her steps makes her take wing and become the Princess of the Enchanted Realm; she poses, *arabesque*, one hand raised to her lips as if calling the Enchanted Blue Bird, then softly dropping to one knee she holds her hand close to her ear as she listens to his song. Gently her head moves from side to side as if she is searching for the Blue Bird in the sky. Now she hears the Blue Bird hovering over her. Nijinsky has appeared onstage in a tremendous leap, *grand assemblé*. He is not seen touching the ground as he comes down behind the kneeling Princess. Standing on half-toe, his wings softly fluttering, he creates the impression of remaining hovering above her.

Princess Florine reaches upwards towards the Blue Bird, from a deep *plié*, *développé à la seconde*. Feeling the tips of the Blue Bird's wings lightly touching her, the lines of her body flow into an *arabesque* as, playfully and teasingly, she frees herself and runs away.

I will never forget the fragile, delicate figure of Pavlova; her hands were so full of life and expression. When the Princess and the Blue Bird danced together, when they played, hovering and flying above the swift tumbling waters of the stream, the lightness of their dancing was unequaled.

Pavlova and Nijinsky both were endowed with the same divine gift, in which music and dance merged into one harmony. I had never seen this *pas de deux* reach such artistic perfection.

—

IN FEBRUARY I had the opportunity to see Isadora Duncan, when she made a return visit to St. Petersburg. Though I had never seen her before I had already heard a lot about her in the School, in the theatre, and at home. She had become quite well-known in our city, and the public was eager to welcome her again.

Following her performance at the Maryinsky Theatre on February 8, a Gala Benefit Performance, she stayed on in St. Petersburg for two more weeks, performing at the Souvorinsky Theatre. Prince Lvov had taken a box for one of the performances, but it was in the middle of the week, either a Tuesday or a Thursday, which meant I would not be able to join them, since students were not allowed to leave the School on weekdays. But then Vaslav came to the School and spoke to the Inspectrice about it. Contrary to the School rules, Varvara Ivanovna gave permission for me to leave the School at five o'clock so that I could see Isadora Duncan and then return the next morning.

It was a memorable evening. I saw for myself the dancing of Isadora Duncan, which I knew was admired by Kshessinska and Pavlova and had also influenced Fokine in his new choreography. I also heard many opinions on the future of ballet voiced by dance critics and artists who came to our box during the intermission.

Prince Lvov had invited Tamara Karsavina and her husband, Vasily Moukhin, to share our box. Karsavina had just been promoted to the rank of *première danseuse* and was popular with the balletomanes, who admired the fact that in *Swan Lake*, just a month before in January, she had dared to be different by dancing not the usual, expected, thirty-two *fouettés* in Act III but a brilliant *variation* of her own.*

Many people came to our box to speak with Karsavina and Nijinsky, both considered innovative young artists, and during the intermission there were loud discussions and arguments about the need for reform in the ballet.

Although I remained silent, I agreed with Vaslav when he said he felt that progress should be achieved not by discarding the classical ballet school in favor of Duncanism but rather by seeking new ideas in the presentation of ballet. But then I also agreed with Karsavina who felt there was room for both forms of dancing—the art of Duncan and the art of classical ballet. Each could only gain and be enriched by observing the other.

I remember how heatedly Vaslav expressed his indignation about those who called the dancing of Duncan an art. "Her barefoot childish hoppings and skippings should not be called an art . . . her performance is spontaneous and is not based on any school of dancing and so cannot be taught . . . it is not Art . . ."

Sometime during the evening, Vaslav whispered to me, "Are they so blinded by their admiration for Duncan that no one seems to notice the absence of one important element—the male dancer . . .?"

I enjoyed the performance very much, but I could not help thinking that the students of the Imperial School would not need any specific instructions to perform the dances mounted by Duncan. But to dance as Isadora Duncan herself had danced, no one could do that; her own artistry was that of a genius.

The next morning when I returned to the School, the Inspectrice and the governess asked me to show them how Duncan had danced. I took off

*She had already shown she was capable of this technical feat when she had danced in *Swan Lake* at the Wielki Theatre on March 25, 1906, and had astonished the audience by her performance of thirty-two *fouettés*—a first for Warsaw. The previous record on the Wielki stage had been Vera Trefilova with twenty-four. (IN/JR)

my shoes and in my stocking feet started to imitate the dances of Duncan. I ran around the room throwing my arms up in a gesture of abandon and then knelt on the floor, assuming various plastic poses. From the hall there were also several advanced students watching me, as well as the Inspectrice and the governess, and they all laughed at my dancing à la Duncan. The Inspectrice and the governess complimented me and thanked me, saying that now they had a good idea what the dances of Isadora Duncan looked like.

In the evening I had to dance again for the other students and another governess. Wearing my nightgown, and with my feet bare, I went into the larger dormitory to show them how I had seen Isadora Duncan. They were all amused as I frolicked and jumped between the beds.

I was also able to show our students how Duncan's pupils had performed on the stage. On her first visit to St. Petersburg, three years before, Isadora Duncan had danced alone, but this time she had brought some of her pupils from her school in Berlin. There were about a dozen of the little girls, aged eight to eleven, and towards the end of the program they had come onstage dressed in white tunics and with wreaths of flowers in their hair and had weaved in and out in endless rounds until Duncan herself came on and danced with them.

Before leaving St. Petersburg, Isadora Duncan came to visit the School and brought the twelve little girls with her, and they watched some of the younger classes in their dancing lessons.

———

THE TIME was approaching for the February Charity Performance that Fokine was mounting in the Maryinsky Theatre, and as all the tickets had not been sold it was arranged that the graduating students from both Fokine's and Kulichevskaya's classes be invited to attend. I was looking forward to seeing Vaslav dancing the Greek slave in the ballet *Eunice*. He had told me just what a difficult character dance number it was, being executed on top of a large leather wineskin filled with water. The dance was a contest between two slaves. Vaslav was the white slave and Rosai was the black slave. The two had to compete with each other in their dance to see who could remain longest on top of the wineskin. As the wineskin was resilient and slippery, it was difficult for them to keep their balance and stay on top as they jumped and rebounded in their dance.

I was also anxious to see the *Divertissement* when Anna Pavlova was to dance the Saint-Saëns "Swan," in which she had created a sensation two months before. Kshessinska and Nijinsky were also to dance "Nocturne," the *pas de deux* mounted for them by Kulichevskaya, which they had first danced at the Maryinsky in November and then at the Bolshoi Theatre in Moscow in December.

Though Vaslav had told me about the mounting tension between Kshessinska and Pavlova, it came as a surprise to us to hear that Fokine had cancelled the *Divertissement* completely. He had not wanted to take part in the dispute between the two ballerinas as to who should appear most advantageously in the *Divertissement*.

Kshessinska was furious when she heard that she would not be dancing the "Nocturne," and she promptly informed Fokine that she would not dance in *Eunice* either. Pavlova immediately offered to dance the title role and to teach Karsavina her own role of Akthea. As time was short, it was decided that Pavlova should retain Akthea's "Dance of the Seven Veils," but perform it in the role of Eunice.

In place of the *Divertissement* and with only three days left before the performance, Fokine quickly decided to mount *Danses sur la Musique de Chopin*. He chose some solos and ensembles from a new ballet he was already working on: *Rêverie Romantique—Ballet sur la Musique de Chopin*. Moritz Keller, the conductor of the Alexandrinsky Orchestra, was orchestrating several piano pieces by Chopin for the ballet, but as they were not yet completed Fokine decided that the accompaniment for *Danses sur la Musique de Chopin* should simply be a piano and possibly also a violin.

With the canceling of the *Divertissement* all the men dancers were sent home and only the girls were kept for rehearsals. This made the men both anxious and angry; they were upset at losing the opportunity of dancing the numbers they had prepared and worked on for some time.

Vaslav was also distressed, but for another reason. When he heard that all the numbers would be mounted to music by Chopin and performed without male dancers, he was reminded of the performance of Isadora Duncan that he had just seen and at which he had been disturbed to note both the ready acceptance by the public and the overwhelming success achieved by a woman dancing alone.

The Charity Performance took place on February 16, and Pavlova was a great success in her interpretation of Eunice in "The Dance of the Seven Veils." Karsavina was beautiful in the role of Akthea and was warmly applauded. Nijinsky and Rosai had to repeat their exhilarating character dance, but like the previous year the biggest success went to "The Dance of the Flaming Torches."

The performance ended with *Danses sur la Musique de Chopin*. The scene opened on a group of ballerinas as seen in the engraved lithographs of the Romantic Period of the nineteenth century. Twenty girls of the *corps de ballet* were dressed in identical costumes copied from the one designed by

Bakst the previous year for Pavlova in *Chopiniana*. With the budget limited for a Charity Performance there had been no funds to make new costumes, so they used the standard white ballet costumes, with the regulation mid-calf skirt length, from the Theatre wardrobe. To get the ankle-length effect that Fokine wanted, each girl wore a costume designed for a taller girl, and then Vera Fokina took lengths of tulle and quickly made a top skirt to wear over the other layers so that the costumes would appear more uniform and of the same length.

For her opening number, Pavlova danced a solo mazurka. As she crossed the stage in a series of *grands jetés,* she seemed to fly. Karsavina in her valse solo was lyrically romantic. Then came the valse *pas de deux* that Fokine danced with Pavlova—that he had first mounted for Pavlova and Oboukhov in *Chopiniana* in 1907. There were also two ensemble numbers, a nocturne and a valse, but my strongest impression is of Anna Pavlova, who evoked for me again the image of Marie Taglioni in *La Sylphide.*

For the next Charity Performance, to take place on March 8, Fokine was mounting another new ballet, *Egyptian Nights,* with music by Anton Arensky, the young Russian composer who had recently died, in 1906.

This ballet, then called *Une Nuit d'Egypte,* with a libretto by Petipa, had been choreographed in 1900 by Ivanov for a performance on Olgin Island at Peterhof in honor of a visit by the Shah of Persia. The ballet had been prepared and all the costumes made when the performance was canceled. So *Une Nuit d'Egypte* had never been performed until Fokine mounted it in 1908 and renamed it *Egyptian Nights.*

The unused costumes had been stored in the Theatre wardrobe for eight years, and Fokine hoped he would find that they were Egyptian, but to his disappointment they were all ballet-style costumes with a few Egyptian ornaments. Fortunately he was able to use some sets and costumes from *La Fille du Pharaon,* and from the opera *Aïda.* Bakst helped him choose them and also advised on the staging and lighting; he designed some of the extra new costumes that were needed. Anna Pavlova, as part of the costume that Bakst had designed for her in the role of Veronica, wore a live snake wrapped around her arm!

The costumes for the other ballet on the program, *Rêverie Romantique— Ballet sur la Musique de Chopin,* were on hand, for they were the same white dresses, à la Taglioni, used in the February Charity Performance. For the set, Fokine and Benois unfurled the forty-yard forest panorama from *Sleeping Beauty* and selected one section that would provide the most suitable background for the "white" ballet.

Vaslav told me that during the rehearsals of *Egyptian Nights* there were live horses on the stage. A messenger on a black horse came to announce the arrival of Mark Antony (Pavel Gerdt), who made his entrance in a Roman chariot drawn by two white horses and followed by Roman legions and Ethiopian slaves. Greek maidens danced with scarves and flowers, and threw petals at Cleopatra's feet as she advanced to welcome Mark Antony.

"I dance in this ballet with Olga Ossipovna [Preobrajenska]. We are the favored slaves of Cleopatra and we perform during the feast to entertain Mark Antony, who is seated, reclining next to Cleopatra."

He laughed as he added, "We dance à la Duncan . . . holding a long wide silk scarf above our heads, and we execute intricate steps, jumping and skipping under the scarf as it floats and undulates in the air above us . . ."

Cleopatra, the Queen of Egypt, was not a dancing role and was taken by Yelizaveta Timmé, a drama student from the dance class of Alexander Shiraev. The two leading roles of Veronica and Amoun were taken by Anna Pavlova and Mikhail Fokine. Fokine painted his body dark brown and asked the other Ethiopian slaves to do the same, rather than wear brown or black leotards.

Vaslav was watching all the rehearsals of *Rêverie Romantique* and was very excited about Fokine's choreography. He was sorry I would not be able to see the ballet; the tickets for this benefit had all been sold well in advance. He told me that the ballet was all classical dance numbers, without any sign of the influence of Duncan. A classical ballet with no plot, it did not give the impression of a *divertissement* but rather was an abstract ballet created with beauty and consistency. The three ballerinas, Pavlova, Preobrajenska, and Karsavina, were the images of Taglioni, Grisi, and Cerrito.

The students were not taken to see the rehearsals, so I was not present to hear Fokine announce that the only male role in *Rêverie Romantique* was to be danced by Nijinsky.

After the rehearsal in costume and makeup, Fokine, who was dancing the leading role of Amoun, found that it took him almost one hour to remove the brown makeup from his body and legs. Vaslav felt this was the deciding factor in prompting Fokine to ask Nijinsky to dance in *Rêverie Romantique*. Fortunately there was no problem about costume, for the one and only costume that Vaslav possessed at this time was the Bakst costume commissioned by Kshessinska for his performance with her in "Nocturne," which was perfectly in accord with the Taglioni costume that Bakst had designed for Anna Pavlova for *Chopiniana*.*

*For non-repertory performances, the artists either had to supply their own costumes or avail themselves of existing wardrobe costumes that might lend themselves to the role. (IN/JR)

35. Bronislava Nijinska in the uniform
of the graduating class of 1908.

36. Bronislava Nijinska in her
graduation gown, May 22, 1908.

Гернецкая Евгения   1908   Чумакова Антонина
Чернашева Лидия Олехина Екатерина   Нижинская Бронислава Дорбулубова

37. Graduation Class of the Imperial Theatrical School, 1908. *From left to right:* L. Tchernicheva,
E. Georgievskaya, E. Olhina, B. Nijinskaya, A. Tchumakova, M. Dobrolubova. Yelizaveta Gerdt also
graduated in 1908, but not being a resident student was not eligible for the official class photograph.

38. Elena Smirnova and Ludmila Schollar, from the official gradution class photograph for 1906. In their Graduation Student Performance Nijinsky partnered Schollar in Kulichevskaya's *The Prince Gardener* and Smirnova in Fokine's *Midsummer Night's Dream*.

39. Cecchetti with three of his students: Lopukhova and Nijinska standing, and Pavlova seated.

40, 41. Bronislava Nijinska in her "white dress," and Vaslav Nijinsky in his practice clothes, at the Krasnoe Selo Theatre, Summer 1908.

42, 43. Olga Preobrajenska in
"Danse Russe" with a sentimental
reminiscence written for Bronislava
Nijinska, and in a dancing pose
from "Bacchanale."

44. Vera Trefilova.

45. Tamara Karsavina as the Spanish
Doll in *Fairy Doll*, in 1910.

46. Costume for the Spanish Doll
in *Fairy Doll*, as designed by Léon
Bakst for Anna Pavlova in 1903.

47. Another costume design by
Bakst for *Fairy Doll* in 1903,
worn by Bronislava Nijinska as
one of the dolls in the toy shop.

48. Léon Bakst, self-portrait. Published
in *Zolotoe Runo*, St. Petersburg, 1906.

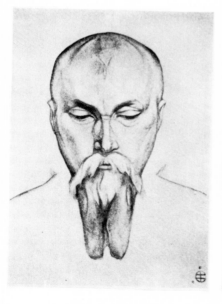

49. Nicholas Roerich, drawing
by his son Sviatoslav Roerich.
Published in New York in 1924.

50. Alexandre Benois, drawing
by Konstantin Somov. Published
in the souvenir program, *Boris
Godounov*, Paris, 1908.

Шаляпинъ. „Жизнь за Царя".

51, 52. Feodor Chaliapin in two of his
most famous roles, as Mephistopheles
in *Faust* and as Sussanin in *A Life
for the Tsar*. Imperial Theatres photographs, c. 1902 and c. 1908, respectively.

Édition
„Richard"
St. Pétersbourg.
386

Шаляпинъ

фотогр.
Императорски
ТЕАТРОВЪ.

Fokine had told Vaslav that he would be dancing in one of the Charity Performances, and at the same time had suggested to Anna Pavlova that she should rehearse the *pas de deux* from *Chopiniana* with Vaslav when they were working together in her studio.

The day before the performance, Fokine asked Nijinsky and Pavlova to rehearse in the Maryinsky; afterwards he kept Vaslav behind, and in just a few minutes he mounted for him his mazurka solo.

The groupings with the *corps de ballet*, the sylphides, were worked out during the intermission of the actual performance. Fokine first placed the sylphides in their positions around Pavlova and Nijinsky, posed in center stage, and then started to show them how to come together for the final grouping. Meanwhile, as Vaslav told me later, Sergei Grigoriev, who was assisting Fokine, kept trying to hurry him up, saying that the audience was getting restive, and warned him, "Soon you will be playing to empty seats." But Fokine simply replied, "I need only one more minute, wait just one minute . . ."

Vaslav, while thrilled to be dancing with the ballerinas, Preobrajenska and Pavlova and Karsavina, was not fully aware of the impact this had on the ballet company.

The news that Nijinsky, officially one rank below that of soloist, had danced the part of the only *premier danseur* in Fokine's new ballet, *Rêverie Romantique—Ballet sur la Musique de Chopin*, hit the ballet company like a bolt of lightning, and rumors soon began to spread. They said that Nijinsky was not ready for such distinction and only owed it to his rich friend, Prince Lvov, because Fokine had needed money for the extra costumes for *Egyptian Nights*, costumes that had been so splendid that they had made the audience gasp. Never before had such an authentic representation of Egypt been seen on the stage of the Maryinsky Theatre, particularly in a Charity Performance without any subsidy from the Imperial Theatres.

I became aware of the extent of the jealousy and resentment that was felt towards Vaslav when Tonya Tchumakova, who had been Vaslav's sweetheart in the School until the incident of the pink letter, and who used to spend all her free time with her sister Olga and Nikolai Legat, told me the harsh things they were saying about Vaslav.

"Nijinsky is not a finished *premier danseur* . . . he is not ready to be dancing with *prima ballerinas* . . ."

The hard feelings of Nikolai Legat towards Nijinsky were understandable. Not only was Vaslav being sought after as a partner by Kshessinska, Preobrajenska, Egorova, Trefilova, and Pavlova, but he was also making it no secret that he found Legat's obligatory morning *classe de perfection* boring. Vaslav avoided them whenever he could join Pavlova in her rehearsals with Cecchetti, and of course was also taking lessons on his own with Cecchetti every day. In addition, Legat resented Vaslav's open admiration for Fokine's choreography. Fokine was emerging as a rival, a direct competitor of Nikolai Legat, the official ballet master and chief choreographer of the Imperial Ballet at the Maryinsky Theatre.

During the next few weeks I did not see much of Vaslav, being busy in the School preparing for the Student Performance on April 6, when I would be one of the graduating students. My teacher, Klavdia Kulichevskaya, was mounting the first ballet in the program, *Danse des Heures* from the opera *La Gioconda*. Fokine, for his class, was mounting *Grand Pas sur la Musique de Chopin*.

I had been thrilled to have Kulichevskaya distinguish me with a *variation*, mounted to show my elevation to advantage as I crossed the stage in *grands jetés* and *jetés entrelacés*, and there were many *pas battus*, at which I also excelled. I was working as well on a *variation sur pointe* with Luba Tchernicheva for the *Divertissement*.

But as the day of the performance approached, I grew more and more depressed. I had not heard anything from Father. Apparently he was not coming to see me dance in the Student Performance. I loved my father very much, even though he had been living apart from us for many years now. I had been hoping that in spite of the quarrel and anger between him and Vaslav he would come and see my graduation performance, or at least write to me.

On the day of the final rehearsal I received a note from my friend Zina Puyman, who had graduated the year before and was now a member of the ballet company at the Maryinsky, asking me to join her during the intermission. We went to one of the loges during Fokine's ballet, so that we could talk on our own.

Zina told me that Vaslav had many enemies in the ballet company. Several of the young dancers who were resentful of Vaslav's success had become friends with Maria Gorshkova and were spreading vicious gossip about Vaslav, saying that the real reason behind his break with Gorshkova was because Vaslav was unable to love a woman. I remembered how deeply Vaslav had been in love with Maria, and how, when he discovered she was only using him in order to advance her dancing career, his love for her had turned to anger. I had known, too, that after he had rejected her, Vaslav had been very gloomy and had kept to himself in the theatre. He had come to distrust women, saying that they used their charms to seduce men for their own selfish aims, and so had declined many invitations to join the boys and girls of the company for supper after the theatre. At the same time, Vaslav had also broken off completely with Bourman and his gambling friends. Zina told me that the boys in the company, the same ones who had played pranks on him during his school years, were now teasing him and daring him to prove to them that he was capable of making love to a woman.

It was during the painful period of his disillusionment and heartbreak with Gorshkova, his first serious love, that Vaslav had met Prince Lvov. As the two of them started going regularly to concerts and theatres together, the boys began to taunt Vaslav about this friendship, and it became the subject of ugly gossip. Some of the rumors about Vaslav and his rich friend reached even me in the School, but I was still childishly innocent and did not understand what was being insinuated. Besides, I knew Prince Lvov as a friend of our family, of Mother and me as well as Vaslav. All I understood was his sincere friendship for our family and his admiration for Vaslav's rare dancing talent. After all, I had long been hearing stories from Mother and Father of the goodness and generosity of admirers and patrons in the theatrical world who bestowed gifts on artists and assisted them financially in their artistic enterprise. I saw Prince Lvov helping Vaslav in his dancing career in the same way that he was promoting many champions for sporting events.

So I was overwhelmed to hear from Zina the nature of the malicious insinuations about the friendship between Vaslav and Prince Lvov. Then Zina begged me to warn Vaslav that according to what she was hearing in the Theatre his enemies were planning some further mischief against him. I had to leave to get ready for the rehearsal of the *Divertissement*, so we could not talk anymore just then.

The Student Performance for 1908 took place the next day, on Sunday, April 6. Though I danced well and had to repeat my *variation* in *Danse des Heures* to shouts of "Bis," this was not a happy day for me.

Father had not come, and there had been no word from him. Mother was accompanied by Vaslav and Prince Lvov, and I felt uneasy in their presence.* I was also worried—Zina had asked me to warn Vaslav, but how was I to do it? I knew that Vaslav would be aware of my unhappiness, for he and I had always been very close. I hoped he would assume it was due to Father's absence.

After the performance, during supper, Vaslav complimented me on my dancing, on the lightness of my jumps and the sharp outline of the *pas*

---

*Bronislava Nijinska's discretion reflects her perceptions at that time. Other biographers have implied strongly that Vaslav's relationship with Lvov was homosexual. The only one to state it flatly was Richard Buckle in *Diaghilev* (1979). "Lvov helped the Nijinskys financially, and it was with him that Vaslav had his first homosexual affair." (AK)

battus, and I told him that I owed much to the lessons he had given me during the summer of 1906.

Mother also seemed happy with my success and was especially proud over the announcement that Frossia Georgievskaya and I were to have a debut in *Paquita* in three weeks. We were to dance a *pas de trois* with Adolf Bolm, who was just completing a successful tour of Europe with Anna Pavlova and a company of twenty artists from the Imperial Theatres.

Though Mama was pleased with my progress, she was critical of Kulichevskaya's presentation of *Danse des Heures.* She knew the ballet herself from the first time it had been performed in Russia in the opera *La Gioconda,* by an Italian ballet troupe supplemented by Thomas Nijinsky and his company of twelve dancers. Father had mounted several dance numbers, and Mama felt that the liveliness of that presentation far surpassed that of Kulichevskaya's.

All three of them, Mama and Vaslav and Prince Lvov, also criticized Fokine for mounting *Grand Pas sur la Musique de Chopin* for the Student Performance only three weeks after *Rêverie Romantique* was seen at the Maryinsky Theatre, which meant that the graduating students could only be compared unfavorably with the ballerinas Preobrajenska, Pavlova, and Karsavina. Prince Lvov, who had seen *Rêverie Romantique,* said that the beauty of this ballet was its simplicity, devoid of all technical display of virtuosity, ". . . and while the most simple *pas* performed by artists is an experience to watch, transporting us to a realm of poetry, when those same dances are executed by students, even graduating students, the interpretation of every dance is so similar that they are boring to watch."

Following the Student Performance, the School was closed for two weeks to celebrate the Russian Easter. Every day I went to the Maryinsky Theatre where Frossia and I were allowed to practice in the big dance hall. We had three weeks to work on the *pas de trois* for our debut in *Paquita.* Since Adolf Bolm would not be returning from his tour until after Easter, we asked one of the graduating students, Arkady Sergeyev, to partner us in the meantime.

I did not see much of Vaslav as he was rehearsing daily with Kshessinska. They were to leave for Paris on April 21, and he was looking forward to going. It was a tremendous opportunity for him, a young dancer performing on the stage of the Paris Opéra, and as the partner of the *prima ballerina assoluta,* Mathilda Kshessinska. We were both so busy that I could not find time to talk to him, as Zina had asked me.

Suddenly, one day when I came home, I found Mama crying. She told me Vaslav was ill. She would not let me see my brother, who was confined to his room.

Vaslav's illness came as a tragedy at home.

Through the wall and behind closed doors I could hear the conversations between the doctor and Mother and Prince Lvov. The doctor was trying to soothe Mother by saying that it was not a serious illness, not dangerous for Vaslav, that he should be well again in a week or two, and that many boys of his age went through such experiences.

From these whispered conversations I learned that they blamed an older friend of Vaslav's who had talked him into visiting a woman of easy reputation frequented by this so-called friend and his companions. From Mama's conversations with Vaslav I learned how the artist, whose name I shall not mention here, had persuaded him by saying, "It is time for you to become a man like us . . ."

From this visit Vaslav had become infected.

He accused his older "friend" of having arranged this deliberately in order to gain favor with Nikolai Legat by ruining Vaslav's chances of dancing with Kshessinska in Paris. I have no idea whether this was true, or whether Vaslav was trying to mitigate his own sense of shame.

Vaslav did not want to see me. He told Mama, "Bronia must not come to see me. I am soiled."

Mama kept praying to God and would look pleadingly at the doctor, as though she expected a miracle. Vaslav was embarrassed in front of Mama, who could not keep herself from remonstrating with him, "I always warned you to be careful and not to find yourself in the company of such women. I told you this so that you would recognize the danger and realize the risks you could run." Sadly, Vaslav answered her, "Now I know, and I am punished."

From books that I had read by the classical Russian authors, Tolstoy and Dostoyevsky, I knew of the existence of such women and had in fact seen many of these unfortunates on the streets of St. Petersburg. But I did not understand what kind of relationship they had with men, though I always felt a sense of revulsion when I saw them accosting men on the streets. I was horrified—how could a man bear to touch them? And suddenly poor Vaslav. . . . The very thought made me feel faint. I must have looked as ill as I felt, for the doctor asked me if I was all right.

All this time Prince Lvov was wonderful. He proved himself more than a friend; he behaved as a dear parent to us. He had immediately called a famous specialist, and noticing that Vaslav was embarrassed and reluctant to be cared for by his mother, Lvov had sent his valet to stay with Vaslav day and night throughout his illness. During the day he would sit dozing in a chair in the hall outside Vaslav's door, ready should he be needed, and at night he would stay by Vaslav's bedside, sitting in an armchair. All the food for Vaslav was specially prepared by Prince Lvov's cook and brought each day. I remember them bringing broth in a bottle, and also a chicken in white sauce. Lvov himself spent nearly every day with us during Vaslav's illness, comforting both Mother and Vaslav.

It was not long before Vaslav was well enough to be up, but he was very disappointed to find that Kshessinska had selected a replacement, and was already rehearsing with Legat.

Lvov was not only thoughtful and attentive towards Vaslav and Mother, but also towards me. I must mention here an incident that happened to me about this same time when, thanks to his thoughtfulness and concern, I was spared from having to undergo a painful operation; perhaps he even saved my leg from amputation.

I was practicing for my debut; my new toe shoes were hard and I soon developed a blister on my heel. I ignored the pain and continued to work intensively, even after the blister broke and exposed the raw flesh. Our rehearsals took place in the big rehearsal hall at the Maryinsky with the other artists, and when the dancers saw my foot they all gave me their advice. One told me to apply a certain medicated talcum powder; the second recommended a special ointment; the third said the best thing I could do would be to cover the open wound with an adhesive plaster to protect the heel. At home I faithfully followed all their advice, and then after cleaning the wound with alcohol I covered it with the plaster.

I did not sleep well that night; my leg ached. By morning it was so swollen that I had difficulty putting on my street shoes. But I was determined to go to the rehearsal, for this was Monday, April 21, the first day we would be rehearsing with Adolf Bolm, just back from his tour. It was also the day when Vaslav wanted to come with me to watch the rehearsal. He had promised to help me, having himself danced this *pas de trois* from *Paquita* earlier that year.

Prince Lvov arrived to take us to the rehearsal and at once noticed my limp. As we were driving along in his automobile, he questioned me about it. I told him about the burst blister on my heel, and Lvov said that instead of going to the rehearsal I should immediately go to see a doctor. Both Vaslav and I tried to convince him that to miss a rehearsal would surely lose me the debut performance, and that it was impossible for me to take time off. But Lvov insisted that as I would not be able to dance at all, the way I was limping, he would take me to see a doctor there and then. Vaslav went on his own to the Theatre to explain why I was not there, and Lvov conducted me to the office of a famous orthopedic surgeon. But the doctor was not there, and so we drove to his clinic where I was taken directly to the operating room. When the surgeon's assistant saw the plaster, he screamed, "What have you done? . . . you should never have put a plaster on an open wound . . . you have caused a bad inflammation . . ." Painfully the foot was cleaned, and after the application of a compress my leg was wrapped in bandages up to the knee. I was forbidden to walk on it, and told to return the next day. By now Vaslav had joined us in the clinic, and he helped me hop across the room.

By the next morning the pain had diminished somewhat. Vaslav helped me return to the clinic, where the surgeon exclaimed, "How lucky you were that you came yesterday! Another day could have caused you the loss of your foot . . ."

Prince Lvov had indeed saved my foot. Without him I would have continued to dance at rehearsals, ignoring the pain. With only a few days before the debut, I would never have taken time by myself to go and see a doctor.

On our way home we bought the *St. Petersburg Gazette* and read the announcement:

On April 26 Kshessinska left for Paris, where her partner will be Legat and not, as previously announced, Nijinsky, who has hurt his leg.

Presumably some reporter had seen Vaslav coming in or out of the clinic and assumed that he had hurt his leg.

I had to stay off my foot, and when I returned to the School I had to spend several days in the infirmary until the foot was recovered enough for me to walk on it. I was not able to make my debut in *Paquita* at the Maryinsky Theatre. I was heartbroken.

The day of my graduation was approaching, and still I did not hear from Father. Nor did he send me any money towards my graduation or my outfitting as an Artist. Mother and Vaslav had been saving up for me during the year, and to this was added a gift from Prince Lvov.

On graduation morning, May 22, 1908, a service was held in the School Chapel. We all attended, wearing our uniforms for the very last time, and after lunch we changed into our graduation dresses. We looked like brides. I had chosen a tea-rose lace and carried a bouquet of yellow roses.

The *Akt* took place as usual in the very large hall in the School, and when the names of the graduating students were read out I received the First Award and the New Testament in Polish, the complete works of Leo Tolstoy, and the one hundred rubles given to each graduating student.

Afterwards, in our beautiful graduation dresses, we drove, as was the custom, to the Islands.

I submitted my application to be admitted to the Imperial Theatres and became an Artist of the Imperial Theatres on May 26, 1908.

There were seven graduating students in the Girls' Division that year: Maria Dobrolubova, Yelizaveta Gerdt, Efrosima Georgievskaya, Bronislava Nijinska, Ekaterina Olhina, Lubov Tchernicheva, and Antonina Tchumakova. All seven of us were accepted by the Imperial Theatres and admitted to the ranks of the *corps de ballet* at a salary of six hundred rubles a year.

27 Summer of 1908: My First Days as an Artist of the Imperial Theatres

As soon as I officially became an Artist of the Imperial Theatres, Mama suggested that since Vaslav and I were both to be working in St. Petersburg we should be thinking of moving to a larger and more comfortable apartment. We agreed with her, and as soon as I was asked to dance at Krasnoe Selo during the summer we told the manager of our apartment that we would be leaving by June 1; we also decided to put the furniture into the same storage where most of it had been since 1904, when we left Mokhovaya Ulitza.

We knew by then that Vaslav would not be dancing at Krasnoe Selo, that he had accepted an invitation from Prince Lvov to spend the summer at Steinbrook Farm, his summer villa on the Islands near Novaya Derevnia at Sestroretzk.

I recall that before telling Mother about the invitation Vaslav had come to me as though seeking my support and approval. He told me that Kulichevskaya had not invited him to dance at Krasnoe Selo before leaving for Paris with Kshessinska (perhaps due to the rumors about his leg injury), which was one reason why he would like to be away from St. Petersburg for a while.

"What do you think, Bronia, should I go?"

I remembered then that Sestroretzk had a small railway station and was in Novaya Derevnia, on the Islands, very close to the villa of the Englunds, where Vaslav used to give dancing lessons. It occurred to me that Vaslav might visit them and that his old friendship with Zina might help him recover himself. They would be able to stroll in the park or on the beach together.

"By all means. It is by the sea, so you can swim and bathe, and Sestroretzk is not far away from St. Petersburg."

Vaslav was delighted with my response, as if he had received my permission as well as my approval. "But what about you and Mama? I expect you will be dancing at Krasnoe Selo. Where will you be staying? I remember how afraid you were last year to be alone at Dudergoth at night."

Vaslav was happy when I told him that Mama would like to be near Stassik at Ligovo, which was midway between Krasnoe Selo and St. Petersburg.

Mama did not object to Vaslav's plan to spend the summer with Prince Lvov. She had found that there were no dachas for rent near Ligovo, which was an area of fashionable summer residences and large beautiful villas owned by the wealthy nobility. However, a young doctor in attendance at the sanatorium had told her that he was staying with his aunt, a widow who accepted paying guests in her villa, if they came with a recommendation, and he had promised to speak to her for Mama.

I had not seen Stassik since December when Mama and I had walked through the snow to his sanatorium, nor had Mama been to see him often through that cold winter and very rainy spring. I told Mama I wanted to visit Stassik on the day after graduation, when it was the custom to visit friends and relatives, driving in an open carriage and wearing another outfit from the "graduation trousseau."

Wearing a new beige day outfit, a suit with a fitted jacket and a slim skirt, I climbed into the open carriage and Mama and I drove out to the country to Ligovo.

When we arrived Stassik looked pale and appeared withdrawn. I believe he was lonely and missed younger people; most of the patients in his new sanatorium were middle-aged or older. We promised that we would come and see him often.

The young doctor then came up to talk with Mama and give her his aunt's address. He said it was just a short walk from the sanatorium on the way towards the station. We soon found the villa—in a garden, behind iron gates. On the large terrace in front of the house several people were sitting, being served afternoon tea by a maid. We were met by a very pleasant lady, the doctor's aunt, who offered us some tea. She explained that she usually took only permanent boarders but would be prepared to rent us a room for the summer. She showed us the room, which was large and airy and nicely furnished with twin beds. We took it, with full board just for Mother, who explained that since I would be going every day to St. Petersburg and to Krasnoe Selo, I would not be able to take all my meals there.

Almost the next day Mama and I moved to Ligovo. Vaslav had already moved out to Sestroretzk.

Three times a week I went to St. Petersburg. In the mornings there was a *classe de perfection* for the Artists. These were held at Teatralnaya Ulitza, No. 2, in the large ballet rehearsal hall. I had several classes that summer with a great teacher, Anna Johannson, the daughter of the famous dancer and teacher, Christian Johannson. At twelve-thirty, following the class, there would be rehearsals for Krasnoe Selo in the same hall. By four-thirty I would be back in Ligovo where, if there was a performance the same evening, I would eat only a light meal before leaving at six to catch the train for Krasnoe Selo.

I danced in many ballets and also had several numbers in the *divertissements*. These were mainly from Kulichevskaya's ballets, so I was already familiar with most of them. Kulichevskaya had not yet returned from Paris at the beginning of the Krasnoe Selo season, so the rehearsals were taken by Georgi Kyaksht, who was also the leading dancer with his sister Lydia. In the *divertissements* Lydia Kyaksht danced many *pas de deux* with Samuil Andrianov.

All three had great success and were offered an engagement in England to dance at the Empire Theatre in London. Georgi Kyaksht had to decline the offer when he was not able to convince the Administration of the Imperial Theatres to give him a three-month leave of absence. He did not wish to aggravate his already tense relations with the Imperial Theatres by insisting on a leave, for he was only two years away from his pension after twenty years of employment as an Artist of the Imperial Theatres.

Adolf Bolm was engaged to go to London instead, and at the end of July Lydia Kyaksht left with Andrianov and Bolm. Though Bolm and Andrianov returned to Russia in the fall, Lydia Kyaksht remained in London, where she appeared with great success in the Empire Ballets. She decided to settle in London and never returned to dance in Russia.

Several afternoons a week we had rehearsals on the stage at Krasnoe Selo and then I would not return to Ligovo until after the evening performance. I would join my friends for tea on the terrace of the Pavillion Restaurant, where there were tables under awnings with a view of the garden. Just before the performance, Kyaksht, or Kulichevskaya when she returned, would give us a short class—a "warm-up class" we used to call it—consisting mainly of *barre* exercises. At the end of the performance I would rush to get ready to go home, for I knew Mother would be waiting for me at the station in Ligovo, to walk home with me. When we got home our landlady would arrange that I always had a hot drink and a snack to eat before going to bed.

I was so busy with the rehearsals and performances at Krasnoe Selo that I was able to see Stassik only a few times that summer, and I often missed Vaslav when he came to Ligovo to see us. Sometimes, after having lunch with Mama, Vaslav would go with her to see Stassik. He told me that several times he had waited until five o'clock before leaving, after Mama had said that I might not have a rehearsal at Krasnoe Selo that day, in which case I would come to Ligovo for tea.

I was also disappointed that during the summer I was able to go only once to Sestroretzk and visit Vaslav at Steinbrook Farm.

I liked Prince Lvov's villa very much. It was far from the center of the little town and away from the noise, and it gave a feeling of extraordinary quiet and serenity. Throughout the villa there was a strong scent from the flowers in the garden mingling with the smell of wax from the highly polished floors.

Vaslav's room was spacious, with a window overlooking the garden. The walls were white; it looked almost monastic. There was a large black lacquered wooden crucifix hanging on the white wall above his bed, and two mahogany chairs were upholstered with black leather. There was just one other table besides the night table, and of course the large wardrobe for Vaslav's clothes, which were taken care of by the servants. There was nothing superfluous in the room, and not a speck of dust anywhere. It was beautifully neat.

Prince Pavel Dmitrievitch was personal secretary to the Minister of Communications and often had to be away, accompanying the Minister on his visits to road or railway construction sites. At some time, I'm not sure when, the Minister was responsible for the Trans-Siberian Railroad. But even though Prince Lvov might be away, Vaslav was free to stay in the villa.

Vaslav showed me the tennis court where he played most days with Lvov when he was home. He also began to teach me to play tennis.

—

WHEN KSHESSINSKA returned to St. Petersburg from Paris she asked Vaslav to dance with her at Krasnoe Selo. At last I had the chance to see Kshessinska and Nijinsky dancing in "Nocturne" and wearing the costumes designed for them by Bakst. Vaslav's costume I had already seen at home hanging in the closet: a black sleeveless jacket worn over white tights, a white silk shirt with wide sleeves, and a long tie of light chiffon that billowed in response to his movements in the dance. Kshessinska's costume was a long white chiffon tunic, in the Duncan style.

Though Vaslav danced well and was recalled several times after his solo, I was disappointed with "Nocturne" and felt that Kulichevskaya's choreography lacked imagination. The dreamy music of Chopin's "Nocturne" was used only for the *adagio*, and a brilliant valse was added so that Kshessinska could display her virtuoso technique *sur pointe* in her *variation*. Kshessinska's interpretation of Chopin's music was quite a contrast from the ethereal and ephemeral image created by Pavlova in *Chopiniana*.

That summer at Krasnoe Selo, Kshessinska and Nijinsky also danced the *pas de deux* from *La Bayadère*, which they had last performed in December. Vaslav was strikingly effective and Kshessinska danced brilliantly. The moment she came onstage the whole theatre was lit as if by a burst of flame. As a child I had seen both Zambelli and Legnani and been amazed by the virtuosity of their technique; but now I saw Kshessinska. Her dance was a dazzling display; in the *prestissimo* of her numerous *fouettés*, she whirled like a fiery ball shooting out tongues of flames.

After Lydia Kyaksht left for England, Kulichevskaya invited Ludmila Schollar to dance at Krasnoe Selo. My own friendship with Ludmila dates from these summer days that we spent together at Krasnoe Selo. Vaslav and Ludmila and I often had lunch together there.

One day Kshessinska came and also joined us for lunch. She told us about Diaghilev's presentation of Russian Opera in Paris, which had taken place during her engagement at the Paris Opéra, and how successful it had been. Mathilda Felixovna recounted an amusing anecdote, an incident that occurred when she went to watch the rehearsal of Feodor Chaliapin in *Boris Godunov*, which was being presented for the first time in Paris by Diaghilev.

There were always many people in the audience for rehearsals in Paris, and of course they did not understand Russian. Chaliapin was not wearing his costume for the rehearsal but was in his ordinary street clothes. In the last act, when the demented Tsar Godunov believes that he sees the ghost of the murdered Tsarevitch, the whole audience rose to their feet in a panic, trying to see what had so frightened Chaliapin, who was gasping for air and trembling with fear as he pointed a finger to the far corner of the stage.

Kshessinska was very friendly towards Vaslav that summer and seemed to love to dance with him. I think this was the time when she asked Ludmila to show her *The Prince Gardener*, so that she could dance it with Vaslav.

Whenever Kshessinska came to rehearsals she was always surrounded by admirers, all expressing their devotion with lavish praise and admiration. Vaslav, however, would keep his distance, trying not to provoke jealousy. He even avoided attending the receptions that she held in her home, where the dancers seeking to be her partner would all strive to attract her attention. Many of these dancers felt that Vaslav was putting on airs, and would say so, sometimes even to Kshessinska.

In the fall, Kshessinska held a housewarming party in her new residence, and it became a much talked of event as all the nobility was expected to be there. Vaslav was invited, too, but he did not want to go, and he didn't know how to get out of the invitation. He took the advice of Prince Lvov and sent a note of apology, a bouquet, and a present: an ikon by Fabergé, carved on mother-of-pearl, showing a group of saints framed by a silver aureole and lighted from behind so as to shimmer with colorful rays.

In her own memoirs, Kshessinska describes Vaslav's gift as "reflecting his nobility of soul." She also says that of all the precious objects she lost during the Revolution, this ikon was the one she regretted most: "souvenir of some of the most beautiful days of my career and . . . a gift from an artist without equal . . ."

28   My First Season at the Maryinsky

IN THE MIDDLE of August we moved back to St. Petersburg, to a much larger and more comfortable apartment that Vaslav had found and rented for us, and where we were to stay for our remaining years in St. Petersburg: Apartment 1 at 13 Bolshaya Koniushennaya Ulitza. Though it was difficult at the time to obtain a private telephone, we were able to get one installed promptly; our number was 112–04.

The new apartment was just as elegant but even larger than our first apartment in St. Petersburg, on Mokhovaya Ulitza, where Mother had been so proud of the beautiful dining room she had furnished from her engagements in the Summer Theatres. When we had moved to smaller apartments it had been necessary for Mama to put the large dining-room furniture and the beautiful pier mirror into storage. She was so happy to find this furniture in good condition after four years, and to see how good it looked in the new dining room.

The drawing-room furniture needed to be reupholstered after ten years of use, and Mother chose a heavy blue silk damask to replace the badly worn and faded pale magenta velours. It was promised to be delivered to the apartment for August 20, the date Vaslav and I had to report to the Maryinsky Theatre.

I now had my own room. I had been saving money from my earnings at Krasnoe Selo, and from that plus the salary I had been receiving as an Artist of the Imperial Theatres since June, I bought furniture for my room. I found just what I wanted—furniture with simple lines, made of solid Karelian birch. Mother reminded me that I also had some money left over from my graduation outfitting, and that I could use it, too. I bought myself a desk; it was of golden bird's-eye birch and matched the other furniture in my room, the first room of my own since we came to St. Petersburg.

Vaslav had two rooms, a study and a bedroom, which Prince Lvov furnished for him. The walls of the study were covered with a dark raspberry, textured wallpaper. The three windows that looked out on the street had dark green velvet draperies. The doors and the wide archway between the two rooms were also draped with the same heavy, dark green velvet. On the floor of the study was a precious antique handwoven rug, which had a decorative black and yellow border and orange and green floral designs in the center.

In the corner, by one window, was a huge mahogany desk. This beautiful desk, the work of a renowned architect named Meltzer, was L-shaped and had numerous drawers that glided open and closed with the lightest touch of a finger. There were also several hidden secret compartments. On top of the desk Vaslav had placed two fine china figures—a French one, Sèvres, of Molière sitting in an armchair, and a Russian one, Popov, of two boys catching crayfish. There was also a bronze cat by the well-known sculptor, Barre.

Against one wall stood a large bookcase with glass doors; on the middle shelf Vaslav had placed a watercolor by Bartels. It represented a young man dressed in a red velvet costume with lace collar and cuffs and a hat with long feathers. On his side he wore a saber. We had had this watercolor for some time; it used to hang in the living room in our previous apartment.

Near the bookcase were several occasional mahogany chairs, a sofa, and two deep armchairs upholstered in green kid leather. In front of the high, white-tiled stove was a small round table with a bronze figure of Narcissus. Between the windows, on short mahogany columns, were two magnificent French bronze candelabra.

In the bedroom, there was a dressing table by the window, also a large, white marble washstand with porcelain bowls and pitchers. In the middle of the wall facing the draped archway leading from the study was a large, ornately decorated brass bed. On one wall was a large wardrobe, and all along another, standing in a row, were at least twelve pairs of elegant shoes, all made to order by the renowned master shoemaker, Korol-kevitch, on Bolshaya Morskaya Ulitza.

One of the things Vaslav had always hated in the smaller apartments was when the odors of cooking reached the main rooms, but in this apartment the large airy kitchen was well to the back, at the end of the corridor beyond the maid's room.

Vaslav also would not allow anyone to smoke in his study. He himself did not smoke, and he would ask any visitor who wished to smoke to leave his study and go to the adjoining living room and smoke there.

About this time Vaslav also acquired a piano. It was a Bluthner, specially brought from Germany. I think he used some of his earnings from Krasnoe Selo to buy it, but possibly Prince Lvov helped him too. I remember how many happy times we had with the piano. Vaslav often played for us, and sometimes they were his own compositions. I offered to write the notes down for two of his pieces as he played them—a virtuoso polka-mazurka and a lyrical valse.

I never knew why, but although music theory was taught in all music classes in the Girls' Division of the Imperial Theatrical School, in the Boys' Division, at least during the years Vaslav was a student, it was taught only in the Lower Classes. In the Upper School the boys had only piano or violin lessons, concentrating on technique exclusively.

Because Vaslav had an exceptionally fine ear for music and was able to play from memory so well, neither his teacher, Alexander Elman, nor the examiners ever discovered Vaslav's secret. Elman was himself an excellent pianist, and at the end of each lesson, having worked with the students on their technique, he would play the next assignment, to be learned and practiced for the following lesson. This was sufficient for Vaslav; he needed only to hear the piece played once and he could repeat it from memory for his teacher, faultlessly, the following week.

When studying for the examination, which required going over all the pieces and exercises learned during the year, Vaslav would ask his friend Leni Gontcharov to play for him those pieces needing to be memorized and to review with him those pieces which had to be played from the music sheets. Then, during the examination, even though he was playing by ear, he would correctly turn the pages as though actually reading the music in front of him. His grade for music was usually 12, the highest mark possible.

One year at the School, I had been given a difficult piece to learn for my piano examination at the end of the year. I was to play from memory a piece for four hands with Maria Elman, the daughter of Vaslav's music teacher in the Boys' Division. She was two years younger than I and was also in a different class. This made it difficult for us to find time to practice together in the School, especially with the great demand for the music rooms and pianos. Maria suggested that she come to my home on Sundays so that we might practice together. I remember how embarrassed I was to have to tell her that we did not have a grand piano at home. "Never mind," replied Maria, "it won't matter if we practice on an upright one." I then had to admit that we did not have an upright piano, either. "You must be very poor indeed if you don't have any piano at all!"

Now I was so happy to have a piano at home.

Many of the biographies of my brother contain fantastic stories about our poverty-stricken life, perhaps because each year at the *Akt* it was read out that Vaslav was the recipient of a Didelot Scholarship. The requirements for the scholarship were always read out in a set way: "A Scholarship for the Poor and Talented Son of an Artist." But this by itself was not enough to give the impression of abject poverty; after all, both Shiraev and Bulgakov also received Didelot Scholarships. The month when Vaslav was punished and was given used and worn-out clothing by the Administration must have made a lasting impression upon his fellow students.

It was only after I became an Artist that I visited the homes of some of our fellow Artists and came to realize that in many instances their circumstances had been poorer than ours.

—

THE SEASON at the Maryinsky began in September. Along with the other recent graduates from the School and new members of the *corps de ballet*, I was very busy learning the ballets in the repertoire scheduled for performance during the 1908–9 season: *Swan Lake*, *La Bayadère*, *Paquita*, *The Nutcracker*, *La Fille Mal Gardée*, *The Humpbacked Horse*, and *Le Roi Candaule*.

As a rule, new girls were seldom assigned to dance in ballet performances; mostly we were used to dance in the operas, though we often found our names posted on the call board as substitutes for the ballet performances. As soon as I knew my assignment I would ask one of the girls already familiar with the ballet to show it to me. My friends Zina Puyman, Ludmila Schollar, Lydia Soboleva, and Antonina Nesterovskaya, all members of the *corps de ballet*, were invariably very helpful towards me and would show me the dance so that I would be ready to take my place at the rehearsal whenever somebody was ill or absent, and if necessary to dance at the next performance. Each dancer was expected to know his or her assigned role before the rehearsal.

During the rehearsal, particularly of those ballets which had been performed for a long time at the Maryinsky, and even if there had been changes of cast, neither the ballet master, Legat, nor the *régisseur*, Sergeyev, demonstrated anything in the dances, nor did they correct the artistic interpretation. They watched only to see that there were no mistakes in the *pas* and that the *pas* came exactly on the musical beat.

They were especially strict in watching to make sure that the even lines of the *corps de ballet* should not be broken, and the arms and legs lifted identically. Each dancer had to place herself exactly on the spot indicated on the stage.

The soloists prepared their parts independently. They could even change some *pas* for convenience, or to be more spectacular, but most performers danced traditionally, not creating anything new in their performances. Nobody was concerned with artistic directions, for neither Legat or Sergeyev were the genuine artistic leaders of the ballet.

Our ballerinas almost always studied the principal parts of a ballet with one of the previous famous performers—Ekaterina Vazem (1848–1937), Anna Johannson (1860–1917), or Evgenia Sokolova (1850–1925). Anna Pavlova studied for two years with Sokolova for the role of *Giselle*.

That season we worked mainly with the assistant *régisseur*, Ivan Ivanov. We liked working with him as he was very musical; he was, in fact, the son of a musician. He supervised most of the ballets that season, for both Legat and Sergeyev were busy working on their own presentations. Legat was rehearsing *Le Talisman* and Sergeyev was rehearsing *Le Roi Candaule*.

Every day, whether or not I had a rehearsal, I would go to the Theatre. I loved watching rehearsals in the Imperial Theatres, even though I did not always like or agree with the artistic renderings. Still, I would not miss a single rehearsal. I was not so much interested in observing the rehearsal to memorize the dance or the *variation*, its mechanics and the sequence of *pas*, as I was absorbed, captivated by the Dance—the interpretation, the movement, the correlation of music and dancing.

On these occasions, Vaslav would watch with great attentiveness to see with whom I was friendly, and would then warn me about those I should avoid, and encourage me to associate with those artists he trusted.

Early in September Vaslav began rehearsals for *The Humpbacked Horse*, an old ballet by Arthur Saint-Léon to music by Césare Pugni, which had been remounted by Petipa in 1895. By October 26 he had to learn the role of Ivanushka, a role that required mime and acting as well as dancing. Ivanushka is onstage in every one of the ballet's five acts.

I was very happy when I learned that I had been assigned to dance in Act II. I was one of the maidens on the Isle of the Mermaids, where the Tsar-Maiden lives and is captured by Ivanushka with the aid of the enchanted humpbacked horse. I was charmed watching Preobrajenska; she was exquisite in the role of the Tsar-Maiden. I thought Vaslav as Ivanushka looked very Russian in his short blond wig; he reminded me of the peasant boys we used to watch as they took the horses to the river.

I joined a small group of dancers from the Imperial Theatres to take lessons from Cecchetti, who had now opened his own studio on Peterhof Prospekt. At the end of our group lesson, Cecchetti would give a private lesson to Anna Pavlova. Now she came to his studio instead of Cecchetti teaching her in her own apartment. Sometimes Anna Pavlova permitted me to work with her, and afterwards, if she was expected at a rehearsal at the Maryinsky, she would take me with her in her elegant two-seater coach drawn by a single horse. This ride with Pavlova seemed magical to me. The inside of the coach was upholstered with soft, light pink, quilted silk. How beautiful Pavlova looked in it!

During the ride to Teatralnaya Ulitza she talked mainly of dancing and of Vaslav—or Vassia, as Anna Pavlova used to call him. She would question me about "the secret" of Vassia's enormous jumps. I took her question as a joke and answered that Anna Pavlova had the answer in her own hands—whenever she danced with Vaslav.

Once during our lesson with Cecchetti, Pavlova told me to take off my dance shoes. "Bronia, you jump so high that I think we should look inside your shoes." She started to examine them carefully. "Now we shall see," she went on, "what secrets Nijinsky shares with his sister . . ."

Cecchetti and I both laughed at Pavlova's joke.

Vaslav was also continuing his lessons with Cecchetti. He told me that although the classes were wonderful in helping to attain perfection in the mechanics of dance technique, yet the ultimate artistic perfection—the feel for the movement and the interpretation of the dance—that, the artist must achieve and create for himself.

On December 14, *Le Roi Candaule* was presented as a Benefit Performance for the Corps de Ballet. The ballet had been remounted by Nikolai Sergeyev, and the leading role of Nisia was danced by Mathilda Kshessinska.

I was dancing only in the first act, where I was a shepherdess, but as Vaslav was dancing with Julia Sedova in the last act, I stayed on in the wings to watch. I was standing with Anna Pavlova, who also had a number in the last act, "The Dance of Diana." It was very crowded backstage, so we could not see the dancers. But we could hear the applause.

Pavlova turned to me. "Do you hear, Bronia, how loudly they are applauding Vassia? . . . They applaud him, I think, more than me . . ."

I smiled at her mock pique, and Pavlova gave me a warm answering smile. I felt how much she loved and appreciated Vaslav; how tenderly she pronounced "Vassia," her special name for him.

———

THAT FALL I was used often in the operas, and whenever I could I would stay in the wings just to listen to Chaliapin. He had returned to St. Petersburg in mid-October and everyone was talking about his successful engagements in New York and Buenos Aires, as well as the Paris performance of *Boris Godunov*. I remembered my "baptism" in the opera in the Imperial Theatres, when I had heard Chaliapin sing

Mephistopheles and been so overwhelmed by his singing and his acting.

But backstage, though I could not keep my eyes off him, I did not want to approach him too closely. I had heard so much from Mother and Father, from the time they had worked with him in the opera in Tiflis, about his unpredictable temper and sudden outbursts of anger whenever he was annoyed over a performance. But I could see the other girls all trying to talk to him and how much he obviously enjoyed their attention. Already there were rumors in the air that Diaghilev was going to organize another season of opera in Paris with Chaliapin, and that this time he might need some dancers for the operas.

We did not see as much of Prince Lvov that fall, as he was often away from St. Petersburg, I believe because of some legal business concerning his estates on the Volga. But two occasions stand out in my memory. He took Vaslav and me to see the very first airplane to come to St. Petersburg. We were excited to watch it fly overhead and land and take off. I also remember the evening he took us to see the fabulous Sarah Bernhardt. I was bitterly disappointed to find that although I had always had high marks in French, I was unable to understand what was being said on the stage. But I was so enthralled watching Sarah Bernhardt—she was so vital and dramatic in her boyish outfit, in spite of her sixty-odd years. I think the play must have been *L'Aiglon*, but I could not bear to take my eyes off her long enough to read the plot in the program.

Towards Christmas I was invited to dance in a Charity Performance some distance from St. Petersburg. I was so surprised and touched to receive onstage a beautiful floral arrangement from Prince Lvov. It was a lovely bouquet made out of gleaming wax, from one of the best florists in St. Petersburg. Pavel Dmitrievitch must have heard my mentioning that I had been invited to dance at this performance and made arrangements well in advance, for he himself was out of St. Petersburg at the time.

Sometimes when Prince Lvov came to visit us he brought a friend, Count Tishkievitch, who was visiting St. Petersburg from Vilno. The Count knew both our parents from the times they had danced in Vilno, where the Count was highly regarded as a patron of Polish artists. Mother and Father had even visited Count Tishkievitch in his palace in Vilno. The Count, however, would lecture Vaslav and me, as if we were both still children. I recall one such lecture to Vaslav: "In company you must always be ready with several topics so that if there is a sudden lull or break in the general conversation you can step in with one of your entertaining, amusing, or interesting prepared topics." He had other instructions for me: "A young lady must not use perfume. Her only scent must be that of the fresh fragrance of clean water and soap."

His advice fell on deaf ears. He certainly did not persuade me to forego my liking for French perfume, and I doubt that Vaslav took time to prepare speeches and memorize topics of conversation. In society, he preferred to listen and remain quiet.

Besides, "company" was a rarity in our home, for neither Vaslav nor I was given to inviting our fellow artists. Only my mother's friends came once in a while, usually for dinner on Sunday. There were three orphaned sisters, daughters of a dancer from the Warsaw Ballet, a former colleague of Father's. Another friend of Mother's, the wife of a friend of her brother's, also came to visit her occasionally. As a child, and while a young student at the Imperial Theatrical School, Vatsa had enjoyed their company, even looking forward to their visits. But now, as an Artist, Vaslav couldn't stand guests and always went out before dinner when people came to see Mother, saying that he did not care "to play host . . ."

I WAS THRILLED when I was chosen by Fokine to dance in *Chopiniana*. The performance was to take place in February.

Vaslav was also to dance in *Chopiniana*, and so we often walked to and from rehearsals together. One evening instead of going straight home we went for a walk. It had been snowing all day, and the weather was cold and nippy. We walked towards Marsovo Polye where the festivities for Carnival took place. But it was evening and most of the show-booths and merry-go-rounds were closed. Marsovo Polye was almost deserted. Vaslav urged me to hurry towards the bright lights at the other end, where he could see that the Ice Mountain was still working. We almost ran to the four-story wooden structure and climbed the steep steps to the top, then paid the operator our five kopeks for a ride. The operator offered to show Vaslav how to steer the sleigh, but Vaslav wanted to do it himself. I remember how my heart sank during the speedy descent; I was sitting in front of Vaslav. Suddenly we hit the wooden edge of the ice-run, making the sleigh tip. I lost my grip and started to roll downwards, my face buried in the snow. Luckily for me soft snow had accumulated along the sides of the run and I did not hit my head on the wooden edge. I rolled from the top of the Ice Mountain to the very bottom, some three hundred feet.

Vaslav was terribly frightened and was waiting for me at the bottom. But after I had reassured him that I was not hurt we made several more rides, though not before Vaslav was given some tips on how to steer the sleigh.

As a student in the School I had seen the first *Chopiniana* in 1907, and then *Danses sur la Musique de Chopin* in 1908. Now, a year later as an Artist of the Imperial Theatres, I had the happy opportunity to dance in *Chopiniana* on the stage of the Maryinsky Theatre. I was so lucky to be privileged to be part of this ideal theatrical performance of a ballet.

The impression of this performance of February 19, 1909, has remained forever in my memory. For the first time I could clearly comprehend the true art in Dance and Ballet. Something was revealed to me; something was born in me and became the basis of my creative work, to influence all my artistic activity.

The extraordinary choreography of Fokine that flowed into Chopin's music . . . the scenery and lighting by Benois, creating the poetic images for Fokine's interpretation of Chopin's music . . . the choreography, the decor, and the music . . . all merged inseparably into a single creation—a masterpiece.

The overture: the pompous "Polonaise" attunes the Theatre. In the audience there is an air of festivity in the anticipation of a brilliant performance. But there is a long pause . . . and then, to the soft sounds of Chopin's dreamy "Nocturne," the mood in the Theatre changes . . . as the curtain is slowly raised an eerie enchantment descends over the Theatre and envelops the spectators and the dancers onstage.

In a moonlight clearing, bathed in soft green-blue lighting, among the ruins of a monastery, stands a group of sylphides in long diaphanous dresses. Everything is so unreal, like a vision, like a poet's dream . . .

The white group comes apart. I dance as if in a trance—sometimes it seems to me that I float above the ground . . . our long skirts during the movements of the dance conceal our feet and brush the floor creating the impression of extraordinary airiness.

Now as I stand in a pose my eyes follow Pavlova and Nijinsky. I can see how Pavlova inspires Nijinsky . . . he is fascinated by the vision of the ethereal Sylphide. I can see how Pavlova is inspired by the poetical rendering of the dance, created by the young Nijinsky; she is charmed by the lightness and airiness of his soaring flights.

Pavlova in her flights upwards is supported by Nijinsky so that they both seem to fly in the air. Nijinsky conceals his every effort in support of Pavlova and at the same time creates for her an ideal balance and a light, airy flight upwards. The great leaps of Nijinsky appear like puffs of wind sweeping Pavlova up in the air, like a leaf . . .

Pavlova lightly touches the ground with her toe; her arms are open. Vaslav gently touches her transparent little wings—he entices the Sylphide in a backwards movement, and when she, in swift small *pas de bourrée*, is on the point of falling backwards, he catches her by the wrists, supporting her with only two fingers. She, as if wishing to free herself from captivity, throws her body low, forwards, while behind her Nijinsky bends over and seems to whisper something to her.

In describing Pavlova and Nijinsky as I saw them in *Chopiniana*, I cannot say "their bodies"; they were weightless and ethereal . . . they were part of the music itself. The harmony of all the movements by these two geniuses of the Dance surpassed everything I had ever seen. . . . What a ravishing accord it was!

I was seeing Pavlova and Nijinsky lifting the ballet to the height of perfection. Their dreamy, poetic interpretation of Chopin's music, the musicality and lightness of the dance, inspired the whole ballet—the dances of Preobrajenska, Karsavina, and the entire ensemble.

That night I had seen the creation of *Chopiniana–Les Sylphides*.

29   Sergei Pavlovitch Diaghilev

I SAW Sergei Pavlovitch for the first time in November 1908 at Fokine's rehearsal of *Le Pavillon d'Armide*. Ever since Diaghilev had returned from Paris there had been great excitement in the Maryinsky Theatre, sparked by persistent rumors that he planned to present a Russian Opera Season the next year in Paris and that dancers from the Maryinsky would be engaged to dance in the operas *Prince Igor* and *Ruslan and Ludmila*. The dancers were in the middle of rehearsing when Diaghilev, Benois, and Krupensky entered the dance hall. Mikhail Mikhailovitch stopped the rehearsal to greet the guests.

All eyes were on Diaghilev. He was an imposing figure: tall, rather heavy, impeccably dressed, carrying a walking cane and holding his hat in his left hand. After the guests were seated, Fokine resumed the rehearsal.

I was not dancing in *Le Pavillon d'Armide* but had come as usual to watch the rehearsal. I was sitting with some of the dancers on a bench at the side of the hall. Diaghilev was seated quite near us on a chair in the center, in front of the mirror. He was broad-chested and had a big, almost square head, slightly flabby cheeks, and a full lower lip. In his big black eyes there was always a look of sadness, even when he smiled. The expression on his face was at once menacing and attractive—like a bulldog's, initially discouraging all friendly overtures. Looking at him, I felt that it would not be easy to become friends with Sergei Pavlovitch.

Vaslav had already met Diaghilev the previous year after the premiere of *Le Pavillon d'Armide* and had seen something of him in the spring when Diaghilev was arranging to take *Boris Godunov* to Paris. Vaslav was greatly impressed by Diaghilev, and he told me what an exceptional and outstanding person he was. Naturally, even as a child, when a pupil in the Imperial Theatrical School, I had heard about Diaghilev. In 1900, my first year in the School, Diaghilev was on the staff of the Maryinsky

Theatre and was supervising the production of Rimsky-Korsakov's opera *Sadko*. Several advanced students danced in *The Underwater Kingdom*, the full-act ballet in the opera. I remember the excitement in the School following each rehearsal when they saw Diaghilev, or "Chinchilla" as he was nicknamed because of the wide streak of silver hair on the right side of his carefully combed, jet-black hair.

"Chinchilla knows everything about all the arts, and he plays the piano better than our pianist . . ."

The opera *Sadko* was a tremendous success, and soon Diaghilev was entrusted with the production of the ballet *Sylvia*. But his suggestion of engaging a young unknown artist, Léon Bakst, to design the costumes and sets met with strong opposition from the Administration and from Prince Volkonsky, the Director of the Imperial Theatres, and Diaghilev's dismissal from the Imperial Theatres in 1901 came as a result of the production of *Sylvia*.

Following that visit of Diaghilev to Fokine's rehearsal, Vaslav began spending a lot more time with Diaghilev and his friends. He told me, "I am meeting such interesting people in his house . . ." Diaghilev's friends were all prominent in the world of art, and among them Vaslav heard conversations about music, art, theatre, literature. "I am learning so much there, and I only wish you could come too. But except for his old Niannia, Dunia, who minds the samovar, there are no women present."

Vaslav tried to convey to me the essence of the conversations, so that I too could absorb this artistic and cultural knowledge which he said would be so useful to both of us in our work.

Not long afterwards I met Diaghilev for the first time, when Mama invited him for tea. I shrank inside myself, so overwhelmed was I by his air of grandeur . . .

In the dining room we had a cage with a small bird, supposedly a cross between a nightingale and a canary. The songbird had become completely tame and rarely stayed in his cage. He usually circled the room, landed on our shoulders, and would peck the crumbs from the table. He would even fly onto our hands and let us stroke his feathers.

During our tea with Diaghilev, the bird landed on the table and spread out his wings, then suddenly ruffled his feathers and, opening his beak, jumped wickedly towards Diaghilev's chest. Even Diaghilev was frightened . . . maybe his monocle had scared the bird.

This scene made such an impression on my mother that she told Vaslav to be on his guard with Diaghilev. "He threatens trouble, even the little bird feels it." But Mama's distrust of Diaghilev did not last long. He soon succeeded in charming her; knowing it would please her, he always called her Pani Nijinska, using the Polish form of address. Though Mama understood Russian she preferred to use Polish at home, and so Diaghilev learned a few Polish sentences to speak with her and this also endeared him to her. Diaghilev, too, I know, sincerely came to love our mother.

Diaghilev's name figures prominently in the history of ballet, but it also has a place in the history of art. He contributed, perhaps more than anyone else in Russia, to arousing the interest of the general public in Russian pictorial art, and to attracting attention and bringing fame to Russian painters, not only in Russia but also worldwide.

It is not my intention to try to evaluate the extensive contributions made by Diaghilev in the world of art but rather to indicate a few phases of his earlier activities, those for which he was already celebrated in Russia at the time I met him. Like most of the other young artists I was overwhelmed by his knowledge, education, and brilliance.

Sergei Pavlovitch Diaghilev was born on March 19, 1872, on the Grusino estate, in the province of Novgorod, where his father, a young officer, was stationed with his regiment in the Selistchev barracks.

Sergei Pavlovitch told me sometime later that his big head had been the cause of his mother's death. Evgenia Nikolaevna Diaghilev never recovered after an agonizing labor and delivery, and died a few days after Sergei was born. His mother's maid, Dunia, and Sergei's aunt Maria Pavlovna, a widow with three children of her own, took care of him, and the two families, the one fatherless and the other motherless, went to live in St. Petersburg where Pavel Pavlovitch Diaghilev obtained the post of Squadron Commander of the Imperial Guards.

Two years after the death of his wife he married Elena Valerianovna Panaeva. She was a wise and warmhearted woman, and Diaghilev said he never met another woman like her. His stepmother loved Sergei no less than her own sons, Valentin and Georgi. He owed his upbringing during his childhood and youth to her; she recognized early his talent and love for music and encouraged his studies on the piano. Both families, the Panaevs and the Diaghilevs, were musical. Sergei Pavlovitch's stepmother sang beautifully, and his father had an excellent tenor voice and was an accomplished musician. He knew whole operas by heart.

The family remained in St. Petersburg until Sergei was ten. His father had been appointed a Colonel and would have taken command of a cavalry regiment but for his numerous debts. His own father, Sergei's grandfather, was descended from ancient Russian nobility and was very wealthy. He offered to pay his son's debts on condition that the family return to live in the ancestral home in Perm. It was considered a great honor in the neighborhood to be invited to the regular music and literary evenings held in the Diaghilev house. Diaghilev was also very proud of his aristocratic ancestors.

At the University of St. Petersburg he studied law and graduated in 1896 at the age of twenty-four. He did not intend to pursue a career in law, for his main interests were music, theatre, and art. He was also a student of Rimsky-Korsakov's at the Conservatory of Music. In 1895 he traveled abroad visiting museums and art galleries and purchasing many paintings. Soon after his graduation he began to organize an exhibition of Scandinavian Art, which opened in St. Petersburg in the fall of 1896 and was followed by an exhibition of British and German Painters in Water-Colors in January 1897.

Diaghilev's third exhibition took place in 1898, at the gallery of the Stieglitz Museum. He organized an exhibition of Finnish and Russian painters that was an event of great importance and magnificent success, an event that attracted attention to Russian art. The works of Serov, Korovine, Levitan, Vasnetzov were shown, as well as the works of young artists such as Somov, Benois, and Bakst.

In 1898 Diaghilev published the first issue of the magazine *Mir Iskusstva* [*The World of Art*]. It was a superb edition and offered a yearly subscription for a fabulously low price of ten rubles for twenty-four issues. The magazine was devoted to Russian Art and the History of Russian Culture, with articles contributed by leading painters, musicians, and writers. Diaghilev was both the editor and the publisher of *Mir Iskusstva*, which was the first quality art magazine to be published in Russia. Following its publication, exceptionally fine editions of books using excellent reproductions began to be published in Russia.

In 1899 and 1900 Diaghilev organized two further art exhibitions under the auspices of *Mir Iskusstva*, in the gallery of the Stieglitz Museum, but in 1901 Baron Stieglitz refused to rent his gallery, and so the annual exhibitions for 1901, 1902, and 1903 were shown in the gallery of the Academy of Art.

Though Diaghilev continued as editor of the magazine during the years when he was appointed to the Imperial Theatres, he handed over much of the work for both the magazine and the art exhibitions to Alexandre Benois. Following his dismissal from the Imperial Theatres in 1901, Diaghilev went abroad and only contributed a few articles to the magazine. In the issues for 1901 and 1902 I could find only two articles written by Diaghilev. One concerned a Paris exhibition and the other an exhibition of paintings in Germany.

In 1904 Diaghilev organized an Exhibition of Historic Russian Portraits. I still have the fifth issue of *Mir Iskusstva* for 1904 announcing the event:

This exhibition will be held in the halls of the Tauride Palace and will consist of portraits by Russian masters as well as those of Russian notables by foreign painters . . .

It is earnestly hoped that those who have such portraits in their possession will notify the organizers and so contribute to both the historical and cultural value of this great undertaking.

Thanks to Diaghilev's effort and his great expertise, this "miracle," as it was called—the Exhibition of Historic Russian Portraits from 1705–1905 —was achieved.

He was such an expert and connoisseur of Russian paintings of the eighteenth century that he could, at a glance, not only recognize the hand of the painter but often also identify the subject of the portrait. The aim of the exhibition was to find Russian portraits painted by half-forgotten Russian masters, portraits hanging in private collections not only in St. Petersburg and Moscow but also in provincial towns and country estates. Only a man of Diaghilev's stamina and inexhaustible energy could have accomplished this gigantic task. There were few railroads in Russia at this time, and often he had to travel over bumpy, unpaved roads, riding on a *telega*, a horse-drawn peasant cart without springs. Using his charm and influence, he persuaded provincial governors or private owners to loan their paintings for the exhibition. He collected more than three thousand.

The Exhibition of Historic Russian Portraits from 1705–1905 opened in February 1905 under the patronage of His Majesty the Emperor and as a benefit "in aid of the widows and orphans of those fallen in battle." It was a tremendous success despite the fact that it took place during the tumultuous days of political unrest and uprisings in St. Petersburg. Many of those who saw the exhibition returned several times during the two months it was open.

Following the success of his exhibitions in St. Petersburg, Diaghilev had hoped to found a permanent national museum there, but the time was not yet ripe for this artistic ambition and his dream was not to be realized. His last exhibition in St. Petersburg was held during the winter of 1906. Two years before, in December 1904, his magazine *Mir Iskusstva* had also had to cease publication, due to lack of funds.

Diaghilev's interests had already turned to Europe. In the fall of 1906 he had organized an exhibition of Russian Art in Paris in the Salon d'Automne. The exhibition, like all his others before it, had been Diaghilev's own conception and creation. It encompassed two centuries of Russian painting and sculpture. Diaghilev had also included a special exhibit of Russian ikons from the collection of L. P. Likhacheyev. Later the entire exhibition was transferred from Paris to Berlin, and in 1907 to Venice.

Because of the tremendous success of the exhibition in Paris and the interest aroused there in Russian culture, Diaghilev began planning "Russian Seasons" to introduce Russian music and theatre to the French public. He had already met many influential people in Paris and made several valuable connections promising support for a series of concerts in Paris in 1907: Russian Music Through the Ages.

These were the concerts repeated in Russia in the Salle de la Noblesse, one of which I went to with Prince Lvov and Vaslav. The public in St. Petersburg was excited at the reports of the success of Sergei Rachmaninoff, and Nikolai Rimsky-Korsakov, Josef Hoffman, and Arthur Nikisch in Diaghilev's concerts. But they were even more excited at the success the following year of *Boris Godunov* at the Théâtre National de L'Opéra, when this opera by Mussorgsky, never before heard outside Russia, was revealed to Paris audiences. The fame of the magnificent and powerful voice of Feodor Chaliapin also had become worldwide following these performances. On his return to St. Petersburg, Chaliapin had been greeted like a hero.

The Paris Season that Diaghilev was planning for 1909 was to comprise several operas. One of them was short and was usually preceded by a music interlude, but Diaghilev was considering using a one-act ballet to complete the evening's program, and the ballet he wanted was *Le Pavillon d'Armide*. Naturally Vaslav was thrilled when he heard that *Le Pavillon d'Armide* might be performed in Paris.

In December Diaghilev went to Paris to conclude the negotiations with the Paris Opéra for the Russian Opera Season. Just before he left, as a mark of their friendship, Diaghilev gave Vaslav a complete set of *Mir Iskusstva* and of the catalogues of all his exhibitions of Russian art. I remember my brother bringing home the packages and how together we spent many evenings looking through them and becoming acquainted with so many artists, sculptors, and architects, both Russian and foreign.

How carefully Vaslav arranged the magazines in a special place he found for them in his library! Already, from them, the legendary personality of Sergei Pavlovitch had taken hold of our imaginations.

Most evenings, and especially after Diaghilev returned from Paris, Vaslav would join the Diaghilev circle of friends and listen to their conversations, discussions, and arguments about the theatre, about art and music. I wanted to hear about those discussions, and about the rumors that Diaghilev was going to include ballet in his next Russian Season in Paris. I would sit up waiting for Vaslav, reading a book in the dining room, where Mama always kept a samovar hot for him. As it grew late I would put my head on my arms on the table, and often I fell asleep.

When Vaslav came he would pick me up in his arms and carry me to my room, where Mama would undress me and put me to bed.

That February, the Grand Duke Vladimir Alexandrovitch died. The performances of *Boris Godunov* in Paris in 1908 had been sponsored by the Grand Duke, and Diaghilev had been depending on his support for the organization of the Russian Opera Season in Paris in 1909. Shortly afterwards, when Diaghilev heard that the Imperial Theatres were not prepared to lend him all the sets and costumes for the operas as originally promised to the Grand Duke, he suggested to the Paris Opéra that he arrange some ballet evenings to replace some of the operas. The Paris Opéra turned down the proposal, and that was when Diaghilev went to Paris to try and sort things out.

When he returned it was announced that Diaghilev would be organizing performances of ballet as well as opera in Paris, at the Théâtre du Châtelet. The excitement among the Artists of the Imperial Theatres reached fever pitch. Everyone aspired to be chosen by Diaghilev and to have the opportunity to travel abroad, to Paris!

At home we talked about nothing else but this remarkable project: performances of opera and ballet by Russian artists in Paris in May and June of 1909. The recompense for the *corps de ballet* was to start at one thousand francs (three hundred seventy-five rubles, more than many earned in half a year at the Imperial Theatres). Several Artists came to me to ask that I mention them to Vaslav and ask him to recommend them to Diaghilev.

The formation of the troupe was conducted with the cooperation of Valerian Svetlov, the ballet critic of the *St. Petersburg Gazette* and Editor of the magazine *Neva*, and Nikolai Bezobrazov, a friend of the Minister of Trade. They provided Diaghilev with lists of recommended dancers. At that time I was not acquainted with either of these balletomanes, and soon I found out that though several Artists had already been offered contracts, I was not on the lists. Vaslav told me that Diaghilev did not intend to engage me in the troupe because, even though I danced well, he thought I was too "set" in classical dance and would not be suitable for the new style of ballets he planned to present.

I felt very hurt. Only a few weeks before, in February, I had been so proud when Fokine himself had chosen me from a large contingent of dancers in the *corps de ballet* of the Imperial Ballet to dance in his ballet, *Chopiniana*. I admired the new concepts of the ballets being prepared by Fokine, Bakst, and Benois for the Paris Season and was receptive to the new ideas, but I did not say anything to Vaslav. I kept my hurt to myself.

Rehearsals for the Paris Season had already begun in the little

Hermitage Theatre when Mama indignantly intervened on my behalf.

"What is the matter?" she said to Vaslav. "They have invited some old dancers who will be ready to retire in a year or two, and the young ones they have chosen do not dance as well as Bronia. Bronia is only eighteen years old, but it is the right time now for her to work in new ballets and to go forward. Vatsa, why do you not speak about Bronia to Diaghilev? . . . She is your sister . . ."

Vaslav was very angry and burst out, "I will not extend any favoritism for Bronia in the ballet just because she is my sister!"

"This time you must talk to Diaghilev about Bronia!" Mother insisted. "Do you think that those not-so-young dancers and the others from the *corps de ballet* that have been invited by Diaghilev for the Paris Season were accepted solely on their own merit? . . . Are they so right for the style, for the new ballets of Fokine? . . . Where would they be without the protection or favoritism of the balletomanes?"

"Mamoussia, you are right. That is the truth."

In a day I had my contract with the Russian Ballet for the Paris Season, signed "Dvoryanin: Sergei Diaghilev [Nobleman: Sergei Diaghilev]."

That was the only time Vaslav had to ask a favor for me in the ballet.

As soon as I had signed my contract and knew that I was to be one of the group of dancers going to Paris, I joined the rehearsals taking place in a small theatre—the Theatrical Club, on the Ekaterinsky Canal—rented by Diaghilev when the Hermitage Theatre was no longer available to him.

We artists were not aware of all the financial problems Diaghilev was facing, and I will not write of them or the difficulties he encountered in his first attempts to organize the Russian performances in Paris; much has been written elsewhere, and after all, everything ended well. Diaghilev overcame all obstacles by his energy and determination. At rehearsals we never saw him looking worried. I only knew about his troubles from Vaslav, who would come home very angry and rail against those who had let Diaghilev down.

Whenever we had a free moment from rehearsals at the Maryinsky we would rush over for our rehearsals with Fokine. Those rehearsals in the presence of Diaghilev, with the painters Bakst, Benois, and Roerich, and the musicians Tcherepnine and Glazounov, were exhilarating. The atmosphere was quite different from that in the Imperial Theatres. It was artistically exciting.

The theatre where we were rehearsing, there on the Ekaterinsky Canal, was the home of a celebrated troupe of artists who called themselves "The Distorting Mirror Company." They performed short comedies and political satires. They also did hilarious parodies of old Italian operas;

everywhere in St. Petersburg people could be heard humming or singing tunes from *Vampuka, The African Bride*. We enjoyed saying that we were going to "The Distorting Mirror" for our rehearsals.

Most of the dancers were already familiar with both *Le Pavillon d'Armide* and *Chopiniana*, which Diaghilev renamed *Les Sylphides* for the Paris performances, so it did not take long to prepare these ballets, and soon we were beginning to work on some of the other ballets for the "Saison Russe." Fokine had previously mounted Arensky's *Egyptian Nights*, which was now given a new ending for the Paris Season, with some of the dances remounted to the music of Glinka, Glazounov, Rimsky-Korsakov, and others. The ballet was renamed *Cléopâtre*, and as soon as it was ready Fokine started to mount *Danses Polovetsiennes* from the opera *Prince Igor*.

Sergei Pavlovitch was preparing to leave St. Petersburg well before the Paris performances. He invited Vaslav to travel with him, since Vaslav was not dancing in *Prince Igor* and Fokine would not need him at the rehearsals.

The news that Vaslav was to go to Paris so soon took Mother by surprise. I recall her frantic rush at home preparing Vaslav for his first long trip abroad. While folding his shirts and suits to pack in his suitcases, she would instruct him how to avoid trouble in a foreign city. He was always to carry the address of the hotel in his pocket and not venture alone into unknown parts of the city at night. All the time she was packing she admonished Vaslav, warning him of all sorts of mishaps that could befall a young man in a foreign city—in *Paris*.

As Mother and I planned for our own journey to Paris I grew more and more excited. I was looking forward to the end of the season at the Maryinsky Theatre, for then, on the very next day, we would be leaving for Paris with the other artists and "The General." (Among ourselves we referred to Nikolai Bezobrazov by his honorary title.)

Though Mother was very happy that both her children were to go to Paris to dance in the Saison Russe, she was disappointed when she heard that Kshessinska was going to dance in Warsaw and was taking Nikolai Legat as her partner. She had always dreamed of the day when Vaslav would dance on the stage of the Warsaw Wielki Theatre, where she and Father had trained as dancers.

And we were all saddened by an incident that occured during the spring of 1909. I have already mentioned that since the previous summer we had seen Prince Lvov only on rare occasions. But one day, that spring, he came to see us. Vaslav was not at home, being in Paris with Diaghilev. Lvov went directly to the dining room where Mother was usually to be found and stayed with her for some time.

I joined him later in Vaslav's study. Lvov was standing in the middle of the room and just looking around. He came close to me and looked straight into my eyes. His own large eyes were full of sadness as he said, "I came to say good-bye to you. I am leaving."

"But when will we see you again?" I asked.

"I do not know. Probably we will not see each other for a very long time." Tears came into Prince Lvov's eyes. It hurt me to look into them, and I turned away. From my heart I wanted to say something, but being so timid I could not find the right words. He kissed my hand and left.

That was the last time I saw Prince Lvov. Later Mother told me that Lvov had informed her that Diaghilev had demanded that Vaslav move away from the sporting world associated with Prince Lvov, and that if he sincerely wished success for Vaslav he should not accompany him to Paris. Prince Lvov had agreed, and had also given Diaghilev money for the Saison Russe in Paris.

After the Revolution, when I was working in London, I asked Diaghilev if he knew what had happened to Lvov. He told me that he believed Prince Lvov was in Edinburgh, Scotland, and was the president of some prominent sporting organization.

30   La Saison Russe: 1909

IN PARIS Mother and I stayed, like most of the other artists, in one of the small modest hotels near the Théâtre du Châtelet, on the Boulevard Saint-Michel.* When Vaslav had first arrived he had stayed at the Hotel Daunou, on the Rue Daunou, a narrow street between the Avenue de l'Opéra and Rue de la Paix—quite near to the hotel where Sergei Pavlovitch was staying on the Rue de la Paix. Vaslav had liked the small, cozy Hotel Daunou—it reminded him of the hotels of our childhood —and so he decided to stay on there for the Paris Season.

Mama never came to watch our rehearsals, and so almost every day Vaslav would come to our hotel to see her. Even if she knew that he would only be able to stay a short time, Mama would always have the tea ready for him. She had a small paraffin burner where she boiled the water. With his tea she would serve buns with ham, cheese, and pâté de foie gras, and she would also have some of his favorite pastries.

Many of the dancers who came to Paris for the Saison Russe were young; I was the very youngest. For us it was all new and tremendously exciting, and we felt ourselves to be very fortunate and privileged to be here in Paris for the first time. We were fascinated and surprised by everything: the Latin Quarter, the student demonstrations, the museums, the boulevards, the cafés, the Eiffel Tower, and the department stores. We couldn't see much of Paris during our first days there as we were very busy at the Châtelet, but nevertheless we had soon made our way to the Galeries Lafayette and chosen the latest fashion in Paris hats.

Right up to the day of the premiere, from early morning until late at night, we were in the Theatre, rehearsing or trying on costumes, or rehearsing with the sets and lighting. We were preparing for the first

*The fact that Eleonora usually accompanied her children to Paris, Monte Carlo, and so forth, was confirmed by both Bronislava Nijinska and Tamara Karsavina in conversations with Richard Buckle for his biography of Nijinsky. (AK)

program: *Le Pavillon d'Armide, Danses Polovetsiennes* from the opera *Prince Igor*, and the *Suite de Danses—Le Festin*. All the ballets and dances had been mounted in St. Petersburg, so for *Prince Igor* we needed only one or two extra rehearsals with the opera singers and the chorus, to learn the *mises en scène* staged by the *régisseur*, Alexander Sanine. The painter, Nicholas Roerich, who had designed the sets and costumes for *Prince Igor*, had come to all our rehearsals in St. Petersburg to work with Fokine and Sanine and the Artists. In Paris he directed the stage lighting and explained our makeup to us.

At the time the Paris program was being planned, Diaghilev had commissioned Anatole Liadov to write a ballet to be called *L'Oiseau de Feu*. The advance publicity for the Saison Russe was prepared, and in it mention was made of "L'Oiseau de Feu," although Liadov had not even started to compose the ballet, much less completed it. Diaghilev decided, in order to take advantage of the advance publicity, that the Blue Bird *pas de deux*, already included in the program, should be renamed "L'Oiseau de Feu." The number was scheduled for *Le Festin*, to be danced by Kshessinska and Nijinsky, but with Vaslav as a Prince instead of the Blue Bird and Kshessinska as an Enchanted Bird instead of Princess Florine.

Then, after Kshessinska withdrew from the Saison Russe, it was announced that Pavlova was to dance the role with Nijinsky. I was looking forward to the arrival of Pavlova, as I particularly wanted to watch them dance together in the "L'Oiseau de Feu" (Blue Bird) *pas de deux*.

I remembered Vaslav telling me in St. Petersburg that he had found himself preparing for a performance of the Blue Bird *pas de deux* at the Maryinsky with Lubov Egorova at the same time that he had been working on his role of the Prince for "L'Oiseau de Feu," and so he had had to change roles in the interpretation of this *pas de deux* from one rehearsal to the other.

The rehearsals for *Le Festin* were not many, and were mainly concerned with the correct tempo for each number. However, a lot of time was spent in rehearsals for *Le Pavillon d'Armide* to achieve smooth changes of sets for the new first and third scenes of the ballet. Alexandre Benois, who was directing the technical rehearsals, was insisting on correct timing. At the end of the new first scene, the platform supporting the groups of dancers in their poses from the tapestry was lifted up through the trapdoor, and the change of lighting had to be very carefully timed to the music.

The Théâtre du Châtelet was well suited for intricate changes of sets, for huge spectaculars requiring lots of lights and special effects, quick changes, and trapdoors were often presented there. The size of the stage was adequate, but the surface left much to be desired for the dancers. It was uneven and had large cracks between the boards. Often during our rehearsals with Fokine the carpenters would be at work on the stage, hammering nails into the floor, adding small pieces of lath to fill up the spaces between the boards, and then planing and smoothing the whole stage.

We soon found that this was not the only problem at the Châtelet. The signal bells to call the artists onstage were often out of order. This made me very nervous; I was so afraid that I should be late for an entrance onstage. There was one advantage to this, however—it taught me to change quickly and to be ready ahead of time, able, if necessary, to run back up to the third or fourth floors to call the artists to the stage.

There was genuine cooperation among all the members of the ballet company, whether from St. Petersburg or from Moscow. We all tried to help each other, pointing out mistakes as we noticed them and together finding ways to correct them. We all worked hard trying to achieve perfection—polishing the proper execution of a certain *pas*, adjusting makeup or hairdressing.

We younger dancers even suggested to the older artists that the Imperial Theatres custom of wearing personal jewelry—earrings, necklaces, and bracelets—would spoil the artistic details of the performance in Paris. We were so thrilled when they happily agreed.

Sometimes our work would be interrupted by a meal call. In the middle of the stage trestles would be arranged, and then long boards covered with white tablecloths would be put on them and we were served with stacks of sandwiches, brioches, croissants, fruit, ice cream, and coffee. The dancers, like a swarm of bees, would gather around the table, and there would be a hubbub of noise and laughter and happy chattering as everyone enjoyed the break. Diaghilev and Fokine also joined us. I liked very much spending our day this way in the Theatre—without leaving it from morning till night, rehearsing, working all day, as if we lived there.

Naturally I saw Vaslav every day at the rehearsals, but our encounters were quite brief, not only because of the pattern we had established in the Maryinsky where in public we were fellow artists rather than brother and sister, but also because as soon as Vaslav appeared for the rehearsal he was surrounded by many people, friends of Diaghilev, whom I did not know. Almost always I saw that Vaslav was accompanied by a young man, about his own height and the same age. The young man was very thin with hollow, rouged cheeks and had thick, black curly hair over a high forehead; his eyes were big and dark. He was always fashionably and elegantly dressed, and in addition to rouge wore lipstick.

I found a moment to ask Vaslav who he was.

"He is a very talented young French poet."

"But why does he wear makeup?"

"That is Paris . . . he advises me to do the same . . . to put some makeup on my cheeks and lips . . ." laughed Vaslav. "This is the poet Jean Cocteau."

For rehearsals Vaslav wore the same dancing costume that he wore in St. Petersburg: his black pants, held with a leather belt and buttoned at the side below the calf, molding his legs, and a white sports shirt with an open collar and long sleeves. When rehearsing he danced at full force, the same as he would for a performance. This attracted much attention from those who saw him . . . even the carpenters would stop their hammering in astonishment to watch Vaslav dancing as he rehearsed his *variation*. He sometimes practiced extra exercises, pretending to be absorbed in his work so as to prevent the friends and guests onstage from occupying him with their conversations.

Each passing day more and more people came to watch the rehearsal. Most of the guests were friends that Sergei Pavlovitch had made during his previous visits to Paris, though some were also new that season. All were the "elite of Paris," considered the authority and "voice" to which the Parisian public listened and whose example they followed when they went to the theatre or an art exhibition, or read a book. These "elite" were seldom wrong in their evaluation of new talent or discovery of genius, but Diaghilev must be given great credit that he was able to arouse their interest and respect.

As the day of the premiere approached our work in the Theatre became even more intensive. No one knew how the Russian artists would be received by the French public, particularly in ballet. For so long, more than a century, France had nourished the ballet in Russia with her choreographers and ballerinas. Suddenly now, we the Russians wanted to astonish the public of Paris with the Russian Ballet.

Every day as we went to the Théâtre du Châtelet by the Seine embankment we saw the huge poster—a sketch in charcoal and chalk on a gray background—Anna Pavlova, airy, flying in an *arabesque*, by the painter Valentin Serov. The poster was so beautifully designed that passing by on the way to the Theatre one had to stop and look at it. The poster seemed to say: This is how you will see Pavlova in the Saison Russe!

Diaghilev was counting on Pavlova and Nijinsky to amaze and delight all of Paris, just as the year before, when he had presented Mussorgsky's opera *Boris Godunov*, Paris had been amazed and delighted with both Mussorgsky's music and the voice of Chaliapin. Now for our Saison

Russe, Diaghilev was bringing more operas—*Ivan the Terrible* by Rimsky-Korsakov, *Judith* by Alexander Serov, Act I of *Ruslan and Ludmila* by Glinka, and Act III of Borodin's *Prince Igor* with the *Danses Polovetsiennes* —and presenting the ballets, *Les Sylphides, Le Pavillon d'Armide, Cléopâtre,* and *Suite de Danses—Le Festin.*

It was the first time such an enormous theatrical enterprise of both opera and ballet, combined from the two largest Theatres in Russia—the St. Petersburg and the Moscow Imperial Theatres—ever went from Russia to a foreign country. The opera artists—Feodor Chaliapin, basso; Vassili Charonov, baritone; and Dmitri Smirnov, tenor—were already well known in Paris for their performances in *Boris Godunov.* They were joined by Felia Litvinne, Lydia Lipkovska, Yelizaveta Petrenko, Konstantin Zaporojetz, and the famous Moscow Bolshoi Opera Chorus. The conductors came: Nikolai Tcherepnine from St. Petersburg and Emile Cooper from Moscow. The ballet artists: the famous ballerinas, Anna Pavlova, Tamara Karsavina, Sophia Fedorova, Vera Karalli, and the celebrated dancers, Fokine, Mordkin, and Nijinsky.

The scenery and costumes for each ballet and opera had been ordered by Diaghilev from the great Russian painters—Benois, Bakst, Roerich, Golovine, and Korovine. From their sketches, the scenery had been painted with great skill by Stelletzky and Anisfeld. The costumes were ordered in St. Petersburg and made by the famous costumiers, Caffi and Vorobiev.

Suddenly a few days before the premiere, it became known that Pavlova would not complete her European engagements in time to join us in Paris for the first performance. We doubted whether without Pavlova, made famous already by the poster of the Saison Russe, there could be a ballet performance in Paris.

However, as scheduled, the *répétition générale* [dress rehearsal] took place on May 18, 1909, at the Théâtre du Châtelet in the presence of many guests and friends invited by Sergei Pavlovitch Diaghilev: the press, eminent painters, musicians, theatre directors, including the directors of the Paris Opéra, as well as many of the patrons of the Saison Russe. The Theatre was filled.

Their enthusiastic mood and expressions of admiration throughout the rehearsal soon dispelled any lingering doubts we had as to how Paris would receive the Russian Ballet.

But I recall how disappointed I was with the costumes, which had been specially made for the Paris performances; they looked beautiful but were too heavy to dance in. I was particularly distressed when I saw the two costumes designed for Vaslav. For *Le Pavillon d'Armide* Alexandre Benois had created a new costume that he wanted to be correct in every detail: a theatrical costume in the style of the designs by Louis Boquet, as seen at the French court in the eighteenth century. It was excessively ornate and was not appropriate to the classical technique of our day, nor to the uniqueness of Nijinsky's dance or Fokine's choreography for this ballet. The coat was too heavy and weighted down by too many decorative details; it was knee-length and flared out stiffly from the waist, being held out by a wire around the hem. I thought it looked like a lamp shade. Under the coat his wide satin pants were gathered by garters below the knee, and over his long sleeves he wore a shorter, second bouffant sleeve, caught at the elbow. For headdress he wore a bulky, stylized turban.

Vaslav's other costume was designed by Léon Bakst for the *pas de deux* from *Sleeping Beauty*, which for *Le Festin* was called "L'Oiseau de Feu"; Vaslav, no longer the Blue Bird of the Maryinsky, was now a handsome Hindu prince, and his costume looked beautiful, richly decorated with gold and multicolored stones, and a large rose embroidered on the front panel of the fitted Hindu coat. But again, it was too heavy and stiff for a dancer. As I saw it, the rich bejeweled costume of the prince with a feather in his turban could not compare with Vaslav's marvelous creation of the Blue Bird.

I did not think that in either of these costumes Vaslav would show his dancing to advantage for the Paris audiences.

The dress rehearsal ended late, well past midnight, but early the next morning I was back in the Theatre. It was dark on the stage, except for a single light bulb placed in the first wing on the top of a high post.

As I walked across the dimly lit stage I was surprised to see Vaslav coming towards me dressed in his costume from *Le Pavillon d'Armide* and holding the headdress in his hand. He looked displeased.

"Vatsa, what are you doing here?"

"Bronia, can you imagine, they didn't even let me sleep this morning. A messenger was sent telling me that I must come immediately to the Theatre and get into my costume for the photographer, who was already in the Theatre waiting for me. But when I arrived there was no one here. The costumier was not in the Theatre. . . . Bronia, please fasten my costume at the back. The hairdresser isn't here. I can't find my wig and the makeup box has been put away and I don't know where to look for it. . . . How will I look on a photograph without any makeup? . . . I'd better leave now . . . "

Just at that moment the photographer walked onstage, and with him several people, including some stagehands. They lit the stage and brought down the black backdrop, and then somebody approached us. I think they must have been sent by the office of the impresario, Gabriel Astruc. Together with the photographer they tried to persuade Vaslav not to leave. At this time we did not really know the language, just a few words that we remembered from our French lessons in the Theatrical School, and so we guessed at what was being said: the photographs were needed for magazines and the press . . . Nijinsky, as he is, is perfect for photographing . . . the publicity is important for the success of the Ballets Russes in Paris—and also for Nijinsky . . .

For the first photographs Vaslav posed somewhat reluctantly, but soon he became absorbed and began to smile, and instead of just standing in different poses he was dancing so that the photographer could try to catch in his photographs the execution of one of Nijinsky's huge leaps.

Until now, Nijinsky had not been familiar with the obligations of an artist to submit to the demands of the press, to give interviews and pose for photographers, for this was not expected of an Artist of the Imperial Theatres. So this was his first experience in such duties of an artist, and the photographs taken that morning, on the day of the premiere of the Ballet Russe, where he is seen wearing the costume from *Le Pavillon d'Armide* but without makeup and without the wig under his headdress, were the first photographs taken of Nijinsky in Paris.

Sometime before the premiere in Paris, Vaslav had presented Mama with a gift of eight hundred francs so that she could buy herself a new evening gown for the theatre. Mama was going to come to the premiere at the Théâtre du Châtelet, as she would to all of our performances in Paris—a custom that she would continue during all our seasons abroad. Before each performance she would go backstage to see Vaslav. She went to his dressing room and there would kiss him and make the sign of the cross over him to bless him for the performance.

On May 19, 1909, the day of the premiere of the Saison Russe in Paris, we were all very nervous and excited in anticipation of the evening. We had an early lunch and then as usual did not have anything else to eat before the performance. Many of us came to the Theatre early; we wanted to be sure that we looked our best and that we should be absolutely and perfectly prepared.

Before the curtain went up everyone waited his turn to peep through the small hole in the curtain to see the public. When my turn came, not everyone was yet seated, and the auditorium and loges seemed to be swaying as some people were moving to their seats while others were sitting or standing. The ladies in their expensive furs and elaborate hairdos were wearing the latest fashion, their décolletages sparkling with jewels. They all looked young and beautiful and were elegantly complemented by the gentlemen in their black tails and white starched shirts.

As the curtain opened for *Le Pavillon d'Armide*, I was standing in the darkness behind the decor of the first scene ready with the others, waiting for the tapestry to come to life, when we were to kneel in a semicircle around the stage with our garlands of roses.

I had a painful sensation of mounting trepidation and anxiety. The whole ballet swam in front of me as if in a fog. I was very worried for Vaslav so I did not pay attention to anyone else that evening. Nijinsky remains forever in my memory, dancing his *variation* in the *pas de trois* with Alexandra Fedorova and Alexandra Baldina . . .

Nijinsky appears onstage in a long prolonged leap, *grand assemblé*, and while he is still up in the air a rumble runs through the Theatre. When Nijinsky descends slowly, barely touching the stage with his feet, a sudden burst of applause erupts and he is unable to start the *variation*. Tcherepnine holds up his baton waiting for the applause to subside. The long white gloves of the ladies and the white cuffs of the men rise in swells over the Theatre like a flock of white doves.

While Nijinsky waits onstage holding his pose, his whole body is alive with an inner movement, his whole being radiant with inner joy—a slight smile on his lips . . . his long neck bound by a pearl necklace . . . a light quivering of his small expressive hands among the lace cuffs. This inspired figure of Nijinsky captivates the spectators, who watch him spellbound, as if he were a work of art, a masterpiece.

Suddenly, from *demi-pointe préparation*, Nijinsky springs upwards and with an imperceptible movement sends his body sideways. Four times he flies above the stage—weightless, airborne, gliding in the air without effort, like a bird in flight. Each time as he repeats this *changement de pieds* from side to side, he covers a wider span of the stage, and each flight is accompanied by a loud gasp from the audience.

Nijinsky soars upwards, *grand échappé*, and then he soars still higher, in a *grand jeté en attitude*. Suspended in the air, he zigzags on the diagonal (three *grands jetés en attitude*) to land on the ramp by the first wing. With each *relentissement* in the air the audience holds its breath.

The next musical phrase is amazing for its dance technique—the modulation of the movement in the air, possible only for Nijinsky, executed on the diagonal from the first wing, *grands jetés entrelacés battus*.

Throwing his body up to a great height for a moment, he leans back, his legs extended, beats an *entrechat-sept*, and, slowly turning over onto his chest, arches his back and, lowering one leg, holds an *arabesque* in the air. Smoothly in this pure *arabesque*, he descends to the ground. Nijinsky repeats this *pas* once more, like a bird directing in the air the course of its flight. From the depths of the stage with a single leap, *assemblé entrechat-dix*, he flies towards the first wing.

Nijinsky's flights in the dance hold the audience spellbound. The intensity of their admiration grows after each movement of the dance. Nijinsky ends the *variation* in the middle of the stage, close to the ramp, with ten to twelve *pirouettes* and a triple *tour en l'air*, finishing with the right arm extended forward in a pose *révérence*. The *variation* has been executed from beginning to end with the utmost grace and nobility.

The public screamed its appreciation and rose to applaud Nijinsky, holding him onstage after his short *variation* (thirty-two bars of music) for a period several times longer than the duration of the dance.

Already in St. Petersburg Nijinsky had amazed the public with this *variation*, but now in Paris, at the first performance of the Ballets Russes, he had surpassed even himself; he had soared away from earth into the realms of space.

Before this apparition of Nijinsky on the stage, the public in the Theatre had been, as one would expect during a Gala Performance, politely restrained in its reception. Nijinsky's *variation* was the first "coup"; it jolted the public from its conventional and restrained politeness. The moment created in the Theatre an unusual ambience and mood of admiration that did not cool for the rest of the evening.

During the remainder of *Le Pavillon d'Armide* each dancer and ballerina had tremendous success in the individual *variations* or *pas de deux*, and as in St. Petersburg the "Danse des Bouffons" with Rosai and the six character dancers won tremendous applause from the Paris audience.

After the intermission, Act III from the opera *Prince Igor*, with music by Alexander Borodin, was given with singers from the Imperial Theatres. In the role of Khan Kontchak was Feodor Chaliapin, basso, while Vassili Charonov, baritone, was Prince Igor, and tenor Dmitri Smirnov was Prince Vladimir. In the role of Kontchakova was Yelizaveta Petrenko, who the previous year had sung a small part in *Boris Godunov*.

Act III of the opera ends with the *Danses Polovetsiennes;* Fokine had created the choreography specially for Diaghilev's Saison Russe, and it was presented in Paris with the decors and costumes executed after the designs by Nicholas Roerich.

Adolf Bolm headed the horde of wild warriors in his role of the barbaric Tartar, a role he created with such intense artistic force and danced with such unrestrained verve and *brio* that he has remained forever unsurpassed in it.

That evening we were all inspired by the excitement in the Theatre and danced burning with the fire and spirit of wild untamed Tartars. In the finale of the *Danses Polovetsiennes*, in the mad rush forwards as we made to "attack" the public, I remember that I had a strong feeling that I must restrain my *élan* on the *avant-scène* or I would be thrown clear into the audience, or at least end the dance in the orchestra pit.

The *Danses Polovetsiennes* was a wild and unrestrained success.

The third part of the program was *Le Festin*, where Nijinsky and Pavlova had been scheduled to dance the *pas de deux* from *The Sleeping Beauty*, now called "L'Oiseau de Feu." Since Pavlova had not yet arrived in Paris, it was Tamara Karsavina who danced with Nijinsky.

All the *pas* were the same as when this *pas de deux* was first mounted by Petipa for the ballet *The Sleeping Beauty*. Then it was danced in a small space encircled by the many guests at the ball, but in Paris it was danced as a separate number in which the dancers had the whole stage to themselves and so had to adapt the *pas de deux* to a larger space.

The roles had been changed without altering the pattern or choreography of the dance. Dressed in the costume of the Hindu Prince designed by Léon Bakst, Nijinsky was no longer the Blue Bird but had achieved a metamorphosis from that image, created by him, into a fairy-tale Prince pursuing his beloved Firebird. His interpretation now was of a Prince so in love with the Firebird that in his enchantment he loses his human form and flies with her. He had incorporated human gentleness and sensitivity into the choreography of the role of the Blue Bird.

Karsavina was astonishing in her portrayal of the Firebird—with large, wide-open, dark eyes, tender and quivering in her dance movements like a frightened bird.

Together, Nijinsky and Karsavina were sublime, and for a long time after this performance Karsavina and Nijinsky danced as partners.

The last dance in *Le Festin* was the *Grand Pas Classique Hongrois*, to music by Glazounov. It was danced by nine couples, led by Karalli and Mordkin, and in this number Vaslav and I danced together.

The triumphant furor at the end of the performance was so great, there are not adequate words to describe the enthusiasm of the audience. They would not leave the Theatre, and their ovations detained the artists for a long time onstage. We felt that the spectators had witnessed the birth of "a living art": the creation of the Ballets Russes. For we artists had ourselves experienced something great being born in us. We felt as though we were walking in the clouds, and this feeling of unreality stayed with us through the entire season.

That evening of May 19, 1909, was a historical date, but none of us at the time realized the importance of this marvelous performance, even while we treasured the joy it had given us.

The next morning all the press and all Paris were talking about the wonderful performances for the premiere of the Saison Russe and the miracle of the Ballets Russes. And about Nijinsky: ". . . the soaring angel."

Later that day, when Vaslav came to visit us, he told Mama and me that after the performance he had gone with Diaghilev and several of Sergei Pavlovitch's friends to celebrate at the Restaurant de l'Opéra. During the evening he had become better acquainted with Misia Sert,* whom he described to us as "a marvelous person and a beautiful woman, the wife of an eminent painter—she speaks Polish and now we are great friends . . ."

Vaslav also told us how they all drank champagne and liqueurs that evening, and how during supper Sergei Pavlovitch had flirted with Misia, kissing her and playfully sticking a banana in the cleavage of her décolletage: ". . . we were all amused and had a good laugh . . ."

The congenial atmosphere of Paris and the success of our performances all merged in our young hearts as one happy experience. I recall how when we walked along the Boulevard Saint-Michel, passing in front of the numerous sidewalk cafés, their tables filled with students, we often heard, *"Ce sont les Ballets Russes,"* and compliments about our youth. . . . We were also recognized in the patisseries and other stores. It is true we must have attracted attention by our appearance, modestly but neatly dressed and, unlike the French girls at that time, without any makeup. Wearing our expensive high-fashion hats from the Galeries Lafayette must have made us very noticeable among the crowds of the Quartier Latin.

Whenever we were free from a ballet rehearsal we would go to watch the opera rehearsals, attracted by the participation of Chaliapin. I wished to see and hear him again and again as Holofernes in *Judith* and as Ivan the Terrible.

Everything about this great artist strongly influenced our appreciation of theatrical art and inspired us in our choreographic art. He made us acutely aware and proud that we were taking part in such a grandiose artistic achievement as Sergei Pavlovitch Diaghilev's La Saison Russe —Opéra et Ballet.

I remembered the very first time I had ever seen Chaliapin—when I was quite young, before I had become a student at the Imperial Theatrical School. It had been when we were in Moscow and Father had gone to the theatre one day, taking me with him. I often thought about Father, too, while we were in Paris. Everywhere there were posters for *La Veuve*

---

*Misia Edwards did not marry the artist José-Maria Sert until August 1920, but according to her autobiography they were living together at the time she met Nijinsky, in Paris. (IN/JR)

Joyeuse. I knew Father had performed in the production of *The Merry Widow* in Russia during the 1906–07 season. I secretly hoped he might be in the production in Paris that spring, and that somehow I might meet him. I knew Mother shared this hope too, when she mentioned she would like to go and see the performance.

But from the time of our arrival in Paris and through the beginning of the season, I was suffering from a severe cough. It was only towards the end of the season that I began to recover. But I never missed a rehearsal and I took part in all the performances—strangely enough, I was never bothered by my cough when I was dancing onstage. My only attacks during the day would come when I was running up or down the stairs. The worst, though, was at night when I couldn't sleep, being choked by the violent coughing attacks. The doctor recommended that I go south, to Italy, to complete my recovery, and so Mama and I began saving for that. She still had some money left from the gift Vaslav had given her at the beginning of the season, even after buying herself a black tailored suit for day wear as well as her fashionable evening gown. We were very economical during our stay in Paris and did not eat out at restaurants, but fixed our meals in the hotel room.

The next program following the premiere of *Ivan the Terrible* was made up of both ballet and opera—Act I from *Ruslan and Ludmila*, and two ballets choreographed by Fokine, *Les Sylphides*, with sets and costumes by Benois, and *Cléopâtre*, with sets and costumes by Bakst. Apart from changes in the music—for *Les Sylphides*, the "Prelude" replaced the "Polonaise" as the overture; and for *Cléopâtre*, pieces by Rimsky-Korsakov, Glazounov, and Glinka were added to the original music by Arensky—these were the same ballets, the same dances, the same choreography as had been seen in the Maryinsky Theatre.

But now, away from the governmental atmosphere of the Imperial Theatres, in the new theatrical atmosphere with Diaghilev, Benois, and Bakst, and the highly artistic surroundings of Paris, an ambience had been created that was conducive to inspired interpretations and dancing—by Pavlova, Karsavina, and especially by the young Nijinsky.

The Diaghilev ballet was highly praised in the Parisian press for its accomplishments. I write from memory: "The performances of the ballet astonish us by a harmony never before seen in the theatre. The painting, the artists, the music, all merge creating a real, great, theatrical Work of Art."

⁓

ANNA PAVLOVA had now joined us in Paris and had danced in *Les Sylphides*, Fokine's choreographic masterpiece. *Les Sylphides* was close to the tradition of French ballet and so did not surprise the Parisians. It was the exceptional execution by the artists that so delighted and completely won the public.

Nijinsky was a revelation. By his artistic achievement in *Les Sylphides* he showed how the *premier danseur* could be more than just a partner of the ballerina. He created a new image for the male dancer, and thereafter ballets were no longer mounted solely for the ballerina. A new epoch began, and many new ballets—*Le Spectre de la Rose, Petrouchka, Narcisse, Le Dieu Bleu*—were created predominantly for the male dancer.

The advance publicity for the Saison Russe had hailed Nijinsky as a new Vestris,* but once the public saw Nijinsky "lifted to heaven, weightless, above a group of sylphs," all comparison with Auguste Vestris vanished. With *Les Sylphides* Nijinsky attained a new height in the esteem of the Parisians. He became the idol of the public. As soon as he was seen onstage, for the beginning of a dance, he caused a sensation. They went wild, screamed, cheered—as one critic put it, "like a frenzy in the theatre."

The second ballet in the program was *Cléopâtre*, newly re-created for Paris from the version of Arensky's *Egyptian Nights* mounted by Fokine at the Maryinsky in 1908. The style of Fokine's choreography for *Cléopâtre* remained unchanged from his first version. To the music by Arensky he added two dances, one by Glazounov and the other by Glinka, and a *finale* to music by Mussorgsky. Glazounov's "Bacchanale," a Greek dance with superb choreography, was mounted after we arrived in Paris. We were led by Vera Fokina and Sophia Fedorova, and the Bacchanale was enthusiastically received by the public. The other number, an Egyptian dance by Glinka, a "duet" for Karsavina and Nijinsky, was the same dance with a veil as in Arensky's *Egyptian Nights*—same *pas*, same poses. The dance was not effective and did not show Karsavina and Nijinsky to advantage. In following seasons it was taken out of the ballet.

The two leading dancing roles in the Paris presentation of *Cléopâtre* were taken by Pavlova as Ta-Hor and Fokine as Amoun. Cleopatra, a dramatic role, was taken by Ida Rubinstein. The scenic presentation—the sets, costumes, and props—was designed by Léon Bakst. He retained the archaic Egyptian style of the first presentation of *Egyptian Nights* but at the same time gave it a completely new appearance with strikingly different colors and designs.

As the curtain opened, the orange-rust hues of the Egyptian stage setting, bathed in a hot African sun, astonished and enchanted the eyes of the spectators. Tall Egyptian columns stood against the blue sky, and

---

*Auguste Vestris (1760–1842) had also been called *"le dieu de la danse"* by the French. (AK)

huge monuments—pharaonic figures—formed a spectacular background. The choreographic effect was to arrange the groupings against this background in a "bas-relief" formation. There were very few dancing *pas* in this dramatic ballet. The dancers, standing on toe or half-toe, or jumping on one leg, would hold the other knee raised high. The arms were extended sideways and were always "flat," like an Egyptian bas-relief with the hands turned stiffly at the wrist, sometimes upwards, sometimes downwards.

The arrival of Cleopatra in the temple was mounted most effectively, and was theatrically striking. The cortege was led by the High Priest, Bulgakov. Eight huge Negro slaves carried a catafalque on which was standing a kind of sarcophagus. The folding screens on each side of the sarcophagus were opened to reveal the mummylike figure of Cleopatra—Ida Rubinstein.

Cleopatra was lifted from the sarcophagus, then girl slaves unwound her body from rolls of precious multicolored veils, deploying the veils across the floor, their colors complementing the decor. At last, amidst the deployed veils, appeared the tall, half-naked figure of Cleopatra. Ida Rubinstein's body was unusual in its strange beauty; she was slim, and the etched lines of her limbs gave her an astonishing and unique individuality. Her gray eyes were elongated by makeup to give her Cleopatra a snakelike gaze. Her whole body, even her face and hands, was covered with a light turquoise-green paint, enhancing her decorative appearance for this dramatic role. With the individuality of her gestures, adaptable only to the structure of her body, one could say that she had created an Ida Rubinstein style of gesture in *Cléopâtre*.

As her favored slave, Nijinsky was always close to her, crouching low as a black panther at the feet of his Cleopatra, her turquoise hand adorned with jewels resting on his black head. Cleopatra, majestic; her slave, on the alert, ready to pounce like a panther if danger threatened. Together they moved towards her regal couch.

The total spectacle achieved by Bakst and by the artists was striking, and the ballet *Cléopâtre* was recognized in Paris as the success of the designer-artist, Léon Bakst, and proved a turning point of theatrical, decorative art in France.

The French critics were quite outspoken in their disapproval of the music for *Cléopâtre*, a potpourri of several composers. They also criticized the orchestration of Chopin's music for *Les Sylphides* by three Russian composers—Glazounov, Keller, and the then unknown Igor Stravinsky.

The Théâtre du Châtelet was sold out every evening during the Saison Russe, and each performance looked like a Gala. The mood of the public remained as wildly enthusiastic as on the first night, and we artists were exuberantly happy. This feeling of exuberance stayed with us not only during the performances in the Theatre but also throughout our days in Paris.

Our heightened perception of artistic achievement continued to the very end of the season and was crowned by a Gala Performance at the Paris Opéra.

—

SUDDENLY AT the end of the season in Paris, Vaslav became ill. He had danced in all the performances at the Châtelet and managed to perform for the Gala at the Paris Opéra, but the next morning a doctor was called to the hotel to examine him. I cannot describe what Mama and I went through when we learned that his illness had been diagnosed as typhoid fever—the dread disease, only too familiar to us from the time when Stassik and I had caught the disease from our Niannia, Klavdia, and been near death for days. Vaslav had drunk some water after a performance, which had come directly from a faucet and had not been boiled. Luckily his illness was caught during the early stages and he did not have any complications; it was not a severe case.

Vaslav was confined to bed for a month in his hotel room. Mama was with him each morning, and a nurse came for the afternoon and another stayed with him at night. During the first few days when Vaslav had a high temperature the doctor did not allow me to visit him.

When the season came to an end there were a few special performances in private parties, but the only one I remember was of *Les Sylphides* in some garden. Most of the artists then returned to St. Petersburg. Mama told me that Vaslav insisted we should not remain on our own in the Quartier Latin, and as we wished to be near him we moved to a hotel on Rue Richelieu, near the Palais Royal and the Hotel Daunou.

When at last I was allowed to see Vaslav he was sitting up in bed wearing his snow-white nightgown. He was cheerful and smiling and looked like a little boy; his head had been completely shaven and he had lost weight. He was eating creamed asparagus soup and kept insisting that I should taste it, trying to convince me that I had never eaten such a delicious soup.

Vaslav seemed to be enjoying his convalescence and all the attention of everybody fussing over him all day long. Laughingly, he told me that throughout the length of his illness Sergei Pavlovitch had never once entered his room but had talked to him from outside, through the door, only slightly ajar. Even now that Vaslav was allowed visitors, Sergei

Pavlovitch kept his distance. Mama and I would not stay much longer, for many other visitors and friends were due to arrive to see Vaslav—Nouvel, Bakst, Cocteau, Misia Sert.

We stayed in Paris a little over a month waiting for Vaslav's full recovery. Every day after my visit to Vaslav I would go and explore Paris, spending most of the day in the Louvre. The first time I went I was overwhelmed by the size of the museum and the number of galleries, and I got lost; I thought I would never find my way out. But soon I became acquainted with the museum, and then on my next day's visit to Vaslav would tell him all about my day and what I had seen, bringing him postcards and reproductions of paintings or sculptures that had particularly enchanted me.

Vatsa, in turn, would tell me who had been to see him the previous day. He was deeply touched by the concern and kindness being shown him. They all talked about Diaghilev, praising him for his achievements in bringing about the Saison Russe. They also spoke of Vaslav's own successes and expressed their admiration for him. He showed me the gifts and souvenirs being given to him by friends and acquaintances. Both his rooms were full of flowers. He was no longer wearing the gold ring with the diamond given him by Lvov. Now he was wearing a massive, new platinum ring with a sapphire, from the jeweler, Cartier—Vaslav's first gift from Sergei Pavlovitch. He never parted with this ring from Sergei Pavlovitch, removing it only just before going onstage for a performance.

We rejoiced with Vaslav and were proud that the Saison Russe had been such a great success, artistically and financially. The large staff of this great enterprise, artists of both ballet and opera, musicians, chorus, and dancers, and technicians had all been paid in full, and all the artists had received their railroad tickets to return to St. Petersburg or Moscow.

It was not until Vaslav was almost fully recovered that I heard from him about the troubles that had befallen Sergei Pavlovitch and the difficulties he had encountered in the settlement of the Saison Russe. Bill after bill kept coming. Bills from the Theatre, from the ateliers, from the advertisements, all rained in on him. On the table in the room next to Vaslav's bedroom was his own pile of unpaid bills, from the doctor and the nurses, as well as the hotel and restaurant. To help Diaghilev, Vaslav never insisted on receiving his full promised salary, but Diaghilev was responsible for paying his bills.

Because of Vaslav's illness Mama and I postponed our departure from Paris. We had been planning to go to Italy, as the doctor had recommended for my cough, and had been very thrifty throughout our stay in Paris. But soon our savings were depleted, and since Vaslav did not have any money either we had to stay on longer. One morning, when Vaslav had quite recovered and Mama and I were with him in the hotel, Sergei Pavlovitch arrived, looking radiant. Things had been settled somehow, and he gave Vaslav a thousand francs for all of us. He also gave me a box of Caramels Marquises. It was a music box, and when opened a ballerina danced on the inner lid. When the chocolates were gone I kept all my letters from Vaslav and Diaghilev in the box, which stayed with me until 1918, when I had to leave many things behind me in Moscow.

Mama and I now went to Italy, to Bocco d'Arne, on the seashore near Pisa, and stayed there until August when we returned to St. Petersburg. Vaslav and Diaghilev stayed on in Paris a while longer to settle everything completely, and then they went to Venice.

We received many letters from Vaslav, both from Paris and later from Venice. He was enchanted with Venice and described the unusual, old city that seemed to float on the water—a fairy-tale city—with canals instead of streets, and where he took a black gondola instead of an *isvostchik*.

It seemed to Vaslav that all of society came to Venice from all over the world, and that Diaghilev knew everyone. Vaslav wrote telling us how at one of Diaghilev's parties he had met Isadora Duncan. He had been seated next to her for supper when she proposed to him: "Nijinsky, we must get married—just think what beautiful children we shall have . . . they will be geniuses . . . our children will dance like Duncan and Nijinsky." Vaslav told us in his letter how he answered her, saying that he didn't want his children to dance like Duncan—and that besides he was too young to consider marriage. I think Duncan was probably joking and that Vaslav in his youth had taken her seriously, for he told me later, "I believe I hurt her feelings . . ."

In another letter he asked me to send him a copy in Russian of the Arabian Nights, *The Thousand and One Nights*. I found a very good edition in Wolf's Bookstore and sent it off without delay.

Afterwards I learned that it was during this vacation in Venice that the ideas for *Schéhérazade* had first been discussed.

31   The Maryinsky: Fall Season
1909

WHEN IN AUGUST we returned to the Maryinsky ready for the fall season, we found that the ballet artists of the Imperial Theatres were divided into two camps: the "Diaghilevtsy-Fokinisty," as we were called by the other party, and the "Imperialisty"—that is, Nikolai Legat and Mathilda Kshessinska and almost all those who had not taken part in the Paris Season, those who were strong supporters of the old established traditions of the ballet and who were in close touch with the Directorate of the Imperial Theatres.

The "Imperialisty" considered Fokine to be their principal foe, and next was Nijinsky, who had become so famous in Paris where the French press had called him *le dieu de la danse;* on his return to St. Petersburg the Russian press had given him a triumphant welcome and feted him for his success abroad. And of course he was also known to be a close friend of Diaghilev. In the past, when Diaghilev had been an employee of the Imperial Theatres, he had found himself in opposition to the Administration, which he considered was not interested in seeing any improvement in the status of ballet nor in artistic renderings of the performances. But after the Saison Russe in Paris, it was as if Diaghilev had proved that under his leadership it was possible to achieve a highly artistic performance of opera and ballet.

Our party of young dancers, Diaghilevtsy, was also known to be critical both of the lack of artistic progress in the ballet and of the not-so-talented choreographer, Nikolai Legat, who as it happened was continuing to work on the restaging of an old ballet to music by Drigo, *Le Talisman (La Fille en l'Air),* at the time we returned for rehearsals at the Maryinsky. Though he was shortening the four-hour-long Petipa version of 1889, the ballet was still being staged in four acts and six scenes in keeping with the old style of long *mises en scène;* it was also designed to show the acrobatic virtuosity of the classical dancers, as demonstrated by the brilliant technique of the ballerina Kshessinska and of Sedova and Vaganova.

As students, in 1905, we had had the opportunity to see Act II of *Le Talisman* on the occasion of its revival for the Twenty-fifth Jubilee of the composer Riccardo Drigo, as performed by Preobrajenska, Pavlova, Karsavina, and Egorova. In that performance of December 18, Nikolai Legat had replaced his late brother Sergei in the role of Zephyr.

In his own version of Petipa's ballet, Legat gave the role of Zephyr to Vaslav, but he renamed it Hurricane. Apart from Vaslav, we other Diaghilevtsy had little to do in this ballet, which was not to be performed until the end of November, after its postponement from an earlier date. Mathilda Kshessinska ceded her role of Niriti to Olga Preobrajenska, and the performance was announced for November 29, 1909, as a Farewell Benefit Performance for Olga Preobrajenska, with Kshessinska scheduled to dance in the ballet in January 1910. Although Vaslav did not care for either the ballet or the choreography, he was a success with the public. One critic wrote that the stage of the Maryinsky seemed to be too small for the magnificent leaps of Nijinsky, while another critic said that Nijinsky—the Hurricane—whirled, so high in the air that his head disappeared in the friezes.

That fall Vaslav was also to dance in one of Nikolai Legat's own ballets, *The Blood-Red Flower*, music by Hartmann and sets and costumes by Korovine. I had seen the ballet when it had its premiere in 1907, with Preobrajenska as Angelica, one of the three daughters of a rich Venetian merchant, Pavel Gerdt. Vaslav was proud that he was to dance the role of the Prince, which had been created by Fokine in 1907.

Legat was also working with Vaslav's friend Asafiev, who had written the music for a new ballet, tentatively called *Poet's Dream*. (Later when it was performed in 1915 at the rebuilt Narodny Dom Theatre with Preobrajenska and Legat, it was called *The White Lily*.) For a Benefit Performance at the Maryinsky for the *corps de ballet* in the fall of 1909, Legat mounted a *pas de deux* for Pavlova and Nijinsky to Asafiev's music from *Poet's Dream*. Vaslav liked the music but not the dance as mounted by Legat. It was called "Papillon." Pavlova was a golden butterfly and Vaslav was a moth; their costumes* were designed by Léon Bakst.

Asafiev wanted to become a musician with the Imperial Theatres, and when he graduated from the Conservatory of Music in 1910, he asked Vaslav to help him to obtain an opening position as pianist at the

---

*The moth costume is still preserved in the Nijinska Collections. Bronislava Nijinska used it for her own concerts in Kiev in 1920 and in Vienna in 1921. (IN/JR)

Maryinsky Theatre. I do not know how much Vaslav's influence helped, but Boris Vladimirovitch Asafiev did receive an appointment with the Imperial Theatres. Vaslav and Asafiev remained friends until Vaslav left St. Petersburg forever in 1911. Asafiev continued to work in Russia until his death in 1949, and became a leading figure in the music world as a musicologist, composer, and active member of the Academy of Science of the USSR. He composed the music for at least two important Russian ballets—*Flames of Paris* in 1932 and *The Fountain of Bakhchisarai* in 1934, both for the Leningrad Ballet. They have remained in the repertoires of the Kirov and the Bolshoi companies.

Most of that fall in the Maryinsky was spent remounting the ballet *Le Talisman*, and we became bored during the rehearsals with Legat. We were dreaming of the spring when we hoped that Diaghilev would again be taking the Ballets Russes to Paris. Before that, however, a long fall and winter season lay ahead. The happy days with the Diaghilev Ballet seemed far off. But there was one consolation. Vaslav was to dance *Giselle* with Anna Pavlova. He had long cherished the desire to dance *Giselle* at the Maryinsky Theatre, and now the Administration had decided that he should dance it with Pavlova.

Throughout the autumn Vaslav worked on his role of Albrecht, on his own as well as during the rehearsals with Anna Pavlova. For some reason the Maryinsky performance was delayed from week to week. Only the artists of the company enjoyed the rare official rehearsals in costume when Pavlova and Nijinsky appeared with the whole ensemble.

It is difficult to describe my impressions of those rehearsals. The unreal quality and beauty of the dance, so ethereal and weightless, charmed the eye and moved one to heartache. In the whole of my lifetime I never saw a ballet performance so supremely right. It was a great gift to us artists that we should be granted the spectacle of those two geniuses of the dance together in a performance of *Giselle*.

I can still see Nijinsky in the second act, a figure of grief wrapped in a cloak of mourning, stepping forward slowly, each step falling upon the earth like a heavy tear, the folds of his long cloak flowing behind him on the ground. In a great white splotch, like the ghost of Giselle, lilies rest on Vaslav's breast—his hand presses the white blossoms to his heart with immeasurable anguish and tenderness, as if they are to tell of his love when they lie on her grave.

It is at once plain that this is Albrecht's first visit to the grave of his beloved. Slowly, his eyes seek one grave after another, searching out the resting place of his Giselle. His whole body weeps in doleful steps until, in the distance, he sees the cross with her name. The cloak is flung wide, the two arms outstretched towards the only visible sign of Giselle on this earth. His entire body, moving forward, melts to his knees; the cloak slips forward; and with the white lilies on his breast he falls on the grave of Giselle.

Nijinsky's interpretation of the role of Albrecht aroused, during these rehearsals, an enthusiasm among the young dancers that often moved them to tears.

In the *pas de deux* of Pavlova and Nijinsky, Giselle is not the living girl, but rather the phantom of Albrecht's thoughts and imagination; she is the Giselle of whom he is aware in another world, the world beyond existence.

In Nijinsky's *variation*, every movement cries of the grief overwhelming his mind. He tries in vain to overtake the phantom of his imagination. Vaslav ends the *variation* exhausted by despair and falls to the ground.

Pavlova in the second act is Giselle's ethereal, chaste shade, summoned from the world of nonexistence. She draws up to herself all the action on the stage in her infinite, tender, moving love for Albrecht. She barely touches the ground with her *pointe*, as if blown by a gentle gust of wind; her *arabesque*, fragile in the perfection of its line, flutters; every movement of her airy dance whispers of another, unearthly world, and of her love, conquering even eternal sleep.

So we saw the dance of Pavlova and Nijinsky.

But during those rehearsals, Pavlova, who had danced the role of Giselle regularly since 1903, did not seem to be arousing as much interest among the artists as Nijinsky. Suddenly, whispers were heard that Pavlova would not be dancing with Nijinsky in *Giselle*. Then came the announcement that Nijinsky was to dance in *Giselle* later in the season, not with Pavlova but with another dancer. I was grieved that *Giselle* was to be performed by each of these geniuses separately, and not knowing what official reason had been given for the change, I asked Anna Pavlova. She was seldom insincere, and also she was kindly disposed towards Vaslav and me. Her answer was candid:

"I do not wish to share with Nijinsky my success before the public. I do not wish to see ovations being given Nijinsky for a performance in which I too dance." She went on frankly. "Let the public that comes to see Pavlova see only Pavlova! Vassia has enough of his own public to fill the Theatre to overflowing . . ."

I think Pavlova realized that the many innovations introduced by Nijinsky in the role were creating his own image of Albrecht, in contrast to those of her regular partners, Gerdt and Legat, and she recognized the impact Nijinsky would have on the public.

Giselle was offered at the Maryinsky with Pavlova on January 13, 1910.

But then Vaslav began to see the possibility of dancing *Giselle* in Paris. He was spending every evening at Diaghilev's, where a circle of friends gathered to discuss arrangements for the Paris Season. He told me that they were almost complete, though for the moment Sergei Pavlovitch was hesitant about *Giselle*, not being sure whether Paris would be interested in seeing their own French ballet.

"But Benois is quite insistent," Vaslav exclaimed happily. "That would be such a joy for me. . . . I think that Sergei Pavlovitch is really teasing and that he has already decided to include *Giselle* for Paris."

I also learned from Vaslav that as Liadov had not fulfilled his commission, Diaghilev had asked instead a young composer, Igor Stravinsky, to write the music for the new ballet, *L'Oiseau de Feu*, for Paris. Vaslav met him quite often at Diaghilev's and told me he had already heard some of the music. He was enthusiastic. "Igor Stravinsky is a musical genius. How wonderful it is that Diaghilev has recognized his talent and has decided to give an unknown musician a chance to realize himself and his work!" Vaslav not only admired Stravinsky, he also liked him very much and enjoyed being with him.

Pavlova was leaving St. Petersburg in February for an engagement in New York, and it was also announced that she would be going to England for an engagement at the Palace Theatre, in London.

When he heard this announcement, which meant that Anna Pavlova might not be available for the Saison Russe, Diaghilev was very upset, for by then he had commissioned Igor Stravinsky to write *L'Oiseau de Feu* for Anna Pavlova and he had also been planning to stage *Giselle* with Pavlova and Nijinsky.

As we waited impatiently for rehearsals to begin for Diaghilev's Saison Russe, a rumor reached us that M. Fokine had agreed to mount a new ballet for a Charity Masquerade Ball sponsored by the magazine *Satyricon*. The ball was organized by the students of the Technological Institute. Soon we learned that the new ballet by Fokine—*Carnaval*, to music by Robert Schumann—was to be mounted with the collaboration of Léon Bakst. Every one of the Diaghilevtsy-Fokinisty was anxious to participate.

The Administration posted a notice in the Maryinsky reminding everyone of the rule that during the season Artists of the Imperial Theatres were not allowed to appear in other theatres in St. Petersburg. But still, all the young Artists wanted to be chosen to dance in Fokine's new ballet, even at the risk of dismissal from the Imperial Theatres. The cast, never publicly announced (to protect the Artists), was imposing indeed: Nijinsky, Harlequin; Karsavina, Columbine; Fokine, Florestan;

Bekefi, Pantalon; J. Kshessinsky, Eusebius; and Meyerhold, Pierrot. Among the young dancers, Fokine gave the role of Chiarina to Vera Fokina, the role of Estrella to Ludmila Schollar, and the role of Papillon to Bronislava Nijinska. I was so proud. I was the youngest of the cast and was prepared to take my chances and participate in the ballet. I did not hesitate to attend the rehearsals. Ludmila and I were sure that at worst a fine for infringing the rules would be imposed, a fine we could easily pay from the honorarium promised for the performance at the Masquerade Ball in Pavlov Hall. We were also sure that the Directorate would never dismiss such artists as Fokine, Karsavina, and Nijinsky.

The ballet was mounted by Fokine in three days, but I was not called for a rehearsal until the day before the performance. That last day Fokine mounted a *valse noble* to be danced by six couples, and then worked with the whole ensemble. When he had finished with the other Artists and only Vaslav and I were left, he started to mount my *variation*. Fokine was tired and in a hurry to end the rehearsal, and he demonstrated the *pas* to me at a slowed-down tempo; then, as soon as I had learned them, he left the hall.

Immediately Vaslav said to me, "Tomorrow is the performance, you must work on your Papillon now and try to dance it to the correct *prestissimo tempo*."

At first I danced at the slower tempo, but then Vaslav made me repeat the *variation* four or eight bars at a time. He watched me intently as I repeated each segment, trying to master the technique. "Bronia, I wish you had more time for your dance, but the performance is tomorrow night. Your technique is good, let's concentrate on your arms and your body, to harmonize the movements so that then you will better achieve the *prestissimo tempo* of Schumann's music."

Vaslav walked to the far end of the studio, assumed the preparatory position, and gave a signal to the pianist to start. He circled the studio like a weightless butterfly, his arms fluttering, even his hands and fingers joining in the aerial dance of his feet. I knew that I would never match Vaslav's technique—he skimmed the floor; his arms, like the wings of a butterfly, seemed to hold him up in the air.

We continued to work, and each time I repeated a phrase Vaslav accelerated the music, until the pianist told us that I had reached the required *prestissimo* in my dance. After the pianist left we worked for several hours alone. Vaslav explained: "Tomorrow at the Pavlov Hall when you dance the *variation* it will be on a semicircular stage that has been built in the ballroom. There are no wings. You enter and leave the stage through slits concealed in the deep pleats of the long curtains that are draped all around the stage. In your dance you must make a full circle and come as close as possible to the very edge of the *avant-scène*, and onstage you must always dance as close as you can to the drapes, brushing them with your fingers as though they are the tips of your wings. Remember, you are a butterfly caught in a room, seeking an opening in the walls to the freedom of the open air, and when Pierrot is about to catch the butterfly with his hat, you turn abruptly, frightened, and whirl across the room. Do the *chaîné déboulé* diagonally as Mikhail Mikhailovitch has mounted it for you, but do not come to a stop on the ramp; do not hesitate, maintain the *prestissimo*, and keep circling around and around the whole stage!"

Vaslav paused a moment and then suddenly, lightly as a butterfly, left the ground and quickly fluttered around the room, his hands opening and closing swiftly with the same brisk musical rhythm of his elastic feet.

"Bronia, this is how I see your *variation* executed. Already you have achieved the *presto* tempo in your dance and your feet do flutter, but your hands must also flutter and move swiftly with the same rhythm as your feet."

After returning home, alone in my room in front of the mirror, I worked on the details of my dance. I concentrated on the movements of the arms and hands. I was up half the night, for I knew I did not have the flexibility in my wrists to imitate the brisk trembling of the tips of the wings of a butterfly.

The next morning I awoke very early and hurried to the rehearsal hall to work on the dance itself. I held before me in my mind's eye the image of Vatsa dancing, barely touching the ground, as if the wings of the butterfly alone were sustaining him in the air. I studied the movements of the whole body in this image.

For hours I practiced my dance, until I knew I was ready and had attained the technique essential for the Papillon that Vaslav had created for me. Though Fokine had mounted the *pas*, he had only shown me the stage pattern of the dance, indicating the various *pas* of the *variation* at a slowed-down tempo without explaining how he wanted the dance to be performed. He had not told me anything about the position of the arms or of the body. It was Nijinsky who had showed me how the forty-five-degree angle of the body during the circular flight of the butterfly would help to achieve the needed *prestissimo* speed, and the importance of matching the rhythm of the hands with the feet in order to capture the fluttering of the butterfly. Now I was ready for the dress rehearsal at the Pavlov Hall.

At the dress rehearsal I was delighted to meet the great artist Vsevolod Meyerhold, who was to play the role of Pierrot. Meyerhold was unforgettable as Pierrot. He made full use of the innovative decor by Léon Bakst, the many folds of the pleated curtains, with concealed slits, draped around the semicircular stage. Pierrot-Meyerhold put these slits to most imaginative use. Each of his appearances onstage produced an effect. First, only his leg would appear through the slit of the drape in a *grand développé*, then slowly the whole white body would emerge, the long arms made even longer by long, hanging, white sleeves. Sometimes Pierrot would simply peer through the openings, showing only his white face beneath the conical white hat. Curious, he looked from side to side, searching for the butterfly that had attracted his attention. Walking cautiously on tiptoes, flapping his long white armlike wings high above his head, he held his little white hat with which he hoped to catch the butterfly, me.

He followed the flight of the butterfly noiselessly, like a whisper. He ran to hide, from one settee to the other, and then unexpectedly his head peeped out, moving from side to side as he watched the flight of the butterfly. Suddenly he rushed after me, but I disappeared from his sight, off the stage. Thinking the butterfly to be on the ground, he covered it with his white hat, and then clapping his hands he jumped with joy. He lay down on the floor beside his hat and very carefully lifted the edge so as not to damage the fragile wings. With his hands the incomparable artist actually imitated the palpitation of a butterfly caught under his hat, while all his being remained full of anxiety in anticipation of at last having a closer look at the butterfly he admired and coveted. There was a look of utter bewilderment and heartbreaking disappointment as he realized that the butterfly had escaped him and was not under the hat. Very sadly he put on his little hat, low down on his forehead, and with his shoulders and his long arms drooping walked away; crossing the width of the *avant-scène* with long slow strides, he finally disappeared from the stage.

Carnaval was a short ballet-pantomime, lasting about twenty to twenty-five minutes. The libretto by Bakst and Fokine had been adapted from the story and characters depicted in "Scènes Mignonnes," a suite of piano pieces by Robert Schumann. It was an uncomplicated libretto of masked guests at a masquerade ball, a succession of romantic interludes, fleeting meetings, light intrigues, and the felicitations and celebrations for the betrothal of Harlequin and Columbine.

All the costumes were designed by Léon Bakst, but were mostly from other ballets. The costumes for Harlequin, Columbine, Pierrot, and Pantalon had been designed in 1908 when Fokine had mounted a harlequinade for a Bal Poudré for the Russian Mercantile Society. Some of the other costumes—the crinolines from the 1840s, a novelty for dancers—came, I believe, from the street scenes of *The Fairy Doll*, also designed by Bakst. I was so happy to learn that among the new costumes he had created for *Carnaval* was one specially for Papillon.* I recall during the fitting how delighted I was with the costume—its ankle-length crinoline of crisp white muslin, and the charming details like the rainbow hues of the transparent wings and the long, brightly colored silk ribbons tied at the wrist.

But after Fokine had mounted my *variation*, I became worried that the wide skirt and stiff crinoline would interfere with the speed of my dance as taught to me by Vatsa. At the dress rehearsal I did indeed realize that I had to increase the speed and force of my dance still more. The crinoline skirt filled with air as I pirouetted and ran around the stage, slowing my dancing movement considerably. But the costume was so beautiful, I never even thought of suggesting any changes. I just tried my best to get used to dancing in the stiff, wide crinoline.

The costume for Harlequin was very becoming on Vaslav. The white and emerald diamonds on the silk tights that extended above the waist underlined clearly every movement of his dancing body, and a white silk shirt with emerald cuff links, a wide, black, chiffon scarf, and a black mask completed his *commedia dell'arte* costume. The slits in the mask were slanted and lines were penciled upwards from the corners of his mouth to emphasize Harlequin's ever-present smile. The whole appearance created by the costume, together with Harlequin's mischievous frolics and the virtuosity of Nijinsky's dancing, expressed laughter and gaiety.

The entrance of Columbine (Karsavina) and Harlequin in their tender dancing poses was an embodiment of laughter and joy. Columbine, in the arms of Harlequin, entered with swift little steps, while Harlequin lifted his legs high and still kept pace with her. Their heads were close together, intimate, tender, moving from side to side as if performing their own dance independently of their torsos, yet still in perfect harmony with the whole gay exuberance of their dancing bodies.

Nijinsky's Harlequin was full of fun and mischief, creating a new image for Harlequin, no longer the blustering and boisterous figure of the *commedia dell'arte*.

A mood of laughing enjoyment filled the ballroom as the masked artists came to celebrate the betrothal of Harlequin and Columbine in a pompous *polonaise*. My partner was Meyerhold, whose exquisite artistry had so

---

*This costume (see Illustration 127) belonged to Bronislava Nijinska and was worn by her for a short solo dance, "La Poupée," that she created in 1915 in Petrograd to the music "La Tabatière" by Anatole Liadov. Afterwards she wore the costume for other performances in Russia and then in Europe, until it was stolen in Paris during World War II. (IN/JR)

heightened my interpretation of the Papillon. It is impossible to describe my state of exaltation to be dancing side by side with him in the *polonaise*, the palm of my hand resting lightly on the top of his hand. For the finale we ran down the steps, leading the artists off the stage to dance the *galop* among the masked guests.

Several members of the Administration of the Imperial Theatres came to the ball, but they chose not to recognize the dancers, incognito in their masks, or report them. And so none of us were fined.

The success of *Carnaval* was exceptional. After the performance, we heard that Diaghilev had decided to include the ballet in the repertoire for his new season.

32   La Saison Russe: 1910

REHEARSALS STARTED in April. All the free time we had from the Maryinsky was spent in rehearsals with Fokine at the "Distorting Mirror" Theatre. Most of it was devoted to work on Igor Stravinsky's ballet *L'Oiseau de Feu*. This was our first ballet danced to his music, and Stravinsky was always present during rehearsals. Sometimes he would play the piano for us, either alone or with the rehearsal pianist.

First of all, Fokine mounted the "Dance of the Enchanted Princesses." There were twelve of us girls who played with golden apples during the dance. Only after our number was finished did Fokine work with the entire ensemble on the scene at the Castle of Kostchei the Immortal. The music now became frenzied, and goblins, monsters, and demons rushed onto the stage to the frantic, discordant sounds, followed by the ugly Kostchei, his body twisted by the evil in him, his soul-less being. All the *corps de ballet* joined in this demonic dance; the whole stage was engulfed in a frightful, horrid, tumultuous commotion as Ivan Tsarevitch found the egg containing the soul of Kostchei the Immortal. Then Ivan smashed the egg, destroying the enchanter and his evil power.

The rhythms and the movements in the dance were new to us. The choreography was intricate and though the dancing steps were not technically difficult, still, it was not easy at first to render the new rhythms correctly. But with the help of Stravinsky and Fokine we began to master their complexities and to dance well. After he had mounted the scene at the Castle of Kostchei, Fokine's work on the ballet progressed quickly, and soon the final scene of the procession and coronation of Ivan Tsarevitch was ready.

Diaghilev often came to the rehearsals, as did the artist Golovine, who had designed the sets and the costumes for *L'Oiseau de Feu*, and both of them admired Fokine's choreography. We were all sure that the ballet would be successful in Paris, but we had doubts whether it would ever be performed in Russia.

The libretto for *L'Oiseau de Feu* was adapted from several Russian fairy tales, and one of them, "Kostchei the Immortal," was controversial. In 1902 Rimsky-Korsakov had written the opera *Kostchei the Immortal* for a private theatre, and the Russian censors had considered his libretto to be revolutionary and had banned the opera. We all still remembered the tragic days in 1905—the disturbances in the streets and the sad news that the private performance of Rimsky-Korsakov's *Kostchei the Immortal*, staged by the students of the Conservatory of Music, had been interrupted and closed by the police on the grounds that it was inciting revolution and advocating the abolition of the autocratic regime (with Kostchei supposedly representing the autocratic ruler and the egg the symbol of autocratic power).* Since then Rimsky-Korsakov's operas had seldom been performed in the Maryinsky. His newest opera, *The Tale of Grad Kitej*, had been performed once or twice at the Maryinsky in 1907, though none of the students at that time saw it or performed in it.

I recall—though I'm not sure whether it was 1909 or 1910—how we had a fright one day when Vaslav was brought home from the Theatre after fainting at a dress rehearsal for *The Tale of Grad Kitej*. The opera was being revived for the first time since the death of the composer on June 20, 1908, and Vaslav had been so moved by its powerful music, which he was hearing for the first time, that he had stayed through the rehearsal, which lasted until seven in the evening. Suddenly he had slumped forward and fallen to the floor unconscious. The Theatre doctor brought him home and Vaslav was put to bed, and the maid was sent to the pharmacy with a prescription. But Mama knew immediately what was wrong with Vaslav. He had left for the Maryinsky early in the morning and had not eaten since breakfast. In the Theatre he had been so absorbed listening to the wonderful music of Rimsky-Korsakov that he had not taken any time for lunch. He was simply tired and hungry. Mama gave him a bowl of broth and a light meal and right away Vaslav was "resurrected" and felt fine, and started to enthuse and rave about the music he had been hearing.

I knew that Sergei Pavlovitch had been a student of Rimsky-Korsakov's at the Conservatory of Music, and now Vaslav told us that for the performances of *Boris Godunov*, in May 1908, Rimsky-Korsakov had revised Mussorgsky's orchestration and had composed, on Mussorgsky's theme, a supplement for the first act, for Diaghilev's presentation of the

Kostchei received favorable reviews at its premiere on December 25, 1902. But on March 27, 1905, its performance by Conservatory students was followed by revolutionary speeches and a police raid. Rimsky-Korsakov's works were banned for two months. (AK)

opera. Vaslav also told us that Diaghilev had seen Rimsky-Korsakov a few days before the composer had gone to Lubens, his home near St. Petersburg, where he had died, June 1908.

It had been in his memory that Diaghilev had produced *Pskovitianka* [*Ivan the Terrible*]—Rimsky-Korsakov's first opera, written in 1873—for the Saison Russe of 1909. For the 1910 season Diaghilev had chosen *Schéhérazade*, the composer's symphonic poem, written in 1880, for a ballet to be choreographed by Fokine after a libretto by Alexandre Benois.

Once he was satisfied that *L'Oiseau de Feu* was ready, Fokine started to mount *Schéhérazade* during our rehearsals at the "Distorting Mirror." The oriental style of this new ballet was unfamiliar to us, and the movements required work and study. Léon Bakst often worked with Fokine and inspired us during the rehearsals; from time to time he would correct us, showing us the proper position of a hand or the movement of an arm, sometimes even demonstrating an oriental pose for us and explaining the way we should move our bodies during the dance. The work was fascinating and challenging; all the more so as it was to the marvelous music of Rimsky-Korsakov. The catchy tunes resounded in our heads and would not leave us even long after the rehearsals were over.

Vaslav was to dance the role of the Negro slave in *Schéhérazade*. He came to watch all the rehearsals, though he did not dance in them. I believe Vaslav worked separately with Fokine and Ida Rubinstein, who was to portray Zobeide. Once or twice Ida Rubinstein also came to watch our rehearsals in St. Petersburg.

Taking part in these rehearsals of the two new ballets by Fokine was for me a most wonderful experience: the inner joy of striving to attain perfection in the dance. Fokine was greatly inspired in his work on *Schéhérazade*, and it was a great happiness for us to transmit his marvelous creation through our dancing. As soon as Fokine had finished mounting *Schéhérazade*, we started rehearsing the other ballets for the season abroad: *Cléopâtre, Danses Polovetsiennes, Carnaval, Giselle,* and *Les Sylphides*.

For *Carnaval*, the excellent mime artist Alexei Bulgakov was to portray Pierrot, and during our rehearsals together we became friends. He told me that his own role of the High Priest in *Cléopâtre* was originally mounted by Lev Ivanov for Stanislav Gillert, for the version of *Une Nuit d'Egypte* that was to have been performed at Peterhof, on Olgin Island, in 1901. We reminisced together about Gillert, who had died in 1907, and I was happy to know that Bulgakov had also admired him, this man who had been my very first teacher in the School and a friend of both Mother and Father.

No one "watched the clock" during rehearsals. On the contrary, we all

53. *Nijinsky* by Modigliani, drawing c. 1912.
Photographic copy given to Bronislava Nijinska
in the early 1920s.

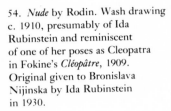

54. *Nude* by Rodin. Wash drawing
c. 1910, presumably of Ida
Rubinstein and reminiscent
of one of her poses as Cleopatra
in Fokine's *Cléopâtre*, 1909.
Original given to Bronislava
Nijinska by Ida Rubinstein
in 1930.

55. Ida Rubinstein in a studio photograph,
c. 1910, in her costume for Zobeide in Fokine's
Schéhérazade. (Stravinsky Diaghilev Foundation)

56. Nijinsky in a studio pose in
Schéhérazade. Studio portrait by Baron
de Meyer, c. 1911. *(Courtesy of the
Dance Collection, The New York Public
Library at Lincoln Center)*

57. Nijinsky in a studio pose in *Le Pavillon
d'Armide*. Studio portrait by Baron de Meyer,
c. 1911. *(Courtesy of the Dance Collection,
The New York Public Library at Lincoln Center)*

58. Nijinsky as Harlequin and Lopukhova as Columbine in *Carnaval*, which they danced together in Europe in 1910 and then in the United States in 1916. *(Courtesy of the Dance Collection, The New York Public Library at Lincoln Center)*

59. Karsavina as Columbine, the role she
created in *Carnaval* in St. Petersburg in 1910.
(Stravinsky Diaghilev Foundation)

60–62. Snapshots by Vaslav
Nijinsky of Diaghilev and Bakst
in the Bois de Boulogne, 1910.

63, 64. Léon Bakst and Vaslav Nijinsky in Carlsbad.
Snapshots by Bronislava Nijinska, 1910.

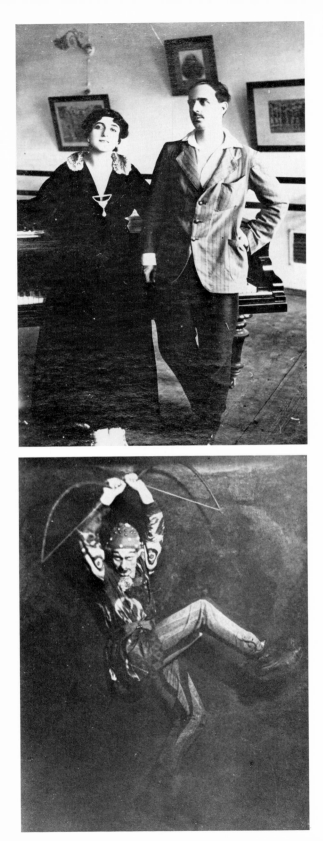

65. Mikhail Fokine and Vera Fokina, c. 1912.
(Stravinsky Diaghilev Foundation)

66. Adolf Bolm as the Warrior Chieftain in Fokine's *Danses Polovetsiennes* from *Prince Igor*. Photograph by Sol Bransburg, 1909.
(Stravinsky Diaghilev Foundation)

wished the work would never end. At least I think that most, if not all, of the other artists shared my feelings. When a rehearsal did last for a long time, we would go to the Theatre foyer where, on a large table, tea would be served with cookies, pastries, and tarts. Around the table we made the acquaintance of the painters and musicians and listened to their conversations with Diaghilev about art and the ballet. This was tremendously interesting for us, and we were all excited as we anticipated our departure for the Saison Russe abroad.

At last we left to go abroad, but this time we did not go straight to Paris. Our first performances were to be in Berlin, in Das Westend Theater in Charlottenburg. Here we gave the premiere performance of Robert Schumann's *Carnaval*, orchestrated by Rimsky-Korsakov, Glazounov, Liadov, and Tcherepnine. New sets and costumes were made for the season, designed by Léon Bakst. Karsavina was still engaged in St. Petersburg and so was not able to come to Berlin. She was replaced in *Carnaval* by Lydia Lopukhova, who had just graduated from the Imperial Theatrical School. The role of Columbine was ideal for the little Lopukhova; she was charming, with a slight figure that seemed to have been created for this role. Léon Bakst was delighted by her performance. In Berlin, Vaslav achieved even greater perfection as Harlequin. He was amazing in this role, and at the same time entrancing. Lopukhova and Nijinsky together excited great admiration, and altogether *Carnaval* was a tremendous success. We hoped that Paris would receive it with the same enthusiasm.

We stayed in Berlin for two weeks, but I did not see much of Vaslav; we were only together in the Theatre, and even there he kept to himself. He was almost always alone now, and seemed to be avoiding people. He looked preoccupied, serious, and absorbed in his own thoughts. I respected his mood and did not want to intrude on his privacy. More and more I felt him to be Nijinsky, "le dieu de la danse," rather than Vaslav, my own brother and dear friend.

While Vaslav, apart from the others, practiced his dance exercises alone, I observed him from a distance. He executed all his exercises at an accelerated tempo, and for never more than forty-five to fifty minutes; that would be his total practice time. But during that time he expended the strength and energy equivalent in other dancers to three hours of assiduous exercises.

During the *barre* and middle-of-the-floor exercises, Vaslav seemed more intent on improving the energy of the muscular drive, strength, and speed than on observing the five positions. Often he did not bother to close the *5ème*, or even to bring his working leg completely down on the heel. He worked on the elasticity of the whole body in the execution of his own movements. Even when holding a pose, Vaslav's body never stopped dancing.

I watched him as he practiced the extension of the legs. In his *adagio* exercises, in the *développé* front, he could not raise his leg higher than ninety degrees; the build of his leg, his overdeveloped thigh muscles, as solid as rock, did not permit him to attain the angle possible for an average dancer.

In the *allegro pas* he did not come down completely on the balls of his feet, but barely touched the floor with the tips of his toes to take the force for the next jump, using only the strength of the toes and not the customary preparation with both feet firmly on the floor, taking the force from a deep *plié*. Nijinsky's toes were unusually strong and enabled him to take this short preparation so quickly as to be imperceptible, creating the impression that he remained at all times suspended in the air.

When we arrived in Paris, all the artists were happy to learn that this time our performances were to take place at the Grand Opéra. We were very pleased to be working and rehearsing in such a magnificent theatre.

Our season in Paris was to open on June 4, and the first ballet in the program would be Schumann's *Carnaval*, and the second *Schéhérazade*. Because *Carnaval* had already been performed in Berlin, all the rehearsals onstage in Paris were devoted to work for the premiere of *Schéhérazade*. This made me very concerned, for I needed as much work as possible on the stage in my crinoline costume for my dance of the Papillon.

Already in Berlin I had realized that I must find the correct equilibrium to adjust to both the slowing effect of the crinoline and the incline of the stage, if I was to cover the whole stage in my flight around the room as Vaslav had taught me in St. Petersburg. When I tried to dance my Papillon for the first time onstage in Paris, in costume, I discovered that I had to increase my speed as I circled the stage to hold a precarious balance at a forty-five-degree angle. With the slightest deviation I would fall over, and so I had to do my dance time and again until finally I had mastered the effect of the incline and was dancing the Papillon on the outermost point of this equilibrium, which contributed so much to my speed, lightness, and freedom of movement.

The atmosphere during rehearsals of *Schéhérazade* was tense and stormy. A contingent of *figurants* had been hired to supplement the dancers and provide the retinue of the Sultan Shahryar. They were all French and did not understand Fokine, and would not follow his directions. They appeared ridiculous among the dancers, and Fokine became furious and often lost his temper. But there was no time to replace the inexperienced *figurants*, who were needed for the last scene in the harem when the Sultan returns unexpectedly and, having discovered the orgy, orders the slaying of the women and of the Negro slaves. The *figurants* had to rush onto the stage with the soldiers, armed with scimitars to take part in the slaughter.

Finally Fokine managed to get the proper Asiatic fierceness from the *figurants*, but now we dancers were afraid of getting hurt as they ran around the stage swinging their gleaming scimitars. And still Fokine was not pleased. During all the rehearsals he seemed dissatisfied with everything and everybody, yelling at us and being rude to the artists, and on more than one occasion he stormed off the stage and left the Theatre without finishing the rehearsal.

We could not understand Fokine's mood—everything about *Schéhérazade* augured success. We knew already from 1909 that Paris admired Fokine as a choreographer and recognized his talent. The artists were wholeheartedly with him and did their best to render each dance and each movement exactly as he wished, to the last detail. But he was difficult to please.

One possible explanation was his anger stemming from the publication of *Comoedia Illustré* on June 1, in which extensive coverage had been given to the Saison Russe. He had been angry because he had seen himself listed last among the performers, with no mention of his being a *premier danseur* or the choreographer. Fokine was very sensitive about publicity, and after that incident had demanded that his name appear in larger letters than anyone else's in the ballet, also that it precede the names of composers, painters, and artists—ahead of Stravinsky, Rimsky-Korsakov, Benois, Bakst, Golovine, Karsavina, Ida Rubinstein, or Nijinsky. Our impresario, Gabriel Astruc, had not complied with Fokine's wishes, having his own ideas about how best to arouse interest and attract the public to the theatre. In the next edition of *Comoedia Illustré*, on June 15, in a special supplement devoted to the Saison Russe, considerable attention was given to the creation of the new ballet *Schéhérazade*, but the emphasis was on the artist Bakst and not on the choreographer Fokine.

He had also been having some difficulty with Diaghilev, for Fokine had insisted that he be allowed to dance in one of his own ballets for each program. It was finally agreed that for the Saison Russe at the Grand Opéra, in addition to dancing Ivan Tsarevitch in *L'Oiseau de Feu*, Fokine would dance Harlequin in *Carnaval* and the Warrior Chief in *Danses Polovetsiennes*.

For the opening night of our season in Paris, June 4, all the tickets were sold out, as they had been for most of the season even before the first night. Many of the St. Petersburg ballet and theatre critics, also many Russian balletomanes, came for the Gala Premiere.

The first ballet on the program was Schumann's *Carnaval*, but the highlight of the evening was the second ballet, Rimsky-Korsakov's *Schéhérazade*, choreographed by Fokine and with sets and costumes designed by Léon Bakst. The leading roles were created by Nijinsky, Rubinstein, and Bulgakov. These three dancers were magnificent, and no matter how many artists later tried to copy their roles of the Negro slave (Nijinsky), Zobeide (Rubinstein), and Sultan Shahryar (Bulgakov), no one has yet succeeded in equaling or even approaching the artistic perfection they so brilliantly created that evening for the first performance of *Schéhérazade*. I would even go so far as to say that unless one has seen their performances, one cannot claim to have seen the authentic *Schéhérazade*.

Bulgakov was an artist of great dramatic talent, and he was majestic and restrained in his pent-up fury when Shahryar discovered that his beloved Queen Zobeide was taking part in the orgy with his other wives and odalisques.

Rubinstein was exotic, and her unusual physical appearance made everything about her seem different; she had a unique beauty, very tall and very slender. Her Zobeide was striking in every movement and gesture.

Nijinsky, as Zobeide's favorite slave, was astonishing in his novel appearance, with blueish-gray makeup over his body, and amazing in his own newly created dance movements—half snake, half panther.

After the departure of the Sultan, all the wives taunt the Chief Eunuch, urging him to open the doors of the harem. Doubtful and fearful, he yields to their demands and with his large key opens the doors of the harem to admit the hordes of black slaves. Then, trembling with fright, he reluctantly complies with the wishes of Queen Zobeide, who orders him to open the door of the gilded cage to free the dark youth who is her favorite.

Nijinsky was a revelation—clad in cloth of gold, the costume created for him by Léon Bakst, with the unusual blueish-gray makeup covering his face and body. He wore loose trousers of gold brocade, gathered above his ankles. Gold bracelets encircled both his arms and ankles; jewels sparkled on his fingers and toes.

This moment of Nijinsky's appearance onstage, framed by the door of the gilded cage, caused a sensation. The whiteness of his gleaming teeth was accentuated by his strange blueish-gray makeup as his bare torso twisted in the fervor and excitement of his newfound freedom, like a cobra about to strike.

Suddenly he sees the seductive Zobeide, reclining on a divan among large, soft, oriental pillows and brightly colored scarves. The youth is transformed into a wild panther; with a huge leap he hurls himself from the depths of the stage onto the divan and like a snake winds himself around her slim body.

> . . . and the night passes in orgy. Boys bring in platters piled high with fruits, odalisques bring wine and incense; there are dancers and tambourines, the women and their lovers join Zobeide in the dancing. The orgy grows wilder; the whole voluptuous throng becomes a whirl of splendid raiment and women's white arms . . . *

Rubinstein was strikingly beautiful in her dance; the slender lines of her elongated body, flexible as a reed, oscillated and swayed to the music. The image created by Nijinsky of the Negro slave in his half-snake, half-panther movements, winding himself around the dancing Zobeide without ever touching her, was breathtaking.

For the final, dramatic scene, upon the unexpected return of the Sultan, mad with rage, ". . . the whole stage frozen, panic-stricken, . . . a moment of paralysis and terror, a vain, frantic flight. Soldiers armed with huge scimitars mow down the women and the slaves."†

The Queen's lover is confronted by the Sultan's brother, Shah Zeman, who with his scimitar inflicts the mortal blow; the dark slave falls, and in his last spasm his legs shoot upwards; he stands on his head and rotates his lifeless body—Nijinsky made a full pirouette standing on his head—before dropping to the ground with a heavy thud.

Only the beautiful Queen Zobeide is alive among the corpses. The Sultan shudders, vacillating, but his brother points to the Queen's Negro lover, lying dead. With averted eyes, the Sultan gives a gesture of command to one of the soldiers. Zobeide forestalls him. She seizes a dagger and stabs herself, and dies at his feet.

With the premiere of *Schéhérazade* Bakst became famous throughout Paris. The unusual range of colors—the greenish-blues, bright yellows, and oranges—and the oriental costumes were the admiration of all. Soon dresses made of brightly colored oriental silks appeared in all the Maisons de Couture, and women started to wear oriental turbans decorated with jewels. *Schéhérazade* inspired Paris fashions. In particular, Maison Poîret gained a reputation for its oriental styles and the bright oriental colors of its dress designs. The Musée des Arts Decoratifs purchased the original watercolor sketches by Léon Bakst of the costumes he had designed for *Schéhérazade*.

Schéhérazade was not only the highlight of that evening but of the whole season—the decor, the music, the choreography, and the artists had all

---

*Taken from the English program notes for the Diaghilev Ballets Russes, 1921. (IN/JR)
†Ibid.

captured the imagination of the audience. The enthusiastic reviews in the press for that performance, and continuously through our 1910 Saison Russe, surpassed those of our first season at the Théâtre du Châtelet in 1909.

The final item in the premiere program was *Le Festin*, already successful with Paris audiences from the year before. The first dance was "Lezginka," which Vera Fokina danced with ten men, with a solo introduced for Nijinsky. Although he danced it well, I felt it to be a strain for him to then have to change in a hurry for the Blue Bird *pas de deux*, which he was to dance with Lydia Lopukhova. This year the name of the Blue Bird *pas de deux* from *Sleeping Beauty* was again changed; now it was called "L'Oiseau d'Or." Between "Lezginka" and "L'Oiseau d'Or" there was only one number, a classical *pas de deux* danced by the two artists from Moscow, Ekaterina Geltzer and Alexandre Volinine. This did not give Nijinsky enough time to exercise or tune his muscles, especially going from a character number to a classical dance.

Concluding the program was the fifth dance number in *Le Festin*, "Finale," to music from Tchaikovsky's 2nd Symphony. Fokine had mounted this dance for his first version of *Le Festin*, but although "Finale" was listed in the program for that first public performance—the Dress Rehearsal of the Saison Russe at the Châtelet, on May 18, 1909—it had been canceled, perhaps due to the length of the program, and was never performed in the 1909 season. So "Finale" was being danced for the first time in 1910 at the Opéra in the new version of *Le Festin*. It was a Russian character dance with sixteen girls and four boys, all dressed in Russian costumes, with the boys also wearing grotesque monster heads.

We had all been pleased to learn that among the visitors from St. Petersburg for the Saison Russe à l'Opéra was Vladimir Arkadievitch Telyakovsky, the Director of the Imperial Theatres. He had arrived for the premiere of *Schéhérazade* and was planning to remain for the premiere of *Giselle* on June 18, and for the premiere of Stravinsky's *L'Oiseau de Feu* on June 25.

Even while still a student Vaslav had dreamed of the day when he would dance in *Giselle*, and as an Artist, during the winter season of 1909 in the Maryinsky, he had worked on the role of Albrecht and rehearsed the ballet with Anna Pavlova. He had been bitterly disappointed when Pavlova had decided not to dance with him.

When Diaghilev had first planned this Saison Russe, he had told Vaslav how much he wished to show Pavlova and Nijinsky together in *Giselle*, but it was only after Pavlova had promised him that she would make arrangements with the Palace Theatre to be free for one week in June, allowing her to come to Paris to dance in *Giselle* with Nijinsky, that

Diaghilev had finally decided to include this ballet in the program for the Paris Opéra and had asked Alexandre Benois to design the sets and the costumes.

Until the very last rehearsals on the stage of the Grand Opéra, Vaslav had expected that Anna Pavlova would come to Paris to dance *Giselle* with him. Both in St. Petersburg and in Paris, even though he was rehearsing with Tamara Karsavina, Vaslav had tried to preserve all the *mises en scène* as he and Pavlova had worked them out together. I recall how unhappy both Nijinsky and Karsavina had been in their rehearsals, their usual friendly relationship somewhat strained. Vaslav had played the role of Albrecht as he had rehearsed it with Anna Pavlova, but Tamara Karsavina had her own ideas for Giselle. She also did not appreciate some of the innovations Nijinsky was bringing to his role of Albrecht.

Now, only a few days before the premiere of *Giselle*, Anna Pavlova informed Diaghilev that she would not be able to come to Paris after all, and so, for his first appearance in *Giselle*, Nijinsky found that he would be dancing instead with Tamara Karsavina.

I do not remember how Paris received this old French ballet, but the Director of the Imperial Theatres, Telyakovsky, was so delighted with the performance of the young Nijinsky that on his return to St. Petersburg he announced that *Giselle* would be performed in the fall at the Maryinsky Theatre with Anna Pavlova and Vaslav Nijinsky.

For the last premiere of the season, on June 25, the program was made up of *Les Sylphides*, *L'Oiseau de Feu*, and *Les Orientales*.

We did not have many rehearsals onstage, and the dress rehearsal for *L'Oiseau de Feu* and *Les Orientales* did not take place until the afternoon of the premiere. I recall the turmoil and the nervous atmosphere, how confused we dancers were by the music. We had rehearsed for *L'Oiseau de Feu* to the accompaniment of a piano, and now we heard Igor Stravinsky's music played for the first time by the orchestra; many dancers missed their entrances.

To the confusion created by the music were added other problems for the dancers because of the quick changes of sets and the many lighting effects during the action of the ballet. Backstage it was crowded —Diaghilev, himself, was directing the lighting—with stagehands trying to learn the quick changes and large numbers of *figurants* in their masks standing in the wings blocking the entrances. Sergei Grigoriev, our *régisseur*, was giving orders to the *figurants*, who were even more confused by the music than the dancers, for they too had rehearsed only with a piano. The conductor, Gabriel Pierné, had worked with the musicians of the orchestra separately.

Fokine was furious not to have more rehearsals onstage with the orchestra before the premiere, but apparently the Grand Opéra could not spare us the stage and orchestra for more than one rehearsal together—the dress rehearsal, on the very day we opened.

Things were made worse by the presence backstage of two horses. At the beginning of the ballet, a horseman dressed in black and mounted on a black horse rode across the stage, to represent night. Later during the ballet, a white horseman would mount a white horse and ride across the stage to represent day.

We were all surprised that Diaghilev allowed Fokine to use horses onstage, for we remembered well the incident in the Maryinsky in February 1910, when Pavel Gerdt and Samuil Andrianov had been thrown out of a chariot drawn by horses during a rehearsal of the ballet *Egyptian Nights* at the Maryinsky. Both Gerdt and Andrianov were injured. Pavel Gerdt, who was celebrating his fiftieth anniversary as an Artist that year, was hospitalized for a month, and Andrianov received many bruises and fractured his right arm. After that unfortunate accident Mark Antony in *Egyptian Nights* no longer made his entrance in a chariot drawn by white horses, and his messenger simply walked onstage instead of riding his black horse. The use of horses in any ballet was discontinued in the Maryinsky after that night.

For *L'Oiseau de Feu* at the Paris Opéra, the horses were used only for the first two performances and then were discontinued.

Towards the end of the intermission following *Les Sylphides*, the artists began to gather in the wings for *L'Oiseau de Feu*. I was standing on the top of the stairs leading from the Castle of Kostchei when I saw Sergei Pavlovitch below me, among the masked monsters, and with him a small man, half-bald, with blond hair and a short beard. Somehow by his appearance, this man merged in my mind with the monsters. Sergei Pavlovitch gestured me over to introduce me. The man was the Italian poet Gabriele d'Annunzio.

I had already read some of his works in Russian translation and to my amazement did not feel as awed in his presence as I usually felt when meeting the "greats" of the arts. When D'Annunzio, hardly taller than I, looked with his pale, faded eyes closely into mine, and then took my hand, I drew it away with a feeling of fear. Since then, whenever reading anything by him, I have always remembered the strange feeling he awoke in me on that first meeting. At that time I was very young, only nineteen, and it is possible that I was experiencing everything too acutely. Sergei Pavlovitch went on to introduce Karsavina to D'Annunzio, and Tamara remained in conversation with him until her entrance.

Whenever well-known artists or personalities were in the audience,

Sergei Pavlovitch wanted us artists to know them, and often he brought them backstage during the intermission to introduce us to them. In those days of the performances of *L'Oiseau de Feu* and *Schéhérazade*, all the famous painters, writers, artists—all the best in the arts and the "beau monde" —came backstage. I disliked our being examined like mannequins displayed in the stores; sometimes they even fingered the material of our costumes . . .

The intermission before Igor Stravinsky's *L'Oiseau de Feu* was over. But Diaghilev remained backstage during the performance that night to direct the lighting, and so did not watch this last premiere from his usual seat in the audience. I cannot say that I was thrilled with this new ballet by Fokine, but I tried to do my best as I danced with the other Golden Princesses in the "Dance with the Golden Apples." The realistic rendering of this Russian fairy tale was foreign to me; I was repelled by the ugly, masked monsters, the skeletons, and other frightful creatures surrounding Kostchei the Immortal, magnificently but terrifyingly portrayed by Bulgakov.

As the Firebird, Tamara Karsavina was absolutely ravishing in her artistic and dancing interpretation of the role. With her beautiful big black eyes and her finely chiseled features, her face framed by a headdress of gold with multicolored feathers, she was truly an enchantress from a fairyland. Karsavina remained irreplaceable in the role of the Firebird.

I did not expect that this fairy tale would interest the audiences, but thanks to the excellent interpretations by Karsavina as the Firebird, Fokine as Ivan Tsarevitch, and Bulgakov in the mime role of Kostchei, also the innovative music by Stravinsky, the marvelous sets and costumes by Golovine, and the strong dancing of the *corps de ballet*, the ballet was a great success.

In *Les Orientales*, which concluded the program, Nijinsky danced two numbers—"Danse Siamoise," music by Sinding, and "Kobold," music by Grieg orchestrated by Stravinsky. Fokine had mounted the two numbers for Nijinsky for a performance at the Maryinsky on February 20, 1910, the same evening as the performance of *Carnaval* at Pavlov Hall.*

When announcing the program for the Maryinsky, the *St. Petersburg Gazette* had noted that the two dances by Nijinsky were technically very difficult and that "It will be the first time that a *premier danseur classique* will appear individually and not as the partner of a ballerina . . ."

---

*Bronislava Nijinska described to her daughter, Irina, how the artists who performed that evening at the Maryinsky had an *isvostchik* waiting outside to take them immediately after that performance to Pavlov Hall. Vaslav laughed as he told her about changing their makeup during the ride and how glad he was to be wearing a mask as Harlequin. (IN/JR)

Nijinsky worked on the artistic rendering of both dances on his own. Fokine had mounted the dances as he usually did, simply showing the *pas* and then leaving the interpretation to the artist. For "Kobold," Vaslav worked closely with Igor Stravinsky, who played for him in rehearsal and explained his orchestration to Vaslav. They worked together on how best to express the unusual tonalities of the music in the dancing.

In Paris, in addition to Nijinsky's two dances, there were three other *divertissement* numbers in *Les Orientales:* Karsavina danced "Danse Orientale," Geltzer and Volinine danced an oriental-style *pas de deux*, and in the last number with the whole ensemble, Rosai and Vassilieva were the soloists.

Our season in Paris was so successful that we were invited to give some extra performances at the Paris Opéra. But before we could, we had to go to Brussels where we had been engaged to give two performances at the Exposition, in the Théâtre de la Monnaie. One of the ballets was to be *Danses Polovetsiennes* from *Prince Igor*. The role of the Tartar Chief had been brilliantly created by Adolf Bolm in the Paris Season of 1909, but he was not with our company this year and the role had been danced by Fokine. However, Fokine was not coming with us to Brussels, having been asked to mount some dances for three operas to be performed by the Paris Opéra Ballet Company in their next season.

When I heard that Nijinsky had offered to dance the role of the Tartar Chief I was very surprised, for I knew Vaslav was usually only interested in dancing those roles which he could create, or which he felt he could re-create by adding his own interpretation. I knew how much Vaslav admired Bolm, and that he considered Bolm to have created this role to perfection.

Bolm's ambition, as was well-known in the company, was to be named a *premier danseur*, and he did not appreciate the fact that he was making a reputation for himself as a character dancer. Bolm had certainly mastered the mechanics of classical technique, but in his physical appearance he was not well suited to the roles of a *premier danseur*. He was robust, well built, and rather heavy; the rugged features of his Asiatic face and his thick curly hair made it difficult to imagine him in a poetic role in *Les Sylphides*, or as a romantic prince in *Giselle* or *Swan Lake*. But his strong appearance was ideal for the role of the savage chief of the Polovetsian Tartars. Even his aggressive and domineering behavior and commanding ways were in keeping with his role. In *Danses Polovetsiennes*, Bolm had found himself. His Asiatic face was enhanced by his makeup, and he truly had the fierce appearance of a Tartar Chief. The taut string of his bow seemed to threaten and vanquish his enemies. All his movements were ferocious as, bareback on a wild horse, he galloped through the vast steppes, whipping his untamed steed with his bow. Undaunted, with his wide, heavy shoulders, his bare neck and chest, he faced the enemy. His enthusiasm inflamed his army, and he led his men as if carrying them over the ramp of the stage and into the audience. The whole structure of the theatre seemed to be under attack, the destruction was left in his wake. That was Adolf Bolm in *Danses Polovetsiennes*.

In Brussels, I saw how right I had been in thinking that Vaslav could not dance the role with the wild fire of Bolm. There was little time for rehearsals, but this did not make much difference, for by his nature Vaslav could not respond completely to the role. His makeup was good, his movements were wild, his dancing surpassed the others, and he was seen leaping above the heads of the warriors. But he was too light, too aerial, and too slender for a fierce Tartar chief. He did not represent the chief of a wild horde; he did not have the warlike strength of a warrior; he was not threatening, nor did he evoke the image of a wild horse galloping across the bare steppes. But still he was a success with the public.

After the performance, Vaslav himself recognized his own mistake in dancing the *Danses Polovetsiennes;* he realized he had not bettered Bolm's performance in any way. For Nijinsky any self-criticism was tantamount to a confession of failure. I could see Vaslav's embarrassment as he said, "Bolm in the *Danses Polovetsiennes* is irreplaceable; it is his perfect creation, and I cannot surpass him in any way."

Obviously Vaslav understood that even a genius has his limitations. As each musical instrument has its own purpose, sound, and tone, so each dancer must remember—and even more important, a choreographer, when choosing among artists for a certain part, must remember—that the body of a dancer is also a musical instrument.

———

In July we returned to Paris from Brussels, though originally it had been planned that we go to London. However, the death of King Edward VII in May had meant, to our disappointment, the cancellation of the London engagement. In its place Diaghilev had accepted some extra performances in Paris. Meanwhile several artists had made arrangements of their own, including Karsavina, who was replaced when we returned to Paris by Lydia Lopukhova for Stravinsky's *L'Oiseau de Feu* as well as *Carnaval*.

Lydia Lopukhova delighted the French audiences as Columbine; she was admired for her delicate features and dainty grace. One critic, after seeing her dance the Prelude in *Les Sylphides*, called her "l'enfant-oiseau," saying that "she runs on the tips of her toes like a little bird." But she surprised all of us when on very short notice she learned the difficult part of the Firebird and danced it with such great success that before our season was over she had signed a contract to dance in America.

For the performances in Paris after the end of our season, Nijinsky again danced Harlequin in *Carnaval*. The portrayal of Harlequin and his dance was one of Nijinsky's greatest achievements. Dressed in the tight-fitting costume and silk tights, each muscle was clearly defined in motion, vibrating with joy. In his short virtuoso *variation*, in a sequence of *pas en tournant*, and small *pas battus* to the accompaniment of clapping hands raised high above his head, the whole body was in perpetual motion, undulating in the air in joyful dance. Nijinsky ended his *variation* in the middle of the stage with a *grand pirouette à la seconde*, followed immediately by countless dazzling *pirouettes en dehors*. On each turn his leg seemed to be driven into the floor with a screwdriver movement, *pirouette en tire-bouchon*, and as he increased the *plié* on one leg, the other leg, beginning at the ankle, was lifted higher and higher with each *pirouette* until it came to rest on top of the knee, now in a deep *plié*. Nijinsky finished the last turn in a sitting position, and then Harlequin, laughing, sat down calmly with his legs crossed, facing the audience.

Instead of wearing a mask as he did for the *Satyricon* Bal Masqué, Vaslav had created a masked image on his own face. The slant of his eyes was accentuated by the glitteringly outlined, slanted slits of the black mask he had painted on his face. Two upward, oblique, thin lines drawn at the corners of his mouth created a constant expression of mischievous gaiety.

During the season in Paris, Nijinsky had amazed the audiences with the versatility of the characters he had created. Each ballet performed in Paris had revealed Nijinsky in a new artistic image: the Negro slave in *Schéhérazade*; Albrecht in *Giselle*; and now, Harlequin in *Carnaval*. The Théâtre Nationale de l'Opéra in Paris was filled to capacity for every performance, and many were turned away, disappointed at not being able to get to see the Ballets Russes and Nijinsky, despite the extra performances.

But our own pleasure in this success was marred when we heard of the death of Marius Petipa, in St. Petersburg on July 1 [N.S. 14], 1910. There was a feeling of sadness among the company, most of whom had known and worked with Petipa. He had been Maître de Ballet at the Maryinsky for so long and had been the choreographer of so many of the ballets we danced in the Imperial Theatres.

The artists were also disappointed and dismayed that in spite of the successful conclusion of La Saison Russe à l'Opéra, Diaghilev did not announce any plans for a future season.

But the main concern of Vaslav and myself was Mother, who was not feeling well. We persuaded her to see a doctor, and he recommended that she take a cure in Karlsbad. Immediately at the end of the season Mother and I traveled to Bohemia, to Karlsbad, while Vaslav remained in Paris for a few more days. During the past weeks he had been posing for the painter Jacques-Emile Blanche, wearing the costume designed by Léon Bakst for the "Danse Siamoise." Blanche wanted to complete the portrait for a forthcoming exhibition of his works, and so Vaslav agreed to stay after the end of the season for some extra sittings.

In Karlsbad, I would accompany Mother early in the morning for her first regimen of the day. The cure consisted of walking back and forth for a certain amount of time while sipping the mineral waters. The throngs of people taking the cure would walk under the arcades of the spa where an orchestra played music by Strauss and Dvořák.

Vaslav joined us towards the end of our stay in Karlsbad, and while Mama was taking her afternoon cure he and I would often walk together under the arcades. He told me that Diaghilev and Bakst had gone to Switzerland to see Alexandre Benois to try and iron out their difficulties. Benois had been delayed in Russia and had arrived in Paris only in time for the premiere of *Giselle*. He had been disappointed and angry to find that the program credits for the libretto of *Schéhérazade* were given solely to Bakst, in fact so angry that he had not stayed in Paris for the additional performances we gave after the official end of the season on July 5.

When Bakst came to Karlsbad he told us that Benois and Diaghilev were reconciled. Vaslav had been invited to join Diaghilev in Venice, so he and Bakst planned to travel there together. Before they left, the three of us made some explorations of the neighboring countryside, and on one of these outings I took several pictures of us with the camera I had bought in Germany.

After Mama had completed her cure, she and I went to Warsaw before returning to St. Petersburg. Aunt Thetya was pleased to see us and hear our news of the Paris Season. We stayed in Poland for a couple of weeks, during which Mother took me to see several historic buildings and monuments in Warsaw, including the Wielki Theatre, where she and Father had trained as dancers, and the Catholic Church of the Holy Cross, where all three of her children had been baptized.

I believe that Mama's decision to visit her sister in Warsaw instead of inviting Aunt Thetya and Cousin Stassia to come and spend a few weeks with us in St. Petersburg was mainly motivated by a desire not to annoy Vaslav. I know Mama was puzzled and grieved by the marked change in Vaslav's attitude and feelings towards our relatives. He had cooled even towards Aunt Thetya and Cousin Stassia, showing nothing of that warmth of feeling towards them with which he had freely expressed his love as a child. When they had come to St. Petersburg the year before for a short visit, Vaslav had not even stayed home to have dinner with them, saying to Mother, "Towards them I no longer feel related. . . . Painters, musicians, writers—these are now my true kin . . ."

During the past year Vaslav had been a regular attendant of the meetings at Diaghilev's apartment near the magnificent Neva Embankment where the plans for the Russian Season in Paris were discussed. Presiding over those meetings was Diaghilev himself, so distinguished and omniscient, and around him sat the great painters Benois, Bakst, Roerich, Golovine, and Korovine, the musicians and composers Glazounov and Tcherepnine, the well-known *régisseurs* Meyerhold and Sanine, and naturally Diaghilev's great friend, Walter Nouvel, who was an expert on music. Among the balletomanes were Bezobrazov and Svetlov, and also the Secretary to the Russian Embassy in Paris, Prince Argutinsky-Dolgorukov. One might say that at these meetings Vaslav was surrounded by the elite of the St. Petersburg intelligentsia.

Not only were all of them older than Nijinsky, but each one had received recognition in his own right. The young Nijinsky immediately appreciated the privilege accorded him by being admitted to Diaghilev's artistic circle. No longer was he surrounded by the greats of the athletic and sporting world of Prince Lvov; now he was in a different world, the world of art. He soon came to the conclusion that this world of art was where he belonged and that he could live only among artists. Naturally, however, Vaslav was not on the same equal friendly footing with them as they were among themselves. He preferred to remain apart and silent, rather than join in their discussions or conversations, though he listened avidly and absorbed everything that could perfect his art.

The next mornings, full of enthusiasm, he would repeat to me in great detail what he had learned. I felt how deeply he had perceived all he had heard and seen at Diaghilev's. On several occasions he expressed to me his own opinions and the comments he would have made if only he had spoken at the meeting. But in the midst of Diaghilev's distinguished companions, the young Nijinsky froze and was not able to overcome his timidity. He did not behave like a famous artist. He did not realize that he had achieved fame on his own merit and that he was great in his own art.

Before he met Diaghilev, Vaslav was quite a different person; he used to be carefree and more relaxed. I had seen him many times in the company of ballet, drama, or opera artists; at small social events he was at ease and unconstrained, and he was particularly popular with young ladies. By nature Vaslav was extremely sensitive and proud; he would be devastated if he felt that he had made the slightest social blunder, feeling embarrassed for days afterwards. Vaslav was always kind and modest, and later after he had achieved fame, he became reserved and never assumed the bumptious airs of a celebrity.

When Mama and I returned to St. Petersburg from Warsaw we had news of Vaslav from Venice. From his letters we learned how much he was enjoying his stay there. He was spending long hours sunning on the beach at the Lido—the meeting place, as he called it, of the "beau monde." He was also swimming a lot; he loved to swim, and he was an excellent swimmer.

His passion for swimming dated from the time when Father had taught him to swim in Novaya Derevnia. I could remember also an outing with Mama, Aunt Thetya, and Cousin Stassia by the river near Cousin Stassia's home in Marijampole. We walked along the riverbank, but Vaslav, about fourteen years old at this time, kept pace with us while swimming in the river. He swam so easily for more than an hour—diving, turning somersaults, swimming on his back, on his side, or disappearing to swim under the water. Vatsa gave us a real performance. So I knew that many of those watching Vaslav in Venice, on the Lido, would also be admiring the extraordinary, beautiful style of his swimming, his strength and endurance in the water, for, whether on the surface of the water or underneath, he was like a fish.

His letters also told us of the admiring crowds who gathered to watch as Léon Bakst painted his portrait. Vaslav posed, standing in his swimming trunks on the reddish sands, against a background of blue sky and blue waters. Vaslav liked the portrait very much, and he told us that he thought it would be shown in St. Petersburg in the *Mir Iskusstva* exhibition.

33　The Maryinsky: Fall Season
1910

OFFICIALLY THE summer leave ended on August 20, and all the artists were expected to return to the Maryinsky ready for the opening of the Season of Opera and Ballet on September 1. I will never forget how thrilled I was when I came to report to the Maryinsky for rehearsals to read on the Theatre call-board: "*Giselle*—September 4. Giselle—Mlle Pavlova. Albrecht—M. Nijinsky." *Giselle* was to be the opening ballet of the season.

But Vaslav had not returned; his letters had stopped suddenly. Mother and I had grown more and more worried about him, for we had not received any replies to our letters. Our worry was indeed justifiable. Vaslav had suffered a sunstroke and for a long time ran a high temperature. He was slow making a recovery, being ill through the end of August. Instead of returning to the Imperial Theatres, Vaslav sent a doctor's certificate, detailing his illness, with the request that his leave be extended until he was completely recovered. The Administration, however, ordered him to return immediately, otherwise his salary would not be paid. Nijinsky replied that he would return only upon fully recovering his health.

But this meant he would not be able to dance in *Giselle* with Anna Pavlova on September 4. When she had returned from London in August to engage dancers in Moscow for her forthcoming tour in the United States, she had promised Telyakovsky that she would delay her departure from Russia for a few days so that she could dance *Giselle* with Nijinsky in the Maryinsky. This was to be Pavlova's only appearance in a ballet in Russia for the 1910–11 season. I was heartbroken when I learned that Vaslav would not be able to leave Venice and that again my wish to see Anna Pavlova and Nijinsky dance together in *Giselle* was not to be granted.

A second performance of *Giselle* was announced for September 26: "Giselle—Mme Karsavina. Albrecht—M. Nijinsky." But Vaslav remained ill all through September, and so he missed his second opportunity to dance *Giselle* at the Maryinsky.

At the beginning of every fall season, the promotions in rank for the ballet artists in the Imperial Theatres were announced. I had been dancing in the Imperial Theatres for only two years, and already in 1909 I had had my first promotion, from the second line to the first line of the *corps de ballet*. Then in June 1910, when Vladimir Arkadievitch Telyakovsky, the Director of the Imperial Theatres, had come to Paris for the Saison Russe, he had come backstage during the intermission at the end of *Carnaval* and, after congratulating me on my achievement in my dancing and on my success as Papillon, had promised me another promotion and a raise in salary.

I was very proud now to learn that after only two years dancing in the *corps de ballet* I had been promoted to the rank of *coryphée*. I was most proud of the fact that both my promotions were based solely on steady progress in my dancing and on my artistic talent and were not due in any way to outside "pull."

A *coryphée* in the Imperial Theatres seldom had the chance to dance a solo role but was usually assigned to dance in groups of four or six dancers. Yet I was to make my debut as a *coryphée* on September 26 as the Goddess Dew, in the short ballet *The Awakening of Flora*, when the title role of Flora was to be danced by Elsa Will.

The Awakening of Flora, music by Drigo, had been choreographed by Petipa and Ivanov in 1894 and first performed at Peterhof with Kshessinska in the title role. Since then the title role had been danced by Pavlova in 1900, Zambelli in 1903, and Karsavina in 1904. And I had seen the ballet performed in 1906 with Preobrajenska, Gerdt, and Fokine. There was one passage I particularly liked when a low chariot drawn by tigers crossed the back of the stage. Later I was disappointed to learn that the tigers were large dogs painted with stripes.

For my role as the Goddess Dew I was dressed in a silver costume and held a shell in the shape of a horn of plenty. As I danced on toe around the stage I scattered small pieces of silver paper from the shell to represent the dew.

The Awakening of Flora was a short one-act ballet, so it was frequently revived when a short ballet was needed to complete the program. During the 1910–11 season it was often performed with the ballet *Giselle*. For the performance on September 26, Tamara Karsavina was to dance the title role in *Giselle* for the first time in Russia. I can recall that night so clearly, for I was hoping and praying up to the last minute that Vaslav would return in time to dance in *Giselle* with Karsavina.

My heart was aching for Vaslav. I could not understand why he was prolonging his stay in Venice; in his most recent letter he had said that he was feeling better, but there had been no mention of when he was expecting to return home. I couldn't understand this in Vaslav, and it saddened me to feel that he was indifferent towards his work, neglecting his obligations towards the Imperial Theatres. Already during January and February of 1910 the public and ballet critics had noticed that on the few occasions when he was scheduled to appear at the Maryinsky he had not displayed his usual brilliance. At first it had been attributed to his recent illness—that is, to his attack of typhoid fever in Paris in the summer of 1909—and many had voiced their concern for the future of this talented artist. But then it was also noticed that for performances of *Le Pavillon d'Armide* and *Chopiniana*, Nijinsky "miraculously recovered and danced superbly . . ." I also remembered how he used to be late regularly for Legat's rehearsals, and that once he had even been fined. It all made me worry about his future, for he seemed to be antagonizing the Administration even more.

In the Maryinsky that fall we were again rehearsing that awful old classical ballet, *Le Talisman*. It was our second year working on this revival by Nikolai Legat, with its endless number of boring tableaux. The whole thing was being cooked up for Mathilda Kshessinska so that once more in her late "youth" she could shine on the stage. *Le Talisman* was scheduled to be performed on November 14, 1910. Though no longer young, this famous ballerina was indisputably talented. She still possessed a great technique, exclusively *sur pointe*, but she did not have elevation. Her style was essentially that of the old classical acrobatic technique. She was vulgar and brusque in all her movements—the very opposite of Anna Pavlova. Yet she demanded that when Pavlova left the Imperial Theatres, being the *prima ballerina assoluta* she should dance Pavlova's roles in *Giselle* and *Chopiniana*.*

Kshessinska had many admirers in the *parterre*. Some were genuinely sincere, like the old balletomanes, but others were seeking only to use her influence as *entrée* into the higher spheres of St. Petersburg society. The "gods"—the balcony and the gallery at the Maryinsky made up of young balletomanes, and the students and admirers of the dancing of Pavlova and Nijinsky and the ballets of Fokine—were opposed to the old guard of

*Kshessinska finally realized this ambition to dance Pavlova roles in the Maryinsky Theatre—in *Chopiniana* on December 11, 1911; in *Giselle* not until April 17, 1916. (IN/JR)

the theatrical public. The "gods" had recently declared war on this famous ballerina and refused to applaud her at all.

On one occasion Kshessinska had said "I spit on the gods." This had so enraged the young theatregoers that they sent her a collective letter, saying, . . . "for us up here, it is much easier to spit down on you than for you to spit up at us . . ."

As a *coryphée*, I was assigned to learn the "Dance of the Four Little Swans" from *Swan Lake* and "Dance of Precious Stones" (Silver, Gold, Sapphire, Diamond) from *Sleeping Beauty*. Though I was happy and proud to have been promoted, I soon found the atmosphere in the Imperial Theatres oppressive and stifling.

I remember one very characteristic incident that will describe the ridiculously unreasonable instructions given to young dancers during rehearsals of the ballet at the Maryinsky. After practicing my Sapphire *variation* I joined the others, and we were rehearsing together when suddenly from the *répetiteur*, Sergeyev, I received a reprimand: "Don't jump so high. Don't jump higher than the others. All four of you must jump to the same height!"

"But," I answered, "I can't regulate my jumps to fit the other three dancers. . . . During the dance it is not possible to guess how high they are going to jump. All my jumps correspond absolutely to the musical beat, and that is the only way I can assess my elevation."

"In that case, it may be necessary to replace you with someone else who does not jump as high as you do!"

This absurd remark reminded me of the discipline of military drill and made me realize how much I missed Vaslav and the excitement and stimulation of the Diaghilev Saison Russe.

But Vaslav was still not home, though he now seemed to be completely recovered, having accompanied Diaghilev to Paris in October. I heard that he had been seen at the opening of Blanche's exhibition of paintings, and I think it was Bakst, when he came to St. Petersburg to design the new sets for *Carnaval* in the Maryinsky, who told me that the name Nijinsky was now well-known to Parisians, even among those who had not had the opportunity to see him dance during the Saison Russe. They had admired his portrait in the Blanche exhibition, fascinated by the pose from "Danse Siamoise"—the enigmatic smile, the oriental features, the expressive, graceful hands.

Yet Vaslav still did not tell us when he would be coming home, and this continued to worry us. He simply wrote that he had exciting news and spared us, then, his anxiety about his military service. When he was lying ill in Venice he had received his draft summons for military service. He had sent the authorities his doctor's certificate, notarized by the Russian Consulate in Venice, and also a letter requesting his complete exemption from military service on the grounds that he, Vaslav Nijinsky, was the sole provider for his mother as his father, Thomas Nijinsky, had abandoned the family, and his elder brother, Stanislav, was an incurable hospitalized in a mental institution. This petition was declared invalid because it should have been made a year prior to the date of induction, and also should have been signed by his mother. However, taking into consideration his illness, he was granted one year's deferment and was not expected to report for military duty until September 1911.

At the end of October all St. Petersburg, in fact all Russia, was anxiously awaiting news of the whereabouts of the eighty-two-year-old Lev Nikolaevitch Tolstoy, who on October 27, on a cold, freezing night, had left his home at Yasnaya Polyana for "destination unknown." On October 31, the news reached St. Petersburg that Tolstoy had been found on a train, gravely ill, and had been taken to the home of the stationmaster at Astrapovo Station.

For the next week all St. Petersburg seemed to stand still as people prayed for Tolstoy. Throngs stood in the snow waiting for the next extra edition of the newspapers, which were immediately sold out.

On November 7, we read in the evening edition that Lev Nikolaevitch Tolstoy had died that morning, at five minutes past six. The death of Tolstoy was felt by everyone throughout Russia not only as the loss of a great Russian genius but as a personal loss. His death was mourned as that of a dear close member of one's own family.

Those were sad days in November with all Russia plunged into mourning, grieved by Tolstoy's death and saddened by the news of his last tragic days. All the cultured world joined Russia in mourning for Lev Nikolaevitch Tolstoy.

At the end of November Vaslav returned to St. Petersburg. He told us how the news of Tolstoy's illness had been received in Paris, where he and Diaghilev had been at the time. People had gathered, standing outside the newspaper offices in Paris, waiting for the news bulletins. Then, when word of his death came, Paris went into mourning. The flags were flown at half-mast, and black crepe was draped all over the city.

Both Vaslav and I had received an eight-volume presentation set of Tolstoy's works as our graduation prizes from the Imperial Theatrical School, and since Tolstoy was my favorite author I had already read all of his works in my set and was now rereading some of his books with renewed interest. Vaslav, too, was spending all his spare time avidly reading Tolstoy, as if he had just discovered him. We often read the same volume at the same time and shared our impressions. Vaslav was always ready to talk to me about Tolstoy, and we were both very proud to possess the works of the great man.

Telyakovsky was very lenient towards Vaslav upon his return to St. Petersburg. He did not even reprimand him for returning late or for missing the performances of *Giselle* with Anna Pavlova and Karsavina in September. Instead, he immediately announced that there would be another performance of *Giselle* with Karsavina and Nijinsky. And then, when Vaslav told him he needed time to work on his dancing and to practice his exercises before starting to rehearse for such an important ballet, Telyakovsky agreed and announced that the performance of *Giselle* with Karsavina and Nijinsky would take place January 23, 1911.

This announcement infuriated Kshessinska, who had asked Vaslav to dance with her on February 13 for her Benefit celebrating her twenty years as an Artist of the Imperial Theatres. He had refused on the grounds that he needed more time to get back into shape, and now she heard that he had agreed to perform in *Giselle* at the end of January, three weeks before her Benefit.

Vaslav was then regarded as a member of "the innovators," as we Diaghilevtsy called ourselves. We "innovators" considered Kshessinska as the epitome of the old classical technique that had outlived itself. In our aspirations for new creativity in dancing we were also fighting the old attitude by which one's only aim and interest was the furtherance of one's career.

For her part Kshessinska had threatened that she would find a way to ensure the dismissal of several of us from the Imperial Theatres. Nijinsky would be the first—he had refused to dance in her upcoming Benefit —and ". . . next will be his sister, for her revolutionary propaganda among the Artists of the Imperial Theatres."

Telyakovsky showed himself to be more sympathetic to the ideas of the "innovators." He had disliked Kshessinska intensely for a long time, as she had caused him endless trouble. The rift between them had widened when, following the departure of Pavlova, Telyakovsky had announced the second performance of *Giselle* for September 26 with Tamara Karsavina. Kshessinska was angry because she herself had always dreamed of dancing Giselle and had particularly wanted to do it this season to prove to Diaghilev and Fokine that she could dance in the Romantic ballets.

Telyakovsky was also becoming more and more disappointed in Legat as a choreographer, and so he had included ballets by Fokine in the repertory of the Maryinsky Theatre—*Chopiniana* and *Egyptian Nights*, the latter with new sets designed by Allegri and costumes by Zanin. Telyakovsky had also scheduled *Carnaval* for February 6, 1911, and had asked Fokine to mount *Danses Polovetsiennes* for the opera *Prince Igor*.

In the time Vaslav had been back in St. Petersburg I had noticed something new, something different about him. He would talk to me about Tolstoy but not about anything else. Otherwise he remained uncommunicative; he seemed more reserved, more pensive and aloof. But there was also a new air of happiness about him, a certain inner glow.

Little by little Vaslav began to open up and tell me about his exciting plans . . . and as I learned about some of Sergei Pavlovitch's projects I found the news was indeed astonishing. "Diaghilev's Ballets Russes," Vaslav said, "had such a great success in Paris, we have become so famous, that we have invitations to perform in all the big theatres in Europe. Everybody wants to see the Ballets Russes. So Sergei Pavlovitch is firmly resolved to create his own permanent ballet company, to engage artists for three years so that we can work almost all the year round, for ten months with two months vacation. This new troupe, Les Ballets Russes, will open with a spring season in Monte Carlo in March, and then we will go to Rome, Paris, and London."

Up to the present time the Russian Ballet had performed only during the summer vacation months as a company made up of Artists from the Imperial Theatres in Moscow and St. Petersburg. The Russian Ballet Seasons abroad had had to coincide with the summer vacations, when there were no performances in the Imperial Theatres.

Vaslav went on to tell me that Sergei Pavlovitch already had in mind which artists he wanted to invite to join his new ballet company.

As we talked, Vaslav and I touched on the many difficulties and troubles Diaghilev would face as he tried to engage these artists, for we doubted whether the Imperial Theatres would grant such a long leave of absence to the dancers he wanted. We found it difficult to conceive of Artists of the Imperial Theatres being willing to submit their resignations and forever lose the title of Artist of the Imperial Theatres, forever lose the security of permanent employment with all its benefits and its assurance of a pension for life. Vaslav and I both believed that such artist "heroes" were to be found only among the young dancers. Diaghilev was not as confident as we were, although he was prepared to offer good salaries.

Diaghilev had ideas for new ballets, and several were already being planned, among them a new ballet by Stravinsky. On hearing Stravinsky's music, Diaghilev had declared the ballet should be about Petrouchka. Vaslav was to dance the role of Petrouchka, and for the Ballerina Doll

Sophia Fedorova was suggested. Diaghilev had asked Benois to work with Stravinsky on the libretto for the ballet, in which they wanted the Ballerina Doll to walk on a tightrope stretched high above the stage.

"Bronia," Vaslav asked me, "would you be able to walk across the stage on a tightrope?"

"If it was required for the ballet, you can be sure that I would learn to do it."

"That is exactly what I said to Levushka [Léon Bakst] and to Serioja [Sergei Diaghilev] in Venice when we talked about *Petrouchka*."

Though Vaslav was excited about the idea of the new ballet, and the new company, the most important news that he had brought back from Venice was still to be confided to me.

"Bronia, what I am going to tell you now no one must know about. . . . For the new season in Paris I am going to mount a ballet. It is going to be *L'Après-Midi d'un Faune*, to the music of Debussy . . ."

Vaslav then began to share with me his general ideas and outline for this, his first choreographic composition.

"I want to move away from the classical Greece that Fokine likes to use. Instead, I want to use the archaic Greece that is less known and, so far, little used in the theatre. However, this is only to be the source of my inspiration. I want to render it in my own way. Any sweetly sentimental line in the form or in the movement will be excluded. More may even be borrowed from Assyria than Greece. I have already started to work on it in my own mind. . . . I want to show it to you . . ."

I was disturbed by this news of Vaslav's. "But what about Fokine? Does he know about it? How will he take it?"

"For now, Fokine must know nothing about my ballet. He will probably mount his three ballets for the coming season. . . . I will work out some of the dances with you, and then we will show them to Diaghilev and to Bakst. If they like the ballet, then that will be the time for Sergei Pavlovitch to speak to Fokine."

Whenever he had a free evening or was not attending rehearsals at the Imperial Theatres, Vaslav worked on his *Faune* at home. This all had to be kept secret, however, and so whenever he worked with me we had to work without a pianist. We already knew the music quite well, for we had heard it played by a good pianist. But to become completely familiar with the music during our rehearsals I would play two or three bars to Vaslav, and he would then dance or demonstrate the movements. I would then repeat those steps as best I could without the music.

To describe the intensity of our rehearsals, I will quote here from my notes of those days:

. . . We are rehearsing in our living room. It is a large room but the only mirror is Mother's pier mirror high on the wall. So I have brought the triple mirror from my dressing table and put it on the floor so that we can really see ourselves. At the very beginning of the ballet the Faune has a series of poses, reclining on a rock, sitting up, or kneeling. We sometimes spend all evening long on the floor in front of the mirror trying out different poses. Vaslav is creating his Faune by using me as his model. I am like a piece of clay that he is molding, shaping into each pose and change of movement.

. . . In our rehearsals together we are completely absorbed in our work and are usually in harmony with each other, but sometimes emotions run high and we lose our tempers with each other. Vaslav is so demanding, unreasonably so. He wants to see his choreography instantaneously executed to perfection. He is unable to take into account human limitations. He is unwilling to realize the tremendous distance separating his vision from the means that are at the disposal of the artist.

. . . He seems to forget that I am, after all, only nineteen and a girl, and naturally I can't grasp at once and render correctly his own choreographic scheme—I find it difficult to express all the nuances of the character of a faune and at the same time find the role of Nijinsky's Faune . . .

. . . I can see clearly the delicate refinement, the precision, the jewel-like work, the finely wrought filigree of his choreography. I realize that the slightest deviation, any undue tension in the rhythm of the movements, any small mistake, could destroy the whole composition, leaving only a caricature of the choreographic idea. I can see all this very well, and even so, it is often impossible for me to master the refinements of each detail of the movement . . .

. . . It is amazing how Vaslav himself, from the very beginning, without any preparation, is in complete mastery of the new technique of his ballet. In his own execution, each movement, each position of the body, and the expression of each choreographic moment is perfect . . .

. . . maybe our work together is made more difficult because we are brother and sister . . . making us impatient with each other. Besides, Vaslav is, as always, unduly demanding with me . . . no different now that he is working on his own ballet, but just as he usually is for my dancing endeavors. . . . But how much I am learning from him . . .

34   Towards a New Life

VASLAV WAS completely engrossed in planning his first ballet and overjoyed at the prospect of this work. For myself, first after the Diaghilev Seasons abroad and now with these exciting rehearsals with Vaslav, I had been finding it difficult to adjust back into the routine of the Imperial Theatres. I was thrilled, however, when, immediately after the first of the year, Fokine called me for the rehearsals of *Carnaval* and told me that I would be dancing my Papillon. I was so proud to have been named to dance this part in the Maryinsky, and I knew there were several soloists of the Imperial Ballet who coveted the role, with its solo *variation*. This would be the second soloist part I had been given since being promoted to *coryphée* in September 1910. My first, the Goddess Dew in *The Awakening of Flora*, I had already danced several times during the season. The ballet was regularly given on the same evening as *Giselle*, and I was looking forward to the next performance in January when, at last, Nijinsky was to dance in *Giselle*.

Vaslav had started to prepare his role of Albrecht and was working together with Karsavina. Since seeing Karsavina with Nijinsky in Paris, I had seen her other performances in *Giselle* in the Maryinsky, and they had made me sadly nostalgic of the deeply moving and inspiring rehearsals of Pavlova and Nijinsky during the winter of 1909. So I wanted to watch Karsavina now with Nijinsky and came to their rehearsals whenever I could spare time from my own rehearsals.

The performance of *Giselle* on January 24, 1911, was attended by all the balletomanes and the high society of St. Petersburg. The Dowager Empress, Maria Fedorovna, along with several Grand Dukes and many of the court were present. Karsavina had her own following in St. Petersburg, and the occasion had all the excitement of a gala night, onstage as well as in the audience. The performance proceeded magnificently.

Unlike the spiritual Giselle of Pavlova, the Giselle of Karsavina was of the earth and had all the charm and tenderness of a woman—so that when dancing with Karsavina, the ethereal qualities of Nijinsky's dancing were enhanced.

Vaslav, in the air, was in his own element. He posed, soared, and hovered in the air, seeming to stay there longer than on the ground.

In the wings during his dancing I could hear whispered exclamations, "magnificent . . . " "a superhuman dancer . . ." "truly the god of the dance . . ."

Vaslav, indeed, surpassed himself in this *Giselle*. He danced as he had never danced before. The success of Nijinsky in *Giselle* is impossible to describe. Each time Nijinsky appeared onstage he was met by thunderous applause, and the orchestra had to stop playing and wait for the interminable ovations to subside . . .

~

THE MORNING following the performance of *Giselle* Vaslav was awakened by a telephone call from the Imperial Theatres. He was asked to come immediately to the office of Alexander Dmitrievitch Krupensky, the Administrator of the Office of the Directorate of the Imperial Theatres in St. Petersburg.

My mother and I were sure that Vaslav had been asked to come to the Theatre so that Krupensky could congratulate him for his excellent performance and for the outstanding success of *Giselle* the previous night. We even hoped there would be a change in his status in the Imperial Theatres. From the age of fifteen Vaslav had been a renowned artist in St. Petersburg and, while the success of the last two summer seasons of the Ballets Russes of S. P. Diaghilev had brought him European fame and recognition, he was working without a contract in the Imperial Theatres. Like the other artists who had graduated with him in 1907, he was receiving a basic salary with routine increases for years of service. In 1909, after his first season abroad, his salary was raised to nine hundred sixty rubles a year, but since then he had not received any increase. And his status in the Imperial Ballet was still a *coryphé*, even though he had been dancing soloist roles, and even leading roles in *La Fille Mal Gardée*, *The Humpbacked Horse*, and now *Giselle*.

Karsavina, by dancing Giselle on September 26, 1910, was now considered a "Prima Ballerina."* Mother and I had often wondered, if

*In her autobiography, *Theatre Street*, Karsavina describes how, following her first performance of *Giselle* in the Maryinsky, "in 1910, I received the title of 'Prima Ballerina' and the Directorate offered me a contract . . . ." However, according to official records the title of

Vaslav had returned in time to dance with Karsavina in *Giselle* then, and if he had not antagonized the Directorate by showing himself in Paris at the opening of the Blanche Exhibition where his portrait in the Bakst costume from "Danse Siamoise" had been displayed, whether in all probability he would not now be the proud bearer of the title of Premier Danseur of the Imperial Theatres.

Tamara had told Vaslav during their rehearsals in January that she had already signed a contract with the Imperial Theatres for three years, with a considerable increase in salary, and that she had promised Diaghilev that she would appear in as many performances abroad with the Ballets Russes as her contract with the Imperial Theatres permitted.

So Mother and I were not at all surprised when Vaslav was called to the Office of the Directorate of the Imperial Theatres. We were expecting to hear wonderful news—but soon Vaslav came back home.

His dark-complexioned face usually had little color, but now it was paler than ever. His beautiful, slanted brown eyes, framed with his long dark lashes, were open wide and shone with a certain determination and excitement.

"Krupensky met me very coldly and began to speak in the stern voice of an official. . . . 'The Director of the Imperial Theatres, Vladimir Arkadievitch Telyakovsky, is away in Moscow. In his absence I perform his duties. I must announce to you, Nijinsky, the orders that I have received this morning by telephone from His Highness Count Fredericks, the Minister of the Imperial Court:* By order of the Dowager Empress Maria Fedorovna, you, Nijinsky, are to be immediately dismissed from the Imperial Theatres for appearing in the presence of her Imperial Highness Maria Fedorovna in the ballet *Giselle* in an indecent and improper costume. This dismissal is to take effect no later than twenty-four hours after the receipt of this order.'

"Krupensky then started to reprimand me on my theatrical costume," Vaslav went on, "but noticing that I was not reacting as he had expected, he softened his tone and suggested that I should turn in a petition to the Minister of the Imperial Court, apologizing for my costume and asking to reenlist in the ranks of the Artists of the Imperial Theatres. 'Undoubtedly, Nijinsky, you would be taken on again immediately,' Krupensky assured me, going on to say that he had already spoken by telephone with

---

Prima Ballerina was not accorded to Karsavina until March 1912, although the contract for three years was signed in January 1911, starting at six thousand rubles a year, increasing to seven thousand rubles the second year, and to eight thousand rubles the third year. (IN/JR)

*Count Vladimir Borissovitch Fredericks, Minister of the Imperial Court from 1896 to 1917, was directly responsible to the Tsar for all matters concerning the Imperial Theatres. (IN/JR)

Telyakovsky in Moscow, who had said that I could submit such a petition.

"There did not seem to me to be anything to say about my dismissal from the Theatre, and as I was preparing to leave the office Krupensky again changed the tone of the conversation. He offered me a contract . . . with the same conditions as for the great Artists of the Imperial Theatres—Chaliapin, Smirnov, Kusnetzova. . . . 'We are prepared to offer you an honorary salary of nine thousand rubles a year for twenty performances. That way you will have some months free each year with the right to perform abroad during that time.'

"After listening to Krupensky's proposal I did not utter a word and again prepared to leave. Krupensky must have thought I was turning down the offer because it was too low, for now he made me a new one. 'Submit your petition to the Minister and the Directorate will sign a contract with you for twelve thousand rubles a year. I hope that will be adequate salary for you.'

"I rose, bowed in silence, and started to walk out . . . but then changed my mind and said to Krupensky, 'A few minutes ago, Alexander Dmitrievitch, you first informed me that I was dismissed from the rank of Artist of the Imperial Theatres, then you suggested that I should submit, with an apology, a petition for reinstatement, and then you make me an offer for an increase in salary. . . . But why did you throw me out first? I, Nijinsky, do not wish to return to the Imperial Ballet from which I was thrown out as if useless. . . . I now consider myself to be an outsider, and if you want me to return to the Imperial Theatres, then I suggest to you, to the Directorate of the Imperial Theatres, that I should be sent an apology for the wrong done me, no matter whether it was due to a mistake or a misunderstanding, and also that I be sent a petition requesting my return. I will consider such a petition and, in due course, will inform you of my decision.'

"I bowed coolly to Krupensky and left the office.

"That is all. . . . I am no longer an Artist of the Imperial Theatres. I am now only an artist of the Diaghilev Ballet. I will telephone Serioja and tell him. . . . I can imagine how happy he will be."

———

BUT MAMA was heartbroken when she heard Vaslav's news. Every hope, every dream, every ambition she had had for her son was shattered. Our mother had always lived with the idea that we should become Artists of the Imperial Theatres—the title coveted by so many great artists in Europe as well as in Russia. Through our childhood she had guided us for our future in the Imperial Theatres, enrolling each of us, Vaslav first, and then myself, in the Imperial Theatrical School. From the age of nine until we graduated, we had lived and studied there, and then following the usual pattern we had applied after graduation to the Minister of the Imperial Court to be enlisted in the Ballet Company of the Imperial Theatres and won the title of Artist of the Imperial Theatres, a lifetime title. And now she was in despair. Vaslav had been dismissed.

———

THE DISMISSAL of Nijinsky from the Imperial Theatres was widely reported in the press and was the talk of St. Petersburg. Nijinsky, already renowned throughout Europe—the god of the dance—had been dismissed. In artistic circles it was said that those who noticed something indecent in the costume worn by Nijinsky for *Giselle*, executed after the sketches of Alexandre Benois, should be mentally examined or have a bucket of cold water thrown over them, and certainly should not be allowed to go to any museum.

The costume Nijinsky had worn in the first act of *Giselle* was not the traditional costume of the Imperial Theatres, which included a pair of trunks worn over the tights of the male dancers. For this performance Vaslav had come onstage not wearing the regulation trunks. He was dressed in an authentic costume of the Italian Renaissance . . . a short brown tunic over tights, a small saccoche hanging from his belt at the side.

It was exactly the same costume that Nijinsky had worn for the performance of *Giselle* presented at the Grand Opéra in Paris by Diaghilev's Ballets Russes. The costume was designed by Alexandre Benois. Nothing in his costume designs could ever be deemed indecent, and I am sure that this design was interpreted correctly down to the last button, to the last detail.

In the press, it was suggested that if the Directorate wanted to make the public believe that there was indeed anything indecent in the costume worn by Nijinsky, they should place the blame where it truly belonged, for it was noted that the Artists of the Imperial Theatres were not responsible for their own attire and that it was the duty of the *régisseur* and the *costumier* to check the costumes before each performance.

A few days later, Count Benkendorff came to see Vaslav. He was the Grand Marshal of the Imperial Court and Count Fredericks's immediate subordinate. He admired and esteemed Nijinsky as a great artist and wanted to find out for himself exactly what had happened and what were the circumstances behind this strange dismissal.

He told Vaslav that when the subject was mentioned in the presence of the Dowager Empress Maria Fedorovna and Nijinsky's dismissal described as being "on her orders," she had declared that this was the first she had heard of any such order.

" 'I did not see anything indecent in Nijinsky's costume,' " Count Benkendorff quoted her as saying. " 'On the contrary, I was full of admiration for him. If I had noticed anything shocking, then as a lady I would hardly have drawn attention to it. It must all have been a joke on the part of those "young boys." ' "

Those "young boys" were hardly young anymore; they were the two Grand Dukes, Sergei Mikhailovitch and Andrei Vladimirovitch,* who were a part of the entourage of that famous ballerina of the Imperial Theatres—Mathilda Kshessinska. Vaslav had already been introduced to one of them, Andrei Vladimirovitch,† and had occasionally met him at the home of the ballerina.

Vaslav then recounted to us how, during the intermission between the first and second acts of *Giselle*, the Grand Duke Andrei had come onstage. He had demanded that Nijinsky should immediately appear before him so that he, the Grand Duke, could check the costume for the second act, for he could not permit Nijinsky to dance again in an indecent costume in the presence of the Dowager Empress, Maria Fedorovna. Such interference by a Grand Duke was unprecedented in the history of the Imperial Theatres. The *régisseur* had come rushing to Vaslav's dressing room to transmit "the order," and was quickly followed by Krupensky, acting in the absence of the Director, Telyakovsky.

Nijinsky was deeply offended, both by the statement made by the Grand Duke that he, Nijinsky, had appeared on the stage in an indecent costume, and by the Grand Duke's order that Nijinsky show himself before him, dressed in the costume for the second act, before the performance could be allowed to proceed.

"Please give the Grand Duke this message. 'I am not dressed at this moment and am putting on my makeup for the second act. It is not possible for me to come onstage now, but if the Grand Duke wishes to see my costume for the second act, then the *costumier* can bring it onstage and show it to him.' "

---

*The Grand Duke Sergei Mikhailovitch was the Tsar's uncle and considered as Kshessinska's "eldest patron." The Grand Duke Andrei Vladimirovitch, the Tsar's cousin, had been living with Kshessinska since 1900. They were married in Cannes in January 1921. (IN/JR)

†Bronislava Nijinska is the first to mention that the Grand Duke Andrei was involved, and to relate this particular backstage sequence of events. Other versions have placed Grand Duke Sergei and, mistakenly, Telyakovsky on the scene, and have stressed Krupensky's reprimand to Nijinsky. The implication that Kshessinska's entourage was involved is strengthened here, but this version still leaves open the possibility that Diaghilev might have encouraged Nijinsky to wear his costume as a provocation. (AK)

Vaslav categorically refused to show himself in his costume to anyone but an official of the Imperial Ballet.

According to the rules and protocol surrounding members of the Imperial Family in Russia, such a response, and especially coming from a regular Artist of the Imperial Theatres, was unspeakably insolent. So Krupensky, on returning to the stage, informed the Grand Duke that Nijinsky would come right away.

But Vaslav was upset, and this slowed down his dressing, to a point where he was not even ready for the scheduled beginning of the second act. At the same time, Krupensky, living up to his nickname of "Tempest," came rushing back to Vaslav's dressing room. First he talked very sternly, but soon switched to a more conciliatory note as he tried to persuade Vaslav not to create an incident. The entr'acte grew longer and longer. The Grand Duke was standing on the stage front, behind the drawn curtains, waiting. It would be impossible to start the second act before the Grand Duke chose to leave the stage.

Some of the other artists had now joined in and were trying to persuade Vaslav to go and see the Grand Duke. Finally Vaslav was dressed; he was ready. By now he was sufficiently calm to feel that it would be unbecoming as an artist, and also an impertinence, to keep the Dowager Empress and all the public waiting any longer.

Vaslav appeared onstage, staying at the back. He was wrapped in a black cloak, pale even under his makeup. He looked at no one, but simply stood motionless near the back wings, a great distance from the Grand Duke. Making no attempt to approach him, he bowed to no one in particular and again stood motionless.

Suddenly he threw open his cloak to reveal the costume for the second act. He turned around with a sweeping gesture, wrapped the cloak back around himself, and threw one end over his shoulder. Then, with no attempt to hide his anger, he strode off the stage. The Grand Duke left to return to his box. The *régisseur* gave the signal for the second act to begin.

After the performance, the Grand Duke, this "young boy," had called Count Fredericks and told him that the Dowager Empress Maria Fedorovna had ordered the dismissal of Nijinsky for wearing an indecent costume onstage for the performance of *Giselle* and had asked him to pass on her order to the Minister.

Vaslav was called several times by the Director of the Imperial Theatres, V. A. Telyakovsky, who urged him to return to the Imperial Theatres. Vaslav's decision was irrevocable.

This departure of Vaslav from the Imperial Theatres seemed to be the deciding factor for the establishment of a permanent company of the Russian Ballet by Sergei Pavlovitch Diaghilev, who now went ahead and signed contracts with artists and made arrangements with the theatres abroad for performances to be given by Les Ballets Russes.

—

AT THE END of January, shortly after Vaslav's dismissal, I submitted my own resignation in writing to the Directorate, explaining that I could no longer remain in the Imperial Ballet or work in a Theatre whose Administration could show such poor judgment in their dealings with a talented artist like Nijinsky, and saying too that I no longer had any faith in the artistic direction of the Imperial Theatres.

Vaslav and I were both in high spirits; we felt that in leaving the Imperial Theatres we were discarding the old and embarking on a new life. A completely new path was opening before us. We were about to live in a world of art, our future uncertain but so exciting. Yet my decision to submit my resignation, as well as Vaslav's dismissal, brought only anguish and grief to our mother.

Mother tried to make me change my mind, and she refused to sign my petition for resignation. I told her that I had already given my consent to Sergei Pavlovitch to join his ballet company. Mother used all the arguments she could think of to try to persuade Vaslav and me to change our decision to join Diaghilev's ballet company and to convince us that we should remain in the Imperial Theatres.

It did not occur to any of us at that time that it was only the Directorate of the Imperial Theatres that could use its influence to spare Vaslav from the obligations of military service. That factor alone might have made him accept Telyakovsky's offer of a long-term contract, giving as it did the right to perform abroad.

Mama was distressed about Vaslav's refusal to reconsider Telyakovsky's offer. She had brought both of us up in the expectation that the Imperial Theatres would be our home for life and throughout our childhood had watched closely over our progress, placing great emphasis on what she considered the moral standards worthy of future artists. Now Mother was also stressing to Vaslav that an artist who has achieved fame has a responsibility towards his public. An artist must be prepared to make sacrifices; his personal life no longer belongs to himself but to his public. His life must serve as an example; he must strive to bring out his best qualities and to cultivate them.

But Vaslav at that time was completely under Diaghilev's influence. Sergei Pavlovitch was impressing on Vaslav that his pride should not allow him to be persuaded by the Director or to sign a three-year contract with the Imperial Theatres; and that he should not forget how he had been insulted or the rude manner in which he had been dismissed . . . as

67. Bronislava Nijinska.
Photographic portrait,
Monte Carlo, 1911.

68. Vaslav Nijinsky.
Photographic portrait,
London, 1911.

69. Nijinsky wearing the traditional Imperial Theatres costume for Albrecht in Act I of *Giselle*, in a studio photographic portrait posed in Paris, 1910. Nijinsky never wore this costume in a performance, though he appeared in it for rehearsals of *Giselle* with Anna Pavlova at the Maryinsky Theatre.

70. The Benois costume that Nijinsky wore in the St. Petersburg performance on January 23, 1911, causing his dismissal from the Imperial Theatres.

71. Mathilda Kshessinska *(circled)* surrounded by her entourage of dukes, balletomanes, and artists. Group photograph taken on the occasion of Kshessinska's Twentieth Jubilee, February 13, 1911.

72. Colonel V. A. Telyakovsky, Director of the Imperial Theatres from 1901 until 1917. *(Roland John Wiley Collection)*

73, 74. Nijinsky as Narcisse, and Nijinska
as Bacchante, in *Narcisse*, Paris, 1911.

75, 76. Nijinska and Fokina in *Narcisse*, 1911.

77. Photographic portrait of Chaliapin,
with affectionate autograph to Bronislava
Nijinska, April 14, 1911, Monte Carlo.

78. The Theatre and Casino in Monte Carlo.
Postcard, c. 1911.

79. *Nijinsky and Karsavina
in Le Spectre de la Rose*.
Painting by Valentine Gross.

80. *Almée in Schéhérazade*. Drawing by Bakst.
This costume was worn by Nijinska in the Monte
Carlo production when Chaliapin remarked
on her performance to Diaghilev.

81. Bronislava Nijinska in Paris,
December 1911.

82. Bronislava Nijinska's twenty-
first birthday party in Paris,
with Tchernicheva, Grigoriev,
and Piltz.

83. Eleonora Nijinska in Monte
Carlo, 1912, wearing one of
the new spring outfits bought
for her by Vaslav in Nice.

if he had committed some kind of crime . . . thrown out as a worthless individual devoid of talents . . .

And of course Vaslav—closely surrounded by Diaghilev's circle of painters, writers, and musicians, and listening to their conversations about all the exciting projects to be created by Diaghilev's future Russian Ballet—was completely enthralled by the exciting prospect of life in this World of Art and Ballet where ballets would be created by great musicians and great painters under the personal guidance and direction of Diaghilev himself. In this world Vaslav was to be a central figure and also participate in the artistic achievements of the ballet.

For Diaghilev, too, it was essential to the formation of his ballet company that an artist like Nijinsky be available for the entire year, and not just during the time off granted by the Imperial Theatres. Vaslav was easily persuaded by Diaghilev that it was for his own good that he should leave the Imperial Theatres and their petty jealousies forever and never return to that tedious world where all the Administration was subordinated to the discipline of bureaucrats, for the most part lacking in culture and having little or nothing to do with art.

But Mother was deeply grieved. Here was Vaslav deciding to quit, to give up a brilliant and promising position in the Imperial Theatres to become a Diaghilev artist. It was not that Mother did not value the Diaghilev Ballet. She had admired the performances of the Russian Ballet abroad and had witnessed for herself the tremendous success of our first season. But she would often say, ". . . it may be that this success and the whole enterprise will only be short-lived. But the Imperial Theatres are forever . . ."

Now she told us, "It has always been my hope to see you, my children, become Artists in the Imperial Theatres. . . . I have suffered much and made painful sacrifices in my own life for you to become Artists of the Imperial Theatres, your future assured with a respected position in life guaranteed by a steady income and a pension. . . . I do not want my children to go through the same hardships that your father and I endured in private companies in Russia. There were endless worries about money, having to think about tomorrow, the lack of engagements, anxiety as to whether the entrepreneur would be able to pay our salaries and, worst of all, being forced to perform in God knows what kind of theatre because, you, the children needed to be fed . . ."

She was also specially saddened by my desire to submit my resignation. "I cannot see how you, of your own free will, can walk out of the most flourishing Theatre in the whole world . . . how you can turn your back on the most privileged title: Artist of the Imperial Theatres.

"Vaslav," she said, "is already famous, and so he can easily return and be accepted back into the Imperial Theatres whenever he chooses. But what will become of you?"

Mama could not understand that all these arguments meant nothing to me. "What is really important," I tried to explain, "is to take part in the creation of new paths in art, in a new ballet theatre, whatever the cost or sacrifice. One must not think only of one's material well-being . . . though, in any case, our well-being will be splendidly guaranteed by our salaries and contracts for the next three years."

One of Mama's arguments against my joining the Diaghilev Ballet was very valid. In the Imperial Theatres I already had the position of *coryphée* and was dancing soloist roles, but in the Diaghilev Ballet I would be dancing as a member of the *corps de ballet*. For Diaghilev had declared, "I cannot have two geniuses of the dance from one family!"

"That means," said Mama, "a theatrical career would be impossible for you in his company!"

"For me, now, my career is not the most important thing, but the ballet is! I want to work and live in a real, contemporary art—our ballet . . . and also to work with Vaslav!"

"There is no need for you to resign and leave the Imperial Ballet forever. I understand your feelings, but you must think of your future. I advise you to reconsider and ask only to be granted a prolonged leave of absence. Isn't that what most of the artists are planning to do, like your friend Ludmila Schollar?"

I had a difficult time before I finally persuaded Mama to sign my petition of resignation; I needed her signature, as I was still a minor, for my petition to be valid.*

—

MEANWHILE, until my resignation was accepted I was still attending all the rehearsals in the Maryinsky for *Carnaval*. When the stage rehearsals began, Fokine was very demanding, particularly when working with those dancers of the Imperial Theatres who were doing *Carnaval* for the first time. He would not proceed with the rehearsal until he had obtained the desired effect, correcting each pose and gesture, making us repeat the whole ballet several times. For myself, I did not mind at all that more

*In writing of these events, Bronislava Nijinska did not discuss her own resignation any further. However, among the letters in her archives was one of April 21, 1971, from the Russian ballet critic and historian, Vera Krasovskaya, which describes how Nijinska's application to resign from the Imperial Theatres was received by V. A. Telyakovsky, the Director. "Telyakovsky was very unhappy and wrote in his diary for 5 February, 1911: 'Krupensky informed me today that Nijinsky's sister has submitted her resignation; her reason being the dismissal of her brother. I advised him [Krupensky] to call her in and talk things over with her.' " (IN/JR)

rehearsals were required, as it gave me a chance to practice my Papillon *variation* on the stage of the Maryinsky.

All the costumes for *Carnaval* were made after the original Bakst sketches designed for Les Ballets Russes in 1910. At that time Diaghilev had insisted that the ballet be presented on a stage draped with pleated blue curtains, as it was first performed at Pavlov Hall. Now at the Maryinsky, Bakst had designed new sets, representing a park and the terrace of a palace. Guests from the Masquerade Ball in the palace came out onto the terrace, dancing or meeting and strolling in the park. It was evening, and lighted lanterns were shining in the park amidst the tall trees behind the white marble balustrade. The set was beautiful, but my dance no longer portrayed a butterfly caught inside, trying to escape into the freedom of the open air. Instead I was now one of the masked performers at the ball, dancing a *variation*—Papillon eluding Pierrot, played by Adolf Bolm.

Schumann's *Carnaval* had its premiere at the Maryinsky Theatre on February 6, 1911, with Fokine in the role of Harlequin and Karsavina in the role of Columbine.

Shortly after the premiere, Adolf Bolm told me that he too was submitting his resignation from the Imperial Theatres to join the Diaghilev Ballet Company. He did not believe that he had any future with the Imperial Theatres. I recalled the difficulty with which he had been persuaded by Fokine to dance the role of Pierrot in *Carnaval*, in place of Bulgakov who after twenty years as an Artist of the Imperial Theatres had retired from the Imperial Ballet Company in 1909. Adolf Bolm had only just been promoted to second soloist from *coryphé*, a rank he had held since 1905, but felt that after his tremendous success in *Danses Polovetsiennes* in the opera *Prince Igor* at the Maryinsky, he should also be given leading roles in the ballets. Because he had replaced Nijinsky as the Blue Bird in *Sleeping Beauty* during 1910, when Vaslav had been away from St. Petersburg, Bolm felt that now that Nijinsky had been dismissed he should replace him in *Carnaval* and dance the role of Harlequin, not Pierrot.

Vaslav was, of course, no longer coming to the Maryinsky, but he was continuing his personal lessons daily with Cecchetti, and he was also busy at home working on his ballet, and with me on the different parts of *Faune*. So far he had mounted the Faune, also the Principal Nymph. I could now dance these segments. I wrote in my diary:

I see that Vaslav has found something new and monumental in choreographic art, and is uncovering a field entirely unknown up to now, in either the Dance or the Theatre. I cannot yet define these new paths and discoveries, but I know and feel that they are there. Not long ago Fokine freed himself from the old classical school and the captivity of Petipa's choreography, and now Vaslav is freeing himself from the captivity of Fokine's choreography so that, again, we enter a new phase in our Art . . .

Vaslav showed Diaghilev and Bakst the work he had done so far, in our home. I performed Vaslav's own part, the Faune, and then the Principal Nymph. Finally, Vaslav as the Faune marked the ballet sequences with me as the Principal Nymph.

Bakst detected many remarkable details in the composition. Diaghilev, on the other hand, was not too impressed with the fragments of the ballet as we showed it to him. He was made uneasy by the unexpected and unusual severity of the composition and the lack of dance movements. Not long afterwards, I heard that *L'Après-Midi d'un Faune* was to be postponed until the next year, and so would not be presented in Paris in the spring.

Sergei Pavlovitch now had some other plans: Wouldn't it be better for Vaslav to start by mounting *Les Nuages* or *Les Fêtes*, also by Debussy? But Vaslav insisted that his first ballet must be *L'Après-Midi d'un Faune;* he refused to consider anything else. Even so, he did from time to time mention to me some of his ideas for *Les Fêtes.*

Possibly Diaghilev thought that it was too early for Vaslav to be presented as a choreographer. It did seem to me that he was young—only twenty-two years old—to be a choreographer. I was also saddened and concerned on Fokine's behalf, as we were all aware that Fokine had signed a contract with Diaghilev and had obtained a prolonged leave of absence from the Imperial Theatres so that he would be free to start the rehearsals in Monte Carlo in March, to teach his "old" ballets to the newly formed company and to choreograph all the new ballets planned for Les Ballets Russes in 1911. Fokine had reluctantly agreed not to dance in his own ballets for that season, as Nijinsky was to be the *premier danseur* of the company, but in return he had received Diaghilev's assurance that proper credits—Mikhail Fokine: Choreographic Director—would appear on all the posters and programs announcing his ballets. I knew that news of plans for Nijinsky to choreograph a ballet for Diaghilev would offend Fokine deeply, so maybe this was also in Diaghilev's mind. In any case, Vaslav agreed to a postponement.

Already at this same time Fokine, Stravinsky, and Benois were deeply engrossed in the preparatory work for *Petrouchka*, and Fokine was also having long sessions with Diaghilev, Bakst, and Ravel. When Diaghilev had been in Paris in October, he had commissioned Maurice Ravel to write the music for a ballet, *Daphnis et Chloë*, and Ravel had then come to St. Petersburg to consult with Fokine and Bakst on the libretto. The score, however, would not be completed in time for the rehearsals in March, so it was decided to go ahead instead with Tcherepnine's *Narcisse*, which had been planned for some time.

Nijinsky as *premier danseur* was to dance in all these ballets, and there was also talk of a ballet to be created specially for him: *Le Spectre de la Rose*. All the ballets were to be choreographed by Fokine.

———

It was the end of the winter season—the last day of Carnival Week, Saturday, February 12, 1911. It was the closing performance at the Maryinsky—*A Life for the Tsar*, with Chaliapin singing Sussanin.

My resignation had been accepted; already I felt myself an outsider in the Maryinsky Theatre. Soon I would no longer be eligible to go backstage, no longer be able to hear an opera from the wings.

My thoughts were sad. . . . *In a week's time I leave for Monte Carlo . . . forsaking forever the right to stand here in the wings of the Maryinsky Theatre, here, backstage, so familiar to me since childhood.*

I could hear Chaliapin's voice, and it calmed my mounting sadness. . . . *There, with the Ballets Russes of Diaghilev, in my new life, everything will be as great and inspiring as the voice of Chaliapin. There I will find what I am seeking in Art.* Slowly my last regrets faded away—my regrets at leaving this familiar home, this Imperial Theatre, my home . . . but where I no longer belonged.

Chaliapin was singing his last aria—"Death of Sussanin"—so moving . . . how deeply he arouses the emotions . . .

I did not stay for the last act; Chaliapin would not be singing in it. I wanted to hold that last aria as my last memory—the essence of my taking leave, forever, of the Maryinsky Theatre. . . . I walked out of the Theatre onto the square, the Ploshchad, where the sleighs stood in rows with their freezing drivers, waiting for the public to leave the Theatre.

A horse-drawn sleigh approached; the proud-looking driver, with a magnificent black beard, asked me, "Young lady, how soon will the performance end?"

"Not for another hour, at least."

"Then, young lady, permit me to drive you wherever you are going, and then I can return in time . . . come along, young lady . . . I shan't charge you much . . . only eighty kopeks . . ."

So many times my brother had reprimanded me for getting into conversation with drivers and coachmen. But I have a kind of empathy with them, and they have such a special way of telling stories about their lives, that I can't resist the chance of talking with them.

This time, though, it was the bearded driver who opened the conversation, and with a subject so dear to my heart.

"Young lady, you just came out of the Theatre. Tell me, is it really true that people sit inside there, in rows from the floor right up to the roof, and that everything is draped in there in red velvet?"

I explained what the Maryinsky Theatre looked like, where the people sat, the arrangement of the stalls, the boxes, the balcony, and the gallery, and that the walls of the Theatre were not covered in red velvet but were white, trimmed with gold, and that the seats were covered in velvet, a light blue velvet.

"The ceiling is like a dome, and in the center hangs a huge crystal chandelier."

"Like in the Cathedral?"

"No, much more ornate, quite different."

Sleigh drivers are always so magnificent that they seem ready to go on parade. But my driver now put aside his official dignity and turned towards me on the rebord of the sleigh. Dropping his hands to his knees, he let the reins hang loosely so that the horse moved at walking pace along Officerskaya Ulitza, and even further, towards the Moika Canal.

"Young lady, there on the Ploshchad, in front of the Theatre, the liveries say that tonight Chaliapin is singing in the Maryinsky Theatre. Tell me, does he really have such a splendid voice that all those people gather there just to hear him sing?"

"Indeed, yes, for Chaliapin is the greatest Russian singer."

"Tell me—for a ruble, would it be possible to go into that Theatre and hear Chaliapin?"

"Well . . . I believe you can get a seat in the gallery for one and a half rubles . . ."

"Is it possible . . . that people pay a whole ruble and a half to hear him sing . . . ?"

I explained that many people pay much more than that.

"Then he must indeed have a splendid voice if they pay that much . . ."

The bearded driver still seemed doubtful, but then went on to say, as if persuading himself, "Well, yes . . . once at the Isakai, there was a deacon . . . he had a bass voice . . . in all St. Petersburg, in all the churches, there was never a voice like his. . . . But him . . . you could hear him in the Cathedral, you didn't have to pay to hear him . . . and what a voice . . ."

From his tone, it was obvious that Chaliapin could not come anywhere near this bass from St. Isaac's Cathedral.

"Petroff was his name, and at the end of the service, when he sang, 'Many Years to the Tsar,' I am telling you, Miss," the driver warmed to his story, "his voice would resound under the cupola with such a strength that it shook all the people and everything would quiver. . . . That was the voice he had!"

He paused a moment, then went on, "When he died—he drank a lot, that's how he died, as I heard it—all the learned gentlemen were filled with curiosity and wanted to find out what had been inside his throat. They took him, dead as he was, to the clinic and cut open his throat. And Miss . . . what do you think there was? That throat, it was all fur, all hairy. . . . They say they still use it in the schools for learning . . ."

He was quiet again for a moment, then added, "Oh, do I love singing. . . . I would give anything in life for a good bass."

"Then you must go and hear Chaliapin. There will not be as much shaking as in the Cathedral, but you will leave satisfied. For one who loves singing there is no one else to hear . . . there is only Chaliapin."

And so, still talking, we reached my house. I started to pay for the fare, but he refused to take it.

"I so enjoyed talking to you, Miss. Please, I will be offended . . ."

I was glad that Vaslav was not at home; if he had been, I would have been tempted to share with him this amusing story of a bearded St. Petersburg sleigh driver—even knowing it would entail the inevitable reprimand and lecture: "It is not becoming in a young lady to engage in conversations with coachmen and sleigh drivers. . . . God knows what they will tell you about their uncouth *moujik* way of life . . . not at all proper for your ears . . ."

Yes, I was happy that Vaslav had already left with Diaghilev, first for Paris and then for Monte Carlo, where I was to join them.

35   First Days in Monte Carlo

THE FIRST SEASON of Diaghilev's permanent company in the spring of 1911 in Monte Carlo was a happy milestone in the history of ballet.

In "Les Ballets Russes de Serge de Diaghilev" as our new company was called, and in the artistic atmosphere enveloping us, we artists began to grow and develop. As we performed in new ballets and created new roles we acquired new artistic techniques distinguishing us as *Diaghilev Artists*.

These pages, extracts from my notes and diaries of those exciting days in Monte Carlo, are only a reflection of some of the moments which, for one reason or another, made my heart beat faster . . .

Pages from the Diary of a Young Dancer*

At last it has arrived, the long-awaited day of our departure for Monte Carlo. The night before we left I hardly slept and was up and ready early. The winter this year had been blisteringly cold, and as we made our way to the station St. Petersburg was under a mantel of snow.

At the station Sergei Leonidovitch Grigoriev, the *régisseur* of the new company, greeted those artists who were traveling to Monte Carlo together. Not all who signed contracts with Diaghilev were able to leave St. Petersburg for the start of the rehearsals early in March. Of the four girls from the Imperial Ballet going to Monte Carlo at this time, I was the only one who had resigned from the Imperial Theatres; the other

*When Bronislava Nijinska composed her continuous narrative of her early memoirs she retained these pages in their original spontaneous note form, distinguishing them from the rest of her text by actually pasting them onto the larger pages of her typescript. In discussing the format of her memoirs she resisted any suggestion that these pages be transposed into a continuous form or that the more personal writings be eliminated, declaring, "The diaries are the soul of my book . . . as my love for Chaliapin has been the inspiration for my work for the rest of my life . . ."

As editors we have respected the author's wishes to retain these pages in their spontaneity and they are distinguished in the present text by being set in extract form. Later in the text where we have inserted other appropriate selections from these more personal writings, such passages are similarly distinguished. (IN/JR)

three, Ludmila Schollar, and the twin sisters, Lubov and Nadejda Baranovitch, had been given one year's leave of absence from the Maryinsky. The nineteen-year-old twins are very pretty. They are good dancers, recently graduated from the Imperial School, and are enrolled in the *corps de ballet* of the Imperial Ballet. There are two other girls joining the Diaghilev Ballet Company who are even younger: Myda Guliuk is only seventeen, and the red-haired Olga Khokhlova [to marry Pablo Picasso in 1918] is just eighteen. They are students of Yevgenia Pavlovna Sokolova. They have never danced in a professional ballet company, and this is their first trip outside Russia. My mother and I promised their parents and Sokolova, the aunt of Guliuk, that we would look after them during the trip, and in Monte Carlo.

My great friend from my last two years at the Imperial Theatrical School, Lubov Tchernicheva, came to the station; she was seeing off her husband, Grigoriev, and was weeping as it was the first time since their marriage in 1909 that they would be apart. She also said good-bye to me, and through her tears Lubasha told me she would be joining us in May.

On the train we six girls all traveled in the same compartment and soon became fast friends. We were all in a happy and excited mood. There was not the usual sadness that one might expect to experience at leaving one's home. We were all delighted at this long journey on the train.

After three days we arrived in Monte Carlo. To get from the railway station to our hotel in Beausoleil, we had to walk across most of the city in our Russian fur coats, our warm hats, and our overboots. The passersby, in their Parisian spring fashions, must have found us a strange sight, still dressed in our winter attire. Luckily for us, it was still early in the morning, and so the streets of Monte Carlo were not crowded.

All of us from St. Petersburg are staying in the Hôtel Français, not far from the Casino Beausoleil where all the rehearsals are to be held. In the room next to mine are the two new girls, Olga and Myda. I have called them "the little ones" and have taken them under my wing. Our hotel is on top of a hill above Beausoleil, and below me from the window of our room I can see the blue sea. After the cold and damp of St. Petersburg, it is so beautiful and warm in Monte Carlo. This is my first time on the Riviera. I am excited and ready to begin my new life as a Diaghilev artist.

Mikhail Fokine and his wife, Vera, are already in Monte Carlo as are Diaghilev, Bakst, Tcherepnine, and Vaslav. Tamara Karsavina and Olga Preobrajenska will arrive later in March, and several other dancers from the Imperial Theatres have also promised Diaghilev that they will be available to dance with us in Paris and London later in the season.

The other members of the company have been recruited from theatres throughout Russia and from the Warsaw Theatre. They have traveled separately to Monte Carlo, and rooms were reserved for them in other hotels in the town. This has divided the company into two groups—those from St. Petersburg and the "outsiders"—and for the time being each group is keeping to itself. But as soon as rehearsals start we will work together . . . and we have lots of work ahead of us. . . . The new artists are unfamiliar with the Ballets Russes repertoire, so they have to learn from us all the ballets staged so far, and then there will be all the new ballets planned for this season, as yet not choreographed.

We have only a short distance to walk from our hotel to the Casino Beausoleil, where we work all day long—starting early in the morning and going on till late at night. We are never free until after midnight. But we always return to the hotel for lunch and for dinner—our only chance to see the beautiful sunshine of Beausoleil. We do not see anyone or anything outside of our theatrical work; but since we are enjoying our rehearsals with Fokine, the work does not seem hard.

Maestro Cecchetti has come from St. Petersburg to be part of our company, and we all have classes with him every day. Fokine welcomes Maestro Cecchetti, who is not only a wonderful pedagogue but also a great artist capable of subtle comedy in his mime roles. Their methods and ideas are widely different. Fokine is a "revolutionary," and Cecchetti is a proponent of the Italian School of Carlo Blasis.

Maestro Cecchetti has faithfully preserved the positions of the whole body according to the geometrical proportions and exact equilibrium developed by Blasis. He also adheres to the rule of six lessons per week, each lesson having its definite set of exercises and sequence of *pas*. And so each week we are repeating over and over again the same lessons to the accompaniment of the same pieces of music, chosen by Cecchetti for each exercise.

The strict routine of this method develops in the student's body an absolute "habit" to assume the correct position automatically and to preserve this correct position not only on the floor but also in the air.

The Opera Season in Monte Carlo has just ended with the performance by Chaliapin in *Ivan the Terrible*, a new opera composed by Raoul Guinsburg, the Director of the Monte Carlo Opera Season. Now everyone is looking forward to our performances, the Ballets Russes, as we move our rehearsals to the Théâtre de Monte Carlo.

In the Imperial Theatres I seldom performed more than ten times in a season, but now in Monte Carlo I am to dance in all the ballets, four times a week. In the Imperial Theatres I was able to dance everything I was given, but in the ballets of Fokine there is still much that is new for me, and I find there is something in myself that I cannot overcome in order to reach what I want in my dancing.

Each new performance in Monte Carlo will be a new trial and test of my abilities. It will be an accomplishment for me even to advance a little bit and to create the tiniest part. I am working to my utmost to achieve a good interpretation, no matter where I am dancing, even in the back row of the *corps de ballet*.

I have two soloist roles with the Diaghilev Company. Besides Papillon in *Carnaval* I also dance a *pas de trois* in *Le Pavillon d'Armide* with Karsavina and Nijinsky. Both these roles I have danced before, in 1910, and since then I have had time to perfect my dance technique in both ballets, particularly the solo *variation* in the *pas de trois* that is technically so difficult. However, of all the dances in the repertoire there is one of which I personally can be proud—the Papillon in Schumann's *Carnaval*. But for Sergei Pavlovitch, the creation of one solo dance is not sufficient evidence of artistic gifts.

"It is true that you have a splendid success with Papillon—but it is due solely to your great classical technique . . . yet in the new ballets of Fokine this same old classical technique is a disadvantage."

Sergei Pavlovitch is right in claiming that the success of my Papillon is due to my classical technique, but he is wrong in calling it an old technique. In my interpretation of Papillon, in order to simulate the fluttering flight, I have had to eliminate from my dance habits formed in the old classical school and achieve a new balance, a new freedom of hand and arm movements.

There is little left in my Papillon of the old classical dance techniques, with their limited span of movements of the body and the arms where all the emphasis is concentrated on the technique of the legs. I want to free my body from the stretched and tense muscles that we worked so painstakingly to develop in our years of training in the Imperial School. I have worked on destroying "bones and muscle" and changing my body into that of a fluttering butterfly.

I am trying to draw from my Papillon this new fluidity so as to dance in the new ballets of Fokine with the whole of my body. Yet when I study the dance of the Odalisques in *Schéhérazade*, I realize how restricted I am in my dance.

Officially I am not rehearsing this dance of the Odalisques, but I want to learn it and am studying it for myself. . . . Very often after a rehearsal, I sit on the floor of my hotel bedroom in front of the mirror and work to attain the correct design and rhythm of each movement of the body and arms. I struggle to free myself of the tension and stiffness in the dance technique imposed by the Imperial School. But I cannot yet find the freedom I seek. . . . I am frustrated that I cannot acquire all at once the new techniques that I need to perform the style and character of this dance.

Unhappily I have to admit to myself that Sergei Pavlovitch is, indeed, right. Yes, I do have only one dance—"Papillon." But there, in my Papillon, I *am* completely free. I have caught it to perfection. Every movement is right to the tip of each finger and toe.

Sergei Pavlovitch has just told me to begin to study the dance of the Odalisques in *Schéhérazade* and that he will let me dance it with Fokina and Schollar in Paris*; meanwhile I am dancing in *Schéhérazade* in the *corps de ballet*.

*According to the program for the opening performance of the Ballets Russes in Monte Carlo on April 9, 1911, "The Odalisques" was performed by Fokina, Schollar, and Nijinska. (IN/JR)

It is the final curtain call of *Schéhérazade*, and we can still hear the applause. We artists are leaving the stage, now only dimly lighted, to go back to our dressing rooms. Sergei Pavlovitch has just come through the audience door onto the stage. He stops me.

"Bronia, tonight Chaliapin was in the audience, and I've just been talking to him. He asked me who the young dancer was who acted so well in the last scene when Shahryar returns to the palace. I realized he was talking about you, and so, Bronia, I told him your name and that you are Nijinsky's sister. Chaliapin admired the way you acted in that scene, your fright at the unexpected return and sudden appearance of the Sultan."

I staged that little *mise en scène*, worked on it alone. No one showed it to me or suggested how I should act it. If among the crowd of artists on the stage in that last scene Chaliapin could pick out my interpretation of this small part, then at last I have achieved something all my own.

Diaghilev is still speaking, "Chaliapin insists that I should pay more attention to you. He declares you are very gifted . . ."

As Sergei Pavlovitch repeats Chaliapin's praise it seems that he also, for the first time, sees me in that scene and is agreeing with Chaliapin about my acting ability. . . . Can it be that at last Sergei Pavlovitch is relenting in his long-held conviction that one family cannot hold two talents? . . .

"Well, Bronia, you must be very happy to hear such praise from Chaliapin."

"Oh certainly, very glad, Sergei Pavlovitch," I answer in a whisper, overcome by emotion.

Diaghilev does not understand my state of mind and looks displeased. "I told you this because I thought you would be overjoyed, and all you can say is 'very glad . . .' Do you understand, Bronia, this was Chaliapin talking about you! Chaliapin, the colossus of the theatre, a genius, and you accept it almost with indifference . . ."

"Oh no, Sergei Pavlovitch, I assure you that I am extremely happy, but I do not know how to express my feelings in words. . . . Usually, it is true, I am not interested in outside praise and seldom even read the critics, but when you, Sergei Pavlovitch, say a few words of praise to me, or, like tonight, repeat the compliment of a great artist, then I am overjoyed. After hearing such praise, far from being indifferent, I am inspired to work even harder and to dance even better . . ."

"Indeed, yes, Bronia," Sergei Pavlovitch encourages, "now go ahead and work harder."

There was no way for me to tell Sergei Pavlovitch of the happiness and excitement that overwhelms me. I am very proud, and already I feel a new confidence in myself.

I run down to the dressing room I share with Ludmila Schollar. I tell her how Chaliapin noticed me dancing in the ensemble and praised me to Diaghilev. There is no pinnacle in the world higher than such a moment of artistic happiness . . .

I leave the theatre, and as I walk past the Café de Paris the music of the Rumanian gypsy orchestra mingles with the happy voices of the throngs of passersby. The tall palms, the sounds of the fountains, the brilliant colors of the flowers in the brightly lit Place de Casino, filling with people still excited from the Casino . . .

I am with Ludmila and two colleagues from the company, Kobelev and Rosai. As we start across the Place I see a tall figure on the Casino steps, waving to Ludmila. It is Chaliapin, and I see that he is hurrying towards us. He extends his hand to Ludmila and asks, "Ludmila, who are you with? Please introduce me."

"This is Bronia; she is Nijinsky's sister."

"How happy I am to know you. I have just admired you in your part in *Schéhérazade* and talked to Diaghilev about you."

I look at him and he seems to be unlike the others . . . he is part of my dream world. . . . I give my hand to Chaliapin. Captivated, I look up into his face, his shining eyes hold me entranced. I do not hear the words he speaks; I hear only a voice, and the sounds caress me like a charming serenade. . . . Now I catch the words:

"Where are you going? May I go with you to the Café de Paris?"

Chaliapin invites all of us to join him.

Soon we are joined by Diaghilev, Bakst, and Vaslav. We all have supper together. I remember a large table with Diaghilev and Chaliapin sitting together across from me. I cannot take my eyes from Chaliapin.

We begin talking about *Schéhérazade*. Half-joking, Chaliapin says he would like to play the role of the Sultan. "That is the perfect role for me!"

We all welcome the idea.

Already I can see Chaliapin in the makeup and costume of the Sultan . . . with one gesture he would be able to say more than is expressed in the long mime scene in the ballet. What a frightening figure he would make in the last scene . . . how superbly he would play the Sultan Shahryar at the moment his beloved but unfaithful Queen stabs herself!

Sergei Pavlovitch is most excited by this idea of Chaliapin's.

"Yes, do please come to Paris and play Shahryar in *Schéhérazade*. It will be an unforgettable performance and a tremendous success! In the opera, in your roles of Holofernes, Khan Kontchak, Sussanin, and the others, whenever you act, every movement of your body, every step, every expression of your face—it is all choreography. I am serious, I am making you an offer, Feodor Ivanovitch."

"Not in Paris, but maybe in London. I shall come for the Coronation and perform in *Schéhérazade*." Chaliapin turns jokingly to me. "But will Broniusha act as well and be as scared then, and will she run away from me with the same dread as she did tonight?"

"With you, Feodor Ivanovitch, everyone will act the scene as never before. Besides, no one in the audience will pay any attention to us; they will see only you . . . and you will create as much dread, fear, and panic as you want the public to feel . . ."

"Thank you, Broniusha. I like the idea. But won't the general public begin to suspect that Chaliapin has lost his voice, that he has to accept acting parts in ballet scenes?"

"No," Diaghilev interrupts, "it will not be so at all. You will be singing during the same season with the Italian Opera at Covent Garden." And he offers to start the necessary negotiations immediately.

"No, please, the public is cruel and one cannot always do what one's heart desires."

The subject is dropped and soon the conversation turns to an incident that has been the talk of the Riviera: Chaliapin was attacked by Russian revolutionaries on the streets of Monte Carlo.

The revolutionaries had been angered by a newspaper headline: CHALIAPIN, FRIEND OF GORKY, KNEELS TO THE TSAR.

In Russia, the names of Chaliapin and Gorky had long been linked together. The revolutionaries were proud of them and their humble backgrounds, claiming that they represented the genius of the Russian people coming to flower in spite of the oppressive rule of the Tsar.

The newspapers were reporting an incident that had taken place in the Maryinsky Theatre during a performance of *Boris Godunov*. Suddenly during the playing of the national anthem—"God Save the Tsar"—the chorus, together with Chaliapin, went down on their knees facing the Tsar, who was present at this performance.

This kneeling to the Tsar the revolutionaries considered a betrayal of Chaliapin's liberal ideals. They felt that by this action he had, in their eyes, also betrayed his friend Maxim Gorky.

As he relates the incident, Chaliapin becomes very serious and angry. "Those revolutionary heroes, they sit here, on the Riviera, and assert their revolutionary ideas by attacking me . . . the other day I was almost killed here on the street. Good thing I had a walking stick with a solid silver handle, so I could fight them off. . . . In Russia they might have found someone more important than I, but here in a dark corner they pick a Chaliapin to make their revolution . . .

"You may ask why did Chaliapin go down on his knees? Indeed, I can't even remember. I am a Russian, maybe I was kneeling before Russia. Suddenly everyone around me on the stage was kneeling. How could I alone, sticking up like a tall post, remain standing? I don't know why I kneeled . . . certainly it was not for personal gain. No one is throwing me out of the theatre . . . I've already sent my resignation to Telyakovsky.* Naturally, now, they all say that I was the first one to go down on my knees, that I had just been waiting for the moment to go down on my knees to the Tsar . . ."

As Chaliapin finishes speaking I can see that he is deeply upset by the incident. . . . I feel as though I have known him all my life. . . . I recall the performance in St. Petersburg when I watched him from the wings of the Maryinsky Theatre, singing Sussanin in *A Life for the Tsar*. It is difficult to believe that we were strangers then, such a short time

---

*The Directorate of the Imperial Theatres asked Chaliapin to reconsider, which he did. (IN/JR)

ago. My conversation with the sleigh driver comes back to me and I think perhaps Chaliapin would enjoy hearing about it. I start to tell my story, looking into his eyes, and feel my tenderness for him growing. . .

As we start to leave the table after supper, Vatsa finds a moment to whisper in my ear: "I didn't know you were such a good storyteller, so clever and so charming." There is a certain pride and happiness in his voice.

As we leave the café, Vatsa continues talking to me: "You know, that was such a clever story that you made up for Chaliapin. Even I could see you were quite pleased with yourself . . ."

"But, Vaslav, everything that I told did happen. How could you think that I could imagine a story like that on the spur of the moment?"

"That is impossible!" Vaslav's exclamation is abrupt. He sounds somewhat annoyed.

There is no time for me to find out the reason for Vaslav's strange reaction. We are all taking leave of each other; Vaslav and Diaghilev are crossing the Place de Casino towards the Hôtel de Paris, where they are staying, while the rest of us will be walking to the Hôtel Français. Sergei Pavlovitch asks Chaliapin if he will return with Vaslav and himself to the Hôtel de Paris. But Chaliapin laughs as he answers, "No, I must see these young people to their hotel. How can I entrust these two young ladies to the care of these two young fellows?"

Vatsa looks very displeased as he walks away with Diaghilev. I am puzzled; what has happened, why is Vaslav so angry with me? Is it because he has just learned that, in spite of his wishes, I entered into a conversation with a sleigh driver in St. Petersburg? I don't think so, somehow; his face is more concerned than angry. Could I, unwittingly, have hurt his feelings in some way? . . .

It is the frown on his face that bothers me. Is he jealous of Chaliapin's fame? Is he becoming overly conscious of a need to create his own artistic fame? This vanity and sense of competition is being instilled and encouraged in Vaslav by Diaghilev on the pretext that it will make him work harder and develop his talent . . .

Though I am puzzled for the moment, the only thing that matters to me as we walk to the hotel is that Feodor Ivanovitch is close beside me. I can feel his hand holding me firmly under the elbow, and I am listening to his voice . . .

As we walk along, Chaliapin asks Ludmila, our two colleagues, and myself to go on an outing with him to Nice, by car, tomorrow. We gladly accept the invitation, for tomorrow will be our very first free day with no rehearsals since coming to Monte Carlo.

We walk slowly up the narrow streets, climbing the hill. At our door Chaliapin wishes all of us good night. He leans towards me and, making a sign of the cross, blesses me and kisses me on the forehead.

"Till tomorrow, Broniusha, sleep well." He smiles his beautiful smile. "I will pick you all up in the morning, here with the car, and we will drive to Nice."

As I enter the hotel I see that the lights are still on in my mother's room, and in the little ones' room. Mama is waiting to kiss me good night and bless me, as she usually does before she goes to sleep. It is a rule that the little ones must return directly to the hotel as soon as the performance is over, and so they are waiting up for me so that we can talk about the performance and about my own evening . . .

I can't sleep. I doze off for a few moments only to wake up with a burst of great happiness in my heart. . . . Finally I decide that it is no use trying to sleep now. It is four o'clock in the morning.

I sit in an armchair in front of the window. I think about the evening and how different it was . . . going over in my mind all the reasons. Was it because my dancing was good . . . because I was complimented . . . or because I met *him* that this feeling stirs my whole being?

The sun is rising. It is the start of a new day. The first gleam of sunshine, and already, so early, the morning feels warm. How wonderful it is to be in Monte Carlo . . . in the spring . . . working in the theatre. . . . And yes, here too is Chaliapin. That is wonderful.

How can I speak of that first enchanted moment of love . . . of this new feeling that seems, as soon as it strikes, to have been always part of me . . . ?

How sad and unfortunate . . . today all the artists are free, and I am the only one called for a rehearsal. Good-bye to the outing with Chaliapin . . . and the morning is so beautiful.

I have been called because Fokine is going to mount the Bacchante for his new ballet *Narcisse*. . . . The part was supposed to be danced by Sophia Fedorova, but she has not arrived in Monte Carlo, and so today's call for the rehearsal means that Bacchante, one of the leading roles in Fokine's new ballet, is being given to me. I ought to be overwhelmed with happiness. But I am not the least bit pleased. As I walk to the theatre, I try all the way to find reasons to be excused and to get out of the rehearsal.

In the theatre I talk to Fokine and Diaghilev, but both are adamant. The rehearsal must take place today, no matter that it is a holiday. *Narcisse* is ready, and starting tomorrow all the rehearsals will be held onstage; only my role is waiting to be mounted. I go to my dressing room to change into my practice clothes. I am sad and have only one thought—that they have all left by now for the outing to Nice with Chaliapin . . . and I shall be on my own for the whole day.

But what is happening to me? Suddenly I realize that the premiere is just over a week away; every hour of work is essential. But I feel resentful: Why does it have to be today? What will be the use of my rehearsing as I know that I will not be able to keep my mind on it and so will neither understand nor dance well? For the first time in my life, I have an almost irresistible urge to run away from a rehearsal.

Finally, reluctantly, I am standing on the stage, in my practice costume, and Fokine is ready to mount the dance for me. I watch him and try to repeat the *pas* he is demonstrating.

Suddenly I see Chaliapin and my friends entering the theatre. How wonderful they are! How could I have thought that they would leave without me and deprive me of an outing. I can see Chaliapin smiling at me as he takes a seat. His presence inspires me, and as never before in my life I immediately catch each nuance of the movements correctly. Everything that up to now has been missing from my dancing is suddenly there. I feel released from the bonds that have imprisoned me, holding my muscles taut.

Something gives me confidence, and strength, and for the first time a new feeling of freedom that creates its own rhythms, its own lines and form in the dance, different from those shown me by Fokine. But I know that what I am dancing is good and right and that I have caught the Bacchante perfectly. And indeed, Fokine is pleased with me. He ends the rehearsal early and lets me go.

Chaliapin comes up from the stalls onto the stage to greet me.

I feel my happiness increasing. Is it the knowledge that the rehearsal was successful, that a dance has been created, or is it his gray eyes now smiling at me? No matter . . . we agree to meet in two hours. I rush to the hotel to get ready. Mama insists that I stay for lunch before setting off. I can hardly wait for the end of the meal. My whole being is in a flurry of excitement. The thrill, the joy of enchantment, the anticipation . . . this is a new, hitherto unknown experience for me. I hold my breath as this new welter of feelings almost makes my heart burst. Mama sits in silence. . . . I will not let myself be troubled by the questions in her eyes.

At last we are in the automobile and on the way to Nice.

Ludmila and I are sitting with Chaliapin while our two colleagues from the Maryinsky, Kobelev and Rosai, are facing us on the folding seats. Chaliapin jokes with us and tells us amusing tales all the way to Nice. It feels so good to be near him.

In Nice we stroll along the Promenade des Anglais in the beautiful afternoon sunshine. We are all dressed in our spring outfits and our mood is springlike to match. I remember nothing of the drive, or even what we had for tea when we stopped at Rumpelmeyers. Just as we are leaving to walk again along the Promenade, I become aware that I have been holding my camera in my hand. Chaliapin sees it too.

"Broniusha, why didn't you say you had a camera? We could have had a picture taken in the sunlight, but now it is already getting dark."

"Yes, Feodor Ivanovitch, I am sorry too. I wanted to have a photograph taken with you, but I was so engrossed listening to you that I forgot all about it."

"Let's try anyway." Feodor Ivanovitch puts his arm around me, and we are photographed on the seashore.

We begin to drive back. The sun is now fast disappearing as we take the return route by the high Corniche. Chaliapin is being very jolly and entertaining as he talks about himself, his family, and the theatre. He shows us photographs of his son Boris. The little boy is holding onto his father tightly with both arms clasped around Chaliapin's neck.

I sit very quietly, listening to every word and absorbed by his stories.

He talks a lot about Gogol, the great Russian writer, and declares that everyone should read him. I am happy to tell him about the opera I heard from the wings of the Maryinsky, one of the last evenings before leaving for Monte Carlo: Tchaikovsky's *Tcherevitchky*, after Gogol's "Night Before Christmas." The opera had not been performed for a long time and had just been revived in a marvelous new version. Now in the sunshine of the Riviera I tell him how when I left the Theatre I was still elated by the music for the marvelous opera and so under the spell of Gogol's story, "Night Before Christmas," that I decided to walk home through the snow. Chaliapin takes out of his pocket a little book that he says he always carries wherever he goes, a little book of Gogol's writings.

The automobile is now carrying us over the mountains. It is my first trip over this magnificent road, but I am completely unaware of the passing scenery as all my consciousness is drawn by the sound of his voice.

Twilight is already covering the countryside when we arrive on the Turbie. We have dinner in a small restaurant on the terrace overlooking the precipice. As dessert is being served, Chaliapin buys some cigarettes and a postcard with a view of the Turbie. On the back he writes for me: "To dear Broniusha, a souvenir of our drive, with the wish that you may remain as long as possible—the pure snowflake."

From the first days of our acquaintance we have spent lots of time together. He is always backstage during the ballet performances, and afterwards we often go to the Café de Paris and sit outside on the terrace. During the daytime, between rehearsals, we are on the beach together, somewhere in Monte Carlo.

During the morning rehearsal I work feverishly. All my being is rushing elsewhere . . . maybe out into the sunshine . . . away from this dark rehearsal hall.

At last the rehearsal is over. With Ludmila I step out onto the terrace and immediately I see Chaliapin walking towards us—and then we all walk together down to the seashore where he teaches me how to throw pebbles. But I can't do it as well as he does. How cleverly Feodor can skim them! For him those flat stones jump several times over the waves.

Suddenly he says, "We'd better catch up with the others. Let's race." And holding hands like children, we race along the seashore.

As we all stroll along together, Ludmila has been entertaining Feodor with flirting eyes and lively conversation, but this in no way casts a shadow over my youthful love, which is as wide as the sea itself . . .

This evening Chaliapin was in a special box backstage during the performance of Schumann's *Carnaval*. In an audible voice he encouraged me . . . admiring my arms, or that last turn. I caught the endearing words he sent me . . . "those little feet, how well they dance . . . so tiny . . ." The voice flowed over me like a wave of music, and the whole of me flew effortlessly—I did not feel my legs, nor the stage under them, and the dance of the Papillon sparkled brilliantly in a frantic *prestissimo*.

This encouragement from a great artist, moreover one who also loves and understands ballet, helped me so much. It created in me an awareness of myself. Whether I am dancing in *Carnaval*, *Les Sylphides*, or *Le Pavillon d'Armide*, I believe in myself, and with each encouragement I am inspired to new creativity.

At the beginning of the Monte Carlo season I received my most important role—to dance the Mazurka in *Les Sylphides*. I dance the part in this ballet that was originally created by Anna Pavlova, except for the *pas de deux* that is danced by Karsavina.

I am receiving many compliments for the Mazurka, and I recall how several people came around after the ballet to compliment me. One of the old balletomanes, an important official from Russia, the Navy Minister, was a great admirer of Julia Sedova. He told me that I reminded him of her, with my high elevation, and that perhaps even she could not have danced in *Les Sylphides* better than I had.

I shuddered, feeling a wave of revulsion at the comparison. Sergei Pavlovitch had to grab my elbow to keep me from protesting. For this balletomane there was no greater dancer in the world than Sedova, and I had to accept his words as though they were the greatest compliment.

It was discouraging to be compared in my dancing with Sedova. Although Sedova has a very high elevation and good classical technique, she is both taller and heavier than I and always dances with full force. I remember her from the Imperial Theatres, and on the relatively small stage of the Maryinsky in her strong, high jumps she always reminded me of a horse. I have never liked her style of dancing.

That bitter compliment has given me a strong resolve to work even harder on the ethereal qualities of the Romantic period; to work on all the nuances and on an even greater lightness in my elevation so that, God forbid, I should never again remind anyone of this famous ballerina of the Imperial Theatres . . .

Sometimes, if only Karsavina and Nijinsky are called for rehearsal by Fokine, Chaliapin will take us out for a long drive in the car. Usually, in addition to Ludmila and myself, there are a couple of our colleagues from the company. We young artists listen fascinated while Chaliapin tells us about the theatre, emphasizing how necessary it is even for the accomplished artist to work hard in order to attain something true in art. He tells us much about the theatre and the everyday difficulties facing the artist; how difficult is the road of the artist.

He also complains about the reputation he has been given, unfairly.

"They all believe and tell God knows what kind of lies about me. 'Chaliapin is a drunkard.' But am I? Who has seen me drunk? No more than five times in the whole of my life have I ever been drunk. . . . Or 'Chaliapin causes scandals.' But do I really create them? Is it my fault? . . . Look, there they were, the chorus. They had ruined my scene with their poor acting. Naturally I was upset. I explained it to them, but to no avail—they still stood there like a stone wall and could not even start with the music. So then, in spite of myself, I could not help but shout out, 'You stand there like a herd of Arabian horses but do not hear the music!' They were insulted. . . . 'Why call us Arabian horses?' So I said, 'If you don't want to be thoroughbred horses, then you shall be green horses.' At this the protests became even louder: 'Why are we green, now?' "

Chaliapin laughs as he goes on to tell us, "They did not notice that they had accepted being called horses. Now they only minded being called green horses. So I said, 'Green horses don't exist, so what is the trouble? . . .' But again apparently I said the wrong thing. 'Why call us green horses if they don't exist?' they asked. 'Very simple,' I said. 'As green horses do not exist in real life, so artists like you should not exist on the stage . . .'

"They called me all sorts of loathsome names, and I admit I lost my temper. So the scandal grows. All I wanted was that the opera should be good. But that is how it always happens. Then they call me a *moujik* and portray me in a bad light, and I have added to my notorious reputation as a wild and unruly character."

No one artist has ever been the object of as much malicious gossip as Chaliapin. Side by side with his fame and success as an artist, there was this other reputation of a wild and unruly character. If he so much as made an observation onstage or during the performance of an opera, this would be cited as an example of his other reputation. The press, of course, was always ready to seize upon such incidents and make lurid reports of them.

For our mother, there could be no excuse for such notoriety. How often as children we had heard her say, "Nothing can be forgiven a great artist; no, no allowances should be made. . . . If you are a serious artist, if you are a great artist, then you must be worthy of your gifts and deserving of your name as an artist. . . . Because you are looked upon as someone special, you must set a good example. The artist must create around himself an 'illusion' "—a wonderful little word of hers—"and must not be like ordinary men, let alone worse."

Chaliapin, for my mother, had other faults—Mama was indignant when she heard it said that someone had seen Chaliapin's wife helping him put on his coat.

"Just think, how rude of him to let a woman, to let his wife help him on with his coat. A big strong man like that."

I doubt if anyone could have changed her mind on this. She would never have considered, for instance, that perhaps his wife was happy to bring his coat for this genius of hers, or whether for Chaliapin this offer to help with his coat was a token of matrimonial care and tenderness, a privilege that he would not allow to any other woman?

The public often knows more about the private life of an artist than about his art. Its curiosity is gratified by reporters' tales of incidents, true or not, and so the portrait of the famous artist, his character and habits, is painted with deeper and more vivid colors than the reality itself; it becomes larger than life. Lucky is the artist whose portrait so created is attractive, but God forbid that due to an unfortunate incident the artist is given an unfavorable image. Then he will never be able to free himself of the distorted or incorrect portrayal. For the public will be resentful if one tries to deprive it of this portrait, once accepted; it will not be told that the artist is any different. Many artists, of course, take advantage of these fabricated images to add even more color to their actions and appeal to the imagination of the public.

Diaghilev felt quite strongly about this.

"Chaliapin is a very clever artist," he declared once. "He always has more press than anyone else, and he doesn't spend a kopek for it. Of course, all these 'scandals' are specially created; he knows the public very well—how curious people are by nature and how they always fall for a scandal. It seems to happen so often that a man can struggle all his life and create something truly outstanding and it will go unnoticed, whereas someone else only has to slap another man on the street, draw a crowd around, and it will be headlines in tomorrow's papers." Then he added, "Chaliapin is well aware of this . . . he is a genius in many ways."

I felt that Sergei Pavlovitch was judging Chaliapin too harshly. After all, Chaliapin is a great artist, a genius. About whom should the papers write if not about such an outstanding person?

I remember one of the stories about Chaliapin that we heard as students in the School. It was told us by a friend of Mother's, the hunchbacked woman who was then employed in the wardrobe department of the Maryinsky.

She told us how Chaliapin had thrown one of his rages and stomped on the costume he was supposed to wear for Ivan Sussanin, in the opera, *A Life for the Tsar*, screaming "I shall not be seen in this attire. Bring me a drab overcoat and a pair of *lapti*. I want to look like a Russian *moujik* and not like a Russian *boyar*."

The director Telyakovsky had to be called before Chaliapin could be calmed. He gave orders to the wardrobe department that they were to comply with Chaliapin's wishes.

Mother's friend told us how shocked the audience was to see the leading man in the opera appear onstage wearing ragged clothes and *lapti* instead of red leather boots. But that night Chaliapin gave an unforgettable performance. The public was deeply moved by his portrayal of Ivan Sussanin, a Russian *moujik* who deceived the Poles and led them into a trap, thus assuring the victory of the Russian Tsar.

Now, as an artist myself, I understand that Chaliapin's so-called uncontrollable temper, his storms and rages, are dictated by his devotion to art and his desire to create a true image of the personage and role he is singing.

Among my friends in the Imperial Theatrical School, the favorite topic of conversation at night, in the dormitories, was about boys, about secret rendezvous and love letters. I had been brought up very strictly, however, and light coquetries and passing flirtations struck me as frivolous pastimes. I was very shy and naïve in matters concerning love relationships, and only from literature was I at all familiar with love. I could not understand why my girlfriends in the School, and later artists even older than I, should confide their "secrets" to me. Listening to their whispered confidences, I heard of love involvements and love affairs, knowing full well that if I myself should ever become involved in such "adventures," I would feel bound forever by love. Love was for me something so precious and sacred that it should not be spoken of lightly . . .

Outwardly, among my friends, I was a happy person. There always seems to be laughter around me. But I was hiding deep inside myself the sorrow of our family. My longing for my father, my mother's love for him and her silent suffering, these were a constant source of pain for me.

The family was sacred for me, and it was the most cruel and despicable thing for a woman to love a married man. But here, in these days, my heart has opened! I forget all my strict upbringing. Now I am in a dream. Everything is changed in me—in my thoughts, my behavior.

Enchanted heart, I cannot hide my feelings.

Only a few days ago the mere thought of my present state of mind would have distressed me greatly, and I would have been angry with myself. But now in these days, I see only Feodor. I sit next to him. I do not feel any embarrassment when I hear my friends say to Chaliapin, "Look at Bronia, her eyes are shining. You have made her fall madly in love with you—she doesn't see or think of anyone but you. She has stopped working. She has stopped eating. She is nourishing herself only on oranges."

"Is it true?" Feodor Ivanovitch asks me.

His marvelous smile lights up his face, and his kind, gray eyes gaze warmly into mine. I forget all else and, unaware of my surroundings, say, "Yes, it's true."

"How sweet you are. I too love you very much. Bronia, kiss me!"

Without hesitation, obediently, I kiss Feodor on the cheek.

"Ah, Bronia, obviously she has never kissed before. Too bad she is not of age yet. Still, I want to teach her how to kiss. But I am very afraid of what Vaslav and Sergei Pavlovitch will say," Feodor Ivanovitch says jokingly to the others, and then he goes on, "I'm not speaking lightly. . . . I have had all sorts of 'scenes' attributed to me, but I have never taken advantage of a young girl . . ."

I do not dwell on his words—what "scenes" or "advantage" is he talking about? All I can think about is which part of his dear face has not been touched by other lips. I console myself that in the corner behind his ear, no one can have kissed him there yet . . .

We are performing four times a week in Monte Carlo and are also preparing new ballets for the later performances in Rome, Paris, and

London. Our days are full of excitement and anticipation.

On the day of the dress rehearsal you can feel the feverish pulsations of creativity. I have always liked the atmosphere of the dress rehearsal, much more than the festive opening night of a ballet. I like to feel that nervous tension, to see the struggle and last-minute strivings to reach perfection, to achieve in reality the creative conception of the choreographer, of the composer, of the designer. All the participants in this creation of a new ballet see their last chance to bring about improvements in these last moments of the final rehearsal . . . each one sees so many imperfections and wishes for more time, regretting now the time that was lost. At the last minute new strokes are added, new details, and even innovations.

To the creators of the ballet, nothing seems to be ready. The sets are not properly hung; the stage lighting does not correspond to the artist's wishes; many mistakes in the costumes and makeup are noticed; and the execution of the dance is far from perfect.

Bakst is to be seen everywhere, no matter where one looks. Now he is near the dressing table, explaining the makeup to one artist; now he is checking over another dancer's costume; he calls the dressmaker, the hairdresser, and shows them the changes he wants. Then Bakst is on the stage, examining the props, showing how they should be placed, or carried, or used. He points out the exact place, in front of which part of the set, he wants a certain group . . . this particular group and no other . . . to achieve the correct relationship between the colors of the sets and the costumes. Then he hurries to the stalls to see from there the interplay of shapes and colors and check how they should be lighted.

The conductor is very nervous; he needs more rehearsals. The composer is worried about every measure of the music. The artists are divided into two groups. The first worries about everything—they want to be helped with their costumes and their makeup by Bakst and Fokine; they get anxious that the conductor will not maintain the correct tempo of the dance. . . . The second is just the opposite—they have an air of nonchalance that makes everyone around them even more nervous; they do not put on their makeup, their costumes are not complete, they only mark the *pas* of their dances; they do not seem to understand how important it is to be "ready" in the dress rehearsal. . . . They simply say, "We know all that has to be done and you will see how well we do it on the day of the performance." They are quite cool and unconcerned.

No one can please Fokine . . . everything is wrong. He is more worried and nervous than anyone else.

Only Sergei Pavlovitch looks calm . . . outwardly. He stands in the stalls, his hands in his pockets. To all questions he mutters, "Well, later, we shall see . . ." and keeps on watching the stage, attentively. We all know that he is more concerned than anyone else about the ballet, but to look at him no one would think so. His calmness, however, does not rub off onto anyone else. They are still feverishly attempting to add something to the ballet, almost as though this is the very first time they have seen it.

But all this agitation is understandable. The premiere is near. . . . And the premiere is like fate. Then nothing can be changed, for the ballet will live exactly as it was created for the premiere, as it is shown to the public at that first performance. After the premiere nothing can be added or changed. If the ballet is a success, then it will remain in the repertoire . . . otherwise it will be scrapped and will disappear forever.

For in the theatre one doesn't try to salvage the ruined reputation of a ballet after its premiere. The public never sees it again. The sets and costumes will be nailed into large crates.

It is time for the dress rehearsal of *Le Spectre de la Rose*.

I go into Vaslav's dressing room, for I want to see Vaslav in his costume for this new ballet . . .

Vaslav is sitting in front of the mirror, already wearing his costume and makeup. Bakst is standing near him and arranging the silken rose petals on Vaslav's head. He brings the petals close around his face and down his neck. Vaslav rises and lifts his arms, curving them around his head. It is a marvelously created pose. Bakst steps back and regards him carefully, then removes one petal from here and adds another there.

Bakst, Vaslav, and I—all three of us look at each other in transports of delight. Vaslav's costume is enchanting in its novelty and fits his body like a glove. The makeup on his arms and chest is a shade lighter than the dusty rose of his tights. Over his tights with light strokes, are painted the leaves and petals of a rose. His face is superbly made up. . . . I seem to be gazing at a work of art . . .

I rush back to my seat in the *parterre* next to Feodor so as not to miss the curtain. I want to see the whole of the new ballet . . .

The orchestra plays Weber's "L'Invitation à la Valse," and Karsavina and Nijinsky dance *Le Spectre de la Rose*.

We are caught in their spell. They make us believe that the young girl has just returned from the ball, still holding her flower in her hand. She breathes the scent of the rose, and in an enchanted reverie she falls asleep in her chair. As she dreams, the apparition of the rose flies in through the open window, coming to rest beside her.

Suddenly, here on the stage in Monte Carlo, all the conventional classical *pas* that I saw Fokine demonstrating to Vaslav during rehearsals in St. Petersburg are changed in the interpretation by Nijinsky into something miraculous . . .

As Vaslav dances around the sleeping girl it seems that the aroma of the rose permeates the theatre and that Nijinsky himself is enveloped by the perfume and is intoxicated by it.

Chaliapin, sitting next to me, is filled with admiration for Vaslav.

"How easily he seems to pose in the air . . . he lives in the air, as though suspended there. To accomplish that, it is not enough to be a good dancer. For that one must also possess the rare qualities of an artist. Bronia, how unique your brother is . . ."

How happy I am at these words! How glad I am that I will be able to tell Vaslav what Chaliapin has said!

Vaslav has always admired Chaliapin. Whenever the ballet students were used in the operas at the Maryinsky or Alexandrinsky Theatres, Vaslav always tried to incorporate Chaliapin's acting style into the *mises en scène*. During the mime and drama classes in the School, he would copy his gestures and mannerisms. Those words from such a renowned artist will surely make him happy . . .

But Vaslav's response is cool . . .

"And so, you were with Chaliapin again. Why don't you do the right thing . . ."

Vaslav and I are very much attached to each other and know each other very well. In the last few days I have seen him only during rehearsals, but apparently I was not good at hiding my feelings. Besides, I did not think of concealing from Vaslav how I feel about Feodor Ivanovitch. While it has not been the habit in our family to talk about one's feelings, even less to question each other's emotions, we have always been able to sense an uneasiness and to understand each other without words.

So I am surprised when he comes to see me in my hotel. As he enters my room, he looks very stern. Without any preliminaries, he asks me, "Bronia, what is happening to you? You have just been given a wonderful dancing role. Sergei Pavlovitch has begun to have faith in your talent. . . . But I don't see you working on the Bacchante. In fact, you are working less than usual, and the performance is only two days away . . ."

"Vatsa, I *will* dance the Bacchante well."

"That is impossible! For that kind of role you should be working on your dance day and night, right up to the very moment of the premiere."

"I know that Vatsa, but it's not entirely my fault. Fokine, just as he did for the Papillon in *Carnaval*, left the solo dance of the Bacchante for last."

I am making excuses for myself. Deep down, I know that Vaslav is right.

"Bronia, I also came to talk to you about something else. I know that you are meeting Chaliapin often, and I have seen you with him several times. What is it all about? Bronia, you are young, so I can understand that in the presence of a colossus like Chaliapin you are wonderstruck. But he is not for you. Tell me, are you serious about him?"

I surprise myself with the frankness of my reply. "Vatsa, I believe I love him."

"That cannot be. And that is why I came to talk to you. You must not meet with Chaliapin anymore. You will soon realize it is only an infatuation with a genius—an artist . . ."

"I don't think so, Vatsa. In the theatre I saw and admired Chaliapin, the artist, and now I am very happy to know *him*. Believe me, Vatsa, Chaliapin is not at all what evil tongues make him out to be. He is a wonderful human being . . . and I knew it the very first time I held his hand and looked into his eyes . . ."

Vatsa explodes. "I forbid you to see Chaliapin! You are talking nonsense. You are not to meet him again. You have been seen too often with Chaliapin."

"What is wrong with my being seen with Chaliapin? We are always in public places; I am never alone with him. When Chaliapin asks me out he always invites other artists too."

"Bronia, I think it best that you stop meeting Chaliapin."

"I do not see anything wrong in our meetings. Chaliapin and I are great friends and we have a wonderful time together. He is a charming man and talks so well about the theatre and music, and about how one must work in the theatre. No, Vatsa, I cannot promise that I will stop meeting Chaliapin."

Vatsa is very upset. "Then Sergei Pavlovitch will have to see to it that you do not meet Chaliapin. You must know all about his reputation —today one woman, tomorrow another—and that all the ladies in town are head over heels in love with him."

"Why do you worry about it, Vatsa? Chaliapin is not in love with me. Let him be with his lady friends, that is another part of his life. I know little about it, and I have no desires there. I love him for himself; I do not want anything in return. Let my love be!"

Vaslav seems relieved. "Then it is not serious. After all, I am your brother, and being older than you I understand more of life. And so I must warn you and protect you."

Realizing that he hasn't convinced me or made me change my mind, Vatsa goes to Sergei Pavlovitch. Together they talk to Karsavina and ask her "to have a word with Bronia . . ."

Karsavina is married and is older than I am—not just in years, but also in her status with the company. Whenever we come in contact she is usually somewhat aloof, though pleasant. She agrees to take on the mission, albeit somewhat awkwardly.

"Bronia, do you know about Chaliapin?"

"Yes, Tamara Platonovna—a little," I reply, jokingly.

"I am talking, Bronia, about his reputation as a man of the world."

"Feodor Ivanovitch, the great Chaliapin, is known all over the world."

"No, Bronia, I am not talking about Chaliapin the artist. I am talking about something else. You have got to realize that Chaliapin's reputation is such that if he is even seen talking to a lady, especially a young lady, that alone is enough to compromise her."

Immediately I protest. "Tamara Platonovna, you are mistaken. This is all nasty gossip. You do not know Chaliapin . . . he is not that sort of person. . . . I have never met anyone more correct or more of a gentleman."

"Bronia, you are young and do not really know what life is like. . . . I hope you are not in love with him!"

Suddenly I feel an urgent need to be as frank with Karsavina as I was with Vaslav. "Yes, I do love him. But do not worry . . . it is very much his tender attentions and his touching concern to protect me from malicious gossip that have most endeared him to me. But you know, I never see him alone . . ."

"Nevertheless, Bronia, be careful."

"I assure you, Tamara Platonovna, Chaliapin himself takes much greater care of my reputation than I ever could."

Almost two weeks have passed since the premiere of *Schéhérazade*, and every day Ludmila and I have met with Feodor. After the rehearsals in the mornings or the afternoons, we go together for a stroll in the Jardins de Monte Carlo, or in the evenings after the performances we go to the Café de Paris.

One night—I am unaware that it is for the last time—we are walking together up the steep hill towards my hotel. Feodor and Ludmila are seeing me home after the performance. Feodor looks as if he is deeply disturbed about something. He looks very sad, and I think he must again have had some sort of unfortunate misunderstanding. All the way up the hill Feodor has been complaining that people can only see the worst in him. "And I am not as bad as they say," he says dejectedly. "Bronia, say what you think."

"You are the best in the whole world."

"Thank you." He pauses, then goes on, "I have stayed too long in Monte Carlo. It is time for me to go to Italy. Bronia, you will quickly forget me."

My heart tightens. "Already? But you are not leaving now?"

"No, I will be here yet awhile. I have some business."

I feel a sudden relief.

At the door of the hotel Feodor says good-bye to me. He takes my head between his strong hands; he kisses me several times, and his voice sounds even more tender and caressing than ever.

"Good-bye, Broniusha. May Christ always protect you." He crosses me several times. "Darling, darling, my dearest little one, be always happy and remain the delicate little snowflake. . . . Now sleep well, and do not think about anything else . . ."

I lift my eyes and look up at him with great happiness, and again he kisses me. Ludmila, who is now staying in a hotel nearer the theatre, also says good-bye to me, and we part.

I hurry up the stairs to my room and go quickly to the window, so that I can watch him as he walks away. I have only one thought: *Tomorrow will be here soon . . .*

It is several days now since I last saw Feodor.

Monte Carlo is a small town where it is easy to meet. So where is he?

The night before Easter . . .

After the midnight church services, the supper is served in our hotel. Most of our fellow artists are gathered together with us. Ludmila tells me she has spoken with Feodor Ivanovitch and that he has told her that maybe he will come. I wait. . . . Today Feodor must come. How I miss him . . .

A delivery boy brings me a large bouquet of red roses with a note . . . "Khristos Voskres! [Christ is risen] Kisses, Feodor Chaliapin."

It means he will not come. . . . A polite Easter greeting, that is all.

I cannot hope any longer that we will greet the Holy Day of Easter together. I must kill any such hope in myself.

A group of artists are arriving and I hear one say, "As we walked past the Café de Paris we saw Chaliapin, Karsavina, and Oblokova, with Baron [Dmitri] de Gunsburg. They were having supper there."

I am torn apart . . . my heart sinks like a stone. An unknown feeling of pain fills my consciousness.

Why does it hurt? Everything is as it was before . . .

But, no, I am not able to soothe the hurt. It is all very simple for him, just a frivolous pastime with young people . . .

I must have been hiding my anguish very poorly. Ludmila comes and hugs me, saying, "Bronia, let's go to the Café de Paris."

"Dear Ludmila, how can we? It is now the middle of the night; if we show up at the Café de Paris, it would be very improper."

"But, Toussia [Karsavina], Ekaterina Alexandrovna [Oblokova], and the Baron are our friends. . . . Tonight is a big holiday and no one sleeps."

"No, Ludmila, let's have a good time right here."

But our celebration soon comes to an end. I return to my room and sit on the balcony until morning.

When I see Karsavina she says to me, "Chaliapin had supper with us last night . . . he is so charming."

I think to myself, *You see, I always said so* . . .

"All the time," she goes on, "he was remembering you, Bronia. He asked me to kiss you for him. He was sorry that you were not with us. He talked about you with great tenderness and wished you a happy Easter. . . . 'Khristos Voskres, dear Bronia, dearest little one.' He wanted to go and fetch you, but then he changed his mind and added in a soft voice, 'Bronia, she must already be asleep. Christ be with her.' . . . But suddenly Chaliapin became very sad. . . . 'Bronia has already forgotten me. She is an angel, so pure, and I am so wicked . . . terrible. . . . I am very guilty towards her. Bronia will never want to see me again.' "

At first, my heart is singing. . . . He remembers, he did not forget. But then my heart sinks. . . . Why does Karsavina have to tell me all this and torture me so . . . ?

I want to ask Karsavina, *Tamara Platonovna, what did Chaliapin mean . . . guilty towards me . . . wicked and terrible?*

The questions rush through my head, but I have no voice to ask them.

I hug Karsavina and kiss her.

"Thank you, Toussia." I also want to tell her that she is good and kind. She knew of my need to hear about him, to bring me a little happiness with his own words. My heart is thankful . . . she knows Chaliapin is "forbidden" to me, and still she wanted to cheer me up.

I feel that I have received a part of the life, of the previous evening, of my Feodor . . .

The premiere of *Narcisse*, the other new ballet we are creating in Monte Carlo in preparation for the seasons in Rome and Paris, is to come after Easter. The music for *Narcisse* has been composed by Tcherepnine, and the libretto is written by Bakst and adapted from the Greek myth of Narcissus. Echo, in love with Narcisse, is rejected by him because she can only echo his voice. She demands vengeance of the gods. It is decreed that he shall fall in love with the next being he sees. . . . Narcisse kneels by a spring, and there in the waters he sees his own image and falls in love with it. In vain he beseeches the image to respond to his passion. Worn out, Narcisse is transformed into a flower, and Echo is transformed into a rock . . .

Karsavina in her role of Echo looks very beautiful. Yet, in her long, dark purple tunic, for me she does not evoke the image of an echo—the voice of Narcisse. But never has Vaslav been as magnificent or looked as handsome as in *Narcisse*, in the short white tunic clasped over his bare shoulder and falling in heavy pressed pleats.

In his dancing for the role of Narcisse, Vaslav has done something new; he stays away from the excessive sweetness of the style recently adopted by dancers to interpret Ancient Greece.

Only I know that all winter long, both in St. Petersburg and here in Monte Carlo, Vaslav has been working on his first choreographic composition, the ballet *L'Après-Midi d'un Faune*, and that the choreographical outlines for *Faune* are ready. But now I am aware that Vaslav's *Narcisse* contains many details that are part of the new ideas and discoveries incorporated in the forms and rhythms of his Ancient Greece, as seen when creating his *L'Après-Midi d'un Faune*. It is an entirely new technique that Vaslav is still working on, but already it has become part of him. Though Vaslav remains in harmony with the whole composition of *Narcisse*, his great artistic individuality predominates and sharply changes the choreographic interpretation of the role of Narcisse.

I too find that after my work with Vaslav on his *L'Après-Midi d'un Faune*, my own technique in *Narcisse* has been influenced. I see how much I have assimilated Vaslav's Ancient Greek style in the poses that Fokine wants for the Bacchante in *Narcisse*.

It is the premiere performance of *Narcisse*: Chaliapin is in the theatre . . . and I feel exhilarated. Now I am onstage, and as I dance the Bacchante I see Chaliapin standing in the wings, backstage.

Bacchante, wearing a wine-colored tunic draped over one shoulder in deep cascading folds, appears onstage supported by two satyrs. On one arm she carries an amphora, and in her other hand she holds a goblet. Her body arches in intoxicated abandonment as she rushes across the stage. Suddenly she stops and holds a pose with the amphora. . . . In one pose after another, the Bacchante yields to the languid tempo of the music. . . . Slowly the tempo becomes more and more animated, and the Bacchante begins the sacred bacchanalian dance . . .

Suddenly I see Chaliapin in the first wing, and each time as I dance on the *avant-scène* he softly whispers to me, "Very good . . . ah, very, very good . . . my dear Broniusha . . . I am so proud of you. . . . My little Bacchante . . . I love you so . . ."

His voice is the sound of my Genius; like music, these whispered words inspire me; I dance for my Genius . . .

I am no longer aware of my own being; before me, as in a vision, is an image of a dancing bacchante. Blindly I follow her. I assume each of her poses and repeat each nuance of her movements. The vision of the dancing bacchante fills my whole being; she reincarnates in me and creates the Bacchante.

First, languorously like a stream of thick wine, the dance moves in a slow tempo; then it accelerates. With intoxicated joy, I dance and sing the Bacchante; the tempo accelerates to the bacchanalian crescendo, and in a frenzy the Bacchante whirls and spins in a wild dance. The rhythm of the dance breaks into a slow wide *adagio*, and languidly the movements flow in dripping, overflowing motions like the slow flow of a thick wine. With each sound of Chaliapin's voice, her dance is more lingering and intoxicating. . . . I experience in each of my dancing movements an unexplainable feeling of triumphal joy, as if by my dance I am solemnly communicating something very sacred to my Genius. In each dance movement, and in each pose, I know I have attained perfection . . . because I have reached and excited the admiration of my Genius . . .

After the dance is over, I am back in my dressing room. All the other dancers are onstage, and I have only a few moments to touch up my makeup—the long red wig that flows over my bare shoulder, and the rouge that Bakst so carefully painted on my heels and bare insteps—before returning for the finale, which I dance with Vera Fokina.

Suddenly I hear a tap and the door opens slightly. Chaliapin slips in sideways . . . softly he whispers, "Broniusha, I am here only for a moment. . . . I had to see you. . . . I followed you from the stage. . . . But don't worry, no one saw me. . . . I had to kiss you . . . my dear, wonderful, little Bacchante . . ."

My heart bursts with joy, and I am in the arms of my beloved Genius. . . . My head rests on his heart, and like a trusting child I accept his kisses. Within my heart the birds of happiness are singing . . .

"Bronia, do you love me?" Feodor holds me in his arms.

"I do love you . . . I do love . . ." My avowal is almost inaudible.

Feodor is gazing so wonderfully into my eyes. . . . He embraces me . . . and kisses me . . . and suddenly, "Good-bye, my dear Broniusha, I must run now . . . no one must see us or they might get the wrong idea . . ."

"No, do not leave yet."

But Feodor says, caressingly, "I must go, dearest Broniusha. You are an angel, my dearest little one. Good-bye."

As silently as he entered the room, Feodor, my beloved Genius, leaves . . .

Despite his very busy schedule, Vaslav always finds time to visit Mama. So it is today; Vaslav has come to see Mama and me. He is very pleased by my success as Bacchante, and he particularly rejoices that Diaghilev has begun to believe in my theatrical gifts.

"Everyone is talking to Sergei Pavlovitch about you with admiration, and now that you have superbly created the role of the Bacchante, Sergei realizes that your creation of Papillon in *Carnaval* was not 'just by chance.' Bronia, you must continue to work hard that this recognition stays with you. . . . In *Narcisse* you had a greater success than I did. One hears only about you . . ."

I know Vatsa wishes to bring me joy with these words . . . but they fail to move me today. My thoughts are elsewhere. Yesterday, the day after *Narcisse*, all day and all evening, I did not see Feodor.

It is so sad, and so hard.

In front of me in a large glass vase, the dark red roses stand amid a lacelike fern greenery, and on the table is lying the white card: "To Bronia—Khristos Voskres! Kisses, Feodor Chaliapin."

Another day Vaslav comes to take me for a walk. We are going towards the Casino when suddenly Chaliapin appears in front of us with two older, rather overdressed women.

Chaliapin sees me and abandons the two ladies; he rushes towards me, speaking in a voice trembling with emotion.

"My little dove, my dear Broniusha, how are you? It is such a long time since I saw you. I am so happy that I have met you. I do not dare to be with you—you are a pure angel, Bronia. I am wicked, forgive me! I am very guilty towards you—Bronia, you will forget me soon."

He begins to speak much faster, and constantly he glances towards the ladies, who are beginning to move away.

"I must run, I must be with them, they are *prima donnas* from the Metropolitan in New York. It is business. . . . I will see you, Bronia, yes?"

And he runs to catch up with the ladies. Ladies . . . is that why he calls himself "guilty" and "wicked"? I do not mind. Only it hurts so much to see Feodor, the great Chaliapin, running after the feathered hats . . .

The conversation I had with Karsavina after she had had supper with Chaliapin comes back to me. I had not really understood it at that time . . . and had thought to myself, *Naturally Feodor is not guilty of anything towards me . . . so Karsavina must have misunderstood his words.*

But now, meeting Chaliapin with the two ladies, I am distressed to hear from him the same words that I heard from Karsavina. There is no need for these words. It seems to me that I am hearing something deliberately exaggerated. I am trying to catch the meaning. . . . Why does he persistently portray himself in a bad light . . . ?

Is it because Diaghilev has spoken to him? Was he trying to impress Vaslav with these words?

And why did he call me a "pure angel"? . . . Only in the family, and by a very close circle of friends who have known me from childhood, am I fondly called "pure angel" . . .

Did Diaghilev in his conversation with Chaliapin call me a "pure angel," and Feodor Ivanovitch "guilty" and "wicked" . . . ?

In despair, I think how it must have sounded to Feodor to have heard such words from Diaghilev. . . . Again the man is misjudged.

After all, it was hardly surprising that Chaliapin had wanted to spend time with me. . . . I am young, quite talented, the sister of the famous Nijinsky, and Sergei Pavlovitch treats me as his own daughter. . . . Chaliapin simply wanted to be polite . . . and after the first meeting, this young girl Bronia looks at him with adoring eyes. . . . How could he not respond to her, not invite her out, and not tell her a few sweet words . . . ?

All it was for Chaliapin was a pleasant interlude, all very simple. But Diaghilev, and maybe Karsavina, built it up into something "serious."

Now I understand why Feodor has been avoiding us, why he has disappeared. He has decided not to spend time with us anymore. He doesn't want unnecessary complications. . . . Besides, what interest could he possibly have with "the little birds" when there are so many beautiful women in whose carefree company there are no troubles . . . ?

I did not see Chaliapin anymore in Monte Carlo after this meeting. A few days later, Ludmila and I both received identical letters from him, with the same message . . . a few sweet words. What? . . . I do not remember.

In later months Serafima Astafieva joined the Diaghilev company. Sima, a dancer from the Imperial Theatres, was a charming, witty, cheerful person, and she and I became good friends.

She had been in Monte Carlo during the spring, probably to arrange her contract with Diaghilev, and I had seen her one day sitting with Chaliapin on the terrace near the Casino.

Six or so months later, after we had become friends, she told me about their conversation.

"Bronia, did you know that Feodor Ivanovitch was talking about you to me? He said he was in love with you, but that Diaghilev had forbidden him to see you, saying that if Chaliapin wished to remain his friend he would have to stop seeing Bronislava . . ."

"That was only a joke, Sima. Feodor Ivanovitch did not mean it seriously."

But how consoled I would have felt if only for an instant I could have believed that Feodor was attracted to me. . . . But still I had doubts. . . . Chaliapin had always behaved so correctly with me, I had no reason to delude myself . . . it was all only a joke . . .

How few were those enchanted days, those spring meetings with Chaliapin! But how much from them has remained with me for life . . .

Ah, dear protectors . . . if only you had not been there . . . at all! . . . Should I thank you for your interference? . . . You meant well . . . you cruel, well-meaning interferers. . . . Why did you not let my love for Chaliapin be as he saw it . . . only a tender smile towards a young girl with lovelight dawning in her clear eyes . . . ?

36   Rome: 1911

FOLLOWING THE Saison de Ballet Russe in Monte Carlo, the entire company left for Rome where later in May we were to perform in the Teatro Constanzi. We traveled all the way together by train, in two passenger cars reserved solely for our ballet troupe.

Before we disembarked from the train, Sergei Leonidovitch Grigoriev, our ballet *régisseur*, told us that we all should be in the Theatre the next morning promptly at nine, ready for rehearsals. He warned us that we would have no time for sightseeing, for in addition to the regular rehearsals for the ballets we were to perform here, Fokine would be choreographing *Petrouchka* for the ballet season in Paris in June and he would continue working on the one-act ballet, *Sadko—Au Royaume Sousmarin*, from Rimsky-Korsakov's opera *Sadko*, which he had already started mounting in Monte Carlo.

Once in Rome we were separated into small groups to stay in different hotels scattered throughout the city. The International Exhibition for 1911 was being held in Rome and most of the hotels were filled to capacity. Ludmila and I were the only members of the company in our hotel, which was near the Teatro Constanzi, in the center of New Rome. This was our first time in Rome, so the next morning, and every morning thereafter, Ludmila and I got up early to try to see a few sights before going to the Theatre.

We had arrived several days ahead of the opening of our two-week ballet season, and immediately we started preparing for our opening night, May 15. At first our rehearsals took place in the basement under the Theatre, in a hall that was not large enough to accommodate all of us, even though we were performing with a reduced staff of ballet artists. The ceiling of the hall was low, and there were no windows. The weather in Rome at that time was hot, and the air in this poorly ventilated room was stuffy.

We had been refused permission to use the stage for our rehearsals during the first week, having been told that the musicians and singers needed the stage for their rehearsals and that afterwards their musical instruments must remain in place on the stage, untouched, ready for their evening performance.

We were surprised and dismayed by this lack of cooperation from Teatro Constanzi, and also by the cool and generally unfriendly attitude of the Italians towards the Ballets Russes. It was as if they were saying "What audacity! . . . How dare the Russians bring their ballets to Italy! Up till now it has been we Italians who have gone to Russia with our Italian companies. Our Italian ballerinas, our Italian choreographers, and our Italian ballet maestros are famous all over the world. What do the Russians think they can show us . . . ?"

This disdainful attitude angered Maestro Cecchetti and made us all the more determined to work even harder. We spent long hours from morning until late at night in the Theatre, leaving us all very tired. We had been supplied with new hard toe shoes in Rome that had to be broken in, but on the carpeted floor in the basement hall we were not able to practice our dances on toe. As soon as we were allowed to work on the stage, which was not until May 13, two days before the premiere, I practiced all my toe dances and *variations* until my toes were rubbed sore.

On the day of the premiere the big toe of my right foot became abscessed. At four o'clock in the afternoon the doctor was called and he lanced the abscess, saying that I should not dance that night. But I knew that I could not miss the performance—with our reduced number of artists in Rome, no one else had been assigned to learn my parts in *Le Pavillon d'Armide* or in *Les Sylphides*. So I had to dance.

I took a cab back to the hotel to rest before the performance, which was not due to start until nine o'clock. Both Ludmila and Mother tried to dissuade me from dancing that night. They said I could get an infection . . . the stage was dirty and the floor had many splinters. As I limped across the room, Mama said, "Look, you cannot even stand or walk. How do you expect to dance?"

I went to my room to rest for a couple of hours while Ludmila returned to the Theatre. She took it upon herself to warn Grigoriev, the *régisseur*, that she did not believe I would be able to dance that night.

I returned to the Theatre in a cab, still limping, trying not to put weight on my ailing foot. Before going to the dressing room I went to look at the stage and was horrified to notice that the floor of the stage was littered with small nails, like upholstery tacks. I found a stagehand. Since I did not speak Italian, I showed him the nails and gestured with my hands that the floor needed to be swept.

I went to the dressing room that I shared with Ludmila, and she was very surprised to see me. She tried again to persuade me not to dance. When I started to put on the toe shoes, the pain was excruciating; they would not fit over the swollen and bandaged foot. Again Ludmila warned me that if I persisted I was risking the loss of my leg from infection. Sitting there in the dressing room and holding the toe shoe in my hand, I remembered the other time, before my graduation in the Imperial Theatrical School, when I had narrowly escaped having my leg amputated, being saved by the kind solicitude of Prince Lvov.

I was still holding the toe shoe when I heard a knock on the door; it was Sergei Pavlovitch.

"Please don't be upset or frightened tonight if you hear hisses or whistles. I have been warned that the Italians are planning some kind of demonstration against our performances in Italy, and I have just now been informed that a claque has been hired and strategically placed throughout the Theatre. So, dance the best you can! It is very important that this performance be seen at its very best. The Italian King may, perhaps, be in the Theatre . . ."

He turned and walked out. Without any further discussion I painfully pulled the toe shoe onto my aching foot.

Before the curtain went up, tacks and small nails were again found strewn on the floor, and the stage had to be swept again before we could start the performance of *Le Pavillon d'Armide*.

At first, as the dancing proceeded, we did not hear any hisses or whistles, but neither did we hear any applause. Little by little the audience became more receptive and began to applaud lightly. Along with the sound of the applause were a few hisses of disapproval.

I danced in the *pas de trois* with Ludmila and Vaslav. Never had Vaslav danced his *variation* so effortlessly. He seemed to float in the air during his amazing *grand changement de pieds*, with each sideways leap wider and lighter than the preceding one. His *variation* ended after his three *tours en l'air* in a pose on one knee, *révérence*, towards the royal box. As he bowed his head and extended his hand, it hardly seemed that he had just finished an exacting dance; he appeared as if he had not yet begun to dance.

After Nijinsky's *variation* the tension was broken; the King applauded and the whole audience joined in.

Then, in the "Danse des Bouffons," Rosai in his solo dance amazed and thrilled the audience. The public by now had lost their prejudices against the Russian Ballet. They loudly applauded the dance numbers and, at the end of *Le Pavillon d'Armide*, there were several curtain calls.

During the intermission Diaghilev came backstage; he looked very pleased. Fokine too was in a good mood. The tension was gone, and we all felt relieved that no incidents had taken place during the performance.

"Now we have nothing to worry about," Diaghilev said with delight. "The King is in the Theatre and he has applauded us. For the Italians this means everything—the King's approval."

After the intermission we danced *Les Sylphides*, and at the end Fokine congratulated me on my performance and dancing. Ludmila then told him that I had danced with an abscessed toe that had been lanced only a few hours earlier.

Fokine did not believe her. "I saw Bronislava Fominitchna dance! No one could have taken even two steps on toe after such an operation, and yet she danced tonight better than ever."

When I told him she was indeed telling the truth, Fokine turned to me. "Bronislava Fominitchna, I'm sorry you had to make up this story to have an excuse not to come to the rehearsals tomorrow so that you can go sightseeing in Rome instead . . ."

I felt deeply hurt and on the spot removed my toe shoe. The toe was bleeding through the bandages and onto the inside of the slipper. I hurried to the dressing room to take care of it and to change into the costume of a Polovetsian girl for the last ballet of the evening.

On stage I forgot all about my foot. How could it have been otherwise, when everything around me was ablaze with enthusiasm? We all danced with verve and gave one of our best performances of *Danses Polovetsiennes*.

—

WE DID NOT perform in Rome every day, and so my foot was nearly healed by the next performance. Three new company members had arrived in Rome to join our rehearsals in preparation for Paris. They were all Artists of the Imperial Theatres—from St. Petersburg were Alexander Orlov and my friend Luba Tchernicheva; from Moscow came Sophia Fedorova who, according to the contract she had signed with Diaghilev, was to dance Bacchante in *Narcisse* in Paris.

All the free time I could find from our heavy schedule of rehearsals I would work with Sophia Fedorova, teaching her my role of Bacchante. Fedorova was a favorite ballerina in Moscow, but her great fame had spoiled her, and she had a hot temper. I had to be very patient with her, for she was slow in perceiving and learning the dance. Fedorova danced with a great force, but she was not able to achieve the form and rhythm of the dance as I saw and felt it. All the movements were strong and wild, but they were unruly. Painstakingly I tried to convey to her all I had done and created with the role in Monte Carlo.

The success of Bacchante had had a decisive influence on my life, and not only on my official position in the company. By creating Bacchante I had suddenly found myself as an artist. The many friendly, sincere comments on my performance by leading figures of the Russian Ballet had opened new vistas for me and given me hope in the future of my art. Though I was indifferent to the voice of the press, I was very sensitive and attentive to words of praise when they came from painters, musicians, and fellow artists. I weighed each word carefully, trying to see clearly what had elicited the praise so that I could preserve and enhance it.

Diaghilev, himself, seldom praised anyone. Once he even told me, "My praise would only spoil the dancer, and later it could cause me considerable nuisance."

But I am sure that this is not true of all dancers. I recall so well how beneficial it was for me to hear these praises, how inspiring it was. Then in my youth, and even later, it would fill me with new ideas and give me the courage to apply these ideas in my work. I felt a deep gratitude to all those great people who shared with me their impressions and who encouraged me not only with their praises for the good qualities in my dancing but also by their criticisms, pointing out my shortcomings and imperfections.

One of the most ardent admirers of my Bacchante was Lev Samuilovitch Bakst. He told me that he wanted to paint my portrait as Bacchante "featuring your dancing feet."* He said, "I have never before seen anyone's feet so alive as yours, Bronia!" Vaslav and Diaghilev did not approve of Bakst painting my portrait in his studio, and so I did not pose for the artist, but I always remembered his words: "Your feet are so expressive, they alone can say more in a dance than other dancers can say with the whole of their body." Naturally after hearing such praise from Bakst I paid particular attention to the technique of my feet. Each dance needed special exercises to develop the flexibility and force of the instep, and I concentrated on them as much as I had on my hands and fingers after working with Vaslav on Papillon.

———

MOST OF the rehearsals in Rome were spent working on Igor Stravinsky's *Petrouchka*. The story for the new ballet had been written by Stravinsky and Benois. Both had now joined us in Rome for these rehearsals.

The ballet takes place at a Russian Fair in St. Petersburg in 1830 and

*Bakst sketched Nijinska as Bacchante during the Monte Carlo rehearsals for *Narcisse*. One of these watercolor sketches appeared on the cover of *Comoedia Illustré*, June 1, 1911. (IN/JR)

tells the story of three dolls—Petrouchka (Nijinsky), the Ballerina (Karsavina), and the Moor (Orlov). The puppets belong to the Old Showman (Cecchetti). To the Fair come merchants, gypsies, street dancers, coachmen, nurses and children, soldiers, drummers, and policemen; every member of the company was used.

I did not take part in the early rehearsals, but as was the custom I had to be present in the theatre to watch with the ensemble.

Many of the artists in the company did not understand Stravinsky's music at all and expressed bewilderment that Fokine was able to mount anything to it. There were a few of us, however, who did admire Stravinsky's unusual and remarkable composition. The others accused us of being ready to like anything as long as it had been discovered or approved by Diaghilev, or Bakst, or Benois.

"This is not music," asserted some of the more outspoken proponents of the old classical ballet school. "It is simply a cacophony. You will see what sort of a failure this ballet will be in Paris."

Only a few days before our departure from Rome, Fokine called me for the rehearsal of the Street Dancer, the role I was to dance in *Petrouchka*.

"Well, what shall I mount for you, Bronislava Fominitchna? The Street Dancer is an acrobat. Do you know any tricks? Can you do the splits and whirl around on one leg while holding the other foot stiffly, high in the air?"

I felt like joking and replied, "If, Mikhail Mikhailovitch, you want to see an acrobat, then I will dance for you the ballerina's *coda* from the ballet *Le Talisman*."

I started to imitate Mathilda Kshessinska, her *cabrioles* and her *relevés* on toe from the last act of *Le Talisman*, the *coda* that was always accompanied by thunderous applause in the Maryinsky.

"That is perfect, it is exactly what is needed." Fokine laughed.

Whenever Fokine was working on the scenes with Karsavina, Nijinsky, and Orlov, I did not have to be in the theatre, and so was free to explore Rome, where everything spoke to me of Art; from all sides the creations of great masters stared at me. I spent all of my free time in the museums, usually on my own. In each masterpiece I could see a path to my own art and recognize a kinship.

One day when the museum guard was nowhere in sight, I could not resist a desire to touch a statue, to feel under my fingers the divine lines chiseled from ancient marble. I dreamed of attaining some semblance of those lines in my dancing body.

The desire to explore the mysteries of creativity in each work of art filled me with awe, and my search to penetrate the depths of art began to exhaust me. Rome came to oppress me terribly. In this city the greatest works of art were gathered all together and seen by everyone as a matter of course, as though they were a common occurrence. I was overwhelmed by the greatness of Rome and not able to handle the continuous flow of new impressions and the immensity of the experience.

It was a surprise to me, after this feeling of oppression, to find when I went to visit Vaslav an unusual lightness in the atmosphere surrounding him. The balcony of his hotel room overlooked the terrace and gardens. On the table was a large bouquet of fragrant white narcissus, and Vaslav also had a narcissus in his buttonhole.

His smile was radiant as he greeted me, asking, "How do you like Rome?"

But, unhappily, I could only reply, "It is very oppressive for me in Rome."

"Why? Don't you marvel at all that you see here? What happiness it is to be here in Rome!"

I could see how relaxed and how much at ease Vaslav was feeling in Rome, as if he had just returned to his homeland.

He was surprised to hear me say, "Rome completely overpowers me. My senses cannot absorb it; I feel swept away. If I could, I would leave immediately, to free myself from the strangely overpowering force of this city."

"Bronia, you are too impressionable; you are very young. You must come back again, later, and stay in Rome longer."

Rome has added crowning touches to my artistic growth . . . but I have a strange feeling from Rome. Rome has brought me pain. . . . I have felt the soul of Art in Rome, and I have been overwhelmed by the depths, the greatness, and the power of Rome.

37   Paris: June 1911

THE SEASON in Rome had ended and now we were again in Paris, with only a few days before our first performance on June 6. Our company had been considerably augmented. At least twenty-five dancers had come from Russia, from the Imperial Theatres; many had danced in the two previous summer seasons in Paris. Among them were Ivan Koussov, Boris Romanov, and Leonid Leontiev. Two good soloists, Margarita Frohman and Maria Reisen, who had graduated in Moscow in 1909, had also joined us, as well as the ballerina Sophia Fedorova.

Though we were working hard preparing for the Paris Season, we were also looking forward to our visit to England. Many of us in the company had been disappointed in 1910 when our season there had been canceled because of the death of King Edward VII. This time we were to dance as part of the celebrations for the Coronation of King George V, and Diaghilev had already mentioned that there would also be many parties and fetes during our stay and that we should be prepared to look our best. I decided to have a gown made by a French couturier, Paul Poîret.

Our premiere was to take place at the Théâtre du Châtelet, which had seen our first success in Paris two years before, in *Le Pavillon d'Armide*. Our program now was to include Schumann's *Carnaval*, already well known to Paris audiences from our previous season at the Paris Opéra, and followed by the new ballet, Tcherepnine's *Narcisse*. On the same program were two other new ballets, *Le Spectre de la Rose*, set to the popular music by Weber, "L'Invitation à la Valse," and *Sadko—Au Royaume Sousmarin*, with its rich and melodious music by Rimsky-Korsakov. Nicolas Tcherepnine, the composer of *Narcisse* and *Le Pavillon d'Armide*, was to be the conductor for the premiere. I was concerned whether *Narcisse* would appeal as much to Parisians as had *Le Pavillon d'Armide* in 1909. I did not like the music of Tcherepnine's *Narcisse*, for I felt it lacked

365

originality and "borrowed" many passages from Wagner and Tchaikov-sky.

Nijinsky and Karsavina were again going to dance the two principal roles in *Narcisse*, Narcisse and Echo. There were many beautiful passages in the ballet, but there were also some weak parts in its choreography. Fokine had mounted *Narcisse* in Monte Carlo, after his disappointment that Ravel had not finished writing the music for *Daphnis et Chloë*, so that ballet again had to be postponed. Bakst and Fokine had been working on *Daphnis et Chloë* in St. Petersburg, and many of their ideas were now incorporated in *Narcisse*. The dances of the ensemble had few innovations and a lot of "Duncanism."

I felt that Karsavina in her role of Echo would not make as great an impression in Paris as she had in her other roles. Perhaps Fokine and Diaghilev had made a mistake in choosing Karsavina. In her dance as the "voice" of Narcisse, her Echo should reflect faithfully, as in a mirror, all the dancing movements and poses of Nijinsky-Narcisse. This was the intent of Fokine's choreography, how he had mounted it for her. But in her repetitions of the *pas* and poses, she did not reflect Nijinsky himself. Nijinsky in his dancing was strong and Karsavina in her dancing was soft. She could not echo or reflect his strength, nor duplicate his extraordinary flights. Karsavina's performance next to Nijinsky's was pale. She was not dramatic enough in her interpretation of the torment of Echo, deprived of her voice. She portrayed simply the suffering of a woman unable to speak of her own love.

I saw the dance of Echo as strong at the beginning, fully reflecting the strength of Narcisse's voice and movements. Then gradually her movements must fade as her voice weakens and she is unable to speak to Narcisse . . . as the voice of Echo fades, so the torment of Echo rises . . . in my imagination I see Echo as a weightless, transparent being, carried through the air on the waves of reflected sounds . . . until finally she disappears, transformed into a rock, able only to repeat dully those sounds which disturb her forest solitude . . .

But Echo as realized in the ballet *Narcisse* was quite different. Even the costume made no suggestion of "a sound." Karsavina was dressed in the costume of a Greek woman—a long heavy tunic, completely enveloping the whole of Echo's figure so that any sound would be smothered and muffled, any dance movements completely hidden.

In Vaslav's dance there was not one movement that might be called "free" or an "à la Duncan" movement. In the figure of Narcisse created by Nijinsky there was something reminiscent of the calm and massive strength of Michelangelo's *David*, and there was the swiftness of the laughing faun. His body of the youth in love with his own image emanated health and the athletic prowess of the ancient Greek Games.

It could have been dangerous to portray in a dance the sensual and erotic Narcisse, driven to ecstasy by his own reflection in the water. Vaslav had so interpreted this scene that all such implications disappeared, dissolved in the beauty of his dance. Each pose on the ground, each movement in the air was a masterpiece.

His makeup, created by Bakst, was also original. Bakst had not chosen the usual makeup to give Nijinsky a suntanned appearance, nor did he use white to make Narcisse appear as if made out of marble. Instead he had created a new tone; to the liquid, lemon-colored makeup he had added only the faintest tinge of ocher. This unusual skin tone, covering the whole body, gave to Narcisse's figure an air of unreality, an illusory appearance. The same makeup covered his face uniformly—no painted lips, no rouge, no eye shadow. The eyes and the eyebrows were only lightly penciled, and the lips were just as thinly outlined.

The light blond wig lay flat; a narrow ribbon encircled the head. Bakst had arranged the short ends of the hair over the forehead and the longer hair framing the face in continuous flat ringlets, like an ornament chiseled from marble.

With his makeup Bakst could transform an artist, could make him unrecognizable. It was as if he had a canvas in front of him on which he painted and created an image as he had envisioned it. Before each premiere he checked every dancer, changed the hairdo or wig to conform with his sketches, and applied the makeup not only to the face but also a few strokes here and there to the body—including rouge to the heels and bare instep. For the men he underlined the shape of their muscles.

Bakst inspired all of us artists with his valuable suggestions. It is difficult to say how much we were indebted to him. Better than anyone else, he could see every detail of the artist's interpretation and could evaluate every fault and appreciate every essential achievement. He participated actively in all phases of the Ballets Russes, and had great influence on Diaghilev. He knew how to defend his own ideas and stand up for his convictions, and in many instances he had the decisive voice.

Everyone in the Ballets Russes loved Bakst. From him emanated an easy, mannered charm, out of a fund of sincere affability and goodness. He was our true friend.

—

DURING OUR rehearsals in Paris I had been teaching the new girls in the *corps de ballet* "The Stream," the dance which Fokine had mounted on me in Rome for *Sadko* so that I could teach it to the new girls. At the same time I was also working with the ballerina, Sophia Fedorova, continuing to show her the role of Bacchante for *Narcisse*.

But on the day of the dress rehearsal Fokine told me that I was to dance Bacchante. He also spoke to Sergei Pavlovitch, demanding that Nijinska, not Sophia Fedorova, dance the Bacchante for the premiere of *Narcisse*.

When Sophia Fedorova found out that she had been taken off the program, she rushed up to the stalls to find Sergei Pavlovitch. He was sitting at the front with several friends and distinguished guests, and she demanded that she be the one to dance Bacchante, saying she had priority as a ballerina from Moscow, whereas Nijinska was still a child and, besides, it had been promised to her in her contract. Sergei Pavlovitch went up onstage and called Fokine over to the side near the wings to talk to him privately, but Fokine answered in a voice audible all over the theatre, "Nijinska dances the Bacchante very well, and Sophia Fedorova doesn't dance at all what I want the Bacchante to be!"

Sophia Fedorova was still in the orchestra stalls, and on hearing Fokine's remark she fainted and had to be carried to her dressing room.

This unfortunate incident was painful for me, and I wished that it could have been handled differently. It would have been simple to say that according to theatrical tradition the dancer who creates a role, dancing at the very first dress rehearsal and the premiere performance, always has the right to perform on an opening night, and therefore Nijinska would dance for the premiere in Paris. I had created Bacchante in Monte Carlo, and since then I had danced in every performance. Sophia Fedorova had always been friendly towards me, and I was sorry that she had been caused distress. But at the same time I was very glad to be dancing the Bacchante in Paris, this dance which for the first time had given me the marvelous sensation of being a creative artist, of realizing the freedom of technique. I was master of the rhythms of its movement, I was able to create the image of the Bacchante as I envisioned and felt it . . . and there was so much more, so many wonderful memories . . . Bacchante is still with me . . .

During the dress rehearsal several photographers took pictures of Nijinsky and Karsavina, both so well loved by the Parisian audiences. They also took some photographs of me in the role of Bacchante, in several different poses on my own and then with Vera Fokina as the Boetian Girl. Some of these were published in the next issue of *Comoedia Illustré*, June 15, 1911, which gave considerable coverage to *Narcisse*. Fokine was very angry when he saw that the centerfold illustration showed the design by Bakst for the postponed ballet, *Daphnis et Chloë*, and described it in the caption as the decor for *Narcisse*.

WE WERE all filled with excitement and apprehension as the hour of the gala performance arrived. The audience in the Theatre provided its own gala performance—sparkling and glittering with jewels, beautiful gowns, and elaborate coiffures, anticipating a thrilling performance from the Ballets Russes. This awareness of the audience's expectations infected the company, and the mingled odors of perfume, plush theatre velvet, and newly painted sets heightened our own anticipation.

Some of the audience were admitted backstage—here were the elite of Paris: patrons of art and famous artists, poets, writers, and critics. During the intermission after *Narcisse*, this great throng filled the space behind the wings, until they were forced to leave because the stagehands were lowering drops and carrying parts of the set from the stage. As the theatre dust and the flakes of fresh paint from the sets began to drift down onto the evening clothes and top hats, the bare shoulders and the silk and satin gowns, the public moved into the corridors and even into our dressing rooms.

I fully realized that the presence of such a large crowd of the elite, backstage on this occasion, indicated the height of our success. As an artist on the stage, I loved the theatre audience. My natural instinct was to seek contact with it. But backstage, I always hurried to leave the crowd, closeting myself in my dressing room to change my makeup and costume for the next ballet. During the intermission Vaslav's room was always crammed with visitors and friends. He changed his costume and created his makeup before their eyes.

I knew how all these visitors interfered with Vaslav; he loved to be alone before going onstage. But he submitted to this "tyranny" as part and parcel of the success of a famous artist. What saved Vaslav, however, was his silence. He spoke to nobody, except for an occasional remark to Vassili Zuikov, an old servant of Diaghilev's, who watched over him like an anxious nurse, wiping perspiration off his face, handing him the soap, turning on the faucet, throwing his dressing gown over his shoulders.

Vassili knew every makeup stick on Vaslav's table. He knew all Vaslav's habits—his manner of making up, his way of dressing. He handed out every item at the proper moment. On days when Vaslav was very nervous, Vassili knew how to keep visitors out of the dressing room. Like Cerberus, he stood guard near Vaslav; in the wings he held a glass of water, a towel, a mirror, a powder box, or some eau de cologne. Vaslav never spoke to anybody before making his entry onto the stage, and Vassili, who could not speak a word of French, usually managed to keep everybody away.

But all Vassili's skill and persistence failed to keep the crowd away from Vaslav after his unforgettable performance in *Narcisse*. The throng in his dressing room could not tear their enraptured eyes from Nijinsky as they watched him prepare for *Le Spectre de la Rose*. It was like watching the creation of a beautiful painting, as the pink was added over his body and the rose petals were arranged in place of the sculpted curls.

At last the curtain rose for *Le Spectre de la Rose*. Karsavina, the girl with the flower in her hand, had fallen asleep in her chair, and in her dream the apparition of her rose entered through the open window and began to dance. It is impossible to convey the fascination exerted by Nijinsky as the Rose. I have never seen more beautiful hand and arm movements —the arms above the head, unfolding like petals. As he approached Karsavina, his fingertips touched her ever so lightly, and gently he drew her into a *valse*. At the first light of morning, he leaped out of the window as airily as a breeze. Nijinsky had taken us all to the land of dreams, and the girl awakened, her crumpled rose petals all that remained of her memories.

As Nijinsky flew away through the open window, an overwhelming explosion of applause and shouts accompanied him. The audience went mad.

Nijinsky, onstage, had soared without effort, after each flight descending to earth, barely touching the stage with his toes. But after his last tremendous, effortless leap through the window, he fell gasping for air into the arms of Vassili. He was exhausted. He could barely stand up. There on the stage, inspired by the dance, he had given the whole of himself, without measure.

Our season in Paris had begun. The success of the evening had been Nijinsky in *Le Spectre de la Rose*.

I was happy for Vaslav and his success, but in my heart the bacchante wept. Chaliapin had not come to the Theatre for our performance.

FOLLOWING OUR first premiere in Paris, all our rehearsals were devoted to preparations for the premiere of *Petrouchka* on June 13. Most of this new ballet had already been mounted in Rome, but there were still many roles to be filled and lots of work for those who had just arrived in Paris. So we were spending all day in the Theatre, from morning until late at night, and did not leave the Châtelet even to eat, but instead had sandwiches in the foyer.

In *Petrouchka*, in the two scenes "At the Fair," a huge crowd on a wintry day is enjoying the entertainments and festivities taking place in St.

Petersburg on Admiralty Square, during the holidays before the beginning of Lent. Many additional rehearsals were needed to teach the *figurants*, the many men, women, and children who had been hired to take part in the various *mises en scène*. Mikhail Mikhailovitch spent many hours working with them and became exasperated when they did not follow his instructions. He lost his temper, screaming at them when they ruined his *mises en scène*. Watching the rehearsal, we artists could not take it all as dramatically as Fokine, indeed we were rather amused by these French *figurants* trying to imitate and portray a Russian crowd. The rehearsal was often interrupted by our bursts of laughter, which of course angered Fokine even more.

How amused we were when the *figurants* came onstage for the costume rehearsal wearing their Russian costumes for the first time! One, supposed to represent a peasant woman selling wares from a vendor's cart, had a fancy hairdo straight from a Parisian hairdresser. Another "Russian" peasant wore a thick wool shawl draped over one shoulder in a Spanish fashion. The French women did not care to wear kerchiefs tied under their chins, babushka-style, but instead tied them on the side and arranged locks of their hair to show fetchingly under their kerchiefs.

For the last rehearsals onstage Fokine was greatly helped by Benois, who had arrived in Paris for the premiere of *Petrouchka*. But despite the most careful inspection and checking by both Benois and Fokine, on the day of the dress rehearsal many of the *figurants* with long beards as Russian *moujiks* were found waiting to go onstage, having forgotten to paste on their mustaches. One bearded *moujik* was caught at the last moment without a wig, his sleek hair parted on the side in the contemporary style.

All the artists who were taking part in the *mises en scène* in *Petrouchka* tried to help the *figurants*, telling them whenever possible to stand near us so that they could imitate our gestures and our characteristic Russian poses.

In *Schéhérazade*, which was also planned for our second program on June 13, the *figurants* were much better at playing their roles, since most of the men had taken part in our performances of the ballet in Paris in 1910. Still, one never knew what to expect from them in the last scene, when on the orders of Shahryar they were to rush onstage and massacre all the women and slaves in the harem. I remember once when I was dancing as Almée, I found myself lying in full view of the audience at the front of the stage, across my corpse a black beard lost by an enthusiastic *figurant* in his zeal to kill me.

Figurants are essential for crowd scenes, particularly in *Petrouchka*, but I deplore their use in a ballet, no matter how well they have been taught.

Inadvertently their presence among the professional dancers in a ballet is an eyesore that gives an amateurish appearance to the whole ballet.

In *Petrouchka*, I became absorbed in my own role of the Street Dancer. I wanted my portrayal to show a poor young girl exploited by a mean organ-grinder. He forces her to dance for a meager pittance even when it is freezing or she has a cold. She wraps an old shawl, full of holes, around her shivering shoulders, blows on her clenched hands to warm her freezing fingers, then carefully rolls out over the snow-covered ground a small rug on which she will dance. She stamps her feet to warm her frozen toes; her face and her whole body express her anxiety. She wants to please the crowd gathered around, whose attention is already attracted to a competitor, another Street Dancer, danced by Ludmila Schollar.

When I have finished my dance and picked up the coins thrown onto the rug, I give them to the organ-grinder and become another little girl in the crowd at the Fair, and in my turn watch with interest the other performers at the Fair, and finally the puppet show.

After the show is over, the Old Showman throws the doll Petrouchka into his box behind the Showman's booth.

For Petrouchka's scene in his box-room, Alexandre Benois painted a portrait of the Magician—the Old Showman—in the center of the wall. The eyes staring from the portrait follow Petrouchka's every move. In this bare room there is no place for him to hide. In vain Petrouchka pounds his wooden, paddlelike hands against the walls and pours maledictions at the portrait; he cannot escape from the power of his master's eyes.

When the sets for *Petrouchka*, which had been executed in St. Petersburg, were delivered in Paris, Benois was completely devastated to learn that some had been damaged during the journey and that the portrait on the wall of Petrouchka's room would need to be repainted. Benois was not able to do the work himself, having suffered an abscessed elbow, and so Bakst offered to retouch the damaged portrait in time for the dress rehearsal, only two days away.

On the day of the dress rehearsal, we could hear from onstage a voice shouting excitedly from the stalls, "I shall not allow it. . . . That is not the portrait as I painted it . . ."

Benois was very angry. Bakst had repainted the portrait of the Showman in profile, thus spoiling the whole idea for the scene in Petrouchka's cell-like room. Now the Showman was no longer holding Petrouchka under the spell of his malevolent eyes.

Valentin Serov was in the audience, and he immediately offered to restore the painting according to the original design by Benois in time for the premiere. Benois gratefully recorded in his *Reminiscences of the Russian Ballet* that "he executed it with touching diligence."

38   Premiere of *Petrouchka:*
June 13, 1911

IN *PETROUCHKA* Nijinsky's body is limp. Petrouchka is a puppet; his soft body has no spine. It is a doll's body filled with sawdust, dressed in a loose shirt and wide pants, loosely propped up inside the Showman's booth.

Petrouchka appears shabby and miserable; one can see right away that he is not one of the Showman's favorite dolls. The Old Showman neglects his appearance, handles him roughly, and once the show is over throws Petrouchka on the floor in a dirty corner of his box.

Petrouchka is piteously ugly, thin, and stooping; the tone of Nijinsky's makeup is ashen; the paint of his puppet-face has flaked away; the lines of his features are faded; on his pale mouth, the outline of the lip has been washed away; of the once bright-red cheeks only a faded trace remains on one cheek; the eyebrows look as though they were hurriedly penciled in, one eyebrow flies up across the forehead; there are no eyelashes on his blank face.

When Petrouchka dances, his body remains the body of a doll; only the tragic eyes reflect his emotions, burning with passion or dimming with pain. The heavy head, carved out of a wooden block, hangs forwards, rolling from side to side, propped on the shoulder. The hands and feet are also made of wood, and Vaslav holds his fingers stiffly together inside black mittens like wooden paddles. His feet are wooden feet in black boots, dangling loosely at the end of sawdust legs. The soft knees bend suddenly under the weight of the body, the knock-kneed legs sway from side to side, and the wooden dangling feet dance freely. Petrouchka dances as if he is using only the heavy wooden parts of his body. Only the swinging, mechanical, soul-less motions jerk the sawdust-filled arms or legs upwards in extravagant movements to indicate transports of joy or despair.

Despite these limitations imposed on his body, these restricted

373

movements of a doll-like character, Vaslav is astonishing in the unusual technique of his dance, and in the expressiveness of his body. In *Petrouchka*, Vaslav jumps as high as ever and executes as many *pirouettes* and *tours en l'air* as he usually does, even though his petrouchkian wooden feet do not have the flexibility of a dancer's feet. He executes the most difficult *pas*, never betraying his doll-like appearance and continually reflecting in his dance all the emotions of the hapless Petrouchka: his love for the Ballerina, his joys, his sorrows, his sufferings, and his clamor for revenge. In the concluding scene of the ballet, mortally wounded by his rival the Moor, the dying Petrouchka lies on the snow-covered ground surrounded by the curious crowd. With great effort he tries to lift his heavy head and piteously bemoans his miserable lot, the cruelty of his foes, his misunderstood and rejected love for the Ballerina. All his dying being reaches out to the crowd. With an agonizing pain and sadness in his eyes, he extends a trembling arm in farewell to the crowd, knowing that only they, the gray, common, Russian crowd, love and understand Petrouchka. The heavy wooden head hangs to one side, and the tragic eyes stare out of the grotesque, still mask of the doll's face.

The suffering of the miserable Petrouchka is infinitely moving.

In the last breath of life, Petrouchka's heart is still filled with love for the Ballerina: he sends her his last, tragic kiss; he presses the palm of his wooden hand to his pale lips and jerkily extends his arm towards the vastness of space.

———

PETROUCHKA, Stravinsky's musical masterpiece, took Paris by storm. Thunderous applause. Triumph for Stravinsky, for Benois, for Fokine. Triumph for Nijinsky, for Karsavina, and for the ballet ensemble. Triumph of course for Sergei Pavlovitch Diaghilev. An unforgettable performance. The magic, the creative imagination, the artistry.

This night our rapport with the audience was perfect. The enraptured public poured behind the wings, into the dressing rooms of the artists, onto the stage. Everyone wished to see us at closer range, our costumes, our makeup, and to express their admiration.

Still happy and excited over the tremendous success of our *Petrouchka*, I was back in my dressing room beginning to get dressed in the costume of the Odalisque, for *Schéhérazade*. Each artist has his own manner of dressing and wearing a theatrical costume. I felt very good about my costume for the Odalisque, and that I had found the correct makeup for the face and body, blending well with the deep rose-pink of the diaphanous harem trousers and the deeper burgundy shade of the silk scarf around my waist, all adhering to the color sketches by Bakst.

Meanwhile the second ballet of the program, *Le Spectre de la Rose* with Karsavina and Nijinsky, had come to an end, and as I was now dressed I hurried downstairs. The stage was crowded and everyone was talking about *Petrouchka* and *Le Spectre de la Rose*. "What a grandiose theatrical performance! Nijinsky—Petrouchka, a puppet . . . Nijinsky—Rose, an apparition . . . What a contrast!" "Nijinsky, not only *le dieu de la danse* . . . a great artist . . ."

And now *Schéhérazade*, which Paris knew from last year but which still excited admiration. Even for us artists as we gathered in the wings for the performance, no matter how many times we had performed *Schéhérazade* we were always inspired by the Bakst decor and the wonderful music of Rimsky-Korsakov.

Here was Shahryar—huge and stern and forbidding. There was Karsavina—looking so striking as Zobeide, with her long black hair framing her beautiful face and her makeup underlining her large dark eyes. She was talking to Bakst and Ida Rubinstein, who was there with Gabriele d'Annunzio. I will never forget Rubinstein as Zobeide, the role she created in Paris in 1910. She was not at all as one would picture a woman in the harem from one of the tales from *The Thousand and One Nights*. Her slim body, so emaciated, unconsciously drew attention to her bone structure. One saw in Rubinstein the angular and curved shapes of an exotic orchid.

Nijinsky as the favorite slave of Zobeide was also unique, quite unlike any other Negro portrayed on the stage. The image he created did not even remind one of any of his other slave roles, neither the brown slave in *Le Roi Candaule* nor the black slave in *Cléopâtre*.

In *Schéhérazade*, Nijinsky's Negro slave was silver-gray. Under this unusual shade of glistening makeup the already prominent muscles of his arms and body were cast in greater relief, making him appear as a steel sculpture. This silvery-grayish skin tone also showed up the burnished gold color of his costume. As soon as he put on his costume Vaslav assumed the character he was to portray. There was something animal, apelike even, in the expression on his face as he drew back his lips to bare his gleaming white teeth.

As I came onstage I saw Vaslav already in the wings. Behind him stood several dancers engaged in conversation. But Vaslav was not speaking to anyone; as usual he was limbering up. I watched, fascinated by his absorption as he worked on the flexibility of his hands. His hands performed their own dance; the brightly colored gems in his rings twinkled and scintillated in the air around his body. His agile fingers moved as lightly and swiftly as a spider, and then as he opened and closed his hands slowly, his fingers twisted with the power and elasticity of an octopus.

Even though I was very familiar with the choreography and the *mises en scène* in *Schéhérazade*, before each performance I liked to go over my solo dance on the stage during the intermission to familiarize myself with the placement of the pillows and small rugs on the stage and to make sure that the wings were not obstructed by any heavy props.

Suddenly, I saw a tall figure walking towards me across the darkened stage.

"I was coming to see you."

Chaliapin took me in his arms and embraced me. "Bronia, you look wonderful."

He told me how much he had enjoyed *Petrouchka*, the music, the ballet, also my own interpretation of the little Street Dancer, and he hummed the tune of my dance, which he had just heard for the first time.

He looked into my eyes, and my eyes must have betrayed my happiness.

Lightly Feodor caressed my neck, my bare shoulder; he kissed my hand and the inside of my elbow. "I want so much to hold you in my arms and to kiss you."

I felt uneasy. There was something new in him, strange and unfamiliar to me.

"Broniusha, you have never been to Maxim's. We will have supper there, with champagne."

A thought flashed through my head: *I must look very beautiful to him now in my makeup and costume, but my evening gown from Poîret's is not ready yet. How can I go out to Maxim's with him looking plain and unattractive after he has seen me as the beautiful Odalisque?*

Feodor must have noticed my hesitancy.

"I have invited Ludmila and her friend S. [no further identification] and there will also be one of my acquaintances with us, a compatriot of yours from Poland. I know you will enjoy his company."

The lights on the stage were gradually coming up and the artists were gathering.

"Bronia, I must go. I must hide." Chaliapin was joking, but I felt a trace of apprehension in his voice as he added, "Sergei Pavlovitch might see us, or he could hear that I had come to see you. And then, again, he will be angry with me."

We were standing in the darker part of the stage, behind the backdrop, and I couldn't see Feodor's face or his eyes. I was enraptured by his voice and the flow of his words. I felt his kisses on my hand, my arm.

Le chef de la scène now appeared on the stage carrying a thick, heavy stick, and according to an old tradition in the French theatre he banged with all his force on the floor, three times: the signal that the performance was about to start and that the stage must be cleared of any visitors who had come backstage during the intermission.

Suddenly the overture of *Schéhérazade* resounded in the theatre. Chaliapin walked away, reminding me again, "I will be waiting for you . . . after the performance."

I hurried to take my place in the first wing and join Vera Fokina and Ludmila Schollar, who were already standing there waiting for the curtain to open for our dance at the beginning of the ballet.

I had had no chance to inspect the placement of the rugs and pillows onstage, nor would have now with Diaghilev standing there, as was his custom before each ballet, to make sure that everyone was present and ready before he gave the signal to raise the curtain. Tonight Sergei Pavlovitch looked very distinguished and elegant in his tailcoat. His eyes did not meet ours, but we could all tell that Diaghilev was very pleased with tonight's performance.

As the curtain rises the three Odalisques run out onto the stage, along the ramp. In the first part of the dance we form a triangle, sitting on the floor before the Sultan with our legs crossed beneath us in the oriental pose. We dance only with our arms and upper bodies, then slowly we rise up, coming close together so that our legs appear as the stem of a single flower. We raise our arms above our heads so that we look like the bud of a huge flower, its petals tightly closed. Then as we open our arms and arch our bodies backwards the flower comes into full bloom. Our arms undulate and our bodies sway from side to side until our fingers, the tips of the petals, brush against the floor.

Later in the ballet we each dance individually, and at the end of my solo, coming down after a high jump, I caught my foot in the fold of a rug. Suddenly I felt something snap in my leg. I had only enough strength to get off the stage and fall into the wings, half dazed with pain and fear for my leg.

"Quick, a doctor," someone called.

The Theatre doctor happened to be nearby. He was bending over my leg to examine my foot just as I heard the end of the music before my next entrance. Seized with a sudden strength, I jumped up as if propelled by a spring to join the final scene and was able to perform until the end.

The performance was over and I was back in my dressing room. I ask Ludmila to explain to Chaliapin that I was sorry but would not be able to join them, having hurt my ankle.

But Ludmila exclaimed, "That is impossible. Feodor Ivanovitch has arranged the whole evening solely for you."

Though my sprained ankle was not hurting so much now, the foot was quite swollen. I explained to her, "I have to take care of the ankle so that I can dance the day after tomorrow for our next performance."

I would have liked to see Feodor again, but not this way . . . I did not feel like celebrating our meeting by sipping champagne at Maxim's in the company of others. Besides, there was something different about Feodor now . . . different from how I remembered my Genius in Monte Carlo.

"No, I shall not go."

My heart was still beating wildly, but all my happiness had gone.

Later in my room I could not sleep. Why had I not gone with Chaliapin? Because of the pain in my leg? I could have overcome the pain.

My heart still longed for him. But I knew I must forget Chaliapin. He was not for me. He was not "my destiny."

At three o'clock in the morning there was a knock at my door, and from Maxim's a basket filled with fruits and a bouquet of violets was delivered. Chaliapin's card had a short note:

> Terribly sorry to hear about the damn accident to your poor little foot. My dear, dearest Broniusha, I think about you all the time and drink to your health. I embrace and kiss my Broniusha tenderly. May God keep you always as you are and bless you, my little dove. Feodor.

39   Our First Season in London

LONDON WAS preparing for the great day: June 22, 1911—the Coronation of King George V. It was my very first time in London. As we were being driven to the hotel, I looked at the imposing gray buildings decorated with flags and portraits of the King and Queen. They were everywhere. We passed under special arches erected over the streets, decorated with garlands and flags. London was overflowing with people from all over the British Isles and the Empire. I was fascinated by the colorful costumes and the diversity of uniforms worn by these visitors from faraway lands.

For this engagement in London our rooms had been reserved well in advance, all in the same hotel—the Premier Hotel, in Southampton Row Road, quite near the British Museum. Not one of us spoke English; we had learned a few words and short phrases from the English guidebook for tourists, but they were not much help to us as no one understood our pronunciation. The waiters, the bellboys in the hotel, the salesmen in the stores, all looked at us puzzled and bewildered. It was the same in the theatre when we asked the way to the dressing rooms, or how to find a dressmaker or hairdresser. But the worst of all was when we tried to hire a taxi and had to explain to the driver where we wanted to be taken. How frustrating it was, especially when we were in a hurry to get to the theatre!

We soon learned to pronounce "Theatre Royal, Covent Garden" without much difficulty. But we all had trouble with the words "Southampton Row Road." Often we would find ourselves being driven across town, out of our way, late at night, instead of to our hotel. So we soon learned to carry a card with the address written on it: PREMIER HOTEL, RUSSELL SQUARE, SOUTHAMPTON ROW ROAD.

Whenever I was free I would go to the British Museum. I was particularly interested in the Oriental and Egyptian Rooms. Nearby were several antique shops and old bookstores, which I would also browse through on my way to or from the museum.

It was an unusually hot summer, and as I walked the few blocks from the hotel to the museum over the melting asphalt, it seemed as though I was walking on a soft plush rug. At night too it was still hot, and during our very first performance, June 21, when we danced *Le Pavillon d'Armide*, *Carnaval*, and *Danses Polovetsiennes*, the makeup ran down our faces.

Several members of the company were invited by the Marchioness of Ripon to a reception. It was a beautiful party held in a garden, and I wore my Poîret dress. I think it was there that I heard that Chaliapin would not be singing in the opera excerpts that were to be presented for the Coronation Gala at Covent Garden. He was unable to come because he was taking a cure at Vichy. I remembered then that I had thought he looked unwell when he came backstage after *Petrouchka* in Paris.

Wistfully I also remembered the happy conversation in Monte Carlo when Chaliapin had talked of playing the role of Shahryar in *Schéhérazade*. But now he would not even see our performances, nor would we hear him sing for the Gala Performance at the Theatre Royal in Covent Garden.

—

THE PROGRAM for the Gala Performance—June 26, 1911—included a selection of acts from three operas and the scene, "L'Animation des Gobelins" from *Le Pavillon d'Armide*.

During that performance in the Theatre Royal, Covent Garden, the lights in the auditorium were not dimmed, and so we could clearly see the Royal Box with the King, the Queen, and the Royal Family. The box was draped with garlands of fresh roses and orchids.

Since my childhood, I had danced in the Imperial Theatres for Royal Galas and had taken part in festivities organized by the Imperial Theatres at the Hermitage Theatre and Peterhof. But what was now before my eyes surpassed anything I had ever seen. The whole interior of the Theatre was decorated with trellises and garlands of flowers. The stalls and the tiers were glittering with diamond tiaras and a myriad of jewels worn with beautiful décolleté gowns. The men wore their sparkling decorations and medals on splendid dress uniforms. In the Grand Tier sat the oriental potentates and maharajas with precious stones in their bejeweled turbans. In the front row I could recognize the Aga Khan, whom I had met in Monte Carlo. His costume was embroidered with many jewels and he was wearing several strings of pearls.

I couldn't help but wonder how the guests would leave the Theatre after the performance, wearing these priceless treasures, and how their carriages would be able to drive through the narrow streets around Covent Garden Market.

—

ALL DURING Coronation Month, the theatres in London were holding special performances by famous artists. Anna Pavlova was dancing at the Palace Theatre. It was not her first appearance in London. England had already seen Pavlova and worshiped her.

I went to the Palace Theatre to see Pavlova dance. How infinitely sad it was to see Pavlova following acts by magicians, clowns, and acrobats. Not that I don't love music halls and circuses. I have great respect and admiration for circus and music-hall artists. Their work is difficult and requires long training.

But, how could one watch the incomparable Pavlova in a music hall? Why was Pavlova here?

I couldn't hold back my tears as I watched Pavlova in her dance, nor could I help but recall her as I had seen her in St. Petersburg and in Paris. Now the daily, routine professional performances in the music hall had changed the unique style of her dance.

This uniqueness, the fascination of Pavlova's dance, was the elusive quality of her movements: her "insecure" balance, her slightly trembling *arabesque*, barely touching the floor. What perfection it was for us to watch Pavlova dance at the Maryinsky! We never thought of the effort or the amount of work involved or of the dance technique; we simply were all under the spell of her dance. After the harsh Italian School, supreme at that time in the Imperial Theatres, embodied by Kshessinska and following the traditions of Brianza and Legnani with all their acrobatic tricks, Pavlova's dance and Pavlova herself appeared to us unreal—like an aroma, a breeze, a dream.

But now here in the Music Hall I could no longer find in Pavlova the qualities I used to love.

40   Late Summer, 1911

IMMEDIATELY AT the end of Coronation Season in London, Diaghilev left for St. Petersburg to begin negotiations and arrangements for our company to have a winter season in Russia.

During May, in Paris, Diaghilev had met with Telyakovsky, who after seeing the premiere of *Petrouchka* had insisted that both Stravinsky's *Petrouchka* and Rimsky-Korsakov's *Schéhérazade* should be seen in Russia. Then, in London, Sergei Pavlovitch and Vaslav had talked to Kshessinska as well as Telyakovsky; both of them felt that it would also be very interesting for the Russian balletomanes to see *Le Pavillon d'Armide*, *Les Sylphides*, *Carnaval*, and *Cléopâtre** performed by the Diaghilev Ballet Company, all four ballets being familiar to them as performed by the Imperial Ballet at the Maryinsky. There were considerable differences between the presentations by the two companies, though all four ballets were choreographed by Fokine.

When the London Season ended on July 31, the company was given two months vacation, with the joyful news that we were to return to London for a further six-week engagement in the fall. Most of the artists planned to return home to St. Petersburg, Moscow, or Warsaw for the vacation. Mother and I were also going home, and Vaslav wished to come to St. Petersburg with us, but because his military-service deferment was due to expire Diaghilev did not want him to return to Russia at this time. "You are no longer an Artist of the Imperial Theatres," he said to Vaslav, "and perhaps now the military authorities will not be as lenient towards you. It is safer for you to remain abroad for the summer and not risk your dancing career."

---

*In the Imperial Theatres *Les Sylphides* was known as *Chopiniana* and *Cléopâtre* as *Egyptian Nights*. (IN/JR)

Diaghilev already knew that Karsavina might not be free to dance in London in the fall, given her commitment to perform with the Imperial Ballet at the Maryinsky for the fall and winter season, and he was apprehensive that if Vaslav went to Russia and was detained there he, Diaghilev, would be without both of his stars for the London Season. So he advised Mother that Vaslav should not return to St. Petersburg before obtaining an extension to his military deferment, and he gave her the name of an attorney in St. Petersburg who would arrange the matter of Vaslav's military-service obligations, or at least secure a temporary extension of the present deferment. He promised to talk to the attorney himself while in St. Petersburg, but meanwhile he asked Mother and me to stay in Venice with Vaslav until he, Diaghilev, returned from Russia.

We happily agreed. We particularly wanted to see the city that Vaslav had described so beautifully in his letters to us, the summers of 1909 and 1910. In Venice, Vaslav stayed at the same hotel where he had stayed before, at the Lido across the lagoon; he liked to swim there in the sea, and he had in the hotel a large hall at his disposal for his daily exercises. Mother and I preferred to be in Venice itself, so we stayed in a hotel on the bank of the Grand Canal. Vaslav often came to see us and was our guide when exploring the city.

We spent several delightful days together in Venice, but Mother tired from our long walks in this city where the only means of transportation was on water, by gondola or waterbus. Mama categorically refused to take a ride in a gondola—she was sure that she would fall off such a narrow boat—though I did take one ride with Vaslav along the Grand Canal.

Our stay in Venice was cut short when Mama received news that her sister, Theodosia, was in the hospital in Warsaw with a liver ailment, and decided we should leave early and spend a few days in Warsaw on our way to St. Petersburg. I was sorry to leave Venice, this ancient city of enchantment built on the water. On our last evening we went to the Piazza San Marco and sat at one of the outdoor tables and watched the sunset over the square. The domes of the Basilica glittered and the four gilded bronze horses seemed to come alive in the blinding rays of the setting sun. Flocks of pigeons squabbled for the crumbs they were thrown on the piazza. I enjoyed feeding them as they walked over our table and even landed on my shoulders.

Vaslav came to see us off at the railway station, and I promised him that I would write often and give him all the news from St. Petersburg.

In Warsaw Mother and I stayed with our relatives and visited Aunt Thetya every day in the hospital. She was happy to see us. She was thinner, but otherwise seemed in good spirits. We were reassured when her doctor told us that she was recovering well, and soon we saw her sitting up in a chair. We spent only a few days in Warsaw and were back in St. Petersburg by August 20.

I had been anxious to get back to St. Petersburg to study with Maestro Cecchetti. A two-month vacation is a long time for a dancer to go without practicing. The hotel in Venice where I had been staying with Mother had not had a room where I could practice.

Sometimes as I went to Maestro Cecchetti's, I asked my cab to proceed along the route over which I used to trudge for so many years from home to the School and back again. After the grandeur of foreign cities I can never have enough of gazing at the delightful views of St. Petersburg. To me it is endlessly tender and soothing.

When Mama and I left Venice, Vaslav was expecting Diaghilev any day. So I was surprised, on our arrival from Warsaw, to find that Diaghilev was still in St. Petersburg. When I met him he was very excited and told me that the arrangements were going well and that we would be performing during the winter season in St. Petersburg, probably in the Narodny Dom Theatre.

The fact that Vaslav was facing the possibility of having to fulfill his military obligations did not seem to bother Diaghilev, who had not been able to see the attorney he had recommended. The man was away on vacation until September, but Sergei Pavlovitch assured Mother that there should not be any trouble in obtaining an extension of Vaslav's deferment, particularly now that Kshessinska, having promised him that she would dance in London in *Swan Lake*, *Carnaval*, and *Le Pavillon d'Armide*, had made it clear that she wanted to dance with Vaslav not only in London but also in St. Petersburg. Sergei Pavlovitch was sure that she would use her influence to enable Vaslav to return to Russia. Meanwhile, though, he urged Mother not to delay in seeing the attorney when he came back to St. Petersburg in September.

We had already received several letters from Vaslav asking if Mother had seen the attorney yet and if the procedures had been started to free him from any military obligation. Mama wrote back to tell him what was happening, promising to see the attorney as soon as he returned to St. Petersburg.

While we were in Venice, I had written a short note to Chaliapin, thanking him for the flowers and fruits he had sent me from Maxim's. I missed Feodor. I wanted to see him . . . to hear his voice. But I had promised myself in Paris that there should not be any more meetings with Chaliapin . . . and so I had not sent my note.

Now in St. Petersburg the posters for the Maryinsky Theatre

announced the beginning of the Opera Season, with performances by Feodor Chaliapin and Dmitri Smirnov.

I said to myself that I really should thank Feodor for remembering me during his evening at Maxim's . . . just a short note. I wrote a three-page letter . . . and gave it to the doorman at the stage door, asking him to give it personally to Feodor Chaliapin.

The next day I read in the newspapers that the performances with Chaliapin had been postponed as he was recuperating in Italy from a recent illness.

I was filled with worry. I had thought Feodor had completely recovered his health, for I knew that after taking the cure in Vichy he had given a few performances there. Two weeks passed and still Chaliapin had not returned to St. Petersburg.

I decided to go to the Maryinsky to see a performance of *Raymonda*. Perhaps there I would be able to find out more about Feodor.

It was my first time back in the Maryinsky since my resignation as an Artist of the Imperial Ballet.

How many times, together with the other students from the Imperial Theatrical School, had I sat here in the first balcony of the Theatre? How many marvelous performances of operas, of ballets had I seen here? How many great artists had I watched, enraptured, on this stage? How many hopes and dreams had I shared with my friends of the day that we, too, would become Artists of the Imperial Theatres?

Before the opening of the curtain my heart was heavy. I was now seated among the public; I was only a spectator in the audience in this Theatre so familiar to me since childhood. Now I was a stranger here.

Last May, in Paris, Vladimir Telyakovsky, the Director of the Imperial Theatres, had seen me dance Bacchante in *Narcisse* and had offered me the position of soloist in the Imperial Ballet with whatever leave of absence I would need to dance abroad. Mother, and even Vaslav, had urged me to return to the Imperial Theatres, and I had promised Telyakovsky I would give him my answer when I came home to St. Petersburg in September. Meanwhile Mama continued to stress the importance and prestige of the title Artist of the Imperial Theatres.

Now, in St. Petersburg, I decided I would serve my Art better by devoting myself entirely to my work with the Diaghilev Ballet. I had just seen Telyakovsky and told him that I could not return to the Imperial Theatres.

Was I correct in my decision? . . . Mother said that I was making a terrible mistake.

But, as the performance progressed, after each act of *Raymonda*, I realized how right I was. After the excitement of such ballets as *Schéhérazade* and *Petrouchka* with Diaghilev's Company, the presentation of *Raymonda* that I was seeing now in the Maryinsky appeared gray and dull. I was appalled by the lack of artistic unity among the artists, even among colleagues who had danced with Diaghilev. Each one seemed to me to be wearing her costume or styling her hair to suit her own figure or face regardless of the style or period depicted by the ballet. I was suddenly aware of glaring artistic blunders.

After having performed in Diaghilev's Ballets Russes and now seeing the performance of *Raymonda*, it seemed to me that the Imperial Ballet and the Ballets Russes were from two different planets.

—

IN ADDITION to studying with Maestro Cecchetti, I was working with Lubov Egorova on the role of Myrtha, Queen of the Wilis, in *Giselle*.

In 1907 I had seen Lubov Egorova dance Myrtha with the Imperial Ballet and had admired her performance and interpretation of the role. At first Sergei Pavlovitch had invited Egorova to dance Myrtha in London, but she was engaged for the fall season with the Imperial Ballet. Then Egorova had come to see one of our performances in Paris, and when I met her she was kind enough to offer to teach me the role of Myrtha in St. Petersburg in September.

I was thrilled to be working with Egorova; she was truly magnificent as Myrtha and has never been surpassed in this role. Working with her, I strove to project the image of the ephemeral Wili, but also to catch the strength and power of Myrtha, the Queen, dramatically commanding the Wilis and Giselle.

I have not heard from Feodor, though I know that he is now back in St. Petersburg. Did he receive my letter?

Today Ludmila Schollar came to see me at home. She told me that she had seen Chaliapin at an opera rehearsal at the Maryinsky. "Feodor asked about you and said that he hopes to see both of us after the performance. . . . There will be two tickets for us at the box office for the first performance of the Opera Season tomorrow night."

Quickly, without hesitation, I said, "Sorry, but I am leaving tomorrow morning for London. Perhaps you can give my ticket to S. . . ."

There were no seats on the trains leaving for Paris for the next few days, but Ludmila's friend S. was able to get me a wagon-lit reservation for the Nord-Exprès leaving for Paris a day later.

I did not see Feodor. Ludmila went with her friend S. to the opera.

41 London: Fall Season, 1911

I ARRIVED in London a week before the start of our rehearsals, scheduled for October 9. There were hardly any other artists from our ballet troupe there yet—only those few who had decided to spend their vacations in England—though I was happy to find Vaslav already in London. We visited the British Museum together and enjoyed browsing through the old bookstores and antique shops, or we would go for long walks in Hyde Park, where one day Vaslav insisted on taking a snapshot of me, saying, "Bronia, you look just like a girl from a Dostoyevsky novel." [See Illustration 97.]

I was looking forward to the beginning of our season, for I was anxious to start working and dancing again, knowing that here in the theatre, only here, would I find my happiness . . . and quell the tumult in my heart.

During the Coronation Season in London our ballet company had numbered seventy-five dancers, but for the fall season our company had been reduced to fifty. Vera Fokina, Biber, Kandina, Rosai, Leontiev, and Khristapson had returned to Russia to fulfill their engagements with the Imperial Ballet in St. Petersburg, and many male Russian character dancers who had been engaged in Paris for the performances at the Châtelet and for the Coronation Season were also gone.

In the *corps de ballet* were some Polish girls who had been engaged from the Wielki Theatre in Warsaw in the spring of 1911 and had remained with us. Since I spoke Polish I often worked with these dancers, teaching them our repertoire, even offering to help them with their hairdos and makeup. I had made many friends among them, including a soloist from the Wielki Theatre, Alexandra Vassilievska, with whom I had enjoyed working in Monte Carlo when together we had been the two soloists in the second act of *Giselle*.

Several artists came from St. Petersburg for the start of rehearsals.

Ludmila Schollar had been granted a short leave of absence to dance in London, and Anatole Bourman had resigned from the Imperial Theatres and had rejoined our company as a permanent member. Another young dancer, Alexander Gavrilov, had just graduated from the Imperial Theatrical School and had chosen to work with Diaghilev's Ballets Russes rather than join the Imperial Ballet.

Vaslav and I were also delighted to see Maria Piltz again. We had both liked Maria from the time she had been a student with us in the Imperial Theatrical School. She had graduated in 1909 and had danced with the Ballets Russes in 1910. Maria and I often worked together, with my teaching her the dances from the ballets that had been added to our repertoire since 1910.

There was one major change in the company for this season in London. Léon Bakst was appointed Artistic Director of the company in place of Alexandre Benois. Benois had been so angry in Paris with Bakst and Diaghilev over what he considered the interference in his set design for *Petrouchka* that he had left the company.

For our opening performance we were preparing *Giselle* and *Schéhérazade*. *Giselle* needed a lot of work, because we had not performed it since the previous spring in Monte Carlo, and I offered to help the Polish dancers. They were all excellent character dancers but were weak in classical technique. For several months, since last March, they had been studying regularly with Maestro Cecchetti and had improved considerably, but as Cecchetti devoted only one class a week to the techniques *sur pointe*, they were still not very strong on toe. The girls were all very pretty and were an asset to our company, dancing very well in *Danses Polovetsiennes*, *Schéhérazade*, *Cléopâtre*, and *Narcisse*, but they had difficulties in performing the purely classical ballets.

Karsavina had obtained a short leave of absence from the Imperial Theatres and would have to return to St. Petersburg to perform there in November, but she was able to dance with our company during October. For the opening night on October 16, Vaslav danced with Karsavina in *Giselle* and *Schéhérazade*. For our second performance on October 17, we performed three ballets already well known to London audiences—*Le Pavillon d'Armide*, *Carnaval*, and *Schéhérazade*.

Anna Pavlova was in London during October and had agreed to dance in a few performances at the end of October and the beginning of November, before her departure for the United States. We were all excited at the news that Anna Pavlova was to return to dance with our company, and I was particularly happy to have the opportunity to see again those two geniuses of the dance, Pavlova and Nijinsky, dancing together.

84, 85. Nijinsky as Petrouchka.
Signed photographic portrait
given to Bronislava by Vaslav
in London, 1913.

86, 87. Scene III of *Petrouchka*, "The Moor's Room," with closeup of Orlov and Nijinsky. *(Courtesy of the Dance Collection, The New York Public Library at Lincoln Center)*

88. Nijinska as the Ballerina Doll, and Kotchetovsky as the Moor, in *Petrouchka*. From *Comoedia Illustré*, June 1, 1912.

M. KOTCHETOVSKY
(*Le Maure*)

Mlle NIJINSKA
(*La Ballerine*)

89. Nijinska, as the Street
Dancer, with Schollar and
Kobelev in *Petrouchka*.
Photograph by Bert, 1911.

90. Benois design for
Petrouchka, Scene I, "At the Fair."

91. Bakst design for *Le Dieu Bleu*. From *Comoedia Illustré*, June 1, 1912.

92. Nijinsky in five poses from *Le Dieu Bleu*.
The center pose was originally in gold coloring.
From *Comoedia Illustré*, June 1, 1912.

93. Nijinska in *Thamar.*
(Stravinsky Diaghilev
Foundation)

94. Nijinska in *Danses*
Polovetsiennes from
Prince Igor.
Photographic portrait,
London, 1912.

95, 96. Cecchetti and Piltz
in *Daphnis et Chloë*. From
Comoedia Illustré, June 15, 1912.

97, 98. Hyde Park, London, Fall 1911. Snapshot of Bronislava by Vaslav, with the face of Maria Piltz showing over Bronislava's shoulder, and of Vaslav by Bronislava.

For her first appearance in London with Diaghilev's Ballets Russes at the Royal Opera House, Covent Garden, Anna Pavlova danced in *Cléopâtre* with Nijinsky. Both appeared in the secondary roles of the favorite slaves, dancing the veil dance *pas de deux*, first mounted to the music of Arensky for Preobrajenska and Nijinsky in *Egyptian Nights* in 1908, and later included in *Cléopâtre* to music by Glinka in 1909. Pavlova also danced the "Bacchanale," to music by Glazounov.

I remember how Mikhail Mikhailovitch had mounted the "Bacchanale" in Paris in 1909, just a few days before the premiere of *Cléopâtre* at the Théâtre du Châtelet. Vera Fokina and Sophia Fedorova had danced it with two satyrs and twelve other dancers—six Greek youths and six Greek maidens—of whom I was one. The number was such a huge success that the orchestra was not able to continue, and we all came forward to take a bow, which greatly angered Fokine who screamed at us "for spoiling the continuity of the performance."

In 1910, in St. Petersburg, Fokine had also mounted this "Bacchanale" for Anna Pavlova and her troupe, and it had become one of the most successful numbers in her repertoire. So Pavlova gladly agreed to dance it with us.

Sergei Pavlovitch asked me to learn the dance number so that later in the season, after Anna Pavlova left (and with Vera Fokina not dancing with us this season), I could perform it. Perhaps Diaghilev gave me this dance to console me, since I would not be dancing the Mazurka in *Les Sylphides* while Anna Pavlova was making her guest appearance with us. For Pavlova was to dance both the Mazurka *variation* and the Valse *pas de deux*, as she had done in St. Petersburg in 1908 and in Paris in 1909. But, naturally, I was more than happy for the wonderful opportunity to see Pavlova again in *Les Sylphides*, to watch enraptured as she danced the Mazurka, the *variation* she had created.

Anna Pavlova danced only seven performances with us, but how memorable they were. She danced with Nijinsky in *Giselle* and *Carnaval* and the Blue Bird *pas de deux* from *Sleeping Beauty*, now called in London "L'Oiseau d'Or."

This *pas de deux* was familiar to London theatregoers from past performances by other guest artists from Russia—by Lydia Kyaksht and Andrianov in 1908, and more recently at the Palace Theatre by Anna Pavlova and Mikhail Mordkin. But Nijinsky astonished the audience in London with the new technique he displayed in his *variation* of the *coda*, introducing a new step, *pas volé*, never seen before, in place of the series of *brisés volés* previously executed by the male dancer.

In the conventional *pas brisé volé* the weight of the body shifts from one leg to the other. Nijinsky felt that the movement of the body from side to side broke the impetus forward and impaired the thrust of the body upwards. In his new *pas* Nijinsky used a *grand battement balançoire* very effectively in combination with a *cabriole (en avant* and *en arrière*), and by developing a supreme coordination and synchronization of movements achieved a perfect balance of the body *en l'air*, rendering himself literally "weightless," high above the stage.

Watching Pavlova and Nijinsky, I was overjoyed to see again how each drew inspiration from the other. The London audiences seemed to feel it too.

—

VASLAV AND DIAGHILEV were again staying at the Savoy Hotel, and I often had lunch or dinner with them in the Grill Room there. One evening Anna Pavlova was with us; we were all having supper together after a performance. Diaghilev wanted her to sign a contract with him and dance with his company, and Vaslav was also trying to persuade Pavlova to join us and tried to lure her with the prospect of new artistic achievements and creations in the Ballet. Finally at the end of the conversation, Vaslav said frankly that an artist must have only one goal, to perfect himself, attain new heights in his art—and a music hall, even if it paid well, was no place for an artist like Pavlova.

"Yes, you will have lots of money . . . but you will destroy yourself."

Pavlova's answer was abrupt: "For me it's more important to have lots of money* . . . With money my art will always be great!"

But how much she could have given us, and how much her own sublime talent could have unfolded even more with the Ballets Russes and with Diaghilev!

—

THAT FALL in London I often felt quite lonely, for Mother had stayed in St. Petersburg trying to obtain the extension for Vaslav's military deferment. Unhappily she wrote that things were not going well. In September, on the due date, the attorney, recommended by Diaghilev, had not gone to the authorities in person but had sent his assistant instead. The military officials had ignored the assistant and had issued a decree declaring that Nijinsky had declined to serve his country.

---

*Because of the failure of several commercial ventures, her manager and benefactor, Victor Dandré, had been arrested and was not able to raise the sum demanded as security for his release from prison. It was not known then that the moneys earned by Anna Pavlova from her English and American engagements were used to secure his release and pay his debts. (IN/JR)

Mother was terrified; she was certain now that even though the Diaghilev Company was coming to the Narodny Dom Theatre, Vaslav would not be able to return to Russia. She was heartbroken, convinced that this was the end of her dream that he might one day dance again in the Maryinsky. She still did not have any faith that the Russian Ballet could last long abroad, away from Russia.

Vaslav, too, was distressed by Mother's news, but Diaghilev reassured both of them that everything would be arranged soon. He hinted that when Mathilda Kshessinska, with her usual entourage of Grand Dukes, arrived in London to dance with Nijinsky later in November, it would all be settled and Vaslav would be freed from the threat of military service.

When Kshessinska arrived with Grand Duke Andrei Vladimirovitch and their entourage, they gave numerous parties that were attended by many Russian officials. Both Vaslav and Sergei Pavlovitch were invited to these parties, but Vaslav never mentioned his military service troubles to any of the highly placed guests. He thought that Sergei Pavlovitch was dealing with the question so that he would be able to dance at the Narodny Dom Theatre in January and February of 1912. But apparently Diaghilev neglected to speak to any of them, depending entirely on Kshessinska's influence to settle Nijinsky's military service status. Vaslav was not unduly worried, for Kshessinska was very friendly towards him during their rehearsals for *Swan Lake*.

Diaghilev also asked me to be very attentive and considerate towards Kshessinska, who would be dancing with our company during our season in Russia and next spring in Monte Carlo. She was also going to watch our rehearsals of *Les Sylphides*. Whenever she came, however, she was very cold towards me, and I soon learned that she had criticized Diaghilev's decision to "let Nijinska dance the Mazurka *variation*." She was claiming that the ballerina who danced the Valse *pas de deux* should also dance the Mazurka as Fokine had first mounted these dances for Pavlova in 1908, and declared that she, Kshessinska, intended to do so when she danced in *Chopiniana* with Fokine at the Maryinsky in December.

I already knew that Kshessinska was going to dance in *Les Sylphides* with our company at the Narodny Dom in February with Karsavina and Nijinsky. But, when Diaghilev told me to learn Karsavina's Valse *variation* I felt he was obviously anticipating difficulties in Russia in persuading Karsavina to share the program with Kshessinska.

At the end of November Kshessinska and Nijinsky danced *Swan Lake*. Though Vaslav was a wonderful partner and performed his role according to the old tradition of classical ballet as choreographed by Ivanov and Petipa, his success was not as great as Kshessinska's. I knew he was disappointed, but I told him that Kshessinska had "all the Russian Court, the Grand Dukes, and the Officials, for her audience," and that she had also enhanced her performance by dancing to the accompaniment of the violinist Mischa Elman, who had been a great success in London with his recent concerts here.

42   My First Quarrel
        with Diaghilev

THAT FALL SEASON in London was marked for me by my first quarrel with Diaghilev. The cause of the quarrel might be viewed as trivial. It had to do with toe shoes.

In the Diaghilev Ballet Company, as was also the custom in the Imperial Theatres, the company furnished the dancers with toe shoes for a specific number of performances. The girls in the *corps de ballet* received one pair of shoes for ten performances while the soloists received two or four pairs. I myself never used the toe shoes furnished by the company; I found them too hard or too stiff. Instead I ordered a dozen pairs each month from Italy, made to my specifications, for a toe shoe has to be cut properly to give full freedom to the instep and must mold the foot like a kid glove—the tip of the toe shoe has to be smoothly rounded and not flattened like a large coin. The shoe must be soft without excessive padding. I often soak my toe shoes for hours in hot water to melt the glue and to soften the cardboard used to harden the tip. The sole has to be pliable enough to let the dancer come down from a jump noiselessly, but still firm enough to give good support to the foot in the execution of the most difficult and technical *pas sur pointe*.

Feet to a dancer are as hands to a pianist.

I always prepared several pairs of toe shoes for each performance and often used two pairs in one night. The toe shoes provided by the company I gave to members of the *corps de ballet*—not that there were many girls who could use them, for my feet are quite small.

The management staff that season was reduced and had its hands full taking care of all the important aspects of the complicated productions, and of maintaining the caliber of our performances in London, and the new pairs of shoes to which the girls in the *corps de ballet* were entitled were way overdue. The dancers had continually reminded the *régisseur* about their toe shoes, but to no avail. They were given only repeated promises that the shoes had been ordered from abroad and would arrive any day.

The Polish dancers were particularly upset and began to complain, even going so far as to accuse the Russian management of negligence and insinuating that it was economizing by skimping on their toe shoes.

On November 30 we had performed *Swan Lake*, a ballet in which the *corps de ballet* has to dance a lot on toe, and then on December 2 we were to perform *Les Sylphides*.

When I went as usual to check on my Polish colleagues, I was shocked to hear them say that they had decided among themselves to dance in *Sylphides* that night on half-toe without mentioning it to the *régisseur*.

During the season, my concern and friendship towards these artists from Warsaw had gained me their confidence and even some authority among them. When one of the girls came to me crying and showed me her shoes, badly worn with holes at the tip, I knew how much they would suffer dancing in such shoes and that they would have to muster all their courage to dance in *Sylphides* on toe in spite of the pain. But I realized too that they would not be persuaded by me. I had only one thought: *How to save the performance?*

I advised them to go to Diaghilev, knowing how Diaghilev, when he wanted, could charm artists. He was the only one who would be able to persuade them of the importance of dancing on toe in *Les Sylphides*, no matter how much they suffered.

The Polish dancers asked me to accompany them; most of them spoke only a little Russian, and they wanted me to explain their predicament to Diaghilev and the validity of their complaints.

But as soon as Diaghilev saw us approaching onstage he started to scream at us: "I am not a shoemaker. I am not responsible for your shoes. That is not my profession."

There was no reason for this outburst, for Diaghilev to yell at these dancers who had approached him politely and not yet said a word about their shoes.

I tried to control my anger as I answered Diaghilev: "Sergei Pavlovitch, you are not a shoemaker,* but somebody in the administration must be responsible for supplying the dancers with new toe shoes, on time. You, Sergei Pavlovitch, are the one who demands that our dancers take care of their toe shoes, that the shoes look neat and clean onstage. These dancers came to you only after repeated requests for new pairs of toe shoes. They

---

*There is a play on words here. *Sapojnik* literally means "shoemaker" but colloquially means "botcher" or "bungler." (IN/JR)

cannot dance *Les Sylphides* in bare feet! Look for yourself. How can a dancer stand on toe in this shoe?" Here one of the dancers lifted her foot to show the hole in the tip of her worn-out toe shoe.

Diaghilev looked straight at me, and as always when he was angry, his voice rose to a high pitch. In front of everyone onstage, he yelled at me.

"You should be ashamed of yourself, Bronia, starting a rebellion in the ballet company and threatening to spoil the whole performance!"

I was dumbfounded and completely shaken by the unfairness of his accusation. Sergei Pavlovitch had hurt me very deeply by doubting the sincerity of my motives and also doubting my true devotion to the Diaghilev Ballet and to my work. Obviously, somebody had already provoked him with words of "rebellion." Was he succumbing to the influence of Kshessinska, who had once threatened to force me to resign from the Imperial Ballet, accusing me of being "a leader of a rebellion-movement"? Was she trying to do the same here?

I was very angry, and I, too, lost my temper. "If you, Sergei Pavlovitch, have so little faith in me that you can believe such malicious rumors, and if it is your opinion that I can only be a bad influence on my colleagues, then I must leave. I shall dance tonight, but tomorrow I will not come to the performance. I am leaving the company."

My innermost feelings had been deeply hurt. Now life no longer had any meaning.

The Dance, the Theatre, that is my life! I was born to dance and now I have left the Ballets Russes. I have nothing to live for.

I shall go to Monte Carlo where I once was so happy and there on the shore of the blue sea, that I love so much for its dear memories, I shall end my life.

Vaslav and Sergei Pavlovitch spent several days trying to calm me and persuade me to change my mind and return to the ballet.

Finally peace was restored.

43 With the Tchaikovskys at Bordighera: December 1911

AFTER THE FALL SEASON in London came to a close, we had almost two weeks free before resuming rehearsals in Paris for the Christmas season at the Opéra. Sergei Pavlovitch had to go to St. Petersburg on business and he suggested to Vaslav that we accompany him to Paris and go on to Bordighera on the Italian Riviera where his "cousins," the twin brothers of Pyotr Ilich Tchaikovsky, were staying.

Vaslav had been worried about me that season, for I had been losing weight and looked tired and strained. He felt that I needed a rest, and so he accepted gladly for both of us.

We left London with Sergei Pavlovitch. The weather was terrible. When the train arrived in Dover and we saw the great waves breaking and splashing over the deck of the boat, Diaghilev suggested, "Wouldn't it be safer to remain in Dover until the storm subsides?"

Vaslav and I did not want to lose even so much as one day that could be spent in the warmth of Italy, but Sergei Pavlovitch dreaded sea voyages, and so we had a difficult time persuading him to board the ship. At last, choosing a lull, we ran aboard quickly over the gangplank to avoid being splashed by the waves.

I left my luggage in my cabin and went up to see Vaslav, who had a cabin on the top deck with Diaghilev and his servant, Vassili. All around me I could hear passengers remarking that this was the worst storm they could remember for a long time. I adore the sea, yet so far all my crossings of the Channel had been smooth, in calm weather. So I was excited at the prospect of crossing in such a rough sea.

As soon as the boat was out of the harbor all the passengers, except for a few hardy men, went below to their cabins, but I stayed with Vaslav, walking to and fro on the deck. As soon as we pulled out into the open sea I began to feel dizzy; my legs became weak and a darkness came over my eyes. I do not remember how I got down to my cabin, but when I opened my eyes a doctor was leaning over me listening to my heart and a nurse was standing beside him. She remained with me until we docked in Calais.

Vaslav alone had experienced no seasickness, and he found our troubles quite amusing. On the train he laughed, saying, "How brave you all were during such a long sea voyage . . . for all the ninety minutes it takes to cross the Channel . . . Sergei Pavlovitch, even while the boat was still at anchor in Dover, went immediately to the cabin and lay down on the bunk. He closed his eyes and refused to say a word to anyone for the entire crossing."

As he mocked us he imitated each of us. For Vassili, he knelt on the floor, showing us how Vassili took a large ikon out of his luggage and placed it in the center of his berth. "He knelt before it and prayed for the whole voyage, crossing himself repeatedly and bowing low before the ikon—so low that in fact his head banged the floor of the cabin several times as the boat was rocked by the waves."

Though Vaslav made fun of the others, he was gentle in his teasing of me.

"Bronia, at first, was like a true sailor. She ran up and down the deck . . . but suddenly I saw her stop and she swayed over. I caught her in my arms and took her down to her cabin and called the doctor."

In Paris we said good-bye to Sergei Pavlovitch and Vassili and took a taxi to the Gare de Lyon. We were afraid we might miss our train and so did not stop to eat, even though we had had nothing since breakfast. There was no dining car on the train for it was past the hour for serving dinner. We stayed up chatting until two o'clock in the morning, waiting for the first stop where we might get something to eat.

"This time I would not mind one of Mama's chickens!" Vaslav said. He told me then about his first trip abroad, with Diaghilev to Paris in 1909. I remembered how Mama had worried that Vaslav would be hungry during the long train journey and had roasted a large capon for him. She had wrapped it first in wax paper, then a large dinner napkin, and put it on a plate surrounded by bread rolls. On the plate she had also put a jar of butter, some oranges, and lastly some cutlery. She had wrapped the whole thing in another large dinner napkin and then made a separate package out of it so that Vaslav could easily unwrap it on his knees.

Vaslav had had a wagon-lit ticket. It was the first time he had traveled this way and he did not know that there would be a dining car for the wagon-lit passengers. He was traveling in the same compartment as Sergei Pavlovitch, his secretary Mavrine, and Walter Nouvel, Diaghilev's friend and an Attaché Extraordinaire at the Ministry of the Imperial Court.

At that time Vaslav was still barely acquainted with Sergei Pavlovitch and his friends, and being quite sensitive and self-conscious, he was afraid that in his youthfulness he might commit a *faux pas*. He wanted to ask the others to share his meal but did not know how to go about it; he only had one plate, one knife, and one fork.

Suddenly Diaghilev rose and said it was time to go to the restaurant car for lunch.

"I was so embarrassed; here was the package with the chicken. What was I going to do with it? I was so scared that at any moment Diaghilev or one of the others would ask me what I had packed so carefully in the package, and that they would then make fun of me for being so naïve as to not know that there was a restaurant car on a wagon-lit train. I felt angry with Mama. I waited for a propitious moment when I was alone in the compartment—then chicken, plate, knife, fork and all, flew out of the window . . ."

Vaslav also told me what he knew about the Tchaikovskys we were going to visit.

"Modeste Ilich and Anatole Ilich are twins," he said. "They are younger than Pyotr Ilich, who was ten years old when they were born."

"But, Vatsa," I asked, "how can the Tchaikovskys be related to Diaghilev? Sergei Pavlovitch asked me to give his love to his 'cousins,' and I also heard him call them 'Cousins Mody and Toly' when he was talking to you."

"They are not related at all, but Serioja knew them as a child when he used to visit his stepmother's sister, Alexandra Valerianovna Panaeva-Kartsova. It was in her home in Kiln that he first met Pyotr Ilich Tchaikovsky. His step-aunt had a beautiful voice and was an accomplished singer. Pyotr Ilich said there was no other singer who could render his songs with the musicality and artistry of Panaeva, and so he wrote songs especially for her. Serioja also told me that whenever he visited his step-aunt Panaeva in Kiln he liked to run next door to see Pyotr Ilich; little Serioja used to call him Uncle Petya. It was probably there too that he became acquainted with Tchaikovsky's younger brothers, the twins. Pyotr Ilich always called them by their nicknames—Mody and Toly—and so Serioja came to call them Cousin Mody and Cousin Toly."

Vaslav also told me that the twins had been only three when their mother died of cholera, and that Pyotr, who loved his younger brothers tenderly, had watched over them all his life, following their progress in school and writing to them regularly whenever he was separated from them.

I had already met Modeste Ilich in Paris during the performance of Tchaikovsky's opera *Eugene Onegin* at the Sarah Bernhardt Theatre. He was very active in the theatrical world as a dramatist, a librettist, and a critic. He had written several pieces for the Alexandrinsky Theatre, and I loved so much the beautiful *Queen of Spades*, his brother's opera, for which he had written the libretto after the poem by Alexander Pushkin.

Anatole Ilich, whom I was to meet for the first time, was in no way connected with the theatre or music. He was a high official in one of the government ministries.

As the journey progressed, I grew more and more apprehensive at the thought of soon being in the presence of close relatives of the great composer, the man whose music for *Swan Lake, The Sleeping Beauty*, and *The Nutcracker* had created new concepts in the ballet. The idea of living for ten days in close proximity with the two Tchaikovsky brothers was quite intimidating. But after Vaslav and I finally got some coffee and sandwiches at one of the stations, my apprehension lessened somewhat and I dropped off to sleep.

I awoke to find that we were passing through Monte Carlo without stopping. I quickly looked out of the window, remembering my happy days there with Feodor . . . and hummed sadly to myself the Prince's aria from Dargomijsky's opera *Russalka* . . . "All here evokes for me the carefree days of my youth . . ."

Soon after crossing into Italy we arrived in Bordighera where we were met at the station by Anatole Ilich and Modeste Ilich. They welcomed us warmly and took us to the hotel where they were staying and where Vaslav and I were given two adjoining rooms.

The twins were not at all alike. Modeste had a longish face and wore no beard, only a mustache like Pyotr Ilich. He was not tall, in fact he was even shorter than Vaslav. His brother Anatole, however, was tall and heavily built. He reminded me of military men when they are dressed in civilian clothes. His head was small and his stiff, short haircut made him look like a porcupine.

The two brothers looked after us well. We always joined them at their table for lunch and dinner, and afterwards they would take us through to the salon for our demitasse of coffee. I couldn't help but be amused by Modeste as I caught sight of him glancing at his reflection in the mirrors as we walked together through the hall. My friends in the School would have had a name for him—"Old Coquette." He would even stop sometimes in front of a mirror and take out the small comb that he always carried in his vest pocket and comb his grayish hair . . . and then with great care and attention he would separately comb the sides of his mustache, and finally fan his face with his perfumed handkerchief. By this time he would have fallen behind us and have to hurry with small, quick steps to catch up and join us to sip his coffee and Chartreuse. There at the table "Old Coquette" would examine his manicured hands and, armed with a file, would then finish his toilette.

On our first morning in Bordighera, Vaslav and I looked for a place in the hotel where we could practice together. The only large room available had a slippery parquet floor unsuitable for us to dance on. Finally we discovered a room in the cellar with a plain wood floor that needed only to be sprinkled lightly with rosin to be adequate for dancing. Its one drawback was a ceiling so low that it was impossible for Vaslav to practice high elevations or to lift me in a *pas de deux*.

Each morning we would begin with regular *barre* exercises, adding new body and arm movements—so essential to the dance—and then after lunch we would rehearse some of the ballets in preparation for the Paris Season at the Opéra. Vaslav also continued to work on his *Faune*, trying on me various movements and poses, all staged *en bas-relief*.

I had always enjoyed rehearsals and danced with the same enthusiasm as for a performance, but Vaslav declared that in daily classes I only went through the motions of the exercises. Perhaps he was right—at least so it must have looked to him, with my not even trying to keep pace with his own intensive work. I have always felt that I attained much more by practicing my actual dances—going over the whole *variation* rather than working on the technique of each *pas* separately in a class routine. I must admit, during the exercises at the *barre* in Bordighera I wasn't working very hard; I used the excuse that the floor was not good for dancing, and besides, I was so fascinated watching how Vaslav worked on his exercises that I kept forgetting about my own. Vaslav would work for forty to fifty minutes each day, all the time at an accelerated tempo.

Though Vaslav was only of medium height, he had great physical strength, equal to that of any of the larger men in the Imperial Theatres, and he continually worked on gymnastics in order to develop it further. During his school days he had been allowed to bring home barbells, and he had practiced with them during weekends and summer vacations until, while still a student, he was able to lift seventy-two pounds with one arm. The muscles in his legs were also tremendously strong, and his thighs were notable for their enormous muscles, the kind grasshoppers and other high-jumping insects have. I remember that tailors had to create a special pattern for the trousers of his suits so that they would fit elegantly with his jackets.

Vaslav's practicing in Bordighera applied maximum tension to every muscle. He would execute each *pas* or movement much more strongly than he ever would onstage, thereby building up a reserve of strength so that, onstage, he could hide all the effort and tension required for his dances and make even the most technically difficult *pas* appear effortless.

During his exercises Vaslav did not bother to observe the strict classical positions but concentrated on the perfection of the movement itself. When practicing *battements*, for instance, he neglected to put the heel of his working leg down on the floor, and he seldom closed to fifth position. But no matter how carefully I watched, I never could see how Vaslav took his preparation for a *pirouette*. During the exercises he would start with five, then seven, then nine, then faster still up to twelve; and often he turned sixteen *pirouettes*.

When we finished our rehearsals we would go for a walk around the little town of Bordighera, which had few visitors in winter. Here and there the fruit and vegetable sellers would be out in the streets. We soon came to recognize them. Sometimes one of the brothers, usually Modeste, would take us for a drive to the mountains or the seashore. All around Bordighera were many orange and tangerine orchards, also some famous groves of palm trees (the special palms of Bordighera are collected each year and sent to the Vatican to be used for the Palm Sunday processions). There were also flower fields on the outskirts of Bordighera, mainly of multicolored carnations. If we went along the seashore we could watch the fishermen repairing their nets or spreading them out on the beach to dry.

Modeste would also come with us on our walks through the town. He was very pleasant and friendly, with a lively disposition. He was about sixty-two but looked much younger. I soon began to feel quite at ease in his company. Modeste and Vaslav would walk around Bordighera arm in arm, and as the sidewalks were quite narrow I would walk along in front of them. I could never really hear their conversations, only their laughter, and later Vaslav would not tell me what had amused them. I would guess that he did not feel it was proper for my ears. (Neither Sergei Pavlovitch nor Vaslav would permit any dubious anecdotes or expressions in my presence even though Diaghilev, in particular, enjoyed them himself very much.)

After dinner in the evenings, around nine o'clock, we would go up to our rooms and write our letters. Talking through the open door, Vaslav would tell me what he was writing to Mother, for as was his usual habit he wrote to her every day. He also wrote sometimes to Sergei Pavlovitch. I would reply to the many letters I was receiving from our colleagues, happy to feel how close we had all become, having worked and traveled together in the company for almost a year. Of course, most of the artists of the Diaghilev Company were from the Imperial Theatres in St. Petersburg, and so I had known many of them from childhood. But over the past year we had also become good friends with the artists from the Moscow Bolshoi Ballet, and so I would write to them as well, saying how much I was looking forward to seeing them soon and working with them again.

One evening, towards the end of our stay, Modeste Ilich invited us to go with him to a small theatre in Bordighera. He promised to show us something very entertaining but would not elaborate. As Vaslav and I got ready, we supposed it would just be a small provincial Italian company. It turned out to be far more diverting than that, as enjoyable and amusing an evening as we had ever known. The artists of the "Distorting Mirror" Company in St. Petersburg could not have invented a better caricature of a theatrical performance. They could never have found actors with the sincerity and simplicity, the naïveté, aplomb, and self-assurance of these amateurs.

The performance took place in a very small theatre, and to see better we found seats on benches in the balcony. As we looked down over the front rows, the most expensive seats, we recognized the waiters, maids, and other employees from our hotel. There was no printed program, but from the reaction of the public to the artists, applauding their entrances loudly and calling each one by name, it was obvious that the public knew what was going on.

The performance was of an operetta we did not know. It began with an overture, played by an orchestra consisting of a clarinet, two large tubas, and a drum. When the clarinetist played a solo, the whole audience welcomed it deliriously.

The curtain went up to reveal several artists onstage, and as we looked closely among the elaborately costumed "ladies and gentlemen" we found we could recognize some familiar faces: the fruit and vegetable vendors, the young butcher from the market. The Prima Donna, as a Lady of the Court, was dressed in a flowered cotton dress with a long train tied around her waist with a wide purple ribbon. On her head she wore a coiffure ornamented with rooster feathers of every color of the rainbow. The leading man, we assumed, was supposed to be an officer of the Royal Guard, but his uniform was strangely reminiscent of the local fireman, even down to his brass helmet and hanging épée, neither of which he removed during the performance, even in the salon of the lady of his heart. She herself had trouble with her train, while he did not know what to do with his épée as he tried to embrace her. His declaration of love was accompanied by exaggerated gestures and unnatural poses aimed at suggesting his aristocracy.

Many of the performers had good voices and sang well, but they had to shriek so as not to be drowned out by the loud tubas and the single drum of the orchestra.

Everyone in the theatre was ecstatic and applauded wildly. We all had a wonderful evening. The next day as we went about the town buying flowers and fruit, we complimented "the artists" on their performances, and they beamed with happiness.

44   Early Months of 1912

VASLAV AND I returned from Bordighera to join the company in Paris. Our first performance at the Théâtre Nationale de l'Opéra was to take place December 24, and as the ballets were to consist of *Les Sylphides*, *Le Spectre de la Rose*, *Danses Polovetsiennes*, and *Schéhérazade*, all of which had been performed the previous season, we did not need much rehearsal time.

It was exciting to be performing again in Paris where the mood during the Christmas season was so festive. I bought a small Christmas tree and invited several friends to celebrate my twenty-first birthday, on December 27, in my hotel on Rue Richelieu. Among my guests were Ludmila Schollar, Maroussia Piltz, Luba and Nadia Baranovitch, Luba Tchernicheva and her husband, Grigoriev. Vaslav and Sergei Pavlovitch also came to congratulate me.

After two more performances in Paris on December 28 and 31, we went to Germany, where for the month of January we stayed in Berlin. No new ballets were to be mounted here, for Fokine was still in Russia, performing at the Maryinsky. Vaslav decided to take advantage of the time available to the company and begin rehearsals for *L'Après-Midi d'un Faune* with the six nymphs. Diaghilev, not wanting to anger Fokine, had not even announced the official rehearsals of *L'Après-Midi d'un Faune* scheduled for Monte Carlo. These first "unofficial" rehearsals with members of the company took place in Berlin during January 1912.

I was already quite familiar with Vaslav's choreography, having worked with him on his ideas in St. Petersburg in 1910, when we were both still Artists of the Imperial Theatres; and then in Bordighera we had worked on my own part, one of the nymphs, particularly on the sudden encounter between her and the Faune when the startled nymph jumps straight up. The difficulty of this jump was that I had to preserve in the air the same pose as when running across the stage—a bas-relief form, with the knees slightly bent. I had to jump high without any additional preparation, and then on landing I had to make an abrupt half-turn without lifting my heels from the ground, before running away to the wing still maintaining the same bas-relief form.

The participants in *Faune*, as we called the ballet for short, were the Faune, the Nymph, and the six nymphs of her entourage. Ida Rubinstein had agreed with Vaslav and Diaghilev to perform the role of the Nymph, and Vaslav had mounted his ballet with her in mind, the tallest among her nymphs and, more important, taller than he would be as the Faune. In both St. Petersburg and Bordighera, Vaslav had mounted the role on me, and in our rehearsals in Berlin I continued to dance it as the understudy. Vaslav was very pleased with my execution of his choreography, but during the first rehearsals with the six nymphs he was nervous and impatient with the other artists, who did not seem to know what was demanded of them. He demonstrated all the steps and poses with great ease, assuring us it was all very simple and easy; he could not understand why the dancers looked so awkward.

The artists were actually applying themselves, were trying their best. In fact as long as they were standing still, holding the pose as shown them by Vaslav, the group was very effective and approached visually what Vaslav wanted. But as soon as the nymphs had to change their poses and move, to form a new grouping or simply resume walking, they were not able to preserve the bas-relief form, to align their bodies so as to keep their feet, arms, hips, shoulders, and heads in the same choreographic form inspired by archaic Greece.

The dancers complained to me that they would never be able to make their bodies assume such unusual positions, no matter how long they worked.

When Vaslav talked to me he also sounded discouraged. "Bronia, look how they are distorting my choreography."

I tried to encourage him, saying, "Perhaps for these preliminary rehearsals it would be enough for the dancers to learn the steps, and then in time they will acquire a feeling of freedom for the performance of these new positions."

Ida Rubinstein came one day and attended only one rehearsal. She was indignant about Nijinsky's choreography and, after that first rehearsal, announced that she would not perform in *Faune*. Possibly she found the part of the Nymph too difficult for her, but more likely she did not want to spoil her friendship with Fokine, who was also her teacher.

Rubinstein had taken private lessons from Fokine in St. Petersburg, and then during the summers she had gone, one year to Switzerland and the following to Italy, to study further with Fokine. In St. Petersburg, in the fall of 1908, Fokine had mounted "The Dance of the Seven Veils," to music of Glazounov, for Rubinstein's role in Oscar Wilde's *Salomé*, to be performed at the Mikhailovsky Theatre, and he had also introduced her to the Parisian public in *Cléopâtre* and *Schéhérazade*. So one could easily assume that she did not want to offend Fokine by taking part in secret rehearsals for a ballet being choreographed by someone else, by a younger choreographer.*

For the role of the Nymph, Lydia Nelidova was engaged from Moscow. She was a young dancer with an interesting and original appearance, and she had a good dancing background, being the daughter of a former ballerina from the Bolshoi Ballet in Moscow. Vaslav was to find working with her quite easy.

For the two smaller nymphs Vaslav had chosen Olga Khokhlova and myself. The other four nymphs he wanted to be taller, though not as tall as the principal Nymph, and for these he chose Tcherepanova, Maichers-ka, Kopetzinska, and Klementovitch.

Whenever we could find time, usually after the other artists had left the theatre, we rehearsed *Faune* piece by piece, in preliminary rehearsals held behind closed doors. But there was not much time for these rehearsals of *Faune*, for though Fokine was still away the artists had to continue rehearsing the currrent repertoire—*Cléopâtre*, *Les Sylphides*, *Carnaval*, *Schéhérazade*, *Le Pavillon d'Armide*, *Giselle*, *Swan Lake*, and *Danses Polovet-siennes*.

During his rehearsals of *Faune* with us six nymphs, Vaslav seemed under pressure and often lost his temper. He would get particularly angry with Michael Steiman, our pianist. Steiman had studied at the Conservatory of Music in St. Petersburg and was also a protégé of Tcherepnine, but he was not familiar with Debussy's score and could not keep to the indicated tempo, sometimes playing too slowly or other times speeding up the beat. Vaslav would get furious. I remember one occasion when he rushed towards the piano and started to hit the young pianist on the hand, beating out the tempo that he wanted.

---

*Many years later when I was working with Ida Rubinstein, in 1928, I asked her why she had refused to perform in such a wonderful role as the Nymph in the *Faune*. She told me about that rehearsal, the only one she had had with Nijinsky. "In my part there was not a single natural movement, not one single comfortable step on the stage. Everything was topsy-turvy. If the head and feet were turned towards the right, then the body was turned towards the left. Nijinsky wanted the impossible. If I had submitted to his direction I would have dislocated every joint in my body and would have been transformed into a maimed marionette!" (BN)

I recall many years later, in Paris in 1931, this same Michael Steiman was the conductor for the Russian Opera Season.* During the orchestra rehearsals Feodor Chaliapin also often lost his temper, and once I heard him scream at Steiman, "Your tempo is as uneven as are the leaves in a head of cabbage!"

My own artistic popularity had been increasing markedly. In London and then in Berlin, I was warmly applauded and praised for my interpretations. Besides performing in all my regular roles, I was replacing Vera Fokina in the "Bacchanale" in *Cléopâtre*, and I also danced the Odalisque in *Schéhérazade*. In London Fokine had remounted the dance of the three Odalisques so that I could dance it alone, for both Fokina and Schollar were returning to St. Petersburg and would not be dancing with us this season.

From Berlin we all expected to return to St. Petersburg, to dance at the Narodny Dom Theatre, but at the end of January we heard the terrible news that the Narodny Dom had burned down. And so our engagement in St. Petersburg was canceled. In its place Diaghilev quickly arranged for us to perform in Dresden, Vienna, and Budapest, before our return to Monte Carlo.

While we were still in Berlin, Fokine had rejoined us. Mikhail Mikhailovitch was especially shocked by the sudden cancellation of our performances in St. Petersburg, for he had made a commitment to present two new ballets, Schumann's *Papillons* and Balakirev's *Islamé*, and to remount *Carnaval* for a Charity Performance he was organizing for March 10 [N.S. 23] in the Maryinsky. Fokine was to appear as Pierrot in *Carnaval* and as the Negro in *Islamé*. Now Diaghilev was expecting him to begin mounting three new ballets for the Paris Season—Reynaldo Hahn's *Le Dieu Bleu*, Mily Balakirev's *Thamar*, and Maurice Ravel's *Daphnis et Chloë*.

The cancellation of our Russian Season also created problems among those artists who had expected to be able to dance with our company while fulfilling their Imperial Theatre obligations. Karsavina, according to her Imperial Theatres contract, had to dance at the Maryinsky during February and March, and so she would not be able to dance with us for all our new engagements in Europe. This in turn affected Fokine in his rehearsals for the new ballets he was mounting for the Paris Season, especially *Le Dieu Bleu*. In Berlin, with Karsavina due to return to the Maryinsky in February, Fokine had to first mount her role, the Young Girl, and also her dances with Max Frohman in the role of the Youth.

---

*Nijinska was the choreographer for this Russian Opera and Ballet Season with Chaliapin. (IN/JR)

Then later in Vienna he worked with Vaslav on the title role. It was not until Budapest that he choreographed the dances for the ensemble and mounted for me my dance of the Bayadère Enivrée.

Even before our Russian engagement was cancelled, Diaghilev had known that Karsavina would not be with us for the beginning of our Monte Carlo Season and had asked me to learn her role in *Petrouchka*, the Ballerina Doll. I began working on it in Berlin, rehearsing whenever I could, often with Alexander Kotchetovsky, an Imperial Artist from Moscow who had been with the Diaghilev Ballet since the spring of 1911 in Monte Carlo. He had been given the role of the Moor.

During the fall season in London I had come to know Kotchetovsky quite well. I had been staying in the same hotel with my friends Luba Baranovitch and her twin sister Nadia and several other colleagues from the Imperial Theatres, including Arkadi Sergeyev and Alexander Orlov. We explored the city together on our free days, and between rehearsals we would often have lunch together and were frequently joined by Kotchetovsky.

Orlov and Kotchetovsky were childhood friends from the time they had studied in dance and drama classes together in Moscow, where Alexander Alexandrovitch Orlov was called Shura and Alexander Vladimirovitch Kotchetovsky was called Sasha. Kotchetovsky had graduated from Moscow in 1907, while Orlov had transferred to St. Petersburg and graduated like me in 1908.

In London, Orlov told me that he had decided not to sign a contract with Diaghilev for 1912 but was returning to the Imperial Theatres, to the Maryinsky, and that Kotchetovsky would be replacing him in many of his roles in the Diaghilev Company. Having been my partner in several ballets, Orlov began asking me to stay after rehearsals to work with Kotchetovsky, to practice the character numbers that we would be dancing together. Often on these occasions, Orlov would himself stay to teach Kotchetovsky his role of the Moor in *Petrouchka*. They were both excellent character dancers and were very funny and amusing in the role—that of a burly fellow, childishly vain of his physical strength and his imposing uniform. Sasha, as I was beginning to call him, would make me laugh, rolling his eyes and smacking his lips with gusto as he put me on his lap, pretending I was the Ballerina Doll.

I spent quite a lot of time in Berlin with Sasha, as we began working together officially on the dances of the Ballerina Doll and the Moor in *Petrouchka*. I found myself enjoying his company, even though I did not think I had much in common with this former Imperial Artist of the Bolshoi Ballet. His dance training and his interpretations and artistic values were different from those of the Imperial Artists from St. Petersburg.

In Berlin, in addition to working with Kotchetovsky, I often stayed after rehearsals to work with Sergeyev, my partner in the classical dances. We were all staying in the same hotel, and we often shared a cab to the theatre for rehearsals. There was an air of romance among us, with Arkadi Sergeyev and Luba Baranovitch very much in love. They had announced their engagement in Paris at a New Year's Eve party. Their romantic mood seemed to have infected Sasha, even in our rehearsals.

When I entered the Moor's room, dancing playfully around the room on toe and playing on a toy trumpet, I did not have to pretend to be frightened when the Moor grabs the Ballerina Doll and kisses her arm with such savage fervor, as though about to gobble it up. Sasha used this excuse to hold me very tightly. I did not care for these demonstrations.

On our days off Luba and Arkadi would take a cab around Berlin and visit the museums or go sightseeing. Sasha and I joined them, and I continued to find him an amusing companion. One day Sasha told me that he loved me and had been in love with me since he first saw me in the spring of 1911 in Monte Carlo. "But, Bronia, you were so much taken with Feodor Chaliapin that you never paid any attention to me."

Even so, I was surprised a few days later, as we were waiting for the train in Dresden after our short stay there, when Sasha proposed to me.

. . . Why do I hesitate? I like being with Sasha, I enjoy his attentions . . . he loves me and wants to marry me. But, can it be I am still in love with Feodor, hopeless though I know that love to be?

I told Sasha I needed time.

———

FROM DRESDEN we went to Vienna, where Sasha told me that in spite of Diaghilev's vehement objection to marriages between his artists, Arkadi and Luba were planning to get married secretly in Prague. They were going there immediately after our performances in Vienna, and he suggested that we might also get married at the same time.

Why do I still hesitate? Sasha knows how I feel for Feodor and he still loves me. Perhaps if we were married I would be able to free myself from this "hopeless love" where there is nothing for me, only grief and disappointment. But I still need more time.

During our last performance in Vienna, Vaslav complained that he did not feel well, although he danced that night as brilliantly as ever. The next morning Diaghilev called me to say he had to leave for Budapest and to ask me to stay in Vienna at the hotel across the square from the Hofoper with Vaslav, who had a slight temperature that morning and could not travel. So while Sasha accompanied Nadia Baranovitch to Prague to attend her sister Luba's secret wedding to Arkadi Sergeyev, I stayed in Vienna with Vaslav.

The following day Vaslav was feeling quite recovered but was kept in bed by Vassili, who looked after him better than any nurse. There were three more days before we had to be in Budapest for the start of our performances, so Vaslav and I stayed on in Vienna, where we enjoyed a pleasant rest. We were often amused by Drubetsky, Diaghilev's new secretary, who was Polish and did not speak much Russian. We had to laugh whenever he called Diaghilev in Budapest and tried to speak to him in Russian. His Polish accent would so distort the meaning that Diaghilev would hang up in desperation, not having understood a word his secretary had said.

I was looking forward to Budapest, where I was to dance Ta-Hor, Karsavina's role, in *Cléopâtre*, but I was also sorry as this meant that I would no longer be dancing the "Bacchanale" in *Cléopâtre*, the part originally created by Fokina in 1909. But the role of Ta-Hor was very challenging and absorbing. I worked out all the details with great care. Karsavina danced the role on toe, but I would dance it in my bare feet.

I also gave a lot of thought to the makeup. I wanted to find a new makeup, not only for the face but also for the body. Karsavina danced the role wearing brown tights to imitate the dark skin of an Egyptian. I wanted to remove the tights and make up the whole body in a dark ocher color. While in Berlin I had visited the Leichner Theatrical Makeup and Hairdressing Shop and had found an unusual liquid makeup, flat and lusterless. It was not greasy, was easy to apply, and it gave the body an unusually theatrical and beautiful appearance.

Knowing that Sergei Pavlovitch did not allow changes in ballets once they had been created, I was afraid and hesitant when I went to ask his permission to wear makeup on my body instead of the tights, and to let me dance the role in bare feet. But Sergei Pavlovitch was delighted with my ideas and not only allowed me to go ahead but also congratulated me on the artistic innovations.

My success in the role of Ta-Hor surpassed all my expectations. I was most pleased because Sergei Pavlovitch, Vatsa, and Baron Gunsburg, and all the artists complimented me not only for my dances and for my makeup, but also for a very touching and dramatic interpretation of Ta-Hor, saying that I had created a new image for Ta-Hor, worthy of a great artist.

My makeup was so successful that Sergei Pavlovitch gave the order that the black slaves in *Schéhérazade* and the Egyptians in *Cléopâtre* should no longer wear their colored tights and jersey tops but should make themselves up using the liquid makeup. Ten flat basins were bought for the artists so that after each performance they could wash off their body makeup. The basins were to be transported with us and kept with the props and sets during our tour. The artists did not like having to remove all this makeup after every performance, when they were tired, and blamed me for their inconvenience. They were not really angry, but grumbled in a friendly way.

Sergei Pavlovitch told me that even when Karsavina returned to the company, I would continue to dance Ta-Hor, alternating with Karsavina.

I was ecstatic; there was no limit to my joy.

Diaghilev had invited Mathilda Kshessinska to dance with us in Budapest in *Swan Lake*, *Les Sylphides*, and *Le Spectre de la Rose*. When she joined us she came with her usual court of admirers and balletomanes from St. Petersburg. They were all present for our performances, and many of the balletomanes supported my successes. For each performance I received bouquets and baskets of flowers.

Among my own admirers were the Grand Duke Gavryil Konstantin-ovitch and his young wife, Antonina Rafayilovna (Nesterovskaya). She had always been kind towards me in the Imperial Theatrical School and I gratefully remembered how she had helped me on the day of the Student Performance in 1906. Now she was sincerely happy for my success, calling me her daughter and sending me flowers for each performance. Grand Duke Gavryil often invited Sasha and me to join them for dinner, and even Kshessinska was much more friendly towards me now, and included me in several invitations to her parties.

I had another success in Budapest that was very significant for me, both artistically and personally. When I danced the "Czardas" in Act III of *Swan Lake*, the public gave me an ovation. I was enormously proud of this reception from the Hungarians for my performance of their national dance, and I remembered too how proud Mother had been when she told us, as children, of a similar ovation she and Father had received in the Caucasus for their dancing of the "Lezginka," the national dance of the Caucasus.

My artistic happiness fills my whole being. I am so happy here in Budapest. I know Sasha loves me and I feel I have come to love him too.

I have given my consent. But I want to wait before fixing a date for our marriage.

Most of the company were going straight from Budapest to Monte Carlo, even though our rehearsals there were not to start for another week, with Fokine away in St. Petersburg to present his Charity Performance at the Maryinsky. Whenever Mother was away, Vaslav took it upon himself to look after me, and as most of my friends from the Imperial Theatres were returning with Fokine to St. Petersburg, Vaslav did not want me to go to Monte Carlo on my own. He was also worried because I was looking pale and thin. He told me that he, Igor Stravinsky, and Diaghilev were going to Venice where they might be joined by Roerich, who was collaborating with Stravinsky on the libretto for the new ballet, *Le Sacre du Printemps*, and he suggested that I go with them.

I wanted to go to Venice. I needed to be alone, away from Sasha for a while, and I also did not want to be in Monte Carlo during the Opera Season with Chaliapin. I was not yet ready to meet Feodor casually, or to tell him of my engagement to Sasha, but neither did I want to stay with Vaslav and Diaghilev at the Lido. Both Vaslav and Sergei Pavlovitch disapproved of my decision to marry Sasha.

Vaslav would not hear of my staying on my own in a hotel, but he agreed when I told him that I would be in Venice with Nadia Baranovitch. Nadia had never been to Italy and wanted to see Venice, being on her own now that her sister, Luba, was returning to St. Petersburg with her husband, Sergeyev.

After only three days, I left Venice to rejoin the company in Monte Carlo. I had to admit to myself that I missed Sasha.

45   From My Notes and Diaries

Just a short while ago everything appeared so clear. I knew I should never love Sasha as I once loved Feodor . . . my love for Sasha is different . . . but Sasha loves me as I loved Feodor. . . . I have given my consent to marry Sasha. . . . I am his fiancée.

But what shall I do now? . . . What terrible mistake have I made? . . . I must tell Sasha about my meeting today with Feodor.

I should have walked away right after our unexpected meeting. I had no right to remain with Feodor. It was wrong on my part. Vatsa was with me, it is true, and it was he who accepted Chaliapin's invitation to go to the Hotel de Paris for tea.

But how happy I was to see Feodor!

I forgot about everything else . . . and during tea I should not have promised Feodor that I would meet him later this evening in the Baccarat Room at the Casino.

How strangely it all happened. This time Vaslav did not "protect" me. He did not stop me, when . . . how unlike me it was! Why did I so obediently take the gold coin from Feodor as a token, as an assurance that I would meet him this evening in the Casino?

Again Vaslav, usually so stern with me, did not say a word and did not object. He even seemed to approve when I gave Feodor my small camera because Feodor admired it.

I was not conscious of all that was being said, only of the great happiness that once again filled my heart . . .

In the evening, at the time that I had promised Chaliapin I would be in the Casino, I met Sasha in the Casino park, on the terrace overlooking the sea. I told Sasha about the meeting and I should have told him then the full truth, that I love Feodor as much as before. When I saw him today, it all came back; I love Feodor and shall love him forever.

But all I said was, "Sasha, we must part. It was all a mistake. I shall never love you as I once loved Chaliapin."

I felt sorry for Sasha. I could not tell him how my heart yearned for Feodor, that I wanted only to see Feodor, that all I wanted at that moment was to walk towards the Casino where Feodor was waiting for me. But instead I said, "Sasha, please leave me now. . . . Perhaps in time I shall forget Feodor."

"Bronia, believe me, you do not love Feodor, you cannot yet understand what love is all about. You have already told me about your love for Feodor. I did not believe you then and I do not believe you now. There was nothing between you. It was a childish infatuation! Besides, Chaliapin is a married man."

"Please understand me, Sasha, I expect nothing from Feodor. I am well aware how hopeless are my feelings. I will do everything to forget him. But how can I be your wife if I believe that I love another?"

"You do love me. I know that better than you do yourself. You told me that you felt lonely without me in Venice. You missed me, and after only three days there you left to rejoin me in Monte Carlo. And we have already told your mother that we are in love."

I had to admit to myself that I had indeed missed Sasha in Venice. Then I had rejoiced at what I thought was a sure sign of my deliverance from my first love. I had welcomed what I thought was a new beginning for me. I wanted with all my heart to believe that I was in love with Sasha, to believe in my new love and make it secure in marriage. I had promised Sasha that we would be married in Paris. Though I knew that Mother would object, I had told Sasha that we would marry, with or without her approval.

I could not tell Sasha that today the truth had been revealed to my heart, that I had mistaken feelings of loneliness for deeper emotions . . .

I am not so much bothered by the fact that I am engaged to a man I feel I cannot marry, even though I care for him deeply, but rather that my heart is grief-stricken, because my love for Feodor can never be the same again. I suffer because I can no longer look into Feodor's eyes as I did before and say to him "I love you." Someone else has kissed my lips. I have lost something that was so precious to me. I have deceived myself, and my grief is of my own making.

To Sasha, though, I could say only, "Perhaps you are right and I am infatuated with an image, and it is all as you say—I am impressed by a celebrity who also happens to be tall and handsome. For my part, I am well aware how hopeless is my love for Feodor and I shall try to forget him. Meanwhile I cannot be your wife believing as I do, that I am still in love with another man."

We were sitting in the dark corner of the park, behind the large aviary, where the Egyptian pigeons were calling softly to each other.

"Bronia, you promised to be mine. I cannot live without you. Do not torment me any longer. I have not known any other woman. I have always been waiting for a true love. For me you are the only one, forever."

His words touched me and drew me closer to him.

"Bronia, for almost a year you have known how I feel about you. How much I love you. If you do not want to marry me then I cannot remain here in Diaghilev's Ballet Company. Where shall I go? I cannot return to the Bolshoi Ballet in Moscow. Where shall I work then? Nowhere else is there real art. Without you, without friends, alone, I could not bear it. I will be lost."

I am tormented. I cannot be so cruel. I, too, have no other place to go. Here, in the Diaghilev Ballet Company, is my whole life. There is no place else for me to work. I cannot force Sasha to leave when he does not want to of his own accord.

We were both weeping now.

"Sasha, do not cry, I am very attached to you as to a friend . . . and maybe in time I shall love you. But you must be patient. If you wish we can get married as I promised, but please wait a little . . . do not hurry me with the marriage."

"In Paris, Bronia. You promised we would get married in Paris."

"No, not in Paris. I promise we shall get married in London . . . three months from now. . . . Sasha, stop crying, wipe your tears, we have to walk back through brightly lit streets."

We walked along the terrace above the seashore and Sasha took Chaliapin's gold coin that I was holding in my hand and tossed it far into the sea.

To myself I made an oath: never again would I walk across the Place de Casino in Monte Carlo, where I would be constantly reminded of Feodor.

46   Monte Carlo: Spring 1912

DIAGHILEV WAS infuriated when he discovered that Fokine had been mounting two new ballets in secret rehearsals in Vienna and Budapest —Schumann's *Papillons* and Balakirev's *Islamé*—working with our artists, not for the Monte Carlo and Paris Seasons, but preparing for a Charity Performance at the Maryinsky.

Fokine had been arranging such Charity Performances regularly since 1906. These were becoming very successful and were attended by wealthy patrons willing to pay more than a thousand rubles for a loge in the theatre. Last December, in St. Petersburg, he had arranged to present a Charity Performance with many of our artists, to follow our performances in the Narodny Dom Theatre. When it was learned that the Ballets Russes performances in St. Petersburg had been canceled after the Narodny Dom fire, all the tickets for Fokine's Charity Performance at the Maryinsky were quickly sold out. So instead of coming with the company to Monte Carlo after Budapest, Fokine and several artists had returned to St. Petersburg for the performance at the Maryinsky on March 10 [N.S. 23], only joining us in Monte Carlo ten days before our opening night.

Naturally Diaghilev was extremely concerned over the delay this meant for the beginning of our rehearsals in Monte Carlo, especially since Fokine had not yet finished mounting Hahn's *Le Dieu Bleu*, with still two other ballets, *Thamar* and *Daphnis et Chloë* to be choreographed for the Ballet Russe Season at the Châtelet in Paris.

Karsavina would not be joining us from St. Petersburg until the middle of the Monte Carlo Season, so Diaghilev invited Lydia Kyaksht to dance *Carnaval*, *Le Spectre de la Rose*, and *L'Oiseau de Feu*.

Stravinsky's *L'Oiseau de Feu*, with Bolm and Kyaksht, had been scheduled for our opening night in Monte Carlo, April 8, and Stravinsky's *Petrouchka*, with Nijinsky, Nijinska, and Kotchetovsky, for April 18. Both ballets were being performed for the first time in Monte Carlo. *Petrouchka* had not been given by the company since the premiere performances in Paris in 1911, and *L'Oiseau de Feu* had been absent from our repertoire since its first performances two years before in the Ballet Russe Season of 1910.

In that 1910 season in Paris, Maria Piltz and I had taken it upon ourselves to learn all the dances in *L'Oiseau de Feu*, she for the girls and I for the boys. We wanted to preserve Fokine's choreography, at least in our own memories, for it seemed to us that though many of Fokine's ballets were already included in the repertoire of the Imperial Ballet, it was highly unlikely that a production of Igor Stravinsky's *L'Oiseau de Feu* would ever be permitted in Russia, since the libretto included the "Legend of Kostchei" that had been used by Rimsky-Korsakov for his opera *Kostchei the Immortal*, banned in Russia since 1905. It had been an act of defiance on the part of Stravinsky, a former student of Rimsky-Korsakov, to include this legend in the Russian fairy tales he used for the libretto.

When we began our rehearsals of *L'Oiseau de Feu* in Monte Carlo we found that few of the artists from the 1910 season were still dancing with us. And Fokine himself had difficulties remembering his own choreography.

Mikhail Mikhailovitch was very pleased when I told him that I could teach all the dances to the boys, and he was amazed when I danced for him the complicated character dances of the Boleboshki. Maroussia was able to remember the dances of the princesses, so she and I proved quite helpful to Fokine in this revival of his ballet.

But *L'Oiseau de Feu* was not presented for our opening performance in Monte Carlo. The rehearsals with Lydia Kyaksht, who was not familiar with Stravinsky's music, took longer than had been anticipated, and since most of the ballet had to be taught to nearly the entire company, it was decided to postpone the performance.

Vaslav and I knew that Mother was planning to join us in Monte Carlo and had arranged for her to travel from St. Petersburg on the same train as some of the artists in our company. I went early in the morning to meet her at the station, accompanied by Nadia Baranovitch, who was meeting her sister, Luba. When we found Luba, she told me that Mother was not on the train. "Bronia, I have a message from your mother. Eleonora Nicolaevna asked me to tell you that she has been unexpectedly detained in St. Petersburg and that she will be arriving in Monte Carlo in early April."

I was worried and puzzled. Why had Mother postponed her trip? Why had she not given Luba an explanation for her sudden change of plans? Luba tried to reassure me, "I saw your mother only a couple of days ago and she was in good health. She wanted to hear all about our performances and was very happy when I told her about the great success you have had in your new role of Ta-Hor. Bronia, your mother will be here soon. She told me that she did not want to miss your performance as Ta-Hor in *Cléopâtre*, and she wants to be in the theatre when you dance the Doll in *Petrouchka*."

Later, after class with Maestro Cecchetti, I joined Vaslav for lunch, which we had expected to have with Mother. Vaslav too could not understand why Mother had delayed her trip. "In all her letters she always says how much she misses us. I have not seen Mother since last summer when I saw the two of you off on the train for St. Petersburg. And you have not seen her since you left St. Petersburg in October to come to London. We have never before been separated from Mother for so long. She was only staying in St. Petersburg to remain in touch with the attorney who is taking care of my status with the military authorities so that I can return to Russia."

"Perhaps, Vatsa, there are new developments and Mother was advised by the attorney to stay in St. Petersburg. That would also explain why she was secretive and did not tell Luba the reason for her delaying her departure."

Mother arrived in Monte Carlo a few days later. She explained, "Your father was in St. Petersburg and called me on the telephone saying that he had to talk to me. It sounded urgent. When he came to see me he asked me to forgive him, saying that he had never stopped loving me and that he wanted a reconciliation. I told Thomas that it was he who had chosen to leave home, to abandon his wife and children. I forgave him but said that it was now too late . . ."

But I knew Mother still loved Father, and I was glad that she had seen him again. Mother told me that Father had accompanied her to Ligovo to see Stassik. She said that Stassik had apparently failed to recognize his father, whom he had not seen for many years. "I believe Stassik was disturbed and perhaps even frightened by Father's visit. Stassik let me kiss him but he jerked away from Thomas. Poor Stassik, he backed away to the farthest corner of the room and stood there facing the wall. When Thomas reached towards him and asked him to look at him, Stassik turned around abruptly and pushed his father away. Stassik was trembling and looked frightened. I had to ask Thomas to leave the room. Alone with me Stassik calmed down and eventually even smiled."

Mother visited Stassik regularly when she was in St. Petersburg—once or twice a month, weather permitting. Her hearing had deteriorated, and she now missed much of what Stassik was saying. She said he would mutter in a barely audible voice, usually just a few words that she thought were Polish.

I had last seen Stassik in September 1911 when I was in St. Petersburg. That day he did not talk at all, but I knew he recognized me and was happy to see me. The doctor told me that Stassik's mental state was unchanged but that he was now seldom talking and that when he did speak it was quite incoherent. I believe also that Stassik did not always understand what was being said to him, for he had never really understood Russian, with all of us speaking only Polish at home.

Mother told me that Father had been interested in hearing all about me and Vaslav. "I showed Father all your recent photographs and the magazine and newspaper clippings that you and Vaslav sent me," and then she added, "I also showed your father the letter you wrote with Sasha from Budapest telling me of your plans to marry." It was the first time Mother had mentioned Sasha or our engagement. "Father was not happy to hear that you wanted to get married, and I told him that I would never give Bronia my permission to marry a dancer."

For the next few days Mother tried to dissuade me from marrying Sasha, saying that marriage between artists would only produce the sort of unhappiness that she had suffered with Father. I reminded Mother that I was now twenty-one and did not need her permission to get married, and I insisted that Sasha and I were going to get married in London.

We had now begun to rehearse Fokine's second new ballet, *Thamar*. I was fascinated by Balakirev's music in this ballet. In Vienna and Budapest I had already heard passages from his "Islamé," which our pianist Steiman had often practiced on his own after our rehearsals. Steiman had told me that Balakirev's "Islamé" was one of the most difficult and complicated pieces ever written for the piano; it had been the favorite piece of Franz Liszt, who often gave it as an assignment to his pupils.

The libretto for the ballet *Thamar* had been written by Bakst, and the story was set in the Caucasus. Vera Fokina had now joined her husband in Monte Carlo, and at one of our rehearsals for *Thamar* Vera and Mikhail Mikhailovitch demonstrated to us some of the dances from the Caucasus. They had spent a summer holiday near Tiflis, where they had studied Georgian and Circassian dances from the native people.

Nikolai Kremnev was my regular partner for character dances and in *Thamar* we were the leading couple in the "Lezginka," performed with its traditional steps. Watching the men dance, I could virtually see Father before my eyes, the way he had danced the *lezginka* for Vaslav and me in the Boys' Hall in the School when he visited us for the last time in 1906. I remembered how Father had found a pair of boots in the dressing room and borrowed them for his dance. He had amazed us by the virtuosity of his technique and his mastery of the incredibly difficult steps.

For the season in Monte Carlo there was a great gathering of the fashionable public. Kshessinska had arrived with her entourage and was to dance in *Swan Lake* and *Les Sylphides*. She continued to be friendly towards me and did not seem to mind that I was dancing the Mazurka in *Les Sylphides*.

Our repertoire for this season included *Cléopâtre*, in which I was again Ta-Hor, dancing with Bolm. The performance of *Cléopâtre* was a great success with the Monte Carlo audience. The next day, Sergei Pavlovitch told me that the Russian painter Konstantin Somov had been in the Theatre and had seen me as Ta-Hor. "He was deeply moved by your performance. Somov seldom comes to see a ballet, and I know that he does not care to paint for the theatre, not even for me, though we have been friends for years. But Bronia," Diaghilev smiled, "I am happy to tell you that Somov found you to be a great artist."

I was so happy at Diaghilev's words. What more could I wish for myself? Somov was not only a great artist but also one of Russia's most refined and cultured painters. It was so good to know that what I had been striving for in my work evoked a response from such an artist. That knowledge was dearer to me than all the applause from the audience and all the bouquets or baskets of flowers.

The only shadow over an otherwise exciting and happy Monte Carlo season was Fokine's sudden change of attitude towards me. It hurt me very deeply when he chose not to use me in his new ballet, *Daphnis et Chloë*. It was a ballet with many scenes, and of the entire ballet company only I was not taking part in it.

I could not understand it. Fokine had been one of my first teachers in the Imperial School; for three years I had been his student, and always he had been well disposed towards me. I remembered how impressed he had been during the 1910–11 season in St. Petersburg when, on the very evening of a performance at the Conservatory of Music, Rosai had called in a few hours before curtain time to say he could not go on that evening and I had offered to replace him in the dance, "Kozachek" [the little Cossack]. I had worn the costume that Bakst had designed for Rosai, for we were about the same height, and had danced all the difficult steps of the *trepak* with great success. After that Fokine was often heard to say, "Bronislava Fominitchna will try anything. If I ask her to stand on her head she will do it."

But what hurt most about Fokine's rejection was that in the Imperial School, and later as an Artist of the Imperial Theatres, I had been one of a small group devoted to Fokine and his new choreographic ideas. Furthermore, I had given up my career in the Imperial Theatres for the opportunity to dance in Fokine's ballets as a Diaghilev Artist, in spite of my mother's deep disappointment.

Although I was not called for the rehearsals of *Daphnis et Chloë*, I was dancing in Fokine's other two new ballets, *Thamar* and *Le Dieu Bleu*, and was also taking part in Fokine's rehearsals of the various ballets in the current repertoire. These rehearsals with Fokine had become strained and tense. He was angry with Diaghilev for having decided that *Daphnis et Chloë* would not be performed until the end of the Paris Season, and then suggested that it might even be postponed for another year. Angry outbursts against Diaghilev could often be heard from Fokine, and soon the discord between the two men had bred rumors that Fokine was about to leave the Ballets Russes.

My main personal concern in Monte Carlo, however, was my preparation for the role of the Ballerina Doll in *Petrouchka*. Fokine was too busy with all the other rehearsals to work on the role with me, and so Vaslav, Sasha, and I rehearsed together on our own.

47   The Ballerina Doll
in *Petrouchka*

DIAGHILEV HAD entrusted me with Karsavina's role in *Petrouchka*, the Ballerina Doll, and I recognized the great responsibility this placed on me, with its opportunity to show all my creative and dancing qualities. I realized that I would have to work hard and carefully on the role.

I was not concerned with trying to do better than Karsavina, for there was no point in trying to compete with her. Karsavina had created this role and was much admired by everyone. Most of all, though, she was a ballerina of the Imperial Theatres and the *prima ballerina* of the Diaghilev Ballet. She was a renowned artist throughout Europe, and I was a novice, just a beginner.

Besides, we were so different physically. Karsavina was a brunette with beautiful, expressive dark eyes. I was blonde with slightly slanted, green-blue eyes. Karsavina was very feminine, whereas my build was boyish. I had a high elevation, and Vaslav defined my natural tempo as *prestissimo* or *adagio largo*, while he defined Karsavina as *andante lento* or *allegro moderato*.

In other words, we were completely different, and it would be virtually impossible for me to duplicate Karsavina in the role. But already I had some notion of a different image for the Ballerina Doll.

Ever since Diaghilev had told me that the role was mine, I had been pondering in my mind how to re-create it. I had to formulate from within myself a different conception of the role, to use the individual qualities of my own dance technique within the choreographic composition of the ballet. But I was bothered by the image of the Ballerina Doll already created by Karsavina. Even as I tried to forget her, I was still seeing Karsavina, so femininely pretty in her doll makeup, her deep décolletage, her long pantaloons under her crinoline skirt, and the cute hat posed charmingly on her curly locks.

In the first tableau, in the Showman's booth at the Fair, Karsavina's dances were doll-like, both with Petrouchka and the Moor. But in the two subsequent scenes, in Petrouchka's room and then in the Moor's room, Karsavina abandoned her limited doll-movements; she came to life and was no longer a doll.

Perhaps this was also how Fokine saw the role. The doll in these two scenes was a classical ballet ballerina, not to be limited and restrained by doll-like movements. Karsavina's Doll was gracefully attractive with soft movements, all the attributes of a traditional ballet technique to be expected from a classical ballerina.

But what was so admirable in Karsavina would be missing in my performance. I was trying to free myself from this image of a ballerina in Karsavina's Doll. She reminded me of a French porcelain doll, very pretty and graceful. Her Doll, to my mind, would be foreign to the Russian crowd gathered on a square to see a Petrouchka Puppet Show. In my portrayal of the Doll I wanted to approach an image that would be closer to the understanding of an ordinary Russian crowd.

First of all, though, I wondered why a doll in a show booth should be called Ballerina Doll. According to an old tradition in ballet companies, the title "ballerina" is one of the highest ranks attained by an artist, usually after many years of great achievement in the ballet. But this term is known in this way only to professional dancers and followers of ballet. Among the more general public "ballerina" is not understood as a distinguishing title for an artist. For them, no matter how well or badly a dancer dances, as long as she wears a tutu and dances on toe she is a ballerina.

I'm sure that it was in this everyday use of the word *ballerina* that the name Ballerina Doll was used in *Petrouchka*, and so I was able to see her as an amusing character understandable to Russian fair-goers. She had to be equally appealing to everyone in the crowd. Karsavina's Ballerina Doll was more for an adult and sophisticated audience. My Ballerina Doll would be recognized by children and adults alike, by the ordinary crowd that gathers in the square when a fair is in town.

I saw the soul of the Doll as being uncomplicated, drawn to anything simple and straightforward; such was her romance with the Moor. She was not cunning, a *mechante coquette*. She was primitive, frivolous, and empty. The Moor was pompously dressed; he was amusing. Petrouchka, on the other hand, frightened her with his amorous sufferings. He was never happy; he grieved over something all the time. He looked neglected and poor. Petrouchka was too complicated for her.

I now saw very clearly what kind of doll my Ballerina would be. She would be far removed from the concept of the graceful, brilliant *prima ballerina*.

My Doll would be a handcrafted doll. The legs, in a turned-out ballet position, should appear to be sewn to the body of the doll—the whole body held tense and stretched, the feet arched *sur pointe*, lightly and sharply touching the floor.

Watching Karsavina and Nijinsky in *Petrouchka*, I had seen two dolls fabricated by two different doll-makers. My Ballerina would be a doll from the same workshop as Petrouchka, from the hands of the same craftsman. Like Petrouchka-Nijinsky, I would hold my fingers together like two small wooden paddles. The makeup would be very simple—two round red spots on the cheeks, the brows highly arched, and the eyes in a fixed stare with the lashes painted on the face. The hair would still be in curls but it would be stiff-looking and not so prettily arranged. The small hat would sit carelessly on the head, as if put on in a hurry, with its tassel dangling absurdly. Although one should be able to see that the Showman takes better care of this doll than of Petrouchka, and that she is dressed with greater care—in silken pantaloons and a crinoline skirt—still, her costume should be amusing and hang loosely on my body, as on a puppet.

I would have liked to shorten the crinoline and to have worn a high-necked jacket instead of the open décolletage, but I could not change the design of the costume without asking Alexandre Benois. Since his trouble with Bakst and Diaghilev in Paris last year, he had left our company and I had not seen him since. So I would dance in the costume as he had designed it for Karsavina. We were about the same size though she appeared taller than I, since her legs were somewhat longer than mine.*

All the time I was dancing I had to remember that the Doll had no musculature in her body. It was necessary for me to conceal all effort, to dance as if there were not a single muscle in this doll-like body, with its movements limited to the joints. A doll does not breathe, and so I had to conceal my breathing, to dance holding my breath. Despite this constraint, I had to deploy the brilliancy of the dance technique.

From time to time I wanted to strike an absurd pose, an unnatural balance of the human body, and such a pose had to be both amusing and appropriate for a doll. The Doll also had to maintain fixed, immobile expressions on her face, changing abruptly to fear or surprise or amusement for as long as the action in the scene demanded.

*When Bronislava Nijinska mounted her own version of *Petrouchka* in Paris in 1931, Benois designed a new costume for her Ballerina Doll (see Illustration 128), as she had wanted. (IN/JR)

It was my understanding of the role of the Ballerina that for the whole of the ballet she lives in the body of a doll, and not for a moment does she leave that state, not even when she dances and acts in Petrouchka's or the Moor's room, where the dolls live their private lives and where the drama of their loves takes place. Like Petrouchka, the Ballerina's soul is enclosed in a doll, and she remains a doll even when reacting to very human feelings.

—

MY FIRST performance in the role of the Ballerina Doll in *Petrouchka* took place on April 18, 1912, in Monte Carlo.

After the performance, Igor Stravinsky told me that he agreed completely with my interpretation of the role and that he wished that I would always dance it.* Just then we were joined by Diaghilev. Sergei Pavlovitch praised me highly and said that he had decided that even when Karsavina was back in the company I should continue to dance the Ballerina, alternating with her in the performances. "You are completely different from Karsavina in this role. In your interpretation, both the role and your dances are very individual. It will be interesting for the public to see what Karsavina has created and also what you have created."

Later that month Karsavina returned to Monte Carlo and danced in a performance of *Petrouchka*, and then on April 30, I shared the program with Kshessinska and Karsavina. That evening Karsavina only danced *Le Spectre de la Rose* with Vaslav. In *Les Sylphides* Kshessinska danced with Vaslav and myself, and then finally in *Petrouchka* I danced the Ballerina.

Vatsa liked my portrayal in *Petrouchka* of a handcrafted doll-puppet, and found me to be a very Russian doll. He said that I gave an excellent performance and that he preferred my interpretation to that of Karsavina.

Fokine, however, did not.

He was, I was told, standing in the wings during my performances in *Petrouchka* and protested all the time against everything I had created in the role. He said loudly that he had never mounted what Nijinska was doing on the stage and that Karsavina danced and interpreted the Ballerina just as he, Fokine, saw the role and had mounted it. Which was to say that when the Ballerina was in either Petrouchka's or the Moor's room, she should abandon the image of a doll and become a woman, graceful and coquettish.

*In an interview with the *St. Petersburg Gazette* (October 1912), Stravinsky also expressed his admiration for Bronislava Nijinska as a dancer, declaring she was "extremely talented, a fascinating ballerina, fully the equal of her brother, and when she and her brother dance together, all others pale by comparison." (IN/JR)

I do not believe that Fokine was reacting only to my interpretation of the Ballerina. I had danced exactly what had been mounted by Fokine and had strictly adhered, as I always did, to his choreographic score. But ever since it had become known that Nijinsky was mounting *L'Après-Midi d'un Faune* for the Paris Season, Fokine had changed in his attitude towards Vaslav, and this was now reflected in his attitude towards me, Nijinsky's sister. I am sure it was this that prevented him from seeing my Ballerina as validly different from that of Karsavina, like different interpretations of the same piece of music when played by two different pianists.

48   Rehearsals of
L'Après-Midi d'un Faune
in Monte Carlo

VASLAV BEGAN his official rehearsals for *Faune* in Monte Carlo at the same time Fokine was rehearsing *Daphnis et Chloë*. The *Faune* rehearsals were usually held immediately before or after Fokine's rehearsals, and they never lasted longer than an hour. More often than not, that was all the time Vaslav was given. In spite of this, towards the end of April 1912, Nijinsky had finished his *Faune*. The preparation had taken ninety rehearsals—which may seem a lot for a ten-minute ballet. Yet the number of rehearsals was not excessive if one takes into account the ballet's completely new technique of presentation, and if one also remembers the marvelous level of execution finally achieved by the artists.

It was the first time that a ballet had been mounted and rehearsed in the same way that a musical score is performed by an orchestra. In this new technique Nijinsky truly demonstrated his choreographic genius: he conducted his ballet, seeing each choreographic detail in the same way that the conductor of an orchestra hears each note in a musical score.

Up to then the ballet artist had been free to project his own individuality as he felt; he was even expected to embellish it according to his own taste, possibly neglecting the exactness of the choreographic execution. The artists simply had to comply with the following rules: keep a line straight or a circle round; preserve the groupings; execute the basic *pas*.

Nijinsky was the first to demand that his whole choreographic material should be executed not only exactly as he saw it but also according to his artistic interpretation. Never was a ballet performed with such musical and choreographic exactness as *L'Après-Midi d'un Faune*. Each position of the dance, each position of the body down to the gesture of each finger, was mounted according to a strict choreographic plan. One must remember that the majority of dancers in this ballet could not understand

Vaslav's composition. They did not like the choreography at all. They felt they were restricted and would often complain, saying such things as "What kind of ballet is this? . . . There is not a single dancing *pas*—not a single free movement—not a single solo—no dances at all. . . . We feel as though we are carved out of stone."

So it is even more amazing that Nijinsky achieved the results he did.

Company members not dancing in the ballet often peeped into the rehearsal hall to watch Vaslav and his "seven collaborators." They were amazed and could understand nothing. Their own ignorance of Nijinsky's work—new in ideas, form, and technique—meant that for them Nijinsky had embarked on a futile task. They predicted certain failure. It was the first time in our company that I had ever heard such condemnation in advance of a new work.

There were other factors contributing to the unhealthy atmosphere. At that time few of the artists regarded the art of Fokine as the pinnacle of innovative achievement in ballet; the majority were still devoted to the Italian School and even considered the official classical Petipa school as an innovation. But, now suddenly, still a newer "window" towards the unknown: the revolutionary choreography by a young artist, Nijinsky. The ardent supporters of Fokine in the company saw this new ballet as a provocation, a challenge to their "master." They would say, "Nijinsky is a wonderful artist and dancer . . . but why is he trying to steal the laurels from our genius of a choreographer? Let Nijinsky dance and let Fokine choreograph."

One day when Vatsa stopped by the hotel where Mother and I were staying, as he often did, he looked very upset and tired.

"Bronia, I can trust you. Please tell me frankly, what do you think of my ballet?"

"Vatsa, if you have any doubts about *Faune* it is because you cannot see the quality of your own work. Don't listen to the others, and don't give up what you have created."

"Don't worry, Bronia. I have no doubts of the merits of my ballet. I know that I have created *L'Après-Midi d'un Faune* exactly as I see it . . . so correct in all its details that I cannot add or cut a thing."

Vaslav was very agitated as he was speaking, and I had the feeling that he was not telling me all.

After a moment of silence, he asked, "Do you think the public will understand *Faune*?"

"Paris will understand, Vatsa, of that you can be sure. But as for our dancers, naturally it is difficult for them to grasp it . . . they have seen so little as yet, they have so much more to learn about Art. Your work is too new for them, they still have to let go of the old school, part of their life in the ballet, and reject their traditional ballet in order to understand your work.

"Besides," I went on, "it is also difficult for them. The transition from Petipa to Fokine was already too much for them; many do not even accept Fokine yet, refusing to recognize him as a choreographer, and you expect them to be sympathetic to your aims and ideas?"

Vatsa interrupted me indignantly, "I can accept that the artists are not ready to comprehend my work . . . but not Sergei Pavlovitch! Only think, he dared to tell me today that I must change the whole ballet. . . . Even if in truth the ballet is all wrong . . . it is my work and I will not change my choreography. . . . I believe in my ballet and I am responsible for it!"

It was painful for me to see how hurt he was, even though he was trying to conceal his feelings, and how hard he was taking this difference of opinion with Diaghilev. I knew how important, how dear to him was the approval and recognition of Sergei Pavlovitch, and now for him to see Diaghilev, who had first suggested the ballet *Faune*, rejecting it and not recognizing its value . . .

Angrily Vaslav continued, "In fact, during all the time that *Faune* was being rehearsed Diaghilev liked everything. He admired every detail and the whole composition. But now that the ballet is finished, only a few days before our departure for Paris and the premiere, Sergei Pavlovitch says that everything must be changed. . . . Everything from start to finish!"

When I heard that, I began to understand, and I too was very upset.

But however I tried, I was not able to calm Vaslav. He went on, "I will leave everything and quit the Ballets Russes. Tomorrow I will go away. But I will not change my ballet!"

"Vatsa, no one can force you to change your *Faune*, so why are you in such a rage? Don't lose your temper."

In the moments between his angry outbursts I tried to make Vaslav listen to me. "I do not think you are fair to Diaghilev. You must understand that Sergei Pavlovitch cares very much and takes to heart your first choreographic work. Naturally he is nervous and listens to people around him. If he has been carried away by a negative atmosphere it is only because he worries for you. You must understand that."

"No!" yelled Vaslav. "Diaghilev has no right to be infected by this destructive atmosphere. He should only be influenced by considerations of true Art."

I had to admit to myself that Diaghilev could be swayed by rumors and was prone to listen to adverse opinions and then to make quick judgments. But I also knew that once Diaghilev was convinced that the artist would win the hearts of the public and be supported by famous members of the artistic world, then he ceased to have any doubts and would stand strong as a rock beside his collaborator.

I walked with Vaslav to the Hôtel de Paris and on the way managed to calm him somewhat. At the hotel he promised me he would lie down and rest.

Returning home I met Sergei Pavlovitch; he was as disturbed as Vaslav. Right away he started to talk about their misunderstanding and to complain how impossible Vaslav was.

"Bronia, you must talk to Vaslav. It cannot go on this way any longer. I will disperse the whole company. I do not want to have a ballet company where I have no voice and cannot make decisions."

My heart sank. This was the first time I had ever seen Diaghilev in such a state.

"You should have heard what scandal Vaslav caused today in the Ciro Restaurant in the presence of Bezobrazov. This is a debut for Vaslav as a choreographer. He must understand that he might be wrong. Vatsa is still a boy. He is only twenty-one [he was actually twenty-three] but he refuses to listen to a single word about his ballet."

Diaghilev pursed his lips, dropped his monocle from his eye, and took another from his pocket; it was one of his nervous habits.

"During lunch Bezobrazov said to Vatsa, 'Your *Faune* is not a ballet, and such a performance will not appeal to or be successful with the public.' He thought that the ballet should be started anew. I wish you could have heard, Bronia, how Vaslav spoke to Bezobrazov, the old man who in his lifetime has seen not a few ballets. Vatsa categorically announced that he would not change a thing, not even a single measure."

I knew how highly Diaghilev regarded General Bezobrazov, a longtime friend of his who had been one of the "artistic committee" supporting Diaghilev in his plans for the first Saison Russe in Paris, and had then helped him found a permanent ballet company. The General was also an influential person in the Ministry of Commerce.

Diaghilev could hardly go on. His voice, as always when he got excited, had risen to a high pitch. People around us began to stop and were wondering what was happening, but Diaghilev did not pay any attention to them. Finally, he firmly announced to me, "I will not give that thing in Paris! Vatsa had better believe that! This is not a ballet, and I cannot give it in Paris. I will dismiss the company. You can tell that to your brother, and I do not wish to argue with him anymore!"

Until then, for me, everything that Diaghilev affirmed in the ballet was like law, and here now I was forced to take Vaslav's side against him, not solely because of our close relationship as brother and sister, but because I inwardly admired what Vaslav was doing. As I started my attempt to come to Vaslav's defense, I felt equally sorry for both of them, for Vaslav and for Sergei Pavlovitch.

"I believe, Sergei Pavlovitch, that you are mistaken. *L'Aprés-Midi d'un Faune* is a great accomplishment, but in a rehearsal hall, without costumes and sets, it is difficult to imagine the range of this ballet. And the dancers are still not free in their movements. Even I who have worked with Vaslav for a long time still find my part difficult."

Sergei Pavlovitch was abrupt in his answer. "Let us see what Bakst will say when he sees this thing."

———

BAKST SAW the rehearsal of *L'Aprés-Midi d'un Faune* as soon as he came to Monte Carlo.

He watched the whole ballet with sincere admiration, and at the end he got up and came to Vaslav and kissed him. He was quite open about his enthusiasm and said in a loud voice to all present—to the artists, to Diaghilev, and to Bezobrazov—"You will see . . . how wild Paris will be for this."

A few days later, Diaghilev spoke to me again. "You know, Bronia, I have never seen Bakst so enthusiastic. Levushka said that *L'Aprés-Midi d'un Faune* is a 'super-genius' creation and that we are all fools not to have understood it."

As he went on, Diaghilev seemed to be radiating happiness, but then he added, half-jokingly, "Still, we shall have to see it. . . . But you can imagine Bronia, how triumphant Vaslav is. Now it is all over and he will never listen to me again!"

———

BAKST'S PREDICTION came true.

Vaslav had found himself as a choreographer.

But his independence and self-assertion marked the beginning of the break with Diaghilev.

49   Paris and London: 1912

OUR SEASON in Paris opened on May 13 at theThéâtre du Châtelet with the premiere of Hahn's *Le Dieu Bleu*, rather than Ravel's *Daphnis et Chloë*, which the French public had been waiting for years to see. There was prolonged applause, however, when the curtain opened to reveal Bakst's extraordinary decor for *Le Dieu Bleu:* a huge bright orange rock, enormous pythons looped lifelessly around two poles protruding from the rock. Against this background Bakst had placed the dancers in groups wearing predominantly white costumes.

My dance of the Bayadère Enivrée took place at the very beginning of the ballet. I felt that there was little that I could contribute to the part; also the solo dance was very slow, consisting of a series of steps and poses in a pseudo-Hindu-Siamese style. I did not like the dance or the costume; the latter was white decorated with a few patches of bright colors worn over a long-sleeved tan jersey. The headdress was heavy and decorated with long strings of pearls. There were no shoes, but Fokine and Bakst insisted that I wear dark tan tights to simulate a dark skin. They would not allow me to dance with bare feet and to paint my body as I always did for Ta-Hor.

One of the more original dance numbers in the ballet was performed by Serafima Astafieva carrying a peacock on her shoulder; the vividly colored feathers of the bird's tail brushed the floor as she performed her oriental dance.

But there was little applause during the ballet, not even for Karsavina, the favorite ballerina of the Parisian public who that same evening had great success dancing *L'Oiseau de Feu* with Adolf Bolm and *Le Spectre de la Rose* with Nijinsky. It was the Bakst decor rather than Fokine's choreography that appealed to the public. There was an air of mystery created by the lighting and the stage effects, and as night descended for the second scene the outline of a pagoda was visible against a dark blue, star-spangled sky. A pool lit up, and from the waters appeared the Lotus Goddess, Nelidova; and then, suddenly, the rock wall split apart to reveal a golden stairway. The public applauded loudly at the apparition of the Blue God, Nijinsky, seated at the top of the golden stairs. The head of the Blue God was crowned with a high, elaborate headdress. He wore a short-sleeved yellow oriental costume, richly decorated, and blue makeup covered his body. But as the ballet progressed even Nijinsky's leaps among the demons and monsters failed to arouse the public.

The ballet had a cool critical reception and was deemed a failure by Diaghilev even though Robert Brussel, the critic of *Le Figaro*, praised Karsavina and said that Nijinsky never appeared more marvelous than in this role of the Blue God. I was proud that Brussel also praised me for my interpretation of the Bayadère Enivrée.

The public was more receptive to the premiere of *Thamar* on May 20, but even so the ballet was not an outstanding success, despite Bakst's magnificent settings for Queen Thamar's castle, the authenticity of the Caucasian costumes, and Fokine's faithful reproduction of the Caucasian-Georgian dances set to Balakirev's superb score.

Karsavina and Bolm were warmly applauded and were highly praised in the press the next day for their gripping interpretations of their dramatic roles. Karsavina as the cruel Queen Thamar looked stunning in her richly decorated red caftan; her big dark eyes appeared enormous in her bloodless white face framed by long black hair braided with strings of pearls.

Despite the praise of the critics we were disappointed that *Thamar* had failed to repeat the sensation created by *Schéhérazade* in 1910.

The third premiere of our season in Paris was to be Nijinsky's *L'Après-Midi d'un Faune*, on May 29. As the time for the performance approached the atmosphere among the company became even more tense. Fokine had been angered to find that Nijinsky's *Faune* was to be performed in Paris before his own third new ballet, *Daphnis et Chloë*, which was now scheduled for June 8 and which Diaghilev had even suggested might be postponed for another year.* Fokine had been incensed, saying that he

---

*Fokine had been working on *Daphnis et Chloë* since 1904, when he delivered to the Imperial Ballet a memorandum and draft for a two-act ballet based on Longus's *Daphnis et Chloë*, to music of Kadletz. Some of the choreographic ideas in that memorandum he used in *Acis and Galatea* for the 1905 Student Graduation Performance, and then in 1910, when Diaghilev asked him if he had any ideas for a new ballet, Fokine showed him his libretto for *Daphnis et Chloë*. Diaghilev was enthusiastic and commissioned Ravel to write the music. But to Fokine's great disappointment the score was not ready as planned for 1911, and Ravel had only just completed it for this 1912 season. (IN/JR)

had not had enough rehearsals in Monte Carlo to mount his ballet in three tableaux, and furthermore blaming Nijinsky's many rehearsals for *Faune*, "a seven-minute ballet," as interfering with his mounting of *Daphnis et Chloë* in Monte Carlo. Even now, he insisted, he was having difficulties at the Châtelet holding complete daily rehearsals because of the dancers who were taking part in *Faune* and who were still rehearsing with Nijinsky.

Then, after seeing most of Nijinsky's *Faune* in rehearsal, Fokine angrily claimed that Vaslav had copied the style of dancing from his own *Daphnis et Chloë*. Of course I knew that in fact Vaslav had started to mount and create his *Faune* as long ago as November and December of 1910, when he had shown it to Diaghilev and Bakst, and that he had worked on the ballet, either alone or with me, during 1911. Early in 1912, in Berlin, when Fokine was in St. Petersburg, long before he had begun to mount his *Daphnis et Chloë*, Vaslav had mounted all the parts for the six nymphs and for the Principal Nymph in *L'Après-Midi d'un Faune*.

Actually it was Fokine who used some of Vaslav's ideas for *Daphnis et Chloë*. I already knew how predisposed Fokine was to making a parody of a dance, from the time when he had been very pleased with my caricature of the dance by Kshessinska in the *coda* of *Le Talisman* and had told me to dance it as the Street Dancer in *Petrouchka*. So it came as no surprise to me when I was told that Fokine had also appropriated the style of *L'Après-Midi d'un Faune* when mounting the dance of the three nymphs in *Daphnis et Chloë*.

During the rehearsals in Monte Carlo, Fokine had been informed step by step of the progress of Vaslav's work on *Faune* and had felt encouraged by the sarcastic mood prevailing among the Fokine artists dancing in *Faune*, so that when he mounted the dance for Adolf Bolm as Darkon in *Daphnis et Chloë*, Fokine had not hesitated to make a travesty of Nijinsky's choreography, using the form and style and rhythm of the movements from *Faune*. This "Dance of Darkon" was to prove the most successful number in *Daphnis et Chloë*.

Following our lukewarm reception in Paris for Fokine's two new ballets, *Le Dieu Bleu* and *Thamar*, and also because of the negative atmosphere throughout the company towards Nijinsky's first choreographic work, I was concerned about our performance. I felt that such an atmosphere and lack of confidence could damage *Faune* and affect the success of Nijinsky's debut as choreographer. It is strange how the mood backstage influences the public. Nervousness and doubts in the wings before a premiere reach out into the auditorium, to the public, and can lead to catastrophe.

I knew that we were well prepared. Through ninety rehearsals, never had a ballet been mounted with such precision; Vaslav had attended very carefully to every detail—every gesture of each finger had to be exactly as he had shown us. Being a dancer in the ballet myself, I had not been able to see our performance as a whole, from the front, nor had I seen Vaslav's own part, which he had only marked during our rehearsals. It was only because of this antagonistic atmosphere in the company that I was very nervous about our approaching performance.

ON WEDNESDAY, May 29, 1912, the elite of Paris gathered in the Théâtre du Châtelet to see Nijinsky's first ballet. The program stated that the libretto was not Stéphane Mallarmé's *L'Après-Midi d'un Faune*, but rather the poem's short preamble, quoted directly after the credits.

> L'Après-Midi d'un Faune,
> a choreographic tableau by Nijinsky,
> decor and costumes by Bakst,
> music by Claude Debussy.
>
> *Un Faune sommeille;*
> *Des Nymphes le dupent;*
> *Une écharpe oubliée satisfait son rêve.*

Le rideau baisse pour que le poème commence dans toutes les mémoires. . . .

There was no immediate reaction from the audience when the curtain came down; they were stunned. Then as the public began to applaud, a few boos could be heard. As the applause increased, so did the protests. We were waiting onstage for the curtain to be raised, ready to take our bows, when Diaghilev came up and told us to return to our places and to repeat the whole work.

We danced the *Faune* again from the beginning and were loudly applauded. At the end of this second performance Vaslav also took several curtain calls, alone, as the choreographer. The ballet was a success.

Auguste Rodin, who had also been present for the dress rehearsal, stood up in his box applauding loudly and calling "Bravo, Bravo." He came backstage during the intermission to congratulate Vaslav. Rodin was an old man in his seventies and had to be helped up the few steps leading to the stage. He embraced Nijinsky emotionally, saying, "The fulfillment of my dreams, you have brought them to life. I cannot but thank you."

The next morning, May 30, the newspapers were almost unanimous in their praise of the performance. We particularly looked forward to reading the review by Robert Brussel in *Le Figaro*. Brussel had been a longtime supporter of Diaghilev and had encouraged him to organize the Concerts of Russian Music Through the Ages, in Paris in 1907. He had assisted Diaghilev in the choice of music for those concerts and had also been responsible for the publicity. Over the years Brussel had become a great friend and admirer of Vaslav as well as Diaghilev.

But, Gaston Calmette, the editor and owner of *Le Figaro*, had eliminated Brussel's review and instead had written an extraordinary attack and published it on the front page of the paper.

A FAUX PAS

Our readers will not find in its accustomed place under "Theatre," the criticism of my worthy collaborator Robert Brussel, upon the first performance of *L'Après-midi d'un Faune*, choreographic scene by Nijinsky, directed and danced by that astonishing artist.

I have eliminated that review.

There is no necessity for me to judge Debussy's music, which, besides, does not of itself constitute a novelty, as it is nearly ten years old. . . .

But I am persuaded that all the readers of *Figaro* who were at the Châtelet yesterday will not object if I protest against the most extraordinary exhibition which they presumed to serve us as a profound production, performed with a precious art and a harmonious lyricism.

Those who speak of art and poetry apropos of this spectacle make fun of us. It is neither a gracious epilogue nor a profound production. We have had a faun, incontinent, with vile movements of erotic bestiality and gestures of heavy shamelessness. That is all. And the merited boos were accorded the too-expressive pantomime of the body of an ill-made beast, hideous, from the front, and even more hideous in profile.

These animal realities the true public will never accept.*

The next day, the public was surprised by an article on the front editorial page of *Le Matin*, signed by Auguste Rodin.

LA RENAISSANCE DE LA DANSE

During the last twenty years, dancing seems to have set for itself its task of making us love the beauty of the body, movement, and gesture. First there came to us from the other side of the Atlantic the famous Loïe Fuller, who has been justly called the rejuvenator of dancing. Then came Isadora Duncan, teacher of an old art in a new form, and today we see Nijinsky, who possesses at the same time talent and training. The intelligence of his art is so rich and so varied that it approaches genius.

In dancing, as well as in sculpture and painting, flight and progress have been smothered by routine laziness, and inability to rejuvenate. We admire Loïe Fuller, Isadora Duncan, and Nijinsky, because they

*Translation from *Rodin* by Anna Leslie, Prentice Hall, 1937. (IN/JR)

have recovered again the soul of tradition, founded on respect and love of nature. This is the reason they are able to express all the emotions of the human soul.

The last of them, Nijinsky, possesses the distinct advantage of physical perfection, harmony of proportions, and a most extraordinary power to bend his body so as to interpret the most diverse sentiments. The sad mime in *Petrouchka* seems, in the last bound of the *Spectre de la Rose*, to fly into infinite space, but in no part is Nijinsky as marvelous and admirable as in *L'Après-midi d'un Faune*. No jumps, no bounds, nothing but attitudes and gestures of a half-conscious animal creature. He stretches himself, bends, stoops, crouches, straightens himself up, goes forward and retreats, with movements now slow, now jerky, nervous, angular: his eyes search, his arms extend, his hands open and close, his head turns away and turns back. The harmony between his mimicry and his plasticity is perfect. His whole body expresses what his mind dictates. He possesses the beauty of the antique frescoes and statues; he is the ideal model for whom every painter and sculptor has longed.

You would think Nijinsky were a statue when he lies full-length on the rock, with one leg bent and the flute at his lips, as the curtain rises, and nothing could be more soul-stirring than his movement when, at the close of the act, he throws himself down and passionately kisses the discarded veil.

I wish that every artist who truly loves his art might see this perfect personification of the ideals of the beauty of the ancient Greeks.*

Calmette, infuriated by Rodin's praise of Nijinsky, attacked the sculptor in a further editorial in *Le Figaro*.

I admire Rodin deeply as one of our most illustrious and able sculptors, but I must decline to accept his judgment on the question of theatrical morality. I have only to recall that, in defiance of common propriety, he exhibits in the former chapel of the Sacré Coeur and in the deserted appartments of the excellent nuns at Hôtel Biron, a series of objectionable drawings and cynical sketches, which depict with great brutality and in further detail the shameless attitude of the *Faune*, who was justly hissed at the Châtelet. And, now that I am speaking my mind, I may say that the morbid mimicry represented by the dancer on the stage the other evening moves me to less indignation than the spectacle offered every day by Rodin in the ancient convent of the Sacré Coeur to regiments of hysterical women admirers and self-satisfied snobs. It is inconceivable that the State—in other words the French taxpayer— should have purchased the Hôtel Biron for 5,000,000 francs simply to allow the richest of our sculptors to live there. Here is the real scandal, and it is the business of the Government to put a stop to it.†

* Ibid.
† Ibid.

Rodin replied simply,

> I have no time to waste on answering M. Calmette's attack on me. I admire Nijinsky's work, and consider him a marvel of harmony. He is a dancer of genius. I wish so noble an effort as the faun could be understood in its entirety and that all artists could come for instruction to this spectacle of beauty.*

The battle continued in the press between the supporters of Rodin and the supporters of Calmette. Many of the most eminent names in France were enlisted on one side or the other. Diaghilev was happy that *Faune* had aroused such a glare of publicity, worldwide, from our Paris Season.

Vaslav was moved by Rodin's appreciation of his work and agreed that during the summer he would return to Paris and pose for the sculptor.

There remained one more premiere for Paris, Fokine's *Daphnis et Chloë* on June 8, only a few days before the end of our season there. Three days before the first performance there were still twenty pages of the score that had not yet been mounted, and again Diaghilev suggested a postponement to Fokine. He refused and quickly mounted the dance for Darkon and also the dances for the three nymphs, finishing them on the very day of the opening. Fokine had been displeased the year before when one of the sets already designed by Léon Bakst for *Daphnis et Chloë* was used for *Narcisse*. Now he was furious when he found that Diaghilev had failed to have all new costumes made for *Daphnis et Chloë*, and that many costumes from *Narcisse* had to be used instead. With all the publicity and furor over *Faune*, Fokine had become even more angry with Diaghilev, saying that Diaghilev was much more interested in Nijinsky's *Faune* than he was in *Daphnis et Chloë*.

After the performance of *Daphnis et Chloë*, the rumors that had been running through the company since Monte Carlo were confirmed. Fokine declared that he could no longer work with Diaghilev.

———

FROM PARIS we went to London where Fokine's new ballet *Thamar* was again presented and was warmly received. I do not remember whether Fokine came with us to London or whether he stayed in Paris.

A few days after the start of our season in London—on Monday, July 15, 1912—I was married to Alexander Vladimirovitch Kotchetovsky. The ceremony took place in the Russian Orthodox Chapel in the Russian Embassy. Sergei Pavlovitch, standing in for my father, led me down the aisle to the altar. Vaslav was the best man and during the ceremony held the heavy gold crown above my head. I was married in the tea-rose lace

* Ibid.

gown that I had worn for my graduation, with the precious pin of rubies and diamonds in the shape of a flower on a stem given me by Prince Lvov on that same day.

It is the custom in Russian Orthodox weddings for the mother of the bride to give her an ikon, placed on a small stand in front of the altar during the ceremony and then taken by the bride to her new home. Mother was disappointed that my wedding was to be Russian Orthodox, but she liked this custom. She gave me the antique silver Catholic ikon that had been in her family for generations and in our home as long as I could remember. Before leaving the hotel, Mother blessed me and we prayed together, kneeling before this ikon of the Miraculous Virgin of Czestochowa.

After the wedding ceremony, the priest, as was the Russian custom, gave me the ikon to take to my new home, but I wanted Mother to have her family ikon back; she insisted, however, that I keep it, and it wasn't until a year later, when Sasha and I returned to St. Petersburg in 1913 and stayed with Mother, that the ikon was returned to its usual place on the wall in the dining room of our apartment.

Following the wedding ceremony there was a small champagne reception for us at the Embassy, and then later that day Diaghilev and Vaslav invited Sasha and me, with Mother and a few friends, for supper at the Savoy. As a wedding present Vaslav gave us one thousand rubles.

Our season in London was to continue until the end of the month, when the company would have a vacation before the start of our fall season. Sasha had made reservations for us to go to Vevey, and we planned to leave immediately following the London performances. Most of our colleagues were returning home for the summer to St. Petersburg, Moscow, or Warsaw. Mother was planning to travel with them and stop for a few days in Warsaw before going on to St. Petersburg. Wanting to be near Stassik, she had again made reservations in Ligovo for the summer.

Suddenly we learned that our vacation was to be postponed for three weeks. Diaghilev announced that we were to give five performances in Deauville, on the coast of Normandy in France, on the occasion of the opening of the Théâtre de Casino. Deauville was to be a new resort center in France, and the Casino there was owned by the same person as the Monte Carlo Casino. Many social events were being arranged to attract the cream of European society. Alternating with our Ballets Russes performances were to be Opera performances with Feodor Chaliapin and Dmitri Smirnov. I hoped with all my heart that I would not see Chaliapin in Deauville. I still did not believe that I was ready to meet him casually, just as an acquaintance.

One of our first days in Deauville, just over two weeks after my marriage, Sasha and I were walking along the Promenade when in the distance I could see Chaliapin and his wife, Maria Valentinovna, walking towards us. Abruptly I turned around, pulling Sasha by the arm, and took one of the side streets. Again I resolved to myself that I would not seek a meeting with Chaliapin and would silence in myself any lingering thought about him.

A great sorrow oppresses me.

How did it happen . . . ?

During the intermission I was changing with several artists in our tiny dressing room. A knock at the door and a friend says, "Bronia, someone wishes to see you."

I step out into the narrow corridor; Chaliapin is standing before me.

"Broniusha, I hear that you got married. I come to congratulate you. Are you happy?"

Life seems to flow from my heart. I muster all my willpower to remain outwardly calm and force myself to say, "Yes, I am very happy."

We both are silent, then, "Bronia, do you love me?"

"Yes, I love you forever."

Suddenly Feodor takes me in his arms, and as he kisses me my heart sinks in his embrace. . . . "My Broniusha, my dearest."

Feodor rushes away without looking back at me, down the stairway . . . away . . . forever . . .

50   With Vaslav
in Monte Carlo

I REMEMBER how sad Vaslav looked when we saw Mother off at the station in Deauville. I knew how he longed to return to St. Petersburg, but with his deferment having elapsed a year ago, Vaslav was now facing serious charges should he ever go back to Russia. Mother promised him that she would speak with the attorney again. Ever since our performances at the Narodny Dom Theatre had been canceled, and with no further urgency for Vaslav to return to Russia, the man had not been making any effort to straighten out Vaslav's status with the military authorities. I have never been able to understand why Diaghilev, who must have been aware of how worried and disturbed Vaslav was over this matter, did not do more. He simply advised Vaslav again that he should not risk returning to Russia for the vacation.

Sasha and I were going to Vevey for a month as we had planned and I asked Vaslav where he was going for the summer. He replied that he had no time for a long vacation, as he had to be in Paris in September to hear Claude Debussy's music for his new ballet, *Jeux,* and while in Paris he would also be posing for Rodin. I was to be one of the three artists taking part in *Jeux,* so Vaslav asked me to come to Paris at the end of September so that he could start to mount my part in the ballet, before joining the company for its next engagement, which had been announced for Cologne.

Before Sasha and I left Deauville I promised Diaghilev that we would be in Paris in a month's time so that I could work with Vaslav. During our stay in Vevey we received a card from Vaslav, also signed by Diaghilev and Stravinsky, from Bayreuth. Then at the end of September Diaghilev called from Paris to tell me that there had been a change of plans and that Vaslav was in Monte Carlo, waiting for me to start the rehearsals of *Jeux.*

From Vevey we went directly to Monte Carlo and were met at the station by Vaslav, who was pleased to see us and took us to the hotel where we were all staying, the Riviera Palace in Beausoleil. The first thing I noticed in Vaslav's room at the hotel was the number of art books. Several of the artists whose works had been reproduced in the books were unknown to me. At that time Vaslav was completely captivated by contemporary French art—Modigliani, Matisse, Cézanne, and particularly Rodin and Gauguin. One of the books was obviously well-thumbed; Vaslav started to show it to me, an edition of Gauguin with many illustrations in color. He was fascinated by Gauguin's works and greatly admired the artist. He wanted me to share that admiration. I pointed out what seemed to me to be a studied primitiveness in Gauguin's paintings. But this quality was what most excited Vaslav's admiration. He liked Gaugin's portrayal of native women with no hint of European airs and graces. Gauguin's Tahitian woman was part of the nature of the island, her body blended with the color of the sands, burned by the sun.

"If I ever marry, I want to marry a native girl, and then our children will have such golden bodies . . ."

At Vaslav's words I rolled a piece of paper, and using it like a brush I dipped it in a bottle of ink, and drew a head of a young woman with long black hair loosely framing her face. The drawing turned out quite well and resembled one of Gauguin's maidens. Vaslav laughed at my joke, but he remained captivated by Gauguin, affirming that this was the new path in art, a return to the primitive. Soon I came to share Vaslav's enthusiasm for Gauguin. I did not at that time know that my brother was preparing to mount Stravinsky's *Le Sacre du Printemps* and that he saw the source of his inspiration for the choreographic work in Russian "pagan" primitiveness.

We started each morning in Monte Carlo with a practice session —Vaslav and I working on the dances and *pas de deux* in the repertoire of the Ballets Russes. Nijinsky did not have any regular pupils but he liked to work with me, so I was both his pupil and his assistant, the human material for his choreographic experiments and research for new forms of dancing and artistic expression.

I must admit that I often protested silently at what I thought were Vaslav's unreasonable demands. Dancing with ballerinas like Pavlova, Karsavina, and Kshessinska, Vaslav was an attentive partner . . . he did not experiment with them. But dancing with me he would say, "Bronia, you are my sister and must dance differently from them. I am not a *porteur*. I dance too. You must stand on toe by yourself and not rely on me. You must turn alone in your *pirouettes* without my assistance. You must jump high and then come down softly. I can only be in harmony with you and reflect your dance. Even if the *pas de deux* is mounted in such a way that the sole purpose of the male dancer is to be a supporter or *porteur*, we must dance these *pas de deux* differently. We must conceal all the supports so that the *pas de deux* will be an artistic choreographic art form and not, as it is now, an acrobatic circus act."

As Nijinsky tossed me up in the air I felt as if I were flying up from his arms. It was much higher than my natural elevation. "Bronia, you must come down now by yourself." He was teaching me to use all my strength to come down as lightly by myself as I would with a partner's support, and not like a bundle. This way Vaslav avoided the ugly *plié* always necessary when catching a partner. For such an unassisted landing the dancer had to have strong legs, with strong tendons of the knees and the back.

"In the *pas de deux* that we dance together, our movements must blend and complement each other. We must be in harmony like a chord in the orchestra."

Vaslav seemed to be demanding technical miracles from me, but when dancing with him in *Les Sylphides* I saw how far Nijinsky had come in his dancing technique from the traditional classical partner.

Nijinsky was using an entirely different technique of support of the ballerina than was used in the old Petipa ballets. In these practice sessions with Vaslav, I discovered a new choreographic world.

I enjoyed working in Monte Carlo with Vaslav for another reason. He reminded me then of his old self before he met Diaghilev.

With Diaghilev and his entourage, it seemed to me that Vaslav was never himself. There was always an inner tension in him, and lately he seemed tired as well. I recalled how whenever he had come to see Mother or me in Monte Carlo, and then later in Paris and London, he would often lie down on the bed and no sooner had his head touched the pillow than he was asleep. Possibly this is what happened in Paris when he was working on his new ballet with Debussy, and was also spending much of his time posing for several artists. Once when posing for Rodin he had fallen asleep in the sculptor's studio. Diaghilev had been so angry to find Vaslav asleep on the couch with the seventy-one-year-old Rodin, sitting on the floor also asleep, with his head resting on the couch at Vaslav's feet, that he had not let the sittings continue.

As Diaghilev himself was leaving Paris and traveling to Russia to make further preparations for the next season, he arranged for Vaslav to come to Monte Carlo so that he could work on *Jeux* away from the social distractions and parties of Paris.

Vaslav seemed so much freer and more relaxed in his conversations with us in Monte Carlo, away from Sergei Pavlovitch; he was expressing so many creative ideas. I was anxious to hear the music composed by Claude Debussy for *Jeux*, but we needed a pianist for our work. Monte Carlo was deserted at this time. Everyone who had been working during the spring season in the orchestra, in the Théâtre de Monte Carlo where we began our inquiries for a pianist, had left. The doorman at the stage door was pleased to see me, however, for he had been holding a letter for me that had arrived after we had left in June.

The letter was from Father and had been written after Mother had told him of my plans to marry Sasha. He was upset and hurt that I had not written to him myself, and that Sasha had not formally asked him for his daughter's hand in marriage. I suddenly felt very guilty that we had not informed Father of our wedding in London. Sasha and I immediately sat down and composed a letter to Father.

For our very first rehearsal for *Jeux* we were without the services of a pianist. Vaslav was mounting the part of the choreography he had composed in Paris when he had first heard the music. With his unusual talent of being able to hold perfectly in his memory a piece of music he had heard only a few times, he had begun to mount those parts of the music that Debussy had played for him.

Meanwhile Sasha was still looking for a pianist, in Monaco as well as in Monte Carlo. And it was in Monaco that he was fortunate enough to discover a piano teacher. When Vaslav showed her Debussy's music she told us that she was not very good at sight reading, but we all talked her into studying Debussy's *Jeux*.

There are three participants in *Jeux*: the Youth, Nijinsky, and two Young Girls, to be danced by Karsavina and Nijinska. Karsavina was again in St. Petersburg for the fall season at the Maryinsky, so Diaghilev had arranged for Alexandra Vassilievska to work with us in Monte Carlo. I was glad to see Alexandra again, for she and I had often danced together as soloists in *Swan Lake* and *Giselle*. Shura, as she was called, was very talented, a pleasant person who was easy to get along with, so I knew that Vaslav would have no trouble working with her.

Vaslav did not explain the libretto of the ballet during our rehearsals, but only showed us the dances and our groupings with him. All the time he held a tennis racquet in his hand, seeking movements with it to include in the choreography. Often instead of a rehearsal we would go to the nearby tennis courts and watch tennis being played. Vaslav studied the movements of the body and paid close attention to the technique of striking the ball, also the positions of the arm and the grip holding the tennis racquet.

At the beginning of the ballet the two Young Girls come onstage from opposite sides. Shura and I walked towards each other from the first wing with tiny steps, *pas de bourrée*, but instead of the turned-out position, our legs were in the normal first position. Our bodies faced the audience, but our hands remained facing each other; both arms were bent up in a half-circle, to one side, with the fingers lightly clenched and the wrists bent. We met in the center of the stage and bowed to each other, then started to dance together with classical dance *pas*, but again not in turned-out positions.

For Karsavina's role, Vaslav mounted on Shura a slow valse tempo solo. He showed me my solo, bringing out in the dance the qualities of my elevation, then joined me in the dance. We crossed the width of the stage in prolonged leaps executed with great force and in a sportive manner. Vaslav told me to practice the steps we would be dancing together, for he could only show me part of my dance; he was not able to get the pianist to play the appropriate *allegro* tempo.

The mounting of the ballet seemed to proceed slowly, and Vaslav appeared to be discouraged. Often he canceled our rehearsals, which led me to feel he was not too interested in the work. I saw what we were doing in Monte Carlo as preliminary sketches towards the final choreographic composition. Even so, I noticed new achievements and discoveries in the positions of the arms and the body, and in the creation of the groupings for three dancers.

Everything in the choreography was new—free movements and positions of the body applied to classical ballet technique. *Jeux* was the forerunner of Neoclassical Ballet.

51   Fall and Winter Season:
1912–1913

WHILE WE WERE in Monte Carlo, Diaghilev was in St. Petersburg recruiting opera artists and trying to obtain permission from the Imperial Theatres to use the sets and costumes for *Boris Godunov*, *Khovantchina*, and *Prince Igor* for a Russian Opera and Ballet Season he was planning for Paris and London, May through July 1913.

He was still in St. Petersburg when we joined the company in Cologne, Germany, on October 25, 1912, a few days before the start of our performance there. When we arrived in Cologne there was no one from the Administration to take charge, not even to make arrangements to transport our costumes and sets from the railroad station to the theatre. We found several notices in the theatre saying that unless they were collected immediately from the station they would be returned to Paris. I was the only one among the company gathering in Cologne who had any money, having saved from the salary that Diaghilev had paid me for the month I had worked with Vaslav in Monte Carlo. So it was I who came to the rescue, saving the situation by paying for the transporting of the sets and costumes to the theatre. Thus I was able to spare Diaghilev the possible embarrassment of having no sets or costumes for our opening night, since he himself did not arrive in Cologne until the eve of the performance.

With Fokine having left the company, his friend Grigoriev, our *régisseur*, had returned to St. Petersburg with no intention of continuing to work with Diaghilev. Adolf Bolm had then been asked to act as *régisseur* and been put in charge of rehearsals.

I knew that Vaslav was not happy with this choice, for though he had always admired Bolm's interpretation of the Tartar Chief in Fokine's *Danses Polovetsiennes*, he felt that he lacked the talent to visualize the interpretation of the *mises en scène* in other ballets. Bolm was prone to exaggeration, to overact so that his performance could border on a caricature. Such slips in the artistic rendering of a role were very distressing and offensive to Vaslav, who had been extremely annoyed during the rehearsals of *Schéhérazade* watching Bolm working on the *mises en scène* with the *figurants*.

Our first performance in Cologne was on October 30, and just before the curtain went up for *Schéhérazade* Vaslav received a telegram. It was from Mother telling him that Father had died suddenly on October 15 [N.S. 28], in Kharkov in the Ukraine. Vatsa knew how attached I was to Father, how much I loved him, and so he tried to spare me the shock by waiting until the end of the performance before telling me the tragic news. But the news of Thomas Nijinsky's death had already reached other members of the company, and as I came onstage one artist detached himself from a group and came to me to express his sympathy. It was Adolf Bolm. At that moment Vaslav also came onstage and, seeing me talking to Bolm, guessed that he was telling me of the death of our father. Vaslav looked angrily at Bolm and, calling him an idiot, took me gently by the hand to move away from the other artists. Vaslav was concerned and worried about Mother, alone in St. Petersburg at this time. "We must send Mama a telegram immediately and ask her to join us."

After the performance a ballet critic from Odessa came backstage. He told us that he had known Father and wanted to express his sympathy. "I met your Father many years ago. He was a great *maître de ballet* and *metteur en scène*. Tonight, during this performance of *Schéhérazade* that I came specially from St. Petersburg to see, I was reminded of another ballet performance, Nijinsky's *The Fountain of Bakhchisarai*. I saw it in Odessa. Your father staged a magnificent ballet. I still remember the breathtaking wild scene of attacking hordes, and the enthralling beauty of the oriental dancers and the dramatic *mises en scène* in the harem. In my opinion, Nijinsky's *The Fountain of Bakhchisarai* was a forerunner of *Schéhérazade*, preceding it by many years."

I could not keep the tears from my eyes as I too remembered the happy days of my childhood when I saw my first ballet, Father's *The Fountain of Bakhchisarai*,* in a performance in the Theatre-Circus at Narva, 1896.

I was grief-stricken over the news of Father's death. When Mother had told me about meeting Father again I had been so happy, hoping that this

---

*Bronislava Nijinska's archives show that in 1892 Foma Nijinsky produced in Kiev a grand ballet in two acts and an apotheosis entitled *Jertva Zavisti (A Victim of Jealousy)* based on Pushkin's poem "The Fountain of Bakhchisarai," and in 1893 he staged the same ballet under the title *The Fountain of Bakhchisarai* for the Odessa Opera Theatre and in 1896 for the Theatre-Circus in Narva. (IN/JR)

might mean that I too would see him again. But I also felt guilty, remembering the hurt letter Father had written me. Had he felt that I too, his only daughter, had rejected him like both Vaslav and, more recently, Stassik? I could only hope and pray that he had received the reply from Sasha and me before his sudden death, which I was later to learn was caused by the perforation of an abscess in his throat.

We arranged a memorial service for Father in Cologne Cathedral. Sergei Pavlovitch suggested the choice of music for the service that was attended by many of the company.

—

AFTER COLOGNE we went to Frankfurt, Munich, and Dresden, for two or three performances in each city. During this fall tour in Germany, Vaslav was not planning much more work on *Jeux;* I believe he was waiting for Karsavina to join us in the spring so that he could work with both artists who would be dancing with him in the performances in Paris in May 1913, Karsavina and myself.

Instead he was going to concentrate on another new ballet, Stravinsky's *Le Sacre du Printemps*. Vaslav had been very excited when he told me that he had been given this ballet to mount, a ballet originally planned for Fokine as choreographer. Vaslav had been present at many of the early discussions at Diaghilev's between Roerich and Stravinsky, who had been working together on the libretto since 1910.

Vaslav had met Nicholas Roerich first in 1909, when Roerich was designing the decor for *Danses Polovetsiennes*, for the Saison Russe. They had become great friends since then and met often in Paris and in St. Petersburg.

In 1910, Roerich wrote the story for a ballet that he entitled *Supreme Sacrifice* and described in an interview with the *St. Petersburg Gazette*, August 28, 1910:

> The new ballet will depict several scenes of a sacred night of the ancient Slavs. At the start of the ballet it is a summer night, and it ends with the sunrise, with the first rays of the sun. Strictly speaking the choreographic part comprises the ritual dances. This will be the first attempt to reproduce antiquity without any explicit story.

As Stravinsky and Roerich worked together on the ballet, this first idea of Roerich's became the "Danse Sacrale" in the second scene of *Le Sacre du Printemps*. Already in Monte Carlo and now in Germany, Vaslav often talked to me about his friendship with Roerich, whom he sometimes referred to as "Professor." When I asked Vaslav if he knew how Roerich got this title, he explained, "Roerich has studied archaeology and held the position of Academic Professor and is a Member of the Archaeological Society. Roerich is not only a great artist but also a philosopher and a scholar. His studies of the Stone Age are of scientific importance. In his numerous excavations and cave explorations he has discovered vestiges of primeval ages. The beauty of the tinted stones and the wall paintings of the cave dwellers have inspired his own art. . . . Bronia, you must remember some of Roerich's paintings that we saw together at the Art Exhibition by *Mir Iskusstva* in St. Petersburg?"

I recalled how we had both admired not only the magnificent beauty of the colors but also the spirit of Ancient Russia so well captured in Roerich's paintings, depicting the life and rituals of those ancient tribes.

"Now that I am working on *Sacre*," Vaslav went on, "Roerich's art inspires me as much as does Stravinsky's powerful music—his paintings, *The Idols of Ancient Russia*, *The Daughters of the Earth*, and particularly the painting called, I think, *The Call of the Sun*. Do you remember it, Bronia? . . . the violet and purple colors of the vast barren landscape in the predawn darkness, as a ray of the rising sun shines on a solitary group gathered on top of a hill to greet the arrival of spring. Roerich has talked to me at length about his paintings in this series that he describes as the awakening of the spirit of primeval man. In *Sacre* I want to emulate this spirit of the prehistoric Slavs."

In the early weeks of November Vaslav began to mount *Le Sacre du Printemps*, working first on the second scene, in which I, in the role of the Chosen Maiden, had a solo dance, "Danse Sacrale."

At this time Stravinsky was in Russia—in St. Petersburg, I think—still working on the score of *Le Sacre du Printemps*. He finished it on November 4 [N.S. 17], 1912, but I remember that it was sometime before that date that Vaslav had already received from Stravinsky a score for part of the music, including the "Danse Sacrale" in the second scene.

The pianist for our rehearsals—I believe it was Steiman—had to decipher Stravinsky's handwritten orchestral score and transpose it for piano. Vaslav, who had already heard this part of *Sacre* played on the piano by Stravinsky, probably in Bayreuth during the summer, was able to assist the pianist.

Vaslav asked me to come to join them during these early sessions, for he wanted me to become well familiarized with the music before he started to work with me. I was happy that this gave me the opportunity to see Vaslav's initial work on his choreographic composition. Vaslav listened attentively to "Danse Sacrale" repeated several times, then told the pianist to play the whole piece again, indicating that this time he wanted to hear each musical phrase separately. Vaslav would stop the pianist in the middle of a phrase and ask him to play a few measures over and over again, until he had thoroughly comprehended the rhythm. Vaslav and the pianist worked on the music of "Danse Sacrale" until Vaslav was satisfied that he had assimilated it.

Vaslav did not explain the story of *Sacre* before starting work with me; he simply told me that the solo he was about to show me was a ritualistic sacrificial dance. It was his own dance, inspired by the music; he followed the "breath" of the music to create his choreographic composition. I followed him in the dance. The rhythm of the movements created by Nijinsky had never been used before by a choreographer, but still I had no difficulty in performing steps and movements that were all novel to me. The exciting rhythms of Stravinsky's music and the precision of rendering these rhythms were challenging. I was inspired by the innovations in the music and in the choreography.

As I danced I imagined above me the dark clouds in the stormy sky, remembered from the painting by Roerich. Around me I pictured the calm of nature before the onslaught of a hurricane. As I envisaged the primitiveness of the tribal rites, where the Chosen Maiden must die to save the earth, I felt that my body must draw into itself, must absorb the fury of the hurricane. Strong, brusque, spontaneous movements seemed to fight the elements as the Chosen Maiden protected the earth against the menacing heavens. The Chosen Maiden danced as if possessed, as she must until her frenzied dance in the primitive sacrificial ritual kills her.

This work with my brother proceeded fast and easily. Perhaps it was because I saw, understood, and executed accurately, each movement, correctly rendering the inner rhythm. During the sessions when I had listened with Vaslav to the pianist playing the music, I too had assimilated this inner rhythm, the mood and spirit of the music. It had taken Vaslav only two rehearsals to create the solo for me. In the third I performed the dance alone, and as Vaslav watched me he was radiant. I could see that he was pleased both with his own work and with my rendition of his creation.

In *Faune*, and now working with me on the "Danse Sacrale," this part of the choreography of *Sacre*, Vaslav did not "graphically" render each musical note by a physical movement, nor did he have recourse to counting the beats aloud, as he did in later rehearsals with the company after he had come under the influence of the Dalcroze System.

⁓

IT WAS Prince Volkonsky, the former director of the Imperial Theatres, who first interested Diaghilev in the Dalcroze System of Eurhythmics.

Prince Volkonsky had highly praised the system during one of our previous tours in Europe. He had written several articles about it, and in his view it was essential to apply this system to choreography.

In 1901, after their disagreement over the production of *Sylvia*, when Diaghilev had wanted to engage unknown artists like Bakst, Volkonsky had dismissed Diaghilev from the Imperial Theatres. (Not long after that Volkonsky himself had also resigned.) They did not speak to each other for ten years, until, in 1911 in Rome, Prince Volkonsky had come backstage after one of our performances and congratulated Diaghilev on the success of his artistic enterprise. With that their friendship had been renewed. Sometime later, Prince Volkonsky had recommended to Diaghilev that he should pay Dalcroze a visit the next time he was in Germany, and see the newly opened Dalcroze Institute at Hellerau near Dresden.

I had heard about the Dalcroze System when Diaghilev and Vaslav had visited the Institute, the last time we were in Dresden. Now Diaghilev invited Bolm, Baron de Gunsburg, and me to visit it with them.

We went by automobile from Dresden to Hellerau. The morning was damp and chilly, but by the time we arrived the sun had broken through the rain clouds and was shining on the russet-colored leaves of the tall trees along the road. I was enchanted by the view of the park around the Institute, and I also remember the marvelous smell of damp earth and fallen leaves.

We were met at the door of the Institute by Jaques Dalcroze. He was a distinguished-looking man of medium height and somewhat stout. He had a goatee and reminded me of a provincial doctor.

We entered a huge hall with high ceilings. The walls were draped from ceiling to floor with gray, deep-folded curtains. At the end of the hall was a raised platform, a stage, and Dalcroze demonstrated to us the multicolored lighting for it. We were amazed to see how the intensity of the light and the colors changed with the volume and the inflections of the tonalities.

A group of young girls came onstage. They followed each other in a long chain, led by an older student. The girls walked to the 2/4 beat of the music; at the same time one arm was gesticulating to a 3/4 time and the other was marking a 4/4 time. Diaghilev declared himself impressed by the musicality thus displayed by Dalcroze's pupils, and Bolm and Baron de Gunsburg shared his opinion. I was not impressed by what seemed to me to be a pseudomusicality, acquired by long training. It reminded me of the skill acquired by jugglers who practice for hour after hour to be able to juggle bottles, plates, or balls, to perfect their circus acts.

Dalcroze, himself, in his conversation with us, never claimed or even hinted that his system of Eurythmics had any connection with choreography. He simply told us that he had developed a series of exercises set to music. Besides being beneficial to health, he felt that his system of Eurhythmics developed in children a sense of rhythm and coordination.

During our drive back to Dresden, Sergei Pavlovitch told us that he was concerned that our artists would not be able to master the difficult rhythms in Stravinsky's *Le Sacre du Printemps*, the new ballet that Vaslav was soon to mount with the company, and that he had invited Dalcroze's best pupil, Miriam Ramberg whom we came to know as Marie Rambert, to teach us Eurhythmics.

I was burning with indignation and protested loudly, "I cannot see what a Dalcroze pupil can teach our artists. We are already familiar with Stravinsky's music, having danced in his two ballets, *Petrouchka* and *L'Oiseau de Feu*, where we had no trouble with the rhythms of his complicated scores." Diaghilev did not let me continue but interrupted me abruptly, "Bronia, you are too young to speak this way."

I was not to be silenced, and continued firmly but politely, "Rhythm cannot be taught, it can only be developed. There is not a single ballet artist who does not have an innate sense of rhythm, otherwise he would be a freak and would hardly be dancing in a ballet company. The Dalcroze Institute is a sanatorium for children who need help to develop their coordination of the body and their sense of rhythm."

Sergei Pavlovitch did not reply at all but only looked at me angrily, and for the rest of the drive back to Dresden there was no further discussion about the Institute. I was surprised that Vaslav made no comment one way or the other.

It turned cold again in the evening and was raining by the time we arrived back in Dresden. The next day when we were to leave for Berlin I was feeling quite chilled, and on the train I began coughing. Vaslav also complained that he had a cold. We must have caught cold during the automobile ride back from Hellerau.

We arrived in Berlin with two weeks before the start of our performances. Vaslav was anxious about *L'Après-Midi d'un Faune*, which was scheduled to be presented for the opening night, particularly when we learned to our great distress that one of our colleagues, Tcherepanova, had died of pneumonia. Vaslav had to find another dancer to replace Tcherepanova and teach her the role as one of the nymphs. Grigoriev had now rejoined our company permanently, and Vaslav chose Grigoriev's wife, Tchernicheva, to dance the role.

Mother had joined us in Berlin at this time and was upset to find both her children in bed with colds. She immediately talked to the doctor, who

99–101. Costumes for *Le Sacre du Printemps*, paintings of early designs proposed by Nicholas Roerich, c. 1912. *(Stravinsky Diaghilev Foundation)*

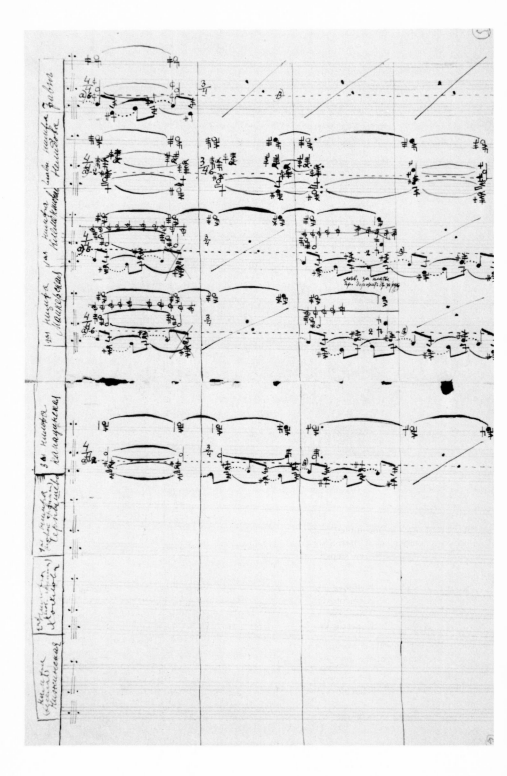

103. Nijinsky and Nijinska in *L'Après-Midi d'un Faune*.

102. *Facing page:* An incomplete page of
Nijinsky's notations for *L'Après-Midi d'un
Faune*, showing the first few steps for:

Faune
Principal Nymph : Nelidova
1st Nymph : Klementovich
2nd Nymph : Maicherska
3rd Nymph : Kopetzinska

The remaining lines are not completed; the
dancers are named but the steps are not marked:

4th Nymph : Tchernicheva
5th Nymph : Khokhlova
6th Nymph
  (Joyful Nymph) : Nijinska

The names are all written in Russian, so
the three Polish names—Nijinska, Maicherska,
and Kopetzinska—are written as Nijinskaya,
Maicherskaya, and Kopetzinskaya. The name
of Tchernicheva as the fourth nymph dates this
manuscript as probably having been written
early in 1913, in either Berlin or London,
after Nijinsky chose her for the part originally to be danced by Tcherepanova, who died
in the fall of 1912. Photograph of original
document in the Nijinska Archives.

N.1.

STRAND FRONT.

SAVOY HOTEL, LONDON.

Le 18 Juillet 1912

Mon cher maître

Si vous n'aimez pas le "Dirigeable" –
supprimons le. J'ai évidemment
compris l'aéroplane comme un
panneau décoratif, peint par
Bakst, qui traverserait au
fond de la scène et qui par
ses ailes noires pourrait don-
ner un effet nouveau. Comme
l'action du ballet est placée dans

l'année 1920 – l'apparition de cette
machine ne devrait intéresser nullement
les personnes sur la scène. Ils ont
seulement peur d'être remarqués
du dirigeable. Mais enfin – je n'y
tiens pas trop là-dessus. Seulement
"l'averse" ne me satisfait pas non
plus, et je trouve, qu'on peut tou-
jours finir sur le lever
côté disparition de tous les trois
dans un bond final.
Quant au "style" du ballet – Nijinsky dit qu'il voit surtout de
la "danse" – Scherzo-valse – beaucoup
de pointes – pour tous les trois. Grand
secret – parce que jusqu'à présent
jamais un homme n'ait dansé
sur les pointes. Il le ferait le premier
et je pense que ça peut être très

104–107. Letter from Diaghilev to Debussy
explaining the concept of *Jeux*. Original
letter in the Nijinska Archives.

SAVOY HOTEL, LONDON.

STRAND FRONT.

.......................19.....

108. *Jeux* (Schollar, Nijinsky, and Karsavina).
Watercolor drawing by Dorothy Mullock, London, 1913.

109, 110. Two 1912 snapshots
of Diaghilev, one alone in
typical pose, the other with
Nijinsky and Stravinsky.
Both given to Nijinska by
Diaghilev.

111. Nijinsky in London, 1914.
Snapshot by Nijinska.

112. Nijinsky with Maurice Ravel,
during the visit to Ravel's apartment
in 1914 described by Nijinska.
*(Photograph from the collection of
Boris Kochno, courtesy of the Dance
Collection, The New York Public
Library at Lincoln Center)*

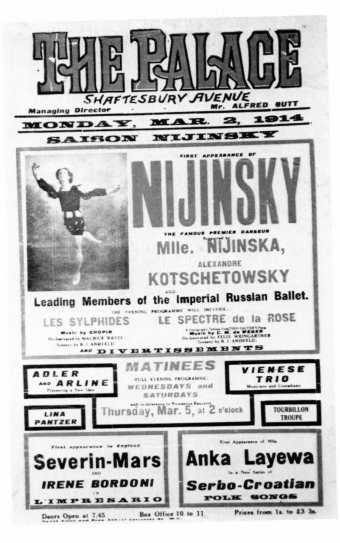

113. Poster announcing Saison Nijinsky
at the Palace Theatre, London, 1914.
Original poster in the Nijinska Archives.

told her that Vaslav had pneumonia and that I had pleurisy, and that we should both remain in bed. Mother was very worried about us, particularly me. I had a temperature, my chest was congested, and I was coughing a lot. She looked after me day and night, and was very angry with Sasha for not having made sure that I always had a hot bowl of soup at night. "Bronia never eats anything," she told him. "You have to make sure she eats enough. Look how pale and thin she is."

Mother also blamed herself for delaying her own departure from St. Petersburg. When we had first asked her to join us after Father's death she had written that the attorney had advised her to stay and submit a petition asking for the release of her son from his military service obligation. He said she could do this on the grounds that she was now widowed and her eldest son had been committed to a sanatorium since 1902, and that she depended entirely upon her son Vaslav Nijinsky for her financial support. When she arrived Mother told us that she was very hopeful that following the new petition Vaslav would be freed from all military service obligations and would at last be able to return to Russia.

But in Berlin Mother got to worrying about Vaslav and me, for neither of us was recovering from our colds, and then we both got up sooner than the doctor wished to prepare for our opening performance. I could tell how ill Vaslav was feeling—he was so irritable with Bolm during the rehearsals for *Cléopâtre* and *Carnaval*—and on the day before the performance I was running a temperature and coughing badly. Mother insisted that we should stay in bed, until Diaghilev arrived to tell us that Kaiser Wilhelm was going to attend our performance, "and colds or not, you must both dance."

For our opening night in Berlin on December 11, we danced *Carnaval*, *L'Aprés-Midi d'un Faune*, *Cléopâtre*, and *Danses Polovetsiennes*. Kaiser Wilhelm came backstage and congratulated Diaghilev on the performance of *Cléopâtre*, and he spoke with Vaslav for a long time about *Faune*, being extremely interested in antique bas-reliefs of which he had a great collection. The following day he sent Vaslav a copy of one of his own rare bas-reliefs in a similar style to that used by Vaslav as the inspiration for his choreography of *Faune*. The Kaiser also sent scholars to study our performance of *Cléopâtre* so that they might learn from it about Egypt.*

During our rehearsals in Berlin Vaslav continued to be irritable and nervous. I particularly remember one incident when we were rehearsing *Les Sylphides*. I had received several pairs of new toe shoes in Berlin that

---

*Years later when I was working in Hollywood with Max Reinhardt, choreographing the ballet scenes for his film, *A Midsummer Night's Dream*, he told me that he had been present that night in Berlin and how much he had admired Vaslav's *Faune*. (BN)

needed to be broken in before our performances, and so I wanted to wear them during rehearsals. But ever since my early lessons with Vaslav during the summer of 1906, when we were both still students in the Imperial Theatrical School, he had always refused to work with me in hard toe shoes, making me wear instead soft men's shoes to dance on toe.

Because I had been ill, I had not had time to soften the shoes before the rehearsal. Dancing together with Vaslav in *Les Sylphides*, my balance was not as sure as usual, and Vaslav became very impatient with me when he realized I was wearing toe shoes. "I hate toe shoes, why do you have to wear them?"

It was never his custom to assist me in the *pirouettes;* he never stood close behind me, so I did the *pirouettes* and finished on *arabesque* on my own, Vaslav barely touching my waist with his two fingers. But in this rehearsal, because I was still weak after my illness and was not as sure of my balance in my new shoes, I could not hold the *arabesque*. Bolm, who was conducting the rehearsals, would not let us proceed but asked us to repeat it. Vaslav was annoyed at this "interference" by Bolm, and when it came to my *grand jeté*, where Vaslav had to toss me higher than my natural elevation, this time in nervous exasperation he tossed me even higher than usual, and I could not gather enough strength to land easily on my own. I stumbled and fell, and Bolm stopped the rehearsal, saying to Vaslav, "You must apologize to Bronia. That is no way to treat your sister."

Vaslav was so angry that he walked out of the rehearsal and declared that he would not dance in the performance that evening.

Diaghilev, as he usually did whenever he wanted to calm Vaslav down, asked me to go and see him. I had a hard time before I was able to persuade Vaslav to dance that evening. I told Diaghilev that Vaslav was not fully recovered from his cold, also that he found working with Bolm an impossible strain. Diaghilev could see that I too was not well and insisted that I should see a doctor immediately.

The doctor, using the new X-ray techniques, told me that both my lungs were affected and that I must stop dancing. He recommended that I go to Switzerland, to a sanatorium in Davos. When I protested, the doctor said that although he could not force me to go to Davos or stop me from dancing, he could and did warn me that if I did not follow his advice, he believed I had no more than six months to live.

I replied, "If I go to Davos and stay in a TB sanatorium, then I know I shall be infected and will not come out alive."

From Berlin we went to Budapest where Marie Rambert, Dalcroze's student, joined us. Diaghilev announced that she was to teach a daily lesson in Eurhythmics to the whole ballet company. To register my protest at this project, I did not attend the first lesson. Despite Diaghilev's strict order that the whole company attend these classes, only half the members showed up for "Rythmitchka's," as we had nicknamed her, second class, and the third was attended only by Adolf Bolm, who had long been a supporter of the Dalcroze System, and two other artists who did not wish to displease Diaghilev. So the project to initiate Dalcroze lessons in rhythm for the company was abandoned after only three classes.

Diaghilev also wanted to make use of Marie Rambert as a dancer, despite the fact that she had not been trained or prepared for ballet performances. Soon after she joined us, Sergei Pavlovitch asked me to show Marie Rambert my solo in the "Bacchanale" in *Cléopâtre*. I protested, "Why me? Why are you replacing me?" But Diaghilev countered, "Bronia, I cannot recognize you. This is not like you. You must know better than anyone else that I always like to give a chance to young artists."

Bolm was working with Marie Rambert to prepare her for this first solo in a ballet performance. But she was not able to effect the syncopation of Glazounov's music, which accented the weak beat of the measure instead of the strong beat. She danced this role for only one performance, when she herself realized she was not ready. After watching our classes with Maestro Cecchetti she began to study with him. Soon she was dancing well in the *corps de ballet* in ballets mounted in the Duncan-Fokine style.

I liked Marie Rambert, whom we called Mim for short. I enjoyed her company. She was a cultured person and well-read; she was interesting to talk to, and she told me that she had studied with Duncan and had taken a few lessons in Paris with Madame Rat of the Paris Opéra.

In January 1913 we came to Vienna, the most musical city in the world and the birthplace of so many great composers. Nowhere in the world is there a better orchestra than that of the Opera Theatre in Vienna, and it was this orchestra that was playing for our ballet performances.

During the first orchestral rehearsal of *Petrouchka* the musicians, after only one look at the notes placed in front of them, refused to play Stravinsky's music, saying they considered it an insult to perform such a piece of music where each note was in disaccord with the laws of harmony.

The Vienna Opera Orchestra consisted of many respected figures in the world of music, including professors from the Vienna Conservatory of Music; they were all fine musicians, and our conductor, Pierre Monteux, had no authority to force them to play, or even to listen to him. The presence of Igor Stravinsky in the *parterre* did not bother them in the least.

As we artists began to come onstage, ready for our first rehearsal with the orchestra, we grew more and more anxious as we followed the increasingly heated arguments among these gray-haired, distinguished musicians. Was it possible that *Petrouchka* would be removed from the program? *Petrouchka*, which had become our favorite ballet.

At last Sergei Pavlovitch arrived. I can see him now as he stood in the *parterre* behind the barrier of the orchestra pit. His imposing figure and the look of contempt on his face had an immediate effect on the musicians. The pounding and tapping of violin bows on the music stands lessened as he spoke up.

"Shame. I cannot believe that I am in the Vienna Opera House among the members of a world-famous orchestra and not among some shoemakers* who do not know a thing about music." He fitted his monocle to his eye and then sternly continued: "Stravinsky is a musical genius, the greatest contemporary musician, and you are refusing to play his music? Stravinsky has been recognized and his music admired by musicians throughout Europe—in Paris, in Leipzig, in Dresden, in Berlin. Stravinsky is a young man, but in his music he is older than any of you. And all of you here must be lacking in culture if you do not understand Stravinsky's music. There was a time when Vienna accused Beethoven of violating the rules of harmony. Do not show yourselves to be as ignorant again. Play the composition before you pass judgment. Please, let's start the rehearsal."

During this entire scene Stravinsky had been nervously pacing the floor in the *parterre*, looking like a sparrow in winter, his shoulders hunched up, his scarf wrapped around his neck up to his ears.

After Diaghilev's harsh words, the noise and bow-rapping completely stopped; no longer were any protests heard. The musicians took their places and began to play. As the rehearsal progressed, the musicians became more and more enraptured by the music, and when they had finished playing *Petrouchka* they applauded Pierre Monteux and gave a standing ovation to Igor Stravinsky.

Stravinsky, who was very sensitive to applause, was now beaming, his shoulders straightened, his head held high, and his scarf hanging loosely around his shoulders. Diaghilev, like the victor of a great battle, was smiling his most charming smile and had let his monocle fall from his eye so that it was swinging by its black cord.

*See note, page 394. (IN/JR)

456

52   Preparation of
Le Sacre du Printemps:
London and Monte Carlo

WHEN STRAVINSKY joined us in Vienna he brought with him the completed orchestral score for *Le Sacre du Printemps*. The manuscript was dated November 4 [N.S. 17], 1912 and signed Igor Stravinsky.

From Vienna we went to London where Diaghilev had arranged that during our six-week season at Covent Garden Theatre, Vaslav would have the use of the Aldwych Theatre to hold his own rehearsals for his two new ballets without interruption. I was called for some of the early rehearsals with a few other dancers, but most of the time was taken by Stravinsky explaining to Steiman what to play on the piano from his orchestral score. Vaslav stood by listening to the music as Steiman played, and to my dismay I noticed Mim standing beside the piano apparently explaining something to my brother. I wondered: "What can Marie Rambert, who hardly knows how to dance, teach Nijinsky?"

I did not say anything to Vaslav, but I must have made my feelings obvious to the other artists. I soon noticed that Vaslav was avoiding me, and then he did not even call me for rehearsals of the "Danse Sacrale." So whenever I had the chance to use the stage or the rehearsal hall I worked on the dance on my own. But realizing that Vaslav was angry with me, I went to talk with him and clear matters between us. He reproached me for criticizing his method of work to others, saying that I obviously did not care for his new choreography.

This was so unfair. It was true that I did not approve of applying the Dalcroze System to a choreographic composition, but I felt that whatever I had said had been deliberately distorted by the "Dalcrozians" trying to make trouble between Vaslav and myself.

Vaslav and I continued to talk over tea at a Lyons Corner House, and gradually he began to tell me more about *Sacre*, saying that he was inspired not only by the music but also by the libretto as written by Roerich and Stravinsky, and that he was being greatly encouraged in his creative work by Roerich. "He perceives and understands my work. But Bronia, I am often exasperated by Igor Feodorovitch. I have a great respect for him as a musician, and we have been friends for years, but so much time is wasted as Stravinsky thinks he is the only one who knows anything about music. In working with me he explains the value of the black notes, the white notes, of quavers and semiquavers, as though I had never studied music at all."

"But Vaslav, you know he does that to everyone. He even teaches Steiman how to read notes when they play together on the piano, and Steiman is not only a pianist but also a conductor."

This did not console Vaslav. He went on sadly, "I only wish I could hear the music without so many unnecessary breaks. I wish he would talk more about *his* music for *Sacre*, and not give a lecture on the beginning theory of music."

The score of Stravinsky's *Sacre du Printemps* was so complicated that even great conductors could not immediately follow it, and during later rehearsals with the orchestra it was necessary for Stravinsky to stand next to the conductor to assist him.

I was not dancing as many leading parts during the London Season, since Karsavina had again joined us. On February 4, the opening night in London, I danced in *Les Sylphides* with Karsavina and Nijinsky, and as I leaped in a *grand jeté* in the Mazurka a black cat crossed the stage in front of me.

What a bad omen!

In the intermission following *Les Sylphides* I learned that Diaghilev had invited Sophia Fedorova to dance with us again and she would be dancing Ta-Hor in *Cléopâtre*, on February 17.

I went to Diaghilev and asked him, "Why are you replacing me? I have been dancing this role with great success. You, yourself, have always praised me for it." He simply replied, "I need a *ballerina* for the London Season!" I recalled then how in Berlin, a few weeks before, Diaghilev had asked me to dye my hair red and to "dress more like a *ballerina*." But I had refused. I felt that dyed red hair would make me look like a *rizhi* [a red-haired clown] and what concerned me about my appearance was how I looked onstage, not how glamorous I could make myself for a social event.

During our season in London I had been feeling indisposed and experiencing occasional dizzy spells. Nevertheless I had continued to take part in the performances, and by the end of our season I was feeling much stronger.

From London we went again to Monte Carlo for our usual spring season there, and on our way south we stopped at Lyon, where we gave one performance before proceeding on to Monte Carlo. Because both Karsavina and Fedorova had returned to Russia, I was again to dance the Ballerina Doll in *Petrouchka* and Ta-Hor in *Cléopâtre*, as well as my usual roles of Papillon in *Carnaval*, Bacchante in *Narcisse*, and Mazurka in *Les Sylphides*. Bolm was to replace or alternate with Vaslav in several of his roles to give Vaslav more time to work on his two new ballets. The general rehearsals were now conducted by Grigoriev, and I was kept busy attending those as well as the full rehearsals for *Sacre*. However, as the Chosen Maiden does not appear onstage until the second scene, I was able to watch how Vaslav was creating his new ballet.

As he had in *Faune*, Nijinsky in *Sacre* took the ensemble as a whole and in his choreographic composition manipulated the artists as one unit. In Nijinsky's choreography the symmetrical arrangements and repeated patterns of the *corps de ballet* no longer existed. Fokine had preserved the traditional patterns of Petipa's delightful *Swan Lake* in his own masterpiece *Les Sylphides*, and even in *Danses Polovetsiennes*, when the wild hordes leap around the stage, forming a well-centered perfect circle, then crisscross the stage keeping an even distance from each other in the same fashion as the symmetric designs of Petipa's ballets.

In Nijinsky's choreography these even, symmetrical, repeated patterns were not seen. Perhaps in the ballet they reminded Vaslav of trained animals, or horses and elephants in the circus, or of the maneuvers of the army regiments during our childhood. Be that as it may, the theme of *Sacre*, depicting the primitiveness of the pagan rituals in Russia in the pre-Christian era, excluded the possibility of such orderly formations and the invariable preservation of symmetrical patterns in choreographic composition.

The men in *Sacre* are primitive. There is something almost bestial in their appearance. Their legs and feet are turned inwards, their fists clenched, their heads held down between hunched shoulders; their walk, on slightly bent knees, is heavy as they laboriously straggle up a winding trail, stamping in the rough, hilly terrain.

The women in *Sacre* are also primitive, but in their countenances one already perceives the awakening of an awareness of beauty. Still, their postures and movements are uncouth and clumsy as they gather in clusters on the tops of small hillocks and come down together to meet in the middle of the stage and form a large crowd.

Nijinsky's creation of a novel structure in the choreography and his innovative movements and poses demanded an exactness of execution to the minutest detail. All this was strange and unfamiliar to the artists brought up in the traditions of the old classical ballet, in which, though used to maintaining an even distance between the dancers, whether dancing in straight, parallel, diagonal, or circular lines, they had always been allowed a certain freedom in the execution of the ballet. They resented and did not understand Nijinsky's demand for exactness in every detail and protested at what they considered unreasonable demands.

Sometimes when they were so tired and exhausted by the long rehearsals they refused altogether to work with Nijinsky. One must possess a strong conviction in his truth and a strong willpower to be able to proceed and work in such a hostile and negative atmosphere.

Often Diaghilev had to intervene, mostly to calm Nijinsky, who did not understand that certain of his created *pas-mouvements*, which he demonstrated with such ease in a huge jump, were not possible for the average dancer. Nijinsky was indignantly angry, believing that this inability of an artist to repeat the *pas-mouvement* after him was a deliberate act of obstruction, and he accused the artists of wanting to sabotage his ballet.

I remember one particular incident during the early rehearsals in Monte Carlo. Nijinsky demonstrated a *pas-mouvement* in the choreography to the musical count of 5/4. During his huge leap he counted 5 (3 + 2). On count 1, high in the air, he bent one leg at the knee and stretched his right arm above his head, on count 2 he bent his body towards the left, on count 3 he bent his body towards the right, then on count 1, still high in the air, he stretched his body upwards again and then finally came down lowering his arm on count 2, graphically rendering each note of the uneven measure.

Nijinsky worked in this manner on each measure, accenting the beats for the artists, and would not proceed in his composition until he obtained from each artist the exact execution. This took considerable time and created the impression that Nijinsky himself was proceeding at a slow pace in creating his composition. This was far from the truth, as could be seen when Vaslav worked with those few artists who understood him and with whom the work went fast.

Over the years, being always in the company of Diaghilev, Vaslav had kept to himself and rarely seen his colleagues outside the theatre, and now that he was working with them as a choreographer he was not able to establish a contact with them, to create a favorable atmosphere among the *corps de ballet*, loyal for the most part to Fokine. He was unable to reach them personally and obtain their cooperation, so that they might believe in him and be supportive of his work and ideas, so essential during the process of creation, especially in the realization of a choreographer's aspirations.

Many of Diaghilev's entourage, the balletomanes and critics from prominent Russian newspapers who came to Monte Carlo for the ballet season, did not even try to conceal their disapproval of Nijinsky's choreography when they came to watch his rehearsals. Of course many had already had great difficulty in accepting the innovations in Fokine's choreography. Now, they could not begin to understand Nijinsky's choreographic composition. They would be heard to say, "What kind of ballet is this? Without the skill of the classical dance there is nothing harmonious to the eyes. These heavy movements, the legs turned inwards, have nothing graceful about them."

Only Roerich supported Vaslav. He often came to the rehearsals and encouraged Vaslav, who would listen attentively. The only time Vaslav appeared relaxed during rehearsals was when he was with Roerich. Vaslav often told me how much he liked to listen to Roerich talking about his studies of the origin of man, describing the pagan rites and the prehistory of the tribes "that roamed the land we now call Russia."

In London, when Vaslav and I had talked in detail about *Sacre*, he had explained more to me about my own role, telling me that he wanted me to portray the fanatic strength of the maiden who is ready to sacrifice her life to save the earth by dancing in a frenzied delirium until falling inert to the ground, killed by her own dance.

I had been coming to all Vaslav's rehearsals in Monte Carlo, even though he was working with the artists of the first scene and did not need me yet. Soon after arriving in Monte Carlo I had gone to see a doctor who confirmed that my recent indisposition was not due to ill health as everyone else thought, but because I was pregnant. He told me that the baby was due in October. I wanted to keep my condition secret from the company, for I was feeling quite strong and able to dance in all the ballets for the Monte Carlo Season. But Mother said that Vaslav should be told immediately . . . "So he does not demand that you dance at full force during the rehearsals. During the first weeks of pregnancy you could risk a miscarriage."

But I knew that Vaslav was demanding perfection in the execution of each *pas-mouvement* and would not proceed until he saw each one executed correctly and performed with the proper rhythm and force. I did not think he would let me simply mark my solo. So I had to tell Vaslav that not only could I not dance at full force for the rehearsals in Monte Carlo, but also he should think of someone to replace me in my solo in case I couldn't . . .

He did not let me continue but screamed at me, "There is no one to replace you. You are the only one who can perform this dance, only you, Bronia, and no one else!"

I tried to explain that it would be detrimental to his choreography if I did not perform adequately and that he could hardly expect me to dance with complete abandon just now and throw myself violently to the ground. Valsav did not seem to hear a word I was saying. He yelled, "You are deliberately trying to destroy my work, just like all the others."

Mother tried in vain to calm Vaslav, telling him this was not so. "There is nothing unusual in a married woman having children, but you must understand how critical the first weeks are for the welfare of the mother and child."

I was trembling and crying when Sasha, who had been in our room next door and heard the screaming and yelling, burst into Mother's room. Vaslav turned on my husband and looked ready to strike him. He called Sasha an uncouth *moujik* with no consideration for his wife who was recovering from a serious illness.

I had agreed with Mother that Vaslav should be told of my pregnancy, but had been apprehensive about his reaction, for lately Vaslav had been extremely nervous and tense during his rehearsals of *Sacre*. But I was completely unprepared for this violent outburst of uncontrollable temper.

During the rest of the time in Monte Carlo I tried to avoid him, even keeping away from him when he came in the afternoon to see Mother. I found something frightening in Vaslav and was afraid that his seeing me would provoke further outbursts of rage. I would have liked to be able to tell him how much I admired his choreography for *Sacre*, and that I knew how exhausting and fatiguing it was for him to be surrounded by uncooperative artists and try to create a ballet in such a hostile atmosphere. It was painful for me to realize just what an effort it cost him to obtain from the artists such exactness in the execution of a choreography they did not understand.

Finally Vaslav selected Maria Piltz to replace me as the Chosen Maiden. She had already danced with Vaslav in *Le Spectre de la Rose*, replacing Tamara Karsavina when the latter had returned to the Maryinsky to fulfill one of her engagements there.

Maria Piltz was one of the few artists who was sympathetic towards all of Vaslav's work; she even seemed to me to be a little in love with him. I showed Maroussia my solo, and later Nijinsky himself rehearsed with her. I think he adapted some parts of the dance for her, as Piltz was taller than I and did not have my high elevation and strong movements, nor my dance technique. She was, however, very musical, cultured, and even-tempered. She was also completely aware of the responsibilities entrusted to her in this solo dance and worked hard on it until she achieved a high artistic execution.

53

Paris:
Saison d'Opéra et Ballet,
May 1913

OUR 1913 SEASON in Paris was to be presented in the Théâtre des Champs Elysées, newly opened that April. The beautiful building was decorated outside with sculpted bas-reliefs by Emile-Antoine Bourdelle and inside with large murals, frescoes, and a gilded bas-relief by Maurice Denis.

Vaslav had already told me that Bourdelle had used Isadora Duncan and himself as the inspiration and models for *La Danse*, the bas-relief for the façade of the Theatre. Bourdelle had seen Vaslav and Isadora dance together during a soirée in Paris sometime the previous year. In his notes concerning *La Danse*, Bourdelle wrote:

> The Dance is perhaps pretty, but it is also grave. It is like a meditation, at least I would like it to be so.
> Isadora, bending and throwing back her fine head, closes her eyes to dance within in her pure emotion.
> Her hands lightly touch the marble sky. They seem to die and their life pass away in well-arranged planes.
> He, the dancer, a Nijinski [sic], tears himself away with a wild leap from the marble still holding him fast. His bony feet are lifted far from the earth but the block will retain this man who carries within him the winged genius of the birds.*

The opening of the Theatre had been marred by the news of the tragic death of Isadora Duncan's two children and her withdrawal from the world. Vaslav had been very distressed at the news, for he had come to know her children, and he was very grieved for Duncan. His sorrow brought us closer again as he talked to me about Duncan and her children. This tragedy cast a depressing shadow over our season in Paris, the first theatrical engagement in the new Théâtre des Champs Elysées.

Diaghilev had planned a season of opera and ballet performances to

---

*Translation taken from "Isadora in Art," in *Dance Index*, vol. 5, no. 3, March 1946. (IN/JR)

open with Chaliapin in the opera *Boris Godunov*. The first new ballet to be presented in Paris would be *Le Sacre du Printemps*, having its premiere performance on May 29. *Jeux*, the other new ballet, would be presented later in the season.

Sometime while we had been in Monte Carlo, Diaghilev had gone to Russia to continue his negotiations with the Imperial Theatres in Moscow and St. Petersburg for artists, sets, and costumes for the operas he was planning. When he rejoined us in Paris he told us that since many of the opera singers would not be free to join us until May 20, he was changing his planned program. Instead of *Boris Godunov* he was arranging for ballet performances to open our season, and suddenly he announced that *Jeux* was to have its premiere on May 15, 1913.

But *Jeux*, originally planned for June, was not ready. After his early work on the ballet with us in Monte Carlo at the end of the summer, in 1912, Vaslav had not called any further rehearsals with Vassilievska and myself. Perhaps he was waiting for Karsavina to return from Russia so that he could work with her and myself in preparation for the Paris premiere the next year. When it was arranged for Vaslav to hold rehearsals in the Aldwych Theatre in London in February, Diaghilev expected that he would apply himself to both *Jeux* and *Sacre*. But Vaslav was working with Stravinsky at the time and concentrating on *Sacre*, which was expected to be premiered in Paris first. He wanted to finish that ballet before resuming rehearsals for *Jeux* (though he may also have worked occasionally on *Jeux* in London, either alone or with Karsavina).

I did not take part in the final creation of *Jeux*. I was replaced by Ludmila Schollar, who had rejoined our company in Paris. Vaslav had problems in his work with both Schollar and Karsavina. Both were critical of their roles and worked reluctantly.

In her *Memoirs*, as published in Russian, Karsavina wrote about these rehearsals, complaining that Nijinsky

> never could explain what he wanted of me and it was extremely difficult to learn a role by the mechanical process, blindly imitating those poses shown to you. I had to have my head turned to one side and keep the arms twisted and the hands clenched as though I had been maimed from birth. If I had understood the purpose of these movements the work would have been noticeably easier. Being in complete igno-rance, I would from time to time resume a normal position, and Nijinsky decided that I was deliberately refusing to submit to his direction.
> Being the best of friends both onstage and off, we always argued when rehearsing our roles. On the subject of the [two girls in the ballet]

our arguments were more heated than ever. As I could understand absolutely nothing I had to learn all the movements by heart. Once I asked "What's next?" and Nijinsky said to me, "You should have known yourself a long time ago! I will not tell you!"*

As a dancer and choreographer myself, I wonder why Karsavina objected to the "mechanical process" in her rehearsals with Nijinsky. No choreographer ever explained movements to us with words. He showed us the consecutive *pas*, one after the other, exactly as the dance was composed, and by mechanically copying the choreographer we memorized all the *pas*. And then, inspired by the choreographic design, we ourselves created our roles. Why should it have seemed so unusual to Karsavina in her rehearsals with Nijinsky to learn the movements mechanically, repeating what Nijinsky showed her?

I remember that Fokine never explained anything to us in words; often he was not even exact concerning the nuances of the movements. I took part in all of Fokine's new ballets except *Daphnis et Chloë*, and I remember that he simply showed us the *pas*, and was not even precise in his demonstrations. Of course it is true that many of these *pas* were already familiar to us from our ballet classes in the Imperial Theatrical School.

Taking part in Nijinsky's ballets—*L'Après-Midi d'un Faune*, the early rehearsals of *Jeux*, and the Chosen Maiden solo in *Le Sacre du Printemps*—I never thought to ask about the meaning of the dance that I was executing. I was simply trying to interpret as perfectly as I could the choreography that Nijinsky was creating. And it was as I did so that I began to feel in each of my movements the meaning and the image created by Nijinsky.

Later, as a choreographer myself, how could I explain my treatment of the Blue Girl in *Les Biches?* Why does she walk on toe this way and not any other? Why does she hold a certain free position? One might as well ask a painter what comes next. The evolution proceeds naturally in the process of creation. And choreography is a *silent* art: the choreographer creates his images, not in words but in plastic positions and rhythmic movements that can only be explained as inspiration, the choreographer's creative intuition.

When I was mounting *Les Biches*, Vera Nemtchinova had difficulty in applying her academic classical technique to my new mechanics in the dance, but as she assiduously strove to reproduce without question the

*Bronislava Nijinska quoted this Russian text making the one alteration in the phrase we have bracketed, i.e., text reads "two ballets," which Nijinska corrected to "two girls in the ballet." Translation directly from Nijinska's copy of Karsavina's Russian text: *Teatralnaya Ulitza*, Leningrad, 1971. (IN/JR)

poses and movements mounted for her she obtained a novel image, thereby achieving great success for both herself and the whole ballet.

Nijinsky did not find this support or cooperation from his two soloists in *Jeux*, Karsavina and Schollar.

I first saw the complete ballet on the occasion of the dress rehearsal and was immediately disappointed by the sets and costumes designed by Bakst: a huge open stage, a pale gray-green garden. The stage appeared deserted and the three figures of the participants could hardly fill this void; they appeared as lonely figures wandering lost in the desert. I became concerned for the success of the ballet. The decor did not seem to me to contribute to Nijinsky's choreography. For this ballet it should have been a more intimate decor—a corner in the garden, and not the whole wide space of a deserted park. The costumes, themselves, sports dress for tennis made by Maison Paquin, were good in their simplicity and contemporaneity. Nijinsky wore a white shirt with an open collar above a wide red tie, with his sleeves rolled up to the elbows. His white flannel trousers were after the same style that Vaslav wore for practicing, tight around the calves with a row of buttons at the side. The girls wore short white sports skirts and tight knitted tops with short sleeves. Usually Bakst's costumes had been part of the scenic decor, but in *Jeux* the brightness of the white did not go well.

On the eve of the premiere of *Jeux* in Paris, an article appeared in *Le Figaro* describing a lunch attended by Hector Cahusac with a group of French and Russian artists in the Bois de Boulogne in the spring of 1912. Among those present were Diaghilev, Bakst, Cocteau, Blanche, Debussy, and Nijinsky. The conversation centered on choreographic art and the difficulty of finding a good subject for a ballet. Some asserted that only history offered material for a good dancing performance; others felt that it was never possible to maintain an accurate rendering of a historical style and at the same time be in accord with contemporary choreographic ideas.

Cahusac quoted Nijinsky's own comments in *Le Figaro*:

The man that I see foremost on the stage is a contemporary man. I imagine the costume, the plastic poses, the movement that would be representative of our time. . . . By attentively studying polo, golf, tennis, I have become convinced that sports are not only a healthy pastime but also create their own plastic beauty. From studying them I derive the hope that in the future this contemporary style will be considered a characteristic style as we now consider those of the past.*

Le Figaro, No. 134, May 14, 1913.

In a letter to Debussy a few months after this spring luncheon, Diaghilev attributed ideas to Nijinsky that suggested that the style of the ballet *Jeux* would be rather different.

Savoy Hotel, London
18 July, 1912

My dear 'Maître,'

If you do not like the "dirigible" we will delete it. I had evidently understood the aeroplane as a decorative panel, to be painted by Bakst, which would move across the back of the stage, its black wings giving a novel effect. As the action of the ballet takes place in the year 1920—the apparition of this machine will be of no interest whatsoever to the persons onstage. They will only be afraid of being watched from the dirigible. However I shall not insist too strongly on this. Only the "downpour" does not satisfy me either and I think we could quite well finish on the kiss and the disappearance of all three in a final leap.

As to the "style" of the ballet—NIJINSKY says that he sees above all—"*the dance*"—Scherzo-valse—lots of *pointes* for all THREE. Great secret—because up till the present *never* has a man danced on toe. He would be the *first* to do so and I think it would be very elegant. He sees the dance from the beginning to the end of the ballet, as in "Spectre de la Rose." He says he will try to ensure the same design of the dance for all three of them to unify them as much as possible. There, then, is the general style and as you see it will have nothing in common with the ideas he expressed in "Faune." I think this information will be sufficient and we are awaiting a new masterpiece from you. I hope you have already begun! Time is short. I expect to be in Paris for a day next Tuesday and hope you will reserve a quarter of an hour for conversation with me. I will call you on the telephone as soon as I arrive in Paris.

Please remember me to Madame Debussy and accept, dear Maître, the assurance of my most respectful greetings,

S. de Diaghilev*

I do not know how much Diaghilev later discussed these ideas with either Debussy or Nijinsky. But Debussy did not write valses for *Jeux*, and Nijinsky did not dance on toe.

In Paris Debussy had come to watch the rehearsals, but I do not remember him participating in the work with Vaslav. He always remained politely silent and did not engage my brother in discussions about the ballet or the designs of his complicated music; nevertheless, there was a genuine feeling between them, and I know that my brother was a sincere admirer of Debussy's music.

*For original, see Illustrations 104–107. (IN/JR)

After seeing Nijinsky's choreography for *Jeux* for the first time, Debussy, in a letter to his friend Godet, condemned the Dalcrozian theories in the strongest terms. He deplored the fact that,

Nijinsky has given an odd mathematical twist to his perverse genius. This fellow adds up semiquavers with his feet, proves the result with his arms and then as if suddenly struck by paralysis of one side listens for a while to the music, disapprovingly. This it appears is to be called the stylization of gesture. *How awful! It is in fact Dalcrozian and this is to tell you that I hold Monsieur Dalcroze to be one of the worst enemies of music! You can imagine what havoc his method has caused in the soul of this wild young Nijinsky!* *

The ballet was not a success, and after a few performances in Paris and London *Jeux* was dropped from the repertoire of the Ballets Russes.

It had seemed to me that during the year Vaslav had lost interest in this ballet and did not carry out his initial ideas that he had shown me in Monte Carlo in 1912. I also felt that one reason for the lack of success of *Jeux* was the decor by Bakst.

But *Jeux* did live on for me. When the critics indicated the influence of *Faune* in my choreography of *Les Noces*, they were wrong. I was formed as a choreographer more by *Jeux* and *Le Sacre du Printemps*. The unconscious art of those ballets inspired my initial work. From them, I sought to realize the potential of my brother's creativity in terms of neoclassical and modern dance.

———

After the premiere of *Jeux* came the premiere of *Le Sacre du Printemps*.

The dress rehearsal went smoothly, irreproachably, an ideal execution, with perfect harmony between stage and orchestra. All of us and particularly Vaslav were confident about the performance. There were, of course, the usual background grumblings, mainly among the men, who

---

*When this letter appeared in an English translation in *Debussy: His Life and Times*, vol. 2, by Edward Lockspeiser (London: Cassell, 1965), it was brought to Bronislava Nijinska's attention by Vernon Duke (Vladimir Dukelsky), the composer and a longtime friend of Nijinska's who had also been one of the four composers—with Georges Auric, Francis Poulenc, and Vittorio Rieti—playing the four pianos for the performance of Nijinska's ballet, *Les Noces*, in London in 1926.

Duke disagreed with the Lockspeiser translation from the French, which has been quoted extensively by biographers of Nijinsky. Nijinska and Duke worked together in 1968 on their own translation, which we have quoted here, in italics, from the transcription made at that time by Irina Nijinska.

Bronislava Nijinska wanted to emphasize that Debussy was not condemning Nijinsky, as is so often stated, but rather the Dalcroze System. (IN/JR)

were unhappy about the makeup, the beards, the heavy hats, and who knows what else.

The historic day arrived: May 29, 1913, the first performance of *Le Sacre du Printemps:* A tableau of pagan Russia in two acts, music by Igor Stravinsky, book by Igor Stravinsky and Nicholas Roerich, sets and costumes by Nicholas Roerich, choreography by Vaslav Nijinsky.

The Théâtre des Champs Elysées was filled and Mother had a seat in the front row. I remained back in the wings, more to be near Vaslav than to watch the action on the stage.

The orchestra sounded, the curtain opened, and suddenly from the audience came a cry of outrage. Vaslav turned pale. The noise from the public was drowning the orchestra, making it difficult for the artists to hear the music. I could see that Vaslav was in a state of extreme anxiety lest the artists miss their execution. He appeared on the point of rushing onstage to restore some kind of order in case the artists went to pieces. I wanted to grab Vaslav to prevent him from running out, but fortunately this was not necessary. From somewhere Diaghilev yelled out to the audience, "Let them finish the performance!" Standing in the wings I had felt weak and my legs had failed me. My heart was tight, not so much for the fate of the ballet as for Vaslav.

The noise and tumult continued, and it was not until near the end of the ballet, when Maria Piltz began to dance her solo, that the public quieted down.

Mama told me afterwards that it was the first time in her whole life that she had witnessed such a violent storm of protest. "I must have fainted," she said, "because I don't remember how this scandal ended."*

—

AN AWARENESS of the need for fearless self-expression—of the original, of the individual, of the unknown in art—awakened that night.

At last the mantle shrouding classical ballet, with all its old preconceived notions of "grace" and "beauty," was lifted and discarded.

---

*But Eleonora became accustomed to such "scandals." In 1925 at the Paris premiere of Nijinska's *Romeo and Juliet*, music by Constant Lambert, a group of demonstrators in the balcony who claimed to be "surrealists" and objected to Joan Miró and Max Ernst working for Diaghilev, the "capitalist," interrupted the performance with boos and stampings and showered the stalls with leaflets. When the curtain was lowered and the police cleared the demonstrators, Eleonora simply shrugged her shoulders and said to her granddaughter Irina, "Oh, not again—another scandal to get Diaghilev a front-page review . . ." (IN/JR)

Nijinsky's new discoveries in choreography were a revelation. They marked the beginning of a new era for the ballet and for choreography.

—

IN 1967, four years before he died, Igor Stravinsky spoke with Yuri Grigorovich, the choreographer of the Bolshoi Ballet, during a visit of the Bolshoi to New York. He said: "Of all the interpretations of *Sacre* that I have seen, I consider Nijinsky's the best."*

*This conversation was repeated to Bronislava Nijinska by Grigorovich when he visited her in Pacific Palisades, California, during the Bolshoi's engagement in Los Angeles. (IN/JR)

54   Towards the
        Break with Diaghilev:
        July–August 1913

EVERY TIME apparently irreconcilable differences arose between Diaghilev and Nijinsky, Sergei Pavlovitch would ask me to intercede. He would urge me to talk to Vaslav and use my influence to try to appease him or calm him down. And so it was, towards the end of our season in London in 1913, during the last days of July, that Sergei Pavlovitch asked me to come and see him at the Savoy Hotel.

When I arrived I found Diaghilev deeply disturbed; he met me with a stream of reproaches directed towards Vaslav.

"I can no longer endure Nijinsky's unpredictable behavior and his violent outbursts. It is impossible to talk to him. With each passing day it becomes more and more difficult to reason or deal with him. This is the end. I must part with Nijinsky! Concern for the affairs of the Ballets Russes compels me to make this decision!"

I had heard such words from Diaghilev before; it was not the first time he had seemed driven to a point of desperation in his anger at Vaslav. This time, however, his threats seemed more than idle words born of irritation or annoyance. Diaghilev spoke in earnest.

"I had to tell Nijinsky that his ballet *Jeux* was a complete failure, and since it has not had any success it will not be performed anymore. The same also applies to *Sacre*. All the friends of the Ballets Russes—from Paris, or London, or St. Petersburg—all agree that *Sacre* is not a ballet and it would be a mistake to follow this path of Nijinsky's. They say I am destroying my ballet company! Bronia, can you imagine Nijinsky's reaction and his response? Me, Diaghilev, to be so insulted by this young man. He is no longer a boy . . ."

I interrupted Diaghilev. "But, Sergei Pavlovitch, many critics in Paris did appreciate *Sacre*. Vaslav is a great artist. He deeply believes in his work and he defends his creations."

"A painting or a piece of music might be misunderstood at first and remain unappreciated for a long time, maybe for a hundred years . . . but a ballet must be well received by the public today and tomorrow, otherwise it is doomed to obscurity."

Again, very tactfully, I tried to intercede on Vaslav's behalf. "Perhaps you are right, Sergei Pavlovitch, and Nijinsky's choreography is not for today and may not be understood by everyone in the audience. But what Nijinsky has created in his ballets is not doomed to obscurity—it is the future of the Ballet!"

"But you must know, Bronia, how much I have done for Nijinsky. He has already choreographed three ballets. And *Jeux* and *Sacre* are not the kind of ballets that can sustain the success of the Ballets Russes. You must understand that I have a great obligation both to the financial support of my ballet company and to the needs of the theatres. The Théâtre de Monte Carlo, the Grand Opéra in Paris, and the Theatre of Covent Garden in London do not want to risk their box-office receipts. They cannot afford to be 'sponsors' for Nijinsky's researches. They want to be assured of a brilliant performance. These are the conditions I am given in my negotiations for contracts."

And now Diaghilev began to tell me the main reason why he wanted to talk with me. He was in the process of negotiating a contract with Covent Garden Theatre for a season the following year. According to the terms of the contract, Diaghilev was obligated to produce two new ballets, and both were to be choreographed by Mikhail Fokine. One of the two was to be to music by Richard Strauss, *La Légende de Joseph*. My heart fell. I knew this ballet had been promised to Nijinsky and that he had already begun working on it. And now Diaghilev had been forced to entrust its realization to Fokine.

"Nijinsky is still young and his future as a choreographer is still ahead of him. But for now I must bring Fokine back to our company. I did not want to talk about this with Nijinsky. Please, Bronia, tell him what you have heard from me and try to appease him. I myself do not want to talk to him about it."

I left Diaghilev with a heavy heart. What a situation! How could it be resolved? I was desolated to realize how much Diaghilev had come under the influence of the ballet critics and balletomanes from St. Petersburg. They had blinded him to Nijinsky's art. And I had so little time to tell Vaslav of my conversation with Diaghilev and influence him in such a way that he would be able to accept Diaghilev's intentions. The London Season was to end on August 15, and later that month the Ballets Russes was scheduled to leave for a long tour to South America. I was expecting the birth of my child in October, and Sasha and I were planning to return to Russia at the end of the London Season; so we would not be traveling with the company and would be separated from Vaslav.

When I went to see Vaslav he met me affectionately and apparently calmly. But as soon as I mentioned that I had seen Diaghilev and he had talked with me about him, Vaslav's whole attitude changed. He thrust his hands into his pockets and flung his shoulders back aggressively. He went pale and threw his head back; he stood tense, facing me, as if he were confronted by Diaghilev rather than his sister.

The more I related of my meeting with Diaghilev the angrier Vaslav became. He drew his hands out of his pockets and, clenching his fists, paced back and forth across the room, his voice from time to time rising to a shout.

"Why is Diaghilev deceiving me all the time, making up all sorts of nonsense about my ballets? Why doesn't Diaghilev speak to me himself about all this? Why does he transmit it through you? He is a coward. He is not sincere with me. He is dishonest and is afraid to tell me of his intentions."

There was no way I could calm Vaslav's angry tirade, and I was beginning to appreciate why Diaghilev himself had not wanted to talk to him.

"The matter as it stands now is that Richard Strauss and I together have already worked out the program of the music and the entire project for the ballet *Joseph*. I have been creating the ballet. . . . Let Diaghilev give it to whomever he wishes . . . to Bolm, to Fokine. I do not care about that. . . . But it does matter to me that Diaghilev has become a servile follower, a theatrical lackey, and is destroying everything that is the heart of the Ballets Russes."

Vaslav continued to throw out accusations, blaming Diaghilev for all sorts of crimes against art. It became clear to me why Diaghilev no longer wished to face Vaslav and be subjected to his anger, but for all Vaslav's resentful tirade against Diaghilev I also realized how justified Nijinsky's protests were at Diaghilev's return to Fokine.

As the days passed I became more and more worried. I knew that Vaslav had only a few friends in the ballet and that in Diaghilev's close circle he had many enemies. I felt that Fokine's supporters were launching an earnest attack not only on Nijinsky's choreography but also on his renown as a dancer.

During our next meeting Diaghilev first spoke to me about my own contract with him for 1914, stressing the need for me to sign it right away. I was shocked. To talk about my own contract just when everything seemed so terrible for Vaslav. . . . When Diaghilev handed me the contract I did not read it but put it on the table and turned the conversation to Nijinsky.

Diaghilev told me more about his plans and was quite open on his negotiations with Fokine. I had been anxious to hear what Diaghilev would say about the rumors circulating among the artists that Fokine wanted to dance all of Nijinsky's roles in his own ballets.

"That's a possibility."

"But what will Nijinsky then do in your ballet company?"

"Oh, *Giselle, Swan Lake*, and Blue Bird."

"But Nijinsky would have more to dance in the Imperial Theatres."

"Well, something has to be arranged. Nijinsky cannot return to Russia. Perhaps he should simply leave the Ballets Russes and not dance for a year."

The existence of the Ballets Russes without Nijinsky! I could not believe my ears. Nijinsky who had been at the heart of its creation and of everything that had been created in it! Impossible, I could not believe it. I wanted to believe that Diaghilev was saying all this to "tame" Nijinsky. Yet I felt strongly he was also making a great mistake in not being frank with Vaslav about his negotiations with Fokine.

I realized that Diaghilev's personal friendship with Nijinsky was over.

During my last few days in London before my departure for Russia, I spent considerable time with both Vaslav and Sergei Pavlovitch. I had become increasingly aware of Vaslav's heightened state of nervousness these past few months, as if he felt that a net was being woven around him and was about to envelop him. I tried to divert Vaslav from his concerns, talking to him about his forthcoming trip to South America, telling him that I was sorry I would not be with him during the ocean voyage and the performances in Buenos Aires, Montevideo, and Rio de Janeiro. I advised him not to worry about the future, not to concern himself with work on new ballets, but to enjoy the ocean and to become closer acquainted with the artists and make friends and not be alone so much. I also tried to convince Vaslav not to engage in "spats" with Diaghilev but to take himself in hand and remember that he was an artist.

Diaghilev continued to share with me his concern as to what to do with Nijinsky. "If he will not accept my conditions, I shall have to part with Nijinsky." At the same time he continued to insist that I should sign my own contract. I did not sign it; my thoughts were too concerned with Vaslav. Diaghilev then told me that he himself was not going with the ballet company to South America and that Baron Dmitri de Gunsburg, as his administrative co-director, would be going instead.

In my last meeting with Vaslav I was distressed to see that he was still in the same nervous state. He shouted, "I have had enough of the Ballets Russes and of Diaghilev with his mercenary commercial enterprise. I shall return to Russia to the Imperial Theatres."

I reminded Vaslav that he could not return to Russia, but as I said good-bye to him, I told him, "Dearest Vatsa, please remember that no matter what the future holds I will always be with you."

I was happy to see that my words seemed to bring some solace to his torment.

—

THE DAY OF our departure arrived. I was sitting with Sasha in the train, and just before it began to pull out of the station, Kamechov, a stagehand for the Ballets Russes, jumped into our compartment holding my still unsigned contract and a pen in his hand. He told us that he had missed me at the hotel and that Diaghilev had ordered him, "to catch Nijinska before she crosses into Russia." Kamechov showed us his ticket to go as far as the German-Russian border as he tried to persuade me to sign the contract.

Still unwillingly, but not wanting to believe that Diaghilev was trying to alienate me from my brother, halfheartedly and under pressure from my husband, I signed the contract with Diaghilev for 1914–15.

The train was one of those in which each compartment had a door opening to the outside, so Kamechov was able, as soon as I signed the contract, to jump out of the slowly moving train back onto the platform.

55   Autumn 1913

FROM LONDON I went with Sasha to Moscow to meet my husband's family, his mother and his sister.

We stayed in Moscow just under three weeks, and when we arrived in St. Petersburg we found several letters from Vaslav, the last one postmarked from Cherbourg, written just before he boarded the S.S. *Avon* to join the rest of the company already on board from Southampton. He said that Diaghilev had not come to see him off. I was worried. Did this mean that Vaslav and Sergei Pavlovitch were even further from a reconciliation than when I had left them in London? Was it possible that their long friendship was indeed ended forever? Vaslav did not mention the subject at all in his letters.

The summer vacation in Russia was over by the beginning of September, and all the officials were back at work. Now Mama and I could go to see the attorney. From him we heard the good news: Vaslav was completely exempt from military service. All the papers were in order and officially approved; they needed only the signature of the War Minister. The attorney suggested that it would be helpful if I could find some influential person in the War Ministry to receive him, so that when he came with the papers they might be signed in his presence and not have to be left to lie about at the bottom of a pile on some clerk's desk.

We wanted to keep the matter as confidential as possible, so when we got home I tried to think out carefully just whom I could ask to help us. The first one who came to mind was the ballet critic, Valerian Yakovlevitch Svetlov. I knew him quite well, and among the balletomanes of St. Petersburg he was the friendliest towards the Ballets Russes. A few days later I went with Svetlov and Ludmila Schollar to visit General Vintulov, the Adjutant of the War Minister, who was also a long-standing balletomane with a regular season ticket in the front row for all the ballet performances at the Maryinsky Theatre. Both Ludmila and Svetlov knew Vintulov well, and we had a friendly conversation while tea was served in his apartment. We told him the favor I was seeking, a plea to speed up the signature for Nijinsky's papers. The General was leaving the next day for Ufa, but promised that as soon as he returned he would take care of the matter and arrange everything.

The next day Ludmila, Svetlov, and I went to the station with a bouquet of flowers. The burly General was amused, saying that we were seeing him off like a *prima donna*.

Mama and I were happy that we now had the support of such an influential person in the War Ministry, and even though we did not yet feel completely reassured, we wrote to Vaslav telling him of the possibility that he might be able to return to Russia for the Christmas holidays and spend them in St. Petersburg at home with us.

Vaslav, as was his usual custom, was writing to Mother every day, but we received the letters from the boat in packages. The next lot came from the Island of Madeira. He was enthusiastic about the ocean voyage and sounded cheerful and relaxed, telling us about a beautiful girl he had met with flaxen hair and blue eyes. "She is also alone and we are often together."

We were happy that he was in such a good mood and thought it might be due to the shipboard atmosphere of his first long ocean voyage. I remembered too how quickly Vaslav would become infatuated with someone on first acquaintance, how he would endow her with a wealth of imagined qualities, and then just as quickly become disenchanted.

Suddenly, one morning, sitting at breakfast, I opened the newspaper and saw in bold print: NIJINSKY MARRIED.

On 10 [N.S. 23] September in Buenos Aires, Vaslav Nijinsky and Romola de Pulszky were married in the Catholic Church of San Miguel.

This newspaper dispatch brought me great joy, and I deeply wanted to share this happiness with Vaslav. Now everything that Vaslav had felt in his heart against my marriage would disappear.

But Mother's feelings were different. The news of Vaslav's unexpected marriage to an unknown woman was a terrible shock for her. She burst into tears. "Why didn't I get a telegram from Vaslav himself about his forthcoming marriage? How could he get married without his Mother's blessing?" She did not want to believe the news. "Maybe it's a hoax—a publicity stunt?"

After three days of worry and anxiety, a telegram came from Vaslav acknowledging his marriage—signed "Vatsa, Romushka"—and finally

Mother was convinced. But it was impossible to console her. Vatsa, her beloved son, who for years had written to her almost every day and was always so solicitous of her peace of mind—now suddenly he had not even advised her of his intention to get married but sent only a belated telegram about his wedding.

Mother had old-fashioned ideas about marriage, and she predicted great unhappiness for this one.

"How could any girl from a good family get married without parental blessing? . . . How did a lonely 'socialite' happen to be on board among the ballet troupe? . . . Why the urgency for a well-brought-up girl after such a short acquaintance with Vaslav to force a wedding in South America, somewhere on the other side of the world, and not wait for their return to Europe among family and friends? . . . How did they get permission to get married so quickly, foreigners newly arrived in a foreign country? . . . How did they bypass church and civil requirements? Who arranged it for them, certainly not Vaslav himself? I am afraid to think. Vaslav is surrounded by enemies who must have played into her hands."

I heard everything Mama said as a reflection of a mother's hurt and even jealousy. I wanted to believe that Vaslav and Romola sincerely loved each other. I could see nothing wrong in their marriage, I even rejoiced in it, and I was looking forward to meeting Vaslav's wife soon and becoming friends with her, as close as a sister.

In her distress Mama recalled, "I am sure now this is the same young woman who in Paris came to sit next to me during an intermission. She tried to open a conversation with me but I didn't even look at her." I myself then remembered how disturbed Mama had later been in London when she noticed the same young woman sitting next to her at Covent Garden, and after the performance had told me, "Can you imagine . . . she was here again. What do you think she wants from me?" For the next performance Mother told Baron de Gunsburg, "I would appreciate it if you did not seat me next to this young woman. She always tries to engage me in conversation and I do not understand a word she says."

I also recalled seeing this "young woman"—at least I assumed she had to be the same one. The incident came back to me vividly. It had been in the winter, at the end of our second engagement in Budapest, when the company had been assembling backstage ready to leave. We had been told to come to the wardrobe workshop to receive our pay and our train tickets. When I got there our wardrobe mistress and dressers were carefully packing all the costumes inside their large wicker hampers. I was very surprised, which is no doubt why I remember it, to find a young woman whom I'd never seen before, sitting, her legs crossed, on top of one of the hampers, looking very much at home and nonchalantly chatting with Adolf Bolm.

The custom had been established among the artists of the Diaghilev Company that we were all responsible for seeing that rules were observed and that we artists should behave correctly, as if guests in the theatre.

When Bolm walked away from this stranger I asked him, "Who is she and what is she doing here?"

"She is the daughter of a famous Hungarian actress and would like to study ballet. She came to see Maestro Cecchetti to arrange to take lessons with him."

"But she must be at least twenty-one or twenty-two, a little late to start to study classical dance. Anyway," I added, "please tell her that no one is allowed to sit on top of the hampers. She could crush the valuable costumes that are packed inside."

As Bolm turned back to her I noticed how politely he offered her a chair, saying that she would be more comfortable sitting on it than on top of a basket.

It was well known in the ballet company that Diaghilev objected to his artists being married. We were concerned as to how Sergei Pavlovitch would take the news of Vaslav's marriage. But we could not possibly imagine that Diaghilev, like us, had found out about Vaslav's marriage from the newspapers. Wouldn't Vaslav have sent a telegram to Diaghilev to announce his forthcoming marriage? But then he hadn't to us, and it was something I could not understand, knowing how much Vaslav cared for Mother and how considerate for her he had always been. It appeared most unusual and strange.

Much later, Romola told me, "I am not stupid. To give advance notice of our wedding plans to Diaghilev or to Vaslav's family and risk you stopping us . . ."

———

ON OCTOBER 7 [N.S. 20] my daughter, Irina, was born. We sent a telegram to Vaslav and from Rio de Janeiro received a joyful telegram of congratulations with Vaslav's blessings for our little one.

Ludmila Schollar came to visit me in the clinic and pinned to the baby's crib a very pretty ikon of St. Michael, the Archangel, and later when I came home she brought me a gift from General Vintulov—a beautiful large, Orenburghsky wool shawl, so fine and light that it could fit, folded, into the palm of my hand.

I wrote a thank-you note to the General and asked Ludmila to get in touch with Svetlov and ask him to talk with Vintulov, reminding him about Nijinsky's dossier and informing him that our attorney would be calling on him soon to find out when it would be convenient to bring the papers for signing by the Minister. A few mornings later our attorney told us that he had been given an appointment at the Ministry that noon.

We waited by the telephone into the afternoon. The news horrified us: the petition was turned down.

"It would have been better if you had not asked anyone to help you in this matter," the attorney said.

We rushed to see him, and he described what happened. "I arrived at the War Ministry building at the appointed time and then had to wait half an hour in the waiting room until a lady, elegantly dressed in expensive furs, came out of the Minister's office. I was then asked to come and see an aide-de-camp, who hardly looked at the papers in front of him. He told me that the Minister had been informed about Nijinsky and that there was no further need to review this case. Nijinsky's petition was denied!"

The attorney then told us that when he pointed out that this petition now submitted by Nijinsky was a new one, based on the law that as the son of a widow he was her sole support, her elder son being mentally ill and confined to a sanatorium, the aide-de-camp merely smiled and said, "All Nijinsky can do now is to return from abroad and serve his term in the military service. And besides, I have just learned that Nijinsky is very wealthy and that he has ample means to support his mother well enough during the three years he would be in the service, and that her daughter is also an artist and receiving a good salary."

Although he felt insulted at being received by an aide-de-camp, the attorney could hardly raise an objection and antagonize the Minister or his Adjutant, General Vintulov, by saying that a decision based on such information was illegal!

The attorney felt that he had been insulted by this reception and was sure that the woman who had come out of the Minister's office had been responsible for the "information" given to the Minister. So, after a period of three years the appeals and petitions over Nijinsky's military service came to an end.

But I knew how hard those three years had been for Vaslav; how he had yearned for Russia; how it had affected him psychologically not to be able to return . . . his feelings of guilt, like a criminal exiled from his own country, and the threat of military service that stood like a wall, an obstacle to his return to his homeland.

The Imperial War Ministry had acted cruelly towards Nijinsky, being undoubtedly motivated by information received from "private sources," arbitrarily following orders from a higher authority. I was never able to discover the identity of the mysterious woman in expensive furs who seemed to have played a role in this tragedy, with its malicious similarities to Nijinsky's dismissal from the Imperial Theatres in 1911.

Not long after the denial of Nijinsky's petition an article appeared in the *St. Petersburg Gazette* with the headline: NIJINSKY—DESERTER.

Strangely enough, Diaghilev's arrival back in Russia coincided with this announcement, and a few days later was followed by a telegram sent to Nijinsky: LE BALLET RUSSE N'A PLUS BESOIN DE VOS SERVICES. NE NOUS REJOIGNEZ PAS. SERGE GRIGORIEFF.

Insultingly, this telegram telling Nijinsky not to rejoin the company had been signed not by Diaghilev himself, but by Grigoriev, the *régisseur* of the company.

What a terrible net had now tightened around Nijinsky!

Even now, as I write these lines long after the events took place, my whole being revolts with deep hurt and amazement at the injuries to which my brother was subjected. What Vaslav must have gone through. How could all this have come about?

Here, I feel it is important to write of things that were already known to me in London in July of 1913 and to relate the subsequent events and consequences that became known to me in St. Petersburg, 1913–14: events that were to disrupt my brother's whole life—both his personal and his artistic life.

The serious quarrels during the London Season of 1913 had revealed Diaghilev to be disenchanted with Nijinsky's talent and disappointed in him as a choreographer. Diaghilev had made it clear to Nijinsky that he did not want to entrust him with the choreography of any new ballets.

At the same time, I knew from my conversations with Vaslav that their close friendship had been over for some time, though Vaslav was far from suspecting that his theatrical work with Diaghilev was about to end.

Such a terrible blow for an artist, to be dismissed from the Ballets Russes! The dismissal of Nijinsky who for so many years had worked so unstintingly for the renown of the Ballets Russes . . . "The Wonder of the Dance" Diaghilev had called him; *"le dieu de la danse"* the public had called him. And now Nijinsky had been ruthlessly cast out.

Simultaneously with the telegram sent to Nijinsky dismissing him from the ballet company, it became known in St. Petersburg that Diaghilev and Fokine had reached complete agreement. Fokine was to join the Ballets Russes not only as choreographer but also as *premier danseur*, taking all Nijinsky's roles in his, Fokine's, own ballets.

In interviews with various St. Petersburg newspapers after his dismissal of Nijinsky, Diaghilev praised highly the talent of a young dancer,

Pyotr Vladimirov, an Artist of the Imperial Theatres who was enjoying great success with the public at the Maryinsky. It had already been announced that Diaghilev was conducting negotiations with Vladimirov, trying to persuade him to leave the Imperial Theatres and join his own company. Diaghilev was claiming in the press that he would show Paris and London a new genius who would surpass Nijinsky.

Vladimirov had graduated from the Imperial Theatrical School in 1911. He was an excellent dancer of the old classical school and had a good theatrical appearance. He declined Diaghilev's offer, choosing to remain with the Imperial Theatres where he had a good position, enjoying the complete support of Mathilda Kshessinska and her circle. Later in the year he did agree to dance with the Diaghilev Ballet Company during the Imperial Theatres' summer vacation.

I want to add here an excerpt from *Materials on the History of the Russian Ballet—1738–1938*, Vol. 2, edition of the Leningrad Government Choreographic School, 1938.

P. Vladimirov in 1914 had obtained leave to dance abroad in the enterprise of Diaghilev. During the same year, 1914, he had been called to serve in the military service; following a request from the Direction (of the Imperial Theatres) he served nominally, not interrupting any of his artistic activities . . .

From the above excerpt it is evident how easily Vaslav, as an Artist of the Imperial Theatres, could have received leave of absence from the Imperial Theatres to perform in the Diaghilev Ballet and like other dancers could also have obtained, upon a request from the Directorate of the Imperial Theatres, an exemption from military service.

If Vaslav had returned to Russia in 1910 and 1911 in time to report to the military authorities for duty, and if he had not broken his ties with the Imperial Theatres, all under pressure from Diaghilev, he would not have been in his present predicament. But one must also remember the long antagonism between Diaghilev and the Directorate of the Imperial Theatres, and what a trophy Nijinsky was for Diaghilev when he was organizing his permanent ballet company in 1911.

But now in 1913 Nijinsky had become a problem. Diaghilev was negotiating contracts in London and Paris for his ballet company for the 1914–15 seasons, and the theatres were demanding four new ballets in the repertoire and that at least two of them should be choreographed by Fokine. At the same time it became known in the company that Diaghilev was also negotiating with Gunsburg for an important investment of his considerable capital in the Ballets Russes enterprise. One of Gunsburg's conditions was the return of Fokine to the company as choreographer.

And in order to produce four new ballets Diaghilev was financially dependent upon Baron de Gunsburg.

Naturally Gunsburg, who had been seeing Fokine often since the latter had left the Ballets Russes in 1912, was well aware of the only conditions under which Fokine would agree to return to work for Diaghilev. These conditions were that Nijinsky would no longer be in the company, either as choreographer or as a dancer, and that Fokine should replace him in both capacities. Gunsburg supported Fokine absolutely in these demands and made it clear to Diaghilev that his financial backing depended upon Diaghilev acceding to them. So Diaghilev had no choice, no other alternative, being forced by financial pressures for the success of his enterprise and the future of the Ballets Russes. He had to agree to engage Fokine and accept his condition that Nijinsky be dismissed.

Diaghilev now faced another dilemma: how to explain the dismissal of Nijinsky, how to justify to the public in London and Paris the absence of Nijinsky from the ballet performances. He needed to "save face" and accuse Nijinsky of something, of some scandal to justify his dismissal. It would be best arranged during the South American tour, when Baron de Gunsburg, an interested party in the matter, would be assuming the position of Director of the Ballets Russes in Diaghilev's absence.

———

WHEN SOME of the artists returned to St. Petersburg in December, I learned from them what had happened on board ship on the way to Buenos Aires.*

"We were all very surprised to see Romola de Pulszky among the artists, the young socialite who under the pretext of wanting to learn dance had followed the Ballets Russes from Monte Carlo to Paris and London. What was she doing in the company?"

On board ship the artists from the *corps de ballet* and some of the administration had had second-class cabins. "Romola de Pulszky then received a second-class ticket from Gunsburg, just like the *corps de ballet*. But what dancing could she do? After only four months of occasional lessons with Maestro Cecchetti?"

From her own funds she had then added the difference to get a first-class ticket for herself. This had given her the opportunity to get to know the important artists and high members of the administration.

Bolm, of course, she had known since our first engagement in Budapest, and then in Monte Carlo she had met Gunsburg. It was Baron

---

*While there is no identification of these artists, or attribution of the quotes that follow, in Bronislava Nijinska's manuscripts, it is known that they included Bourman, Kovalevska, Bolm, and Tchernicheva. (IN/JR)

LIBRO DE MATRIMONIOS

Parroquia de *San Miguel*

AÑO DE 1903

En diez de septiembre del año del Señor de mil novecientos *tres,*

sobre el matrimonio que libremente como consta del Boleto N.º ... intentaba contraer Dn. *Vaslav Nijinsky* de *veinte y tres* años de edad, natural de *Rusia* de estado *soltero* domiciliado en *Av. de Mayo 1509* ... legítimo de Dn. *Tomás Nijinsky* y de Dª *Leonora Bereda* natural de

natural de *Austria-Hungría* con Dª *Romola de Pulszky-Lubocsi-Cselfalsa* de estado *soltera* de edad *de veinte y dos* años, domiciliada en la calle *Av. de Mayo 1509* hija legítima de Dn. *Carlos* y de Dª *Emilia de Markus* natural de

y no habiendo resultado impedimento alguno canónico

y estando hábiles en la

doctrina cristiana   enterado de su

libre y expontáneo consentimiento ...

... les despué por palabras de presente IN FACIE ECCLESIE, según la forma del ritual, siendo testigos

de   años de edad, natural de

domiciliado en

de   de   años de edad, natural

de   domiciliado en

Y en señal de verdad lo firmaron

El Cura de la Parroquia

Testigo   Testigo

114. Certificate of marriage of Vaslav Nijinsky and Romola de Pulszky at Church of San Miguel in Buenos Aires, on September 10, 1913. Photographic copy given to Bronislava Nijinska in Buenos Aires in the 1940s.

115. Romola and Vaslav Nijinsky at their wedding reception in the Majestic Hotel in Buenos Aires. *From left to right:* E. Oblokova, Baron de Gunsburg, J. Kovalevska, Romola, Vaslav, Mme Rhené-Baton, and Rhené-Baton.

116. Alexander Kotchetovsky in makeshift costume for "Danse Polovetsienne," London, 1914. Snapshot taken on the stage of the Palace Theatre by Bronislava Nijinska.

117. Kotchetovsky wearing Vaslav's costume for "Danse Siamoise" during the Saison Nijinsky. Wrongly identified in other publications as Nijinsky.

118. Bronislava Nijinska with her daughter, Irina, on the latter's sixth birthday. Kiev, 1919.

119, 120. Vaslav Nijinsky with daughter Kyra, and Romola Nijinsky with daughters Kyra and Tamara. Both photographs taken in Budapest, 1923.

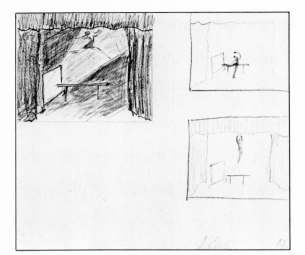

121–123. *Impressions of Nijinsky:*
In School, Le Spectre de la Rose,
Le Sacre du Printemps.
Drawings by Bronislava Nijinska.

124–126. *Impressions of Nijinsky: Jeux, L'Après-Midi d'un Faune*. Drawings by Bronislava Nijinska. These are of the Saison Nijinsky; the one for *Faune* shows the new set designed by Anisfeld.

127. Nijinska in "La Poupée,"
the number she created in
Petrograd, 1915, wearing the
costume designed by Bakst
in 1910 for her in the role
of Papillon in *Carnaval*.

128. Nijinska in the costume
designed for her version of
Petrouchka by Benois, in 1931.
Photograph by Lipnitzki.

129. Chaliapin and Nijinska with ballet cast
after dress rehearsal of Nijinska's *Princesse
Cygne*, Paris, 1932. Photograph by Lipnitzki.

130, 131. Nijinska's *Les Noces*. Artists
of Diaghilev's Ballets Russes rehearsing on
roof of Théâtre de Monte Carlo, 1923.

132. Nijinska, at age seventy-four, demonstrating the *adagietto* from her ballet *Les Biches* to Georgina Parkinson of the Royal Ballet. Photograph by Dominic.

133. Portrait of Bronislava Nijinska, Hollywood, 1934. Photograph by Fryer.

de Gunsburg and his mistress Ekaterina Oblokova who introduced Romola de Pulszky to Nijinsky. In Monte Carlo, Oblokova had been jealous of Romola, whom she saw flirting openly with Gunsburg, and so now she joined him in encouraging the shipboard romance with Nijinsky. During the voyage Josefina Kovalevska, an attractive young artist from the Warsaw Wielki Theatre, who to Vaslav's annoyance would persist in speaking to him in Polish, was seated at the same table as the Baron, Oblokova, and Nijinsky, and either she or some of the other artists told me how benevolently Gunsburg and Oblokova watched over and encouraged the budding romance between Nijinsky and Romola de Pulszky, until so recently a stranger to him.

The matchmaker, Baron de Gunsburg, on the day before arriving in Rio de Janeiro, proposed in Nijinsky's name, asking Romola de Pulszky to marry Vaslav Nijinsky.*

In the harbor of Rio de Janeiro, Romola and Vaslav became engaged, and for the first time during the voyage she sat at the same table with Vaslav, Gunsburg, and Oblokova. The announcement on the boat of the forthcoming marriage of Nijinsky and Romola de Pulszky was received by the artists with bewildered astonishment.

From Rio the ship sailed to Buenos Aires, arriving there on September 7, four days before the first performance at the Teatro Colón. Immediately, however, Baron de Gunsburg made arrangements for the marriage to take place in three days' time.†

Ten days had elapsed between the betrothal in Rio de Janeiro and the wedding in Buenos Aires, but Vaslav's mother had not been informed about his forthcoming marriage. Equally strange, both Vaslav and Gunsburg failed to notify Diaghilev.

It would seem that Gunsburg, as well as casting about to find ways to remove Nijinsky from the Ballets Russes, was also trying to widen the rift between Nijinsky and Diaghilev. Perhaps Gunsburg felt that Diaghilev might later try to persuade Fokine that Nijinsky should dance at least in such ballets as *Swan Lake* and *Giselle*, and wanted to make the break between them complete and irrevocable.

---

*This evidently occurred on the day before Nijinsky himself approached Romola in an incident recounted in other biographies and described to Irina Nijinska by her aunt Romola in 1974: how Nijinsky, on the deck of the boat, pointed to the ring finger of his left hand and inquired, "Voulez-vous avec moi?" (IN/JR)

†By contrast, Richard Buckle in *Diaghilev* reports that Gabriel Astruc and Diaghilev himself felt Gunsburg engineered the marriage in order to head a new troupe with Nijinsky. Romola Nijinsky's own account places herself in the center as prime mover in the event. (AK)

IN ONE OF his letters to Mother from Paris, before he went to Cherbourg to board the S.S. *Avon*, Vaslav had told her that Sergei Pavlovitch had promised that in South America he would receive a large portion of the money that Diaghilev still owed him.

But no such money was paid, either in Buenos Aires or in Montevideo. Nijinsky felt that the only way to force Gunsburg to pay him at least part of the back salary due him was to refuse to take part in a performance in Rio de Janeiro. Gunsburg made no secret of the reason why Nijinsky did not appear onstage, saying that he had no money to pay Nijinsky even if he used the artists' last salaries. Nevertheless, on the following day, in spite of his statements to the company, Gunsburg managed to find enough money to pay Nijinsky, who then danced for the remaining performances. He had only missed one performance, his place having been taken by Alexander Gavrilov.

When I first heard about the incident I was shocked by Vaslav's behavior, so unbecoming to an artist and so different from his usual conduct concerning his salary, especially since he must have known of Diaghilev's financial difficulties. But, once I calmed down and got over my initial emotional reaction, I understood: the time had come for Vaslav, now that he was married, to think of his new responsibilities and expect to be paid his regular salary—as did Karsavina, Bolm, all the other artists, and the administrative staff.

I believe, too, that before Vaslav left for South America Diaghilev had advised him to be firm in demanding that Baron de Gunsburg pay him the money due for the several years he had worked in the Ballets Russes. Diaghilev wouldn't have dismissed Nijinsky with an easy conscience, unless he was sure he was reasonably provided for.

Nijinsky's refusal to dance and his demands to be paid a considerable sum, due to him for several years of work with the Ballets Russes, created hostile feelings among the company. Many artists were afraid that they would not receive their own final salaries before leaving South America. Others were afraid that Diaghilev's quarrel with Nijinsky, exacerbated by news of his marriage and now his refusal to dance, thereby missing a performance, would so anger Diaghilev that he would not want to continue and would simply close down the Ballets Russes.

Nobody in the company suspected or even thought it possible that Nijinsky, during all the time since the formation of the permanent ballet company in 1911, had not been receiving his salary. Diaghilev had agreed to pay Nijinsky two hundred thousand francs for ten months work, about one hundred performances. Karsavina and Fokine were each paid the same amount but for only six months each year. All during 1911, 1912, and 1913, Nijinsky had not received his full salary. Much of it had been used to defray different expenses incurred by the ballet company, sometimes even other artists' salaries. Nijinsky was always provided with a room in the same hotel where Diaghilev was staying and his restaurant bills were paid out of his salary, as were his bills for clothing, including his dancing shoes; Vaslav used a new pair of dancing shoes for each performance. Also, a regular sum of five hundred francs was sent to Mother each month to pay her living expenses and cover the rent for the St. Petersburg apartment. This was a modest amount to take care of all her expenses, but she never asked Vaslav for more, though I also contributed a share for the St. Petersburg expenses. Whenever Mother came to join us in Monte Carlo, Paris, and London, Vaslav always paid for her traveling expenses, and then Mama would stay in a modest hotel with me. Often I paid for our hotel bills and for our meals in restaurants. Vaslav himself did not have many expenses beyond his dancing shoes, but often he would ask me to buy socks or handkerchiefs for him, and sometimes he would borrow a hundred francs from me for pocket money.

Now Vaslav was rightfully demanding to be paid what was due him for his work for the Ballets Russes over the years, after allowing for the expenses of the luxurious hotels and restaurants. His refusal to appear onstage in Rio de Janeiro until he was paid what was owed him provided a "scandal" that could be used as the excuse to break his contract.

56   My Meeting
with Diaghilev: St. Petersburg,
January 1914

VASLAV WAS IN Budapest when he received the telegram from Grigoriev dismissing him from the Ballets Russes. After expressing his initial disbelief, his letters to us were full of resentment and even hatred towards Diaghilev. He wrote that he could perfectly well work without Diaghilev and that in fact he would even be better off, both materially and artistically; he described Diaghilev as behaving like a "mischievous boy" trying to destroy Nijinsky's image.

With what had happened to Vaslav, I could not see myself returning to the Diaghilev Ballet Company, although I was bound by the contract I had signed on the train just as we were about to leave London in August. And Sasha had a contract with Diaghilev effective until March 1914. We were at a loss concerning what to do next. We had already been six months in St. Petersburg without work, and all our savings were gone. Our friends among the artists of the Ballets Russes who had returned from the South American tour were preparing to rejoin the company in Prague in January for the 1914 season.

About this time I encountered Maria Piltz, who had not gone with the company to South America; following her success in Nijinsky's *Le Sacre du Printemps*, she had had several engagements in Europe and did not return to St. Petersburg until Christmas. She had been very distressed when she heard the news, both of Vaslav's marriage and then of his dismissal. When I asked her if she was rejoining the Diaghilev Ballet Company, she told me she did not wish to do so now and instead would sign a contract with the Imperial Theatres. I realized how heartbroken she was, knowing how much she had adored Vaslav. Both her mother and my mother had often talked together about "Vaslav and Maroussia," whispering among themselves, "those two ought to get married." Vaslav was acquainted both with Maroussia's mother and her aunt, who was an operatic artist, a contralto in the Imperial Theatres; he had often been invited to their home in St. Petersburg. But following Vaslav's marriage Maroussia never returned to the Diaghilev Ballet. As Mama would say, "She was not Vaslav's destiny."

I also met several artists who told me how Diaghilev had reacted to the news of Nijinsky's marriage. I could easily imagine the fierce rage into which Diaghilev flew when he heard the news. Anna Fedorova, an Artist of both the Imperial Theatres and the Diaghilev Ballet, told me how for some time afterwards Diaghilev had not wanted to see anyone, avoiding people and even going into hiding. Shortly after the news of Nijinsky's marriage had become widely known, she had seen Diaghilev in Montreux, Switzerland. He was sitting alone, at a café table on the terrace of the hotel on the shore of the lake. The table in front of him was empty. Diaghilev appeared deep in thought, his chin resting on his hands folded on top of his cane. "When I approached to greet him," she told me, "he lifted his head and I was frightened to see his face so distorted by grief . . . he did not say a word, he did not answer me." She went on to say that the following day when she stopped by the hotel in the hope that Diaghilev might see her, she was told that he had left.

Such demonstrations of grief were, I believe, sincerely felt, notwithstanding the fact that what had happened was the result of Diaghilev's own plotting and planning with Gunsburg. Evidently it was one thing for Diaghilev to make a decision to part with Nijinsky for one year, as he had suggested to me in London, but it was a different matter to face the drastic unforeseen results.

My own heart was filled with indignation for Diaghilev's ingratitude and his cruel, vengeful behavior towards Vaslav. How could I possibly return to dance with his ballet company or even meet Diaghilev face to face?

The time to make a decision was approaching . . . suddenly the telephone rang, and I heard Diaghilev's voice, "Bronia, I must see you and talk to you and Sasha. Come and have dinner with me at the Hotel Astoria."

In spite of everything, Diaghilev still had over me the same magical strength and power to make me respect his command. I promised him that we would come to the Hotel Astoria.

It was with a heavy heart that I set out with Sasha, through the snow, for our rendezvous with Diaghilev.

The Astoria was a luxurious hotel newly opened in St. Petersburg on St. Isaac's Square. Diaghilev met us in the lobby and invited us to his room before dinner. Never in all the years I worked with Diaghilev, either before that night or later, in the 1920s, did I see him display so strongly his legendary irresistible charm. His eyes reflected a genuine love for me and a joy at seeing me again.

For dinner we came down to the elegant dining room, brilliantly lit with crystal chandeliers. Sergei Pavlovitch ordered the choicest items on the menu, beginning with lobster and concluding with strawberries, fresh strawberries in January, with champagne. All during dinner Sergei Pavlovitch continued to assure me that I had always been very dear to him, that he loved me as if I were his daughter, and that I was equally dear to him as an artist. I felt that Diaghilev's feelings were stronger towards me now than in the past, as though he saw in me a part of Vaslav. I could also feel how painful for him had been the break with Vaslav. He told me how hurt he had been, how insulted he had felt.

"He did not find it necessary to inform me of his marriage."

I then told Sergei Pavlovitch about Mother and how she was still suffering, feeling so deeply offended by her son's negligence in not informing her, either, of his wedding. I asked Sergei Pavlovitch, "What was Baron de Gunsburg doing through all this? Why did he fail to inform you of events on board the ship?"

His reply was short. "Gunsburg did not see fit. But how could Nijinsky agree to get married in this fashion?" Sergei Pavlovitch then told us that he had received a letter from Vaslav later, written sometime after his marriage. "Not once in the letter did he call her by name. He called her only 'my wife' or 'she.' Apparently he does not care for her very much if he does not at least show respect when talking about his wife."

I started to ask about the incident in Rio de Janeiro when Nijinsky had refused to dance. Sergei Pavlovitch replied angrily, "Only Gunsburg was harmed by that; he was counting on South America to be reimbursed for part of the money I owe him."

I also wanted to know how the young woman, now Vaslav's wife, happened to be on the ship as part of the ballet company, not being herself a dancer. "That, too, was the doing of that idiot Gunsburg," Diaghilev declared.

I thought to myself that this so-called idiot was not so naïve. After all, he had insisted that Fokine return to the company to choreograph the new ballets, knowing all the while that Fokine would not return as long as Nijinsky was in the Diaghilev Company. And now, Nijinsky was dismissed.

When we talked about the coming season Sergei Pavlovitch told me that he had already signed contracts with both Mikhail Fokine and Vera Fokina. "But all your roles and parts, naturally, will remain yours."

I had already heard from reliable sources that Fokine had also demanded my expulsion from the company, and had even tried to tie this condition to his own acceptance of his contract with Diaghilev; but Sergei Pavlovitch had protested saying that he had a contract for 1914 with Nijinska and could not break it.

The remaining time at dinner Sergei Pavlovitch used to try to persuade me to remain with his ballet. "Bronia, will you promise me that you will come to Prague for the beginning of our 1914 season?" However often he asked me this, he never once reminded me that I was bound by a contract that I had signed with him.

When we parted he embraced me several times, and as he helped me on with my fur coat he looked deep into my eyes. Suddenly he took my *botiki* [felt overboots] from the hall porter, and as gallantly as a youth he bent on one knee to help me put them on. That was too much for me. I took my *botiki* from him and gave them to Sasha. I hugged Sergei Pavlovitch and said, "All right, I shall come to Prague!" And so we parted that evening, but were not to meet again for many years.

—

In spite of my contract with Diaghilev and the promise that I had given that I would go to Prague, it still seemed impossible to consider working in the ballet company from which my brother Nijinsky had been expelled. I was also oppressed with doubts and worry about Vaslav, wondering how he would be able to live independently. Up till now he had always been protected from everyday worries. I was somewhat reassured by the fact that Vaslav was not alone; he had a wife at his side, though we knew so little about her. In my letters to Vaslav I repeated to him my promise given in London that I would always be with him and that if he needed me in his work, or for moral support, or even just to ask my advice, then I would leave everything and come to join him.

Not long before the Ballet Russe Season was scheduled to begin, while Sasha and I were still in St. Petersburg, I received a letter from Vaslav advising me to rejoin the company. From his letters we learned that he himself had received several offers from the directors of different theatres and from various impresarios, but that most likely he would sign a contract with the Grand Opéra in Paris. He had been offered an engagement as choreographer and *premier danseur*, at a high honorarium, with the privilege of leave of absence to dance in other enterprises. In his latest letter Vaslav wrote that he was preparing to go to Paris and negotiate the contract for the fall season with Jacques Rouché, the newly appointed director of the Paris Opéra.

Sasha and I prepared to go to Prague, leaving our little daughter in St.

Petersburg in the care of my mother and a wet nurse. While I was in the clinic it had been determined that I was too weak to nurse our daughter myself, and so we hired a wet nurse for her.

Diaghilev was in Paris when we arrived in Prague, and in his absence Baron de Gunsburg was again acting as Director. When I came to the theatre for rehearsal I felt half a stranger among the dancers. In the dressing room no one expressed any joy at seeing me. It had already been announced officially to the company that Fokine had been engaged, not only as choreographer but also as *premier danseur*. I knew that Fokine's attitude towards Nijinsky had always been reflected in his attitude towards me, which in turn had affected the other members of the company. This did not augur well for my prospects of artistic work with Fokine.

Neither Mikhail Fokine nor Vera Fokina had yet arrived in Prague. Grigoriev, the *régisseur*, was conducting rehearsals with the company. It was *Cléopâtre*, in which I had been dancing the role of Ta-Hor during the 1912–13 season, but Grigoriev immediately told me that I would now be dancing my old solo part in the "Bacchanale" and that the role of Ta-Hor would be danced by Vera Fokina, who had never before danced in that part. From this it became obvious that the promises made to me by Diaghilev that I was to retain all my parts in the ballets would not be kept.

Our stay in Prague was very short. We received a telegram from Vaslav asking whether Sasha and I would consider leaving the Ballets Russes and going to work with him. Immediately we wired our consent, and that same day I announced to Gunsburg that my contract with Diaghilev had been broken, as certain agreements had not been kept, and that I was leaving the Ballets Russes. Gunsburg asked me to wait for the arrival of Sergei Pavlovitch and to talk to him before making any decision.

When we received a further telegram from Vaslav, dated January 27, 1914, offering us a two-year contract, eighty thousand francs a year for me and forty thousand francs a year for Sasha, half to be forfeited for breach of contract, we got ready to leave Prague immediately. Gunsburg saw us to the station still trying to make me change my mind, repeating urgently, "Do not leave yet. Sergei Pavlovitch arrives from Paris later today. How will I tell him that you have left, and how will I be able to explain to him that I did not keep you from leaving?"

Diaghilev was indeed on his way to Prague from Paris, and on the very day that Sasha and I were leaving Prague to join Vaslav in Paris. The coincidence I am about to describe is so unlikely as to seem beyond belief.

All the way from Prague to Berlin I was thinking about Diaghilev, worrying whether in his vindictiveness he would prosecute me for breach of contract . . . our train was standing at the platform in Berlin . . .

when suddenly a train going in the opposite direction pulled into the station and stopped, on the platform opposite us . . . and in one of the windows I saw Diaghilev. He seemed to be staring fixedly at me. I quickly pulled back from the window and only breathed freely when our train pulled out of the station and we were again on our way to Paris.

57   With Vaslav in Paris: January 1914

OUR MEETING with Vaslav in Paris was joyous. I was immensely happy to
see him again, and he assured me that from then on we would always be
together. He introduced us to his pretty wife, Romola, and then wanted
to know about Mother. He was sorry that she had not come with us from
St. Petersburg, but I explained that Mother had not wanted to leave her
baby granddaughter in St. Petersburg, entrusted to the care of a wet nurse
and a maid. As we were showing Vaslav and Romola the snapshots of our
little daughter they confided in us that they too were to become parents,
in June. Sasha and I embraced them and congratulated them. Vaslav now
seemed so much more mature than when I had last seen him, six months
ago in London. He was self-assured and conscious of his new responsibilities as a married man.

Vaslav and Romola were staying in the Hotel Scribe, not nearly as
luxurious as the hotels where he had stayed with Diaghilev. I remember
sitting and talking in one of the rooms in their suite, a long room with high
ceilings and gray walls. There was only one window and the room was
somewhat somber. Soon our conversation turned to ballet and Vaslav's
plans.

He told us that he had signed a contract with Alfred Butt, the owner of
the Palace Theatre in London, the music-hall theatre where Anna Pavlova
had been performing regularly for several years. The contract was for
eight weeks, to present a one-hour program, and for that Nijinsky was to
receive the not inconsiderable sum of one thousand pounds a week.

I was astonished at the news and wondered how Vaslav could have
signed a contract with a music hall. His strong views on this were well
known to me. He had always spoken out passionately, protesting that it
was not worthy of a great artist to perform in theatres such as music halls,
as did Anna Pavlova and Sarah Bernhardt, on the same bill with

magicians, acrobats, ventriloquists, clowns, jugglers, and even animal acts.

It was no less surprising for me to learn that the ballet program Vaslav was planning for the Palace Theatre consisted almost entirely of ballets choreographed by Fokine and currently in the repertoire of Diaghilev's Ballets Russes. I knew that Fokine had protested in 1911 when Theodore Koslov had restaged *Les Sylphides*, *Cléopâtre*, and *Schéhérazade* for Gertrude Hoffman's company in New York, and I was apprehensive about Vaslav's program considering the strained relations between Nijinsky and Fokine.

As it turned out the contract specified that Nijinsky was to appear at the Palace Theatre in the ballets that had made him famous. Vaslav also explained to me, "I am planning to present these ballets in my own choreographic versions. After all, these ballets can hardly be credited solely to Fokine. *Les Sylphides*, I feel, is as much a creation of Benois as of Fokine. *Le Spectre de la Rose* is Théophile Gautier, Bakst, and Nijinsky. All the *pas* that Fokine showed me for that ballet were simple, academic, and classical. As for *Carnaval*, that is entirely Bakst's ballet; Harlequin, I created that role myself, not Fokine." Then he pointed out to me, "You yourself danced the Papillon that Fokine showed you in less than an hour at the end of a rehearsal, quite differently after you had worked on it, first with me and then by yourself. *You*, Bronia, created Papillon."

Though Vaslav felt that he could have given a performance dancing with just Kotchetovsky and myself and perhaps two or three other dancers, he said that he wanted to engage a small ballet troupe so as to create a truly artistic performance. In the program for the "Saison Nijinsky," Vaslav was planning to present *L'Après-Midi d'un Faune*, *Le Spectre de la Rose*, and his own choreographic versions of *Carnaval*, *Les Sylphides*, and to mount various short dance numbers.

The performances were to begin on March 2. There were only four and a half weeks to opening night, and Vaslav had not even started the work. To sign a contract with such a short time for preparation seemed to me to be pure folly, but it was too late to talk about it, least of all with Vaslav.

Now, hard work and quick action were needed: to find artists for the ballet troupe, to order sets and costumes, to find music already orchestrated for some of the dance numbers or arrange for new orchestrations.

We decided that the very next day, the day after our arrival in Paris, Kotchetovsky and I would return to Russia and engage artists in St. Petersburg and Moscow, and also find orchestrated materials published in Russia.

Before my departure Vaslav asked me to go with him to see Maurice

Ravel, who had already agreed to make some orchestrations. Nijinsky had decided to mount *Les Sylphides* anew, using other pieces of music by Chopin different from those used by Fokine, and Ravel had already begun to work on the orchestrations for this new version of *Les Sylphides*. Vaslav wanted to make the final choice of the different Chopin compositions with Ravel and myself.

I remember well our visit with Maurice Ravel. His apartment was on the top floor, looking out over Paris—I believe it was on the Champs Elysées. Ravel greeted us affectionately and was very pleasant with us. He soon seated himself at the piano and played a selection of Chopin's works—mazurkas, nocturnes, preludes, and valses. From time to time he would stop and indicate those pieces he thought were suitable for *Les Sylphides* and which were also adaptable to his orchestration.

That day the music for *Les Sylphides* was selected. I listened entranced and had the fleeting vision of ethereal sylphides. I knew then that Vaslav could create his own *Les Sylphides*.

Towards the end of our visit a photographer came to take some pictures. He took some of Ravel and Nijinsky sitting together at the piano, and then of the three of us standing together on the balcony of the apartment.

Sasha and I then set off on our task, knowing that to assemble even a small troupe would be extremely difficult. We knew how often the Diaghilev Ballet had been forced to engage a certain number of ill-prepared or theatrically inexperienced dancers to make up the numbers called for in a contract. We could find no one among the artists in either St. Petersburg or Moscow who wanted to leave their permanent work in the theatre and travel abroad for an eight-week engagement.

The task was made more difficult because at that time private ballet schools were almost nonexistent. In Moscow there was only one private school, that of Lydia Nelidova from the Bolshoi Ballet, but there we were happy to find Bonni [spelling taken from the program for the Saison Nijinsky], an accomplished dancer whom we knew from 1913 when she danced with the Diaghilev Ballet. We also found three good students, though without previous stage experience, and then in St. Petersburg we found two more students. We set off with them for London where Vaslav was waiting for us.

There, in London, we found four experienced male character dancers —Kojuhoff, Abramovitch, Morozoff, and Kaweki—and also four girls, good classical dancers. Three of them were English and were given Russian names, so Johnson became Ivanova; Jacobson, Yakovleva; and Doris became Darinska. Vaslav gave contracts to each of the dancers for eight weeks with the option of extension for a year. The four men and the three soloists, Bonni, Ivanova, and Darinska, were to receive seven pounds ten shillings, and the other seven girls five pounds, per week for the performances, and all were also to be paid for the rehearsal weeks at a reduced rate.

And so the company for the Saison Nijinsky was completed, consisting of ten women and four men with Bronislava Nijinska and Alexander Kotchetovsky, and headed by Vaslav Nijinsky.

58   The Saison Nijinsky:
London 1914

For our eight-week engagement Vaslav planned to prepare four programs, each to last two weeks. The first was to include the two ballets, *Les Sylphides* and *Le Spectre de la Rose*, and between them, as an interlude, "Danse Orientale" (the "Danse Siamoise" Nijinsky had first danced in 1910, and which was now to be danced by Kotchetovsky).

I had strongly advised Vaslav that he should present his *Faune* in the first program, but Romola and one of her influential London society friends insisted on *Les Sylphides*. They both tried to persuade Vaslav to return to the classical dance and perform ballets that were more appealing to the general public, rather than continue on the way of *Sacre*. They disapproved of both *Jeux* and *Faune*, though Vaslav did plan to include them in the Saison Nijinsky.

The rehearsals began, and Vaslav mounted his *Les Sylphides* with rare enthusiasm and freedom. I watched in amazement at how his work proceeded, so strikingly different from his mounting of the two Debussy ballets, *L'Après-Midi d'un Faune* and *Jeux*, and also Stravinsky's *Le Sacre du Printemps*. There his efforts with the Diaghilev artists had proceeded so slowly, measure by measure, as he searched to create the Dance of Nijinsky, each *pas* so completely unfamiliar to the others. Now Vaslav was showing us each dance only once or twice, and after demonstrating parts of the choreography would proceed immediately to another part of the ballet. We were spending all day from morning to midnight in rehearsal with the ballet company.

The work proceeded well, but the further it progressed the more convinced I became of what a folly it was for Vaslav to have taken upon himself such a tremendous task, and one that was completely unfamiliar to him, an artist who had never had any administrative experience. Kotchetovsky, who spoke some English, not badly, and also had some business ability, was able to help Vaslav by dealing with dressmakers, hairdressers, and stagehands, while I tried to help Vaslav as much as possible in the rehearsals by working with the dancers on what he had already mounted. I watched very carefully when Vaslav demonstrated to us, and I memorized all the *pas* in case he lost any as he moved on, so quickly, in his choreography.

As the time for our opening night drew nearer, Vaslav became more and more nervous. But the first program was already completed, also parts of the second.

To design all the sets and costumes, Vaslav had invited the artist Boris Anisfeld, who had so artistically painted the sets for *Schéhérazade* in 1910 from Bakst's sketches. For *Les Sylphides* Anisfeld designed a backdrop to be framed by the black velvet curtains that were the permanent setting for the stage of the Palace Theatre. Against the background of a night sky Anisfeld painted tall, slender, gray birch trees, finely outlining the white bark and the lacy silvery foliage.

Anisfeld also conceived and admirably executed the decor for *L'Après-Midi d'un Faune*. On the backdrop were two huge bunches of grapes in a blue-lilac color, with dark gold and purple leaves, arranged so that when the curtain rose the grapes held by the Faune, reclining on a rock, blended with the decor in one beautiful tableau.

When the sets were hung for the first rehearsal with lights, the firemen came onstage. One of them lit a match and, bringing it close to the backdrop for *Faune*, declared that it had not been coated with a fire-preventive treatment and so would have to be removed from the stage. After some negotiations, the firemen went off and returned carrying cans of fireproofing liquid, and to our horror were about to pour it over the backdrop. We had a hard time persuading them to apply the liquid only to the reverse side of the sets, not on the painted side, facing the public.

Even so, the fluid soaked through the newly painted backdrop and in some places the paint ran and the colors changed hue. The sets for *Faune* were ruined.

Vaslav was distraught. It was frightening to see him trembling and the perspiration pouring off him. From then on, things went from bad to worse, as though a maliciously planned campaign had been launched to undermine the success of the Saison Nijinsky.

It is common knowledge that an artist and his performance can be influenced greatly by the box office. A full house, all tickets sold, lifts the spirit of the performer and also affects his standing with the management of the theatre, especially a music-hall theatre. Long before our first performance, stories began to appear in the newspapers that over ten thousand pounds worth of seats had been sold and that all the tickets for the first two weeks had gone. We knew this was not true, not even for the first night, when it was possible to buy tickets at the box office right up to curtain time, as was also the case on following nights. It is difficult to say whether these newspaper stories were misguided publicity or were intentionally worded so as to discourage the public from trying to buy tickets for the Saison Nijinsky.

But there was other mischief ahead.

Our first performance was to be on March 2, and the dress rehearsal was arranged for the morning of the same day. When I arrived at the Theatre I found the stage-door entrance blocked by a policeman. He handed me a court order prohibiting me from entering the Theatre and a summons to appear in court that very morning.

Diaghilev had instigated a suit against me for breach of contract, claiming that Bronislava Nijinska, an artist in his ballet company, had a contract with him, signed in London, for the 1914 and 1915 ballet seasons.

All contracts signed in England were subject to the jurisdiction of the English courts. An artist who signed a contract in England was not allowed to appear in another English theatre until he was free from his current obligation or before the expiration of his contract, not even if he paid or was willing to pay the forfeit for breach of contract usually included in artists' contracts.

The dress rehearsal took place without me. Meanwhile a well-known lawyer, George Lewis, filed a countersuit on my behalf against Diaghilev, claiming that it was Diaghilev who was guilty of breach of contract with Nijinska, who had gone to Prague to work with the Diaghilev Ballet Company only to find there that all the leading parts she was supposed to dance, according to her agreement with Diaghilev, had been given to another dancer.

The judge pronounced Diaghilev guilty of breach of contract with Nijinska, and so I was allowed to return to the Theatre and was able to dance in the premiere performance with Nijinsky that night.

When I went to see Vaslav just before the beginning of our performance, I found him extremely upset. A telegram had been delivered to his dressing room just minutes before.

CONGRATULATIONS BEST WISHES TO MUSIC HALL ARTIST. ANNA PAVLOVA

This was a spiteful message from Pavlova, who apparently had never forgiven Vaslav for something that had happened several years before. In 1911, at a banquet in Paris, when Vaslav had just learned from Diaghilev that Pavlova had finally declined his invitation to join his company permanently, Vaslav had said to Pavlova, "I cannot believe that you,

Anna Pavlova, have chosen to be a music-hall artist rather than a *prima ballerina* of the Diaghilev Ballet."

To which Pavlova had replied coolly, "Yes, I do prefer to perform in my own Pavlova Ballet and to be known as an artist of the Imperial Theatres rather than as 'Pavlova, a Diaghilev Artist.'"

I remembered how sad Vaslav had been the following day when he returned from the farewell lunch Diaghilev had arranged for Pavlova and told me, "I did not realize until this morning that I had so offended Anna Pavlova. During lunch she spoke to Sergei Pavlovitch and to the others at the table, but she did not say a word to me, and she turned away from me when I wished her 'bon voyage.'" Anna Pavlova had left later that day for London, and apparently she never forgave Nijinsky.

We were about to begin our performance of *Les Sylphides*, and as the last notes of the overture sounded the curtain opened. Vaslav and I were standing in a pose in the center of a group of sylphides, Vaslav's hand on my waist and my head almost touching his shoulder. Usually I never pay any attention to the audience, but this evening as I looked towards the conductor to watch for his signal to the musicians my eyes were drawn to a white spot in the front row, illuminated by the conductor's light; it was the white evening shirt of a man seated immediately to the left of the conductor. Diaghilev was in the Theatre. He was seated so that even in the dimly-lit stalls we would notice him at once, nonchalantly sprawled in his seat, his large head leaning to the right, his lower lip protruding with great self-assurance in a sardonic smile.

I felt Vaslav's fingers tighten nervously on my waist, and his shoulder jerked, touching my head, as his body straightened up. He took a deep breath and entered into his dance, the first *pas* of his *Les Sylphides*. I watched Vaslav and listened to the "Nocturne" in Ravel's new orchestration, so perfectly in harmony with Nijinsky's new rhythms. From time to time I would tear my eyes from Vaslav and glance at Diaghilev, who was intently following Vaslav in his dance, his eyes never leaving him. I could feel an inner battle being waged between them, a personal struggle that I knew Vaslav must win, by his dance and his creative genius.

Our nerves were stretched to the utmost, but the performance proceeded beautifully. The "Étude," danced by Ivanova and the six sylphides, had an exceptional success. They danced on toe, *pas de bourrée*, following each other, their hands touching in an unbroken chain, weaving in and out in a continuous, linked pattern. By the time the ballet came to its closing group, Diaghilev's body had seemed to shrink in his seat and his arms were tightly crossed. I do not believe that he applauded once, not during *Les Sylphides* and not at the end.

Whenever I was not dancing onstage, I was able to watch Vaslav's composition. Against the airy decor, the moonlight, the night sky, and the delicate trees, the white figures of the sylphides were lightly silhouetted. *Les Sylphides*, framed by the dark velvet curtains, appeared as an engraved picture, and Nijinsky in his dark short-sleeved costume was its artist, his dance penciling lightly or tracing boldly to create the designs of his new *Les Sylphides*. He brought the engraving to life before our eyes.

We were warmly applauded for *Les Sylphides* and took several curtain calls.

For the second item in the program Kotchetovsky danced the "Danse Orientale" to great success.

The last ballet of our program was *Le Spectre de la Rose*, which I danced with Vaslav. During our *pas de deux* I had another glance at Diaghilev, who was now sitting very erect, his arms crossed on his chest, looking straight at Vaslav and me. As usual, his hands were clenched to hide his short fingers inside his fists; he had once told me, "My crooked fingers are the most unattractive part of my body." Throughout *Le Spectre de la Rose* he never moved or unfolded his arms.

Le Spectre de la Rose met with a storm of applause and ovations. Nijinsky received many flowers and after the performance was surrounded by his English society friends and other admirers from the public.

The next day Nijinsky was notified that Fokine was demanding that performances of *Le Spectre de la Rose* be stopped. But the ballet remained on the program for the whole of the first two weeks of the Saison Nijinsky. Vaslav was not concerned by Fokine's protest. He had told me some time ago how a great many people in Paris had thought that Diaghilev was ruining the Ballets Russes with "his Fokine," and then later, when he heard that in Prague and on tour of Germany Fokine had danced his, Nijinsky's, roles, Vaslav had told me, "Now Fokine has finally succeeded in getting rid of Nijinsky from the Ballets Russes, so that he can satisfy his yearning to show the world that Nijinsky was merely an artist who faithfully reproduced onstage what he, Fokine, had created. But his schemings have not worked. I keep hearing his ballets are failing to achieve the success he predicted and that his own interpretations of the roles and dances have been a disappointment to the artists in the ballet company as well as to the public."

Most of our time in London I saw Vaslav only in the Theatre, during rehearsals or performances. Once in a while we had supper together late at night in a small restaurant near the Theatre and discussed his plans for the remaining programs. Vaslav was very hungry after a performance and would eat a whole young chicken by himself and order a half bottle of red wine. I had never before seen Vaslav drink wine with his meals. Usually he had mineral water, or sometimes at home, if he had a glass of red wine, it would be largely diluted with water.

Vaslav and Romola were staying at the Savoy Hotel for the Saison Nijinsky, and they invited Sasha and me there to meet Romola's mother, Emilia Markus, and stepfather, Oskar Pardany, who had come from Budapest for the premiere. They were very pleasant and we had an enjoyable visit together. Our business meetings to discuss our future programs were also held in the Savoy Hotel, and on these occasions we were sometimes joined by F. Zenon, who had been engaged by Vaslav to look after the administrative concerns of the company. Zenon was well informed about the business side of the theatre, having been employed by several Russian enterprises performing abroad. He spoke English and French well and during February and March had made several trips between London and Paris to bring the costumes and to fetch some of the music, collecting the orchestrated materials for *Les Sylphides* from Ravel and also obtaining from the music publishers the full score for *Faune* and for *Jeux*. One of the other ballets we planned to present was *Carnaval*, not with an orchestral accompaniment but to the original piano pieces by Schumann.

Once, as we were leaving the hotel after one of our meetings, Vaslav and I were walking along the Strand when we almost collided with Levushka Bakst, our longtime friend. Vaslav and I both moved towards him, but Bakst gave us a quick glance and, turning away, walked quickly past us.

I was deeply distressed. Bakst had always been so encouraging after my early success in Monte Carlo with Bacchante. I remembered seeing him in the spring sunshine of Monte Carlo, not extravagantly dressed like Stravinsky, but always neatly turned out, wearing a white shirt with pink stripes, a dark pink bow tie and, of course, always the flower in his buttonhole. His prominent blue-gray eyes looking out over the pince-nez, which he rarely removed, his red hair carefully combed over his small, round, balding head, with that pompous mustache beneath his large, arched nose. One could not call him handsome, but beneath his attractive individuality one sensed the artist.

And now Lev Samuilovitch Bakst, whom we had always regarded as our true friend, had turned away from us. We were cut to the heart. It was as if our friend had lashed us with a whip.

"This is all Diaghilev's doing," said Vaslav.

On the morning of March 4, the third day of our performances, Alfred Butt, the director and owner of the Palace Theatre, called Nijinsky to have him come to see him in his office. It was Vaslav's opinion that if Butt had anything to say to him, he should have asked Nijinsky to receive him at his hotel. We had a difficult time persuading Vaslav to keep this appointment. Since Sasha spoke English, he accompanied Vaslav to the Palace Theatre, and then afterwards he described the dramatic meeting for me.

"When we came into the office, Butt was sitting at his desk, with his back to us. He did not turn around but simply raised his hand to his shoulder and waved two fingers at us. Vaslav approached the desk and slapped away Butt's hand, then asked in French what he wanted. Butt immediately began to criticize Nijinsky's performances. 'You, Nijinsky, are a Russian dancer, but in your program you do not dance any Russian dances, which is what the public expects.' Butt then went on to insist that Nijinsky should include something authentically Russian in his performances. Suddenly Vaslav squatted down and performed two or three *pas* of the *prissyatka*, screaming angrily, 'Is this what you want to see from Nijinsky?'"

Sasha then told me how he had grabbed Vaslav by both arms, afraid that he was going to attack Butt, but then Vaslav had pulled himself up straight and, with a nod of his head, walked out of the office.

Vaslav gradually calmed down after this stormy interview with Butt, and by the evening's performance there was no sign of tension in his dancing. However, he told me to come the following morning for a rehearsal with the four male character dancers, and he then mounted for us a character dance number to Borodin's music from *Prince Igor*, from Act III, immediately preceding *Danses Polovetsiennes*, and not used by Fokine.

I do not know if Vaslav decided to add this number to satisfy Butt's demand for something Russian in the program, or in order to give himself more time to change his makeup and costume between *Les Sylphides* and *Le Spectre de la Rose;* Kotchetovsky's "Danse Orientale" was too short for that, and often the audience began to show signs of impatience, having to wait up to ten minutes for *Le Spectre de la Rose*. Normally the public would be entertained by the orchestra during an entr'acte, with the Theatre brightly lit. But Vaslav had insisted that for his program the lights be turned off, not only during the performances but also during the entr'acte. The Theatre regulations could not permit this, and so the house lights could only be dimmed for Vaslav's program. The regular music-hall audience did not like to remain seated in a darkened theatre during the entr'acte.

For the second week, beginning March 9, we continued the same program, but now with the addition of "Danse Polovetsienne." Since I could not change from this costume in time for *Le Spectre de la Rose*, one of the soloists, either Bonni or Darinska, danced with Vaslav.

"Danse Polovetsienne" had been beautifully mounted by Nijinsky for the four male character dancers and myself. I enjoyed performing it and we had several curtain calls with shouts for "Bis," but we could not repeat it due to the strict timing of our program. We began at nine o'clock at night and had to be finished in fifty minutes to allow for the next music-hall performance after a ten-minute intermission.

During the day we were now rehearsing for the second program. Vaslav was working with the four men and four girls on *Carnaval*, mounting their dances for them. In this ballet I was to dance Columbine, but Vaslav had not yet mounted the part for me, though we were practicing the Blue Bird *pas de deux* together and Vaslav was also working with the girls on their dance for *Faune*. He looked tired during rehearsals, and it was painful to see how he was being diverted from his real aim, artistic creation, by having to deal with business affairs and to fit his program to the demands of the music-hall theatre. He was becoming impatient with the dancers and had less and less time to work with me. I was worried: How would I be ready to dance for the performance? I needed quite a bit of work with Vaslav on both *Carnaval* and the Blue Bird *pas de deux*. Often when we rehearsed together Sasha would reproach Vaslav for not being polite or civil towards me—demanding that Vaslav "show respect towards my wife"—and then Vaslav would become angry with Sasha. The rehearsal would usually end abruptly with me in tears and Vaslav and Sasha arguing loudly.

But however tired Vaslav looked during rehearsals, or in his dressing room before the start of the performance, onstage there was no visible sign of exhaustion or fatigue. He danced as superbly as ever. But even so I noticed that the usual spark, the enthusiasm that always filled his being, the elation felt in each dancing movement, was no longer there.

Saturday, March 14, was the last day of our first program, with a matinee performance in the afternoon. For the first time during the Saison Nijinsky all the seats were sold out.

During the matinee, when he took the stage during the entr'acte just before *Le Spectre de la Rose*, Vaslav was very upset to hear a loud outcry in the Theatre and a stamping of feet in the audience; the public was protesting the long entr'acte and expressing displeasure at having to sit in a darkened theatre without the usual entertainment by the orchestra.

Vaslav was so on edge that I was afraid he would break down and not be able to perform.

But as soon as the first notes of the music for *Le Spectre de la Rose* were heard, all noise in the audience stopped and Vaslav began to dance, and after his performance he was repeatedly called back onstage.

For the evening performance all the seats were again sold out. Maurice

Volny, the manager of the Theatre, realizing how disturbed and annoyed Vaslav had been at the matinee, and wanting to avoid a repetition of the loud protests, asked the conductor, Herman Finch, to play something suitable in the entr'acte between "Danse Polovetsienne" and *Le Spectre de la Rose*. When, in his dressing room, Vaslav heard "Valse des Fleurs," a Tchaikovsky valse, being played just before he was to dance to the music of Weber's "L'Invitation à la Valse," he became infuriated and refused to get dressed. Sasha called me to come and talk to Vaslav, whose screams could be heard through the corridors and backstage, demanding to know who was responsible for the wretched choice of music. When I came into Vaslav's dressing room I found his Rose costume on the floor. I pleaded with him to dance and finish the performance. My words seemed to have an effect on Vaslav, for he then sat at his dressing table and put on his Rose wig, retouched his makeup, and asked the dresser to help him with his costume.

Vaslav completed the performance and danced *Le Spectre de la Rose*. But that night, March 14, was to prove to be Nijinsky's last performance in the Saison Nijinsky. And though I could not know it then, it was the last time I ever danced with my brother Vaslav, and the last time I was ever to see Nijinsky, *le dieu de la danse*, perform onstage.

The next day, Sunday, Romola called us and said that Vaslav had been running a fever since the performance. His temperature now was over 100, and it was out of the question for him to be at the dress rehearsal the next morning. But this was the dress rehearsal, Monday, March 16, for the new numbers in the program—*Carnaval*, "Danse Grecque," *L'Après-Midi d'un Faune*, and "L'Oiseau et le Prince" Blue Bird *pas de deux*. After telling us that Vaslav would be unable to attend the rehearsal, Romola also notified the management of the Theatre that Nijinsky would be unable to dance that evening.

The rest of us would have to continue the performance without Nijinsky. But it was out of the question for us to give *Carnaval* or "L'Oiseau et le Prince" without Nijinsky. So we retained *Les Sylphides* from the first program and asked Finch to make some cuts in the music—Nijinsky's Mazurka and some other parts he had danced. Then we retained Kotchetovsky's "Danse Orientale" and used the "Danse Grecque" danced by the six girls, as planned. Our program was completed with "Danse Polovetsienne," where we extended the music by various repeats to fill in our assigned time.

At the beginning of "Danse Polovetsienne," as Vaslav had mounted it, I had a solo as a Polovetsian Girl. To a repeat of the music I worked out further dance sequences so as to give Sasha time to change from his "Danse Orientale" costume and join me onstage . . . to dance a solo as a wild Tartar Youth, which he improvised that very morning. Following his dance, the four men and I did the number as mounted for us by Vaslav, and then, in a repeat of the music, Sasha rejoined us for the finale.

We rehearsed and worked on our dances through the day and almost up to curtain time at nine that evening.

Though many of the public were disappointed not to see Nijinsky and the new program, nevertheless our program went well. "Danse Polovet-sienne," in the new version choreographed by Vaslav, Sasha, and myself, was a huge success. The "Danse Grecque" was also effective, as the nymphs danced against a black background in their white tunics from *Faune*.

As Vaslav understood his contract, he was able to miss three days' performances during the season because of illness. The London newspapers were publishing daily bulletins informing the public of his progress. For three days—Sunday, Monday, Tuesday—his temperature remained high, but by Wednesday he was feeling much improved. However, understanding that he was entitled to miss three days of performances he told me to inform the Theatre manager, Volny, that he would be returning to dance on Thursday evening. When Sasha and I came to the Palace Theatre early in the morning to give Volny Vaslav's message, he informed us that the Saison Nijinsky had been canceled and that our program had been replaced.

Simultaneously Vaslav received at the Savoy official notification that his contract had been terminated, as Nijinsky had breached its terms by not performing for three consecutive days.

Vaslav immediately instigated a countersuit through his attorney George Lewis.

Outwardly, despite this unbelievable action by the management of the Palace Theatre, Nijinsky remained calm. I felt he was even happy to have parted with the Palace and to no longer have to dance in a music hall.

I have never been able to understand how his wife, Romola, who from the very beginning of their marriage had shown herself to be so clever in business and financial dealings, and who also spoke English fluently, was able to allow Vaslav to sign such a difficult contract with a music-hall theatre. Nijinsky himself did not read or speak English, and so could not read the contract before signing it. It must also be mentioned that this was his first official contract, quite different from the friendly agreements he had had with Diaghilev.

After the sudden cancellation of our performances, all Nijinsky's theatrical properties were ordered to be removed immediately from the Palace Theatre, and so all the sets, costumes, and props, even the music from the Saison Nijinsky, were hurriedly packed, and it was arranged by

F. Zenon that they be stored temporarily in a warehouse in London.*

Vaslav paid all his artists one month's salary for the two weeks and the odd days that they had performed at the Theatre, as well as the agreed amount, half pay, for the rehearsal time before the opening of the Saison Nijinsky, and their return fare back to Russia. All the artists were quite satisfied with the money settlement and returned home hoping to work with Nijinsky again.

I knew that Vaslav had not suffered major financial losses with the cancellation of the performances, for he had been given a considerable advance to finance the Saison Nijinsky on signing the contract with the Palace Theatre. So when he offered Sasha and me one month's salary, a sum equivalent to the salary we would have received with the Diaghilev Company, we readily accepted. We also decided to stay on awhile in London and see what plans Vaslav might make for future engagements.

Not long after the cancellation of the Saison Nijinsky, I remember Vaslav making arrangements with someone, I don't know who it was, for the publication of the marvelous series of photographs taken by Baron de Meyer of *L'Après-Midi d'un Faune*. They were talking in French and discussing a deluxe edition, and Vaslav wrote a check for one thousand pounds for the costs of publication.

Vaslav did not stay long in London. Soon he and Romola decided to leave. Sasha and I went to the station to see them off, and I remember that a couple of Vaslav's English friends were also there, and that Vaslav wrote them a check for quite a large amount as a loan, which they promised to repay shortly. This I found reassuring. Obviously Vaslav still had some money left, and for the time being there was no need for me to worry about him and Romola. Apparently they had enough money saved to pay for the expenses of their first child in June.

Kotchetovsky and I then left for St. Petersburg to rejoin our little daughter and my mother.

---

*I met Zenon again in 1921 when I returned to London from Russia to join the Diaghilev Company, where Zenon was also working. He told me that all the Nijinsky theatrical properties had been sold because of nonpayment of the warehouse fees during the war. The sets had been bought by different theatres as canvases for their productions, and the costumes had been bought by several artists whose names he did not recall.

I wanted to find out about the music, especially the Ravel orchestrations. One of the most exciting memories from the Saison Nijinsky was *Les Sylphides* as orchestrated by Ravel. Chopin's familiar piano pieces had sounded so unusual and beautiful, and I had been enchanted by that music rendered to perfection in Ravel's orchestration.

In answer to my further questioning about the music I heard Zenon say, "Yes, there was a big package of papers—perhaps the scores—but the papers were so damaged that they had to be thrown away . . ." (BN)

59   St. Petersburg: Summer
1914

FROM VASLAV'S letters in May we learned that he had been to Spain to give a special performance at a royal wedding and on his way back had stopped in Paris where he had met with Diaghilev. He had agreed to dance in London for a few performances with the Ballets Russes at the Theatre Royal, Drury Lane.

I was happy to hear that Vaslav had agreed to dance with the Ballets Russes again. However angry Vaslav might have been towards Diaghilev, the bond between them was very deep. It had been from Diaghilev that Vaslav had perceived that an artist can only live in Art and for Art, an awareness that I too, through Vaslav, had learned from Diaghilev. I knew how much Vaslav dreamed of creating his own ballets with his own artists, but for that one must have the indefatigable energy of a Diaghilev, his tremendous persistence and talent for organization. These strengths and qualities my brother did not have, and I felt that Vaslav himself was recognizing this.

By June Vaslav was back in Vienna, from where he wrote to tell us that Romola had given birth to a daughter on June 19. He sent us snapshots he had taken of the baby when she was barely a week old, on June 28, calling her simply "the little one," for she had not yet been christened Kyra. Then in early July he sent us a telegram asking if either the both of us or Sasha alone could join him in London to help with the negotiations for future engagements after the Diaghilev Season, which was to end on July 25. Sasha left immediately, but since Vaslav would be dancing only during the closing week of the season, Sasha did not travel by train, but took the slow packet boat from St. Petersburg to London.

He arrived a few hours too late, to find that Nijinsky had checked out that very morning. At the Savoy Hotel he was given a letter Vaslav had left for him. With the letter was a telegram from Romola with the short message: RETURN IMMEDIATELY. In his brief note Vaslav told Sasha that he was worried about Romola, fearing complications following her childbirth, and that he was sorry he could not wait to see him but had to leave immediately for Austria. Vaslav also asked Sasha to go to the Drury Lane Theatre and explain the reason for his sudden departure. When he got there Sasha found Vaslav's dressing room filled with flowers and many messages of greeting welcoming Nijinsky back to London.

———

I WAS IN St. Petersburg and, of course, not knowing that Kotchetovsky had missed Nijinsky, was looking forward to hearing about the plans for future engagements with Vaslav. I was happy simply to be back home.

The beauty of my city is unique; it is not like any other city in the world. There is a touch of Venice in it. Many of the architectural monuments have the look of being closely related to Italy. Nevertheless, in all its soul, its atmosphere, and its vistas, it is wholly ours, a city of Northern Russia.

As we ride slowly down Nevsky Prospekt, past the Anichov Palace, over the bridge with its famous statues of dismounted horsemen curbing their steeds, we roll along beside the Fontanka River and turn into Mokhovaya Ulitza, the street where we lived during our first years in St. Petersburg.

I can never have enough of gazing at its different views, and sometimes I hire a cab and drive through the city for many hours. I pass the Imperial Theatrical School, going down one of the most beautiful streets in all St. Petersburg, Teatralnaya Ulitza. It looks like a long yellow hall with columns of white pillars on both sides leading to the Alexandrinsky Theatre. Of the same architecture as all Teatralnaya Ulitza, it is a fascinating Russian version of the Empire style.

The horse's hooves rap softly on the wooden paving as we emerge into the square in front of the Theatre, continue down Nevsky Prospekt, and come out onto the Neva Embankment. I tell the driver to proceed slowly so as to stay a while longer amid the beauties of the Embankment. So many times as a child I strolled with Vaslav along this beautiful river. Every corner here is an intimate part of my childhood and youth. We go along the English Quay, past the Admiralty, the Palaces, and the Summer Garden.

Through the wonderful railings, so tall and light, I stare into the Summer Garden, recalling the countless days spent there. I know every path, every statue, every flowerbed. I know the willow that bathes its branches in the little pool and the stone vase on the edge of that pool. I remember the spring fragrance of the blossoming lindens. I remember, too, my childish joy when after the long winter I was allowed at last to take off my heavy winter coat, my galoshes, and my many woolen scarves. In my memory I step out again in the blue spring coat with the velvet collar that Father brought me from Paris, and I am wearing a soft felt hat, with a pom-pom and a light gauze scarf tied in a bow around my neck. How delightful it is to step over the crunching sand of the garden walks in my boots, unhampered by galoshes!

The Summer Garden does not have any overgrown shady paths, but how beautiful everything is. In the spring when the wooden boxes protecting the statuary are removed, you walk down the main path among marble figures from Ancient Greece, feeling that you are in a royal park in antiquity. In the autumn when the leaves have fallen and the black twigs of the trees lace the lowering gray sky of St. Petersburg, everything is wrapped in mist—the garden railing, the marble statues, the trees, the symmetrically laid-out avenues; the whole park, the entire Summer Garden, has the look of an old engraving.

Vaslav and I were fond of strolling in the Summer Garden, down one of the avenues paved with flagstones and hedged with trimly cut shrubs bordering the River Fontanka. There is where the little Palace of Peter the Great looks out onto the Fontanka; close at hand is the monument of the fabulist, Grandfather Kriloff, the La Fontaine of Russia. We knew every minute detail of the various stories from Kriloff's fables depicted on the plinth. Particularly we loved "The Monkey and the Spectacles." I remember how outraged we were when somebody broke off and took away many of the Monkey's spectacles.

Quite near the Summer Garden are two museums—the Baron Stieglitz and the Alexander III—not far from the house on Mokhovaya Ulitza where we lived as children. In winter when the weather was bad Mother would often take us to the museums, and from those childhood visits was born our love of museums. During the summer vacations, when we were old enough to go out on our own, Vaslav and I would often wander down the Neva Embankment, and from there we would visit the Hermitage Museum and become acquainted with more great works of art.

We loved the walk along the Neva at all times of the year. In winter, when the river was locked in ice to a depth of two or three feet, sleighs would dash across it from one bank to the other. These were special sleighs; they were made like armchairs set on runners and were pushed by men on skates. The path for the sleighs was cleared of loose snow, which would be piled up at the sides. Fir trees were then mounted in the piles of snow so that it seemed as if one were driving along a snowbound country road. The deep river flowing right under the ice gave rise to a slight sensation of fear, but it was a great joy to be tearing through the falling snow, against a strong wind, seeing neither horse nor coachman, as if moving under one's own power. The pleasure of being pushed over the ice cost five kopeks per person, each way. We children were delighted to spend our winter savings in this manner. I must allow, too, to loving this ice-sleighing even when I grew up.

When we walked along the embankment in the summer, Vaslav and I often stopped by the broad, massive granite parapet to gaze at the river. We enjoyed watching the steamers, the tugs, and barges that went past, while we dreamed of long voyages. Occasionally Vaslav would decide to do a little fishing. Then we climbed along the barges, jumping from one to the next in order to get as close to midstream as possible. Vaslav would unwind his homemade line, and we would sit beside each other on the deck of the barge, our legs dangling over the side. This would have been a forbidden pastime if Mother had known anything of it.

As far as I can recall, Vaslav never caught a fish. Whether this was due to the strong current in the river or to our loud talk and laughter, frightening the fish away, I do not know. But the failure to catch anything never troubled us. It was marvelous to sit close to the deep, transparent water, flowing past with great speed, while in the hot sunshine the barges gave off the delightful fragrance of birch logs.

"Would you like a real fast drive, Miss?" the coachman interrupts, jolting me back from the world of memory.

He drives madly up the Kamenostrovsky Prospekt to the Islands and the open seashore.

—

THE WORLD WAS on the brink of war.

Sasha remained in London for a few days after missing Vaslav and then returned through Germany on the last train to cross the Russo-German border.

War was declared and I was not to meet my brother Vaslav for seven years.

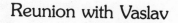

60   Reunion with Vaslav

DURING THE war, and then during the early years of the Russian Revolution, I tried every possible way to join my brother. From his letters, sent from America and Switzerland, I knew he was planning his own new choreographic enterprise and wanted me to join him.

All postal service between the Soviet Government and countries abroad was suspended in 1918, and after that we heard nothing from Vaslav. However, towards the end of the year we received a letter from Emilia Markus, Romola's mother, from Budapest. We were in Kiev at the time, which was then under the control of Hetman Skoropadsky, a Cossack leader supported by German forces. She told us that Romola, Vaslav, and their daughter, Kyra, were in Switzerland and were awaiting us in their villa above St. Moritz, where they had rooms ready for us.

But this was not the time for us to leave—I was seven months pregnant with my second child; the Hetman government and the German forces were evacuating Kiev; and Petlura and his rebel forces were already attacking the suburbs and were soon to occupy the city. It became increasingly obvious that we would not be able to leave for some time, though I continued to plan for the days when I would again dance and work with Vaslav. Already I had begun to develop my own theory of the dance, and in February 1919, three weeks after the birth of my son, Leo, I opened my own Ecole de Mouvement to train artists for Nijinsky's choreography.

We did not receive any letters from Vaslav or Romola until the middle of 1920 when a pilot who had flown into Kiev from Vienna smuggled in a letter for me. The letter was from Romola, written by another hand in Russian, telling us that Vaslav had been mentally ill for a year and a half and that it was essential for his recovery that Mother and I be with him.

We could not accept this tragic news. With all our hearts we wanted to believe that Vaslav was well and that Romola had been advised to send this letter, and had had it written formally in Russian, to assist us in obtaining the documents necessary for us to leave Russia under the pretext that our presence was necessary for Nijinsky's recovery. The pilot who had brought the letter offered to fly me out of the country in his twin-seater plane, but I had to refuse. I could not leave Mother and my two children behind in Kiev, where they would have been alone, for I had been separated from my husband for over a year.

During the following months I explored every legal way to leave the country and join Vaslav.

In April 1921, a newspaper dispatch from Budapest announced that Vaslav Nijinsky was hopelessly ill and had been committed to a mental institution in Vienna.

I decided we would have to leave the country illegally.

In May 1921, with my mother and my children—Irina, aged seven, and Leo, aged two—I made my way to the Polish border. Our journey was long and difficult. Without permits or documents we ran the risk of being arrested by the Cheka. Six weeks after leaving Kiev we arrived in Vienna, where Romola met us at the station and took us to the Hotel Bristol. There we stayed, and shortly met Vaslav's two children—Kyra, who had just turned seven, and the baby, Tamara, one year old.

The next day we saw Vaslav in the Steinhof Sanatorium.

When we entered his room Vaslav was sitting in an armchair; he did not get up to greet us. Mother rushed to embrace him, but Vaslav showed no emotional reaction on seeing his mother. He remained withdrawn into himself, also when I embraced him. Throughout our visit in his room he had an absent look, staring into space and not uttering a word.

Later during that first visit we walked out into the garden. I was overwhelmed by a deep sorrow. In spite of my grief I tried to appear relaxed and even to engage Vaslav in conversation. I talked about the dance and the theatre. I told him of my work in my Ecole de Mouvement and about my students there who were now ready to take part in Nijinsky's choreography. I went on to describe how, without having seen him dance, they all had a great admiration for him, and that I knew they would be devoted to him and would understand his dance. My words did not seem to reach him; he remained impassive, but when I said, "Would you believe, Vatsa, that with them I have already devised two ballets?" Vaslav suddenly turned his head and looked straight into my eyes.

He said very firmly, as if instructing me, "The *ballet* is never devised. The *ballet* must be created."

Vaslav's beautiful eyes were sparkling, the sound of his dear voice rang in my ears, my heart brimmed over with hope. Words rushed from me; I was as excited and overjoyed as if a miracle had taken place before my eyes . . . but the spark of consciousness suddenly died. Vaslav was again staring into the distance, indifferent to everything around him.

For many years I continued to believe that Vaslav would recover completely.

Whenever a conversation around him touched on the Dance, one could see a sudden spark of consciousness. That part of his consciousness that lived in his vision of Art was preserved, and I knew that in this Vaslav remained completely sane.

For Nijinsky, the Dance was credo, life, and soul.

Without the theatre Nijinsky withdrew into himself and closed the door to the realities of life, to abide in his own inner world of the Dance.

Afterword

VASLAV WAS not only a brother; he was also, for me, a great friend. I was two years younger, but the difference in our ages and the fact that I was a girl did not interfere with the close bond of friendship that linked us from childhood. We had everything in common: our games, our mischief, our sorrows. We grew up together, at home and in the Imperial Theatrical School. We had the same upbringing, we shared the same impressions, we were attracted by the same fantasies, we had the same dreams.

During our childhood years it seemed to me that I knew everything about Vaslav, my brother . . . until that happy day I "saw" Nijinsky dance.

Before my eyes was *le dieu de la danse*. . . . Nijinsky is onstage, and as he extends upwards, a barely perceptible quiver runs through his body; his left hand close to his face, he seems to be listening to sounds, only heard by him, which fill all his being. He radiates an inner force that by its very radiance envelops the theatre, establishing a complete rapport with the audience.

Since then, and with each passing year that we spent in theatrical work, though much of him remained close and known to me, I was aware less and less that he was my brother. His art became for me a dancing discovery: seeing him dance, I was filled with awe, captivated by his art.

I wanted to understand the fascination Nijinsky exerted on the public, a fascination that so captured the imagination, there were those who claimed that in his dance Nijinsky's feet never touched the ground. I wanted to understand those qualities of his dance that I felt depended not so much on his huge leaps, his extraordinary elevation, or the amazing virtuosity of his dance technique, but rather the nature of the Dance, living in him, body and soul.

I would watch my brother preparing for a performance, standing in the wings, immersed in silence and concentrated in himself. He seemed unaware of anything around him, as if in a meditation, gathering within himself an inner soul-force that he could carry onto the stage and offer wide to the audience.

There are those who say that to dance like Nijinsky one would have to have Nijinsky's body, which they liken to a Stradivarius violin. Certainly Nijinsky was endowed with exceptional physical qualities, but that was not what made his dancing exceptional. The Stradivarius violin can produce enchanted sounds only in the hands of a great musician. When Nijinsky danced one not only saw but also heard with one's eyes the melody of his dancing body, infused with subtle musical qualities.

Nijinsky is always with me, he has inspired me as an artist. Even now as I write, I can see Nijinsky dance, feel the breath of the rhythm of each movement.

Remembering the perfection of his created images I feel the same exaltation I experienced on seeing the works of Praxiteles and Michelangelo. What those masters in their God-given inspiration brought to life, creating masterpieces out of a block of marble, so Nijinsky, in his God-given inspiration, created in the line and music of the dancing body.

November 27, 1971

Bronislava Nijinska: Highlights of Choreographic Career

Bronislava Nijinska began her choreographic work in Kiev in 1919 and 1920 by mounting dances and choreographic sketches for her *Ecole de Mouvement*. In 1920 she created two "libretto-free" ballets, *Twelfth Rhapsody* and *Mephisto Valse*, both by Liszt, and considered these ballets to be a foundation of much of her later work.

1921–1925. On leaving Russia in 1921 Nijinska rejoined the Ballets Russes. She was engaged by Diaghilev both as dancer and choreographer. From 1921 until 1925 Nijinska was the sole choreographer for the company. Her first assignment was to stage all the action scenes and to mount several new dances for the revival of Petipa's *The Sleeping Beauty* to be presented in London. This was also her first collaboration with Igor Stravinsky, who orchestrated both "Aurora's Variation" and "The Three Ivans."

Nijinska soon established herself as a versatile choreographer—from her re-creation of Petipa's classical works to the creation of her neoclassical ballet, Poulenc's *Les Biches*. Her deft touch with light comedic themes was revealed in Stravinsky's *Mavra* and also in his ballet *Le Renard*. It was to a very different Stravinsky score that Nijinska created her powerful *Les Noces* with its architectural formations and rhythmic movements.

In the Diaghilev Ballets Russes Nijinska worked with the artists: Braque, Ernst, Gontcharova, Juan Gris, Larionov, Laurencin, Laurens, and Joan Miró.

1922: *Aurora's Wedding* (d'après Petipa)	Tchaikovsky	Diaghilev Ballets Russes
1922: *Le Renard*	Stravinsky	Diaghilev Ballets Russes
1922: *Mavra*	Stravinsky	Diaghilev Ballets Russes
1923: *Les Noces*	Stravinsky	Diaghilev Ballets Russes
1924: *Les Biches*	Poulenc	Diaghilev Ballets Russes
1924: *Les Tentations de la Bergère*	Montclair	Diaghilev Ballets Russes

1924: *Les Facheux* (comedy-ballet from Molière by Boris Kochno)	Auric	Diaghilev Ballets Russes
1924: *La Nuit sur le Mont Chauve*	Mussorgsky	Diaghilev Ballets Russes
1924: *Le Train Bleu* (scenario by Jean Cocteau)	Milhaud	Diaghilev Ballets Russes

(During the 1923 and 1924 seasons Nijinska mounted all the ballet scenes and acts in more than a dozen operas, including *Tales of Hoffmann*, *Aïda* and *Schumann's Faust* with Diaghilev Ballets Russes, for the Monte Carlo Opera.)

―

1925–1931. After leaving Diaghilev's Ballets Russes, Nijinska choreographed new ballets for the Théâtre de l'Opéra in Paris and the Teatro Colón in Buenos Aires. In Buenos Aires, Nijinska also choreographed all the ballet scenes for the Teatro Colón operas; these included *Le Chant du Rossignol* by Stravinsky, *Le Coq d'Or* and *Tsar Saltan* by Rimsky-Korsakov, and Prokofiev's *Love of Three Oranges* (the music for which she had first heard some years before in Russia when Prokofiev himself had played it to her in the early days of the Revolution).

In 1926, at the Teatro Colón, developing the choreographic ideas she had first used in Kiev, Nijinska created *Etude-Bach*. This first abstract ballet, inspired by the spirituality of the music, was choreographed to an arrangement of the six Brandenberg Concertos and was the first ballet to be mounted to the music of J. S. Bach.

In 1928, Nijinska became artistic director and choreographer of the newly formed Ida Rubinstein Ballet and worked with that company through 1931, using both classical and contemporary music for her ballets. She collaborated on the selection of music with the composers Honegger, Tcherepnine, and Milhaud, who orchestrated works of Bach, Borodin, and Schubert and Liszt for her. She also worked with Stravinsky and Ravel. For the performances of his *Bolero* and *La Valse*, Ravel conducted the orchestra, as did Stravinsky for the premiere of his new ballet *La Baiser de la Fée*.

1925: *Les Rencontres*	Ibert	Paris Opéra
1925: *La Naissance de la Lyre*	Roussel	Paris Opéra
1926: *Romeo and Juliet*	Lambert	Diaghilev Ballets Russes
1926: *Pomona*	Lambert	Teatro Colón
1926: *Etude-Bach*	Bach	Teatro Colón
1926: *Guignol*	Lanner	Teatro Colón
1926: *Momento Japonés*	Lucas	Teatro Colón
1926: *Cuadro Campestre*	Chabrier	Teatro Colón
1927: *Ala y Loly (Skif Suite)*	Prokofiev	Teatro Colón
1927: *Impressions de Music Hall*	Pierné	Paris Opéra
1927: *Daphnis et Chloë*	Ravel	Teatro Colón

1927: *La Giara*	Casella	Teatro Colón
1927: *Petrouchka*	Stravinsky	Teatro Colón
1928: *La Valse*	Ravel	Ida Rubinstein*
1928: *Bolero*	Ravel	Ida Rubinstein*
1928: *La Bien-Aimée*	Schubert & Liszt	Ida Rubinstein*
1928: *Le Baiser de la Fée*	Stravinsky	Ida Rubinstein*
1928: *L'Amour et Psyché*	Bach	Ida Rubinstein*
1928: *La Princesse Cygne*	Rimsky-Korsakov	Ida Rubinstein*
1928: *Nocturne*	Borodin	Ida Rubinstein*
1929: *Paysage Enfantin*	Kristkoff	Olga Spessiva Ballet
1931: *Etude-Bach* (2nd version)	Bach	Nijinska Ballets†
1931: *Capriccio Espagnole*	Rimsky-Korsakov	Nijinska Ballets†
1931: *La Valse* (2nd version)	Ravel	Ida Rubinstein*

*The ballets created for the Ida Rubinstein Ballet had their premiere at the Paris Opéra and were included in the 1929 seasons at Théâtre de Monte Carlo; La Scala, Milan; the Opera House, Vienna. They were also performed at Covent Garden, London, in 1931.
†The ballets created by the Nijinska Ballets were presented in Paris during the Saison d'Opéra Russe at the Théâtre des Champs-Elysées.

~

1932–1937. In 1932 Nijinska formed her own company, Ballets Nijinska, Théâtre de la Danse, reviving several of her own ballets and creating two important new ballets—*Variations*, a choreographic symphony (Thème Pyrrhique, Thème Pastorale, Thème Pathétique) composed on Themes and Variations by Beethoven, and *Hamlet*, to music by Liszt, a choreographic poem inspired by Shakespeare's tragedy.

Following seasons in Paris, Barcelona, and tours in France and Italy, she joined her company with the Ballets Russes of Col W. de Basil in Monte Carlo for the whole of the 1934 Opera and Ballet Seasons. In December 1934, Nijinska was invited to Hollywood to compose the ballet scenes for the film *A Midsummer Night's Dream*, working during 1935 with director Max Reinhardt, for whom she had already staged the ballet scenes for the opera *Tales of Hoffmann* in Berlin (1931).

After the American premiere of her ballet *Les Noces* with the Ballets Russes in New York in 1936, Nijinska went to Buenos Aires where she presented her ballet *Baiser de la Fée* in a Stravinsky Festival with the Teatro Colón.

In 1937 as the artistic director and the choreographer of the newly formed Polish Ballet, she created five new ballets that were first performed at the Paris Exposition Internationale of the same year. The Polish Ballet was awarded the Grand Prix and Nijinska also received the Grand Prix for choreography.

1932: *Les Comédiens Jaloux*	Casella	Théâtre de la Danse
1932: *Variations*	Beethoven	Théâtre de la Danse
1932: *Les Biches* (reprise)	Poulenc	Théâtre de la Danse
1933: *Les Noces* (reprise)	Stravinsky	Théâtre de la Danse

1933: *Le Baiser de la Fée* (S. American premiere)	Stravinsky	Teatro Colón
1934: *Hamlet*	Liszt	Théâtre de la Danse
1935: *Les Cent Baisers*	D'Erlanger	Ballets Russes (London)
1936: *Danses Slavs et Tziganes*	Dargomijsky	Ballets Russes (New York)
1936: *Les Noces* (American premiere)	Stravinsky	Ballets Russes (New York)
1936: *Le Baiser de la Fée* (reprise)	Stravinsky	Teatro Colón
1937: *Beloved (La Bien-Aimée,* reprise)	Schubert & Liszt	Markova-Dolin Ballet
1937: *Les Biches* (reprise)	Poulenc	Markova-Dolin Ballet
1937: *Concerto de Chopin*	Chopin	Polish Ballet*
1937: *La Légende de Cracovie*	Kondracki	Polish Ballet*
1937: *Le Rappel*	Woytowicz	Polish Ballet*
1937: *Le Chant de la Terre*	Palester	Polish Ballet*
1937: *Apollon et la Belle*	Roszycki	Polish Ballet*

*Premiere at Exposition Internationale (Théâtre Mogador, Paris) followed by European tour 1937–38—London, Berlin and thirty-three cities in Germany, Warsaw and ten cities in Poland.

—

1938–1966. Nijinska returned to the United States in October 1939, and for the inaugural season of Ballet Theatre (later American Ballet Theatre) in 1940 she choreographed *La Fille Mal Gardée.* That same year she presented *Bolero, Chopin Concerto* and *Etude-Bach* in a performance at the Hollywood Bowl to an audience of twenty-two thousand. She was invited to the Jacob's Pillow Festival as choreographer and resident teacher in 1941, and for the opening of Ted Shawn's new theatre there she presented her *Chopin Concerto* and *Etude-Bach.* She had already established her own school in Hollywood and was also continuing with her choreographic work, reviving her own ballets as well as creating new ones with the Ballet Theatre and the Ballets Russes de Monte Carlo, and later with Ballet International of Marquis de Cuevas, for whom in 1960 she mounted *The Sleeping Beauty.* The title role in Nijinska's choreography was danced by Rosella Hightower, who later staged *The Sleeping Beauty,* d'après Nijinska, with the Ballets de Marseilles in 1968 and with the Stuttgart Ballet in 1977.

In the mid-sixties Nijinska herself was invited to revive *Les Biches* and *Les Noces* for the Royal Ballet in London; both have continued in their repertoire to the present.

1940: *La Fille Mal Gardée*	Hertel	Ballet Theatre
1942: *Beloved* (American premiere)	Schubert & Liszt	Ballet Theatre
1942: *Snow Maiden*	Glazounov	Ballets Russes
1942: *Ancient Russia*	Tchaikovsky	Ballets Russes

1942: *Hitch Your Wagon to a Star*	Glazounov & Tchaikovsky	Ballet Repertory (Chicago)
1942: *Vision*	Brahms	Ballet Repertory
1944: *Brahms Variations*	Brahms	Marquis de Cuevas
1944: *Pictures at an Exhibition*	Mussorgsky	Marquis de Cuevas
1949: *In Memoriam* (centennial of death of Chopin)	Chopin	Marquis de Cuevas
1953: *Rondo Capriccioso*	Saint-Saëns	Marquis de Cuevas
1960: *The Sleeping Beauty*	Tchaikovsky	Marquis de Cuevas
1964: *Les Biches* (reprise)	Poulenc	Royal Ballet
1966: *Les Noces* (reprise)	Stravinsky	Royal Ballet

During the years 1966–1972 Nijinska was repeatedly invited to revive several of her ballets. Following a performance of *Les Biches* in Rome in 1969, she returned to the United States and mounted *Brahms Variations* and *Les Biches* for the Jacob's Pillow Festival. Early in 1970 she mounted *Les Biches* in Florence and then returned to the United States to mount *Chopin Concerto* and *Les Biches* for the Washington, D.C., Shakespeare Festival. In August 1970 she was invited to London where she met the Kirov Ballet to whom she demonstrated her brother's *L'Après-Midi d'un Faune*. She then returned to her home in Southern California before her next engagement in Venice, where she was to mount *Les Noces* for performances in January 1971. Nijinska celebrated her eightieth birthday, onstage, at the Teatro Fenice in Venice during rehearsals for her ballet *Les Noces*—the first major work she had created for Diaghilev in 1923.

IN/JR

Index